Winston and Archie

WINSTON AND ARCHIE

The Letters of Sir Archibald Sinclair and Winston S. Churchill 1915–1960

Edited by
Ian Hunter

POLITICO'S

First published in Great Britain in 2005 by Politico's Publishing, an imprint of Methuen Publishing Limited
215 Vauxhall Bridge Road
London SW1V 1EJ
www.politicos.co.uk/publishing

10 9 8 7 6 5 4 3 2 1

A CIP catalogue record for this book is available from the British Library.

ISBN 1 84275 040 2

Printed and bound in Great Britain by St. Edmundsbury Press, Bury St. Edmunds, Suffolk.
Designed and typeset in Bembo and Franklin Gothic by Duncan Brack.

Contents

Illustrations

Introduction

This book collects together the personal and professional correspondence between Winston Churchill and Sir Archibald Sinclair (later Lord Thurso). The former requires little introduction; his colourful career and character have been heavily researched and legions of books and articles have been published on all aspects of his unparalleled political journey.

The latter is a much lesser known entity. Sir Archibald Henry MacDonald Sinclair was born in 1890. Sixteen years younger than Churchill, this age gap, as well as very different personalities and ambitions, shaped their long-term friendship. Sinclair was born into a wealthy landowning family with massive estates in Caithness in northern Scotland. Both his parents died before his fifth birthday and his grandfather and other relatives bought him up. He was educated at Eton and Sandhurst and was commissioned into the 2nd Life Guards in 1910.

Sinclair was never a Conservative by principle or inclination. He was well connected in the Liberal political world, knowing the Asquith family and being friendly with other leading Liberals. Churchill, then a Liberal Cabinet Minister, and Sinclair were first introduced by Maxine Elliott, an American actress and grande dame of late Edwardian and inter-war international society. Maxine had a home at Maidenhead, near Sinclair's uncle. Although of different generations, Sinclair and Churchill shared much in common. Both had American mothers and both had experienced unsatisfactory upbringings. Both were also enthusiasts for polo, flying and politics.

Whilst their friendship pre-dated the First World War, it was in 1916, when Churchill appointed Sinclair as his second in command to his own battalion of the Royal Scots Fusiliers, that the roots of their lifelong friendship were formed. After the armistice Sinclair worked directly for Churchill as his personal private or military secretary at the War Office (1919–21) and then the Colonial Office (1921–22). Whilst at the War Office Sinclair played an important and secretive role in the British attempts to nip the Bolshevik revolution in the bud. In 1922 Sinclair was elected as the National Liberal MP for Caithness and Sutherland, his home constituency. He held this seat until the 1945 general election.

While Churchill returned to the Conservative Party after 1924, Sinclair remained true to the Liberal colours and slowly ascended the party hierarchy. In 1930 he became Liberal Chief Whip at a particularly challenging period, as the party split into three different factions the following year. Whilst erstwhile Liberals moved either to the left or right of the political spectrum, and it became increasingly apparent, especially after the 1929 election, that the party was no longer a serious contender for power on its own terms, Sinclair remained committed to ensuring Liberal independence.

With the formation of the National Government in August 1931, Sinclair, a dedicated Scottish Home Ruler, became Secretary of State for Scotland, joining the Cabinet in November 1931. When the National Government formally abandoned free trade, the small group of Liberal ministers, led by Sir Herbert Samuel, resigned and later went into opposition. With Samuel's defeat at the 1935 general election, Sinclair was asked by David Lloyd George to lead the parliamentary Liberal Party, by then reduced to twenty-one MPs.

As Liberal leader Sinclair made his mark as an early opponent of appeasement and a principled supporter of the League of Nations and collective security. He consistently believed that a Liberal revival was imminent and through the remainder of the 1930s worked to ensure the survival of an independent Liberal Party. From 1936 he called for an acceleration in the speed of rearmament, arguing passionately for a Ministry of Supply to be formed by Chamberlain to mirror the effectiveness of the Ministry of Munitions during 1916–18. He was a leading opponent of the Munich agreement and suffered much abuse both inside and outside the House of Commons as a 'warmonger'.

When war broke out in September 1939, Chamberlain offered Sinclair an office of Cabinet rank but outside the War Cabinet. Not wishing to serve under Chamberlain in what he believed was a discredited government, Sinclair declined. In May 1940, he was one of the principal speakers in the Norway debate which brought Chamberlain down and, like Attlee and the Labour Party, made it clear in the immediate aftermath of the debate that the Liberals would refuse to serve in any coalition under Chamberlain.

When Churchill was appointed both Prime Minister and Minister of Defence he offered Sinclair the post of Air Minister, reporting directly to him. Sinclair occupied this post with considerable success throughout the rest of the European war, leaving office on the collapse of the coalition in May 1945. He was considered and approached to be Ambassador to Washington in 1941 and Viceroy of India in 1942 but preferred to remain at the heart of the war effort. His commitment to the Royal Air Force was remarkable and he was respected and well-liked by most of his senior service staff – although there were a few exceptions, such as Dowding and Harris, who regarded him as being too subordinate to Churchill.

In the 1945 election Sinclair's failure to cultivate his constituency during the war resulted in the loss of his seat. Although he stood again in 1950 he was never able to resume his political career as an MP. When Churchill returned for his third premiership in 1951, Sinclair was offered a seat in the Lords, becoming Viscount Thurso. In early 1952, however, he suffered a severe stroke which prevented him from taking his seat in the Lords until 1954. In 1958 he suffered a much more severe attack from which he never recovered, becoming gradually more bedbound and dependent on others. He died in Twickenham in June 1970.

Sinclair's ill-health during the 1950s and 1960s prevented him from writing any autobiography or war memoirs. He is, therefore, one of the few senior politicians or servicemen who led the country through the Second World War not to have given their side of the story. Furthermore, his personal and professional papers were mainly destroyed in two incidents: the first when the headquarters of the Liberal Party was destroyed by a bomb in 1942 and the second when his personal archive was badly damaged by a fire at his home in Thurso. Consequently, his opinions and views have been hard to gather, and his role and importance has often been overlooked or discounted.

A short biography of Sinclair was published in 1993[1] but its author did not have access to the full archives now available at Cambridge and at Kew, which substantially add to our knowledge of Sinclair's role, responsibilities and close relationship with Churchill. By compiling a comprehensive view of the letters that passed between Churchill and Sinclair, especially during their periods in government in 1919–22 and 1940–45 I hope that I have, at least partially, begun to redress the balance and give a clearer picture of the contribution that Sinclair made.

The letters cover the full extent of Sinclair's and Churchill's personal and professional relationship between 1915 and 1960. This is not, however, an exhaustive collection. Although the vast majority of their personal correspondence is reproduced here, I have had to be more selective over their professional papers, due to the sheer volume of documents produced, especially in the 1919–21 period and during the Coalition Government of the 1940s, when Sinclair and Churchill were in almost daily contact.

This is not a formal history of their relationship. My goal has been to allow the letters to speak for themselves, with a little light editing to provide a basic explanation of the context and the people who are mentioned. If the end result allows the friendship that existed for over fifty years to have its voice then the objective of this work will have been achieved.

Editorial note

The text presented here is essentially faithful to the source with some concessions to increase comprehension and intelligibility. Date and address formats have been harmonised and placed at the start of the letters. Grammar, spelling and punctuation that might have confused the sense have been amended but without changing the meaning. Original spellings, for instance for Russian names, have been retained but their modern versions given in the explanatory footnotes.

An attempt has been made to identify all individuals appearing in the text, and to provide brief biographical information; this is included in a footnote where the individual first appears in a letter, and repeated in Appendix B for ease of reference. If no biographical information is given for an individual, it is because I have been unable to discover any. When referring to Sinclair and Churchill their titles have been given as they

[1] Gerard J. De Groot, *Liberal Crusader: The Life of Sir Archibald Sinclair* (London: Hurst & Co., 1993)

were at the date of the letter. For example, Sinclair is Sir Archibald Sinclair until 1952, after which he is referred to as Viscount Thurso.

The work of editing these letters was eased considerably by the vast mine of information, references and footnotes on people and events in Sir Martin Gilbert's main biographical and companion volumes of the official biography of Winston S. Churchill. It would be inappropriate not to pay full tribute to this invaluable reference work and the help it has provided in the preparation of this volume.

Acknowledgements

I would like to thank the staff at the Archive Centre at Churchill College, Cambridge for their cheerful and efficient help; in particular, the efforts of Rachel Lloyd and Jude Brimmer were much appreciated. I would also like to thank Katharine Thomson for her help in translating Churchill's handwriting. My thanks also to the archivists and counter staff at the National Archives in Kew.

The help I received from my brother, Chris, and my sister, Deryn, was very much appreciated. I am particularly grateful to Penny Hunter for her flexibility and incredible accuracy. The speed with which she was able to turn large piles of photocopied documents into a professional manuscript was awe-inspiring. I am grateful to Judy Parkinson for her efforts in the early stages of researching this book.

This book would not have been possible without the support and encouragement of Iain Dale and Sean Magee of Politico's and Methuen. I would also like to thank Duncan Brack for his Herculean efforts in ensuring that this book has far fewer errors than it otherwise would have.

I am very grateful for the kindness of Archie Sinclair's grandson, John Thurso MP, for permission to use the Sinclair Papers held under his copyright. My formal thanks is due to Tim Padfield at the National Archives, and to Her Majesty's Stationery Office, for their permission to publish documents subject to crown copyright held at the National Archives. Andrew Roberts, Lady Soames and Professor John Vincent made valuable comments on earlier versions of this book and I am thankful for their input and advice.

Lastly, I would like to dedicate this book to Emma and Liberty who have tolerated my incoherent ramblings about dead politicians, trips away, and regular absences in the study over the last two years with grace and understanding.

Ian Hunter
June 2005

Part 1

The First World War 1915–1918

Introduction

The series of letters between Sinclair and Churchill sent between January 1915 and July 1918 offer a fascinating insight into both high politics and life in the trenches on the Western Front. Sinclair, as a serving cavalry officer, was mobilised and moved to France soon after the start of hostilities. He was to serve on the Western Front throughout the conflict. His Liberal Party connections, as well as support from Churchill, meant that when Jack Seely, the former Secretary of State for War and commander of the Canadian Cavalry Brigade, was seeking a new aide-de-camp (ADC) in early 1915, Sinclair was an obvious choice.

Sinclair took up his new appointment on 19 February 1915, at the age of twenty-five, and proved to be a great success. He got on well with the Canadian troops and was universally known to all ranks, according to Seely, as 'Archie'. He was also to prove a capable officer in the field, Seely commenting to Churchill that he was cool under fire. At the battle of Festubert in May 1915, Sinclair was appointed acting Brigade Major and took a leading role in consolidating captured enemy positions – a particularly dangerous and unpleasant responsibility. Seely was keen for Sinclair to be confirmed in the Brigade Major position but six weeks later he was informed that a Captain from the 19th Lancers was to be appointed instead. Sinclair was sanguine about this disappointment, noting to Churchill on 26 July that it was ridiculous to think that he could be confirmed in the appointment as he had neither the staff college training necessary nor the years of experience that was typically expected.

In contrast to Sinclair, Churchill was only to spend six months in the trenches before returning to the political mainstream. Churchill entered the war in his pre-war post as First Lord of the Admiralty, but the resignation of Lord Fisher (the First Sea Lord), the Dardanelles misadventure and the formation of a coalition government with its influx of Tory and Labour ministers, saw him relegated, in May 1915, to the Chancellorship of the Duchy of Lancaster – a post still in the Cabinet but with very few official responsibilities and little power.

In late October and early November 1915, Asquith reconfigured the government creating, in effect, a small War Cabinet, but with no seat for Churchill. Excluded from the inner sanctum, Churchill resigned, announcing that he was leaving to serve in Flanders as a Major in the Oxfordshire Hussars. He made his resignation speech on 15 November and on the 18th crossed to France. Arriving at Boulogne he was driven to British General Headquarters at St Omer to meet the Commander-in-Chief, Sir John French. French offered Churchill the choice either of joining his staff as ADC, or of taking command of a brigade at the front with the rank of Brigadier General. Churchill chose the brigade.

On 20 November 1915, Churchill joined the 2nd Battalion, Grenadier Guards and moved to their front-line HQ at Neuve Chapelle. His commanding officer, Colonel Jeffreys, did not offer him a warm welcome: 'I think I ought to tell you that we were not at all consulted in the matter of your coming to join us'.[2] Although expecting to be given command of a brigade (of four battalions) he was eventually offered a battalion after Asquith intervened, driven by fear of parliamentary criticism, the Prime Minister suggesting to French that 'perhaps you might give him a battalion'.[3] Churchill was deeply disappointed and offended. He also felt personally wounded by Asquith and from this point on moved away from the circle of Asquithian Liberals in his political allegiance. 'Asquith will throw anyone to the wolves to keep himself in office', he wrote to his wife Clementine.[4]

In December 1915, French was replaced by General Douglas Haig as Commander-in-Chief. Haig was much less inclined to look favourably on a politician turned soldier, and refused to contemplate giving Churchill command of a brigade until he had shown that he could bear responsibility in action as CO of a battalion. On New Year's Day 1916 Churchill learnt that his battalion was to be the 6th Royal Scots Fusiliers, part of the 9th (Scottish) Division and part of Kitchener's 'New Army'. With the rank of Colonel, Churchill took command on 5 January.

The 6th Royal Scots Fusiliers was composed of around 30 officers and 700 men (mainly Lowland Scots); the unit had been badly mauled in French's offensive at Loos in September 1915, during which more than half the men had been killed or wounded and three-quarters of the officers shot. Morale was low. Churchill requested from Haig that he be allowed to bring in Jack Seely and Archie Sinclair to assist him in pulling the battalion together before it returned to the front line. Haig declined to release Seely but agreed that Sinclair could join Churchill as his second-in-command.

The Fusiliers did not warmly receive the news that Churchill was to be their new commanding officer; his reputation as a warmonger and adventurer did not please his new troops. Churchill did little to endear himself to his new officers at their first lunch together. As one of them, Hakewill Smith, later recalled: 'It was quite the most uncomfortable lunch I had ever been at. Churchill didn't say a word: he went right round the table staring each officer out of countenance. We had disliked the idea of Churchill being in command; now, having seen him, we disliked the idea even more. At the end of the lunch, he made a short speech: "Gentlemen, I am now your commanding officer. Those who support me I will look after. Those who go against me I will break. Good afternoon gentlemen." Everyone agreed that we were in for a pretty rotten time.'[5] He further deepened the troops' foreboding on his first full inspection, when he insisted on shouting out cavalry orders which none of the infantrymen understood.

---

[2] Quoted by Churchill in *Thoughts and Adventures* (Thornton Butterworth, 1930), p. 101.

[3] Martin Gilbert, *Winston S. Churchill, Vol. 3, 1914–1916* (London: Heinemann, 1971) p. 625.

[4] Letter from Churchill to his wife dated 20 December 1915, quoted in Gilbert, *Winston S. Churchill*, Vol. 3, p. 617.

[5] Quoted in Gilbert, *Winston S. Churchill*, Vol. 3, p. 632.

However, from this poor start relations between Churchill and his battalion soon improved. His energy, resilience and willingness to share the conditions with his men improved perceptions, and confidence in his leadership abilities rose. Working with Sinclair, Churchill made efforts to understand the duties of the battalion members and paid great attention to detail. He also made sure that everyone clearly knew what was expected of them. One of the means through which Sinclair and Churchill won the respect of their troops was by paying attention to the personal cleanliness of the soldiers. Using brewing vats as bathtubs, the battalion declared war on lice, and Churchill also ensured that his men got fresh uniforms and equipment.

The Fusiliers returned to the front line on 20 January, to a sector near the village of Ploegsteert – known as 'Plug Street' to the British troops – just within Belgium on the Franco-Belgian border. The routine was six days in the front line followed by six days in the support line. Sinclair and Churchill set up their headquarters in a small battered farmstead named Lawrence Farm. Throughout January and February the routine remained the same – inspecting trenches, improving defensive positions, training the troops and holding the front. Both front and support trenches came in for frequent shelling and machine-gunning, and the Lawrence Farm HQ was hit on at least two occasions.

In early March 1916 Churchill took seven days' leave and returned to London. On learning that Balfour was to introduce the Navy Estimates in the Commons, Churchill decided to speak in the debate. Churchill had mended his bridges with Lord Fisher and was convinced that for the Navy to succeed the most important factor was the return of Fisher and himself to the Admiralty at the earliest opportunity. On 7 March he spoke in the Commons to urge the return of Fisher, his demand being met with almost unanimous incredulity from all sides of the House. Less than four months earlier, in his resignation speech, Churchill had attacked Fisher for neither supporting nor guiding him during critical moments in the Dardanelles crisis; it was unbelievable that he was now arguing for his reinstatement. Many MPs agreed with the Tory backbencher who concluded that 'we all wish him a great deal of success in France, and we hope he will stay there'.[6]

Churchill still believed, however, that he had an opportunity to return to the centre of government, and on 9 March requested that Kitchener relieve him of his command. A meeting with Asquith, together with pressure from Clementine, persuaded him, however, that he risked destroying his career by laying himself over to charges of opportunism and inconsistency, and he agreed to return to France.

For the rest of the month Churchill pondered over whether to return to London or remain in the Army. He came to the conclusion that he had no real prospects in the military and that he should return to parliament to take up a front-bench position with His Majesty's Opposition. He was particularly attracted by the political turmoil brewing around the issue of compulsory conscription, with Liberal and Conservative ministers starting to fall out over the need for compulsion. He believed that the Tories in the coalition, led by Carson, would launch an open challenge to the Prime Minister over

---

[6] *Hansard*, 7th Series, vol. 80, cc. 1442–43 (7 March 1916).

the issue, and that there was every chance that Asquith would lose the premiership. When Asquith called a secret session of parliament to debate the proposed compromise (whereby the current scheme was extended but fell short of compulsion) Churchill requested leave to attend. Wishing Churchill luck in the debate, Sinclair urged him to stay in London if he felt he could best contribute to the war's success by being there. However, when Asquith introduced his compromise bill Churchill was recalled to the Royal Scots Fusiliers and did not take part in the final debate. Asquith failed to convince the House of his proposals and was forced to withdraw the bill and bring in new legislation for full compulsory service.

During May 1916, daily losses through shellfire led to moves to consolidate the various battalions along the Ploegsteert section of the front. The depleted 6th and 7th battalions of the 6th Royal Scots Fusiliers were amalgamated, and the Colonel of the 7th was senior, rendering Churchill's position redundant. He quickly took the opportunity to leave military service and return to parliamentary and public duties. On 6 May he gave a farewell lunch to his officers and left for England on the 7th. Sinclair decided to take some leave and he too returned to England in mid-May.

Churchill attempted to find a staff role for Sinclair in the War Office, but as a young, physically fit and unwounded officer, Sinclair felt that it was his duty to remain in the field. After spending his leave in London and Caithness, he returned to France to a post with the Household Cavalry – which ensured that he avoided the Battle of the Somme that summer and autumn, as Haig insisted on keeping the cavalry units out of the combat, ready for the breakthrough when they would come into their own in the open country behind the enemy lines.

Sinclair became increasingly frustrated with the inactivity and boredom and with the lack of prospects within the cavalry. He toyed with the idea of joining the Royal Flying Corps (he was an experienced pilot who had flown regularly before the war) but was urged by Churchill to remain with his squadron. Churchill anticipated Lloyd George would call a general election in the spring of 1917, and was keen to find Sinclair a safe Liberal seat.

In April 1917 Sinclair came down with appendicitis and returned to London for treatment. He was sorely frustrated that his squadron, after all the months of waiting, was moved to the front line at the same time. After his operation he was passed as unfit for active service and had to accept a staff officer's position with General Trotter at Windsor Barracks. Here he remained for the rest of 1917. In May, after a six-week romance, he married Marigold Forbes.

During late 1917 and early 1918 Sinclair attempted to transfer into the newly formed Tank Corps, but the War Office decided that the whole of the Household Cavalry should become a unit of machine gunners. This decision again saved Sinclair from further front line action as he was away being trained to operate and manage machine gun units during the initially successful German spring offensive in 1918.

From May 1916 to mid-July 1917 Churchill remained a backbench MP, speaking in debates and urging greater effort and leadership to pursue the war to a favourable conclusion. He regularly hoped and expected to be recalled to high office, but the hostility of the Tories kept him out. In early December 1916, the increasing dissatisfaction with Asquith's gentlemanly and relaxed style of leadership led, after agitation by senior Conservatives, to his replacement as Prime Minister by Lloyd George. Lloyd George indicated that he would like to help Churchill return to the Government but that he needed to wait for the Conservatives' attitude towards him to cool down.

In March 1917 the report of the Dardanelles Commission was published. The report failed to refute many of the public charges laid against Churchill over the fiasco, but, more importantly, allocated no blame to him, leaving him better positioned for a return to the Cabinet. In mid-July Lloyd George, without consulting his coalition partners, offered Churchill the post of Minister of Munitions, which he held for the remainder of the war – perhaps following his aunt's advice to 'stick to Munitions, and don't try and run the Government'.[7]

After completing his training Sinclair was given command of a machine gun company positioned ten miles behind the lines. In July 1917 he was moved to be second-in-command at battalion headquarters, where he stayed for the remainder of the war, despite toying with the idea of moving to a tank unit or the Flying Corps. In early autumn 1918 Churchill offered him the role of military liaison officer at the Ministry of Munitions, but Sinclair declined the offer, fearing that his fellow officers would regard it as a soft posting and feeling, once again, that his duty required him to remain in France.

With the announcement of the armistice on 11 November 1918, Sinclair was finally able to turn his attention to his own political future and, at Churchill's request, was quickly released from his military duties. Churchill had consistently held out the prospect of a constituency being found for Sinclair, as long as he agreed to stand as a Coalition Liberal in support of Lloyd George. Sinclair was keen to run in the 1918 election but, despite his and Churchill's best efforts, he failed to find an appropriate seat at short notice and travelled instead to assist Churchill at Dundee. When the coalition won a landslide victory Churchill was appointed to the War Office by Lloyd George, and Sinclair went with his mentor to be Churchill's personal military secretary.

1915

The opening of 1915 found Sinclair serving on the Western Front with the 2nd Life Guards. Churchill was entering his seventh year as a Liberal Cabinet minister – his fourth as First Lord of the Admiralty – and was beginning to undertake detailed planning for the ill-fated Dardanelles campaign.

[7] Gilbert, *Winston S. Churchill, Companion Volume IV*, Part 1, p. 101.

Sir Archibald Sinclair to Winston S. Churchill
25th January 1915

My dear Winston,

This is just one of a few scribbled lines written from the wilderness of Flanders to prepare the way before me on my return to the blessed oasis of London – the only oasis, it seems to me, in a world wide wilderness. I said I would send you one, which is my only if inadequate apology for inflicting it on you.

Nothing attempted, nothing done! But I am going to get another bit of leave unless the gods dispose on the 3rd February. So I shall look you up soon after. It will really require much bracing of the nerves to leave this safe and restful abode for London and the R.A.C.[8] (where I intend to fix my headquarters, so close to the War Office & Admiralty) in view of the recent Zeppelin trail trip.[9] I had hoped when I read the earlier accounts that they might pass over the Riviera or the Lengadime on their return journey – unhealthy localities for Zeps just now! Hope they'll get hit next time. The chief danger to London seems to me to lie in their uselessness to the Germans. As they are no good on the battlefield they won't mind risking them, costly as they are and long as they take to replace.

Archie

In early 1915 Churchill paid a short visit to inspect the British front line in Flanders. His enduring belief in the chivalry and gallantry of war are evident in the note he hastily scribbled to Sinclair on his return to London. Churchill continued to show an interest in sponsoring Sinclair's budding political career by offering to use his influence to find Sinclair a promising seat.

Winston S. Churchill to Sir Archibald Sinclair
Admiralty, Whitehall
3rd February 1915

Archie my dear,

I was so sorry to miss you on my flying visit. But 'Plugstreet',[10] Hill 63, Vermelles and Cuinchy, all of which I did thoroughly, occupied every moment of daylight; and after dusk I had much business to attend to.

Good luck to you in the trenches this spell. I wish I could share it with you. My thoughts are often with the firing line and the gallant life they lead. Afterwards come over here and stay with us; and I will fix up a constituency for you. Write and let me know how you get on.

[8] Royal Automobile Club, Pall Mall.

[9] 1915 was known as the 'year of the Zeppelin' with a total of nineteen raids on the UK.

[10] Ploegsteert – a Belgian village very near the front line which became a maze of soldiers' billets, dugouts and canteens; the 6th Battalion of the Royal Scots Fusiliers established their HQ there during 1915.

Next time I come I must try to see the cavalry section of the front.

Yours ever
W

Sinclair's patience with the life of a cavalryman in the trench warfare of Flanders was beginning to pale. Sinclair had been flying his own private plane since 1913 and with the emergence of the Royal Flying Corps, was attracted to the glamour of life in the air.

Sir Archibald Sinclair to Winston S. Churchill
17th February 1915

Winston,

I am an utter fraud. I've never been near the trenches or even left the peaceful inglorious seclusion of this one-housed village. They only took up about two-thirds of the regiment in motor buses while the 2nd in command of the regiment from each squadron was left behind to look after the horses and the remainder of the men. It was really the last straw. To be kept away from London to go to live in a ditch for ten days was bad enough but to be left behind in this backwater of desolation was the limit. They had great luck in the weather, too, were left alone by the Germans, had no shelling at all and spent the second half of the time in reserve in Ypres, sight-seeing and looting.

What an interesting time you must have had out here. Of course I had no idea until I got your letter that you had been. It is characteristic of life in this part that even you might live for a month within five miles of the place before one got to know about it!

However, I am getting a little tired of 'work' out here, our wounded at Windsor are clamouring to return and I think the hour is propitious for transferring to the Flying Corps as soon as – but not before – I get my leave paper for next weekend signed. I'm really going to tackle the Colonel seriously about it. I went in to see Col. Sykes[11] the other day and he was exceedingly kind and promised to put my application through as quickly as possible in spite of the long waiting list they have.

I hope to be in London on Wednesday or Thursday, probably the latter but will 'phone you immediately. Am in the middle of your splendidly spirited, defiant and determined speech.[12]

Archie

---

[11] Colonel Frederick Hugh Sykes (1877–1954): Chief of Staff, Royal Flying Corps, 1914–16; air commander for the Dardanelles campaign; Assistant Adjutant-General, War Office 1916–17; Chief of Staff, Royal Air Force 1918–19; Controller of Civil Aviation 1919–22; Conservative MP, Sheffield Hallam 1922–28, Central Nottingham 1940–45; Chairman British Broadcasting Board 1923–27; Governor of Bombay 1928–33.

[12] Churchill's speech to the House of Commons on 15 February 1915 on the British Navy's command of

Between February and June, Sinclair transferred from the Life Guards to work as aide-de-camp to Churchill's former colleague and friend Jack Seely, commander of the Canadian Cavalry Brigade.[13] Seely had been Liberal Secretary for War until sacked by Asquith for mishandling the Curragh mutiny. Churchill, in the mean time, had been moved from the Admiralty to the Chancellorship of the Duchy of Lancaster on 26 May as part of the price the Conservatives demanded for joining the new coalition Government under Asquith. Many at Westminster held Churchill responsible for the failure of the initial phase of the landings on the Gallipoli peninsula in March. Sinclair was not supportive of the new Government's appointments.

Sir Archibald Sinclair to Winston S. Churchill
3rd June 1915

My dear Winston,

I have been thinking so much and so anxiously about you lately that I have hesitated to put pen to paper lest it should cover innumerable sheets to your intense boredom and to the detriment of my little job here.

What an appalling blunder this 'National Government' is![14] Bring in Balfour,[15] Austen,[16] Carson,[17] F.E.[18] if you will but why half a dozen others of less ability and vastly less experience than those they displace? With regard to the amazing decision

the sea, during which Churchill referred to two British naval victories: the Falklands (8 December 1914) and Dogger Bank (24 January 1915).

[13] In early June 1915 Seely wrote to Churchill applauding Sinclair's performance in battle: 'At the most critical time, when I was in command of a section of the line, committed to the attack in co-operation with the people on my right and left, with a big force of artillery against us, and suffering heavy casualties, my brigade major was taken away, and I appointed Archie to act. Quite new to the technical part of the business, he rose to the occasion in the most astonishing way. Soon passed the methods of communication, and issuing of orders, and at the right moment went up to the front line; and right along it, not a particularly pleasant job in a newly captured position, straightening things out and encouraging everyone. When the stress was over he slept for 18 hours at a stretch, and is now very fit. I promise you to take care of him as he deserves, and I cannot put it higher.' Quoted in letter from Jack Seely (later Lord Mottistone) dated 7 June 1915, held at Churchill College Cambridge (Ref. CHAR 2/67/4).

[14] On 15 May Fisher, the First Sea Lord, resigned in opposition to the Dardanelles campaign, having decided that he could no longer work effectively with Churchill. Bonar Law picked up rumours of the resignation and told Lloyd George that this development, combined with the munitions 'shell scandal', meant that the Opposition would push for a vote of confidence if the government were not fundamentally restructured. During May 17–22 Asquith buckled under the pressure from senior Liberal colleagues, led by Lloyd George, and agreed to form a coalition government with Bonar Law's Conservatives.

[15] Arthur James Balfour, 1st Earl of Balfour (1848–1930): Conservative MP from 1874 and Leader of the Conservative Party 1902–11; Prime Minister 1902–05; First Lord of the Admiralty 1915-16; Foreign Secretary 1916–19; Lord President of the Council 1919–22 and 1925–29.

[16] Sir Joseph Austen Chamberlain (1863–1937): son of Birmingham mayor and Liberal Unionist leader Joseph Chamberlain, older half-brother of Neville Chamberlain; elected as Liberal Unionist MP 1892; Chancellor of the Exchequer 1903–05; Secretary of State for India 1915–17, resigned over mismanagement of the Mesopotamia campaign; rejoined War Cabinet 1918; Chancellor of the Exchequer 1919–21; Lord Privy Seal and Leader of the Conservative Parliamentary Party 1921–22, resigned after

to remove both the leads of that Department which has been most successful in the conduct of its share in the war – certainly the most important Department of all and the only one which has achieved a measure of success which has really exceeded everyone's expectations and astounded the world. I may be biased, I am certainly ignorant of the circumstances, but I am honestly bewildered. But the sacrifice of Lord Haldane[19] is another amazing concession to ignorant popular clamour and the petty intrigues of a few mud-slinging, self-advertising, soulless journalists and newspaper proprietors.

Often you have told me that the papers are of no account – that you pay no heed to what they say, but now Harmsworth[20] seems to be King of England: he makes Cabinets, appoints ministers, even creates new offices: decides what minister is to go, and who may stay. For weeks he is permitted to publish information forbidden to other newspapers, to conduct an agitation for national service by methods which involve a direct incitement to eligible men not to have regard to K's[21] appeal if they are married or above a certain age (vide Daily Mail) and finally the 'authorities' only manage to screw up their courage sufficiently to bell this wild cat of English journalism by the scandalized protests of the French. Rome when in peril submitted to the absolute will of a dictator. We still cling to our constitutional forms but the ultimate repository of power is apparently Harmsworth.

But perhaps you could explain it to me. But aren't you too a little surprised? But I have much comfort in knowing you are still in the Cabinet. I was so much afraid you would yield to the temptation to chuck it altogether and come out here. But it was stupid of me to think you would do anything so unwise and unpatriotic though you used to say yourself that you would.

Carlton Club meeting in October 1922 voted to end the Coalition; Secretary of State for Foreign Affairs 1924–29; First Lord of the Admiralty 1931.

[17] Edward Henry Carson (1854–1935): Irish Unionist leader; Attorney General, 1915; First Lord of the Admiralty, 1916–17; member of War Cabinet, 1917–18; created Lord of Appeal, 1921.

[18] Frederick Edwin ('F.E.') Smith (1874–1930): Solicitor General, 1915; Attorney General, 1915–19; Lord Chancellor, 1919–22; Secretary for India, 1924–28; Created Baron Birkenhead, 1919, Viscount, 1921, Earl, 1922.

[19] Richard Burdon Haldane, Viscount Haldane of Cloan (1856–1928): Liberal MP for Haddingtonshire 1885–1911; Secretary of State for War 1905–12; ennobled 1911; Lord Chancellor 1912–15; dismissed by Asquith at Conservative insistence when the coalition government was formed in May 1915, following a press campaign to smear him as pro-German – in large part because of his taste for German philosophers; joined the Labour Party and became Lord Chancellor again in 1924, and leader of the Labour peers until his death in 1928.

[20] Alfred Harmsworth, Viscount Northcliffe (1865–1922): founded *Daily Mail* in 1896, *Daily Mirror* in 1903; created Baron Northcliffe in 1905, the same year in which he purchased the *Observer*; in 1908 secured control of *The Times*; his papers, particularly the *Daily Mail*, were instrumental in exposing the army's shell shortage and in campaigning for the creation of a separate Ministry of Munitions; headed the British war mission to the United States in 1917; ennobled 1918.

[21] Herbert Kitchener, 1st Earl Kitchener (1850–1916): field marshal; Secretary of State for War, 1914–16, during which he organised manpower on a vast scale (the 'Kitchener armies').

But enough of my un-informed and perhaps rather impertinent reflections: they must bore you. We haven't been doing very much yet. We had 3 or 4 days in the trenches and lost rather heavily, making some yards of ground in the direction of La Barsee at a pace which would have made a snail rock with laughter. Our Brigade Major went sick and the General was good enough to let me try my amateurish hand. Luckily I had skilled technical assistance from the Staff Captain and as no great demands were made upon me, no disaster resulted. The General was splendid – mostly refreshingly unorthodox. The men are devoted to him and greatly appreciated his rather too frequent visits to the trenches. It is a very great thing that everyone in the brigade knows about our general – that however tight a hole we may be in, he will be there and he will be cool and collected if no one else is.

Please give my warmest respects to Mrs. Churchill[22] and love to Eddy[23] & Masterton[24] – I hope they are still with you. I do so much hope that you will find time to drop me a short line.

Yours ever,
Archie

Churchill wrote to Sinclair sharing his dissatisfaction with the new Cabinet position and his puzzlement at Fisher's resignation from the Admiralty, which was partly responsible for forcing Asquith to form a coalition with Bonar Law. In one of his less prescient statements Churchill assured Sinclair that all was finished between him and Lloyd George.

Winston S. Churchill to Sir Archibald Sinclair
Duchy of Lancaster Office
9th June 1915
Very Private

My dear Archie,

It was very nice to get your letter. One must try to bear misfortune with a smile. You might look at a speech I made at Dundee – which is the best that is in me.[25] But the hour is bitter: and idleness – torture. Here I am in a fat sinecure very well received and treated by the new Cabinet who have adopted my policy and taken all the steps that I was pressing for and more. From a political standpoint the situation

[22] Clementine Ogilvy Churchill (née Hozier), Baroness Spencer-Churchill (1885–1977): married Churchill on 12 September 1908; provided invaluable, though far from uncritical, support to her husband; remained a life-long Liberal even after her husband returned to the Conservative Party in 1924.

[23] Eddie (Eddy) Marsh (1872–1953): Churchill's private secretary from December 1905 – November 1915; became private secretary to Asquith when Churchill left to fight in France.

[24] James Masterton-Smith (1878–1938): Private Secretary to the First Lord of the Admiralty 1910–17.

[25] On 5 June Churchill delivered a speech in his Dundee constituency. Ostensibly a review of the war, in effect this was his first public statement defending his position following his demotion from the Admiralty to be Chancellor of the Duchy of Lancaster following the formation of the Coalition in May 1915.

is very favourable. I thought it my duty to stand by the National Government at the outset, and especially until the grave decisions about the Dardanelles have been taken. But now all that is settled and I cannot endure sitting here to wait for a turn of the political wind. I do not want office, but only war direction: that perhaps never again. Everything else – not that. At least so I feel in my evil moments. Those who live by the sword –

Fisher[26] is a mystery. Was it a nervous breakdown or a coup d'etat? Or more likely than either both combined. And synchronising with this Lloyd George[27] striking out for power in alliance with Northcliffe:[28] and Asquith[29] affectionate but weak and indolent and seeking self-preservation at all costs.

I am profoundly unsettled: and cannot use my gift. Of that last I have no doubts. I do not feel that my judgements have been falsified, or that the determined pursuance of my policy through all the necessary risks was wrong. I would do it all again, if the circumstances were repeated. But I am faced with the problem of living through days of 24 hours each: and averting my mind from the intricate business I had in hand – which was my life. I do not think I can go on here.

I am not yet decided what to do or which way to turn. When I see clear again I will write to you.

I have felt very anxious about you and Jack[30] in the trenches and have watched the lists of casualties in the Canadian Mounted Brigade. I am so glad you have done so well. He had a bad time to go through, but now at any rate he has a good clean-cut job.

Take care of yourself and don't let him run unnecessary risks. A wise and thrifty use of one's slender store of luck is one of the aptitudes of a modern Brigadier.

The political grouping and situation gives me now I think a clear run after a few years. But I do not feel at all attracted by our political prospect and am repelled by the political game. Between me and Ll G tout est fini.[31]

---

[26] John Arbuthnot 'Jackie' Fisher, Admiral of the Fleet Lord Fisher (1841–1920): entered Royal Navy in 1854, rising to Rear-Admiral in 1890; held a succession of senior positions before becoming First Sea Lord (1904–10); brought out of retirement by Churchill to become First Sea Lord again in 1914, but quarrelled with Churchill over the Dardanelles operation and resigned in May 1915.

[27] David Lloyd George, 1st Earl Lloyd George of Dwyfor (1863–1945): Liberal MP for Caernarvon Boroughs 1890–1945; President of the Board of Trade 1905–08; Chancellor of the Exchequer 1908–15; Minister of Munitions 1915–16; Secretary of State for War 1916; Prime Minister 1916–22; Leader of the Liberal Party 1926–31; ennobled 1945.

[28] Alfred Harmsworth, Viscount Northcliffe – see n20.

[29] Herbert Henry Asquith, Earl of Oxford and Asquith (1874–1928): Liberal MP for East Fife 1886–1918, Paisley 1920–24; Home Secretary 1892–95; Chancellor of the Exchequer 1905–09; Prime Minister 1909–16; Leader of the Liberal Party 1909–26; created Earl of Oxford and Asquith 1925.

[30] John Edward Bernard ('Galloper Jack') Seely, Baron Mottistone (1868–1947): a Unionist free trader who followed Churchill in crossing the floor of the House of Commons to join the Liberals in 1904; Secretary of State for War, 1912–14, resigned over the handling of a potential mutiny of senior army officers at the Curragh in July 1914; commanded Canadian mounted brigade 1915–16; Under-Secretary of State to Churchill, Ministry of Munitions and Deputy Minister of Munitions, 1918; Secretary of State for Air, 1919; ennobled 1933.

I want a breath of fresh air. God bless you.

Yours always,
W

PS. I was so glad you have been acting Brigade Major. I hope you will be able to keep this work.

Sir Archibald Sinclair to Winston S. Churchill
26th July 1915
Private

My dear Winston,

When I got a message from the 'ADC to the GOC in C, GHQ' (the language of militarism!) to be at St Omer at 12.30pm the following day, I know it could be for one of only two reasons. Either Sir John[32] wished to consult me on the strategical situation or you were coming out and had angelically sent for me to meet with you: instinctively, I guessed it was the latter. Agog with excitement at the thought of seeing you again, my brain whirling with messages from the General (Seely), I rushed off in a car which I had wheedled out of the Canadian Division (ours having long ago been taken from us) to a hairdresser in St Omer where so much hair was removed that what with my close cropped skull and khaki uniform I presented what the newspapers call 'quite a soldier-like appearance'. And then after all this when I finally entered the den very nearly punctually at the hour named, I found Watt, the only lion then at home, who told me you weren't coming after all and who politely intimated that I could sit and talk to him for a bit of the lunch with Sir John and General Lambton[33] who would probably be speechless with rage.

As ill-luck would have it Sir J. had apparently arranged a series of inspections etc for that day and when he got your message about your proposed visit, the whole programme had been altered, and your telegram that morning hadn't arrived in time to catch him before he left St Omer. At about one o'clock, General Lambton strode into the room and Sir J. appeared in the doorway and there followed such a storm of wrath that I quailed unnoticed in a corner of the room. Watt hurried off to order lunch muttering something about the importance of quickly 'feeding the brute' under these circumstances, and soon afterwards Sir J. returned full of smiles, damning the politicians and saying we must forget our sorrows in lunch and revive sweet memories of the 'Enchantress' and the 'Swift'.[34]

[31] Within six weeks Churchill was prepared to see a future working alongside Lloyd George – see letter dated 30 July 1915.

[32] Field Marshal Sir John Denton Pinkstone French, Earl of Ypres (1852–1925): Commander of the British Expeditionary Force deployed to Europe in the opening days of the war; relieved of his command in December 1915; Commander British Home Forces 1915–18 (in which position he dealt with the Easter Rising in Ireland in 1916); Lord Lieutenant of Ireland 1918–21; ennobled 1922.

[33] Sir William Lambton (1863–1936): Military Secretary to Sir John French, Commander-in-Chief, British Expeditionary Force, France 1914–15; Commander, 4th Division 1915–17; retired 1920.

Altogether it turned out to be a very pleasant and most interesting lunch and Sir J. was quite expansive. He hinted that the principal subject of conversation might have made your visit rather less of a pleasure than it would otherwise have been but added 'but of course I should have loved to see Winston again'.

Your letter gave me much to think about but mine is more likely to be opened than yours so I won't comment. I hadn't shown it even to the General but as you assumed in your letter to him that I had done so, we exchanged letters and I was thrilled to see that your star was rising again.

Dundee was splendid[35] – it was a tonic to the jangled nerves of the millions who look out upon the world through the distorted spectacles of Northcliffe and his minions.

But what of the outlook at home? If the 'gentleman' whose interest in wireless telegraphy[36] so nearly brought him to disaster and who owed so much to you, has played you false at this crisis no wonder you say 'tout est fini'. I hope the Tories get him.[37] You speak of new groupings, fresh concentrations. But you, you still remain with the Armies of the Left? You won't go over to the right where the leaders are old, irresolute and purposeless, their objects short-sighted and selfish, and the rank and file apathetic, inert and reactionary? You will stay and direct the forces that mean to go forward so that when the great struggle of nations is finished, the victory shall be not merely that of a nation but that of humanity, progress and democracy – not merely that of one people over another so that one extends its boundaries and the other loses territory, but a victory of right and enlightenment over wrong, militarism and unscrupulous imperialism.

You told me you would write when you saw your way clearer but after all it is perhaps unwise to put too much in a letter which is subject to censorship. Is it true that you are going for a long voyage for a holiday? I am rather hoping to get a bit of leave during August but I've not yet approached the General. Three months in the country is supposed to entitle one to make the request. Would there be any chance of seeing you then?

If you find time to write again do tell me something about the Chancellorship of the Duchy – what your official duties are etc. Lucky it has great advantages from the point of view of 'war direction'? Your hands are free and you can see the war as a whole without being compelled – at any rate officially – to adopt the view of the War Office, the Admiralty, the Colonial Office or the India Office. And I am wondering, too, where you are living: please let me know your address.

---

[34] The *Enchantress* and the *Swift* were Admiralty yachts that Churchill made great use of during his tenure as First Lord.

[35] A reference to Churchill's speech at Dundee on 5 June – see letter dated 9 June 1915.

[36] Lloyd George – a reference to the Marconi share scandal of 1912.

[37] Sinclair was to change his mind about Lloyd George and, in due course, to come to like and respect him. Sinclair was first elected to parliament in 1922 as a Lloyd George 'National Liberal' (rather than an Asquithian Liberal) and was to serve Lloyd George as Chief Whip. It was Lloyd George who proposed Sinclair for the parliamentary party leadership in 1935.

Would you care to go up to Caithness for part of your holidays to shoot and fish for a bit? I suppose you might think it rather far away in these strenuous times but it would do you a power of good for a week or two.

Are Eddy and Masterton still with you? I do hope you haven't had to part with either of them. Give them my love if they are with you.

The General gives me many messages for you. I believe he very kindly wrote you about me when I was superseded as Brigade-Major. Of course it is always rather a blow to go down lower but I suppose it was really ridiculous to think for a moment that I could be confirmed in an appointment for which I had no training whatever and which is generally given to men of 35 and 40 and often older than that with great experience and always with a Staff College training ...

The General also wants me to tell you that he has now been in the trenches 200 days and that we have been in now just one month on end. He himself goes in every day. I know you would agree with me that he ought not to expose himself as much as he does but it is a good fault as faults go and the trenches here are as safe as Piccadilly. If this is really the melting pot into which the destinies of European nations have been flung, we are in a funny little cool corner where the fuel consumption averages only about one man a day per regiment in the trenches – we have two regiments in and one out.

The General also wishes you to know that his interest in the political situation is unflagging and sends you an expression of his bitter hostility to and exasperation with the Northcliffe Press. With unabated love of paradox, he declares that while we are spending £1,000,000,000 a year we should spend an extra £10,000,000 on social reform, thus making a new heaven and a new earth in England at a time when all purse strings are open and if he is wounded, he is coming home to advocate this policy.

I am truly grateful to you for getting me this job. It has been a great experience and enables one to see the war in much truer perspective. The perpetual imminence of danger, and the constant discomfort of regimental life in billets behind the line, undoubtedly distorts the vision of regimental officers ... Later on I shall hope to get back either to my own or to an infantry regiment and in the meantime have quite grown accustomed to the idea of an interminable war and to this topsy turvey life in which it appears that Englishmen were created to kill Germans and Germans to kill Englishmen and those who do well are the sheep and those who don't are the goats (the latter is true anyway.)

Well, you will have to read this effusion (if you read it all) like a calendar, a page a day as spare time permits. I hate settling down to write but when I do my pen just runs on and after all you needn't read it.

Please congratulate Miss Stanley and Mr. Montagu[38] from me if you see them.[39] I thought of writing to Miss Stanley because she is so very charming and interesting

[38] Edwin Samuel Montagu (1879–1924): Liberal MP for Cambridgeshire Chesterton 1906–18, Cambridgeshire 1918–22; Private Secretary to Asquith 1906–10; Chancellor of the Duchy of Lancaster

and I do so sincerely wish her good luck. But I wasn't quite certain if she would remember who I was and I'm not quite sure that I like the idea of her marrying Mr. Montagu: he has always been very nice to me but isn't he ugly and not so brilliantly attractive either.

Please give my warmest regards to Mrs. Winston. I do hope I shall be able to see you both again soon.

Yrs ever,
Archie S

By the end of July Churchill was beginning to hope that he could play a part in pulling the Dardanelles campaign back to a successful conclusion. He was also feeling very pessimistic about the capabilities of the new cabinet. Churchill also looked ahead to rejoining his regiment and playing a front-line role in the war.

Winston S. Churchill to Sir Archibald Sinclair
Duchy of Lancaster Office, Lancaster Place, Strand, W.C.
30th July 1915
Private

My dear Archie,

It was very nice to get your letter & I wish you would write to me more often.

I have been watching over the fortunes of the Dardanelles enterprise which was so seriously jeopardised by the late upset;[40] & I have succeeded by hard and continual fighting in getting very large forces and abundant supplies directed upon that vital point. I now await results. The painful part of the situation is that it takes so long to get the necessary action taken & so many people have to be persuaded that the enemy has time to bring up reinforcements from all parts of his Empire so that what was originally sufficient for victory may now be insufficient. Still I am hopeful – though anxious. Also I have now much time on my hands and can feel thoroughly every twinge. It is a horrible experience remaining here in the midst of things, knowing everything, waiting passionately conscious of capacity for service, yet paralysed nearly always. It is

1915–16; Minister of Munitions 1916; Secretary of State for India 1917–22; in 1919 he was responsible for the Government of India Act, which provided India with wide powers of self-government.

[39] Venetia Stanley, Asquith's close confidant, had recently announced her surprise engagement to Asquith's friend, the Liberal MP Edwin Montagu. Asquith was very badly affected by this news, which occurred at the same time as the crisis participated by Fisher's resignation.

[40] The attack and landings on the Gallipoli peninsula commenced on 25 April 1915. Progress had not been as planned and by early July the War Cabinet were considering sending further divisions to supplement the ground troops. Churchill had been badgering Asquith to send him to Gallipoli to investigate the situation. Bonar Law and Carson opposed Churchill's mission and prevented him from going. From mid-July onwards the British and Allied troops suffered heavy bombardment from the Turkish guns and lost some ground to a Turkish offensive.

like being in a cataleptic trance while all you value is being hazarded. But I have managed to bear it so far. It will comfort my soul to come out for a few months and serve with my regiment, & my mind turns over and over in its malaise to that. But till our victory is made at the Dardanelles my part is plainly here.

This government of able men and opposed parties does not develop any of the qualities required for war. The personal and party elements neutralise each other. There are many opinions, much politeness, unlimited decorum but little action. The predisposition towards the negative is very marked. Meanwhile, there are restless undercurrents, which I watch attentively without joining.

L.G. is necessary to the State. He has the war-making quality. I do not intend to allow any personal feelings to prevent my working with him. But distrust based on experience is a terrible barrier.

It is strange to look back on a year ago and the tremendous exertions of that cataclysm. Now slaughter has become commonplace and destruction the order of the day. My part in events is woefully shrunken. But I still think I shall have work to do – though not for many months. The war must be fought to the bitter end. Any half measured peace would only be a truce. We must at all costs have a decisive result. We are not doing all we should. Would you believe it – I pass my days painting. It keeps my mind at peace. These people here are mostly played out, and no new figures appear on the scene.

You, at least, [engaged] in honourable definite real, though circumscribed, activities may feel content. You have done so well. If you survive you will always look back upon these months as the true and glorious period of your life, & I trust they may also prove to be in the history of the country.

I have a small farmhouse beautifully placed in Surrey.[41] Do come please – & let me know the earliest moment. Don't think of coming to England without warning me. Letters will find me here at 21 Arlington Steet.[42]

Nellie[43] pursues her training in the hardest of schools – the London Hospital, & is on the verge of being made a regular military staff nurse duly paid £20 a year & board and lodging. Clemmie is very well and busy organising Y.M.C.A. huts for munitions workers.

Do not let my letters fall into the hands of the Germans when they storm your trenches. The swine will rejoice. You can always write through Freddie Guest[44] who takes this. It is better to burn letters.

Always your friend,
W.

[41] Hoe Farm, Godalming, Surrey, a Tudor farmhouse that had been converted into a country residence by Edwin Lutyens. Rented by Churchill for the summers of 1915 and 1916. It was here that he first took up painting.

[42] Churchill's residence during June and July 1915 – just off Piccadilly, this was the London home of his cousin, the 2nd Baron Wimborne.

[43] Nellie Hozier (1888–1957): Clementine Churchill's sister.

[44] Frederick Edward Guest (1875–1937): cousin of Churchill's and close political friend; Liberal MP,

Sir Archibald Sinclair to Winston S. Churchill
8th August 1915

My dear Winston,

I was so delighted to get your letter and hasten to answer since you so request ...

I think much of you at this tremendous crisis[45] and each morning as I wake up I think 'Is it to-day?' I know what great things depend for you upon its solution and I realise if only imperfectly how fatal our success would be in every respect, military, diplomatic, economic, to the hopes and plans of Germany. At such a time conventional phrases of hope and confidence seem out of place: perhaps in days to come we shall talk it all out in the Turkish Bath at the R.A.C.[46] and laugh over our hopes and fears of which the equilibrium now weighs me down with anxiousness, and over your skilful, Herculean efforts to overcome the colossal moment of inertia of the National Cabinet!

But above all things, don't come out here. You would be wasted, your position would be hopelessly anomalous and difficult, you would see so much of which you would strongly disapprove and which you would be powerless to alter, your seniors in rank would not trouble to exercise much politeness or unlimited decorum in dealing with you here and on the contrary there would be a tendency to show you that out here a Privy Councillor and an ex-Minister is no better than any other Major ... The Army is a jealous Army!

On the other hand at anytime your influence may decide a Cabinet Council on some vital question of policy. No orator has at the present time a greater hold on large sections of public opinion. Your value to the country out here is incomparably smaller than your value in England.

As I write there is a great battle in progress at Ypres and I keep listening to the heavy reverberations of the guns. Distant guns sound even more terrible and menacing than when they are fairly near.

I understand from Freddy [Guest] that you have made it up with L.G. and this your letter more or less confirms. Your generous appreciation that he is necessary to the State is obviously true and for the present your 'working agreement' is evidently patriotic and necessary.

Freddy tells me that he has your tacit support in his conscription campaign: if so, why not come out strong? Personally I am hostile, because if there are figures which prove it necessary, I don't know them. But you have the means of judging and if you think it necessary, as Freddy says, what is exactly your attitude?

1910–22, 1923–29; Conservative MP, 1931–37; Chief Whip, Coalition Liberals, 1916–21; during the 1930s Guest was one of the small band of Churchill supporters in the House of Commons.

[45] On 6 August 1915 further landings at Suvla on the Gallipoli peninsula took place in an attempt to achieve a flanking advantage. Unfortunately this action did not achieve the desired breakthrough and by mid-August it was clear that stalemate persisted.

[46] The Royal Automobile Club, Pall Mall.

What of the general situation? It seems to me that there is much to be thankful for – that the Russians evacuated Warsaw before it was too late, that their armies are still in being, great formidable masses of men which only require guns and munitions to be transformed into unconquerable armies, that the Germans are losing men at the rate of between 200,000 and 300,000 a month and above all for the wind which blows constantly from the West. Please congratulate Miss Hozier from me on her splendid pluck and perseverance in sticking to the London hospital until she becomes a real paid nurse. It really is inspiring to think of people like her putting their shoulders to the wheel and helping to shove.

You never told me if Eddy and Masterton were still with you.

Ever yr devoted
Archie S

By late September Churchill was returning to consider how to best assist Sinclair in entering Parliament at the next election (which many observers felt was likely sooner rather than later due to strains between Asquith and the Tory leadership).

Winston S. Churchill to Sir Archibald Sinclair
Duchy of Lancaster Office
28th September 1915

My dear Archie,

I will speak to the PM and to Gulland[47] about Stirling Burghs.[48] It would suit you admirably and I am all for it. You would march with Dundee[49] and I could come and help you. During the war you would get in without difficulty, if an opportunity arose. But the whole field of politics is obscured and no issues define themselves.

I am relieved to learn you are not in the forefront of this battle.[50] The tactical opening seems good and promising: but whether strategic alterations will be effected is not yet clear.

These events and the Bulgarian and Balkan situations make it very difficult to see plainly. All the reactions are entangled. I never saw things so puzzling – and yet so cogent. In a few days it will be easier to decide – then – perhaps too late. The course of events has drifted off the lines on which I would like to have seen them kept.

---

47 John William Gulland (1864–1920): Liberal Chief Whip 1915–16.

48 One of a number of seats that Churchill was keen on Sinclair fighting (Perth being another) at the end of the war. Eventually Sinclair decided not to stand in the 1918 election and waited until 1922, when he was elected at the first attempt to his home constituency of Caithness & Sutherland, a seat he held until 1945. In a nice twist Sinclair's grandson, John Thurso, won the seat for the Liberal Democrats in 1997 (although it had been held by Robert Maclennan for the SDP and then Liberal Democrats since 1981).

49 Churchill's parliamentary constituency until 1922.

50 The Battle of Loos, 25 September – 16 October 1915. 800 British officers and 15,000 men were killed. The Germans lost around 5,000 in total.

Naturally I have been thinking constantly of the possibility of escaping to simpler and more congenial tasks. But since we parted political events have laid hold of me, and I must abide their issues. Perhaps this new War Council of 8 of which I am to be a member may be an improvement. I feel bound to serve as asked unless or until convinced that my presence is useless. But I am resolved to see that all necessary measures are taken if I am to bear a defined share of these formidable responsibilities.

We spent the Sunday at Maxine's:[51] and we thought much of you and hoped all was well. She has returned to her barge in Flanders.[52] Diana[53] is much better and the Roentgen rays do not show any break.

I told Bendor[54] myself. He is very trustworthy. But all my plans are 'clouded with a doubt'. Presently we shall see clearly and then I shall know exactly what to do and where my duty leads me. I shall try very hard to do what is right.

My heart is all with the army now fighting so well against such difficulties, and also with our poor friends in the Dardanelles. So near and yet so far from results which would save months of slaughter.

Good fortune guard you. Love to Jack.
Yours always,
W

Sir Archibald Sinclair to Winston S. Churchill
23rd October 1915
France

My dear Winston,

I don't suppose you have any idea what an event is the arrival of a letter from you: you should see me pounce eagerly upon it or hear the general[55] say with a kind of deep purr which always signifies glad and profound satisfaction 'Ha! I've got a letter from Winston!'

Well, we've been marching a long, long way along the road of War since I wrote you last, and now a new vista comes into sight as the road bends towards the South East, but still no sign of that turning to Tipperary! At least recent events both in the

[51] Maxine Elliott (1868–1940): American actress and grande dame of late Edwardian and inter-war international society; lived at Maidenhead and Chateau de l'Horizon, Golfe Juan; Maxine Elliot was a stage name, although this was what her friends called her – her real name was Jessie Dermot.

[52] Maxine Elliot had, in 1914, organised a Belgian refugee relief barge which fed and clothed more than 350,000 refugees over the course of fifteen months.

[53] Diana Spencer Churchill (1909–63); Churchill's first child; married Conservative politician Duncan Sandys in 1935 (divorced 1960); served as an officer in the Women's Royal Navy Service in London 1941–45; suffered declining mental and physical health from 1953, and took her own life by an overdose of sleeping pills in 1963.

[54] Hugh Grosvenor (1879–1953): 2nd Duke of Westminster.

[55] Jack Seely – see n30.

Balkans and on the Western front furnish a tremendous vindication of those who have urged the vital importance of prompt and vigorous action in the only theatre of war where a definite decision was obtainable, and where if the decision were favourable we could find new and powerful allies: but the vision of our military pundits appears to have been blinded by mists of strategic formulae and generalizations; and the lessons of the battles of Arras and Ypres last year where the French and ourselves were on the defensive against overwhelming numbers and a predominant artillery, lessons repeated through various minor offensives culminating in the winter battle in the Champagne and Neuve Chapelle, seem to have been ignored and the delusion was still cherished that, given sufficient shells and artillery we could drive the Germans before us like sheep across the Rhine. Souchez and Festubert seem to have made no difference in their appreciation of the strategic situation and this pathetic and fantastic belief that some staggering development was possible on this Front no doubt prompted much of the unimaginative and ignorant criticism of the Dardanelles expedition.

So now people at home are depressed. They were told that it was only because the whole of the wretched quantity of munitions available was being sent to the Dardanelles that we failed to sweep the Germans out of France and Belgium and I am getting terribly depressed letters from home.

Moreover, although in the Army perfect confidence prevails, for we know that the great object is to disarm the German army, and that lots of Germans are being killed and otherwise disarmed in Russia and on this front, to say nothing of Serbia and Italy, and so although an offensive on this front seems to me a slow, stupid, expensive method of beating the Germans, given the necessary munitions it is bound to tell in the long run. But all this confidence will be undermined if we continue to read in the papers and hear from people who have been on leave of pessimism, vacillation and dissension in high places at home. I am so glad and thankful that you are still at home, Winston. I don't suppose that you are as oil on these troubled waters. Indeed I have heard something about some of your recent activities with the pen! But I know your influence makes for vigour and resolution and that you at least would not resign your seat in the Cabinet from petty reasons of pique or wounded pride. I don't wish to pre-judge Carson's resignation[56] or the circumstances of which one knows so little but when a lawyer resigns on a question of strategy, he would seem to be lacking either in patriotism or a sense of humour.

Of the strategic problems involved, I know nothing, but I do hope, if there is a reasonable chance of saving Serbia, that we shall risk everything in that endeavour. England, as the protector of small nations, has already in the case of Belgium given the enemy cause to mock. Are we truly powerless to save our loyal and gallant little ally in the South East. Here too we strike at a pestilent litter of Kings: here indeed is a War of Liberation: de l'audace, more de l'audace, toujours de l'audace! Let us hurl

[56] In fact Carson did not resign from the Coalition as Attorney-General until October 1916. Possibly at this stage he was threatening resignation, but if so it is not clear why.

at their feet a gage of battle – the throne of Greece! If there were a Danton now in England; a Carnot at the War Office, a Hode or a Moreau in the field! Heaven be praised for that we have you, Winston!

The best piece of news I have heard recently, is that I am going on leave on Saturday or Sunday so much that I have to tell you will keep till then. The Canadians are not quite such a happy band of fearless brothers as they were. Intrigue is eating deep into their efficiency, undermining their discipline, shaking their cohesion …

Since writing the above I have been having lunch and have seen the papers with the announcement of Miss Hozier's engagement, I shall write to her at once and offer my congratulations and most hearty good wishes though I don't know Colonel Romilly.[57]

I had a delightful letter from Eddy (Marsh) the other day with a capital story of poor Charlie Mills whom I hardly knew. I heard a characteristic anecdote of Foch which probably isn't true but may amuse you. After the gas battle at Ypres in April he is supposed to have wired to Joffre[58] – forgive my ignorance of genders etc: 'Mon droit est detourné, ma centre est enfonceé, ma gauche n'existe plus – J'attaque!'[59]

I do hope Diana is well again: please give her and Mrs. Churchill and Randolph[60] and Eddy my love.

Yrs ever,
Archie

Sir Archibald Sinclair to Winston S. Churchill
Undated – but written early November 1915

My dear Winston,

It is joyful news indeed, Winston, that you are really coming to see us, and the general is writing to Mrs. Churchill to ask her to come too either for Sunday night or, as we hope, for both Saturday and Sunday. As far as I can understand your message on a most indistinct telephone, I am to be outside the Admiralty at 5pm on

[57] Bertram Henry Samuel Romilly (1878–1940): Churchill's brother-in-law (married to Nellie Hozier, Churchill's wife's sister); soldier, served in Sudan, the Boer War, and France in the Great War.

[58] Joseph Jacques Cesaire Joffre (1852–1931): Chief of the French General Staff from 1911, Commander-in-Chief 1915–16, but blamed for the French Army's lack of preparation at Verdun and in December 1916 was appointed Marshal of France with only ceremonial duties.

[59] Ferdinand Foch (1851–1929), marshal of the French army (and in 1918 commander of the Allied armies) in fact sent the message during the first Battle of the Marne, in September 1914: 'Mon centre cêde, ma droite recule, situation excellente, j'attaque' ('My centre is giving way, my right is retreating, situation excellent, I am attacking').

[60] Randolph Frederick Edward Churchill (1911–68); Churchill's only son; Conservative MP, Preston 1940–45; intelligence officer in the Middle East and Yugoslavia during the war; author of several controversial books, including *The Rise and Fall of Sir Anthony Eden* (1959) and *The Fight for the Tory Leadership* (1964); his well-received historical study of Lord Derby (1960) convinced Churchill to give him permission to write his official biography, and by his death he had published two volumes: *Youth, 1874–1900* (1966) and *Young Statesman, 1901–1914* (1967).

Sunday next with my open car. Expect me therefore at that place and that hour but if I'm wrong or if you have to change your plans, will you please send me a wire to Masefield Park, Uckfield.

As regards the drink problem, I may remind you that we take our stand on the sacred principle of the liberty of the individual so don't be afraid of having to conform to the example of our supreme War Lord George![61]

Yours ever,
Archie

On 11 November a War Committee replaced the Dardanelles Committee and Churchill was not invited to join. It was apparent that the Gallipoli landings were a failure and the political tide was turning strongly toward evacuation. Being excluded from the inner councils of the War Committee was the final humiliation for Churchill and he resigned from the government. He made his resignation speech in the Commons on 15 November, where his reference to Gallipoli as a 'legitimate war gamble' was not well received. At that time it seemed that his political career was beyond repair. Churchill indicated in his resignation speech that he would be leaving England to serve on the Western Front. Sinclair welcomed this announcement and offered his services to help Churchill in the trenches.

Sir Archibald Sinclair to Winston S. Churchill
15th November 1915

My dear Winston,

I'm so glad that you have taken the plunge and that you are coming to join us out here. Some day when the situation permits of plain speech, and searching investigations, men will be bewildered at your treatment by the Pooh-bahs and some will say that the gods had decreed that the country should suffer a long and severe trial for its own good and had stopped the ears of our leaders to the voice of our wisest counsellor. You could never have endured to remain in 'well paid inactivity' and to watch the ship of state lumbering along with LG as its solitary bit of canvas and a whole shipload of ballast.

If brilliant projects inspired by your lonely imagination had not failed for want of speed and vigour in their execution you would now be directing the whole policy of the war (which might indeed be coming to an end!). But since the appeal is to the final and awful but certain arbitration of attrition, you have the knowledge

[61] In January 1915, the Chancellor of the Exchequer, David Lloyd George, launched a campaign against alcohol, claiming that Britain was 'fighting Germans, Austrians and Drink, and as far as I can see the greatest of these foes is Drink'. He persuaded leading national figures to take the pledge that they would not drink alcohol during the war; in April, for example, King George V promised that no alcohol would be consumed in the Royal household until the war was over.

that you struck the decisive blow of the war when you set in motion that Naval Machine which you have brought to such a pitch of power and efficiency as not even the British navy had known before your administration. What Englishman who has figured in this war so far threatens to eclipse your fame?[62]

Do write and tell me your plans. If there is a difficulty about a higher formation surely the command of a Kitchener battalion would be a better position than that of 2nd in command of a yeomanry regiment which in common with the rest of the cavalry can only work dismounted? Why not get a battalion – no-one could object to that on any grounds? A Scotch one as you are a Scotch member for the Scotch divisions of the King's armies (9th and 15th) have fairly eclipsed the others.

I know nothing whatever about infantry drill and organisation but I know a bit about conditions out here and if I could be of any service and if my General would spare me you know how proud and eager I would be to serve under you in any capacity.

Always your devoted friend,
Archie S.

1916

In January 1916 Churchill was appointed Colonel, in charge of the 6th Royal Scots Fusiliers, a battalion of approximately 30 officers and 700 men. On Churchill's request Archie Sinclair was released from the Canadian command to assist him in pulling the battalion together before it returned to the front line; Sinclair became Churchill's second-in-command. In early March Churchill briefly returned to the House of Commons while on leave and made an ill-judged speech which, to the incredulity of the House, finished by urging the reappointment of his nemesis, Fisher, to the Admiralty. On his return to the trenches, with Sinclair now on leave in London, Churchill reflected on his current position.

Winston S. Churchill to Sir Archibald Sinclair
6th Royal Scots Fusiliers
22nd March 1916

My dear Archie,

Bar a shrapnel which saluted McDavid[63] and I at almost 20 yards distance near left company Headquarters – no adventures. They shelled the town yesterday, &

[62] Lloyd George, though born in Manchester, was of course Welsh.
[63] Jock McDavid (1897–1972): a Lieutenant in the 6th Royal Scots Fusiliers.

the Norfolk Ave. extension today. Last night the bomb boy did no good. He is very sticky. I took him out myself to almost 20 yards beyond the outer listening post and descanted to him in the bed of the Warnave on the fascination of no man's land: but in the end he only got about 30 yards further than I took him. Today a sergeant and a private from Vancouver have arrived from Lipsett.[64] They are first class men. I have taken them around and explained everything, and they both go out tonight to hunt. I hope to get some real information out of them. Really I am surprised at the lack of enterprise and daring that these young officers show. It is so unusual to have to press superior officers. I have never come across it before. None of the younger men are for it. They all want to live forever.

Furse[65] and Trotter[66] both came around this morning and I took them in charge. They were very affable and appeared pleased with everything. Trotter is I think coming to dine tomorrow night to do a moonlight walk. I went over the ground last night very pleasantly and easily. The bullets have taken to falling in our courtyard on the way to the minor establishments. Checked regiment wounded in Lancs S Farm last night and a sentry in Burket sub 7 was killed this morning. Otherwise no damage.

I can almost hear you and Clemmie arriving by the most noble of arguments at the conclusion that I must inevitably stay here until the day of judgement.

NO NO – 'That were some love, but little policy'

I am not so lonely without you to grouse to as I had expected: nevertheless come back ere long, fattened, refreshed & exhilarated.

You might, I think, sidle artistically into your discourses with the P.M.[67] my natural reluctance to enter upon a course of political action which could lead me into increasing friction with his govt. Mind you write and tell me all about it. I am quite resolved what to do.[68]

Yours ever,
W

[64] Louis James Lipsett (1874–1918): Brigadier-General, attached to the Canadian Expeditionary Force; highly regarded by Churchill who described him to Beaverbrook as 'exceptional in his judgement and flair'.

[65] William Furse (1865–1953): Major-General commanding the 9th (Scottish) Division during 1916.

[66] Algernon Trotter (1870–1945): Lieutenant-Colonel, 2nd Life Guards, during 1916.

[67] H. H. Asquith.

[68] On 7 March 1915 Churchill made a disastrous speech in the Commons where he attracted widespread ridicule and incredulity for his demand that Lord Fisher be restored as First Sea Lord. He was urged by Asquith, at a private meeting on 8 March, to be less impulsive and to return to France. Churchill returned to the front on Monday 13 March but had already made his mind up that he wanted to quit military life and return to Westminster.

Winston S. Churchill to Sir Archibald Sinclair
6th Royal Scots Fusiliers – In the field
23rd March 1916

My dear Archie,

They have just finished giving us 40 shells of the fizz-bang variety this morning – 5 direct hits – only casualty Corporal Walls whose arm was broken in the new cook house. The traverse in the court-yard was hit directly and by many splinters. The orderly room, the store near it, the end of the barn, the staff latrine all got their dose. We tested the efficiency of our new defences by remaining at breakfast – all except the bomb boy who lurked in the dugout. He thinks too much.

The Canadian scouts went out all last night and report:
No listening posts and no enemy patrols
Trenches far more strongly built than ours
Sentries awake and looking out all night
They fire back when we fire as a general rule
Ground north of the river – very bare and unsuitable.

Canadians go out again tonight south of the river. The regimental scouting system must be thoroughly reorganised. These Canadians are a different breed of animal altogether.

The young artillery officer – Nicolls, has been much tormented by me, and shows abysmal ignorance under examination. He did not know what 'calibre' meant, or what weight of shell his guns fired, or that shrapnel bullets travel forward after the burst. He thinks he will go with the flying corps. But I have deprecated the squandering of so much accumulated expert knowledge. Cigars have arrived.

Yours always,
W

PS The working parties on the new aid post and on the so called 'slits' were caught by 2 salvoes of crumps. Altogether 8 casualities today – 4 Fusiliers. This evening a beautiful pink coloured shrapnel arrived. He is the first of his kind.

Winston S. Churchill to Sir Archibald Sinclair
6th R.S.F. – In the field
24th March 1916

Archie,

Deep snow still falling and thawing. Trench conditions damnable for the men: no shelling possible.

The Canadians made further scoutings last night. They say the line is very strongly held and many sections are kept awake by order. The enemy are sure of themselves, do not require to go out in front. They court an attack. The wire is weaker in front of us than in front of Lipsett, but the sentries much more numerous and the watch more thorough. The Canadians also declare that there are a number of slits diagonally cut all along the enemy's trenches on the front which look like sally ports. They have never seen anything like this elsewhere. We are studying this attentively as you may imagine.

Altogether the prospects of our doing any good here are very small. The ground is most unpromising – the river line is the only possible approach and that is a bad one. I will tell you the only sort of plan that would have a chance when you come back. But the general outlook is strongly negative.

I have proposed to Brigade the enclosed reorganisation of the scouting, sniping and sentries.

Dixon[69] arrived this morning to see our blessed McD.[70] And complained of 4 or 500 shells directed at the convent end of the town yesterday. Some very big ones – he declares. 12 fired from far away and 5 fell very erratically: 4 within 50 yards of our new home. He was himself blown back into his dugout by one which burst only 30 yards off while he was waiting to see if it hit the town. This carelessness on the part of the Hun is most reprehensible.

Work is getting on pretty well.

Yours always,
W

I enclose you a note I have received from one of your supporters.[71]

Winston S. Churchill to Sir Archibald Sinclair
25th March 1916

Archie,

If, as is probable, P.B's[72] minor stunt comes off tonight, we are to remain an extra day in the line to get the benefit of any retaliation, and to avoid a relief at a disturbed moment.

Everything is quiet – and the day is clear. No mail – nor newspapers. But tomorrow I shall hope to have news of you and also possibly to receive other communications.

I do hope you are enjoying yourself and that the change and rest is doing you good.

Radcliffe[73] & Trotter are dining tonight.

---

[69] The medical officer.

[70] Jock McDavid – see n63.

[71] Document not found.

[72] Henry Pelham Burn (1882–1958): Lieutenant-Colonel, Argyll & Sutherland Highlanders during January to April 1916.

[73] Percy Pollexfen de Blaquiere Radcliffe (1874–1934): Brigadier-General, General Staff, 1915–17; Director of Military Operations, War Office, 1918–22; appointed to mission to Poland in 1919 where he assisted General Weygand in reorganising the Polish Army; finished service as Commander-in-Chief, Southern Command, 1933–34.

I am greatly looking forward to your news. I remain here like the genie in the bottle in the Arabian Nights – thinking a lot but unable to say anything – what shall I do to the knight who removes the seal of Golden Soldau by which I am confined?

Yours always,

W

Winston S. Churchill to Sir Archibald Sinclair
41 Cromwell Road[74]
26th March 1916 (Stamped 'Passed Field Censor 135')

Archie,

P.B's show failed last night. The ammonal tubes worked well; but the trench when entered was full of wire. 1 officer and 2 men missing – 4 killed – 1 officer and 7 men wounded. 15 out of 36. No result. Enemy retaliated for our artillery barrages (which were considerable) with about 60 shells on our battalion front line and communications [line] – 2 hit. We are remaining in the line today – owing to change of plan. I am asking for 7 days out as compensation for our lost days, and then 2 spells of 5 to put it square.

Trotters & Radcliffe dined last night. Dinner was quite good – sustained by one of your salmon. Afterwards I took them up the line via the shrine and across the fields. There was much more sniping than usual and I began to be quite anxious for our guests. However, all was well and they were delighted with their jaunt.

I expect this is the last letter that will catch you before you return. I have received no news at all but perhaps today's mail will bring me some. I do hope my dear you have had a good time and are really benefited. You have had a very long spell out there. I like to think that my incursions into your affairs will have added a little variety to your work, and given you a wider scope – if a more dangerous station. You have been a great comfort to me and I shall always be on the qui vive where your interests are concerned. I shall have a very difficult task at home, and time and patience will be needed as well as other rarer qualities. But I do not feel unequal to the undertaking. The war goes ill: & I think the move against Russia is now developing. We have no plan – no vision – no drive. But the allied nations are magnificent and their strengths greatly superior.

I rather expect my affairs will be settled in about a week or ten days (Asquith going to Paris may be a cause of delay). Bring back plenty of good things with you.

Always your affectionate friend,

W

PS They keep on shelling the artillery line across from the wood here. But they seem to be very accurate and careful and we are not molested so far.

Churchill left the front in early April and returned to London. He was soon active once more in high politics. Sinclair remained in Flanders.

Winston S. Churchill to Sir Archibald Sinclair
41 Cromwell Road
18th April 1916

Archie,

A big situation here is at full tension: & I am involved in it deeply.[75] The outlook is hopeful. The debate is postponed through repeated Cabinet disagreements and may now hold over to Monday or Tuesday. Very likely there will be a new conscription Bill – or else a smash and either may detain one. I cannot tell. I am just off to dine with Carson and Lloyd George, and have been able to unite various powerful forces who were criss-cross.

All my friends are very cordial and confident.

Most tiresomely my haversack was left behind. Please take care of all the papers. I don't want any of them except the Grigg[76] letter. Post this in another envelope addressed to Clemmie without delay.

I have read the enclosed message from you. It is cryptic and does not tell me what I want to know – viz: Can I on my own responsibility and at my own risk use the information in debate without queering Furse's pitch. Please telegraph on this through the same channel. Be explicit and don't boggle at the necessary words.

Good luck to you my dear. I reproach myself with having been a tease and burden sometimes to you. If I come back I will be more considerate. If I stay here I trust I shall have the power to provide for your fortunes in a satisfactory manner.

Yours affectionately,
W

Sir Archibald Sinclair to Winston S. Churchill
19th/20th April 1916

My dear Winston,

It is just midnight & I have returned from prowling round the line, supervising an exercise in Gap E., & a visit to the Wamove listening post, to find your telegram laid out on my bed no doubt by the faithful Gibb. So with gummy eye, I search for

[74] Churchill was using his headed paper from home even though he was in the field.

[75] The coalition government was spilt over whether to introduce a general conscription bill for compulsory military service. There were rumours that Lloyd George had decided to resign from the government if a bill were not agreed.

[76] Edward Grigg (1879–1955): served in the Grenadier Guards 1914–18; Churchill served at the front with him.

my languid pen instantly to comply with your request. I suppose you got my wise "action taken & secret letter".

My information, however, is not detailed merely that the two H.L.I.[77] battalions in this division are to be amalgamated with two sister battalions in the XVth Divn., the 8th Gordons with the 10th Gordons and ourselves with the 7th R.S.F. in the 15th Divn. The S.A.[78] brigade is to replace the 28th Bde. which is to be entirely broken up – General Lerase Dickens who has commanded them from the beginning will presumably get some other brigade. The C. in C. only returned to this country three days ago & so probably Furse hasn't yet had his interview.

Moreover the S.A. Bde. is not yet in this country. Of course the Bde and Division staff are speechless with rage, and doubt whether Furse's representations will be successful. No hint has yet been vouchsafed as to the disposal of the officers but we were asked to recommend N.C.O.s as instructors for the Second Army school, with explicit reference to the circumstances of this amalgamation which of course implies that there will be a great many Othellos weeping for their vanished occupations.

No date is yet assigned to the perpetration of this ingenious scheme for the most effective utilisation and encouragement of Scotch & South African patriotism but it cannot be for two or three weeks yet.

Your telegram makes me sad to say the least for I fear you can't be returning if you ask me to write. Of course I have no knowledge of what went on yesterday & today in Parliament but I have never ceased to think of you playing a great perhaps <u>the</u> great part in this tremendous crisis.

Good luck to you, and if you find your strength has returned, stay where you can most effectively contribute to the damnation of the philistines.

As for my part, my thoughts turn more & more towards my regiment. I should like to command a battalion, but that is out of the question, & there are few people I shall care to serve under among strangers in this deadening, monotonous life.

There is some excitement to report as some hundreds of Germans were seen by the F.O.O.[79] advancing down their communication trenches carrying what looked like rugs. Nevertheless, there has been a good deal of shelling on our left, & Lawrence Farm and area 1875 were shelled with 5.9″ to-day & almost 40ft of the railway were blown up. Then one to three searchlights are reported to have been flashing in the Bosch lines behind the Birdcage, and a Bosch patrol was caught prowling about there last night. So we remember with something of an effort that we are at war & that our placid monotonous nights may in fact be disturbed by the trumpet's brazen blast, or the rumble of a mine. But one remembers that exciting deductions are frequently made from similar evidence and nothing ever happens except bombardments & then one wishes nothing had happened and one

---

[77] Highland Light Infantry.

[78] South African.

[79] Forward Observation Officer or Outpost.

longs for peaceful monotony instead of the nerve rending routine of life in the salient, Verdun etc.

We've had an ancient captain & major from the 48th Divn. staying with us for three days; they return the day after to-morrow. Under considerable pressure, they have declared that it is their one wish to live in the trenches, so having put them up for one night here, I have sent them up to one of the dug-outs in the central trench. But I've taken them round by day & night twice & shown them everything myself. They seem a little unused to shells & bullets – but no wonder though the Captain is a South African & was with Botha[80] in German SW. The major & he were both in the S.A. War. I took them out to-night to the listening posts where a man was shot in the line last night. Poor fellow, he has little chance of life the doctor says. Five casualties since you left. I think I had better address this to Mrs. Winston as she will know what to do with it. Please give her and Lady Goonie[81] my love. Do write if you have time.

Yours always,
Archie

Sinclair's letter updating Churchill on the reorganisation plans for the battalions overlapped with a letter from Churchill seeking to know what was happening. Churchill recognised that the amalgamation of units offered him the perfect opportunity to return to active politics. He was also keen to find a safe staff position for Sinclair, though Sinclair, feeling that it was his duty to remain on active service, refused Churchill's offers until the conclusion of hostilities in 1918.

Winston S. Churchill to Sir Archibald Sinclair
20th April 1916
Private

Archie dear,

I am expecting to hear from you regarding the position of the battalion: when is it going to be amalgamated; what is the process; what will happen to the officers. I presume I move on to the unemployed list preceding a new appointment: and I daresay it will be convenient to delay this till the compulsion crisis and the necessary legislation are settled. That is the view I am suggesting to Vesey.[82]

Our leave has been extended to cover the postponed debate i.e. Thursday next will be the day on which I should in the ordinary course return. Shall I find you

[80] Louis Botha (1862–1919): Commandant-General of the Boer armies 1900–02; Prime Minister of South Africa, 1907–19; offered immediate military assistance to Britain in August 1914, and in 1915 launched an invasion of German South West Africa (now Namibia).

[81] Lady Goonie was the universally used nickname of Lady Gwendoline Churchill, wife of Churchill's brother Jack.

[82] Ivo Vesey (1876–1974): Major, GHQ France, 1915–16.

then at the old place, or will the amalgamation actually have begun? You must answer these questions as far as you can.

The situation here is most obscure: but I believe the Government will, against the convictions of the majority of them, be forced to propose general conscription at the last possible moment and in the worst possible way. Then will follow a series of bills, in all of which I shall be deeply concerned. I cannot look further than that.

I have seen the AG[83] about you. His view is that after 20 months of service at the front, you should have a spell of staff employment at home: and you will, I think, be offered a staff captaincy under the War Office or in the company of an interesting and responsible character. I hope that unless something much better is in your reach you will be guided by me and accept this. An election at no great distance is possible and I must have you home for this and other contingencies. Let me know.

I am working in the closest accord with Carson: and indeed find myself as much in the centre of things as I have ever been. The lack of faith and clear leading is frightful to witness.

Will you show these letters to General Furse as it will explain to him how my affairs stand.

Yours affectionately,
W

It is quite hopeless to stop the disbursement. All has been settled for weeks by the War Office and GHQ.

Sinclair wrote passionately about the threat to the Coalition posed by the debates over the rights and wrongs of the Conscription Bill then passing through the Commons. Many Liberal MPs were totally opposed to conscription whilst for many Tory MPs the debate was more about whether married men should be included rather than whether the Bill was required or not. However, the Conservative leader, Bonar Law, was not prepared to force the issue just yet for fear that the Liberal members of the Coalition would resign.

Sir Archibald Sinclair to Winston S. Churchill
22nd April 1916

Winston,

So the expected seems to have happened and the PM has secured a renewal of his lease of No. 10. Presumably the Government refused the water jump at the last minute and B-L[84] decided after taking everything into consideration and weighing this against that and having due regard to the wishes of each of the various sections

[83] Adjutant General – Sir Neville Macready.

[84] Andrew Bonar Law (1858–1923): Leader of the Unionist (Conservative) Party since 1911; Colonial Secretary 1915–16; Chancellor of the Exchequer 1916–18; Lord Privy Seal 1919; Prime Minister 1922–23.

of his party and the difficulties of any alternative course of action that it is best to maintain the unity of the Cabinet especially as we are bound to lose the war in any case. And all these rigid convictions so long and tenuously held, according to Lord Lansdowne[85] (or Crewe[86]), by individual ministers seem after these last few days of furious thought to have been discovered really to have been identical all the time.

How curious that these misunderstandings should have subsisted throughout all these months of 'anxious consideration', should have resulted in a complete deadlock involving the repeated postponement of a debate of unparalleled importance, and should then be completely dissipated in a day! What a commentary on the stern patriotic resolution of the dissenting ministers not to stick even at the sacrifice of the deepest convictions when their minds have long been irrevocably made up in order to avoid the supreme national disaster of the break-up of the Cabinet.

But where do you stand in all this? Perhaps I am wrong in my estimate of the situation, but if I am right I suppose your war station will be the Front opposition bench hand in hand with C.[87] But not G.[88] Of course as Tuesday is a secret session you will speak on all matters without restraint: in any case you need have no fear of queering Furse's pitch as his interview has been refused on the grounds that the plans are settled and cannot now be altered. Have one try to preserve the threatened battalions.

We expect you back Wednesday or Thursday. Do come to say good-bye to everybody. I am a little troubled as to my future but I might be not very happy with or interested in a strange battalion or might not get on with the C.O. Moreover, I have been thinking lately that the regiment may very likely be full and I may not be allowed to go back to them. However, I shall write no more until things are quite settled. My love to Mrs. W. and Lady Goonie.

Ever your devoted
Archie

[85] Sir Henry Charles Keith Petty-Fitzmaurice, 5th Marquess of Lansdowne (1845–1937): Governor-General of Canada 1883–88; Viceroy of India 1888–93; left the Liberal Party for the Conservatives in 1893; Secretary of State for War 1895–1901; Foreign Secretary 1901–05; Minister without Portfolio 1915–16.

[86] Robert Offley Ashburton Crewe-Milnes, 1st Marquess of Crewe (1858–1945): Liberal politician; Lord President of the Council 1905–08 and 1915–16; Secretary of State for the Colonies 1908–10; Liberal leader in the Lords 1908–22 and 1936–44; Secretary of State for India 1910–15; President of the Board of Education 1916; Ambassador to France 1922–28; Secretary of State for War 1931.

[87] Carson.

[88] Lloyd George.

Winston S. Churchill to Sir Archibald Sinclair
41 Cromwell Road
25th April 1916
Private

Archie,

G.H.Q. reply that they will extend my leave for a fortnight till 27th April, and then either a further extension or reemployment according to circumstances can be considered. I am applying officially.[89]

I will write more fully after the debates of today and tomorrow.

God bless you all.

Yours affectionately,
W

Sir Archibald Sinclair to Winston S. Churchill
Ploegsteert
25th April 1916

Winston,

I wrote you a long letter this morning by post but as it may not reach you before you return & as I hear Gallie is going on leave to-day, I am writing this in answer to the questions which you put to me in your letter of the 20th received yesterday afternoon.

2½ battalions of S.A. – are at Steenwerck: the other 1½ are at Marseilles in quarantine owing to typhus having broken out among them. If there is no other case before Friday next, they should be up here on Sunday and the change would probably take place about 10 days thereafter i.e. in about a fortnight. Two things however may occur, one which would tend to delay & the other to accelerate developments. In the first place the 1½ battalions may be detained by the outbreak of further cases of typhus: in the second place the 15th Division which is howling for reinforcements may prevail upon G.H.Q. to demand that we should be sent away sooner. But in no case could the amalgamation take place within the next 6 or 7 days, so do return on Thursday, if only for the week-end to bid everyone "Good-bye". There will be a divisional car at Boulogne on Thursday taking down two Staff Officers. The division, if you wire them at once to that effect, will order the car to await you: it is a quicker route back than Dunkirk, & you will have the car to yourself on the return journey. We shall be at Lawrence Farm.

Furse, who was very agreeable yesterday, assured me that the Army Corps Commander who he had seen only yesterday, could give him no information with regard to the disposal of the officers but Trotter tells me that the O.C.[90] 7th battalion is junior to you but you could verify that in London – he wasn't quite sure.

[89] Churchill was applying officially to be released from military service.

[90] Officer commanding.

I tried in my last letter (this is the fifth I have written you or Mrs. Churchill since you left – I am wondering how many you have received) to express – haltingly and at great length – some of the great gratitude I feel for your kindness in thinking of me and my future in the middle of these great events. Also my keen longing to serve you in politics – more humbly but more energetically than I have been able to in war. However, I can't believe that it can be right for me young, physically fit and unwounded to leave the field at this juncture. Probably, however, they will not be able to find employment for me immediately and I should dearly like to have 3 weeks or a month's leave in the meantime. If there were then to be an election or other political crisis, I should then be at hand. Moreover, I should then still feel that I was a soldier and belonged out here. You want every man to strain every nerve, to brace every sinew and to concentrate his whole mind on doing his best to beat the Bosch. So do I. That is the policy for which, as I understand it, you are contending. We must each of us apply the test to ourselves. According to it you must return to Parliament and I must obviously stay out here.

Yesterday a German aeroplane carrying a Lewis gun was brought down in the field adjoining brigade H.Q. The pilot & observer were both killed. The Bosches on the other hand got two direct hits on the 6″ gun with a 5.9″ howitzer, & though they didn't pierce the barrel, they dented it & destroyed the elevating & traversing machinery. 25 shells, two hits and the furthest crater not 40 yds from the gun & several craters within 10 yds – some shooting!

Picture me writing this sitting on the lawn between Smith[91] and the doctor, the sun shining brightly in our faces and the Bosches shelling Ploegsteert. The day before we came in the Bosches dropped a 4 inch howitzer shell in the lawn, and one plump into the armstrong hut which was the orderly room: part of it (the hut) alighted in the Warnave and part in the trees on the other side of it.

Au revoir, Do come back Thursday, write me – or 'adjutant' - more official might clear the line better![92]

Archie

During May 1916 Sinclair achieved his wish for a long home leave and returned, via London, to his estate in north Scotland.

Sir Archibald Sinclair to Winston S. Churchill
Thurso Castle
Tuesday [late May 1916]

My dear Winston,

[91] Hakewith-Smith, an officer in the 6th Royal Scots Fusiliers.

[92] i.e. pass the censor.

Comment ça va? I hear little of you and nothing from you – yet so far as one can measure a force by superficial manifestations – as one can detect an invisible shell by its whistle in the air or locate an unseen fish by the swirl of the surface water – so by certain agitations in the Press, the Spectator's apprehension that you may be cast for the role of St. Patrick to stamp out the reptiles, I gather that already you have – albeit silently – made your presence felt.

I am so very happy now I am at home again and, gazing into my shaving glass as I perform my morning lacerations, I see I'm getting browner & fatter day by day or even hour by hour. The fishing is topping. My first day I got 7 fish (of which I sent Mrs. W. one): that was Friday. Saturday was a beastly day cold & raining and, as I had much to do in doors, I took advantage of its beastliness and spent but a short time in the river and caught nothing.

Sunday I meant to write to you but after rising slothfully & dressing hurriedly for Church, I was so much occupied with religion exercises and social gaieties, that I had not a moment to myself until at midnight I bowed out the Parson, the Provost, the Sheriff and the Senior Naval Officer, a jolly old sea dog of the Beresford type who thoroughly disapproves of your friend, "the old devil".[93]

Yesterday I fished again, and again caught 7 fish of which I sent one to Lady Randolph – so wherever you are I hope you ate one of mine. I was out from 8.30 a.m. till 8.30 p.m. (including motoring to and fro). Oh this is life! No pistols, belts, or stifling Jaeger underclothing or communication trenches! But one just strides freely where one will in kilts and shoes, instead of thick muddy breeches in which one has slept & big thick boots. And without your English Daylight saving we have broad sunlight here till 9 o'clock or later and one can see to read the paper – I tried it just for fun – out of doors at tea and even after eleven there is a faint white light in the west – a kind of reflection, I suppose, of the sun. I only wish you could be here for a few days – and damn the needs of the Government or anything else you wished to damn!

At present I am intending to be back in London on Monday – staying with Lidney at St James Palace. When do you intend to make your speech to your constituents? Do tell them the facts in true proportion: interpret to them the passage of events. If the Government is "a-feared to tell the worst, then will the worst untold fall on our heads". Folk here seem to me to be afflicted with most unhealthy opinions on the war – a compound of unreasoned optimism and cynical pessimism. No doubt there is great weariness of the war and the sheriff – a radical & stalwart friend of yours whose business takes him a great deal into all sorts of society here & in Edinburgh – tells me he thinks there is such war weariness that the Government will be compelled into an inconclusive peace to avoid another winter's war. I told him that was dangerous nonsense and that if this Government showed itself too sensitive to the pressure of an unenlightened public which can see nothing but a deadlock in the battlefield, there would arise another Government of more rigorous spirits to

[93] Probably a reference to Lloyd George.

re-kindle their enthusiasm. He was interested and though he owes his position to the Government, and though you refused to appoint him to some position in the colonies where you were Under-Secretary, although Haldane recommended him, and he considered you scandalously favoured the Irish & the English as against the Scotch in making your appointments, yet I think he would be glad to see a change of Government though he thinks it is too late.

But now I am going out to fish again so fare thee well.

The defenders of the [unreadable] have apparently followed the path of glory to its logical conclusion & now apparently Lawrence Farm has been the centre of a certain liveliness – I hope not to the detriment of that comfortable little residence.

Au revoir, my love and duty to Mrs. W., Lady Goonie & Lady Randolph.[94]

Yours always,
Archie

Winston S. Churchill to Sir Archibald Sinclair
41 Cromwell Road (Addressed to Sinclair at Thurso Castle, Caithness)
16th May 1916

My dear,

Come to see me as soon as you return. The War Office are on the point of offering you a staff captaincy at home. I told them to hold on till you came south.

I am so glad you are enjoying yourself and having good sport. I am getting into the collar here: but now of course at times I look wistfully over the channel. What a fool I am! Well it's lucky for me everyone has not seen my folly at as close quarters as you. This is the penalty of office and friendship.

Best love,
W

Winston S. Churchill to Sir Archibald Sinclair
41 Cromwell Road to AS 2nd Life Guards, Cavalry Barracks, Windsor
22nd June 1916

Archie dear,

I am watching these complications very carefully. They are exceptionally interesting.[95]

[94] Lady Randolph Churchill, née Jennie Jerome (1854–1921): Churchill's mother; socialite, magazine editor (*Anglo-Saxon Review*) and journalist; married (1874) Lord Randolph Churchill (died 1895), (1900) Captain George Cornwallis-West (divorced 1913), (1918) Montagu Phippen Porch, colonial administrator.

[95] It is likely that Churchill is referring to the political manoeuvring following Kitchener's death when his ship hit a mine en route to Russia on 6 June 1916. Churchill was hopeful that Lloyd George would be moved to replace Kitchener as Secretary of State for War and that in turn he could replace Lloyd George

I am going away for the Sunday. I am sorry you are going so soon to France: but if you are, surely you can get leave meanwhile. Why not come Monday evening at 6.30, and dine with Clemmie and me for our long deferred sing-song.

I have written a flatterer to Zetland.[96] It will be published either tomorrow or next day.

Yours always,
W

Winston S. Churchill to Sir Archibald Sinclair
41 Cromwell Road
23rd June 1916

My dear Archie,

Where have you been? What have you seen? I have been looking for some signs of activity on the part of the Daddy long legs: but not a whisker has stirred.

I had a line from Spiers[97] who is all right so far. I gather that the fighting has now settled down into the attack on small fronts after intense preparation. There is no harm in this: & I should like to see it develop in more than one part of our front. I do not expect the Life Guards will have much charging to do – at any rate I hope not.

I think the Germans have again got control of the situation in the East. Altogether it seems likely that no marked change will happen this side of winter.

Here Parliament has finished for the time: & I am off to Blenheim for a week and thence to Herstmonceux.[98] I am busy with the Dardanelles Commission, about which I feel hopeful. I write and paint – and ponder. From my cottage at Herstmonceux I can hear the guns better than at St Omer. They induce sombre reflections.

Do write to me and tell me all the news. L.G. is getting on well with Robertson.[99] I am to dine with them both this week. The Admiralty dozes placidly.

Yours affectionately,
W

as Minister of Munitions. In the end, although Lloyd George did get the War Office, Edwin Montagu was moved to Munitions, principally because Asquith was not prepared to appoint Churchill in the face of almost united opposition from nearly all Tories and a significant slice of the Liberal Party. Churchill felt deeply resentful.

[96] Unclear who this is.

[97] Major General Edward Louis Spiers (changed surname to Spears) (1886–1974): Liaison Officer with French 10th Army 1915–16; based in Paris immediately after the war as head of the British Military Mission; National Liberal (Lloyd Georgite) MP 1922–24, Conservative MP 1931–45; remained a close friend of Churchill's throughout his life.

[98] A castle in Kent; Churchill had access to a cottage in its grounds from which he could practise painting.

[99] William Robert Robertson (1860–1933): Chief of the Imperial General Staff 1915–18.

Winston S. Churchill to Sir Archibald Sinclair
41 Cromwell Road
15th September 1916

Archie,

I am glad to think you have not heard a shell since our parting 'dud' at Le Gheer. Drilling is good for the young and inculcates humility and other virtues of that order.

You are right about Roumania.[100] That is Hindenburg's[101] proper coup, and I believe a manageable one this year. I felt it the moment she came in. But of course all these things are very speculative. It would be hard enough to forecast events if people acted wisely. But folly has no laws or processes.

The tanks are to be filled prematurely I fear. It would have been worth waiting. I wonder whether they will be rightly used.

LG returned last night from his tour. He thinks a lot; but so far has done nothing.

I am occupying myself with the Dardanelles Commission which is now about to begin. The case is an extraordinary one. I don't think anyone realises the full significance of the story which is to be told. The Admiralty have simply put in the plans of Jackson[102] and Oliver.[103] These Admiralty papers on what is now the highest naval authority are the foundation of my case. They have behaved very well in taking so much upon themselves. But of course I shall assume the fullest responsibility.

I am looking about to buy a country seat, and am just off to Sussex to examine one which has been offered. I wish to find a place to end my days amid trees and upon grass of my own! Freed from the penury of office these consolations become possible. Soon we shall correspond as between one landlord and another![104]

Poor Garvin[105] comes to see me sometimes to talk about his boy. This gallant lad on being mortally wounded, observed in a collected voice 'Tell Mr Porter to carry on with the company' and expired without a sigh. My heart is very full of all these things – and I have much pain and mortification at my impotence enforced on energies of which I feel the throb.

[100] Romania had declared war on Germany and Austria on 19 August 1916 and had proceeded to invade Hungarian-held Transylvania. The German High Command decided that all other campaigns in the west and the east would be put on hold while Germany threw her main weight against Romania; the Austro-German offensive began on 3 September and the Romanian armies were routed, with more than 25,000 Romanian prisoners taken during the first three days of the counterattack. Sinclair had obviously been sceptical about the capabilities of the Romanian war machine and Churchill acknowledged this.

[101] Paul von Hindenburg (1847–1934): Chief of the German General Staff, 1916–18; second President of the Weimar Republic 1925–34; appointed Adolf Hitler as chancellor in 1933.

[102] Henry Jackson (1855–1929): First Sea Lord, replacing Fisher, May 1915 – December 1916.

[103] Henry Oliver (1865–1965): Chief of the Admiralty War Staff, 1914–17.

[104] Churchill eventually (in the spring of 1917) purchased a country home, the small manor house of Lullenden, East Grinstead.

[105] James Garvin (1868–1947): Editor of the *Observer & Pall Mall Gazette*; his only son was killed in action.

God bless you my dear. Your letters are a great pleasure to me: so don't cut them off.

Yours always affectionately
W

PS. Last night I dined in the middle of the Government – Asquith, McKenna,[106] Curzon.[107] All very caressing. But you cannot make rivers run backwards.

Winston S. Churchill to Sir Archibald Sinclair
41 Cromwell Road
29th November 1916

Archie –

Although I owe you a letter, still I think you are a pig not to write more often. You will reply in the jargon of the day that in that case I am a super-pig. But I put off writing you from time to time on the chance that I may have good news to send – and something definite to say – and that chance lingers on the road. You on the other hand have no such excuse – though I do not doubt your ability to manufacture any number and express them at any length.

Well, events are taking a sombre course and you may imagine the feelings with which I watch the remorseless unfolding of the terrible Balkan tragedy[108] combined with the realisation of my forebodings in the west. The consequences of these latest episodes will be far-reaching. The internal condition of the Government is explosive, and its action paralytic. Northcliffe is its bitter foe, but continues to keep a side portion of venom for me. The Generals have had sole direction of events; and now it is the 'politicians' who are to be blamed! The forces which make for an inconclusive peace are gathering from every quarter and will, I do not doubt when the hour is ripe, receive encouragement from within the government itself.

I gather the Russians will make a sort of Chinese wall across Roumania from the mountains to the sea and try to hold the Germans there. Bucharest lies far outside their line. When the fronts are thus shortened, the enemy will either strike on with massed artillery into Russia (Odessa) or turn sharply back on to Sarrail.[109] I expect the latter as Constantine[110] no doubt has definite pledges. A fresh vista of misfortunes opens then.

[106] Reginald McKenna (1863–1943): Liberal MP for North Monmouthshire 1895–1918; President of the Board of Education 1907–08; First Lord of the Admiralty 1908–11; Home Secretary 1911–15; Chancellor of the Exchequer 1915–16.

[107] George Nathaniel Curzon, Marquess Curzon of Kedleston (1859–1925): Conservative MP for Southport 1886–98; Viceroy of India 1898–1905; Lord Privy Seal 1915–18; Foreign Secretary 1919–24.

[108] The military disasters that had befallen Romania. By November 1916 the capital, Bucharest, was under threat from the German and Austrian forces and the government was forced to relocate to Jassy in the north. Romania eventually surrendered to the Central Powers in May 1918.

[109] Maurice Sarrail (1856–1929): Commander-in-Chief of the Allied armies at Salonika.

[110] King Constantine I (1868–1923): King of Greece 1913–17; opposed Prime Minister Venizelos' support

These events will it seems certain entail changes in the Government: but I cannot tell their form or extent. The Admiralty is already reconstituted. You will know before you get this. But further alternations in the governing instrument are unavoidable, unless disaster is to end our efforts.

Everything I hear about the Dardanelles Commission encourages me. The interim report cannot now be long delayed and I have good hopes that it will be a fair judgment. I should like to have it out as soon as possible. But the days slip away.

When will you be home again? I am going to Blenheim for Christmas and if you could get away I am sure you would be welcome there for a visit. FE[111] will be there.

Let me know my dear – if you are in need of anything.

Spenser Grey[112] is rather offended at your not answering one of his letters. Don't say I said so – but put it right.

I rejoiced to read of the glorious achievements of the RND.[113] The heroic Freyberg[114] is here in hospital. They ought to make him a general.

Now write soon and often to your affectionate friend.

W

Lloyd George replaced Asquith as Prime Minister on 6 December 1917. Churchill was hopeful that this would enable him to return to office, but Lloyd George was not able to oblige, due to continued Tory opposition; Churchill was crushed and disappointed. Ironically he remained on the Opposition front bench, along with many of his former Liberal ministerial colleagues who followed Asquith out of office, and proved to be one of the most effective critics of the Government he so strongly wished to rejoin.

---

for the Allies, but in June 1917, with Venizelos planning to march on Athens with Allied support, handed over the throne to his second son, Alexander, who reigned until dying from a monkey bite in October 1920; a plebiscite in December 1920 voted overwhelmingly for Constantine's return, but his popularity rapidly waned after the Turkish defeat of the Greeks in Anatolia and Smyrna, and in 1922 he was forced to abdicate; died in exile in Sicily in 1923.

[111] F.E. Smith, Lord Birkenhead – see n18.

[112] Spenser Grey (dates unknown): Squadron Commander who at this time was a test pilot for the experimental flights of early versions of flying boats; led the first successful British air attack on Germany in 1915, when two Sopwith Tabloids of the Royal Naval Air Service attacked Zeppelin airship sheds at Dusseldorf, destroying Zeppelin L9.

[113] Royal Naval Division.

[114] Bernard Freyberg (1890–1963): Lieutenant, Royal Naval Division; awarded the Victoria Cross when commanding the *Hood* battalion in an attack on a German strongpoint on the western front in November 1916.

Winston S. Churchill to Sir Archibald Sinclair
41 Cromwell Road
10th December 1916

Archie dear –

I am indeed your debtor for a long and vividly interesting letter,[115] and this is the moment when it is very pleasant to receive the messages of a friend. The papers will have apprised you of the course of events, and you will have learned from them of the downfall of my hopes and desires. These have not been unworthy, for I had an impulse and a gift to give to the war energies of the country. But my treasure is rejected. If I could reconcile the turn of events and of newspaper opinion with the true facts and the true values I should be hopelessly downcast. But I am sure that these judgments are unjust and I have a good conscience and am confident of my record. Still you who know me so well will understand how unpleasant it is to me to be denied all scope in action at this time of all other times.

Of course I have every right to complain of LG who weakly and faithlessly bowed to Northcliffe's malevolent press. But this is not the hour when personal resentments however justified must influence conduct or colour opinion. I shall remain absolutely silent!

It was unlucky that the Dardanelles report should have been delayed until after the crisis; for I am still hopeful that it will give a turn to public opinion. But everything has turned out ill for me since the war began. Perhaps we are now at the nadir.

It will be odd now on the Front Opposition Bench with all the furious ex-Ministers arriving. I expect they will soon be very anxious to be civil to me. But I intend to sit in the corner seat in a kind of isolation.

The Liberal party will now gradually develop pacifist tendencies. Their resentment against LG is fierce and concentrates upon his personal conduct and probity. The fact that no Liberal colleague would serve with him is of course a serious testimony.

He may force an almost immediate dissolution with a view to securing a Parliament more in personal sympathy with him. If so I shall have to make a very difficult decision which it is not worthwhile anticipating. The new Government is a weak one, – so far as ability is concerned and largely inexperienced. Political considerations alone have ruled the formation of the War Council, and except LG not one of its members possessed any aptitude for war or knowledge of it. The exclusion of the Admiralty and War Office from the War Council shows an utter lack of comprehension of the interplay of forces. The difficulties before them are enormous, and only disaster lies ahead for many months. The position of Sarrail's army and the imbecile Salonika enterprise (of which LG, Carson and BL are the principal initiators) is one of very great danger. No measures which can be taken now can relieve that danger. Events will move rapidly there. One can only wait developments.

---

[115] No copy has survived.

If an election comes I shall perhaps be in a position to secure you a seat. But the future though imminent is obscure.

Yours always,
W

Winston S. Churchill to Sir Archibald Sinclair
41 Cromwell Road
20th December 1916

Archie,

Yours of the 17th:[116] and I am very grateful for all the kindness you show me.

Secret – 10 days ago LG sent G Riddell[117] to tell me he was keeping the Air Board for me at the first possible moment. Since then I hear this arrangement bruited in various secret and well-informed quarters. I have not seen him however, tho' he threw a note across the floor last night asking me to come. I do not want to have a chatterbox talk. Unless I am really wanted I do not want to join them. However painful it is not to have work to do against the enemy, one must just wait. There is nothing to be gained by eagerness. The matter now hangs I suppose in the balance. I have seen nobody except FE since the crisis culminated – nor shall I seek to do so.

I hang heavy on his[118] conscience and on his calculations.

But for the war nothing would induce me to take office.

I look back a great deal to our Plugstreet days, and wish I could have cut myself more adrift from London and its whirlpools and been more content with the simple animal life (and death) which the trenches offered. When I am absolutely sure there is no prospect of regaining control or part of it here, I shall turn again to that resort and refuge: and after all I have learned in disillusionment I think I could do better. It is a mellow picture in retrospect. But I was always tormented by the idea that great opportunities were slipping by at home.

And this is a fret. If I had stayed Chancellor of the Duchy and shut my mouth and drawn my salary, I should today be one of the principal personages in direction of affairs. That was a costly excursion. Still I cannot regret it. Under a fair pretence of fine words, there is a great deconsideration of all who wear uniform. They are discounted as persons 'under the law'. Not one of these gallant MPs who have fought through the Somme at the heads of their battalions, stands a chance against less clever men who have stopped and chattered at home. This is to me the most curious phenomenon of all. It is quite inexplicable to me. Fancy putting Mond[119]

[116] Again, no copy has been retained.

[117] George Riddell (1865–1934): Chairman of the *News of the World* newspaper; Liaison Officer between the government and the press, 1914–18; close associate of Lloyd George.

[118] Presumably Lloyd George.

[119] Sir Alfred Moritz Mond, 1st Baron Melchett of Blandford (1868–1930): Liberal MP for Chester

and Crawley[120] in a War Government as representative Liberals, while excluding Jack Seely.

Young Blandford[121] has had a desperate operation for appendicitis, and till his fate settles itself (I hope for the best) our Blenheim plans hang in suspense. He is really charming – such a bright life. Assuming all is well, I shall go there on the 23rd and shall stay there over the New Year. You will be most welcome from the moment you arrive on the 30th. You have only to telegraph to me that you will come and I will arrange the rest. FE will be there and my little lot – whom you know. If au contraire Blandford's condition continues critical or the needle dips to the magnet, you will find us all here: and very welcome you will be. Telephone or telegraph on your arrival (588 Kens)

Dardanelles report though mottled is I understand a document which will greatly benefit me. Publication is imminent on the 'inception' phase: but poor old Cromer[122] is prostrated by his exertions and may never rally.

I have been enveloped in courtesies by the ex. Liberal Ministers: But I remain quite unattached.

Always your affectionate friend,
Winston

1917

Unfortunately no copies of Sinclair's correspondence during 1917 have been found, so the evolution of their relationship can be followed only through Churchill's hand. While Sinclair remained a serving officer on the Western Front, Churchill's fortunes undertook a dramatic improvement when Lloyd George overrode Conservative opposition and appointed him to the Ministry of Munitions in July 1917. Churchill held this office until January 1919.

In early 1917 Sinclair became increasingly disillusioned with life as a cavalryman, and continued to harbour ambitions to join the Royal Flying Corps. Churchill urged him to stay put.

1906–10, Swansea Town 1910–18, Swansea West 1918–23, Liberal and Conservative MP for Carmarthen 1924–28; First Commissioner of Works 1916–21; Minister of Public Health 1921–22; joined Conservatives in 1926; helped to create ICI in 1926.

[120] Frederick Crawley (1850–1937): Chancellor of the Duchy of Lancaster 1916–18.

[121] John Spencer-Churchill, Marquess of Blandford (1897–1972): son of Churchill's cousin, the 9th Duke of Marlborough.

[122] Evelyn Baring, Earl of Cromer (1841–1917): Chairman of the Dardanelles Commission of Enquiry 1916–17. Died 29 January 1917.

Winston S. Churchill to Sir Archibald Sinclair
33 Eccleston Square
22nd March 1917
Private

Archie dear,

I was delighted to get your letter and to have news of you. The war weighs heavy on us all and amid such universal misfortune and with death so ubiquitous and life so harsh, I find a difficulty in setting pen to paper. I have liked to think you have been bored and not in danger, and I hope this condition will continue. I share it – so we are fellow sufferers. I remain inactive and useless on the edge of the whirlpool. I see a good deal of LG and hear how things are going. But otherwise I keep clear of the whole governing machine except FE. The Asquithians are all very civil and friendly: but here again I keep a separate dwelling.

You will be glad to hear that the House of Commons is coming to hand again. The three speeches I have made this year have all been very well received. The Dardanelles debate especially was very successful to me personally. The grouping of forces in the House are proving increasingly favourable. The Dardanelles report has forced all who care about Kitchener's memory (and they are many) to join with all who adhere to orthodox Liberalism in defence of that operation: and I thus have strong bodies of public opinion between me and the malevolence of the Tory press.

This is likely to govern my affairs. I fear that LG will seek to force an election although there is no justification for it in the attitude of the House. But victory at the polls is easier than in the field. I am doing all I can to prevent such a disastrous event both by supporting the government in the prosecution of the war, and by protesting against such a course. It would grieve me to be drawn into such a struggle now. If it comes I shall I think be able to find you a good seat. Scotland is very stable.

When is the next blow going to fall? There is the dominant question.

Please stay where you are with your squadron. It is much too late for you to go into the Flying Corps.

Yours always,
W

PS. We are slowly getting in to Lullenden.[123]

Winston S. Churchill to Sir Archibald Sinclair
33 Eccleston Square
11th April 1917

My dear –

[123] The house that Churchill purchased in early 1917 near East Grinstead. The family lived there until 1919.

I am so sorry to hear of your illness and I know how vexed you will be to be out of the fight. Never mind. Cavalry have no role on the Western front. There will be no galloping through and even catastrophe will be prevented by the unfailing interposition of preliminary hard facts.

This battle seems to have been well organised and the Artillery (fed by the abused LG and other 'politicians') has proved once again overwhelming on the limited area exposed to its attack. But the secondary stages are very costly, and the forward movement must be gradual – i.e. step by step. Meanwhile there is much to cause anxiety. Russia! The Submarines!! The German reserve Army!!! (if it really exists). All these are factors of fundamental uncertainty.

It is very joyous reading of this brilliant episode.[124] 11,000 Huns glad to accept life at the hands of our small army. One likes to dwell on it, although I fear the tendencies are no longer so favourable as they used to be. Still America – dear to your heart and mine, is please God a final makeweight.

Do not fret or chafe. Just do what is your appointed task and may Heaven protect you till better days dawn and even after that – is the prayer of your sincere friend.

W

Winston S. Churchill to Sir Archibald Sinclair
33 Eccleston Square
21st June 1917

Archie dear,

Very many thanks for your letter and for the salmon. Its succulence revived memories of our banquet to 'Windy Bill'[125] at Lawrence Farm.

I am going on Thursday for a visit to the French and English fronts and expect to be away the best part of a fortnight. Thereafter we will meet in London town, and I will tell you a good many things which are now too secret to put down even in a letter to you.

Yours always,
W

Winston S. Churchill to Sir Archibald Sinclair
29th December 1917
Private

My dear Archie,

---

[124] The Battle of Arras, under way during the first ten days of April. On 9 April British and Canadian forces took the strategically important position of Vimy Ridge. Although newspapers reported over 11,000 prisoners, in reality the number was nearer 6,000.

[125] Major-General Furse; see n65.

I have been anxiously looking for a letter from you and was delighted to receive one.

The cavalry myth is exploded at last and there is every prospect of these splendid regiments being given a fair opportunity on the modern field. I am strongly pressing that the cavalry should be put by regiments into the Tanks both heavy and chasers and this view is meeting with a great deal of acceptance. I advise you to apply for Tanks, and I will assist in any way I can to further your wishes. It would be a thousand pities if the cavalry were simply dispersed as drafts among the infantry. The future life of this arm after the war depends upon their discarding the obsolete horse, and becoming associated with some form of military machinery having a scientific and real war value. It is not fair to blame the cavalry. I blame those who assign impossible task and absurd conditions to brave men.

It looks as if the failure of the Submarine attack as a decisive factor must leave the Germans no resource but a great offensive in the west. In spite of their reinforcements from the Russian front they will be inferior in (a) number, (b) morale and (c) ammunition and (d) reserves. I wish them the joy of it. An elastic defence with strong 'one-day battle' counter blows at other points, and tank-led counter attacks on the flanks of hostile salients; a good army of manoeuvre behind our front; and a steady influx of Americans ought to make in combination a singularly cheerless outlook for the Hun general staff. Thank God our offences are at an end. Let them make the pickets, let them traipse across the crater fields, let them rejoice in the occasional capture of placeless names and sterile ridges: and let us dart here and there armed with science and surprise and backed at all points by a superior artillery. That is the way to break their hearts and leave them bankrupt in resources at the end of the 1918 campaign. I look forward with good hopes to the coming clash; and to the opportunity of a good peace at the end of it.

We must not be done out of our world victory by wordy generalities. France has got to win and know that she has won, and Germany has got to be beat and know that she is beaten. I do not think there will be any weakness here or in America. For me Alsace Lorraine is the symbol and test of victory.

Arm yourself therefore my dear with the panoply of the modern science of war. Make catsmeat of these foolish animals, who have broken your hearts so far. Embark in the chariots of war and slay the malignants with arms of precision.

I will try very hard to see you when next I come to France: or give you rendezvous in Paris. At present I am submerged by labour difficulties – and have to fight for breath. I hope they are looking after Salonika, which might otherwise well be a cause of offence.

We are Christmasing here with the children at Lullenden and I go each day to town. Clemmie sends her love and so does Goonie, and so as you know does your sincere and devoted friend

W

1918

Churchill continued to build a reputation as a competent and credible Minister of Munitions during 1918. His personal relations with Lloyd George were restored to robust health with the two men achieving something akin to their pre-1914 levels of trust and mutual respect.

1918 was also a pivotal year in Sinclair's life. In March he met Marigold Forbes, who was helping to run a canteen with her mother in Flanders, and in May they were married.

As the war continued and an Allied victory seemed increasingly likely, especially after the failed German offensive in March–April 1918, Sinclair's thoughts began to turn to his political future and in particular to whether he should stand in the election expected soon after the war ended.

Winston S. Churchill to Sir Archibald Sinclair
Ministry of Munitions of War
Whitehall Place, SW1
8th March 1918

My dear Archie,

I spoke at once to Paul Elles who commands the Tank Corps, and who is now over here to confer with me. He will, I am sure, give you a warm welcome to the Tanks and will write to you himself as soon as he returns to France at the end of the week. You should be able to write to him quoting me, I am sure this is the best thing to do.

I very nearly secured the Household Brigade en bloc for the Tanks. Surely that would have been much better for them than what has now been settled?

Please let me know if there is any way in which I can help you to overcome the difficulties of leaving the Regiment and inform me what happens.

Yours affectionately,
W

Winston S. Churchill to Sir Archibald Sinclair
16th May 1918

My dear Archie,

I am very sorry indeed not to be able to present myself at your wedding on Saturday. I have no legitimate official reason for crossing before Tuesday.

My dear this is a splendid event in your life and I wish you from the bottom of my heart lasting happiness. That you may be preserved through the dangers that surround you is my intense desire and I have also good confidence in your fortune, and that this joyous event will renew it. God Bless you both and guard you always is my prayer. May you both see many golden summers together in the North and may all your life be lighted by true love and sweet companionship.

I have been casting about in my mind for some token to mark this occasion, but I have decided to wait till you both return to these shores and can help me to find something that you would like to keep and use in your home.

Clemmie sends her very best love and sincerest good wishes. She looks forward so much to meeting Marigold.[126]

With every wish of friendship and wish every hope of fortune my dear friend believe me ever

Yours affectionately,
W

Sir Archibald Sinclair to Winston S. Churchill
3rd July 1918

Winston,

I feel deeply ashamed of myself that I have never written to thank you for the perfect letter which you wrote me when I got married: I missed you awfully at the wedding but I knew you would have been there if you could.

Now we have got a quite delightful little flat at Le Touquet.[127] Next time you are over here, you must go and see Marigold and our little home – Les Aeroplanes,[128] Paris Plage, only half an hour's drive from Montreuil.

I want to see you, too. I heard of you quite close by the other day and reproached you silently for never coming to see me. If you were to appear in a large and luxurious automobile on a Friday or Saturday very early, I might be able to take you down to Le Touquet to see Marigold.

I was hugely interested to see that your mother had married again.[129] Please give her my best love and heartiest good wishes: please remember to do that, Winston. Does one call her Mrs. Porch or Lady Randolph now? Do you like Porch? I've been simply working all day long and have just had to ignore every single one of my marriage letters – yours is the first I have answered. The Battalion is going strong and when we get our motors we shall be as proud as peacocks. I'm delighted with my company and should like to show it to you at work one of these days.

There is much I should like to say about politics and the war but it would take too long and it would be futile unless I heard your reply, but the Government still

---

[126] Marigold Sinclair (née Forbes) (1898–1975): married Sir Archibald Sinclair on 18 May 1918. Unfortunately Marigold and Clementine Churchill never saw eye to eye and did not become friends.

[127] La Touquet was close to the British camp at Les Etaples and Marigold's mother ran a canteen there for troops and civilians.

[128] The name of the flat in Le Touquet.

[129] On 1 June 1918 the sixty-four-year-old Lady Randolph had made her third marriage, to Montagu Porch, a member of the Nigerian Civil Service, who was three years younger than Winston. This age difference would account for Archie's 'huge interest'.

seem to be in hot water about manpower, in a terrible mess over Ireland and without any policy in Russia. I should like to see a few of the Ulster rebels sent to join the Sinn Fein 'rebels' and a belated but generous measure of Home Rule given at once. As soon as it was working you could demand your recruits or conscripts but not before. The Government wants new blood, and good, strong, Radical blood too of the John Simon,[130] Samuel[131] and Arthur Henderson[132] type, more in sympathy than the present Cabinet with the democratic aspirations and ideals of America and the Dominions as well as of this country, and it's high time you went to the War Office or Downing Street. You are hiding your light under a bushel with hardly a crack in it, through which any light ever escapes.

I'm so glad that Jack Seely has joined you – please give him my love – also to Clemmie and to Randolph and Diana and Sarah[133] – bless them; I wish I could come down to Lullenden for the week-end!

Yours always,
Archie

PS. Do write, if you have time.

Sir Archibald Sinclair to Winston S. Churchill
July 1918

Winston,

I've been reading your 4 July speech[134] – I haven't had time till last night – and though I don't flatter myself that my opinion interests you very much, I feel that I

---

[130] Sir John Allsebrook Simon, 1st Viscount Simon (1873–1954): Liberal MP for Walthamstow 1906–18, Liberal and Liberal National MP for Spen Valley 1922–40; Attorney-General 1913–15; Home Secretary 1915–16; split from the Liberal Party in 1931, and joined National Government; Foreign Secretary 1931–35; Home Secretary 1935–37; Chancellor of the Exchequer 1937–40; Lord Chancellor 1940–45.

[131] Sir Herbert Samuel Samuel, 1st Viscount Samuel (1870–1963): Liberal MP for Cleveland 1902–18, Darwen 1929–35; Chancellor of the Duchy of Lancaster 1909–10, 1915–16; Postmaster-General 1910–14, 1915–16; President of the Local Government Board 1914–15; Home Secretary January–December 1916; High Commissioner for Palestine 1920–25; Chairman of the Commission of Inquiry into the Coal Industry 1925–26; Leader of the Liberal Party 1931–35; Home Secretary 1931–32; ennobled in 1937; Leader of the Liberal peers 1944–55; a leading New Liberal in his youth, he became a popular panellist on the radio programme *The Brains' Trust* and wrote several works of philosophy.

[132] Arthur Henderson (1863–1935): Labour MP for Barnard Castle 1903–18, Widnes 1919–22, Newcastle-upon-Tyne East 1923, Burnley 1924–31, Derbyshire Clay Cross 1933–35; Chairman Parliamentary Labour Party 1908–10, 1914–17; President Board of Education 1915–16; Paymaster-General 1916–17; member of War Cabinet 1916–17; fell out with Lloyd George in 1917 and resigned from government; first Labour Home Secretary 1924; Foreign Secretary 1929–31.

[133] Sarah Millicent Hermione Spencer Churchill (1914–82): the Churchills' third child, nicknamed 'Mule' because of her stubbornness; actress and dancer; served in the Women's Auxiliary Air Force during the Second World War; married three times, and suffered long term problems with alcohol.

[134] Churchill spoke at the Central Westminster Hall to the Anglo-Saxon Fellowship, where he argued the case that one of the principal benefits of the war had been the reconciliation of Britain and the United States. He also argued that the Germans, once beaten, should be treated with wisdom and justice and that

must write and tell you what a splendid utterance it appeared to me to be and how absolutely I agree with almost every word you uttered and every sentiment you expressed.

I remember sounding you upon the possibility of drawing closer to the States on that first walk we took together at Maxine's years before the war. How delighted I was when you treated the idea seriously and not as an impracticable dream. It was certainly absolutely true of all Englishmen and Scotsmen with recent American connections and probably of the vast majority of thinking men in our country that they will be willing to regard the complete understanding and co-operation with America as our highest reward – 'the lion's share'.

Next to that sentiment I like best the insistence on the necessity of victory and the impossibility of compromise: and especially I was delighted (and not a little surprised, I confess!) at the declaration that the principles, for which we are fighting, will be Germany's (and Russia's, Winston!) protection when the final peace comes to be made. Of course, I remember you used to say that 'Germany for the Germans' was our battle cry, but lately I have thought that you had gone over to the camp of the 'practical statesmen'. This splendid declaration of democratic ideals thrilled me. It is the best counterpart of the President's utterances which has proceeded from Europe. Just off to my little home in Le Touquet, so in haste.

Archie

Winston S. Churchill to Sir Archibald Sinclair
11th July 1918

Archie dear,

I was delighted to get your letter. I tried very hard to see you when I was at the HQ of the 57th Division. I could not discover your squadron, though sections of the 2nd Life Guards were within the command.

I will come to see you, if it is possible – on my next visit – I hope week of 20th.

I have been allocated a small chateau at Verchocq[135] by the C-in-C as a permanent lodging – a little maison-tolere. But I expect if you can escape for an evening you will want to go nearer to the sea. I will try to let you know my movements in good time. Is there anything you want?

I flew all my journeys last time, and very nearly finished an eventful though disappointing life in the salt water of the channel. We just fluttered back to shore. I have had better arrangements made for a good flight for communications purposes now. It only takes 1 hour from Lullenden to GHQ! But one must have careful engine supervision.

---

the war was a fight between Christian civilisation and scientific barbarism.

[135] Situated near Agincourt, around twenty-five miles from the front line.

I will try to organise a plan by which you can be transported for a few hours nearer to your hearts desire. The life and death struggle will begin again soon. Here mainly stress and talk. I hope you were pleased with my Independence day speech. If all goes well England & US may act permanently together. We are living 50 years in one at this rate.

Best love.
Yours affectionately,
W

PS. We will talk also about a constituency.

Winston S. Churchill to Sir Archibald Sinclair
General Headquarters British Army in The Field
(Undated but probably late summer 1918)

My dear Archie,

I have not had a chance to see you during this exciting and truly memorable visit here: and I never saw you to bid you God speed.

This I now do and send you and your gallant chief all my most heartfelt wishes for your success and safety.

I shall always feel very anxious about you two – daring being in some ways instrumental or at least a link in the chain – which brings you to this fierce conflict.

God bless you.

Your sincere friend,
W

Part 2

Fighting the Bolsheviks 1919–1923

Introduction

After the 1918 general election Lloyd George appointed Churchill Secretary of State for War and Air, and Sinclair joined him as his personal Military Secretary.

During the period 1919–21 both men became preoccupied with what they saw as the threat to the European political order posed by Bolshevism. Churchill feared that the Russian Revolution would follow the same course as the French Revolution a century and a half earlier, and he strongly supported the anti-Bolshevik White Russian forces during the Russian Civil War. He overestimated, however, their capabilities, cohesiveness and strength, and by spring 1920 it was clear that the White Russians were doomed to failure.

After Lenin had withdrawn Russia from the war with Germany in the spring of 1918 Lloyd George had initially agreed to provide British troops to support the anti-Bolshevik forces, in the hope that they would defeat the Bolsheviks and recommence resistance to the Central Powers. There was great optimism amongst British Intelligence representatives at the War Office that the injection of a small number of professional troops would help fashion a credible fighting force out of the White Russian armies, and by March 1918 nearly 200,000 Allied troops had been deployed around Murmansk and Archangel. The Armistice of November 1918, however, removed the original rationale for their presence, and on New Year's Eve 1918 the Cabinet decided that British troops would not, after all, be used to assist any counter-revolution. Instead, Lloyd George expected Churchill to take charge of the process of extricating British armed forces from Russia while ensuring that the White armies were provided with adequate supplies to continue the war.

Once in office, however, Churchill seemed to depart from the agreed Cabinet line, and began to look for opportunities to maintain and even enhance the British forces deployed in Russia, especially in the Archangel region. As Philip Kerr, an advisor to Lloyd George, stated in a message to the Premier, 'in my opinion Mr Churchill is bent on forcing a campaign against Bolshevik Russia by using Allied volunteers, Polish and Finnish and any other conscripts that he can get hold of, financed and equipped by the Allies ... I think you ought to watch the situation very carefully, if you do not want to be rushed into a policy of a volunteer war against the Bolsheviks in the near future.'[136]

[136] Kerr to Lloyd George, 15 February 1919, Lloyd George Papers, quoted in David Carlton, *Churchill and the Soviet Union* (Manchester University Press, 2000), p. 11.

Throughout 1919 Churchill manoeuvred constantly to prolong British military involvement in Russia. He was ably supported by Sinclair who spent much effort acting as liaison between his Secretary of State and representatives of the White Russian generals and wealthy émigrés and other opponents of the new Bolshevik regime. Sinclair was closely enmeshed in the security services at this time and exchanged correspondence with leading figures in Military Intelligence (MI1 and MI5) and met a number of their leading operatives, including the 'ace of spies', Sidney Reilly, with whom he built a close relationship.

Lloyd George became increasingly irritated by what he saw as Churchill's myopic focus on Russia. Both the Prime Minister and Austen Chamberlain, the Chancellor of the Exchequer, sought to cut back public spending, including the rapid demobilisation of Britain's large conscript army. On 22 September 1919 Lloyd George wrote an angry letter to Churchill stating:

> I wonder whether it is any use my making one last effort to induce you to throw off this obsession, which if you will forgive me for saying so, is upsetting your balance. I again ask you to let Russia be, at any rate for a few days, and to concentrate your mind on the quite unjustifiable expenditure in France, at home and in the East, incurred by the War Office and the Air Department ... The reconquest of Russia would cost hundreds of millions. It would cost hundreds of millions more to maintain the new Government until it had established itself. You are prepared to spend all that money, and I know perfectly well that it is what you really desire. But as you know you won't find another responsible person in the whole land who will take your view, why waste your energy and your usefulness on this vain fretting which paralyses you for other work?[137]

Churchill did not relinquish his hopes for the success of the counter-revolutionary White Russians. It was not until the military defeats of General Denikin over the winter of 1920 in southern Russia, and the capture and execution of the leader of the Siberian-based forces, Admiral Kolchak, in February 1920, that he was finally persuaded that the game was up.

It was during this period that Churchill made some public statements verging on the edge of anti-Semitism. A number of the briefing notes that passed between Sinclair and Churchill focused on the leading part played by Jews in the Bolshevik Revolution (four out of seven members of the first Politburo were Jewish). In an article published in the *Illustrated Sunday Herald* on 8 February 1920, entitled 'Zionism versus Bolshevism – A struggle for the soul of the Jewish people', Churchill referred to 'this world-wide conspiracy for the overthrow of civilisation and for the reconstitution of society on the basis of arrested development, of envious malevolence, and impossible equality'. In late 1919 Sinclair read a copy of the anti-Semitic *Protocols of the Elders of Zion*, and recommended that Churchill read it too, even though he questioned both its providence and its basic arguments. When conclusive field reports came into the War Office proving that Jews were being murdered and mistreated by the White Russians, Churchill spoke

[137] Lloyd George to Churchill, 22 September 1919, quoted in Carlton, *Churchill and the Soviet Union*, p. 18.

out in support of the rights of Jews in Russia to go unmolested in the areas controlled by Kolchak and Denikin.

As the White generals' chances waned, Churchill turned to Boris Savinkov, a former anti-Tsarist revolutionary and now anti-Bolshevik plotter, regarding him as the best hope for an effective leader of a new Russia.[138] But Savinkov lacked men and money and after a number of setbacks he was forced to retreat to Poland and organise terrorist resistance from outside Russia's borders. In 1924 Savinkov was tempted back to Russia with a promise of a role in the government; he was arrested, subjected to a show trial and sentenced to death. He died in May 1925 after falling from a window in Moscow's notorious Lubyanka prison.

Sinclair's role in Churchill's anti-Bolshevik war was pivotal. Churchill relied on him to build and maintain links with all the major players, to collect and assess intelligence reports about the Bolsheviks and their White Russia enemies, and to help coordinate the War Office's activities in support of Denikin and Kolchak throughout 1919 and early 1920. Sinclair was almost certainly a member of Military Intelligence, often writing to 'C', the head of Military Intelligence, preparing evaluations of intelligence reports for Churchill and following up on his responses. [139] Sinclair also acted as the contact point for swashbuckling spies, like Reilly, who were keen to influence Churchill's thinking about Russia and to use his political clout to win backing for their own aims.

The letters that follow capture the uncertainty and excitement of the period, when it appeared far from certain that the Bolshevik regime would survive and there seemed to be major political and military stakes to play for. Unlike the correspondence from the trenches these letters and memorandums are more formal in tone and less chatty in content. There are also far fewer replies from Churchill. Typically Churchill and Sinclair worked together in the office each day. While Sinclair presented his thoughts and information in written form for the hard-pressed War Minister to digest, Churchill's responses were frequently reduced to short sentences scrawled in red pencil in the margin or at the end of a paper.

The vast majority of the material relates to their experiences in dealing with the Russian Civil War. In February 1921 Churchill was moved to the Colonial Office and spent the next eighteen months dealing with the difficult situation in Iraq and the Near East and, though not a Colonial Office issue, the Irish problem. Although Sinclair transferred to the Colonial Office with Churchill, only a small number of their personal and professional papers from this period have survived. The letters that have been located relate to Churchill's plans for transferring Mesopotamia's (Iraq) defence responsibilities to the RAF in order to cut the costs of policing the region.

[138] Churchill was so impressed with Savinkov that he included him as one of twenty-one profiles in his book *Great Contemporaries* (Butterworth, 1937).

[139] Proof of Sinclair's membership of military intelligence during 1919–21 is held in a file (CHAR 16/77) in the Churchill archives which contains Sinclair's invitation from military intelligence, in 1921, to attend a farewell dinner when he left both Military Intelligence and the War Office to follow Churchill to the Colonial Office.

Towards the end of the period the letters resume a more informal tone, with much discussion of Sinclair's political career and which parliamentary seat he should stand for. In the November 1922 general election, Sinclair and Churchill had very different experiences. Although both, as supporters of Lloyd George, stood as National Liberals, Churchill lost his Dundee seat by a wide margin whilst Sinclair comfortably beat an Asquithian Liberal to win the Caithness & Sutherland constituency. He was to hold this seat without serious challenge until 1945.

1919–1920

During this period Churchill was Secretary of State for War and Sinclair his personal Military Secretary. Churchill required Sinclair to focus on building and nurturing contacts both in the various military intelligence services and with the eclectic White Russian anti-Bolshevik forces; he expected Sinclair to act as a go-between with the major players and to collect and assess intelligence relating to what was happening in the émigré Russian communities and within Soviet Russia itself. Sinclair worked long hours filtering material from an astonishingly wide variety of sources, preparing his own analysis and précising reports for Churchill. He also followed up Churchill's requests for further information and passed on the Secretary of State's requests to the head of Military Intelligence and others.

Along with this strategically important work in the Soviet sphere, however, Sinclair also performed many mundane duties. The first surviving letter of 1919 finds him advising Churchill of the possible embarrassment likely to be caused by Sir Douglas Haig's insistence on remaining in Scotland rather than meeting the US General Pershing.

Sir Archibald Sinclair to Winston S. Churchill
7th May 1919
Very Confidential

S. of S.

It is understood that Sir Douglas Haig[140] intends to remain in Scotland for the rest of this month and would therefore be absent from London during the whole of General Pershing's[141] visit from the 22nd to the 25th May. There is reason to believe that Sir Douglas Haig's absence would make a most important impression on General Pershing and the seven Army Commanders and High Staff Officers who are accompanying him. These men on their return to America will not only occupy

[140] Douglas Haig, First Earl Haig (1861–1928): served in Sudan and Boer War; succeeded French as Commander-in-Chief British Expeditionary Force in December 1915; pursued strategy of attrition, at enormous cost in British lives; ennobled 1919.

[141] General John J. Pershing (1860–1948): Commander-in-Chief American Expeditionary Force, 1917–19; Chief of Staff, US Army, 1921–24.

the highest posts in the American Army, but also very often will undoubtedly become in due course Governors of States in the Union and are, or even perhaps two of them are, possible Presidential Candidates.

It is felt that there is one ceremony from which Sir Douglas Haig's absence would be particularly wanting. At noon on Friday May 23rd two battalions of Footguards will be drawn up on the Horse Guards Parade and General Pershing will present the American Distinguished Service Medal to a number of officers of the British Army. A very similar ceremony took place at the American G.H.Q. France, a short time ago, as part of the reception accorded to Sir Douglas Haig by the American C. in C., Sir Douglas Haig's presence on this occasion would, it is believed, be greatly appreciated by General Pershing, while his absence throughout the whole of the visit would probably give rise to widespread comment in America.

AHMS

One of Sinclair's tasks was to compile for Churchill's approval the lists of recommendations for military decorations for officers for services rendered during the war. Sinclair's administration was not always up to the standard that the Secretary of State expected.

Winston S. Churchill to Sir Archibald Sinclair
21st May 1919

MILITARY SECRETARY

These papers have reached me in a very inconvenient form. I do not understand why lists cannot be drawn up instead of bundles of separate recommendations. It is further stated that "A" contains recommendations under two headings: on the contrary, "A" appears to be nothing more than a letter from Sir Douglas Haig to the Secretary of State. What is the use of sending "B", "C", and "D" to me when they are merely collections of individual recommendations?

Pray let me have a proper table made out under each of the decorations concerned, showing the decoration or reward which it is proposed to award the officer and the work he has done in the war which is held to justify it. There obviously can be no question of completing these lists in time for the Birthday Honours.

WSC

In May 1919 Churchill wrote to the Chief and Deputy Chief of the Imperial General Staff, copied to Sinclair, to say that he did not expect the War Cabinet to be informed of all the details of the North Russian Brigades. He was following a personal policy of providing only the very minimum of information on the activities of British forces in North Russia and he made it clear that before any issue was passed to the War Cabinet it should be checked with him first. This reflects the increasing extent to which

Churchill was conducting operations in North Russia in a manner at odds with Lloyd George's foreign policy.

Winston S. Churchill to Field Marshal Sir Henry Wilson,[142] *Major-General Sir Charles Harington*[143] *and Sir Archibald Sinclair*
22nd May 1919

C.I.G.S.[144] (to see).
D.C.I.G.S.[145]
SECRETARY

Some time ago I stated my opinion that the formation of Russian Brigades with British officers was a purely administrative measure within the scope of the authority I have received from the Cabinet to form and maintain the strong Military Missions at Kolchak's[146] and Denikin's[147] Headquarters. This is also Mr. Balfour's view.[148]

I did not therefore consider that it was necessary to go the Cabinet on the subject afresh.

I understood that orders had already been given for the necessary action to be taken, and I had supposed that both in North Russia and in Siberia the units were already in process of formation. Unnecessary labour is caused when questions of a departmental character of this kind have to be explained and argued to the Cabinet as if they were great matters of principle. As long as I am available at short notice, I require to be informed before my question is remitted by the War Office to the Cabinet.

Pray report fully on the present position.

Action yourself meanwhile.

WSC

---

[142] Sir Henry Hughes Wilson (1864–1922): Chief liaison officer with the French Army January 1915; commanded Fourth Corps 1916; Chief of the Imperial General Staff 1918–22; assassinated by Sinn Fein on the steps of his London house, 1922.

[143] Sir Charles 'Tim' Harington (1872–1940): Deputy Chief of the Imperial General Staff 1918–20; Lieutenant-General Commanding the Army of the Black Sea 1920; Commanding Officer of the Allied Forces of Occupation in Turkey 1920–23; Governor and Commander-in-Chief Gibraltar 1933–38.

[144] Chief of the Imperial General Staff (Wilson).

[145] Deputy Chief of the Imperial General Staff (Harington).

[146] Alexander Vasilevich Kolchak (1874–1920): Russian admiral; Commander of the Black Sea fleet during World War I; after the October Revolution became leader of the anti-Bolshevik White forces in Siberia, and in October 1918 proclaimed himself 'Supreme Ruler' of Russia; captured and executed by the Bolsheviks at Irkutsk in 1920.

[147] Anton Ivanovich Denikin (1872–1947): Russian soldier, rose to the rank of Lieutenant-General in World War I; Commander of the White Russian forces in Southern Russia 1918–20; escaped to Constantinople and then lived in exile in France and the US.

[148] Then Foreign Secretary – see n15.

Churchill was under great pressure to increase the pace of demobilisation. In early 1919 British troops near-mutinied at Whitehall and Calais at the prospect of being sent back to France rather than home. Both the Treasury and the Ministry of National Service were arguing for swift reductions in the size of the retained Army.

Winston S. Churchill to Sir Archibald Sinclair
22nd May 1919

SECRETARY

Draft reply not approved. Write as follows:-

"I am directed by the S. of S. to acknowledge the receipt of your letter of the 6th May, in which you state that 'Sir Auckland Geddes[149] cannot but consider that it is far from satisfactory that so large a percentage of officers is still retained'.

"Mr. Churchill desires me to observe in reply that he accepts the fullest constitutional responsibility for the measures which are taken to demobilise the Army, having regard to the general military situation. He is unable to concur in the adverse opinion expressed by Sir Auckland Geddes, and he regrets that such a statement should have formed the subject of inter-departmental correspondence."

WSC

Churchill's optimism about the possibility of the White Russian forces winning the civil war was increasing in late May 1919. He urged that British forces should do all they could to help.

Winston S. Churchill to Major-General Sir Charles Harington, Major-General Sir Percy Radcliffe and Sir Archibald Sinclair
22nd May 1919

D.C.I.G.S.
D.M.O.[150]
SECRETARY

I do not think this telegram should have been sent without my previous sanction. The situation in North Russia has now reached a most hopeful and critical phase, and the probable speedy junction with Kolchak requires to be assisted by the most strenuous measures.

---

[149] Sir Auckland Geddes (1879–1954): Minister of National Service 1917–19; Minister of Reconstruction 1919; President of the Board of Trade 1919–20; Ambassador to Washington 1920–24.

[150] Director of Military Operations (Radcliffe – see n73).

What is the number and character of British personnel which it is said cannot be collected? I am not prepared as at present informed to recognise the impossibility of meeting the necessary requirements.

I do not agree that General Maynard[151] should be limited to maintaining the Russian forces already mobilised and should be forbidden to mobilise more. The reaction of Russian forces in this theatre is an indispensable preliminary to the execution of our policy of evacuating North Russia when suitable arrangements have been made with the loyal Russian armies. It should be pressed forward by every conceivable means.

WSC

In a highly contentious letter Churchill argued that the use of gas against natives in India or Afghanistan was preferable to high explosive shells.

22 May 1919

Military Secretary

The objections of the India Office to the use of gas against natives are unreasonable. Gas is a more merciful weapon than high explosive shell, and compels an enemy to accept a decision with less loss of life than with any other agency of war. The moral effect is also very great.

There can be no conceivable reason why it should not be resorted to. We have definitely taken the position of maintaining gas as a weapon in future warfare, and it is only ignorance on the part of the Indian military authorities which interposes any obstacle. Having regard to the fact that they are retaining all our men, even those who are the most entitled to demobilisation, we cannot in any circumstances acquiesce in the non-utilisation of any weapons which are available to procure a speedy termination of the disorder which prevails on the frontier.

If it is fair war for an Afghan to shoot down a British soldier behind a rock and cut him in pieces, as he lies wounded on the ground, why is it not fair for a British artilleryman to fire a shell which makes the said native sneeze. It is really too silly.

C.I.G.S. concurs.

WSC

Churchill and Sinclair spent considerable time encouraging and supporting initiatives to open up supply routes to the White Russians via the frequently ice-bound Kara Sea off the Northern coast of Russia.

[151] Charles Maynard (1870–1945): Major-General commanding Allied forces, Archangel, 1918–19.

Sir Archibald Sinclair to Winston S. Churchill
27th May 1919

S. of S.

Note on interview with Mr. Jonas Lied, War Office 18th June 1919.

Kara Sea Route to Siberia

Mr. Jonas Lied called upon me this morning with a letter of introduction from Commander Oliver Locker-Lampson, M.P.[152] He handed me a copy of the Memorandum which was sent to you by Mr. Cox (enclosed with his letter marked X on this file) and he explained that the Department of Overseas Trade had declared that it was not possible to put his scheme through in the time available. He realised that, unless exceptional measures were to be taken, this was the case, as the time is short but he was quite certain, from his own experience in recent years with similar expeditions, that, if exceptional powers were taken and if operations were begun within the next week or 10 days, his expedition would be successful. He was therefore anxious to have an interview with you as he was certain that he could prove to you that his scheme was feasible.

I pointed out to him that you, yourself were already convinced of the expediency from the military point of view of the opening up of the Kara Sea route, but as regards the possibility of doing it in the time available this year or the means to be employed, the decision rested entirely with the Department of Overseas Trade and that you would on no account interfere. He then declared that if he were unable to obtain an interview with you he would abandon his project altogether. I suggested to him that it would be better for him to see the Chiefs of the Department of Overseas Trade or at the Foreign Office before taking a final decision as to the abandonment of his project as the War Office had already expressed its recognition of the value of the Kara Sea route but that the decision as to the possibility of opening it up this year rested with those Departments.

You will observe from the attached correspondence that the Department of the Overseas Trade are helping the Merchant Trading Company to open up the Kara Sea route and that they do not wish to avail themselves of Mr. Lied's services or to encourage competition between his Company and the Merchant Trading Company.

AHMS
18.6.19.

I cannot take this written out of the hand of the proper officials[153]

Throughout most of 1919 Churchill was responsible for the confirmation of medals and awards for officers and men who had served during the 1914–18 war. He took his

[152] 'Oliver' Godfrey Locker-Lampson (1875–1946): Conservative MP for Salisbury 1910–18 and for Wood Green 1918–35.

[153] Note in Churchill's hand at the foot of the memo from Sinclair.

responsibilities seriously and would not hesitate to probe further if he felt someone had been overlooked or not given the appropriate recognition.

Winston S. Churchill to Sir Archibald Sinclair
22nd June 1919

MILITARY SECRETARY

I think you should see Sir Archibald Murray[154] and find out what principle he proceeded upon in his recommendations for the Quatia Oasis fight.[155] It was a very nasty fight, and as nearly everybody who survived was captured, I do not suppose it received very careful attention.

Needless to say, it is not desired that any special favour should be shown, but if this officer is found to have behaved well and gallantly in these difficult and tragic circumstances, something more is required than a mere assurance that there is nothing against him for having been taken prisoner.

WSC

Sinclair and Churchill were keen to explore opportunities to exert economic and financial pressure on the Bolshevik regime. The Foreign Office, however, declined to support the Department of Trade's proposal for a scheme to establish British control and influence over the Russian banking system

Sir Archibald Sinclair to Winston S. Churchill
17th July 1919
Personal

<u>S. of S.</u>
<u>Russian Trade</u>

Mr. Bagge[156] has just been to see me about the position of the Yaroshiuski[157] scheme, referred to in the papers marked X and Y on the attached file. This is the big scheme which has been drawn up by the D.O.T.[158] for the control of the Russian

[154] Sir Archibald Murray (1860–1945): Chief of Staff to the British Expeditionary Force commander, Sir John French, 1914–15; suffered a nervous breakdown in early 1915 and replaced by Sir William Robertson; commanded imperial forces in Palestine and in March 1916 became British commander-in-chief Middle East; after twice failing to take Gaza, he was replaced by Edmund Allenby in June 1917.
[155] It has not proved possible to identify this action but it is likely that it was part of the campaign east of Sinai and the struggles to capture Gaza in March–April 1917.
[156] Sir John Picton Bagge (1877–1967): civil servant with the Department of Overseas Trade; British Consul-General at Odessa; knowledgeable of economic and political conditions in South Russia.
[157] It has not been possible to locate biographical information on this individual.
[158] Department of Overseas Trade.

banks by an Anglo-Russian Corporation which would ensure the predominance of Great Britain both economically and politically in Russia.

The scheme appears to have many enthusiastic advocates such as Sir A. Steel-Maitland[159] and Sir W. Tyrell, but they seem to be somewhat unsuccessful in arousing Lord Curzon's interest, and without his support and encouragement, it is impossible for the promoters of the scheme to form the British Group. If Lord Curzon would go as far as to call a meeting of the principal backers and financiers so that the scheme could be explained to them, the promoters have little doubt that the corporation could be quickly formed and that it would be fairly in its stride in the winter, In that case it would provide a solution for many of the economic and financial problems, which will be pressing upon Denikin and Kolchak still more strongly then, than they are now. Mr. Bagge learns that the pages are in Lord Curzon's office this evening. Will you urge him to interest himself in this question?

AHMS

Sir Archibald Sinclair to Winston S. Churchill
18th July 1919

S. of S.
Russian Trade

This morning the attached pages marked Z arrived at the same time as I received your directions to draft a note to Lord Curzon.

I therefore refrained from carrying out your instructions pending further enquiries, as you would not wish to appear to support the particular scheme of economic reconstruction which is being put forward by the D.O.T. as against that of the Supreme Economic Council.

Bagge is away to-day but I will report to you again on Monday or Tuesday if you approve.

AHMS

Great Britain's interest in Persia (modern-day Iran) had been significantly augmented during the First World War. Early in the war the British Government purchased, primarily on the initiative of Winston Churchill, 51 per cent of the stock in the Anglo-Persian Oil Company (later BP). The company owned the oil concession for the whole of Persia, with the exception of the five northern provinces which, under the terms of the Anglo-Russian Agreement of 1907, were located in the Russian sphere of influence.

This agreement had helped to bring to an end nearly a century of intermittent conflict between the two powers over Persia, which Britain regarded as an area of strategic

[159] Sir Arthur Herbert Drummond Ramsay Steel-Maitland (1876–1935): Conservative MP for East Birmingham 1910–29, Tamworth 1929–35; Secretary for Overseas Trade at the Board of Trade, 1917–19; Minister for Labour, 1924–29.

importance to the military security of India, its jewel in the east. The collapse of Tsarist Russia had thrown the 1907 Agreement into disarray and Britain was keen to prevent the spread of Soviet influence beyond Russia, especially to Persia, which had an extensive border with the British protectorate of Mesopotamia.[160] Furthermore, the Foreign Office hoped to establish a series of independent anti-Bolshevik regimes in countries such as Armenia, Azerbaijan, Georgia and Persia. For nine months up to August 1919 Lord Curzon, the Foreign Secretary, negotiated a treaty with the Persian Government that pledged Britain to respect the independence and integrity of Persia and to supply expert advisers, military officers and equipment; Britain also agreed to lend Persia £2,000,000. Churchill and Sinclair followed the negotiations with interest; any enemy of the Bolsheviks, as the Persian Government appeared to be, was a friend of theirs. Sinclair kept Churchill informed of progress and also queried whether they should ensure that the key participants at the Versailles Peace Conference be kept appraised of developments.

Sir Archibald Sinclair to Winston S. Churchill
24th July 1919

S. of S.

As you are doubtless aware from the F.O. telegrams, the negotiations between Persia and this country for the signature of a comprehensive political agreement which will embrace military questions, are approaching a satisfactory conclusion. Should not Spears[161] either be advised not to pursue his conversation with the Persian Minister and his staff in Paris or be given the full official information as to the present position of the Persian negotiation and the military proposals contained in draft agreement before embarking upon an exchange of views with the Persian Minister?

AHMS

In November 1918, soon after the disintegration of the Austro-Hungarian Empire, Romanian troops crossed the Carpathian Mountains and occupied Transylvania, then part of Hungary; the Allies approved the occupation in January 1919. In Budapest on 21 March, Bela Kun proclaimed the establishment of the 'Hungarian Soviet Republic' on the model of the Russian communist regime, and during late March and early April the Hungarians organised a counter-offensive which was beaten back by the Romanians.

[160] The British had conquered most of Mesopotamia (mainly modern-day Iraq) during the war, and administered a military government until 1920; this was replaced by an Iraqi Council of State under British supervision, and then, in 1921, a Kingdom, though still under British mandate. Iraq became fully independent when the League of Nations abolished its mandate status in 1932.

[161] See n97. Spears had a vast network of contacts and provided Sinclair and Churchill with an alternative source of intelligence than the Foreign Office.

There was much concern about the spread of communism to Hungary and how best to ensure that the Peace Conference's decisions were enforced.

Sir Archibald Sinclair to Winston S. Churchill
24th July 1919

S. of S.
Hungary

Spears rang up to say that he had been speaking to General Bliss[162] who assured him that he was not opposed to the plan of action against Hungary which is under consideration. Spears attached importance to this opinion because it is the Americans who are blamed by the French and the Roumanians for refusing to agree to any plan to compel Hungary to carry out the armistice terms.[163]

Spears states that the situation is the worse confused because Foch, who should have been charged by the Allies with the preparation and, in certain contingencies, the execution of the plan of action against Hungary, was away in Brussels when the Hungarian attack began. The French Minister for War, apparently telegraphed, in Foch's absence, certain instructions to which Foch on his return to Paris chose to resent.

Spears had been talking to many people in Paris during the afternoon and is confirmed in the opinion which he expressed on the telephone this morning, that decisive action should not be any longer delayed. The Hungarian divisions are engaged with the Roumanians; only four – I understood him to say but I won't guarantee the figure – two in reserve, a few days grace would allow the Hungarians to withdraw, and re-group the divisions now fighting the Roumanians. Moreover it is important to settle with the Hungarians before communicating the peace terms to the Bulgarians who are now on their way to Paris.

Towards the end of our conversation the line began to get very faint and we had to break off abruptly in the middle of a sentence which I couldn't understand.

AHMS 8.30 p.m. so please forgive untidiness

Sinclair continued to update Churchill on the proposals to assist the White Russians with the formation of an Anglo-Russian Corporation.

---

[162] Tasker Bliss (1853–1930): American Military Representative on the Supreme War Council, Versailles 1917–19; American Commissioner, Paris Peace Conference, 1919.

[163] The Romanians had been rewarded with significant tracts of formerly Hungarian land in Transylvania by the Peace Conference. Hungary resisted this decision with military force but was soundly defeated, and Romanian troops occupied Budapest on 3 August 1919; Bela Kun's embryonic communist regime collapsed. The Allied powers agreed to the withdrawal of the Romanian forces, which left in stages until April 1920. On 4 June 1920 the Treaty of Trianon was signed between the Allies and the new Hungarian administration, settling the borders as they remain today.

Sir Archibald Sinclair to Winston S. Churchill
28th July 1919
Very Confidential

S. of S.
Russian Trade

Bagge told me in conversation two or three days ago that he was delighted with the events narrated in the memo which I have just received from him. The fact that this assembly of the greatest financiers in Russia, including the financial representatives of Kolchak and Denikin as well as ex-officials like Litonoff-Falysky, not only elected Yaroshiuski President of the proposed Corporation in his absence but also accepted the various conditions for which he stipulated, is striking proof of his pre-eminence in the Russian financial world, and the enhanced prestige which these events will bring him, should greatly assist the development of the Yaroshiuski scheme for the revival of Russian economic life by an Anglo-Russian Corporation, under the wing of the British Government.

Would you care to see Yaroshiuski?

AHMS

During the war the German army occupied Lithuania, but in February 1918 nationalists proclaimed the country's independence under German protection. With the defeat of Germany in November 1918 Lithuania declared full independence. The new state was soon subjected to attacks by Bolshevik troops and by volunteer bands of German adventurers. Leading Lithuanian figures came to London in August 1919 seeking assistance in resisting the Bolsheviks and in preventing Poland from seizing territory.

Sir Archibald Sinclair to Winston S. Churchill
8th August 1919

Secretary of State,
Note of an interview with Comte Alfred Tyszkiewicz, at the War Office on 7th August, 1919

Comte Alfred Tyszkiewicz[164] is in London as the representative of the Lithuanian Government, He asked to see you, but you refused to see him; and the heads of the General Staff Branches concerned were also reluctant to do so as it would have been contrary to their usual practice. On the other hand, he was being interviewed by the heads of the Branches concerned in the Foreign Office and was very anxious to

[164] Alfred Tyszkiewicz (1882–1930): Lithuanian by birth (then part of Russia), served in the Russian army in the Russo-Japanese War (1904–05); subsequently worked in the Foreign Ministry and was secretary to the Russian embassy in London; transferred his allegiance to newly independent Lithuania in 1919, and attended the Paris Peace Conference; Lithuania's minister to Great Britain 1920–21.

see somebody in touch with you at the War Office and, therefore, upon the special representations of General Spiers I consented to see him.

Speaking with much fluency, now in French and now in English, he emphasised the urgency of the supply of equipment to the Lithuanian Government for 25,000 men.

He pointed out that in the month of October, the state of the country begins to preclude military operations on any considerable scale, while on the other hand, there is in Lithuania an ample supply of men who would gladly share in the fighting against the Bolsheviks if equipment were available.

His second point was that they badly needed Staff officers and senior regimental and general officers. They had an ample supply of junior regimental officers, but they felt the need of highly trained Staff officers and Commanding officers.

His third point was the necessity of drawing a fairer line of demarcation between the Lithuanians and the Poles. A line was fixed by the Peace Conference not long ago but only recently it was altered again and was made more unfavourable to the Lithuanians. He considers it of the first importance to the full development of Lithuanian resources against the Bolsheviks that a line would now be firmly and finally fixed. The recent alteration had most unfavourably affected the tranquillity of Lithuania. If a line could be drawn which would satisfy the people of Lithuania, there would be greater production of food and more men would be available to fight the Bolsheviks.

You will remember, however, that reports have come from our Mission in these parts that the Lithuanians have not been tactful or statesmanlike in their dealings with the Polish elements in the country.

In reply to Comte Alfred Tyszkiewicz I pointed out that the questions which he raised in so far as they affected the line of demarcation between Poland and Lithuania would be dealt with by the Foreign Office and in so far as they affected military assistance would be dealt with by the Supreme War Council in Paris.

I assured him of your lively interest in the affairs of the Lithuanians and in the plucky struggle against the Bolsheviks.

AHMS

Sinclair regularly summarised for Churchill reports concerning the plight of the populace in the Bolshevik-controlled parts of the Russia. These reports generally painted a dire picture and encouraged both Sinclair and Churchill to think that the revolutionary regime could be overthrown.

Sir Archibald Sinclair to Winston S. Churchill
8th August 1919

S. of S.

You were considering yesterday the circulation of this memorandum to the Cabinet. Perhaps you will have observed to-day that a slightly altered version of it has been published in the "Times" newspaper. It is presumed therefore that you will not require it to be printed for Cabinet circulation.

AHMS

Memorandum

Colonel Vladimiroff,[165] who has been entrusted with a special mission by General Yudenitch,[166] has just arrived in London from the North-Western front and brings the following information regarding the situation in Petrograd[167] where he stayed until July 10th, and also regarding the state of affairs on General Yudenitch's front, which he left towards the end of the month.

1. THE SITUATION IN PETROGRAD

The whole city has, so to speak, been transformed into one huge military camp, and the remaining population (not exceeding 500,000) are being subjected to a military regime. The town is divided into districts which are rigorously guarded by reliable communists. The system of searching houses and flats at random has been abandoned for one of wholesale requisitions carried out by night by special detachments, partly formed of women. These searches result in requisitions and wholesale arrests of the last remnants of the educated class, the object often being to round up certain categories of the male population such as, for instance, engineers.

Accommodation in the prisons is quite inadequate, and the overflow of prisoners is drafted to other towns, chiefly Moscow. It is hardly necessary to dwell upon the regime of the prisons – it is appalling. People are shot systematically with the utmost cynicism.

The feeding of the population is carried out as follows: supplies for a few days only are brought to the city and a "dinner" consisting of a plate of soup made of local fish called "vobla" and an 8th of a pound of bread is served out to each person once a day. Such a dinner costs 4 roubles. The impossibility of purchasing provisions

[165] Dimitri Vladimiroff or Vladimirov (1896–1952): born into an aristocratic Russian family, originally called Dimitri von Prebsting-Cesarevsky; trained at Moscow's Bolshoi Theatre; an ardent monarchist, he rose to the rank of Lieutenant-Colonel in the Don Cossack Army during the Russian Civil War; fled Russia and moved to Toronto, where he established a successful ballet school.

[166] Nikolai Nikolaevich Yudenich (1862–1933): Commander of the anti-Bolshevik North-Western Army against Petrograd in 1919; arrested by fellow White officers when his offensive failed, but released on British insistence and emigrated to Britain.

[167] Known as St Petersburg until 1914, as Leningrad 1924–91, and now St Petersburg once more.

in the markets and the compulsory reduction of fuel for private persons have resulted in the almost total abandonment of private housekeeping and domestic alimentation, practically the whole of the population being transferred to the communal dining rooms. Mortality is exceedingly high, while conditions in the hospitals beggar description. Burials are a thing of the past for the simple reason that there is nobody to do the work and coffins cannot be made for lack of material.

The population is thus kept in a state of perpetual hunger and terror, while, owing to the system of espionage and violence set up by the Bolsheviks, any internal upheaval is out of the question. The terrorized people's one and only hope is deliverance from outside.

2. POSITION OF LABOUR

The economic, sanitary and technical conditions are infinitely worse than those prevailing before 1917. In this respect the present demands of the workmen are symptomatic: – "down with all summons to join the Red Army", "enough promises", "give us bread and order" etc. They complain of the abolition of the old system of sanitary and technical inspection and detest the Bolshevik political control. An organised insurrection on the part of the workers is impossible for the reasons given above. Only communists are allowed to carry arms. Requisitions among the labourers are carried out in the same way as among the rest of the population, and the discovery of arms in the hands of a non-communist workman leads to his summary execution just as in the case of the other classes. Any attempt to revolt is immediately suppressed by armed force. During the suppression of a strike of the railwaymen on the Nicholas Railway which occurred on July 11th, six workmen were killed and nineteen wounded.

Many branches of Petrograd labour, such as domestic servants, messengers, cabmen (izvoshtchniks) porters etc. have ceased to exist, either of their own accord, or through Bolshevik action. A considerable percentage of the population has consequently lost its earnings and is practically thrown on to the street.

3. MILITARY SITUATION

The efficiency of the military branch of the administration is the cause of the utmost concern and takes precedence over any other consideration. The continual application of violence and terrorism, carefully fostered by the Bolsheviks, yield undoubted results. The Bolsheviks have set themselves two principal tasks: the creation of an absolutely obedient Red Army, and the undermining of the forces of the enemy.

The first object is achieved by a system of intense political espionage carried on within the ranks of the Red Army itself by a body of special communist commissaries and small communist units and also by the ruthless application of capital punishment. An illustration of the severity of prevailing conditions, the following verified fact may be cited: a Red soldier belonging to one of the units stationed at Ropsha (near Petrograd) in the beginning of July was shot by his colonel for having ventured to leave his regiment in order to get some milk in the neighbouring village. In an attack, the communists form the first line, and follow up the bulk of the unit with machine guns which are used for shooting deserters or retreating troops. These measures, together with the harsh treatment meted out to the commanding officers in cases of mass-surrender, or, in general for any reverse, have certainly increased the efficiency of the Red forces. This has been specially noticeable since the month of June when the last simultaneous surrender of 7,000 men of the Red Army took place near Krassnaya Gorka. Since then they have surrendered only in small groups. The Red Army lacks technically educated officers, especially artillery officers who are sought for any and everywhere, and are forced into the army even if unfit or over military age. There is also a shortage of shells.

The second object is achieved through propaganda and latterly through direct and unblushing bribery. Billions of roubles are allotted to this method of persuasion, banknotes being specially printed for the purpose by the Soviet Authorities. 2,500 millions have been set aside in this way for bribery on the Eastern Front. In order to bring about a breach in the enemy's lines a great number of Red guards went over to the Whites, and under the pretence of surrender, distributed huge sums of money to their unsuspecting opponents, thereby causing four entire regiments of Koltchak's army to join the Bolsheviks in the next few days. The net result was a breach which, among other reasons, compelled the Siberian Armies to return very far back. Bribery has become systematised; each fighting unit organizes a group of convinced communists whose duty it is to give themselves up to the enemy for the purpose of propaganda and of causing disruption of his front.

4. POSITION ON GENERAL YUDENITCH'S FRONT

When the recent check took place in the advance on this front, the Bolsheviks decided to defend Petrograd at all costs. Five divisions have been concentrated on this sector, with 100 guns (not counting the Karelian division of 10,000 men with 120 guns) which gives a total of about 60,000 men. There exists here a reserve of 20,000 men (Novgorod and Petrograd). Losses are replaced in a satisfactory manner, i.e. normally about 2,000 men a day.

General Yudenitch's forces on the southern shores of the Gulf of Finland now reach 35,000 men in the fighting line and 15,000 in the rear. Of the former (35,000) barely one third is adequately armed and equipped: two thirds have rifles, but are without sufficient cartridges. There are only 35 guns with 30,000 shells, borrowed from the Finns and the Esthonians. The troops are gradually being organized in the midst of active warfare. Four divisions are being formed. The fighting qualities of these troops have been proved by the fact that in spite of their extremely poor armament and equipment, they have not only succeeded in retaining the line Yamburg–Pskoff, captured from the Bolsheviks, but they continue successfully to harass the enemy.

It would follow from the above that were General Yudenitch's army, which is now being formed, to receive the necessary armaments, and were it to be equipped with the utmost speed, even if only with articles of immediate military necessity, it would be afforded the possibility of abandoning its present semi-defensive operations in order to assume an independent and decisive offensive for the capture of Petrograd.

Requests from White Russian intermediaries for British assistance, in the form of money, supplies and advisors, kept Sinclair busy throughout the summer and autumn of 1919.

Sir Archibald Sinclair to Winston S. Churchill
11th August 1919

S. of S.
Petrograd

On Friday last W.A.B. Stockart, Manager of the Russian Corporation, called upon me at the suggestion of Sir William Sutherland[168] to explain the situation and prospects of General Yudenitch and his committee of White Russian supporters as set out in the attached memorandum, and to ask me to see on Tuesday (25th) or Wednesday (26th) next:–

A. Mr. Jules Hessen, Managing Director of the two principal Russian Steamship companies and a prominent member of General Yudenitch's committee.
B. M. Vladimir Ber, a wealthy and influential Russian business man who has long been resident in this country but keeping in touch with General Yudenitch.
C. And a representative of the Russian Corporation who has just returned from Finland.

Mr. Stockart's object is, of course, to promote the policy of General Yudenitch.

I embodied the information which I obtained from him in the questionnaire which I drafted at your dictation and placed in your box on Friday night and I was waiting till I heard what action if any you were taking on that and what your view was with regard to operations against Petrograd before enquiring whether I should give these further interviews.

But as time now passes will you please instruct me whether:

1. You wish me to see any of the above gentlemen
2. You wish me to see any of them and report to you
3. You wish me to reply that you are fully informed of General Yudenitch's projects which are receiving earnest consideration in relation to the other aspects of the Russian problem.

Representatives of General Yudenitch have come to London in order to get support in their contemplated attack upon Petrograd.

A. Objects

1. The occupation of Petrograd, the moral effect of which throughout Russia would, it is believed, be tremendous – leading almost directly to the overthrow of the Bolsheviks in Moscow by the population itself.

[168] Sir William Sutherland (1880–1949): Private Secretary to Lloyd George 1915–18; Coalition Liberal MP for Argyllshire 1918–24; Parliamentary Private Secretary to Lloyd George 1918-20; Junior Lord of the Treasury 1920–22; Chancellor of the Duchy of Lancaster 1922.

2. The capture of the fleet in the Baltic before it is liberated by the melting of the ice.
3. The seizure of the printing presses which are now producing the paper money as fast as they can be worked and all of which are concentrated in and around Petrograd.

B. Forces

General Yudenitch claims already to have under his command Russian forces adequate for the enterprise. The Finnish frontier is within 25 kilometres of Petrograd and there are few if any Bolshevik troops in the intervening country.

C. Requirements

1. General Yudenitch will not move before he is assured by the allies of an ample supply of provision for Petrograd. It is considered that 30,000 tons of breadstuffs would be sufficient for the first two months.
2. A high military official of one of the Allied Armies to assist General Yudenitch especially in his relations with the Finnish authorities.

What is your view as to:–

1. General Yudenitch's prospects of success?
2. The effect on the general Russian situation of the capture of Petrograd?
3. The desirability of helping him?
4. If it is considered that General Yudenitch's force is too weak to hold Petrograd against Bolshevik counter-attack, would it be desirable to encourage and assist the enterprise if the Finns would co-operate in the defence of Petrograd after its capture?

AHMS

Sir Archibald Sinclair to Winston S. Churchill
9th August 1919
Personal

S. of S.

Dragomirov's[169] Requests

I am informed unofficially with regard to the attached requests:–[170]

[169] General Vladimir Dragomirov (1862–1920): prominent White Russian general, appointed Military Governor of Kiev by Denikin in October 1919; presumed killed by Polish forces following the fall of Kiev in 1920.

[170] The requests were that: (1) surplus stores and all that is surplus at Archangel be sent via the Kara Sea to Kolchak; (2) that General Kolman be directed to send General Denikin's priority wires to Admiral Kolchak via the War Office who should pass them to Kolchak by the quickest route; (3) that General Ermolov, Russian Military Attaché, should have facility to communicate with General Denikin via the

1. General Staff would prefer that North Russian stores should go to Yudenitch, but as no shipping is available except Wilkitzky's and as he is Koltchak's man taking a convoy of ships to him via the Kara Sea, it is most unlikely that he will fall in with the G.S. suggestion which Ironside[171] has been ordered to make to him that he should take the stores to Yudenitch and, in the alternative, Ironside has been ordered to send them on to Kolchak as requested by Dragomirov.
2. If strictly confined to urgent 'Priority' wires there would probably be no objection.
3. There would probably be little or no objection.
4. This matter has already been taken up in the sense desired by Dragomirov and there is a file in your box dealing with it.
5. Colonel MacAlgive, representing the Supreme Economic Council but under the orders of our Foreign Office is already with Denikin. F.O. is taking up the question of a diplomatic representative with the Allies in accordance with recent Cabinet decision, and no doubt some-one will be despatched very shortly.
6. As you will see from General Briggs' notes attached, he is willing to go to Yudenitch but wants three or four weeks' leave first beginning next Thursday night if possible. He would be in Northumberland – less than one day's journey from here if urgently required.
7. General Briggs is taking up this and all the other requests with the branches concerned.

AHMS

Sir Archibald Sinclair to Winston S. Churchill
11th August 1919

S. of S.

Reference the first of Genl. Dragomirov's requests to you, definite orders have now been sent that the surplus Archangel stores are to go to Kolchak via Kara Sea, owing to the impossibility of getting them to Yudenitch.

AHMS

War Office by cipher telegrams rather than having to do so via Paris; (4) that the French Government be approached to put an end to plans for sending 50,000 Russian soldiers who are pro-Bolshevik to Odessa; (5) Mr Savonov requests facility of travel to help send a Mr. Schebeko to General Yudenitch.

[171] William Edmund Ironside (1880–1959): Major-General commanding Allied troops at Archangel 1918–19; Head of British Military Mission to Hungary 1920; Commander British Forces in Turkey 1920, and North Persia 1920–21; Quartermaster-General India 1933–36; Governor and Commander-in-Chief Gibraltar 1938–39; Chief of the Imperial General Staff 1939–40; Commander-in-Chief Home Forces May 1940; one of a small number of men who held general officer rank in both world wars.

From mid-August 1919, Sinclair stepped up his attempts to persuade financiers and the Foreign Office to support the development of trade, commerce and basic financial and banking systems in the areas of northern Russia controlled by the White armies.

Sir Archibald Sinclair to Winston S. Churchill
12th August 1919

S. of S.

Mr. Bagge (ex-council Odessa now of D.O.T.) paid me a visit to-day and handed me attached memo which is worth a glance.

He also tells me that your interview with the Russian Financiers was an immense success and that they were delighted with and greatly encouraged by their reception. Its effect is believed to have been particularly wholesome on M. Bark who has been in the past numbered among the Russians who ardently denied a pro-ally policy and hated being made fools of by the Germans, but, on the other hand, despaired of receiving from this country substantial assistance against the Bolsheviks and were reluctant to commit themselves completely against the Germans.

The organisation of the British Committee also proceeds apace and Lord Farringdon, Mr. Hambro, Mr. Percy (of the British Trade Operation) and the Duke of Northumberland are considering the Yaroshiuski proposals. They only ask for an official assurance from the F.O. that the Government is benevolently – not financially or in any way directly – interested in the scheme and a letter on these lines has been prepared by Bagge and the Head of the Russian Department in the F.O. for Lord Curzon's signature. Sir Ronald Graham is confident that Lord Curzon cannot refuse to sign but as his caution is proverbial and it is therefore necessary to have the greatest possible volume of support behind any proposal for action, the letter has been put in the place to the Treasury for their approval. Bagge was anxious that you should mention to Curzon the visit of the three Financiers, apprise him of your interest in the scheme and urge the importance of it to Denikin, and the whole anti-Bolshevik policy.

I pointed out that there are obvious objections to worrying Curzon too frequently about these matters, but assured him that you fully realised their immense importance and would miss no opportunity of helping.

Bagge also suggested that you might come to see Lord Farringdon and talk to him about the Russian policy of the Government, but I indicated that I doubted very much whether it would be expedient. Of course if you met him casually, you might draw him on and encourage him.

AHMS

Sir Archibald Sinclair to Winston S. Churchill
13th August 1919

The Secretary of State

I received a visit yesterday from the Manager of the North Russian Government's Bank at Archangel, who has a 'Caisse' with £2,000,000 (two million pounds) sterling with which he does not know what to do, and the transfer of which to South Russia he is prepared to consider and to discuss with the Treasury. His name is Mr. G.M.Young. He is a Civil Servant originally belonging to the Board of Education. He then served on the War Cabinet Secretariat and was finally sent to Archangel on Lindley's Staff. There he was apparently transferred to the Service of the North Russian Government, and therefore ultimately of Kolchak, and £2,500,000 (two million, five hundred thousand pounds) was advanced by the Treasury to enable him to begin the operations of his Bank. He has been printing and issuing notes against the reserve of £2,500,000 (two million, five hundred thousand pounds) and his notes are the normal currency throughout the whole of North Russia.

He came to see me to find out whether the evacuation of North Russia was finally decided upon or if there was any hope that either the "evacuation" of British Troops would take place through Petrograd, thus leaving behind a strong North Russian Government in touch with Yudenitch at Petrograd, or whether, in default of an offensive, a certain amount of military assistance would be given to the North Russian Government if they decided to establish themselves at Murmansk. I informed him that I did not think any plan for an ambitious offensive from Archangel and Murmansk would have a chance of consideration and that the policy of evacuation was definitely and finally decided upon; but of course if the North Russian Government decided to hold on at Murmansk it was not impossible that some slight assistance might be given them in the shape of supplies, stores, etc.

He then explained that he was faced with the necessity of making three alternative proposals to the British Treasury. He had just enough money to pay either the Holders of his Notes if they were presented or to repay the money advanced by the British Treasury if it was decided to repudiate the Notes. Therefore, the three courses open to him were:-

1. To repudiate the Notes and repay the money advanced by the British Treasury.
2. To cash the Notes on demand of the Holders, in which case the British Treasury would lose the whole of its £2,000,000.
3. To suspend payment, keep the Bank in being, and move it to Murmansk if the North Russian Government were going there, or to some other part of Russia and hope, when things were more stable, operations could be commenced again and the Notes be eventually honoured and the money repaid to the British Treasury.

I then pointed out to him the great opportunities which General Denikin's vast territory now presented for the operations of his Bank. I showed him on the map the position of General Denikin's Armies and informed him of the high hopes that we held of his eventual success, or at any rate of his ability, to maintain his Armies somewhere in the region of their present front. He seemed to be very much taken with the idea, and said that provided tranquillity was maintained in General Denikin's area he might quite well be able, within a few years, to repay the whole of the money advanced by the Treasury, as well as to build up a substantial reserve behind his Note Issue.

Of course, however, he pointed out that he must be bound by the decision of the Treasury, and if the Treasury demanded their money back and were prepared to ignore the disastrous effects which repudiation of his Note Issue would have on our financial prestige in Russia, he would be bound to comply with their instructions. I then asked him to prepare a memorandum which I could submit to you; I attach it hereto. Do you not think that this matter is of sufficient importance for you to address a letter on the subject to the Chancellor of the Exchequer?

I am putting Mr. Young in communication with Mr. Bagge, late Consul at Odessa, who has an exceptional knowledge of trade conditions in south Russia, and, through his activities on behalf of the Department of Overseas Trade in connection with the Yaroshiuski Scheme, is fully cognisant of the measures which are being taken to revive trade in South Russia and to provide General Denikin's Government with the necessary credits.

AHMS

Sir Archibald Sinclair to Winston S. Churchill
25th August 1919

Secretary of State

1. I attach the memorandum which you instructed me to prepare with reference to the proposal to transfer Mr. Young's Archangel Bank to South Russia.
2. I had prepared a draft memorandum on the same lines the day before we left for Cologne but fortunately it occurred to me that it would be better to wait and see how Mr. Young got on with the Departments concerned before you intervened, and it now appears that the situation has altered to some extent since then.
3. In the first place it appears that only £1,000,000 will be available in any case on the 15th September, when it is proposed to close the Bank. This, however, would in itself be a useful sum and Mr. Young is fully alive to the possibility of supplementing it either by an agreement with the South Russian Banking Agency, to which your attention was drawn in a memorandum forwarded to you by Lord Curzon the other day, or by an agreement with the Treasury, whereby the £1,000,000 or so could be allotted out of the £26,000,000 which is at their disposal for the encouragement of British trade with unsettled countries.

4. So far, Mr. Young's negotiations with the Directors of the South Russian Banking Agency have been fairly promising, and he has had more difficulty in dealing with the Treasury. He feels convinced that if the attention of the higher Treasury officials and particularly of the Chancellor of the Exchequer could be directed to these proposals, their chances of being adopted would be improved.

AHMS

Sir Archibald Sinclair to Winston S. Churchill
27th August 1919
(Attached to a note from Baron William de Ropp to Sinclair)

S. of S.

Baron William de Ropp is a young Lithuanian landowner who served during the war in our Air Service and Secret Service. At one time, when at the Ministry of Munitions, you interested yourself in a proposal of his to fly to Germany and obtain certain information but just as the plans were being completed the Armistice was declared and the project was rendered unnecessary.

Masterton vouched to me for his bona fides and, as he was anxious to pay a visit to his home in Lithuania and at the same time to work for our Government, I sent him across to M.I.[172] who consented to employ him and they tell me that they are very pleased with his reports. I asked him to send in to me a summary of these reports and this memorandum is in response to my request. Quite interesting. Note his estimate of the military value of the Lithuanians – Spear's protégés!![173]

AHMS

Sir Archibald Sinclair to Winston S. Churchill
27th August 1919

The Secretary of State

Proposal to transfer the Caisse D'Emission from Archangel to South Russia.

1. There is in Archangel a Bank known as the Caisse D'Emission, operating under the orders of the North Russian Government by means of money borrowed

[172] Military Intelligence.

[173] Ropp wrote that 'the view is that order and prosperity can only be restored with British help ... The Balts are now chiefly concerned about their economic future in Lajvija and would be willing to agree to a [British] policy as long as their property is safeguarded. The Baltic bourgeoisie is eager to resume the old established trade relations with England ... Bolshevism took a very mild form in Lithuania, murder and the usual outrages were practically unknown and the retreat of the Red Army was hailed with joy by the great majority of the peasants. Their only wish is to return to their pre-war life. Although they disapprove of Bolshevism they, unfortunately, dislike fighting even more and strongly object to risking their lives in any cause ... I have spoken to Russian, Polish and German officers who all agree that the Lithuanian is best employed well behind the fighting line.'

from the British Treasury. The Notes issued by this Bank constitute the only medium of Foreign exchange in North Russia.

2. Now that North Russia is being evacuated by British Troops and it seems likely that the whole of the Archangel region at any rate, will be abandoned to the Bolsheviks, the situation of the Bank on or about the 15th prox. will be roughly as follows:

Sterling at disposal of Bank	£1,000,000	
Owing to Holders of Notes issued by the Bank		£1,100,000
Owing to British Treasury		£700,000
Adverse Balance	£800,000	
	£1,800,000	£1,800,000

3. It would then appear that three courses would be open to the British Treasury.
   I To demand payment of the £700,000 owing to it by the Bank, in which case there will remain to the Bank only £300,000 to meet its liability of £1,100,000 to the holders of its Notes. This would therefore involve repudiation of the greater part of its Note Issue.
   II To allow the Bank to pay on the demand of the holders of its Notes, in which case the British Treasury would lose its £700,000.
   III To suspend payment, keep the Bank open, and transfer it elsewhere so that operations could be begun again.
4. (I) would have disastrous effects to our financial prestige in Russia. (II) would mean a dead loss of £700,000 to the British Treasury. If the third course were to be adopted and if the operations of the Bank in another sphere were to be successful, the Notes could eventually be honoured and the money be paid to the British Treasury.
5. At the same time the General Staff and the British Military Mission to General Denikin have long been urging the necessity of doing everything to revive trade and commerce in South Russia. Lord Curzon recently sent to the Secretary of State a memorandum prepared by the Department of Overseas Trade, pointing out that "in the provision of economic assistance even more than by military means, are we likely to find not only the most effective and permanently satisfactory, but the least expensive solution of the Russian problem".
6. Supposing, therefore, that it was found possible to transfer the Caisse D'Emission to South Russia the advantages might be summed up as follows:–
   I As the Region now occupied by General Denikin's Forces comprises some of the richest provinces in Russia, the Caisse would earn money and might be able after the return of peace to redeem its North Russian Note Issue without calling on His Majesty's Government for further assistance. Eventually no doubt it would be able to repay to the British Treasury the money originally advanced.
   II If the Caisse prospered it would be able to lend General Denikin money up to one-third of its reserve. The importance of this consideration has

been emphasized by the General Staff and by General Holman[174] on several occasions.

III It would supply importers and exporters with an absolutely solid medium of exchange.

IV Being established in a large trading area, it would contribute to the ultimate solution of the currency problem of Russia as a whole.

AHMS

Rumours of Churchill's enthusiasm for British military intervention in the Russian Civil War reached Military Intelligence. The extent to which Churchill came close to running his own foreign policy in Russia, at odds with the Foreign Office's objectives, is an interesting question. He was certainly the most ardent supporter of the White Russians in the Government, and ignored warnings that they were highly unlikely to succeed and that his policies could draw Britain into another costly and risky major war.

Sir Archibald Sinclair to Winston S. Churchill
28th August 1919
Confidential

The Secretary of State

Do you know an officer by the name of Colonel Hunter in the Indian Cavalry? I understand from Morton that he met —[175] the representative of M.I.1,[176] at Stockholm, and stated that you had declared in his presence that now that Parliament had risen, and the Ministers had dispersed from London, you were contemplating the organisation of a grand anti-Bolshevik offensive in Russia.

The impression that this conversation left upon — was that Hunter was trying to pump him and, finding — reticent, had tried to lead him on by affecting to be, to some extent at any rate, in your confidence. He also stated that he was going out to join General Holman's staff in South Russia.

I have enquired from M.I.R.[177] and M.O.5[178] and failed to verify this statement. If he is indeed going out to South Russia, and if you have discussed the plans of the Government with Colonel Hunter, — would, of course, be prepared to exchange

[174] Herbert Campbell Holman (1869–1949): Chief of British Military Mission to South Russia 1919–20, commanding about 500 officers and 2,000 men who trained White Russian forces in the use of artillery and machine guns.

[175] Blanked out in black ink on the original document in order to protect the identity of the Military Intelligence Officer.

[176] MI1 was the office of the Director of Military Intelligence.

[177] Military Intelligence Research.

[178] MO5 was later to be known as MI5 – the branch of the secret service dealing with internal UK security matters.

confidences with him, and it would indeed be useful, and in accordance with custom for him to do so; but, in the meantime, — is inclined to treat his statements with reserve, and I assured Morton that the impression which — had gathered from his conversation with Colonel Hunter of your intentions was completely and fundamentally erroneous.

If you know Colonel Hunter, and if he is merely misrepresenting something which he did overhear you say, it will be quite easy for M.I.1 to stop him talking.

Will you please instruct me?[179]

AHMS

Sir Archibald Sinclair to Winston S. Churchill
29th August 1919
Confidential

The Secretary of State

Yesterday I dictated the note marked "A" and attached hereto,[180] and as the matter is rather a delicate one, and as I was relating the story third-hand, I sent it across to Morton to make quite sure that I had in no way distorted it. I attach his reply marked "B".

Meanwhile I found in your pouch Colonel Hunter's letter to you, marked "C" and attached hereto, with your minute on the back of it.

I have taken no action on the minute in case you may wish to vary your instructions after receiving the information which Morton has given me. I found out, however, from the Military Secretary that, as Colonel Hunter really wants employment in Persia, he should apply to the Military Secretary at the India Office. As he has apparently already had a considerable connection with that country, and as he states that Lord Curzon has found his suggestions useful, he should have no difficulty in obtaining employment from them.

I do not suppose you will wish to pursue the subject matter further, especially as it would make it rather unpleasant for Scale who seems to have behaved well in reporting it. Would you, therefore, like me just to write to Colonel Hunter and refer him to the Military Secretary at the India Office, and at the same time to tell Morton to convey a hint to Colonel Hunter that he should be more discreet in future?

AHMS

(Note in hand of WSC at the bottom of the letter)
Yes, I never said anything that remotely resembled this: neither is it true.
WSC 30/8/19

[179] See Churchill's reply of 6 September 1919.
[180] This is the letter printed above, dated 28 August.

Sir Archibald Sinclair to Winston S. Churchill
September 1919

The Secretary of State

I attach an interesting letter from Spears regarding Alexinsky,[181] and also some comments by MacCallum Scott[182] on the references to his failure to introduce Alexinsky to anyone in this country. As a mater of fact MacCallum Scott met M. Turin who is a representative of Zeminov's in London two days ago, and was told by him that Alexinsky was delighted with his interviews with Scott.

I do not understand the reference to the Russian Ambassador in London on page 5. Of course Nabukoff is still the Russian Ambassador in London, and whatever his limitations he could hardly be described as a weak man.

I cannot get any information about anyone called Naratoff, but an ex-official of the Russian Foreign Office named Neratoff accompanied General Dragomirov on his mission from Denikin.

I have written to Spears to ask for an explanation. Of course MacCallum Scott is quite right in deriding the melodramatic account that Spears gave of Alexinsky's interview with Sylvia Pankhurst.[183] It is quite evident from Basil Thomson's[184] weekly reviews that little importance is attached to her activities by the Home Office.

I think you will find the body of the letter thoroughly interesting.

AHMS

---

[181] Grigorii Alexinsky (1879 – ?): Bolshevik deputy to the Second Duma; fell out with Lenin and aligned himself with Plekhanov, the leading Menshevik (the Mensheviks were the more moderate and democratic opponents of the Bolsheviks within the Russian Social Democratic Party); emigrated to France in 1917.

[182] Alexander MacCallum Scott (1874–1928): Liberal MP for Glasgow Bridgeton 1910–22; Parliamentary Private Secretary to Churchill, 1917–18; in 1924 left the Liberals to join the Labour Party; Churchill's first biographer, publishing in 1905 a flattering account of Churchill's first thirty years.

[183] Sylvia Pankhurst (1882–1960): daughter of Emmeline Pankhurst, the suffragette leader; a passionate supporter of the Soviet Union as a superior form of democracy to the parliamentary variety, she both visited and corresponded with Lenin and was regarded with deep suspicion by the British Government, which particularly disliked her pro-Communist articles in her newspaper *The Worker's Dreadnought.*

[184] Basil Thomson (1861–1939): trained as a barrister and joined the Colonial Office; served in Fiji and Tonga, where he was briefly Prime Minister; on returning to England joined the Prison Service and later served as Governor of Dartmoor Prison and Wormwood Scrubs; in 1913 became Deputy Commissioner of the Metropolitan Police and in 1918 head of the Special Branch; involved in some of the most sensational spying cases of the period and played pivotal roles in the investigations of Mati Hari and Roger Casement.

Winston S. Churchill to Sir Archibald Sinclair
6th September 1919
Private

SIR ARCHIBALD SINCLAIR

You spoke to me the other day about some remarks attributed to me by an officer whose name I have forgotten but who had been talking indiscreetly to someone in the Intelligence Department.[185] Will you please compare what this officer alleges I told him, and what he undoubtedly told to the officer in the Intelligence Department, with the account given in the Bolshevik Wireless of the plan by which 14 States were to advance together on Petrograd against the Bolsheviks this month. There seems to be a very strong similarity between the two versions, and I think you should make very discreet enquiries through your young friends in the Intelligence Department. It is quite possible that an indiscretion has been committed, or again that the officer derived the rumour from the same source as the Bolsheviks. He certainly did not get it from me, as I have never said anything to anyone remotely resembling this.

WSC

Winston S. Churchill to Sir Archibald Sinclair
6th September 1919

MILITARY SECRETARY

With regard to the recommendation of the Selection Board for the command of the Mhow Division in India, I wish all the remaining Divisional Commands which are vacant or are likely to become vacant to be considered as a whole, and I will discuss them with you and the C.I.G.S. in that form.

I cannot think that any of the three officers mentioned by the Selection Board would do justice to the future of the army. We really must think of using the younger men who have made great names and displayed great qualities in the war. I certainly thought that General Kavanagh would retire. The Selection Board appear to be governed almost entirely by seniority. The only result of blocking all the command with the older Major-Generals will be to crush out altogether the talent which the war has revealed among the younger commanders. This is absolutely wrong. All these three officers, viz., Generals Gorringe, Kavanagh and Capper belong to the very class which should be offered special facilities for retiring at the present moment in connection with the clearance of the Major-Generals' list.

WSC

[185] See letter from Sinclair dated 28 August 1919.

Winston S. Churchill to Sir Archibald Sinclair
9th September 1919

Sir Archibald Sinclair

You should tell General Spears to help Alexinsky as much as he can. I presume he is not entirely destitute of resources. If he were, I should like to be informed and I would see whether means could not be found to aid him in that way.

WSC

Sir Archibald Sinclair to Winston S. Churchill
9th September 1919

S. of S.

Colonel John Ward M.P.[186] has just been here. He is anxious to go to Glasgow to-night in order to attend the Trades Union Congress, although he is not a delegate, in order to speak on our policy in Russia. He is particularly anxious to contradict Simon's[187] recent misstatements regarding the size of our army in Russia and the extent of U.S. intervention. He is very strong on the wickedness of abandoning the Russians at this crisis to the Germans or the Japs now that they have served our ends in the big war. He thinks it is probable – I think he even hopes – that he will be personally criticised for the part he has played.

I took him to see D.P.S.[188] who after careful consideration is convinced that there would be no disciplining grounds for objection if John Ward were to address the Trade Union Congress provided that he wore plain clothes. As he is an M.P. a clear distinction could be drawn between his case and that of Colonel Sherwood-Kelly.[189]

Colonel Ward was therefore satisfied to the disciplinary aspect of this proposed visit to Glasgow, but he was anxious that you should have the opportunity of improving your veto on the grounds of political expediency if you saw any objection.

I promised to do my best to get into touch with you, so will you please telephone to me as soon as you get this and I will inform John Ward at the National Liberal Club of your decision. I ventured to urge him to go, if I failed to hear from

[186] John Ward (dates unknown): commanded 25th Battalion of the Middlesex Regiment, who at one time had the poet Wilfred Owen serving under him; the battalion fought on the Western Front for most of the war but in August 1918 was transferred to Siberia; Ward ended his war at Omsk in 1919; one of the founders of the organisation that became the Transport & General Workers' Union.

[187] Sir John Simon (see n130), who had lost his seat as an Asquithian Liberal in the 1918 election, and at this time was preparing to stand in the 1919 Spen Valley by-election – he was unsuccessful.

[188] Deputy Permanent Secretary.

[189] John Sherwood-Kelly (or Sherwood Kelly) (1880–1931): Lieutenant-Colonel, Norfolk Regiment, won the Victoria Cross whilst commanding 1st Battalion Royal Inniskilling Fusiliers in November 1917; served in Siberia 1918–19; court-martialled for publicly saying that he had 'formed the opinion that the puppet government set up by us in Archangel rested on no basis of public confidence and support, and would fall to pieces the moment the protection of British bayonets was withdrawn'.

you in time to convey your desire to him before the Glasgow train leaves at half past nine to-night. He is trying to get into touch with P.M.

AHMS

Sir Archibald Sinclair to Winston S. Churchill
10th September 1919

The Secretary of State,

1. With reference to the attached telegram, I am informed that Goode, the "Manchester Guardian" correspondent, was sent over to Russia by the Foreign Office in spite of the protests of M.I. He was interviewed by the M.I. people before he went, and they found him prejudiced, self-opinionated and cantankerous. They suggested that the Bolsheviks would only show him what they wanted him to see, and that in the best possible light, to which he replied that he was quite clever enough to see through any such tricks, and that he meant to go to Russia and, on his return, to tell the people "the real truth" about what he found there – leaving no doubt in the minds of his auditors what "the real truth" would be.
2. At the same time the Foreign Office were also facilitating the journey of Mr. Keeling, the "Westminster Gazette" correspondent. He was also interviewed by M.I. and made a very much better impression. He said that he had no intention of going where Lenin[190] and Trotsky[191] and their associates took him, but meant to get into touch with the ordinary people in the big cities, observe the conditions in which they lived, and try to discover their real attitude towards Bolshevism and the political future of their country.
3. They started off together, and Goode sent a wireless message to the Bolsheviks announcing their impeding arrival. The Bolsheviks replied that they knew Goode and would be glad to welcome him, but they did not know Keeling, who could not, therefore, cross into their country without further enquiries. However, apparently both men crossed the line somewhere on the Lithuanian, Latvian or Esthonian front, and Goode at any rate reached Moscow.
4. A few days ago Goode returned across the Esthonian lines, and announced that he was the accredited envoy of Lenin: in the first place to the Esthonian

[190] Vladimir Ilich Ulyanov ('Lenin') (1870–1924): led the Bolshevik wing of the Russian Social Democratic Workers' Party (later the Communist Party of the Soviet Union) after the split with the Mensheviks in 1903; returned to Russia from exile in western Europe in April 1917 and led the October Revolution; Chairman of the Council of People's Commissars (Prime Minister) from then until his death in 1924.

[191] Lev Davidovich Bronstein ('Leon Trotsky') (1879–1940): joined the Mensheviks against Lenin in 1903, but returned to Russia in 1917 and aligned himself with Lenin; appointed head of the Petrograd Soviet; military leader of the October Revolution; Soviet Commissar for Foreign Affairs 1917–18 and for Military Affairs 1918–25; expelled from the Communist Party by Stalin in 1927 and assassinated, on Stalin's orders, in Mexico in 1940.

Government and in the second place to England and the other Governments of Europe; and it was apparently he who conveyed to the Esthonian Government the terms which Lenin was prepared to offer and arranged for the Esthonian delegates to meet the Bolshevik delegates at Pskov. He is believed to have similar messages from Lenin for this country, and is said to have announced that he will raise a revolution in England within a month of his arrival. Meanwhile I understand that he has been detained by the S.N.O.[192] at Reval. His return to this country cannot be long delayed. He has been clever enough to telegraph to Moscow for news of his travelling companion, Mr. Keeling, but the Bolsheviks have replied that Keeling came over in defiance of their laws and regulations, and that he must, therefore, stand his trial in Moscow.

5. MacCallum Scott also declares that he has repeatedly been told by friends who have been associated with him in Anglo-Finnish and Anglo-Russian affairs, and by journalists that Goode was sent over by the Foreign Office and he received the same impression from a conversation which he had recently with C.P. Scott.[193]
6. From supplementary information I learn that Goode is plentifully supplied with money and photographs of
    a. Bolshevik wireless messages of which only excerpts have been allowed to be published – presumably relating to Prinkipo,[194] the Baltic Mission,[195] etc.
    b. Atrocities committed by English troops – English officers laughing and smoking while Bolshevik prisoners are shot, etc.

In support of Churchill's search for anti-Bolshevik allies, Sinclair collected intelligence on the situation in Finland. The Finns had taken advantage of the Russian Revolution in 1917 to declare their independence. A left-wing coup in January 1918 resulted in a brief civil war; the right-wing government re-established its authority in May and, after a brief flirtation with a monarchy, Finland became a republic in the summer of 1919. Tensions with its Russian neighbour were never far beneath the surface, however, and many Finnish politicians were keen to forge a good relationship with Britain, which had significant armed forces located in the nearby Baltic states of Latvia, Lithuania and

[192] Senior Naval Officer.

[193] Charles Prestwich Scott (1846–1932): Editor of the *Manchester Guardian* 1872–1929; Liberal MP for Leigh 1895–1906; close friend and advisor to Lloyd George, and highly influential in Liberal circles.

[194] At the peace talks at Versailles the major powers refused to invite representatives from either the Red or White Russian forces. However, when it came to deciding the fate of the new states on Russia's western frontiers the need to involve Russian representatives led to a suggestion that a separate conference be arranged at the Prinkipo (Prince) Islands, in the Sea of Marmara near Constantinople. The Bolshevik Government was apparently anxious for some kind of adjustment, but Kolchak and Denikin, the two leading generals of the White Russian counterrevolutionary forces, refused to enter into discussion, and the whole project fell flat.

[195] It is not clear what Sinclair is referring to here.

Estonia. Sinclair and Churchill's main interest in Finland was the extent to which it could be persuaded to cooperate with the White Russian forces and support an assault on Petrograd (St Petersburg).

In 1920, the Peace of Dorpat (Tartto) with Russia finally recognised Finland's borders.

Sir Archibald Sinclair to Winston S. Churchill
11th September 1919

S. of S.

You will see from Memo, No. 3, which I am sending you along with this, that Alexinsky has joined forces with the Russian Financial Committee and is actively associated with Lavintoff and Routenberg in Paris – I don't suppose they will let him starve! On the other hand it would undoubtedly help him if we were to order a few hundred thousand of his pamphlets at a cost of some hundreds of pounds as suggested forwarded herewith. Spears is on leave in Venice.

AHMS

Sir Archibald Sinclair to Winston S. Churchill
11th September 1919

S. of S.

Reference your instructions to me to tell General Spears to help Alexinsky as much as he could, when A. returned to Paris (just before we returned to London from the Rhine) I thought it would be easier for Spears to help him out to South Russia than for me from London. I thought he would work it through the [unreadable] but apparently he thought it necessary to write to Kell here (MO5). Unfortunately as you will see from his letter to me which I attach, D.M.I.[196] jumped at the opportunity of giving him another slap in the eye.

Do you now wish me to try and intervene from this end that all facilities are given Alexinsky for his journey?

AHMS

Sir Archibald Sinclair to Winston S. Churchill
11th September 1919

The Secretary of State

The letter marked A attached was brought to me this morning by Mr. Stinton Jones.[197] The writer, Colonel Pirie-Gordon is deputy commissioner (under Colonel

[196] Director of Military Intelligence.

Tallents[198]) of the Baltic States, and of course is under orders of the Foreign Office. It was with and through him that Generals Gough[199] and Marsh were working when they formed the North West Russian Government, as Colonel Tallents was at home on leave.

Attached to the letter is a memorandum, marked B, giving details of a scheme proposed by the Activist Party in Finland for operations against Petrograd.

You will see that Colonel Pirie-Gordon hoped that you would be able to give Mr. Stinton Jones an interview. He certainly talks well and to the point in a bluff, down-right way, but I do not think you would care to see him. Colonel Gordon has given him letters to the heads of the Foreign Office, Department of Overseas Trade, the editor of the Times, Sir Basil Thomson and Sir Maurice Hankey,[200] but they all appear to be out of London. I asked Mr. Jones to prepare a Memorandum for submission to you, which he did with commendable promptitude. I attach it, marked C. He is more long-winded on paper than he is in conversation, and I therefore marked certain paragraphs which contain the pith of his information.

His information about Professor Goode bears out what I have told you in Memorandum No. 5 which I am submitting to you to-night. He has not been in touch with anybody connected with the War Office, but he and Morton agree that Goode is plentifully supplied with money, credentials, and messages from Lenin, and photographs.

You will also note at the bottom of page 3 what he says about the alarming extent of German commercial penetration in Finland and even into Petrograd. This is entirely confirmed by what Major Marsh, General Gough's G.S.O.2, told me while you were speaking to General Gough this afternoon. The part of the scheme I like least is the idea that seems to be lurking at the back of his mind that we should support the Activist Military Party against the present Government in Finland, but as is shown in the Memorandum attached to Colonel Gordon's letter, and also in the recent telegrams which have been received from Kennard at Helsingfors, the present Government would not appear to be indisposed to co-operate in an advance, and in this case it would obviously not be necessary to connive at any intrigue against them by military party. He brings out well the reason why Finland may well be disposed to attack the Bolsheviks when he shows that the situation of the country will be very much more serious in the winter when it is cut off from the support of the

[197] Stinton Jones (dates unknown): a British engineer working in Russia 1905–17; a witness to the Russian Revolution, after arriving back in Britain he published *Russia in Revolution* (Nast & Co., 1917).

[198] Sir Stephen George Tallents (1884–1958): civil servant; Irish Guards 1914–15; in 1919 appointed Chief British Delegate for Relief and Supply of Poland, and then British Commissioner for the Baltic Provinces, where he had some success in helping to restore order.

[199] Hubert de la Gough (1870–1963): commanded Fifth Army 1916–18; headed Allied Mission to the Baltic in 1919, retiring in 1922.

[200] Maurice Hankey, 1st Lord Hankey (1877–1963): Secretary to the War Cabinet 1916, Imperial War Cabinet 1917–18 and Cabinet 1919–38; Minister without Portfolio, War Cabinet 1939–40; Chancellor of the Duchy of Lancaster 1940–41; Paymaster General 1941–42.

Allies by the ice, and exposed along the whole of its frozen frontier to the attacks of the Bolsheviks.

AHMS

Sir Archibald Sinclair to Winston S. Churchill
11th September 1919

The Secretary of State
Russian Propaganda

General Spears recently sent me a letter asking if the journey to this country of M. Bourtzev,[201] the well-known Russian revolutionary, could be facilitated. I asked M.I.R. for an account of M. Bourtzev's career for your information before taking action, but in the meantime I have obtained the attached Memorandum, marked A attached hereto, from Lieutenant Reilly,[202] with a specimen of M. Bourtzev's pamphlets.

Do you wish me to take steps to facilitate M. Bourtzev's journey?

Reilly has also sent me a letter and a copy of a Memorandum dated the instant, marked B and attached hereto, which he has addressed to Basil Thomson, regarding the encouragement of anti-Bolshevik propaganda in this country, with special reference to Alexinsky's pamphlets. I asked him what it would cost to produce and distribute pamphlets on a large scale, and you will see that 100,000 pamphlets could be prepared for an expenditure of something between £300 to £500. Would you contemplate devoting a few hundred pounds of the funds which you have obtained for the assistance of General Denikin to the dissemination of a few hundred thousands of Alexinsky's pamphlets?

AHMS

Sir Archibald Sinclair to Winston S. Churchill
11th September 1919

The Secretary of State
Russian Diplomatic Representation

I attached a letter from Spears about the appointment of the new Russian Ambassador in this country, and also a Memorandum by Lieutenant Reilly, on the same subject. You will see that they are both very much to the same effect. If you approve of the views expressed you might have an opportunity in Paris of speaking

[201] Vladimir Lvovitch Bourtzev (1862 – ?): Russian revolutionary; exiled to Serbia in 1885 for his revolutionary beliefs and activities; escaped after twelve months, fled to Geneva and then London; after 1917 an equally strong opposition to the Bolsheviks – who he regarded as unpatriotic – replaced his hatred of Tsarism.

[202] Sidney Reilly (real name Georgi Rosenblum) (1874–1925): of 'Reilly, Ace of Spies' fame; Polish by birth, he spied on Germany and Russia for British Military Intelligence, and was regarded as Britain's most important secret agent; executed by the Russians on 5 November 1925.

to A.J.B.[203] or even Savinkoff[204] on the subject. My information was that M. Sabline has already been appointed to succeed M. Nabukoff, but you will see that Reilly says that Savinkoff has since prevailed upon the Russian Council of Five to cancel this appointment. In Reilly's opinion either a strong general should be appointed to this Embassy or better still an economist, and in this connection he suggested Litvinoff-Falynsky, whose Memorandum on the economic situation in Russia you circulated to the Cabinet a month or two ago. You may remember that he was at one time assistant Minister of Commerce in Russia, and later was one of the strongest men on the War Industries Board.

Reilly gave the same information about Savinkoff's views as to the situation between Denikin and Petlura[205] as Spears gave you in the second paragraph of his letter of the 5th instant.

AHMS

The deterioration in the relations between the White Russian leaders in the Baltic and the growing tensions between General Yudenitch and the British advisors were highlighted by Sinclair in a memo in mid-September.

Sir Archibald Sinclair to Winston S. Churchill
11th September 1919

The Secretary of State

As I reported to you in a Minute which I wrote on a letter to you from General Spears, Colonel Scott's friend, Prince Serge Belosselsky-Beloszersky,[206] recently paid me a visit. He was most anxious, that I should understand that he was only talking

---

[203] Arthur James Balfour (see n15) – the Foreign Secretary, at this time intimately involved with the Paris peace conference negotiations.

[204] Boris Savinkoff or Savinkov (1879–1925): anarchist, writer and anti-Tsarist member of the Socialist Revolutionary Party, he was transformed by the war into an ultra-patriot, becoming Deputy Minister for War under Kerensky in 1917; a bitter opponent of Lenin, he formed the Union for the Defence of the Motherland and Liberty as a White Russian umbrella organisation; his subsequent intriguing with the British and persistent insurgent activities against Soviet Russia ensured that when he was captured (having been tricked into returning to Russia to negotiate with the Soviets) there was little hesitation in arranging for him to fall to his death from a window in the Lubyanka prison.

[205] Simon Petlura (1879–1926): Ukrainian political and military leader during Ukraine's unsuccessful war for independence in 1917–22; assassinated by a Bolshevik agent in Paris in 1926. On 31 August 1919 Ukrainian troops and Denikin's White Volunteer Army, advancing against the Bolsheviks, had both entered Kiev at the same time; hostilities between the two forces were only narrowly averted when the Ukrainian forces pulled out of the city.

[206] Prince Serge Sergeevitch Belosselsky-Belozersky (1895–1978): born in St Petersburg; enjoyed a colourful career including a period in the elite Russian Imperial Horse Guards; fled to Paris via Finland in 1917; became an active organiser of the White Russian forces; migrated to the United States and completed his military career as a Colonel in the US Army Air Force during the Second World War; died in New York in October 1978.

very confidentially and unofficially, and I said that, though of course I should report to you what he told me, he could be quite sure that no use would be made of any information which he might give, which could be detrimental to the prospects of the North West Russian Army. He was obviously afraid lest the General Staff or the Government in this country should resent his criticisms upon the British Military Mission, and should withdraw it with the result that our assistance to the North West Russian Army would cease.

He said it was a great pity that we did not send to the Baltic some officer or even some civilian attached in an advisory capacity to the British Military Mission who had lived in Russia, and therefore understood the Russian people. He said that the only officer on the British Military Mission with any experience of Russia was General Marsh, and his experience consisted mainly in acting as Chief British Liaison officer with the Grand Duke Nicholas in the Caucasus. He said that British officers did not understand the mentality of the ordinary Russian officer and private soldier, and that they were apt to be completely taken in by Russian officers who, from their bluff domineering manner, appeared to have a fine command of men. He said that they were apparently much impressed by the way Rodzianko[207] ordered his men about, not realising that the Russian standard of discipline was much stiffer than ours and that it was not unusual for Russian officers to order men about in a way that would be resented by British soldiers, and that such a manner in no way denoted possession of exceptional qualities of leadership.

Nor could they make any allowances at all for any officer who at any time in his career had shown some disposition to look to the Germans for assistance. They were particularly suspicious of General Arsenieff, who had been Prince B. B.'s old squadron leader and who in Prince B. B.'s opinion cared for nothing but the restoration of Russia. (In this connection I must say that I understood from M.I.R. that Prince B. B. himself lies under some suspicion of having had relations with various German agents abroad, and I understand that it is doubtful whether he will receive permission to remain much longer in this country. I could not help suggesting to M.I.R. that they would be able to keep better watch on him here than if they turned him out of the country, and that he struck me as being the last man who would be capable of subtle and complicated intrigue.)

Prince B. B. then went on to speak of Balahovitch who had been a trooper in one of the regiments in the division which he commanded. He believed him to be a plucky leader of irregular troops, but he had neither the education nor the personal prestige in the Russian Army for high command.

Prince B. B. then referred to the letter which General Gough had sent to General Yudenitch. He said that he himself was a short-tempered man, and that he

[207] Mikhail Vladimirovich Rodzianko (1859–1924): served in the Tsarist army before turning to politics; President of the Duma 1912–17; monarchist and moderate reformer who was deeply opposed to both the Mensheviks and the Bolsheviks, he was an active leader of the White Russian forces in the Baltic area; sought exile in Yugoslavia in 1920 and died in Belgrade.

was afraid that if he had received it he would have replied in the words of a well-known story: "Your letter is before me, etc." As I told you in my Minute on Spears' letter to you, he promised to bring me a copy of General Gough's letter and of the reply which was sent by General Yudenitch. However, he called a day or two later to explain that these papers were strictly official and highly confidential, and that they belonged to General Heroys,[208] who is the official representative of Admiral Koltchak and General Yudenitch in London. He had therefore suggested to General Heroys that he should call himself and bring me the letters.

General Heroys called yesterday and handed me the letters which I have marked A and B. He talks well in fluent French and understands English perfectly. He expatiated upon the superlative merits of General Yudenitch, who he assured me was "un nom". His prestige was unrivalled among the anti-Bolshevik Russians in the North West. His military reputation founded upon his record as Chief of Staff to the Grand Duke Nicholas and afterwards as the Commander of the Russian Armies on the Caucasus front, and caused him to be regarded as a man of "supreme military valour".

General Heroys then referred to the formation of the North West Russian Government. He declared that General Marsh, without previous consultation with General Yudenitch, presented him and his political council with an ultimatum giving them to understand that all military assistance would be withdrawn if they refused to accept his proposals, and allowing them forty minutes in which to decide on their answer. He said that General Yudenitch had only one thought, which was the good of Russia, and he had at once determined to accept the position of War Minister and Commander-in-Chief under the leadership of M. Liasnosoff, who, in General Heroys' opinion, is a very estimable commercial magnate and a moderate politician. But General Heroys considers that it was fatal for the future of the North West Russian Army to insist upon this act of self-abnegation on the part of General Yudenitch, who was the principal asset of the North West Russian Army. Everything should have been done to foster and increase his authority and prestige. Indeed even the British Military Mission could not allege anything against his loyalty to the Entente. Now General Yudenitch has to retire from the front and take up his duties as War Minister in M. Liasonoff's Cabinet, and his prestige must inevitably suffer. Something must be done, General Heroys urged, to repair this blunder. General Heroys then handed me a copy marked C and attached hereto, of the telegram which he had received from General Yudenitch dated the 28th ultimo. He stated that General Yudenitch was still most anxious to work with any British officers whom we might send to the Baltic, but it was useless to disguise the fact (though he wished it to be treated as highly confidential) that recent events had rendered co-operation between General Yudenitch and the British Military Mission more difficult. "Ses Relations sont Gatées" was an expression which he repeated two or three times.

[208] Boris Vladimirovich Heroys (dates unknown): chief of the White Russian Military Mission to London.

Both he and Prince B. B. said that they had heard the opinion expressed that Yudenitch's men will not fight. He said that they had fought their way to within a comparatively short distance from Petrograd, and that they were only compelled to fall back, as you yourself will well remember, owing to the non-arrival of the munitions which have been promised from England. Now many of the officers and men have insufficient clothing, hardly any have great-coats, some are bare-foot, few have enough to eat. Rifles have to be used instead of machine guns in the ranks. "If you will only clothe and feed these men, I will guarantee that they will fight", said Prince B. B.

General Heroys was very anxious to know whether the munitions, which it was understood were going from Archangel and Murmansk, were to be sent to the Esthonians or to the North West Russians. I assured him that they would be sent to neither, but to the British Military Mission, who would distribute them among the anti-Bolshevik forces, with a single eye to the attainment of the victory of the anti-Bolsheviks.

General Heroys was exceedingly anxious to have an interview with you. As you have seen Prince B. B. who is only an unofficial envoy from Yudenitch, at the special request of Colonel Scott, would it not be as well for you to see General Heroys who is the official representative of General Yudenitch in London? You would find him an interesting talker, and you could get from him the Russian standpoint regarding the formation of the North West Russian Government. May I suggest that I should arrange an appointment for one day next week?

AHMS

Sinclair reported further bad news from North Russia from a recently returned British officer; it was becoming clear that the White Russian forces there were likely to be defeated. Sinclair suggested to Churchill that the British should consider supporting the use of cinema films of triumphant White forces as a propaganda tool to arouse popular interest and support for the anti-Bolshevik troops.

Sir Archibald Sinclair to Winston S. Churchill
13th September 1919

Secretary of State

Major Harris, whom you met in the train on your way South when he was returning to London from North Russia, came to see me this afternoon. He brought a large selection of interesting photographs which he had taken both on the Archangel and Murmansk fronts. He also brought some hideous photographs of the effects of frostbite. He is going to make a further selection of these which you have not seen and send them to me for your inspection when you return from Paris.

He talked for a long time about the conditions in North Russia, but as you have already been speaking to him probably on the same subject, I will not repeat what he said. He knew Colonel Sherwood Kelly and had dined with him the night before he left North Russia, but his opinion was as unfavourable as those which reach us from every other quarter.

He made it quite clear that the Russians had no chance of holding out at Archangel after we left, and that none of the Battalion Commanders and Senior Regimental Officers had any confidence in their chance of making a successful defence. Great bitterness characterized the feelings of the North Russians towards the British. It was said that they should not have made a convenience of the Russian people, using them as a weapon against the Germans and then flinging them aside when their usefulness was exhausted – moreover individual officers and men had profiteered in cigarettes, whisky etc., on a scale which in the aggregate was very considerable. He considered that the feeling was so strong that it would militate very seriously against our commercial prospects in North Russia.

He was very strong on the great advantages of the cinema as a medium of propaganda, and it certainly seemed to me that the only possible way of arousing popular interest in the doings of the distant Armies of Denikin and Koltchak, would be to show their troops on the screen in victorious action against the enemy. I invited him to submit a memorandum giving his ideas on the possibility of organizing cinema propaganda on rather more extensive lines than those upon which it is now being attempted. He is now working in S.D.4.[209] and is preparing two films:– (a) showing the work of the Armies of the North Russian Government and also the work of our own troops, though of course less stress is being laid upon the fighting done by our troops than upon that which is being done by the Russians, and (b) a film showing the life of the British Soldier in the most agreeable light in each of the campaigns of the recent war.

He is going to let you know when these films are ready and you will be able to see a private view in the War Office before they are finally published, which will enable you to direct that any part of them should be cut out. He asked me whether he should include views of our troops in North Russia in film (b), as it would only show these troops indulging in sports and other agreeable occupations and as you would have an opportunity at the private view of directing that the Archangel promotion should be cut out, I told him to get ahead and include it in film (b).

AHMS

From one of Sinclair's regular meetings with Sidney Reilly, on 14 September, he was able to update Churchill on some of the wild rumours circulating through the White Russian ranks – one of which was that groupings of irregular German troops were awaiting Churchill's resignation over the failed British intervention in Russia before they

[209] A specialist part of Military Intelligence dealing with propaganda.

crossed into Soviet territory and stormed north to capture Petrograd and then drive south to link up with General Denikin.

Sir Archibald Sinclair to Winston S. Churchill
15th September 1919

Secret
S. of S.
Russia

I am keeping in fairly close touch through Bagge, Reilly and others with the doings of the Russian Financial Committee and with various sources of information about Russia. I am urging them not always to come begging for Government assistance and asking for interviews with you but to get busy on their own account both in the direction of rendering financial and economic assistance to Denikin and with propaganda. I have pointed out the disadvantages of Government propaganda and contrasted the efforts of private individuals and the 22 anti-Bolshevik organisations in this country with the achievements of the anti-Bolsheviks in America, and suggested that the Russian Financial Committee with its properties worth 2 milliard roubles might surely be able to arrange for the printing and distribution of half a million or a million pamphlets at a cost of a very few thousand pounds. Both Reilly and Bagge seemed to agree.

Bagge is very anxious that you should see Yaroshiuski who badly wants to see you because firstly he wants to use our cables to obtain Denikin's authority to compel one of the big Russian banks (which is still run by pro-German directors although Y. has bought the controlling interest) to submit to his authority, secondly he has just returned from Paris and, being full of the latest information from all sources, wishes to discuss the general situation with you and thirdly having been received by all the French Ministers, his amour propre is slightly wounded at finding difficulty in approaching British Ministers.

But I told Bagge to arrange for Y. to communicate with Denikin through the Foreign Office – the Russian Department – with whom of course Bagge is in close touch, and, if they are willing to assist Y. but point out that the War Office line via Denmiss is the quickest means of communication, then I had little doubt that War Office would be glad to help.

Would you like to see Yaroshiuski on the general situation?

Reilly had heard from two Russian sources that Von der Goltz[210] has now got 100,000 men either in Courland and Livonia or just over the German border. He is

[210] Gustav Adolf Joachim Rüdiger, Count von der Goltz (1865–1946): son of Wilhelm von der Goltz, who commanded the Turkish forces in Mesopotamia in the First World War, and defeated the British at Kut; commanded German troops in Latvia (under Article XII of the Armistice, German troops occupying territories of the former Russian Empire were allowed to remain in their positions until ordered to quit; the Allies' intention, obviously, was to use these forces against the Bolsheviks) and hoped to establish a

supposed to be waiting for your resignation to be forced over the question of intervention in Russia and then, when we have finally abandoned the anti-Bolshevik Russians, hopes to march on Moscow, taking Petrograd in his stride, to join up with Denikin in the South, and then to return to Berlin via prostrate Poland.

It sounds preposterous but Goutchkoff,[211] one of Reilly's sources of information, has just returned from Reval with this story, and Litonoff-Falysky has heard it from other sources and believes it implicitly.

I am further told that Colonel Macalpine, the representative of the Supreme Economic Council with Denikin, has returned with a melancholy story of the confusion and disorganisation in Denikin's rear and of the inefficiency and corruption of his administration. He is apparently disposed to recommend peace with the Bolsheviks.

In Reilly's opinion, however, which he assured me was shared by MM. Bark, Litonoff-Falysky, and Yaroshiuski, the best remedy was to help him by supplying British advisers in all branches of the administration.

With regard to the von der Goltz story the Wireless News sheet No. 272 which is sent with this memo in your box to-night, is interesting. If you look at the message from Moscow at the bottom of page 9, you will see that they quote Goutchkoff, estimate the German forces at 100,000 men and conclude somewhat mysteriously with the statement that the intentions of the leaders of these troops are not known.

AHMS

PS. See also P.1. para 2. of Basil Thomas's 'Govt of Revolutionary Movements Abroad' next herewith.

Churchill was keen to complete his 'plan' for awarding all those who had served during the war with both General Service Medals and specific awards for particular battles or periods, such as the 1914–15 Star for members of the original British Expeditionary Force. He instructed Sinclair to pull together the details.

Winston S. Churchill to Sir Archibald Sinclair
17th September 1919

Sir Archibald Sinclair,

---

pro-German government in Latvia from which German influence could radiate eastwards; although his troops captured Riga in May 1919, they were defeated by a combined Estonian-Latvian force in June and withdrew to Germany in December.

[211] Alexandre Goutchkov or Guchkov (1862–1936): fought in the Boer War against the British; leader of the Octobrist Party in the wake of the abortive Russian Revolution of 1905, a moderate figure arguing in favour of constitutional reform before and during World War One; from 1910–11 President of the State Duma and notable public critic of the Tsar and Tsarina's close advisor Grigory Rasputin; appointed Minister of War by Kerensky in March 1917; sought exile in Paris following the October Revolution.

My plan is all before you in the various minutes I have written. Would you kindly have it now reduced to one sheet of print, as follows:–

1. The 1914–15 Star.[212]
2. The rosette and clasp on the 1914 Star.[213]
3. The British War Medal[214] for all who left this country for service overseas in a theatre of war (including India).
4. Battle clasps on the above and the emblem on the ribbons denoting possession of the clasp.
5. The General Service Medal[215] for all enrolled personnel who do not receive the British War Medal, with a clasp for those limited categories which served coast and anti-aircraft batteries under fire or assisted in suppressing the Irish Rebellion.
6. Possible extension of General Service Medal by block grants to certain organisations which have rendered exceptional services, in many cases of a dangerous nature, together with an outline scheme for the above.
7. The Victory Medal[216] with a palm or other device on the ribbon in cases of officers and men mentioned in despatches or receiving a reward for gallantry.
8. The grant of the General Service Medal to the Territorials who had undertaken a pre-war obligation.
9. Asking the Navy to draw a similar line between War Service and Home Service as we draw between the British War Medal and the General Service Medal.
10. Air Force to confirm generally to this scheme, making special arrangements for their peculiar position.

If all the above were reduced to a concise and compendious scheme, it should be possible to arrive at an early decision.

Note. I am, of course, quite ready, if it is generally desired, to drop out the whole of the General Service Medal from the scheme in every aspect.

WSC

---

[212] The 1914–15 Star was awarded to all who saw service in any theatre of war between 5 August 1914 and 31 December 1915, except those eligible for the 1914 Star. 2,078,183 were issued.

[213] The Mons Star was awarded to all officers, non-commissioned officers and men of the British and Indian Expeditionary Forces, serving in France or Belgium on the establishment of the British Expeditionary Forces between 5 August 1914 and midnight of 22–23 November 1914. 365,622 were issued.

[214] This medal was instituted to record the successful conclusion of the First World War but, at Churchill's initiative, it was extended to cover the period 1919–20 and the operations in North and South Russia, the Eastern Baltic, Siberia, the Black Sea and the Caspian. 6,610,000 were issued.

[215] The General Service Medal was never actually issued for service in the 1914–18 war. A General Service Medal was introduced in 1923 and used to cover service in minor campaigns from 1918 to 1962 such as Iraq, Palestine, Malaysia and Cyprus.

[216] The Inter-Allied Victory Medal (generally referred to simply as the Victory Medal) was instituted following an agreement by fourteen Allied powers in March 1919. The medal was awarded to all those who had served in the armed forces, as well as to civilians contracted to the armed services, and to those who served in military hospitals on the various battlefronts during wartime. 5,725,000 were issued.

Sir Archibald Sinclair to Winston S. Churchill
1st October 1919

S. of S.

Reference attached letters from General Spears.

1. It appears almost certain now that Petrograd will not be taken this year, while, if the Baltic States make peace, it will be very difficult to know what to do with Yudenitch's force.
2. It has been suggested that he should be sent to join Denikin but it is hardly to be expected that transport will be available.
3. His strength is only about 15,000 fighting men, with the possible addition of a few thousand men (for whom at present he has no equipment) and perhaps some Russian prisoners from Germany.
4. In these circumstances, if it were decided to adopt Prince Lieven's[217] proposal and to send Yudenitch to join the Poles, it could hardly be expected that he could undertake an ambitious advance on Moscow. On the other hand he might be sent to the Southern Polish flank to join up with Denikin via Gomel or, if that were considered too long a trek, he might surely contain a considerable number of Bolsheviks by operating towards Vitebsk or Mogilev.
5. Moreover the pressure of some Russians on the Polish front might make it easier for Paderewski[218] to justify to the Poles his refusal to make peace with the Bolsheviks and to minimise the share of fighting due by Polish troops; or on the other hand if an advance into the heart of Russia were undertaken, the presence of Russian troops in the van would surely modify the historical and political disadvantages.
6. It is submitted that Spears' letter should not be circulated to the General Staff as it might cause friction if he had not reported to them officially in the same sense.
7. Do you want to see Prince Lieven as suggested in attached letter?

AHMS

Sir Archibald Sinclair to Winston S. Churchill
7th October 1919

The Secretary of State

---

[217] Prince Paul Ivan Lieven (1875–1963): Russian aristocrat, worked briefly as an engineer; senior Red Cross official during the Russo-Japanese War; commanded White Russian forces in the Baltic region 1918–19; increasingly disillusioned by the lack of British support, he turned to the local German commander, von der Goltz, for financial support; after the White collapse in late 1919 he fled to Paris, and subsequently lived in Germany, Belgium, and Ireland.

[218] Ignacy Paderewski (1860–1941): Prime Minister of Poland January–November 1919; Polish Representative at the League of Nations 1920–21.

Note of an Interview with M. Bourtsev at the War Office, 6.10.19

I discussed in particular with M. Bourtsev the letter from Spears which I showed you yesterday. He informed me that he thought that it was a waste of time to try and bring social revolutionaries of the type of Avksentiev[219] into line with the allied policy towards Denikin and Koltchak. He is a follower of Kerensky,[220] and having been exiled from Siberia by Koltchak, he can hardly be expected to give him any support at the present time. Moreover, the Kerensky party is thoroughly discredited in Russia and its prestige is scarcely higher in France or in this country, and in M. Bourtsev's opinion, therefore, it is not of much account.

Fomdaninsky, though he is in close touch with that party, stands more to the right, and it is not likely that he will come out in open opposition to Koltchak and Denikin.

With regard to the Jews, M. Bourtsev's opinion was that as the Bolsheviks lose power there will be a great mass movement on the part of the people of Russia against the Jews. He is quite ready to credit Denikin with the best intentions, and is aware that he has issued orders to his troops to protect the Jews from violence and to regard them in every respect as ordinary Russian Citizens.

On the other hand, he confirms what Spears reported, that rumours of pogroms have reached Paris and it is realised that these rumours will have an unfortunate effect on socialist opinion in Russia and also upon public opinion in France and in the country. A telegram has therefore been sent by the Socialist group, with which M. Bourtsev is associated, to M. Alexinsky who, as you may remember, recently left Paris on a visit to General Denikin, asking him to impress upon Denikin the importance of protecting the Jews and to report what truth there is in the stories of persecution.

You will remember that Spears considered that the emergence of M. Krivoshein[221] as a dominating political personality at General Denikin's headquarters was an ominous portent, but in M. Bourtsev's opinion, although M. Krivoshein was for a long time Minister of Control and served in this important office of State in successive Ministries before and during the war and must be regarded as a conservative and as one who would more naturally welcome the assistance of the Germans than of the Western Democracies, he is an unusually honest and broad-minded

[219] Nikolai Avksentiev (1878–1943): founder member, along with Kerensky, of the Party of Socialist Revolutionaries; served in two senior positions in Kerensky's short-lived government in 1917; opposed the Bolsheviks but also resisted involvement with the Tsarist White Russians; left Russia in 1919 and lived in the émigré community in Paris.

[220] Alexander Kerensky (1881–1970): leading member of the Socialist Revolutionary Party; when the Tsar abdicated on 13 March 1917, a Provisional Government, headed by Prince George Lvov, was formed; Kerensky served as Minister of Justice and later Minister for War, and in July replaced Lvov as Prime Minister; with the deteriorating war situation Kerensky's government fell to a Bolshevik putsch (the October Revolution) and he fled to London; in the 1930s moved to the US and took up teaching.

[221] Alexander Krivoshein (1858–1921): political moderate; Minister of Agriculture 1908–15; dismissed because of his opposition to Tsar Nicholas II's decision to take personal command of the Russian Army; following the October Revolution of 1917 joined the White anti-Bolshevik Volunteer Army in the Crimea; after its defeat he fled into exile in France.

politician whose services will be of real value to Denikin and to Russia. Although he took no share in the Government after the revolution and was undoubtedly looking to Germany to save Russia from the Bolsheviks, it is not expected that he will be reluctant to work with the British if they are going to continue to help Russia.

Before leaving, M. Bourtsev expressed his intense admiration of yourself and his gratitude for the work which you are doing for the assistance of his country.

AHMS

One of the more controversial episodes of the Russian Civil War was the treatment of Jews by the White Russians: there were numerous reports of killing and mistreatment of Jews in the areas controlled by the White Russian forces. Churchill and Sinclair noted frequently the large number of Jews who were leading members of the new Soviet Government. Both men also read, though discarded as unlikely, the famous *Protocols of the Elders of Zion,* which shortly afterwards were proved to be an anti-Semitic forgery (see letter dated 29 November 1919). Lloyd George was so concerned about the reports of mistreatment that on 7 October he wrote to Churchill:

> I wish you would make some enquiries about this treatment of the Jews by your friends. Now that we are subsidising the volunteer army and providing them with weapons we certainly have a right to protest against outrages ... being perpetrated. You may depend upon it that sooner or later a discussion will be raised on the subject and I do not wish to see the British Government placed in the same position as the Kaiser when he kissed the cheek of Abdul Hamed shortly after he had massacred the Armenians. Apart from the iniquity of the proceeding and one's natural repugnance to be associated with it, it provides material for a most disagreeable debate in the House of Commons.

After reading Lloyd George's note and the accompanying report on the troubles Churchill asked Sinclair to investigate further.

Sir Archibald Sinclair to Winston S. Churchill
8th October 1919
Personal and Secret

Secretary of State
Jews in South Russia

With reference to the memorandum regarding the persecution of the Jews in South Russia which you showed me this morning, I think that two broad facts emerge which are completely in accord with the information which reaches us from several other sources.

Firstly, that, as the Bolsheviks lose their grip over the people of Russia, there will be a great mass movement against the Jews which not even the most stable and energetic Government will find it easy to stop. This is evident from the third, fourth and sixth paragraphs on page 10 of the memorandum.

(Note. I have re-numbered the pages consecutively in blue chalk).

Secondly, that General Denikin and his civil and military authorities are doing their utmost to prevent pogroms and issuing the strictest orders on this subject. In this connection the account on page 11 of the interview between General Myevski, the Commander of the Volunteer Army, and the Jews of Kharkov is of the greatest interest and importance, as is also General Myevski's order which is quoted from the Kharkov newspapers.

The Jews whose tragic experiences are related on the first three pages of the memorandum were apparently the victims of the Tchetchens,[222] a wild mountain tribe, some of whom are serving in General Denikin's army while the tribe itself appears to be in a revolt against him in Cis-Caucasia. But it will be noticed near the bottom of page 3 that in at least one case the victim was delivered by soldiers of the Volunteer [White] Army.

It would be useless to deny the strength of the popular feeling against the Jews in South Russia. I have reported to you separately upon my interview with M. Bourtsev, the well known historian and Social Revolutionary, but in this connection he made a great point of the difficulties with which General Denikin's government would be faced in coping with this mass movement against the Jews. He and his political associates were naturally greatly exercised about this question, and they had cabled only a day or two before to M. Alexinsky, a prominent Socialist who recently left Paris on a visit to General Denikin, to ask him to report on the efficiency of the measures which were being taken to project the Jews.

Moreover in this connection it is important to remember that the people in the Ekaterinoslav and Krementschug areas, in which, according to the memorandum, most if not all of the atrocities against the Jews have been committed, have been inflamed against the Jews, not only by their own experiences under the Jewish Commissars appointed by the Bolsheviks, but also by the deliberate and calculated incitements of adventurers of the type of Grigorieff. This was the General who conquered the Ukraine for the Bolsheviks and entered Odessa at their head. Then he grew tired of serving the Bolsheviks and determined to bid for supreme power himself. Unable on the one hand to secure recognition from Denikin or the support of patriotic Russians owing to his criminal antecedents, or on the other hand to outbid the Bolsheviks in their attacks upon property, he decided to adhere to the political and social tenets of Bolshevism but in addition to permit and even to encourage pogroms.

This policy met with such a large measure of success that it was quickly imitated by several other bandits, such as Makhno the ex-convict, and it is chiefly with these criminals and their adherents that Denikin has been fighting in the territory that lies

[222] Now normally spelled 'Chechens' – who continue into the twenty-first century to assert their independence and objections to government from Moscow, with violent and dramatic results.

between the towns of Odessa, Ekaterinoslav and Kiev, and it is the harvest of vengeance which they have sown that Denikin is left to reap.

General Holman reports that he is astonished at Denikin's success in restraining his troops to the extent he has done in spite of the propaganda directed against him by Petlura, who bolsters up his declining influence in the Ukraine by truthfully declaring that the volunteer Army is the protector of the Jews.

It would be interesting to know the source of the memorandum which you gave me. It is evident from General Holman's telegrams that all such information can only be accepted with the greatest reserve. In his I.P.1956 of the 24th he states that he was himself in Poltava immediately after its capture and witnessed an attempt by Jews to spread the report that they were being murdered when nothing of the sort was happening.

General Holman also references specifically to the report of the Zionist representative, Caleb, which he states bluntly is false – not only according to his own conviction but also in the opinion of the correspondents of the "Times", "Daily Express" and "Reuter", and of several British officers who have recently returned from the captured areas. Apparently in connection with Caleb's report, General Holman states that he has himself been in Losovaya, Poltava and Kharkov (all of which are mentioned in the memorandum), that Reuter's correspondent has been in Poltava and Kiev, and that others have been in other places recently captured, and that all testify to the efficiency of Denikin's orders and to the absence of pogroms.

Although it is fully recognised that the Jews of Russia were not as a community responsible for the sufferings of the people under the Bolshevik tyranny, yet it is an undoubted fact that, whatever the explanation may be – perhaps that the proletarian Jews were the most intelligent members of their class – the Bolshevik regime was mainly controlled and administered by Jews and that 80% or 90% of the Bolshevik commissars were Jews. (See General Holman's telegram I.P. 1956 of 24th September.) It must therefore be realised on the one hand that the Jews are identified in the minds of the great majority of the people of Russia with the hideous tyranny from which they are now finding deliverance, and on the other hand that the one man who has the keenest sense of the responsibility of the Government to safeguard the lives, property, & civil liberties of the Jews as citizens of Russia, and is doing this utmost to ensure that that obligation is fulfilled, is General Denikin.[223]

AHMS

[223] This belief was supported by a telegram Sinclair received from Lord Kilmarnock in Copenhagen on 10 October 1919, reporting that he had 'good reason to believe that reports of pogroms by Denikin's troops which are being widely circulated are false and are being put about by the Ukrainians'. Unfortunately the reports turned out to be mostly true.

Sir Archibald Sinclair to Winston S. Churchill
9th October 1919

Secretary of State
Aeroplanes for General Yudenitch

General Heroys, the official representative of General Yudenitch and Admiral Kolchak in London, left with me this correspondence about 18 aeroplanes, which are promised to General Yudenitch, are now packed up but have nowhere to go, on account of the War Cabinet decision that "no further military supplies are to go to the Baltic States". This was perhaps rather a tactless phrase for the Air Ministry to use in a letter to a Russian General as General Heroys indignantly explained that General Yudenitch's Army was not operating in the Baltic States. Apparently there was some understanding, if not an actual promise, that these machines were to go to the North West Russian Army, but I imagine that you will not wish to interfere with the discretion of the General Staff in this matter.

AHMS

Sir Archibald Sinclair to Winston S. Churchill
10th October 1919

Secretary of State

The writer of this letter is Jack Scott's friend, whom you saw recently. I understand that the General Staff would not be indisposed to consider some such scheme[224] on the grounds that if Denikin reaches Moscow this Winter a collapse might well ensure on the Bolshevik Western front with the result that Yudenitch would be able to walk into Petrograd. In this event it would be useful to us to have some troops upon which we could rely to ensure that Yudenitch did not pursue a line of policy that was unwelcome to Denikin at Moscow.

Prince B-B assured me that he had ample financial backing in the City, although he admitted that, once the Brigade was formed, he hoped that the Government would supply the necessary equipment. He has already found a Commanding Officer in the person of Colonel Lecky, a Canadian Officer who has just returned from France, and has many promises of support. He assures me he is quite certain he would find no difficulty in raising a Brigade and in detaining the necessary funds provided that he can receive an assurance that his action would not be regarded as illegal; beyond this, he assures me, he would not require any support or encouragement.

AHMS

[224] Ill-thought-out plans to form an irregular international auxiliary brigade (on similar lines to the 'Black and Tans' deployed in Ireland in 1920) to provide a structure for what would mainly be a force of mercenaries and adventurers opposed to the Communists.

Sir Archibald Sinclair to Winston S. Churchill
14th October 1919

S. of S.

Reference attached, I am informed that the Serbians have been offering the Russians in vague terms a battalion from Serbia to go to Archangel in substitution for the one at Murmansk, but only provided that we would be responsible for transport and supply. We offered to help to make Russian ships available for transport but expressed our inability to be responsible for supply, and asked the Serbian Military Attaché to make a definite proposal in writing. The matter now appears to have been dropped and the impression received is that the Serbians were anxious to obtain the credit for a "blood thicker than water" policy while placing the blame for their inability to carry it out upon us.

AHMS

Sir Archibald Sinclair to Winston S. Churchill
15th October 1919

Secretary of State

With reference to the attached two letters from Spears, he appears to be saturated with the French view of Denikin[225] and the Ukrainian question. Don't you think it might be useful if you were to write him a short note and give him a line to go on? I gather that he does not get very much guidance from the War Office, and I am sure he would welcome a short note outlining your view of our policy towards Russia in general and Denikin in particular.

AHMS

Sir Archibald Sinclair to Winston S. Churchill
15th October 1919

Secretary of State

With reference to the attached letter from Spears and as regards the first paragraph, I did not think that Spears would consider it necessary to inform Prince Lieven that you would not see him, although, of course, I told him that you did not think it worth while for him to come over here in order to discuss his scheme for employment of Yudenitch's army on the Polish front.

I suggested that he might let us know the attitude of the Poles in Paris towards Prince Lieven's project,[226] and it would appear from Spears' letter that it is not very

[225] The republican French government was highly sceptical of the capabilities of Denikin and had withdrawn its forces from Odessa in April 1919, in part to avoid any possibility of being sucked into supporting the White Russian fight to restore the Russian monarchy.

[226] Prince Lieven proposed that Yudenitch's army be redeployed to support the Poles and guarantee Polish

friendly. But what he means by the reception of the Polish troops at Dvinsk and Polotsk I cannot conceive, as the Poles have only been on the outskirts of those places and have never been and are not now in full occupation of them. You will, however, observe that in spite of the general trend of Spears' observations, he suggests that the relations between the Russians and the Poles seem to be "slightly better".

But while Yudenitch is marching on Petrograd, Prince Lieven's project does not appear to be of immediate practical importance.

AHMS

Sir Archibald Sinclair to Winston S. Churchill
17th October 1919

Secretary of State
Jews in South Russia

The following information which reaches me from a reliable source is interesting as showing General Denikin's attitude towards the persecution of the Jews.

Among his strongest and most constant supporters is M. Boris Suvorin, a big Russian newspaper proprietor who was described to me as the Northcliffe of Russia. His best known paper at the present time is the "Vetchernja Vremya".[227] He has also done a great deal of Y.M.C.A. work among General Denikin's troops, and his is the only organisation which is at work on these lines in the South Russian Army. He is, however, a strong anti-Semite and allowed certain anti-Semitic expressions of opinion to be published in his newspaper. After warning him against publishing such articles, General Denikin fined him 3,000 roubles, and when the offence was again repeated, he fined him a further 8,000 roubles. However , in M. Suvorin's absence at Constantinople his paper offended again and this time, although, as stated above, M. Suvorin was one of his most faithful supporters, General Denikin closed the offices of the newspaper, summoned M. Suvorin from Constantinople, and informed him that he would not allow the newspaper to be published until he gave a definite undertaking that no anti-Semitic propaganda would be published.

AHMS

independence; he hoped in return that the Polish army could be persuaded to work with Yudenitch to help overthrow the Bolshevik regime.

[227] Probably 'Evening Times'.

File note by Sir Archibald Sinclair for Winston S. Churchill
23rd October 1919

Note of an interview with General Golyeiushi at the War Office 23/10/19

General Golyeiushi expressed the view that during the transition period between the military collapse of the Bolsheviks and the conversion of the Constituent Assembly, Russia would have to be governed by a Military Dictator. He considered that of the three Chief anti-Bolshevik leaders, neither Kolchak nor Denikin nor Yudenitch would enjoy the necessary prestige for this exalted position, nor would either one command the unquestioning loyalty of the supporters of the other two. A man was required whose personal position would be generally recognised as superior to that of any possible claimant and where occupancy of the position would suffice to safeguard it from the intrigues of rural factors.

In General Golyeiushi's opinion only one man in Russia possessed the necessary qualifications – The Grand Duke Nicholas.

The Secretary of State replied that it was not for him to express any view upon such a delicate, internal question of Russian politics as the choice of a man for the supreme position in the Russian State. He could not speak for the British Government but he could feel no doubt that they would refuse to intervene in such a matter which could only be decided by the unfettered judgement of the Russian people themselves. On the other hand he was quite sure that it was of the first importance that a strong government should be set up in Moscow as soon as it was entered and that certain broad, simple principles of democratic policy which would command the assent of enlightened political opinion in the country, in the United States and throughout the world, should be proclaimed.

These principles should be founded upon a policy of appraisement. The Constituent Assembly should be involved and it should be declared that the Russian Government would in future rest upon the consent of the Russian people. Freedom of religious belief should be recognised and the claims of different acts to State recognition might be reconciled by a policy of concurrent endowments. No man should be punished without trial. Bolsheviks and members of the Government or any other political party should on no account be subjected to wholesale proscription, but where any misdeeds were alleged against individuals, they should be dealt with justly and in due course of law. A generous means of regional autonomy should be conceded to various nationalities within the Russian Empire. Finally it would appear most unwise to attempt to relieve the peasants of the land which they had gained during the Revolution: though it would be fair and just, and probably in accordance with the wishes of many of the peasants themselves, that they should pay a fair price or some form of compensation to the dispossessed owners.

As to the wisdom of such a policy the Secretary of State expressed strong views but he refused to give any opinion whatever upon the form of Government which would be set up because he believed that the Russian people would be quick to react, in a matter which they alone could decide, any attempt, however well-intentioned, to influence their judgement.

N.B. The above notes were made by me after a conversation with the Secretary of State within the minute of General Golyeiushi's departure.

AHMS

Sir Archibald Sinclair to Winston S. Churchill
30th October 1919
Very Confidential

S. of S.

This paper[228] is certainly interesting but the main argument is perfectly familiar to anyone with the slightest acquaintance with Russian affairs while on the other hand the considerable amount of detailed information which it supplies upon the workings of German influence in Russia does not appear to have been sifted and tested: at any rate it is not accompanied by any instructed comment or criticism.

But I have searched in vain for a passage which could in any degree justify D.M.I.'s comment "that it looks as though there were a very pretty plot between the Germans and the anti-Bolshevik commanders". According to this report the Germans have conceived the ambitious policy of fusing the Bolshevik and anti-Bolshevik armies together, after promoting a coup d'etat in Moscow, and they are only waiting until by means of vigorous propaganda the armies of Denikin and Koltchak shall "have become definitely pro-German". There is not the slightest suggestion that I can discover that either Kolchak or Denikin or Yudenitch is plotting with the Germans: while on the other hand it is definitely stated that "the High Command of the Red Army ... is entirely pro-German and that "the Principal Bolshevik heads" are "blind instruments of Germany". The only prominent anti-Bolshevik whose name I can discover is M. Alexandre Goutchkoff in line 8 on page 8. The name is actually spelt "A. I. Gontchkof" but as M. Butilof's name on page 11 is also spelt "PONTILOF", as no one but a man of the very first rank could have saved the German firms in the circumstances described and as none but such a man would have been thought worth a salary of £30,000 a year, it is impossible to avoid the conclusion that it is intended to refer to M. Goutchkoff.

On the other hand, although M. Goutchkoff is well known to have been in close touch with the Germans since the Revolution, the suggestion that he betrayed his country to the Germans for a salary of 300,000 roubles would appear to be quite irreconcilable with his whole war record. It might well be true that he had taken over the administration of these concerns from the Germans in order to ensure that they were conducted in the interest of his own country but it is submitted that the

[228] A report from an anonymous Military Intelligence field officer concerning his belief that German influence was spreading amongst the White Russian forces.

suggestion that he deliberately became a salaried agent of Germany during the war can only be accepted with reserve.

Although a certain amount of the information about German activities in Russia during and since the war may be new, I can hardly believe that the F.O. will share D.M.I.'s naïve surprise at the mention of the names of a few individuals. The latter particularly marks the paragraph dealing with German control of Russian Banks, but I don't think that there is much that is new in that. Most of those mentioned – I think all except two – are now controlled by M. Jaroszynski,[229] and of the two exceptions, M. Jaroszynski certainly holds a large interest in one, the Azov Don Bank, in which the controlling interest is held by M. Kamenko, a member of the Russian Financial Committee which is dominated by M. Jaroszynski's interests. I cannot claim to have made any special study of these questions, but many of the names of pro-German Financiers which are noted in this report are familiar to me. Vchengradski and Chaikevitch are among M. Jaroszynski's most stubborn opponents in Paris, while M. Khari's activities in Odessa are notorious.

The writer's conclusions are pious and his second demand would broadly be satisfied by the Jaroszynski scheme if it were put into operation.

His two main points seem to be:

A That there is a great German scheme for fusing the Bolshevik and anti-Bolshevik Russian Armies into one instrument of immediate revenge upon the Allies.

B That a big financial coup in Turkey is contemplated by a group of Russo-German Financiers in Paris.

Probably nobody could throw more light upon the second suggestion than M. Jaroszynski or Mr. Reilly. Would you like me to make enquiries?

Finally it is submitted that this report should be thoroughly examined and tested not only in the War Office but by the Foreign Office and the economic experts on Russia, such as Mr. Picton Bagge in the D.O.T., and that until this has been done there is no justification either for the value attached to the report by D.M.I. or for the excessive secrecy in its treatment which he enjoins or for his aspersions upon the integrity of the anti-Bolshevik commanders.

AHMS

Sinclair and Churchill were aware that the attitude of the Finnish Government could be critical to the success of General Yudenitch's march on Petrograd. The White Russians were anxious that the Finns should be persuaded to join forces and send troops to support their attack. The Finns, however, had only established themselves as an

[229] Karol Jaroszynski (dates unknown): Ukrainian/Polish banker who purchased a string of banks and finance houses; a close associate of British agent Sidney Reilly, Jaroszynski was the leading advocate of a plan to form an Anglo-American syndicate to invest in post-Bolshevik Russia; considered by the British Consul-General in Odessa, John Picton Bagge, to be a possible 'Cecil Rhodes for eastern Europe'.

independent republic that summer, and with over 40,000 Russian troops still stationed in their country, they were reluctant to join such a risky venture, preferring to seek final peace terms with the Bolshevik Government which would guarantee Finland's borders and her newly won independence. Not all Finns agreed with this reluctance to intervene, however, and the Finnish General Mannerheim encouraged the British and anti-Bolshevik Russians that he could persuade his country to align with the White forces.

File note by Sir Archibald Sinclair for Winston S. Churchill
3rd November 1919

Note of an interview with M. Savinkoff and M. Brunstrom[230] at the War Office on the 1st November

M. Savinkoff, speaking in French, explained that the object of their visit to London was to bring about the intervention of Finland in the operations against Petrograd, without which it was feared that the efforts of the North West Russian Army would prove abortive.

Earlier in the year the Finns had offered to negotiate with the Russians on the basis of the recognition of their independence and the satisfaction of certain other demands. However, contrary to M. Savinkoff's own advice, the Russian Political Committee[231] in Paris had refused to entertain the Finnish proposals. But, now that it was hopeless to expect that the operations of General Yudenitch could meet with success without the assistance of the Finns, the Russians were prepared to negotiate with the Finns, and to accept the principal conditions which the Finnish Government had laid down.

In reply to a question by the Secretary of State, M. Savinkoff declared that Admiral Kolchak had given him practically a free hand to negotiate with the Finns on behalf of Russia.

At the beginning of the interview M. Brunstrom had handed to the Secretary of State a letter of introduction from General Mannerheim[232] and M. Savinkoff now explained that M. Brunstrom was present as a personal friend of General Mannerheim, who was confident that he had only to appear in Finland to rouse

---

[230] An associate of General Mannerheim, otherwise unknown.

[231] The Russian Political Committee was the nearest the various White Russian émigré groupings came to establishing a government-in-exile at this time.

[232] Carl Gustaf Mannerheim (1867–1951): Finnish soldier; Lieutenant-General, Russian Imperial Army; assumed command of white (anti-Bolshevik) forces in newly independent Finland in 1918 and defeated Finland's communists and Russian Bolsheviks; regent of Finland 1918–19, but defeated in Finland's first presidential election in 1919; tried to make Finland participate in the Russian counter-revolutionary military operations, but failed and retired to private life; Chairman of the Defence Council 1931–39; commanded the Finnish forces in the 'winter war' against Russia in 1939–40; joined Germans in attack on Soviet Union in 1941; President of Finland 1944–46, negotiated peace with Soviets in 1944; his greatest contribution was to maintain Finnish independence in the face of Russian aggression and German ambitions in the 1940s.

public opinion so strongly in favour of intervention that the Finnish Government would have no option but to march on Petrograd. But before doing so, he felt it necessary to be assured of a loan, without which it would be impossible to make the necessary military preparations. The minimum sum which he would require would be a hundred million francs, or something less than three million pounds sterling, and of this a half had been all but promised by the French Government if the other half could be raised in England. M. Savinkoff therefore desired the help of the British Government in raising a loan of fifteen hundred thousand pounds.

The Secretary of State replied that, although the British Government would welcome a decision of the Finnish Government to assist actively in the restoration of Russia and the rescue of Petrograd from the Bolsheviks, he could hold out no hope that they would make a loan to Finland for the purpose. But it was, in his opinion, quite out of the question that they would consider putting pressure upon Finland to intervene, or that they would assist any private citizen or any party in Finland in an attempt to force the hand of the Finnish Government. However, he indicated that it was not for him to make a pronouncement upon such a matter of high policy, but that M. Savinkoff should seek an interview with the Foreign Secretary, who would be able to give him an official reply on behalf of the Government.

Moreover, it appeared to the Secretary of State that the time for Finnish intervention had already passed. The Gulf of Finland would probably be frozen over within a fortnight at most, and the co-operation of the British Fleet could not, therefore, be counted upon; and the difficulties of provisioning Petrograd and the supply of the armies after the Gulf of Finland had frozen would be enormously increased.

The Secretary of State agreed with M. Savinkoff that it was no longer possible to hope for the deliverance of Petrograd without the intervention of the Finns, but good service had been rendered to the Russian cause by the offensive of the North West Russian Army, since strong Bolshevik forces had been drawn to that front and the pressure correspondingly relieved on General Denikin at a critical moment. It was in General Denikin's operations that the Secretary of State saw the best hopes of Russia's future, and he besought M. Savinkoff to concentrate his political and financial resources upon the revival of trade and commerce and the improvement of the administration behind Denikin's armies.

M. Savinkoff replied that he realised that officially the Government would be unable to intervene, but he had hoped that the Secretary of State would find it possible to put him and his financial friends and supporters, such as M. Jaroszynski, in touch with financial circles in London which would assist him in finding the money. The Secretary of State replied that he was quite unable to entertain such proposals, which were not in accordance with the conventions by which Ministers in this country were bound. Moreover, he repeated that no one in an official position in this country would be able to co-operate with a private citizen in putting pressure upon the Finnish Government with which the British Government was in friendly relations.

At this point the interview had to be brought somewhat abruptly to a close, and it was arranged that MM. Savinkoff and Brunstrom should call again in the evening.

The discussion in the evening followed the same lines as in the morning. It was opened by M. Brunstrom who stated that he thought that there had been some misapprehension on the part of the Secretary of State who appeared to think that it was General Mannerheim's object to overthrow the present Finnish Government. Such was not the case at all. Minor alterations in the personnel of the Finnish Government might be necessary, but General Mannerheim's only object was to influence the existing Government of Finland in the direction indicated by an enlightened understanding of his country's interests. Nor was it even proposed that this loan should be offered to General Mannerheim while he was still a private individual. It was only desired that General Mannerheim should be in a position to assure the Finnish Government that if they were to adopt the policy of intervention they could rely upon receiving the necessary loan.

The Secretary of State replied that there was no room for misunderstanding between them and virtually repeated the observations which he made in the morning indicating that his judgement was unaffected by the ingenious distinctions which M. Brunstrom had drawn. M. Savinkoff, continuing the conversation in French, then urged that it was not really necessary for the Government to make any loan but all that was required was that, in the event of his being able to interest financial circles in London in the proposition, the Secretary of State should be ready to express to them his interest in the project on political grounds. The Secretary of State in reply expressed grave doubts whether such a personal expression of opinion on his part would have the decisive effect which M. Savinkoff appeared to anticipate, and in any case it would be out of the question for him to take such action unofficially and independently of his colleagues.

M. Brunstrom then withdrew and the Secretary of State discussed with M. Savinkoff the situation on General Denikin's front and the paramount importance of reviving trade and commerce in South Russia and of improving the Civil administration.

M. Savinkoff and M. Brunstrom made an excellent impression by reason of the clearness of their statements, their frankness, their ready recognition of the assistance already given by this country to Russia, and the good humour with which they accepted the failure of their mission. There was indeed some vagueness as to the powers which had been bestowed by Admiral Kolchak upon M. Savinkoff and the Russian Political Committee in Paris to negotiate with the Finnish Government, and also about the extent to which the French Government had committed itself to raise a loan of fifty million francs, but this was admitted with engaging frankness and the conversation at no time reached a stage at which it would have been necessary to press for more precise information. M. Savinkoff in particular appeared to take an enlightened and liberal view of the policy which Russia should adopt towards small nationalities, including the Ukrainians, on her borders, and expressed with evident sincerity his appreciation of the powerful aid which this country had already given to Russia.

AHMS

Churchill met representatives of the Romanian Government in November 1919 and urged them to help Denikin and the other White generals in return for his support for their own objectives in the region.

Sir Archibald Sinclair: notes of an interview at the War Office
10th November 1919

M. Ciugureanu and M. Pelivan spoke no English and scarcely any French and it was therefore arranged at the beginning of the interview that they would speak Roumanian, that the Secretary of State would reply in English and that Colonel Rossetti, the Roumanian Military Attaché, who had introduced the visitors, would act as interpreter.

M. Ciugureanu opened the conversation by stating that he was aware that the Secretary of State took a particular interest in the future of Russia and in the fight against Bolshevism. These problems were of especial concern to Roumania, who, owing to her geographical propinquity to Russia, would be the first country to be exposed either to the infection of triumphant Bolshevism or to the predatory designs of resurgent Tzarism.

At this point the Secretary of State interposed with the remark that his friend was Denikin. He would speak frankly – not in the name of the Government – if his visitors desired an official pronouncement they should address themselves to the Secretary of State for Foreign Affairs – but he would give them his own personal views. He did not admit that the success of General Denikin would entail a complete reversion to the old Tzarist regime in Russia but he felt convinced that whether in a few months, a few years, or after a struggle prolonged over many years, a great united Russian State would inevitably arise. It was not the part of far-sighted statesmanship to set itself to hamper and obstruct the development of forces which it was powerless to control and hostility on the part of Roumania could only prolong the agony and provoke the enmity of Russia. The Secretary of State was well acquainted with the history of Roumania and with the deeds of her valiant army before Plevna, nor was he unaware of the short-sighted and illiberal course of Russian policy towards Roumania in the intervening period. But let Roumania profit from Russia's need of help at this time. Let her not repeat in her policy towards Russia the errors of Russian policy towards herself. The Secretary of State would not go so far as to say that the foes of Denikin were his foes but he would emphatically declare that the friends of Denikin were his friends.

M. Ciugureanu replied that he greatly appreciated the frankness of the Secretary of State and would assure him that he was no less sincere in his abhorrence of Bolshevism, but he desired to raise the question whether the policy which the Allies were pursuing in Russia could not be improved and strengthened. Many small States had come into being on the borders of Russia – many of them such as Finland and Poland had shown themselves as hostile to the Bolsheviks as Kolchak or Denikin. Russia was never a national entity but an agglomeration of nationalities and neither Kolchak nor Denikin would ever unite all these nationalities under the banner of indivisible Russia. On the other hand the spirit of Nationalism was strong in the Border peoples – for Poland, the Baltic States, the Caucasian Republics (the Ukraine was not mentioned) compromise with Bolshevik internationalism was impossible – yet by our support of the champions of Russian Imperialism we were depriving ourselves of the powerful assistance of these ardently nationalist states in the war against Bolshevism.

The Secretary of State appealed for greater frankness. He understood that what Roumania wanted was the final settlement of the Bessarabian question[233] in her favour. He declared that the present situation gave her an opportunity which would never recur. Let her treat with Denikin, let her offer him substantial assistance in his hour of need, and the Secretary of State for his part would undertake to exert such personal influence as he possessed with Denikin to bring about a settlement in harmony with the aspirations of Roumania and to recommend it to the British Government and to the League of Nations.

M. Ciugureanu replied that one of Roumania's principal difficulties was that there was no one with whom she could treat. At one time Kolchak was the Supreme Ruler, then he was succeeded by Denikin – but this statement the Secretary of State was able promptly to deny – but not even Kolchak would give a definite answer to any such question but always declared that he was unable to prejudge the decision of the Constituent Assembly. Nor would the Peace Conference ratify any agreement which they might reach, since it recognised none of the Governments in Russia as legally competent to act in the name of the Russian people.

The Secretary of State admitted that this was true but asked what alternative M. Ciugureanu had in his mind. With whom could he deal if not with General Denikin? Who was more competent than Denikin to dispose of the title deeds to Bessarabia?

At the point M. Pelivan intervened with a somewhat lengthy and not unfamiliar historical argument which tended to prove that the Russia which Kolchak or Denikin would restore would inevitably turn to Germany for guidance and support, but to this the Secretary of State replied that such considerations had already been carefully weighed against other factors in the Russian situation and that a decision had been reached to help Denikin.

[233] Bessarabia, the Moldavian Republic, was the subject of a dispute between Romania and Russia over whose sphere of influence it fell under.

He then turned to M. Ciugureanu and enquired his attitude towards Petlura. But without interpreting this question Colonel Rossetti declared that Roumania was no longer assisting Petlura and that he had already issued an official communiqué upon the authority of his own War Office denying the report, which had been spread by General Petlura's representatives here, that Roumanian officers had been given permission to serve in Petlura's army. This démenti appeared in today's 'Times'.

In conclusion the Secretary of State had spoken with complete frankness but his frankness was based upon feelings of the most sincere friendship for Roumania and of profound admiration of the valiant exploits of the Romanian army even when surrounded and overwhelmed through the treachery of the Bolsheviks. But he was firmly convinced that the true policy for Roumania to pursue was that of helpful friendship towards Denikin.

M. Ciugureanu assured the Secretary of State that he felt greatly indebted to him for the obvious sincerity of the friendly sentiments which he had expressed towards Roumania and also for his candid exposition of his views on the Bessarabian question. He would make a full report upon his conversation with the Secretary of State to his own Government as soon as he returned to Bucharest.

AHMS

Sir Archibald Sinclair to Winston S. Churchill
29th November 1919

S. of S.

I should be grateful if you would tell what you think of these 'Protocols'.[234] They seem to me cleverly written with real passion and purpose but their comments on politics and ethics are so utterly wrong headed that they strike one as sheer, wild nonsense. Inverted wisdom – and it is curious how symmetrically inverted – as though by some professional 'Alice through the Looking Glass'.

It is possible that they were written by some clever old Jew on the borders of Bedlam and read out at the meetings of a lodge of Jewish Freemasons. Is it not equally possible that they were written by a clever anti-Semitic professor in some Russian University as

[234] The *Protocols of the Learned Elders of Zion* is the most notorious and successful work of modern anti-Semitism, drawing on popular anti-Semitic notions with roots in the medieval Europe of the Crusades. The *Protocols* were first published by Sergei Alexandrovich Nilus (1862–1930), successively a lawyer, judge, and Greek-Orthodox monk, in 1905, in the wake of Russia's defeat in the Russo-Japanese War, which triggered a revolution leading to the promulgation of a constitution and the establishment of the Duma. The reactionary 'Union of the Russian Nation', or 'Black Hundreds' organisation, as well as elements of the Tsarist secret police, used the *Protocols* to incite popular feeling against the Jews, who they blamed for the revolution and the constitution. Claiming to summarise the secret plans of Jewish leaders seeking to attain world domination, the *Protocols* were later used by the White armies to incite widespread opposition to the Jews who they were keen to link with the Bolshevik leadership. At the same time, Russian emigrants brought the *Protocols* to western Europe, where the Nilus edition served as the basis for many translations, starting in 1920. In 1921 the *Protocols* were revealed as forgeries in a series of articles in *The Times* by Philip Grave, the paper's correspondent in Turkey.

propaganda? You should read the introduction by Sergyei Nilus. The account of how he came into possession of these papers is not convincing to say the least.

AHMS

PS. In no case could it be suggested that the Bolshevik revolution was the outcome of the policy expressed in these Protocols. In this connection it should be remembered that of the principal Commissars of Soviet Russia only two are Jews – Trotsky and Zinoviev. Lenin is pure Russian. The fact that the great majority of the Commissars in the lower levels of the Bolshevik hierarchy are Jews, is surely more likely to be the result of the higher education and superior intelligence of the Jew as compared to the ordinary Russian 'worker' or peasant, than to be the fruit of a deliberate Jewish plot.

Moreover, it is suggested in the introduction that the Zionists are the chief promoters of the policy of the Protocols. But they have definitely declared their hostility to the Bolsheviks and the Zionist organisation of Russia is the object of Bolshevik persecution and its nationalist policy is in fundamental contradiction to the international policy of the Soviet Power.

AHMS

By December 1919 it was apparent that the end was near for the White Russian forces, and Britain took decisive steps to cut itself free from any further involvement or support. This was not to Churchill's liking, but he was well aware that Lloyd George had run out of patience with him on this matter.

Sir Archibald Sinclair to Winston S. Churchill
31st December 1919

Secretary of State
<u>Final Contribution for Denikin</u>

The chief point at issue is, whether the principle, on which the assessment of the price of <u>Surplus</u> stores is to be made, should be:–

(a) To charge the market price;

or

(b) To charge the higher price (based on the cost price of the articles) which the War Office – but not the Admiralty – has been accustomed to obtain from India and the Dominions.

D.Q.M.G.,[235] who was President of a Conference between representatives of the War Office, Admiralty, Air Ministry and Ministry of Munitions, asks for a ruling.

A.F.S.[236] argues in favour of the second alternative on the ground that it might prove very expensive to us in years to come if we set a lower standard of prices for

[235] Deputy Quartermaster-General.

Denikin than for the Dominions and he points out that the lower scale of charges hitherto adopted by the Admiralty arises from the fact that they have had less chance of finding a market for their goods.

C.I.G.S., however, cannot see why the first alternative should not be adopted and Q.M.G.[237] also declares in favour of the adoption of the Commercial basis in assessing the value of surplus stores.

If these articles were thrown up in the ordinary course, the Ministry of Munitions state that they could not obtain more than 20% of their value for guns and 5% to 10% for ammunition. It is for consideration whether a charge of 100% for new guns and 50% for old guns and 100% for ammunition can be considered equitable.

Moreover it is the custom of the Admiralty to charge only 10% for guns, small arms and accoutrements surplus to their own requirements. If now the cost price of the articles is to be taken as the basis of the assessment, the Admiralty would have to adopt a new principle in disposing of their surplus stores.

However, both Q.M.G. and A.F.S. indicate that the freight charges constitute the principal limiting factor in the final contribution and that a considerable reduction, in the prices to be charged, might only have the effect of rendering more stores available than we had the money to ship. It is submitted, however, that this argument is fallacious.

In the first place, it is apparently forgotten that a sum of approximately £60,000 is still available under Category C. and could be used for additional freight charges.

In the second place, the Russians in this country have considerable sums of money at their disposal. An order to the value of £750,000 was recently placed with Kynochs[238] for Russian S.A.A.,[239] and a further order for £1,500,000 worth of S.A.A. is contemplated. If we tell the Russians that we can supply additional stores to the value of three to four million pounds under Category A, provided they can find up to two hundred thousand pounds to cover additional freight charges, there is little doubt that they would gladly co-operate.

In the third place it is submitted that even if it were to provide impossible to ship all the stores available according to this computation, it would be impolitic and unreasonable to make that a pretext for charging higher prices than are charged to the Lettish and other governments in the open market.

In addition to dealing with this question of principle A.F.S. refers to two important points of detail.

a) He suggests that it would be unwise to re-open the question of the pricing of guns as this would involve an increase in the price of naval guns.

[236] Assistant First Secretary to the War Office.

[237] Quartermaster-General.

[238] Kynoch Munitions Works, at Arklow, on the east coast of Ireland, halfway between Dublin and Rosslare. Prior to the 1914–18 war Kynochs supplied commercial explosives to mining companies in Europe, South Africa and Australia. By 1914 it was one of the world's biggest munitions factories and at its peak level of production, in 1917–18, employed 4,000 workers.

[239] Possibly 'small arms and ammunition'.

It is evident from D.Q.M.G.'s minute 9, that this argument is wholly misleading, as the additional charge for new naval guns would be insignificant in comparison with the saving on part worn land guns.

b) He considers that "100% for ammunition is too stiff" and suggests that 100% should be charged for non-surplus ammunition and 50% for surplus ammunition.

The Ministry of Munitions, however, state that the swap value of ammunition is only 5% or 10% and the charge of 50% of the cost price for surplus ammunition would therefore appear to be excessive.

In conclusion, therefore, it is submitted:

1. That a ruling should be given in accordance with the views of C.I.G.S. and Q.M.G. that the price to be charged for surplus arms, ammunition and accoutrements should represent their market value.
2. (a) That attention should be directed to the fact that £60,000 will be available from Category 'C' to meet any additional freight charges that the shipment of the additional stores may involve, and
   (b) That it should be ascertained as soon as possible whether any further stores will be available for shipment when the money at our disposal for the payment of freight charges has been exhausted, and that General Denikin's representatives in London be invited to arrange for the transport of such additional stores.
3. That it be pointed out that the present charge of 100% of the cost price for surplus ammunition is a particularly glaring instance of harsh dealing since the market value is only 5% to 10% and the stores are of urgent and vital importance to the armies of General Denikin, and it is further submitted that the amended charge of 50% proposed by A.F.S. is unjustifiably high.

AHMS

Sir Archibald Sinclair to Winston S. Churchill
8th January 1920

S. of S.

Mr. Montefiore, an influential and enlightened Jew, believes that the majority of the Bolo[240] leaders are not Jews and that to speak as you did at Sunderland "as if Bolshevism were a purely, or predominately, Jewish movement is false". Mr. Fisher, who forwards the letter, apparently concurs.[241]

[240] Bolshevik.

[241] On 3 January 1920, at Victoria Hall, Sunderland, Churchill delivered a virulent assault on the Bolshevik leadership following the withdrawal of British forces from Russia. He asked: 'was there ever a more awful spectacle in the whole history of the world than is unfolded by the agony of Russia? … they [the Bolsheviks] have driven man from the civilisation of the 20th century into a condition of barbarism worse than the Stone Age, and have left him the most awful and pitiable spectacle in human experience, devoured by vermin, racked by pestilence, and deprived of hope.' (Robert Rhodes James (ed.), *Churchill Speaks: 1897–1963* (Windward, 1980), p. 387.

If you think it worth while to correct him, I can easily provide you with the facts, as far as they can be ascertained, and these would prove the predominance of Jews in the Bolshevik movement beyond a peradventure.

But perhaps you won't think it worthwhile to join issue.[242]

AHMS

Sir Archibald Sinclair to Winston S. Churchill
8th January 1920

Secretary of State

Professor Hart writes to say that "it would appear from your recent speech at Sunderland the Government are contemplating a great publicity campaign in order to instruct public opinion as to the evils and dangers of Bolshevism" and offers his services as Lecturer.

Do you approve – (a) My reply to Professor Hart, of which I attach a copy. (b) Action proposed to forward his letter and enclosures to Sir Basil Thomson at the Home Office?[243]

AHMS

Sir Archibald Sinclair to Winston S. Churchill
8th January 1920

Secretary of State

General Spears forwards this memorandum which, he says, Marshal Foch has seen and considers most interesting.

It is thoughtful and sensible, but long and rather involved. You will get the principal argument if you read from LX on page 7 while the conclusions are summarised on the last page but one.

A good point, which is in accordance with the facts as reported to us by Denmiss, is that Denikin's advance could never have been so successful if it had not been for the popular risings which took place in the rear of the Bolshevik armies, and his present difficulties are partly due to the conviction of the people of South Russia that he is little likely to respect their cultural and political aspirations or to give the peasants their land into their own possession as the Bolsheviks themselves. Nothing but the execrable tyranny of the Bolsheviks could have roused the Russian peasants from their characteristic inertia, but under the illiberal and incompetent administration of Denikin they undoubtedly sank back to bewildered apathy and lost the will to struggle against the Bolsheviks.

AHMS

[242] Churchill added at the bottom of this note that Sinclair should 'write a soother' in reply.

[243] Churchill indicated on the letter that Captain Freddie Guest (Coalition Chief Whip and Patronage Secretary at the Treasury) should deal with the issue.

Sir Archibald Sinclair to Winston S. Churchill
12th January 1920

S. of S.

1. I was saying to D.M.I. (and had meant to repeat to you but you began talking about something else) that it is not necessary to assume that the Bolo message was a meaningless blind intended solely to deceive us. Operations in the east would require immense organisation, especially as Turkistan is ill supplied with railways and would require a serious tax on the material and especially the intellectual resources of the Bolos. (The scarcity of trained Staff Officers.) Other reasons obviously suggest themselves which would tend to make the directing brains at Moscow reluctant to pledge their military resources in support of any wild schemes of a none too firmly seated monarch in Central Asia. In these circumstances it would be possible to send a message which would indicate policy correctly to local agents and at the same time deceive the enemy in the wider sphere.
2. I suggested to my interviewer that according to his account, the Germans were playing a game which might be very dangerous for their own country. He replied that the Germans had only two alternatives to choose from. To support the Allied anti-Bolo policy as far as they were graciously permitted to do and renounce interference in Russia or to thwart the Allied policy, to foster their own power and influence in Russia and to seek to control the Red Army. They calculated that this control was now sufficiently strong to enable them to select the next objective of the Bolo armies. It would be important for them to keep the flames from their own house and they would therefore direct the offensive at the junction between Poland and Romania towards Hungary, leaving Czecho-Slovakia between themselves and the Bolos. If a further advance were necessary to keep the Red Armies in check until the German plans were clear it would be towards Italy and the Balkans.

AHMS

Winston S. Churchill to Sir Archibald Sinclair
25th January 1920

Sir Archibald Sinclair

What is this "Labour Army" the Bolsheviks have started? Is it simply people conscripted and made to do industrial work, or is there some other explanation?

WSC

Sinclair wrote the following response:

S. of S.

No information has been received either here or at the F.O. beyond what has appeared in the Wireless Press viz. that the 3rd Bolshevik army (from the eastern front), of course compiled mainly of conscripts, has been transported into a Labour Army with Trotsky as "President of its Executive Council".

It would appear to be an exceedingly clever move because:–

1. Trotsky in a recent speech has explained that the Labour Army will work under rigid military discipline.
2. The difficulty of demobilisation was that it involved sending men back to towns and villages where no one in the prevailing conditions of economic stagnation would be able to give them work and where clothing, food and fuel are scarce. This would have resulted in widespread malnourishment and anarchy. Under this scheme the Red Army will remain the well clothed, well fed, well disciplined support of Soviet Authority.
3. Demobilization would necessarily follow peace but under this scheme, it will be possible to convert all or a larger proportion of the Red Armies into Labour Armies which will retain their discipline and cohesion.
4. To the Allies the Soviet will say:– "How else can we re-start the normal economic processes of trade and commerce? How else can we get hold of the grain which you so much need?" To the Russian peasants whose grain will be essential to their economic schemes and bargains with the Allies, but who will refuse to surrender it except for payment in goods which will not at first be available and will therefore have to be forcibly coerced, the Soviet will say "The Allies drove us to it. We have to continue to enforce conscription to comply with the demands of the Allies."

AHMS

Sir Archibald Sinclair to Winston S. Churchill
31st January 1920
Personal

Secretary of State

I don't want to butt in on this controversy, especially as I don't know exactly what Mr. Mackinder[244] said, and I am far from suggesting that any accusations which he may have made against the British Military Mission are well founded. At the same time, I do not think that the facts quite bear out the attached rejoinder by the

[244] Sir Halford Mackinder (1861–1947): British High Commissioner in Southern Russia and a key liaison officer with General Denikin's White troops; argued that Britain's interests would be best served by splitting Russia into smaller states, and urged Curzon, the Foreign Secretary, to support the independence of Belarus, Ukraine, Georgia, Azerbaijan, Armenia and Chechnya; also recommended that Southern Russia, governed by the Whites, should be recognised as a separate state.

General Staff. In this connection I would draw your attention to General Holman's report dated 8th July, 1919. Paragraph 9 begins as follows:–

"I also found that the officers selected were in a good many cases unsuitable for the work allotted to them."

Paragraph 57 is to the following effect – "The method of selection of such officers and men as may be sanctioned requires to be greatly improved. It is imperative that their medical history should be investigated and that only those who are perfectly fit should be sent there, where the climate is trying. It is also very necessary that all members of the Mission should know what they are coming out for and the conditions of service."

I attach a letter which Major Sayer of the Tank Corps has sent me. When he returned from South Russia you will remember that you saw this officer and that you were very favourably impressed with him and sent him to see the Archbishop of Canterbury on the Jewish question. He writes to me as recently as the 16th October "General Holman impressed upon me the absolute necessity for careful selection at this end of personnel for South Russia, pointing out that one unsuitable officer may, in a very short while, seriously affect the cordial relations, &c." In private conversation he elaborated this considerably and mentioned in particular that the General Staff here appeared not to realise that it was a serious blunder to send out Jewish officers to South Russia. Several other people who have returned from South Russia to whom I have spoken have remarked that many of the officers who were sent out to South Russia were ill qualified for their duties, and the recent testimony of General Briggs was also quite definite on that point. He said that a great many officers were quite unsuitable and that there were a number of Jewish officers on the Staff of the Mission.

On the other hand, on several occasions when I have been able to recommend officers for employment on the Mission in South Russia, I have been informed that there were no vacancies, and that there were a great many more applicants than the Staff were able to find employment for.

As I have said, I don't know how far Mr. Mackinder's accusations went, and there is a great deal of evidence to show that the great majority of the officers on General Holman's staff are doing splendid work and are immensely popular with the Russians. But I don't think it can be maintained that the selection of these officers has been as strict as it should have been, or that the War Office is altogether blameless in this respect.

It seems to me a great pity that this controversy should have arisen, as Mr. Mackinder is without doubt in general agreement with the policy of the War Office in South Russia.

(Forgive me, if I ought not to have said this but I have headed this note "Personal"!)

AHMS

In early February 1920 Sinclair wrote a short briefing paper for an article by Churchill that was eventually published in the *Illustrated Sunday Herald* on 8 February 1920, entitled 'Zionism versus Bolshevism – A struggle for the soul of the Jewish people'. This article has been widely published by modern day anti-Semitic groups on the internet to imply that Churchill was at one time anti-Jewish and believed in a Jewish conspiracy to take over the world. While the article is reasonably balanced overall, Churchill did use some ill-advised phrases and his concern that Jews were so over-represented in the Soviet leadership had obviously prejudiced his attitudes at the time.

Sir Archibald Sinclair to Winston S. Churchill
6th February 1920

In accordance with your instructions the following notes on your article are submitted:-

1. THE PART PLAYED IN RUSSIA BY JEWS BELONGING TO THE FIRST OF YOUR CATEGORIES.

The loyal Russian Jews, in spite of the disabilities under which they have suffered, have managed to play an honourable and useful part in the national life of Russia. As bankers and industrialists they have strenuously promoted the development of Russia's vast economic resources and they were foremost in the creation of those remarkable organisations, the Russian Co-operative Societies. Their support has been given, for the most part, to liberal and progressive movements, and they have been among the staunchest upholders of friendship with France and Great Britain. Although it was exceedingly difficult for a Jew to play a prominent part in politics under the Czar's regime, their influence was strong in the Cadets Party[245] of which M. Vinaver,[246] a distinguished Jew, found the most adequate means of expressing their views and of contributing to the formation of public opinion and among the newspapers, which were conspicuous for their patriotism and devotion to the cause of the Allies in the Great War, were the 'Russkoe Slovo', the 'Retch' and the 'Bourse Gazette' which were controlled by Russian Jews.

2. THE INTEREST TAKEN BY THE WAR OFFICE/BRITISH GOVERNMENT IN THE RUSSIAN JEWS.

The War Office/British Government has been kept informed by the officers belonging to the British Mission in South Russia about the terrible atrocities committed by the Jewish Commissars, the prosperity of the Jews under the Bolshevik regime, the immunity of their dwellings, synagogues, and other property from the ruthless pillaging of the Bolsheviks, and the consequent mass hatred of the non-Jewish population against the Jews. This hatred was deliberately inflamed by bandits

[245] The Constitutional-Democratic Party, formed in October 1905 and usually called 'Cadets', were reformers who sought to retain the monarchy but establish parliamentary rule in Russia. The Cadets formed the largest party in the Provisional Government that followed the February 1917 revolution.
[246] Maxim Vinaver (1863–1926): Jewish lawyer and one of the founders of the Cadets.

and adventurers of the type of Grigorieff, Makhno, and Petlura, and it was realised that Denikin, who had expressed his determination to prevent the persecution of the Jews, would be faced with a task of almost insurmountable difficulty in giving them adequate protection.

Representations were therefore made to Denikin, with the object of indicating the importance of this question and of strengthening his hands in dealing with anti-Semitic agitation among his own people, and it only remains to be said that our advice was cordially received and loyally acted upon. General Holman reported that General Denikin had a keen sense of his responsibility for safeguarding the lives and property of the Jews as citizens of Russia, and that he was astonished at the success with which this obligation was fulfilled.

AHMS

Sir Archibald Sinclair to Winston S. Churchill
27th May 1920
Very Confidential

SECRETARY OF STATE

Mr. Picton Bagge has been appointed Political Officer and mediator between General Wrangel[247] and the Soviet government at the forthcoming negotiations. He is due to leave on Wednesday next. He has not yet received any written instructions, but he understands that they will be to the effect that General Wrangel asked for the mediation of His Majesty's Government to bring about an agreement with the Bolsheviks on the following basis:–

1. Cessation of hostilities.
2. The Crimea to revert to Soviet Russia.
3. A two months' interval of time to elapse between (1) and (2), providing full opportunities for the evacuation of the Crimea by General Wrangel and his associates.

Mr. Bagge will, therefore, be instructed to endeavour to bring about an agreement on these lines.

On the other hand, his own belief is that these negotiations will never take place. He is convinced that the Polish Government and Military Authorities are confident of the success of their operations, and he heard yesterday from the Polish Consul General that a definite agreement for common action had been reached between the Poles, the Ukrainians and General Wrangel. He also told me that news had just arrived of a considerable success in the region South of Kief, and the Bolshevik wireless today is certainly very reticent about operations in that area. He tells me

[247] Piotr Nikolayevich Wrangel (1878–1928): former Tsarist officer who joined Denikin's forces in 1918, and assumed command of the anti-Bolshevik forces in southern Russia in 1920; launched a final offensive against the Bolsheviks in June 1920, but was forced to evacuate his forces from the Crimea in November 1920, bringing the Russian Civil War to an end; died in exile in Brussels.

that the Poles have issued a proclamation that the land will be restored to the peasants and that, although the Polish landlords in the Ukraine will receive full compensation for the loss of their estates, the Polish Government had undertaken that they will not be allowed back into the country. He is therefore confident that the popular risings will grow in number and strength, and that a junction will soon be effected between the Ukraines and General Wrangel, which will put negotiations between the latter and the Soviet Government out of the question.

However, if Mr. Bagge does leave the country on Wednesday next, would you care to see him on Monday or Tuesday? He did not ask for an interview with you, but I have no doubt that he would be very much gratified if you would give him one.

AHMS

Sir Archibald Sinclair to Winston S. Churchill
25th June 1920

S. of S.

I have read the attached précis and several passages in the original report. The writer who evidently possesses a complete mastery of this subject, is convinced that the Commission of Control[248] is up against a determined attempt on the part of the German General Staff to repeat the achievement of Stenin and to save sufficient material out of the war wreck to reconstruct the framework of the German Army.

He makes out what appears to me in most respects an unanswerable case for the immediate enforcement of the classes of the peace treaty relating to the reduction of the German Army to the strength of 100,000 men but he shows little recognition of the appalling difficulties with which the German Government is faced in its efforts to maintain internal order against the revolutionary factions both of the Right and of the Left, while there is no reference at all in his memorandum to possible external dangers and the genuine alarm which must no doubt be spreading in the minds of German soldiers and statesmen as they watch the westward advance of the Bolshevik armies.

His most telling points are – First, that the legal obligation to universal service has not yet been repealed so that if call-up notices were issued to-morrow, every man of military age in Germany would be under legal obligation to obey them. Secondly that if the Germans are allowed to postpone the formation of an army of 100,000 men to an "ulterior date" and meanwhile to enlist the men on short term engagements of a few months or a year's duration, a reserve of 800,000 men maybe built up in two years. And Thirdly that the present organisation includes a large number of unauthorised staffs which enable brigade and divisional staffs to be established all over Germany according to the precise pattern of the pre-war Corps and

[248] The Commission of Control was set up by the Allies to police the terms of the Treaty of Versailles.

Divisional commands in all of the old military districts outside the Neutral Zone and the various plebiscite and occupied areas.

On the other hand the Commission of Control has recommended an increase by one third in the strength of the police as laid down in the Treaty and would be prepared to recommend a further increase if satisfied that the police force will be a genuine Constabulary armed and organised after the pattern of the R.I.C.[249] and kept under local control.

My impression is that the German Government should be told that this police reorganisation should be completed by a certain date, that a generous increase in numbers should be allowed (over those laid down in the Peace Treaty which are admitted on all hands to be inadequate) and that they should be told to cut down their Army to 100,000 men by the same date. This would give time for the political and military situation on the Eastern frontiers of Germany to develop. Meanwhile all short term enlistments should be stopped.

I am less clear about the necessity for the immediate repeal of the Conscription Laws. If disarmament and the destruction of war material is carried out thoroughly, we should have little to fear from mobs of ill-armed German conscripts. On the other a crisis may arise when it will be well for the natives of Western Europe if the Germans are able to repel an invasion from the East which would probably be accompanied by Bolshevik risings and strikes all over Germany. The legal power of conscription might in the hands of the German Government be a decisive factor in such a situation. Notwithstanding the lack of artillery, aeroplane, tanks, gas etc., the German conscripts would be formidable to the Bolsheviks.

AHMS

The defeats of the White Russian armies in eastern and southern Russia persuaded Lloyd George and Curzon that there was no merit in continuing political, military or economic support to the surviving anti-Bolshevik forces led by General Wrangel in the Crimea. Despite Churchill's protests, the Cabinet agreed on 28 May 1920 to open negotiations with the Bolsheviks with the aim of resuming trade between Russia and the British Empire. On 3 June the Government wrote to Wrangel to inform him that he could expect no further support from Britain. On 23 July Churchill received a letter from Savinkov painting a very dark view of the Whites' chances of recovering their position and asking him to bring pressure to bear on Wrangel to work more closely with Savinkov.

[249] Royal Irish Constabulary – which, unlike the British police, was armed.

Winston S. Churchill to Sir Archibald Sinclair
23rd July 1920

Sir Archibald Sinclair

You should write to Monsieur Savinkov and say that in view of the decisions of policy come to by His Majesty's Government I regret I cannot intervene in the matter in any way.

WSC

In August Sinclair turned his attention away from the excitements in Russia to the more mundane issues around the proposals for improvements and repairs to military barracks in the London area.

Sir Archibald Sinclair to Winston S. Churchill
16th August 1920

Secretary of State

I saw General Jeffreys[250] this afternoon about the improvements and repairs to the Foot Guards Quarters at the various Barracks in the London District.

He remains strongly of the opinion that the Foot Guards are not so well catered for in this respect as Battalions quartered at Aldershot or Salisbury, and in this connection it would be interesting to call for a return, on the lines of General Jeffreys' own return, which I have flagged, of the Barracks contained, for example, in the Marlborough lines at Aldershot. In calling for this return it would be important to state that only a statement of the normal accommodation was required because, while a great number of Battalions are on service overseas in places where wives are not allowed to accompany the troops, the Married Quarters of the battalions remaining at home are proportionately but temporarily congested.

General Jeffreys considers that the proposed improvements at Wellington Barracks are of paramount importance, but even when these are carried out there will still remain a whole battalion out on Wimbledon Common. You will see that Q.M.G. proposes that this battalion should be sent to Aldershot or to Woking, but surely there are strong reasons why this should not be allowed and why you want the battalion here in London? Apart from other reasons, it should be remembered that the training of the ordinary Infantry soldier is now far more severe than before the war. He has still to be proficient in ordinary Infantry tactics and also with his rifle, but in addition every man has to be an expert light machine gunner and bomb thrower, and a rifle grenadier and therefore it is also important from the point of view of training to concentrate as many Guards Battalions as possible in London, so

[250] General Sir George Darrell Jeffreys, 1st Baron Jeffreys (1878–1960): infantry division commander in the 1914–18 war; Conservative MP for Petersfield 1941–51; Colonel of the Grenadier Guards 1952–60.

that the exceptional ceremonial duties which are thrown upon them shall be made as light as possible. At the present time every man has to go on guard about once a week, and every time a man goes on guard he loses two days' training. General Jeffreys, therefore, attaches great importance to his scheme for converting the Duke of York's School into a Barracks for the accommodation of this extra battalion. This would involve only a small charge on Public Funds as, of course, the buildings are already public property. He is about to submit a definite scheme.

The other battalion which is out on Wimbledon Common will be accommodated in Wellington Barracks as soon as the new improvements have been completed.

Q.M.G. states that authority has now been obtained for the purchase of a site in York Street, but he remarks that no provision has been made for the reconstruction of these Barracks in the Estimates for 1920–21, and he gives no indication of the date upon which it may be possible to undertake them; and until the work is completed a battalion will be on Wimbledon Common in huts which the local authority desire to remove.

The next most important proposal is the scheme at Caterham, with regard to which General Jeffreys will shortly make an official submission.

But of almost equal importance to these two schemes is his proposal for the housing of the unmarried officers of the Foot Guards. It is quite true, as Q.M.G. states, that it has never been the custom hitherto to provide quarters for these officers, except for a very small proportion, and such quarters as are provided are scarcely habitable. On the other hand, there are a large number of officers in the Foot Guards now who are less able to afford to find accommodation of their own outside the Barracks. An officer who had £250 a year before the war was better off than one with £500 a year now, consequently this matter has become one of extreme urgency, and General Jeffreys hopes that his scheme for the acquisition of Belgrave Mansions will be taken into serious consideration, although it is strongly criticised in Q.M.G.'s note. The latter indicates that it would be more desirable to buy a freehold property than this 35 years leasehold, but General Jeffreys says, "Where is it possible to find accommodation within reasonable distance of the Foot Guard Barracks which could be bought freehold for a reasonable sum of money?" Belgrave Mansions, on the other hand, is situated at the corner of Grosvenor Gardens and Buckingham Palace Road, just opposite Victoria Station and is therefore on the direct route between Chelsea and Wellington Barracks and within two minutes walk of the Underground Station by which the officers could proceed direct to the Tower. It would be impossible to find a more convenient site, nor would the purchase price of £100,000 for a 35 years lease with a Ground Rent of £423, against which a rental of £2065 for the shops on the Ground Floor should be set off, providing accommodation for 100 officers, be considered excessive. Not only this, but as this block of buildings is the property of the Duke of Westminster, it is not impossible that special consideration would be given by the vendor if it was desired to purchase the property freehold.

Confidential

You appeared to be considerably struck by the amount of work that was being done by Q.M.G's department on the improvement of these quarters, and thought it possible that General Jeffreys was not aware of the progress that had been made. I would point out, however, that both with regard to the scheme for the improvement of Wellington Barracks and that for the purchase of four houses in Belgrave Road to provide married quarters, Treasury sanction is stated to have been obtained – in both cases – on the 30th July last. General Jeffrey's visit to you took place on or just previous to that date, and it was known in the Q.M.G's department about a week or ten days before that, that he was coming to see you.

AHMS

Winston S. Churchill to Sir Archibald Sinclair
25th September 1920

Archie dear,

Would you be able to meet me in Dundee between 14.15.16 for meetings etc. If so I should like it very much – not just but also to sort your own plans out.[251] Get the programme from the office.

Yours ever,
W

Sir Archibald Sinclair to Winston S. Churchill
29th October 1920

Secretary of State

Major General J. Bagratouni, member of the Armenian Delegation, and Chief of the Military Mission, called to see me this afternoon. He is very anxious to have an appointment with you in order to bring before your notice the dangers to which Armenia is exposed on account of the concentric Turkish and Bolshevik attack.[252] He pointed out that, as far as the Bolsheviks were concerned, the objects of the operations were to effect a junction with the Turks and to threaten British interests in the Middle East, and that they were only incidentally aimed at the unhappy Armenians who had the misfortune to stand across their path. He promised to be

[251] Churchill was keen to help Sinclair to find a suitable parliamentary seat adjacent to his Dundee constituency.

[252] Armenia, previously divided between the Ottoman and Russian empires (and suffering, in 1915–18, the first modern genocide, in which at least a million people were killed by the Turks), took the opportunity of Turkey's defeat in the First World War to declare independence, on 28 May 1918. In the autumn of 1920, however, Turkish and Bolshevik forces overran the region and signed the Treaty of Moscow (March 1921), which ended dreams of an independent Armenian state until the collapse of the Soviet empire in 1991.

brief, speaks English well and lost a leg in the war, and I thought it possible, therefore, that you would consent to give him a few minutes.

AHMS

In November 1920 Churchill sought Sinclair's opinion about how he would feel about representing Churchill at the regimental dinner of the Royal Scottish Fusiliers, the unit in which they had both served on the Western Front. Sinclair was not at all attracted to the idea.

Winston S. Churchill to Sir Archibald Sinclair
3rd November 1920

Sir Archibald Sinclair,

I think it very likely that this will devolve on you, but before writing to Trenchard[253] I should like to know what you feel about it.

WSC

Sir Archibald Sinclair to Winston S. Churchill
3rd November 1920

S of S

As you are good enough to ask me to express my feelings, I feel bound to do so frankly.

1. During the last period that I served with the 6th R.S.F., if would be much truer to say that I was attached to you than to the battalion. I came with you & left with you.
2. I thoroughly enjoyed my association with the battalion, but I never entered into the life of the regiment & I have never ever been invited to their regimental dinner.
3. I know from experience of my own regimental dinners that these functions are very much in the nature of family parties, & I should suggest that one of the family should be appointed to represent you.
4. A minor point is that I have no Fusilier uniform in which to attend the two military ceremonies, one of which is the consecration of the Colour at which your representative is particularly desired to be present & at which it is obviously essential he should wear the uniform of the regiment.

[253] Hugh Montague Trenchard, 1st Viscount Trenchard of Wolfeton (1873–1956): commanded the Royal Flying Corps from 1915; Chief of the Air Staff January – April 1918, when he helped establish the Royal Air Force, but resigned from office after a quarrel with Lord Rothermere, the Air Secretary; in February 1919, invited by Churchill to return as Chief of the Air Staff, a position he held until his retirement in 1929.

Consequently I feel bound to say that you could hardly suggest to me a duty which I should feel more reluctant to undertake. I know little or nothing of the regiment and I should feel awfully out of place.

I would therefore request that you should authorise me to write in the first place to Gibb & ask him to represent you &, if he is unable to do so, that I should ask General Stewart, the Chairman of the Dinner Club to nominate an officer who served in the 6th R.S.F. There were plenty who lived in or near Glasgow.

AHMS

Events in Turkey in late 1920 were of concern to the British Government. In August 1920 the Turkish and Allied governments signed the Treaty of Sèvres, by this the Turkish government renounced all claims to non-Turkish territory. The kingdom of the Hijaz, and Armenia, achieved independence, Syria became a mandate of France, and Mesopotamia (with Mosul), and Palestine, of Britain. In Asia Minor, Smyrna and its hinterland were to be administered by Greece for five years, after which a plebiscite was to be held; the Dodecanese and Rhodes went to Italy, while Thrace and the remainder of the Turkish islands in the Aegean were assigned to Greece. The Straits were to be internationalised and the adjoining territory demilitarised. Istanbul remained Turkish, as did the remainder of Anatolia.

A revolt in Turkey, led by Mustafa Kemal, later known as Atatürk,[254] Churchill's old adversary from the Dardanelles, led to a repudiation of the Treaty; during 1922, the Greeks were driven out of their new possessions, with those Greeks who failed to get on to the boats leaving Smyrna being massacred by the victorious Turks. When the Turks swept on towards the Dardanelles, they came up against a small British force at Chanak, guarding the area of the Straits which had been neutralised under the Treaty. Lloyd George's willingness to threaten military action against the Turks was seen by many Conservative MPs as dangerous sabre-rattling, and triggered the famous meeting at the Carlton Club in October 1922 which was to break the coalition and force Lloyd George from office. Conflict was avoided, but as a result of Atatürk's successes the Treaty of Sèvres was ultimately replaced by the Treaty of Lausanne.

Sir Archibald Sinclair to Winston S. Churchill
12th November 1920
CONFIDENTIAL

Secretary of State

[254] Mustafa Kemal Atatürk (1881–1938): commander, Ottoman 19th Division at Gallipoli, prevented Anzac troops from gaining possession of a strategic ridge; emerged as leader of the attempts to retain Turkey's territorial integrity and independence after the war; elected President of the new Republic of Turkey in October 1923; known since 1934 as Atatürk ('Father of Turks').

Mr. Aneurin Williams,[255] failing to obtain an interview with you today, called to see me.

He informed me that at his last interview with you, he had discussed the question of the occupation of Trebizond which he considered was one of the principal bases of the Kemalist Army operating against the Armenians. In reply to his questions, you had admitted that the possibility of its occupation by the Greek army had been considered, but you had indicated that the principal difficulty was finance.

The following day he called on the Greek Minister whom he described as being so much agitated over the supply of arms to Mustapha Kemal by the Italians as to make it difficult to get a word in. Moreover, when he at first broached the question of Trebizond, the Minister relapsed into reticence, but when Mr. Williams informed him, without mentioning your name, that he had heard on high authority that financial difficulties were deterring the Greeks, the Minister replied that that was not so.

M. Venizelos[256] would certainly not take the initiative in proposing the occupation of Trebizond, but would expect to be invited to act by the Great Powers. If it was a matter of putting two or three battalions into Trebizond at a cost of a couple of hundred thousand pounds, he did not think that the Greeks would hesitate to comply with the wishes of the Powers in view of their strong sympathies with the Armenians.

Believing that this information was of the utmost consequence, Mr. Williams proceeded yesterday to Downing Street where, in the absence of the Prime Minister, he saw Mr. Philip Kerr,[257] who declared that the Prime Minister fully realised the unhappy plight of the Armenians, but suggested to Mr. Williams that he should see Lord Curzon. Mr. Williams appears to have protested that he understood that the foreign policy of the country was largely in the hands of the Prime Minister himself, and to have hinted that he believed that Mr. Philip Kerr had no little influence in these matters, but I gather that Mr. Kerr replied that Lord Curzon took a particular interest in Eastern affairs and that in such matters as Armenia he still remained the principal adviser of the Cabinet. Indeed, Mr. Kerr went so far as to say that he thought that such a little matter as the occupation of Trebizond might hardly require a Cabinet decision at all, but I assured Mr. Williams that he must have misunderstood him on this point.

---

[255] Aneurin Williams (1859–1924): barrister; Liberal MP for Plymouth January – December 1910, Durham Consett 1918–22.

[256] Eleftherios Venizelos (1864–1936): Greek Prime Minister 1910–15, 1917–20, 1924, 1928–32, 1933; dismissed by King Constantine after inviting the Allied forces into Salonika, he established a provisional rival government and, with Allied support, forced the King's abdication in June 1917; at the Versailles Peace Conference, Greece won substantial territorial gains from Bulgaria and Turkey.

[257] Philip Kerr, Lord Lothian (1882–1940): Private Secretary to Lloyd George 1916–21, where he was active at the Paris Peace Conference, 1919; Chancellor of the Duchy of Lancaster August – October 1931; supporter of appeasement until 1939; Ambassador to US 1939–40; died in December 1940 following a common viral illness, his belief in Christian Science leading him to refuse simple medical treatment that would almost certainly have saved his life.

Mr. Williams then proceeded to the Foreign Office, where he found that Lord Curzon had gone down to the country to attend the funeral of his brother-in-law, but he was received by Sir John Tilley.[258] Sir John Tilley explained the objections to the occupation of Trebizond on political and military rather than financial grounds. He said that if the Greeks were once allowed into Trebizond, they would want to stay, to which Mr. Williams naturally replied that he saw no objection in view of the fact that Trebizond was an ancient Greek city with a large Greek and Armenian population. Then apparently Sir John Tilley went on to say that when this occupation was last discussed, the objections were military and not financial at all. This information Mr. Williams found difficult to reconcile with what you had told him.

I replied that although I had no knowledge of these matters and was not competent to express either your views or those of the General Staff on the question, it appeared to me that it was not difficult to reconcile what Sir John Tilley and you had told him. It seemed to me hardly possible to dump two or three battalions, as Mr. Williams had suggested, in Trebizond and leave them there all alone to face any troops that Mustapha Kemal might detach to attack them, and to take no further action to support them on any part of the front in Asia Minor. Consequently it was probably found that the occupation of this city would entail costly military operations elsewhere, or alternatively the strong reinforcement of the original two or three battalions. Mr. Williams seemed quite satisfied with this explanation, but urged that the question should be reconsidered in the light of the information which he had elicited from the Greek Minister, and that M. Venizelos should be invited to undertake the occupation of Trebizond by the Allied Powers.

Mr. Williams then went on to inform me that M. Aharonian, who represented the Armenians at the San Remo Conference and signed the Treaty of Sèvres on behalf of his country, was not in London. He proposed raising 15,000 Armenian volunteers for the occupation and defence of Trebizond, and he suggested that we should supply the officers and equipment for these volunteers, and that 10,000 other volunteers should be raised in Europe to reinforce. I ventured to indicate to Mr. Williams that I did not think this proposal would meet with an encouraging reception here. However, he was exceedingly anxious that you should see M. Aharonian, who he declares is a man of great charm and striking intellectual attainments, and is particularly anxious to have the honour of an interview with you. He would be accompanied by General Bagratouni, the Armenian Military Representative who lost a leg in the war. They promise not to occupy more than few minutes of your time.

AHMS

[258] Sir John Anthony Cecil Tilley (1869–1952): career diplomat who served the Foreign Office in Constantinople before the First World War; became a Privy Councillor in 1920 and served as British Ambassador to Japan 1926–31.

Sir Archibald Sinclair to Winston S. Churchill
14th December 1920

Secretary of State

With reference to the attached minutes of the Allied Conference:–

1. The first subject under discussion was the admission of Armenia to the League of Nations. The decision, of which you are aware, was reached with complete unanimity.
2. The next subject was the Treaty of Sevres. In this connection M. Leygues[259] pointed out that in influential French political circles there was a strong growing demand for a drastic revision of the Treaty, but he declared that this was not the view of the French Government. That Government, he declared "Thought that in the circumstances the better course was to maintain the Treaty as a whole but to amend it in certain respects to meet the new situation which had arisen in the Near East".

He did not advocate the return of Smyrna to the Turks in the sense that the Turks should resume their sovereignty as in pre-war days, but he did think that Smyrna should be placed under some form of Ottoman sovereignty, but at the same time given some kind of local autonomy or possibly being placed under international control. He was convinced that peace could not be attained so long as the present arrangement at Smyrna continued.

Count Sforza[260] declared that from some points of view it was to Italy's advantage to have the Greeks in Smyrna, and he instanced the Tripartite agreement which he did not desire re-opened in any respect. But the broader question was to secure a peaceable solution in the Near East, and he thought that some way out of the difficulty could be found without making concessions of substance to "the unspeakable Turk".

Mr. Lloyd George said that in the view of the British Government, any discussion on this question at the present time was premature. If Constantine[261] returned he would either have to carry out his pledges and demobilise the Army, in which case Mustapha would drive the Greeks out of Smyrna, or he must maintain the Greek Army, in which case the Greeks would turn against him, and he would be unable to redeem his pledges about demobilization. This situation, however, had not as yet arisen. The Powers would be discrediting themselves if they forced back under Turkish rule any of the lands which had recently been freed from Ottoman mal-administration, and he could not assent to any proposal which involved putting

---

259 George Leygues (1857–1933): French politician during the Third Republic; Minister of Education, then Interior; Minister for the Colonies 1918–20; President of the Council of Ministers September 1920 – January 1921.

260 Count Carol Sforza (1873–1952): Italian diplomat; Minister for Foreign Affairs 1920–21; Italy's ambassador to France 1922; resigned after refusing to serve under Benito Mussolini; a strong anti-fascist, lived in voluntary exile in Belgium until 1939 and in the US 1940–43; returned to Italy after World War II to serve in various government posts, including Minister of Foreign Affairs 1947–51.

261 King Constantine I (see n110).

Smyrna again under the Turk with Allied assistance. But if the Greeks themselves like to allow the Turks to get back into Thrace and Smyrna, then the responsibility and the consequence must rest with them. He added that he was no believer of international control which, in fact, was no control at all. He trusted, therefore, that no decision to modify the Treaty would be taken until the allies knew what the Greeks were going to do, and until the return of the Mission which the Turkish Government was about to send to Mustapha.

"If the Allies began pulling the Treaty of Sevres to pieces without knowing what they proposed to put in its place, they would be initiating a fearful conflagration in the Near East."

President Wilson's[262] views about Armenia[263] could not possibly be accepted, nor could the Allies undertake to fight the Turk to enforce such a scheme.

Count Sforza had only one remark to make on Mr. Lloyd George's views

"That he could not regard the return of Smyrna to the Turks under proper safeguard as amounting to an infamous act on the part of the Allies."

M. Leygues referred to Mr. Lloyd George's view that it would be better to take no decision until they saw more clearly what was likely to happen in Greece, but he (M. Leygues) indicated that during the last fortnight the relations between the Nationalists and the Bolsheviks had been drawing closer.

"If these two hostile elements were to make common cause, it would be the Allies that would have to bear the shock. He felt strongly that they must do all in their power to prevent this unholy alliance, and he thought it was most dangerous … To take no steps to stop the junction of these two forces … An honourable peace should be offered to the Turkish Nationalists."

He did not wish to insist on any decision being taken that day, but the situation in Asia Minor was full of the gravest perils and he and the French Government felt that it was essential to make peace.

Mr. Lloyd George said that he feared

"the difficulties of view between himself and the French were rather more fundamental and deep-rooted than he had imagined".

The British information regarding Mustapha Kemal was absolutely opposite to that which was in the hands of M. Leygues. The British report was that in the last

[262] Thomas Woodrow Wilson (1856–1924): 28th President of the United States (1913–21); creator and leading advocate of the League of Nations, for which he was awarded the 1919 Nobel Peace Prize; suffered a paralytic stroke while seeking American public support for the Treaty ofVersailles (October 1919) which incapacitated him for the rest of his term of office; in 1919 US Senate failed to ratify the Treaty by seven votes.

[263] The 1920 Treaty of Sèvres, which partitioned the defunct Ottoman Empire and recognised the Armenian Republic that had emerged in 1918 from the collapse of the Russian Empire, delegated the responsibility for resolving the boundary between Armenia and Turkey to President Wilson. After a US military mission to the region had observed the dangers Armenia faced from Turkish and Russian ambitions, Wilson sought to give it greater security through access to the Black Sea. Turkish and Bolshevik armed forces, however, simultaneously invaded the Armenian Republic in November 1920 and partitioned its territories before Wilson's boundaries could be implemented.

few days the Bolsheviks had become convinced that Great Britain and the French were stirring up Mustapha against them, and that the latter intended to capture Georgia, Azerbaijan and Batum and

"it seemed quite likely that war would break out between the Bolsheviks and the Nationalists".

Mr. Lloyd George's view was

"that the Turkish idea was to carry out the old Pan-Turanian scheme"

They meant to extend to the East, they wanted their own home land, for instance Turkestan, and they were not thinking of Smyrna and Thrace. Consequently the Nationalists regarded the Bolsheviks as the danger and their enemy, as they stood between them and their Eastern ambitions. It was curious to see in Russia the old racial feeling once more emerge out of the communism which had been imposed upon it.

"The Turks were thinking more of Batum than they were of Smyrna. Supposing the Allies offered Smyrna and Adrianople to the Turks, no doubt they would gladly accept them, but their mind was concentrated in the East. He sincerely trusted that at a time when the mind of the Turk was fully engaged elsewhere, the Allies would not ask him to turn back West ... He was not in the least disposed to ask Mustapha Kemal to turn back to the West when all his thoughts were concentrated on the East".

M. Leygues referred to a series of observations which Mr. Lloyd George had made about the treachery of the Turks as compared to that of the Greeks, and said that it was certainly not his (M. Leygues') wish to eulogise the Turks. They were in complete agreement about the Turkish character, and he was far from forgetting all that they had suffered at the Turk's hands. However, he maintained his view about the approaching rapprochement between the Nationalists and the Bolsheviks, and if, as was the British view, the Bolsheviks and the Nationalists were on the point of coming to blows so much the better for the Allies, but they were bound to prepare for all eventualities. He assured Mr. Lloyd George that there was no real divergency of opinion.

Count Sforza stated that M. Krassin[264] had been to see him the day before, and after making certain complaints had said –

"I am all for peace, but you will not have peace, and you are forcing the Bolsheviks and the Turks to form an alliance against the Entente.

M. Berthelot[265] thought that if the Nationalists got into actual contact, the situation would be dangerous.

[264] Leonid Krassin (1870–1926): close ally of Lenin; Commissar for Foreign Trade 1918–22, sent to London to re-establish trade relations.

[265] Henri Mathias Berthelot (1863–1931): head of the French military mission to Romania in 1917 until the country surrendered to the Central Powers; appointed as Commander-in-Chief of the Danube Army when Romania re-entered the war in October 1918; in February 1919 visited Odessa to meet Denikin; he was not impressed by the White Russian leadership and predicted that Denikin's forces would be defeated; appointed governor of Metz in 1920 and awarded a seat on the French Supreme War Council.

Mr. Lloyd George stated that this was not his view!"

At the next sitting of the Conference the final draft about the admission of Armenia to the League of Nations was approved.

As soon as the discussion on the Treaty of Sevres was resumed, Lord Curzon informed the Conference that the mission from Constantinople to Mustapha Kemal was starting that day, and that the Turkish Government had announced its intention of ratifying the Treaty on the day (say December 14th) on which the mission actually arrived at Angora.

M. Leygues enquired what would be the position if Turkey ratified the Treaty but France did not ratify it.

Mr. Lloyd George replied that France would then be at war with Turkey and the position would be similar to that now existing between the U.S.A. and Germany.

M. Leygues said that the representatives of the French Government had come to London in order, if possible, to arrive at a full understanding with the British Government.

"It would be most difficult for him to return to France and tell the French Parliament that no alteration of the Treaty was possible ... It was at least necessary for him to be able to say that the Powers were not closed to possible adjustments ... So as to secure the lasting peace which everyone desired."

Lord Curzon's view was that

"those adjustments and concessions could only properly be discussed after the result of the meeting between Mustapha Kemal and the mission from Constantinople was known."

His opinion was that Mustapha Kemal was most anxious to reach some modus vivendi with the Central Turkish Government, partly on account of his fear that Enver Pasha[266] might supplant him, and partly on account of a genuine feeling of distrust and apprehension about the progress of the Bolsheviks.

In these circumstances Lord Curzon thought that any questions of concessions and adjustments to be made in the matter of the Turkish Treaty by the Allies must be based on the terms of the agreement reached between the Turks themselves.

M. Leygues replying to some observations from Mr. Lloyd George declared that France did not for a moment refuse to honour her signature to the Treaty, and that he himself was anxious to have joint action with the Allies

"and that he was opposed to any drastic revision of the Treaty!"

But it would be of great assistance to him if the British representatives would admit the possibility in the future of making adjustments and concessions.

M. Berthelot said that

[266] Enver Pasha (1881–1922): Turkish War Minister and Commander-in-Chief during World War One, instrumental in bringing Turkey into the war on the side of the Central Powers; fled to Germany after the war; travelled to Moscow in 1919 seeking support for a campaign to overthrow Mustafa Kemal's new government but was met with deep suspicion by the Soviet regime who refused to assist his plans; killed in August 1922 while fighting the Red Army in Turkestan with the Whites.

"if Mustapha, who was obviously ill at ease, could be persuaded to negotiate with the Allies, it might be possible to come to some amicable arrangement with him about Smyrna which would lead up to general peace."

Mr Lloyd George observed

"that it was a great mistake to think that Mustapha Kemal was mainly interested in the proceedings of the Allies."

In point of fact he was looking to the East and to the possibility of a revival of the historic enmities between the Russian and the Turk. Whenever the Turks had quarrelled in the past with Russia they had been forced to turn for assistance to the Western Powers. One of the great principles in dealing with Orientals was to let them make the first offer. He (Mr. Lloyd George)

"was all for concluding peace with Mustapha Kemal, but it would be fatal to proclaim this to the world as the object of the Allies. If this were done, Mustapha's price would immediately rise and his terms would become impossible."

Mr. Lloyd George had just had luncheon that day with a person who had recently returned from Greece, whose views were worthy of attention, and he had told him that in his opinion the effect of the Allied declaration issued yesterday would be that the Greeks would not vote for Constantine.[267]

He had also received a message from M. Gounaris[268] to which he had contented himself with the reply that he could not believe anything that M. Gounaris said. But the mere fact that this man had communicated with him showed that he realised perfectly well that Constantine could not rule in Athens if the allies were against it. He therefore urged once again that

"the Allies should wait and see what policy Greece proposed to adopt and secondly what results, if any, followed from the meeting between the Constantinople mission and Mustapha Kemal."

M. Leygues said that he found himself in agreement with Mr. Lloyd George on nearly every point, and was particularly impressed with the necessity for the allies keeping their proposals to themselves and leaving Mustapha Kemal to make the first offer. He also agreed with Mr. Lloyd George's opinion of Gounaris, who would betray the Allies on the first convenient opportunity.

He was prepared to accept the British draft proposals which were before the meeting, subject to certain modifications.

A discussion then ensued on the wording of the draft, which was finally agreed upon in the form which has already appeared in the Press.

The principal point at issue was whether any reference should be made to the fact that the Allies were waiting to see what would be the result of the

[267] During December 1920 the Greek plebiscite on the return of King Constantine to the throne took place; the result was an overwhelmingly positive vote for the return of the King – see n110.

[268] Dimitrios Gounaris (1866–1922): Prime Minister of Greece March – August 1915 and April 1921 – May 1922.

Constantinople mission to Angora, and it was finally agreed that to refer publicly to that mission would have the effect of putting up Mustapha Kemal's terms.

A discussion then took place on the situation which would arise in the event of ex-King Constantine being recalled to the Throne of Greece, and the possible methods which should be adopted by the Allies in dealing with it. It was agreed that the surest method of exercising pressure was by withdrawing financial support from the Greek Government, and eventually it was decided to object to the note issue of a further amount of two hundred million drachmas which the Greek Government had recently made. It was considered that such a step was far more effective than simply recalling the Allied representatives from Athens.

AHMS

1921–1923

In January 1921 Sinclair visited Paris to attend the preparations for the Paris Conference designed to establish German reparation payments. Sinclair wrote frequently to Churchill about information, gossip and insights that he acquired through his contacts.

Sir Archibald Sinclair to Winston S. Churchill
10th January 1921
Personal & Secret

Dear Secretary of State,

I am informed that Krassin is very much perturbed about the sale of his Russian gold. He is informed that the big banks of Europe and America are issuing circulars forbidding the purchase of gold of Russian origin. In the meantime he is satisfied that the only method of fighting this plan is the independent sale of gold in Reval, and he considers that Solomon is managing this plan very successfully, but he is afraid that with Solomon's recall and the appointment of Litvinoff,[269] all these operations will fall through. He has pointed out to his Chiefs in Moscow that they are risking, by the recall of Solomon and the appointment of Litvinoff, the loss of enormous sums because every unprofitable sale not only spoils the purchase for

[269] Maxim Litvinov (1876–1951): appointed in November 1918 as the Bolshevik Government's representative in Britain; arrested by the British Government and held until exchanged for Bruce Lockhart, the British diplomat imprisoned in Russia; then employed as the Soviet Government's roaming ambassador; it was largely through his efforts that Britain agreed to end its economic blockade of the Soviet Union, and he also negotiated several trade agreements with European countries; Commissar for Foreign Affairs from 1930; in 1933 persuaded the United States to recognise the Soviet government; Ambassador to the United States 1941–43.

future deals but lowers their political prestige. On the other hand he has received instructions in the form of a resolution of the "Political Bureau" not to carry on negotiations in London with the Italian Representative as discussions have already commenced with an Italian Representative at Reval. This looks as if the task of reaching an agreement with Italy was being taken away from Krassin and entrusted to Litvinoff.

In this connection also I may mention that two Russians are proceeding from Tuapse on the board the notorious steamship "Ancona" to Italy.

The French Political and Military Missions in Riga still take a very serious view of the situation, but I understand that the opinion of the American Mission is that while the British are unduly optimistic, the French are over anxious.

Yours sincerely,
Archibald Sinclair
Personal & Secret

Sir Archibald Sinclair to Winston S. Churchill
12th January 1921

Dear Secretary of State,

M. Krassin has been receiving complaints from the Secretary of the Peoples Commissariat and from Comrade Tchitcherin[270] himself that many of the long bulletins which are sent daily via Petrograd to the "Herald"[271] remain unprinted, and Krassin has been enjoined urgently to find out whether they are not held up. In addition to these daily bulletins, bi-weekly "Bulletins of Occurrences" are sent to Krassin. In addition to this, M. Tchitcherin complains that forged copies of the Pravda are being printed containing articles which are falsely ascribed to Lenin and Trotsky which are being reproduced in the Foreign Press. Krassin is to see that the 'Herald' publishes this scandalous fact and exposes the forgery. Of course, it will be very easy for the Bolshevik authorities, whenever an article or speech is reproduced from the Pravda of a nature unpalatable to the British public, to declare that it is a scandalous forgery, and doubtless the "Herald" will be instructed suitably to prepare the ground for such explanations.

The Latvian diplomatic representative at Moscow has just returned to Riga, and states emphatically that there is no organization now in Soviet Russia capable of

[270] Georgi Vasilyevich Chicherin (1872–1936): member of the Social Democratic Party 1904-14; arrested in London due to his perceived 'enemy associations' after the Russian armistice with Germany following the October 1917 revolution; released in January 1918, returned to Russia as Trotsky's aide and soon succeeded him as foreign commissar; ended the diplomatic isolation of the USSR by gaining formal recognition from European nations.

[271] The *Daily Herald*, launched in 1911 as a strike sheet for the London printing unions, grew into a daily newspaper specifically for workers; in 1922 it was taken over by the TUC and in the 1930s became the world's top-selling popular daily newspaper. After years of declining sales, however, in the 1960s it became the *Sun* and was sold to Rupert Murdoch's News International.

overthrowing the present Government or administering affairs if the present regime is overthrown. The only hope is in the Army. This at present is well disciplined and on the whole loyal. There is no real split among the Communist leaders, whose common aim is world revolution. Concessions will undoubtedly be confiscated after exploitation. War with Poland is certain; probably in February, and the Border States will be attacked about the same time or perhaps earlier. Mobilization is proceeding secretly. The only aim is world revolution and Treaties, whether political or commercial, with bourgeois Governments are not considered binding. The leaders feel confident that they can last out at least another year, during which time they will reinforce their influence of world wide propaganda and revolution.

With regard to the League of Nations, I am informed that the Chilian Delegation are much impressed with the importance of improving their liaison with European and Asiatic countries, in particular with the small countries whose combined vote in the Assembly will be important to them when questions relating to the Pacific come up for discussion. In particular they are impressed with the importance of getting on good terms with the Japanese and the Chinese and also with Canada, whose Delegates exercised well merited influence in the Assembly. The Brazilian Delegation, on the other hand, is rather disconcerted at the amount of ground that their country has lost in South American politics, although they believe that the recovery of their prestige by activity of policy is not impossible. Their relations with the Peruvians were cordial and their conversations with the Chilian Delegation created a good atmosphere, but it is understood that the President of the Brazilian Republic holds firmly to the opinion that the United States is the only Great Power upon which they can rely to safeguard their traditions and to champion their international interests.

With regard to the visit of Marshal Pilsudski[272] to Paris, the Roumanian Minister, I am informed, has been explaining to the French Prime Minister that he would render a signal service to the cause which is so dear to him if he got Marshal Pilsudski in favour of a definite agreement between Poland and the Czechs. In spite of the disturbance caused by the Greek affair to M. Jonescu's[273] plans, he is still devoted to his central ideas of foreign policy. He wishes to conclude two separate agreements one with Poland and the other with Czecho-Slovakia and Servia with reference to the treaties of Trianon and Jeuilly, for while Roumania and Poland cannot by themselves cope with the danger in Eastern Europe, Roumania without the Czechs and Servia will never have her elbows free. M. Jonescu has good reasons for knowing that he will never succeed in establishing confidential relations with Hungary and that even Bulgaria, despite the declarations of her Prime Minister, is unrepentant. For example, M. Stambulinski spoke at Warsaw on the Southern Dobrudja which he claimed was due to Bulgaria from Roumania if friendly

[272] Jozef Pilsudski (1867–1935): leader of the Polish Socialist Party from 1892; declared Poland's independence in 1918, President of Poland 1918–22; Minister of War 1926–35; Prime Minister 1927–28 and 1930.
[273] Take Jonescu (dates unknown): former Romanian Prime Minister.

relations were to be established. Consequently it is evident that it is impossible to establish real friendly confidential relations between Roumania and Hungary or Bulgaria. Pilsudski, on the other hand, of all the men in Warsaw, is the most unsympathetic towards Czecho-Slovakia since he has preferred the friendship of Hungary, and it is essential that the French Government should make him understand the importance of fraternal relations between Czecho-Slovakia and Poland. One method of winning over Pilsudski would be to promise him powerful support over the question of Upper Silesia and also modification of the Russian-Polish Frontier.

It would seem that the prospect of the conclusion of a Treaty between Persia and Russia has caused considerable perturbation in Teheran.[274] A recent meeting of the diplomatic corps under the Presidency of the American Minister, decided to evacuate the foreign colonies in the course of the next few weeks in the direction of Baghdad, but to this meeting the German Minister was not invited and I understand that he is alarmed at the prospect that the German Colony will probably be prohibited from going to Mesopotamia.

The Americans, in view of the fact that the American people seem to take a lively interest in the possibilities of "certain natural resources" of Persia, appear to hold the view that the present moment furnishes an unrivalled opportunity of giving this interest practical form. It strikes them that the most pressing need of the Persian Government is a number of military officers to take the place of the Russians recently dismissed. The Persians are determined not to employ our officers and our Minister has stated that even if we were now asked we would not accept, and the suggestion has been made that 30 experienced American officers should be sent to reorganise and command the Persian forces in order to prevent disturbances locally and to save the country from the Bolsheviks. These officers would have to arrive not later than April, that is just before the British evacuation is complete, and it is considered that such a step, which would in no manner involve the American government, would produce a powerful moral effect on account of the confidence which Persians still have in America, and would probably rally sufficient enthusiasm to bring new life into the body of the Nation. Moreover, it would supply a useful test of the sincerity of the Bolsheviks in promising non-interference provided the British leave the country. It is recognised that the Persian Government has also need

[274] After the First World War, because of Russia's preoccupation with its own revolution, Britain became the dominant influence in Tehran. Under the Anglo-Persian Agreement of 1919 Iran was provided with a British loan and with advisers for the army and virtually every government department – making the country effectively a British protectorate. The Iranian prime minister, Vosuq od-Dowleh, and two members of his cabinet who had received large financial inducements from the British, supported the agreement, but it aroused considerable opposition, and the Majlis refused to approve it. The agreement was already effectively dead when, in February 1921, the Persian Cossacks Brigade officer Reza Khan, in collaboration with prominent journalist Sayyid Zia ad Din Tabatabai, marched into Tehran and seized power. His government renounced the agreement with the British and entered into an agreement with the Soviet Union allowing Soviet forces to operate on Iranian soil in order to suppress White Russian activities. In 1925, Reza Khan became Reza Shah Pahlavi, and adopted a policy of modernisation and development; his son, Mohammad Reza Shah, was overthrown in 1979.

for financial and technical assistance, but the most urgent demand is for the military officers to maintain discipline during the critical moment of transition.

Moreover, it is believed that there would be no objection raised by us, as we have virtually decided to abandon Persia to her fate.

PS. I have just received information that at the end of last month M. Krassin discovered a new source of anxiety and of indignation against France. He learnt that the French Government had issued through the Poles to Savinkov, Lebedeff, Zenzenoff (a Social Revolutionary leader and a colleague of Kerensky) and Tchernoff (another Social Revolutionary leader who was President of the Constituent Assembly at its only sitting before it was dispersed by the Bolsheviks) fifty million francs for a new Anti-Bolshevik Army. As a matter of fact I can not help thinking that M. Krassin is mis-informed, as these social revolutionaries have declared against intervention from outside Russia and in favour of political agitation inside Russia, which they secretly intend to supplement by terrorist activities, nor are they particularly in need of money, for they have large funds which were looted from Koltchak in his retreat by the Czecho-Slovaks under an arrangement with their leaders. This is one of the principal reasons why they have their headquarters at Prague. M. Krassin is also annoyed that Wrangel has paid his debt to France in Russian ships, and considers an official protest necessary. I am further informed that messages are constantly passing between Koop in Berlin and Krassin on the one hand, and the Communist International on the other, on purely party business. This surely is in contravention to the undertaking with regard to propaganda and makes it quite certain that similar use will be made of the facilities which will be afforded under the Russian Trade Agreement to the official agents of the Soviet Government.

I understand that there is reason to believe that Suritz is not at all satisfied with the agreement which Djemal proposes to conclude with the Afghanistan Government.[275] He considers that it will involve lengthy activity on the frontier which must be regarded from not only the military but also from the international and political points of view. Nor does he consider that Djemal is prepared to give the Soviet Government sufficient guarantees for control in the reorganization of the Army, the defence of the frontier, and the distribution of assistance among the tribes. He considers that Djemal's programme should be carried out according to an agreement which should be concluded between Russia and Afghanistan. He points out Djemal is not connected with the general policy of the Soviet Government and that the Indian Central Executive Committee can only exist if the real revolutionary

[275] In May 1921, the Afghan and Soviet Governments signed a Treaty of Friendship, Afghanistan's first international agreement since gaining full independence in 1919. Afghanistan became one of the first states to recognise the Soviet government. The treaty was not warmly received by the British Government, which feared Soviet attempts to advance its influence on a state bordering India.

element and "our (the Soviet Government's) Indian Communists" participate, and not if it is solely directed by Djemal.

Hopner is believed to be keenly desirous for Suritz to sanction the immediate despatch of the Indian revolutionaries to Kabul, as Roy insists on sending them independently of Suritz, denying the latter's competency in Indian matters and regarding him only as a diplomat. Hopner, however, is hoping to receive the views of Suritz regarding the issue of passports to Mohamed Ali, to whom Roy has issued 20 thousand roubles in gold, and another Indian revolutionary, and it appears that no Indians are willing to work with Roy, but that a mutinous feeling exists among them. The Bokora Government is sending an envoy to Afghanistan in the hope of establishing friendly relations with that Government and finding in it a true ally in the struggle against bloodthirsty British Imperialists.

There is strong reason for believing that the Japanese Delegation were very favourably impressed with the results of the recent meeting of the League of Nations at Geneva. In their opinion the Majority of the representatives make it their ideal to represent various aspects of civilisation and thought in the interests of the far reaching objects of the League, and that the representatives of quite small countries have been respected if endowed with individual capacity and loftiness of view. Consequently, success has been dependent upon personal merit and friendship.

Therefore the members of the Delegation have expressed the view that it will not suffice for the Japanese Government to concentrate solely on the protection of their country's interest, but it will be essential for it to come forward in a spirit of rendering general service to the league with concrete proposals on all questions. To this end it will be important for the Government to pave the way for the presentation of constructive proposals by Japan by fostering expert knowledge upon such subjects as the International Court of Justice, Finance and Economics. Reduction of Armaments, Insurance and the Revision of the Covenant, and at the same time arrangements should be made for the appointment of Japanese representatives of intellectual and linguistic attainments to serve on the several expert organizations established by the League.

The Delegates at the first Assembly developed a spirit of conciliation and co-operation with the result that the meeting must be admitted to have borne better fruit than was expected, and in the near future the initiation of a movement to do away with the fundamental principle of the unanimous vote may in the opinion of certain members of the Japanese Delegation be fairly anticipated, and the League, having now surmounted its initial experience, should advance as a real identity with the ideals of an international Court of Justice and the Limitation of Armaments as its central features.

AHMS

Sir Archibald Sinclair to Winston S. Churchill
17th January 1921

Note of an Interview at the War Office with General Bezobrazoff, 14.1.21

General Bezobrazoff, at one time commanding the Guards Division and later a Group of Armies on the Russian Front, came to see me with a letter of introduction in most cordial terms from General Knox[276] to the Secretary of State.

He told me that he was convinced that Koltchak, Denikin and Wrangel (whom he had visited during last Summer) had failed because their armies were not founded upon the rock of moral principle. Their troops understood little of the cause for which they were fighting and were uninspired by feelings of patriotism and loyalty. He had travelled a great deal in Europe during the past two years and whenever he came across any of his old comrades in arms they appealed to him to put himself at their head and lead them in a crusade against the Bolsheviks.

Consequently he had formed a plan for the formation of a new anti-Bolshevik army for which he required no money or arms or equipment from us, but only an understanding that we would not interfere. I hastily enquired whether this army was to be formed in England and he assured me that was not his intention, but that he intended to select a "neutral" country. He had discussed his plans with Marshal Foch and with members of the French Government but, while they were munificent in their assurances of sympathy, they had told him they could give him no undertaking unless he could win over the British Government. I replied that in the first place the Secretary of State for War was not the Minister for him to see, as he could neither assist nor impede the formation of such an army in a neutral country. If he desired an official reply from the British Government, he should address himself to the Foreign Secretary. But I did not conceal my conviction that he would be unable to extract any undertaking in the sense that he desired from the British Government. I pointed out that when we had supported Koltchak, Denikin and Yudenitch, we had done it openly before the whole world, and that when General Wrangel had disregarded our advice we had withdrawn our support again quite openly and publicly. Now, as everybody knew, we were negotiating with the Bolsheviks for a commercial agreement which would involve the cessation of hostile propaganda by both parties, and it was inconceivable that the British Government in such circumstances would give a secret undertaking to the organisers of an anti-Bolshevik army.

In reply to an enquiry from the General, I said that if the trade Agreement should be rejected by the Bolsheviks, it might be worth his while to re-open the question although, even in that case, I could hold out no hope of an answer favourable to him, but if so the Foreign Secretary was the Minister whom he should approach.

---

[276] General Alfred Knox (1870–1964): British Military Attaché in Petrograd from 1911; spoke Russian fluently and on the outbreak of the First World War became liaison officer to the Russian Army, working closely with George Buchanan, the British Ambassador; Chief of the British Military Mission to Siberia 1918–20; Conservative MP for Wycombe 1924–45.

The General was particularly anxious to see Mr. Churchill personally, but I replied that although I felt sure that Mr. Churchill would be most happy on personal grounds to make his acquaintance, I felt it would be quite impossible for him, in view of the policy of the Government, to give him even a semi-official interview on the subject of the formation of an anti-Bolshevik army.

I was not anxious to discuss the details of the General's plan, consequently I did not enquire upon what particular moral principles his army was to be founded, but from the general trend of his conversation, I should be willing to hazard a guess that they would be monarchical in character.

AHMS

Sir Archibald Sinclair to Winston S. Churchill
17th January 1921
Personal and Secret

Dear Secretary of State,

I have recently been receiving a good deal of information from a most reliable source about Kopp, the Soviet Agent in Berlin, which is a new and interesting development. I understand that he has an Agent in Poland of the name of Lapinsky who is employing as informer the notorious Colonel Orloff, who was at one time the head of Denikin's counter espionage and is believed to have been to some extent in the confidence of M. Savinkov. Of course there is a possibility that there may be a confusion of names, but it is likely that the facts are as stated.

Contrary to the opinion which I have reported to you as being expressed by M. Krassin, Kopp believes that the French have finally renounced the idea of supporting the Russian reactionary Chiefs in their campaign against Soviet Russia, and he considers that they are more likely to devote their efforts to strengthening Poland as the principal factor in maintaining the balance of power in Eastern Europe. He understands that the Polish Minister of Finance has obtained the consent in principle of the Polish Cabinet that, in exchange for a loan in dollars, American financiers be granted the right to introduce a number of important monopolies including tobacco, matches, salt, sugar and oil, although the Left is opposed to the grant of such vast concessions and is afraid of America obtaining too great an influence in Polish affairs. I am also informed, according to information that Kopp has received from the source indicated above, that Pilsudsky has finally decided to entrust to France the solution of the Lithuanian question, and in so doing has incurred the hostility of Zeligosky, who believes that the Lithuanian Government will in no circumstances recognise the Polish character of the Vilna district and seems to be preparing for armed action against Kovno. Pilsudsky recently despatched a General to Zeligosky to induce him to renounce his plan. Pilsudsky is also at loggerheads with Balohovitch who, contrary to his undertakings, has been negotiating with the Chief of the Roumanian Military Mission and M. Stambulinksy. Balohovitch is preparing to go to Belgrade and M. Savinkov is reported to be going to Paris.

It is understood that M. Kopp, as Trade Representative, has been recognised by the German Government and will be confirmed officially when he presents his credentials, but before doing this he is demanding further instructions from the Soviet Government and he categorically insists that it will be necessary to admit the German Trading Commission into Russia.

I understand that the American consul at Viborg has been expressing the view that the Bolsheviks are distributing considerable numbers of troops on the frontiers of Poland and the Baltic States, but in no such numbers as to indicate that immediate action is intended and considerable amount of long leave has been granted. Nevertheless a general mutiny in the Red Army is feared. If this discontent grows some minor military activities may be undertaken, of which the nature and objective are not yet clear. The Extraordinary Commission is now fully occupied in the search for over 130 social revolutionary agents which are supposed to have been sent to Petrograd by M. Savinkov for propaganda among workmen and soldiers, but they do not appear to have been discovered so far.

I learn that the greatest difficulty is being found in agreeing upon the appointment of the representative of the Soviet Government at Stockholm. Count Wrangel is to discuss this subject with M. Krassin when the latter passes through on his return to Moscow. The Soviet Government are insisting on Kerjentseff's candidature. I reported on this gentleman to you some weeks ago when his name arose in connection with the Russian Trading Delegation in London. He is an exceedingly clever and active propagandist and has held high office in the Soviet Government in Moscow and, with the exception of Radek, he is probably the most brilliant publicist in Russia. The Swedes have already turned down not only Litvinoff and Rothstein, but also two other Bolsheviks, whose names are quite unknown to me.

I hear that the Roumanians in London have been intimidated by Krassin into the view that in order to avert the danger of a conflict it will be necessary to negotiate with the Soviet Government. They have been assured that their treasure is still intact at Moscow and that the Bolsheviks are prepared to settle this question in "a most satisfactory manner". Moreover, assurances have been given that the question of Bessarabia would be definitely solved at the conference in accordance to the Roumanian wishes. On the other hand, hints have been thrown out that Roumania is deliberately held up by the Bolsheviks as the last hope which the French have of maintaining the struggle against Russia in order to maintain the morale of the Bolshevik army, and Krassin has expressed the view that the Roumanian refusal to open peace negotiations can only be explained on the assumption that the Roumanians are pursuing the French policy. He indicated that Russia had said her last word in a friendly spirit, and that it only depended on the Roumania to decide the course of her relations with Moscow.

It appears that General Wrangel has been proposing to the Japs that his army should be transferred to Siberia but his offer has been politely rejected on the grounds that although keen sympathy is felt with Wrangel's purpose of prosecuting further operations against the Bolsheviks, it is considered that his shortest road lies rather in the prosecution of such operations from European Russia. The transport difficulties were also pointed out and regret and sympathy were expressed.

I am informed that an American of the name of Mr. Tuck, who is apparently a Consular Official, has arrived in Constantinople from Samsun. He reports that Americans have no trouble in leaving or going to Samsun and the interior, and their relations with the Turks are cordial, but permits for travel have to be obtained. On the other hand Bolshevik influence is hostile to the Americans and it is calculated that about 3,000 Russian Bolsheviks are in Samsun and it is thought that some have reached Angora. Mr. Tuck had an interview with Bekir Sami, Kemal's Foreign Minister, who stated that the Nationalist Turks are very antagonistic to the Bolsheviks.

It would seem that the Italians have been advising the Turks to ratify the Treaty of Sevres, pointing out that if they are too obstinate, England might definitely line up with Constantine.

I understand that when the French ambassador communicated the note of his Government to the Italian Government about German disarmament, the Italian Foreign Minister replied that it was not in the interests of either France or Italy that the restoration of peace in Europe would be delayed, and that the Ambassador appeared to be impressed with the force of the Minister's arguments, which he is transmitting to Paris.

Yours sincerely,
Archibald Sinclair

Sir Archibald Sinclair to Winston S. Churchill
17th January 1921

Dear Secretary of State,

I was asked by General Prince Belosselsky-Belozersky, who recently sent you a picture of the Great Duke of Marlborough, to receive General Besobrasoff who at one time commanded the Russian Guards Division and subsequently a Group of Armies on the Russian front. He brought with him a letter of introduction to you from General Knox.

He was exceedingly anxious to have an interview with you on the subject of the formation of a new anti-Bolshevik army, but I made it quite clear that it would be impossible for you, in view of the declared policy of the Government, to give him even a semi official interview.

I attach a note of the conversation which took place between us.

Yours sincerely,
Archibald Sinclair

Winston S. Churchill to Sir Archibald Sinclair
22nd January 1921

Sir Archibald Sinclair,

I have received also a letter from General Knox which I enclose. I do not think there is any advantage in my seeing General Besobrasov, but I should be glad if you would handle the matter politely on my behalf and also write to General Knox to answer his letter.

WSC

In early January 1921 Lloyd George asked Churchill if he would be willing to move from the War Office to the Colonial Office to take charge of the new Middle East Department, with responsibility for Iraq (Mesopotamia) and Palestine. After considering the offer for a week Churchill decided to accept and wrote requesting that Sinclair transfer with him. He also requested that Sinclair be allowed to retain his active commission until he was promoted to major (which Churchill expected to happen in 1922) after which it was Sinclair's intention to retire and seek a seat in Parliament.

Winston S. Churchill to Sir Henry Wilson, Sir Archibald Sinclair and one other (unknown)
22nd January 1921

SECRETARY
C.I.G.S.
MILITARY SECRETARY

Before I exchange seals, I have decided immediately to make a change in the commander-in-chief in Mesopotamia. This does not imply the slightest reflection on General Haldane,[277] who had done extremely well in most difficult circumstances, and who I am pledged by my telegram of a year ago to provide for in the event of a shrinkage in the Mesopotamian command. It is, however, necessary to appoint an officer of much lower rank, in view of the fact that the army there must be greatly and rapidly diminished in strength. I contemplate an attempt to hold the country with a force which will not exceed 15,000 men, though some of them will be very high-class troops. The sooner a new man takes charge the better. He will realise that his command will only be a moderate one and he will immediately address himself to getting the rest of the troops out of the country. The officer I wish to select for this most important post is General Ironside. Another capable officer will have to be found to take command of the Kasvin brigade. I wish to make this appointment during the course of next week and to notify Haldane accordingly. I

[277] J. Aylmer Lowthorpe Haldane (1862–1950): served in the Boer War and was imprisoned with Churchill in Pretoria; knighted and appointed Lieutenant-General 1918; Commander-in-Chief Mesopotamia 1920–22; appointed General 1925.

must find a Lieutenant-General's command coming vacant within the next twelve months for Haldane. Gibraltar occurs to me as being vacant in the near future. Please advise me as to what is possible.

WSC

Sir Archibald Sinclair to Winston S. Churchill
31st January 1921

Secretary of State

I attach a letter which I have received from Colonel Trower, whose case, you will remember, General Jeffries was very anxious that you should look into personally with a view to his appointment as Colonel of the South Wales Borderers with the honorary rank of Major-General. The Military Secretary, however, advised you strongly against this course, in spite of the gallant services which Colonel Trower had rendered, on the grounds that he had never commanded any higher unit than a Battalion, except a Brigade for short periods, that his promotion would bear very hardly on those officers who held the rank of temporary Major-General for less than six months during the late war and consequently were not allowed to retain the higher rank on demobilization or retirement, and that there were at least three other fully qualified officers belonging to the Regiment who might be given the appointment of Colonel if the present colonel were to retire. You concurred in the views which M.S. expressed and I informed General Jeffries accordingly.

Colonel Trower writes to me asking me to lay his "last appeal" before you to grant him the honorary rank of Major-General. Alternatively he desires "to be recommended for advancement to the rank of K.C.M.G." in special recognition of his voluntary service during the war and the number of times he was mentioned in despatches.

There is no dispute about the gallant service which this officer has rendered, beginning at Isandhlwana and Rorke's Drift in 1879 and finishing with the Great War during which he served throughout in the trenches and was six times mentioned in despatches and six times placed in command of a Brigade in the front line, although he was debarred from permanent promotion on account of his age, which is over 60.

On the other hand I am not sure what view you will take of his personal application for these alternative honours, and I have therefore not spoken to M.S. until I should hear from you. I have, or course, briefly acknowledged Colonel Trower's letter.

AHMS

Sir Archibald Sinclair to Winston S. Churchill
31st January 1921

Secretary of State,

With reference to Deputy Director of Military Intelligence's Minute 8 on the attached file, and the draft letter which it is proposed to send to the India Office, I would like to add for your information that Mr. Ackerman was sent here with a letter of introduction to you from Mr. Marcossen, who particularly asked that you should see him. As a matter of fact you were too busy, and I saw him instead.

He was of the somewhat boisterous loud-voiced type of American, but he was obviously intelligent and apparently disposed to be most friendly. He told me that the American Press had been receiving cables from their Correspondents in Europe and the East to the effect that we were trying all kinds of new forms of Aerial warfare on the natives of Mesopotamia, and furthermore that we were not only rigidly excluding well accredited American newspaper correspondents, but even refused to allow an American Attaché to accompany the forces in the field.

You are, of course, aware of the reasons for the latter decision, and I explained them to Mr. Ackerman. I further reassured him about the nature of the warfare which we were conducting in Mesopotamia, but he pointed out that the only effective method of counteracting the harm which these stories were doing to Anglo-American friendship in America was to allow an American correspondent to go there and see for himself what was going on and relate the true facts to the American public in his own words. He appreciated the reasons which I advanced for not extending an invitation to an American Attaché to accompany the troops, but if we had nothing to conceal he could see no grounds for excluding a duly accredited American Journalist.

Perhaps you would like to see Mr. Ackerman yourself as he has a letter of introduction to you from Mr. Marcossen and as he is already disposed to take an interest in the regions for which you are accepting special responsibility. Would it not be better to do this before deciding to send this draft letter to the India Office?

AHMS

Winston S. Churchill to Sir Archibald Sinclair
7th February 1921

SIR ARCHIBALD SINCLAIR

I have no objection to his having a K.C.M.G.[278] You might see what the Military Secretary says about it. You need not show his own letter, but put it on General Jeffries' recommendation.

WSC

[278] See letter dated 31 January.

Sir Archibald Sinclair to Winston S. Churchill
8th February 1921

SECRETARY OF STATE

Colonel Trower made a personal appeal to you and as the matter is of some delicacy, I should be glad if you would glance at the letter to him and the minute to M.S. which I have drafted and attach hereto.[279]

AHMS

10th February 1921

SECRETARY OF STATE

I attach a letter which M. Savinkov has sent to you enclosing a copy of a declaration which he has transmitted to M. Bartoum, the French Minister of War (both the original French and an English translation).

Pages 1 to 3 of the letter to M. Bartoum consist of a profession of political faith on behalf of the Russian Evacuation Committee in Poland – Land, Peace, Liberty and Equality, and implacable hostility towards the Bolsheviks on the one hand and the representatives of the old regime on the other.

Pages 3 to 6 consist of a description of the apparatus of revolution which the Committee is setting up within the borders of Sovdeia. Communication has been obtained with the detachments of Makhno[280] and with Budenny's staff, besides various corps of partisans and secret societies in the towns and countryside. On page 7 it is lamented that money, the essential motive power of the apparatus, is scarce.

On pages 8 and 9 it is contended that although it is not possible to wage civil war in Russia at the present time or to maintain large anti-Bolshevik armies such as those of Generals Denikin and Wrangel, it is possible to make a revolution but that an essential adjunct of a revolution would be a small regular army of about five thousand bayonets and swords which would form the nucleus of the revolutionary force and would be able to restore order after a successful revolution. This army would be formed out of the remnants of the armies of Generals Bulak-Balachovitch and Permykin which are now interned in Poland, but here again money is required and at present the funds of the Committee are almost exhausted.

[279] Colonel Trower did not get his wish. Sinclair wrote back on 8th February 1921: 'The Secretary of State desires me to acknowledge receipt of your letter of the 23rd instant but in view of the fact that he can give no decision which could become operative during his term of office as Secretary of State for War, he will be compelled to leave your case in the hands of his successor.'

[280] Nestor Makhno (1889–1934): Ukrainian revolutionary and anarchist; jailed in 1908, released after the February 1917 revolution; returned to Ukraine and began organising against landlords and capitalists; when Ukraine was handed to Germany under the Treaty of Brest-Litovsk in 1918, formed partisan resistance groups, who united into the Revolutionary Insurrectionary Army of the Ukraine, also called the Black Army (fighting under the black flag of anarchism); successful against Germans, Ukrainian nationalists and Russian Whites in 1918–21, but defeated in 1921 by his former allies the Bolsheviks; fled into exile in France.

M. Savinkov concludes with an appeal to France on page 10, not to supply millions of francs of equipment for an army of a few hundred thousand men, but not entirely to forget those who have remained steadfastly faithful to the Allies, who have never carried on negotiations with Germany, who have worked indefatigably in the consolidation of Russian–Polish relations, and who represent the sole but real, if small, anti-Bolshevik force which has not yet laid down its arms.

The whole letter is very interesting and is well worth a glance.

With regard to an acknowledgment –

(a) will you write to M. Savinkov yourself; or
(b) shall I write on your behalf; or
(c) do you think it wisest to take no notice of his letter?

AHMS

A note at the end of the letter records: Agreed with S. of S. message to be sent via Spears – no sympathy or encouragement in plans. AHMS 12/2/21.

On 12 February 1921 Lloyd George appointed Churchill as Colonial Secretary; Sinclair accompanied him to his new post. From then until the 1922 general election Churchill concentrated on issues in Mesopotamia (now Iraq) and Palestine rather than the usual Colonial Office concerns of India and Africa, aiming to reduce the manpower and financial costs of managing Mesopotamia. Basing his approach on a suggestion of Lord Trenchard, Chief of the Air Staff, Churchill proposed to hand over control of security to the RAF and use a combination of aeroplanes and light armoured cars to defend Britain's interests. He also spent considerable time working with Lloyd George to resolve the crisis in Ireland, even though it was not a Colonial Office responsibility.

In 1920 Palestine, Iraq and Arabia cost the British taxpayer £37 million, the equivalent in 2004 prices of approximately £885 million. Lloyd George had tasked Churchill with cutting this sum by half. To achieve this goal Churchill proposed setting up an Arab Government at Baghdad which could develop the country without making undue demands on Britain. Sir Percy Cox, the High Commissioner of Iraq, proposed an Arabian Prince, the Emir Faisal, to rule Iraq under the Mandate.

Winston S. Churchill to Sir Archibald Sinclair
15th June 1921

Military Secretary

I am strongly in favour of the introduction of representative institutions in Palestine, and I consider it impossible to deny them to that country while little backward places like Trans-Jordania are given them. We really must face the practical facts of the situation. And so must the Arabs. The franchise can be devised in many ways so as to secure responsible representatives and fair representation of minorities. But of course the instrument of Government creating the elective institutions must provide for the execution of our pledge to the Zionists. As long as it continues within certain limits, immigration must be ultra vires,[281] and I should hope that this constitutional basis would be reinforced by an agreement with the leading Arabs as to the proportion of Jews to be admitted.

WSC

Winston S. Churchill to Sir Archibald Sinclair
9th July 1921

Military Secretary

All this seems very complicated and I do not think we ought to bombard the High Commissioner with these elaborate instructions. It is quite true that I am responsible for approving all the telegrams that you have sent. In the main, however, I think it much better to leave matters to Sir Percy Cox,[282] who alone knows the local situation and who has the greatest possible interest in bringing out a satisfactory result.

There is also too much talk about 'Mandates', 'Mandatories' and things like that. All this obsolescent rigmarole is not worth telegraphing about. It is quite possible that in a year or two there will be no mandates and no League of Nations. Something quite different may have taken their place.

Do let us keep the practical salient points of the policy in our minds and only check Sir Percy Cox when he diverges from them:–

(1) To get another large wave of troops out of the country and so reduce the expenditure to the British taxpayer.
(2) To get Faisal on the throne as soon as possible.
(3) To make whatever arrangements are most likely to conduce to the above objects in regards to Basra (about which I have a perfectly open mind) or Kurdestan (about which the only principle is that we do not put Kurds under Arabs).

I suggest that we repeat these dominant needs to Sir Percy Cox in a telegram and ask him to submit proposals for action.

I am rather worried by all these lengthy detailed telegrams going out in my name and at so many being sent. I am sure they must impair the effectiveness of messages which I send myself personally.

281 Beyond the powers (of the new institutions).

282 Percy Zachariah Cox (1864–1937): Political Resident in the Persian Gulf 1909–14; Chief Political Officer with the Indian Expeditionary Force to Mesopotamia 1914–17; Acting Minister to Tehran 1918–20; High Commissioner and Commander-in-Chief Mesopotamia 1920–23; plenipotentiary for negotiations with Turkey over the Iraq frontier 1924; Indian representative at Geneva conference on control of arms traffic 1925.

Anyhow let us talk about it at 12.30 to-day.

WSC

Winston S. Churchill to Sir Archibald Sinclair
16th July 1921

See General Haldane's letter, which is very important and very satisfactory. The great question we now have to decide is whether we shall go to the Cabinet on the basis of getting the War Office out of the country from the beginning of the new financial year. In this case we should have entire control of everything done in Mesopotamia, the necessary white personnel being entirely under the Air Ministry, who will certainly work with us. Although in my negotiations with the War Office I am holding out for the two white battalions settled in Cairo, I should be prepared for a satisfactory settlement to take four white battalions and to assume that they will be in Mesopotamia for four or five years. I will only do this if they will help us in other ways and accept the limited responsibilities defined in my letter of the 23rd June.

If it is decided to bring the Air Force scheme into operation as from April 1st, it will probably be best for General Haldane to go on continuously till then, and I will have to explain matters accordingly to General Ironside. There is no doubt that General Haldane has greatly assisted the cause of economy, and having committed himself to the practicability of the change he ought certainly to remain and carry it out.

The first step for us to take is to discuss details with the Air Ministry and let us see exactly how they would propose to take over and carry on. For this purpose you should send a copy of the extract from General Haldane's letter dealing with the air to Captain Guest and Air Marshal Trenchard. Also send a copy of the telegram in which armoured cars are described as useless by the General but light caterpillar vehicles as invaluable, together with the excellent reasons for this opinion. We have got to get these light caterpillar vehicles made as quickly as possible by somebody, and whoever makes them should undoubtedly be run by the Air Force from the RAF workshops.

I shall be ready to have a conference next week with the Air Ministry. I had better have a talk with Air Marshal Trenchard beforehand. I could see him on Monday at 5 o'clock.

If it is decided to take the plunge to air from next year, all the preparations must be begun now. I do not exclude the possibility of my visiting Bagdad at the end of October or November. I shall be actually in the neighbourhood of Rome in October, and apparently it would only take about three days to Bagdad from there by ship to Alexandria and aeroplane on. As soon as I have discussed matters with the Air Ministry and arrived at definite conclusions, I will put them to Sir Percy Cox.

There is another matter of very great importance which you must deal with promptly. The most I can spare for Mesopotamia next year is six millions. If therefore there are any barracks to be built they must be built out of savings on the present year's expenditure. I must also know about the terminal charges which will fall due after the present year. It is far better to have everything in this year. There must be large savings this year, because of the fall in the rupee. Vernon is responsible for knowing exactly where we are and for guarding against all surprises in the sense of heavy sums coming suddenly upon us. If he is in any doubt about any point he must come to me and let me know in good time so that I may take what measures are possible.

WSC

In August 1921 Marigold ('Duckadilly'), Churchill's three-and-a-half-year-old daughter, died from complications following a chest infection.

Undated but probably 25th or 26th August 1921
Post Office Telegraph

Mrs. Churchill, 2 Sussex Square, London.

Cannot possibly express how grieved we are to hear of your terrible sorrow.

Marigold and Archie

Sir Archibald Sinclair to Winston S. Churchill
Dalnawillan,
Altnabreac,
Caithness
Sunday, 28th August 1921

My dear Winston,

We are so unhappy about poor little Marigold. She was such a lovely, sparkling, winning little child that we were already completely captivated and we can't bear to think what her loss must mean to you & Clemmie.

What a wonderful & terrible year this has been for you – full of political triumph & material good fortune but crossed with too much sadness!

Jack writes me that you are going to Loch More this coming week. Do come on to us if you would like a few days quietly painting. The few people we are able to put up in this tiny house will have left by then and we shall be alone for ten days at any rate. We should be so delighted to welcome you & Clemmie here & we could easily motor round to fetch you.

Yours always,
Archie

In September 1921 Churchill wrote to Sinclair agreeing that the responsibility for the defence of Iraq should transfer from the army to the air force.

Winston S. Churchill to Sir Archibald Sinclair
11th September 1921

I am quite ready to agree to the 1st October 1922, as the date for the Air Force taking over, and as soon as a reply is received from Sir Percy Cox to my telegram of September 7th I will communicate with General Haldane accordingly. You had better inform Sir Percy Cox that the Air Ministry will not be able to take over in any case till October 1st, and that General Haldane will carry on till the change.

WSC

Although Sinclair remained working for Churchill at the Colonial Office until the 1922 election he found plenty of time to visit his Scottish estates and to find himself an appropriate seat at the pending election.

Sir Archibald Sinclair to Winston S. Churchill
Dalnawillan,
Altnabreac,
Caithness
2nd October 1921

Winston,

Just a line of belated but most hearty congratulations on your splendid Dundee speech[283] – the reports were excellent, Caird must have played his part well, and the classes of praise in the Press from the loud plaudits of the Tories to the grudging & embarrassed comments of the Nation & the Manchester Guardian must have astonished you yourself. It must have been a desperately difficult & delicate test and you achieved a wonderful success.[284]

I am wondering so much what your plans are & whether you are going to Washington – surely a great deal depends upon whether the P.M. goes? The contretemps last spring seems to have turned out for the best after all – you go from triumph to triumph, winning general & hearty approval for your Mandatory & Colonial policies while a rash man flounders in a morass at the Treasury.[285] But don't

[283] Probably referring to a speech given at Caird Hall, Dundee on 24 September, covering the issues of Ireland and Russia. Churchill outlined his deep opposition to an Irish Republic in any form.
[284] *The Times* declared, under the headline 'An Essay in Statemanship': 'the country will be grateful to Mr. Churchill for the breadth and lucidity of his speech … Whether men agree with him or not, Mr. Churchill's able and calm review of the situation helps to restore confidence.'
[285] Sir Robert Horne (1871–1940): Chancellor of the Exchequer 1921–22.

risk it again – don't get stranded for months in Washington if L.G. stays at home at the centre.

I am thinking of starting South about the middle of next week. The chairman of the Glasgow Coalition Liberals has asked me to meet him as Sutherland[286] has given him my name: I shall try & avoid committing myself before consulting you. At the same time I have been approached on behalf of a number of local Tories & Liberals to stand against Harmsworth here.[287]

Yours ever,
Archie

Winston S. Churchill to Sir Archibald Sinclair
12th November 1921

Repeatedly I have asked for calculations to be made on the savings that must have accrued in this year's estimates on the Cairo Conference basis in Mesopotamia from the more rapid diminution of the Garrison and from fall in the exchange value of the rupee. I have never received any answer to these requests. It is imperative that I should have these facts before the end of next week.

What progress has been made in the Sketch Estimates for 1922–23 for Mesopotamia. There is no excuse for our not knowing at this date what the forecast of expenditure will be.

WSC

Winston S. Churchill to Sir Archibald Sinclair
25th November 1921

What is all this talk about 9 millions for Mesopotamia next year? There is absolutely no question of anything over 7. Not one farthing more than 7 will be asked for by me, together with 2.5 for Palestine. Everything has got to be cut down to this level by any means that you like and at any risk or cost.

WSC

Winston S. Churchill to Sir Archibald Sinclair
3rd December 1921

We must have some of these light Tanks before we take over in October. If the War Office cannot produce a company themselves we must ask the Air Force to

[286] George Granville Sutherland, 5th Duke of Sutherland (1888–1963): Under-Secretary of State for Air 1922–24; Paymaster-General 1925–28; Under-Secretary of State for War 1928–29; represented the Colonial Office in the House of Lords at the date of this letter.
[287] i.e Caithness & Sutherland.

organise a unit. It is absolutely essential that at least a dozen of these tanks should be in Mesopotamia properly organised. I have no doubt the War Office tanks are much the best, but if we cannot have them we must try our best to purchase elsewhere some vehicle which can be utilised till better ones are available.

Anyhow please let them know that if they will not help us in the matter, for which help we are willing to pay the full cost in relief of Army Estimates, we shall have to make other arrangements.

WSC

Sir Archibald Sinclair to Winston S. Churchill
Thurso Castle
Thurso
15th April 1922
Personal

My Dear Winston,

I have just had a long telegram from Eddie informing me that, if invited by a strong committee of local Liberals, you are prepared to address a meeting in Perth on my behalf on the 5th of May.

I can't tell you how grateful I am for offering to return so soon to Scotland to do this for me and, of course, if your stipulation is fulfilled, I shall be more than willing to attend and play any part that is allotted to me in the proceedings. At the same time, I am a little bewildered, as I am ignorant of the developments which must have occurred while you were in Dundee. Hitherto, Mr. Munro, the ex-secretary of the Liberal Association, has not expressed to me any confidence in the strength of the Coalition Liberal forces in Perth.

Moreover, just before I left London I saw in your box a letter from Atholl[288] claiming the Coalition candidature in East Perthshire for the Conservatives. I am, naturally, curious to know how you answered him and what has passed between you since.

In the meantime, I find that my prospects up here, although exceedingly uncertain, are not at all bad. More than twelve hundred electors, mostly Liberals, have signed a requisition definitely pledging themselves to support me if I come forward and there are still some signatures to come in. After all, as you emphasised when we last talked this over, I can't expect to get a safe seat and here at any rate I have a little army of 1200 supporters, who have pledged themselves to me without my having made a single political speech. I enclose a copy of the requisition so that you can see that the pledge is definite as required. The numbers of this little army would almost certainly be doubled the moment I come out into the open, for a great many people

[288] Duke of Atholl, who was heavily influential in the allocation of Scottish parliamentary seats amongst Coalition Conservatives.

have expressed themselves as being strongly favourable to my candidature, but as disliking the method of requisition, and have declared that they must await a declaration of my views before committing themselves to my support.

I am writing to the Coalition Headquarters in Edinburgh to ask what their plans are about this seat. If they don't do something they will certainly wake up one day to find they have lost it, just as they nearly lost Inverness-shire and as they lost all control over and even touch with the Liberal Association in Perth. The feeling against the Government is just as strong here as it is all over the rest of the East and North of Scotland, and several people have advised me that I should have a much better chance if I stood as an Independent Liberal than as a Coalition Liberal.

I don't ask for a safe seat, nor even for a seat where I can get a unanimous adoption, nor would I necessarily be discouraged by a failure to obtain a clear majority in a Liberal Association, but if I am asked to take on a constituency where the Coalition Liberals are only able to mobilize eleven supporters in the local Association and to go down – as was suggested in the last letter I had from the Coalition Headquarters in Edinburgh – and address a public meeting in one of the smaller halls to "help to" break down the existing apathy which is now prevalent in the "constituency" can I be blamed for preferring to accept the invitation which more than twelve hundred pledged supporters are to extend to me here within the next week or ten days?

This is very far from being a safe seat, but I believe I have a chance of saving it for the Coalition and I am told that nobody else could. Of course I should need all the support I could get if I were to take it on. In the first place, I should, of course, need yours most of all. I should also hope to get Munro[289] to speak for me, as he was for some time Member for the Wick Boroughs and has considerable influence in Wick. It would also be important to get Ian Macpherson, whose constituency marches with Sutherland, to help me, and of course I should need a letter from the P.M. If, on the other hand, the Coalition are not going to take my candidature seriously, but regard it merely as the indulgence of a personal whim, my chances of success would be considerably lessened, but, even so, I should have a straight fight with a united and enthusiastic body of supporters on my side, whereas in Perthshire I and my eleven disciples stand to be shot at from all quarters, not excluding His Grace of Atholl!

I have, therefore, telegraphed to-day to the Coalition Headquarters saying that I shall be ready to speak at a meeting on the 5th of May only if I am invited by a representative committee of local Liberals and that I am unwilling to bind myself to come forward as a candidate in East Perthshire unless I receive beforehand assurances of support from the Conservative Wing of the Coalition. Further, I am writing to them to-day in strong terms about Caithness & Sutherland.

I shall know how I stand here when I receive the requisition and make my speech in about ten days' time. I shall, of course, avoid committing myself definitely

[289] Robert Munro, Baron Alness (1868–1955): Liberal MP for Wick Burghs 1910–18, Roxburgh and Selkirk 1918–22; Lord Advocate of Scotland 1913–16; Secretary of State for Scotland 1916–22; created baron 1934.

to coming forward here and by that time the position in Perth may be clearer and it may be possible to ascertain the strength of the Coalition Liberal forces there and the Tories will, I hope, have made their position clear.

Forgive this long egotistical letter – if you have a few spare minutes, I would be so grateful if you would let me know how you regard the situation. Have you given any further consideration to your own proposal the night you left for Dundee to trade off East Perthshire against Dunbartonshire with the Tories?

Warmest congratulations on Dundee.

Yours ever,
Archie

Winston S. Churchill to Sir Archibald Sinclair
18th April 1922

My dear Archie,

I have arranged with Austen Chamberlain that the Conservatives will give us a month or so to see whether we can produce a sufficiently strong Coalition Liberal Association in Perth in support of your candidature before they bring out a Conservative candidate. Sutherland has seen Gilmour on the subject and matters are arranged accordingly. I have told the Perth people, some of whom visited me in deputation at Dundee, that if a strong enough committee is formed I should be willing to address a meeting in Perth introducing you. The Perth Coalition Liberals have an option on the Town Hall for the 5th May. They are now engaged in trying to form their association, and we shall be able to see in the next week or so what support they get. Meanwhile, of course, you ought not to commit yourself in any way to Caithness, and you should delay your answer until the Perth situation resolves itself one way or the other.

Your answer to the Coalition Headquarters is quite satisfactory so far as it goes. There can be no question of your standing for Perth unless a good strong Liberal Coalitionist Committee is formed plus the Conservatives, in support. In these circumstances, against a Labour opponent you will have a very good chance of winning, and the inclusion of a Wee Free[290] candidate will in my opinion make very little difference. Do not, therefore, commit yourself in any way to Caithness until after Perth has been settled one way or the other.

I hope you have had good sport. When are you coming back here?

WSC

[290] The 'Wee Frees' were originally the members of the minority of the Free Church of Scotland who refused to be joined with the United Free Church in 1900. It later became a popular way of referring to the Asquithian Liberals who refused to follow Lloyd George into coalition with the Conservatives in 1916.

On 2 June 1922 Lloyd George sent by telegram to Sir Auckland Geddes, the British Ambassador in Washington, a summary of information relating to the Bolshevik armed forces which had been collected during the Genoa Conference[291] from pronouncements made by Rakowski, the leading Italian diplomat there. This highlighted the facts that Russia was spending 24% of its income on maintaining the Red Army and that its current strength was 1,450,000 men. Rakowski also claimed that the Western powers underestimated the capabilities of the Red Army and that it was a 'formidable instrument of war', and warned that the deteriorating conditions in Russia made it increasingly likely that she would turn to seeking relief from famine and pestilence through armed incursions into foreign territories. Lloyd George closed the telegram by stating that 'this is the essence of the argument which has impelled His Majesty's Government to regard the Russian problem as one in which the possible disadvantages of forcing the pace towards a solution is greatly less than the certain dangers to be apprehended from indifference and delay'. Sinclair did not agree with much of this intelligence and wrote a critical note to Churchill.

Sir Archibald Sinclair to Winston S. Churchill
7th June 1922

Dear S. of S.,
Notes on attached telegram.

- The estimate which I gave you before the Genoa conference of Red Army strength was based on the Bols figures and amounted to 1,300,000 for the Red Army and 1,590,000 for all armed forces. At that time the P.M. was on quite a different line and discounted these figures as grossly exaggerated!
- Some Western estimates of comparative fighting power of Bols and anti-Bols armies were incorrect, but they were always given by responsible authorities, and understated reserves. On the other hand there is no reason to suppose that the Red Army could stand any sort of comparison with any well trained and equipped Western Army. At Archangel the Bols never recorded the slightest success against the polyglot army opposed to them except when there was a mutiny among the Russian contingents; while as for the Poles, they completely falsified the predictions of those who anticipated the triumphal entry into Warsaw of the Red Army.

[291] The 1922 Genoa Conference bought together the representatives of thirty-four nations to attempt to reconstruct European finance and commerce; it was the first conference after World War I in which Germany and the Soviet Union were accepted on a par with other nations. The creditor nations – all represented except the United States – demanded recognition of the Tsarist debt, compensation for confiscated property, and guarantees for future contracts; the Soviets offered to recognise the debt in return for cancellation of the Russian war debt, compensation for damages inflicted by Allied forces in their intervention after the revolution, and extensive credit for the Soviet government. The divergent purposes of the former Allies and the distrust caused by the announcement of the Treaty of Rapallo between Germany and the Soviet Union, however, made agreement impossible, and the conference adjourned without agreement.

– It is apparently contemplated that negotiations should continue with the Bols not only under the shadow of the military menace described in this telegram but with the primary and well advertised object of buying off the Bols – a reversion to the diplomacy of Ethelred the Unready!

AHMS

Sir Archibald Sinclair to Winston S. Churchill
8th July 1922

Secretary of State,

M. Krassin's remarks at the close of this meeting of the Private Property Commission of the Hague Conference are particularly interesting.

In the meetings of the various commissioners and sub-commissions, in private conversations with the principal statesmen at Genoa, in conversations and meetings which he has had with the British Delegates since he returned to London, the Prime Minister has laid particular stress on two observations by the Russian Delegates at Genoa.

The first is Litvinoff's remarks that it would be much easier to agree in practice than in principle, and the second was Krassin's later remark that 90% of the foreign-owned private property in Russia could be handed over to the previous owners and that in only 10% of cases would it be found that the properties had been so cut up or embodied in larger properties that it would be impossible to extricate them and hand them back in their old state to the proprietor, and that in these 10% of cases compensation could be arranged. Indeed, I think it would not be too much to say that this was one of the foundation stones of the case for the meeting of the experts at the Hague and, if it interested you, I could give you several extracts from Genoa meetings showing what stress was laid on this alleged remark now repudiated by Krassin.

AHMS

Sir Archibald Sinclair to Winston S. Churchill
Dalnawillan,
Altnabreac,
Caithness
13th September 1922
Personal & Confidential

My dear Winston,

At Jack Wodehouse's request, I am making enquiries about wintering your ponies.[292] I have sent mine to a different place this year for reasons of personal

[292] Churchill had injured himself in a polo fall and had to retire from the sport for the rest of the season. He had asked Sinclair if he could arrange to stable his ponies.

convenience – not because I was dis-satisfied with the wintering last year – but in the meantime I happen to have grooms both in the new place and in the old place and I have told them to write direct to Jack and to tell him the best terms they can obtain for your ponies.

I am sorry to hear that your ponies are being turned out so soon. I am afraid it means that your Mimizan plans[293] are off and you must be full of anxiety for your tender Arab plant in Iraq with this furious storm raging on – and threatening to spread from – the Asia Minor horizon.

At such a time, I feel truly diffident about troubling you with my little personal affairs, but as you took the principal part in introducing me to the Liberals of Perth and in rallying them after their reverse in the initial advance guard action I venture to ask you to read the copies which I enclose of two letters which I have received from the very capable and energetic secretary of the National Liberal Council in Perth.

It is evident that we are up against the determination of the Duke and Duchess of Atholl to assert their political influence in Perthshire, and they probably look upon me as the harbinger of your influence encroaching upon their preserves from the neighbouring constituency of Dundee. It is apparent from Munro's letter to me that some of the Conservatives present were not indisposed to accept the proposal of arbitration and I have little doubt that, if the opposition of Atholl and his Duchess could be overcome, the rank and file could easily be won round.

Meanwhile, the National Liberals who have been encouraged from headquarters to come out and form their own Association will feel badly let down if they fail to receive the support which they were invited to expect when their Association was formed. Men like G.K. Smith, who accepted the presidency of the new National Liberal Council, and Munro, the secretary, will not be content to play second fiddle to the Conservatives and you will see from the concluding sentence of Munro's last letter to me that they demand stronger support from Headquarters in London. If they are defeated in Perth their resentment will undoubtedly, carry them into opposition, and their fate will excite widespread sympathy and concern among Scottish Liberals. I am enclosing a spare copy of this part of my letter in case you may care to forward it to MacCallum Scott. Munro is obviously most grateful to him for his personal support at the recent Conference in Perth.

There is one other matter I want to tell you about. Edwin Montagu who is staying here happened by chance to mention that Fred Cripps[294] had been a fellow-guest with him at Beaufort. I naturally enquired about his Moscow venture and was delighted to learn that it already appears to be in serious jeopardy and that Cripps is blaming the Government – the Board of Trade and the Prime Minister in particular. His case is that the Board of Trade is completely in the hands of the Dudley Docker clique and the Federation of British Industries and that Leslie Urquhart, being hand

[293] Churchill was planning a painting holiday at Mimizan on the Landes coast in South-West France.

[294] Frederick Cripps (dates unknown): brother of Stafford Cripps; Director of the Russian and English Bank in Petrograd before 1914; served in Gallipoli, Palestine and France in the First World War.

in glove with them, has received all their favours, while he has been refused even the courtesy of an interview by Lloyd Graeme and Sir William Clark.

The point is that Edwin advised him to go and see you and ask your help. I don't want to prejudge his case and I am not in full possession of all the relevant facts, but I do know that Leslie Urquhart has engaged with patience and resolution in a series of contests against the Soviet Government and that he has been recognised by the Bolsheviks as one of their most formidable enemies. I have not of course seen the contract which he has recently signed in Berlin with the representatives of the Soviet Government, but from the accounts in the newspapers, it appears to safeguard the principles upon which private enterprise is founded and which must in the long run prove fatal to Bolshevism in Russia.

I have no figures or papers to refer to here but I understand that most of the British holders of property in Russia are, like the bondholders, formed into associations for the protection of their interests and that Leslie Urquhart has come to be looked upon as their principal champion.

Fred Cripps, on the other hand, at a time when the Board of Trade was formulating its policy in consultation with the British interests involved in Russia before the Genoa Conference, went off at a tangent on his own with a casual blessing from the Prime Minster and with Kenworthy as his companion to Moscow, where he made a contract with the Soviet Government which included no provision for the compensation of the private owners of the property handed over to Cripps for exploitation and which was loudly proclaimed to the world by the Bolsheviks as the type of contract they were making with prominent British capitalists. In short, it looked like an attempt to nip in front of his fellow British holders of property in Russia, who were trying to drive a bargain with the Bolsheviks at Genoa, with a get-rich-quick speculative venture.

Therefore, I implore you, if you see Cripps at all, not to commit yourself to his support or against Leslie Urquhart until thorough investigations have been made. I had the best of the argument with Edwin this morning from my point of view, but I knew nothing of the case from his standpoint which was that the Board of Trade is under certain influences which make it difficult for small competing firms and individuals to obtain fair play. That may or may not be so but, while I am quite open to conviction and have no means here of verifying the statements which I have set out and which I believe to be true, I doubt very much whether Cripps' case can be regarded as lending any substance to this allegation.

If Mimizan has fallen through I wish so much that you could come up here for a week or ten days. From the all-round sporting standpoint the end of September or the beginning of October is the best time of the year here. The salmon fishing is sure to be good, the snipe are coming in to the bogs – Edwin & I shot 16 in 1½ hours yesterday and the light was bad or we could have had many more – stags are coming on to the ground, and we go after the grouse with dogs or drive them according to the weather. Do come if you can. Love to Clemmie and Eddie.

Archie

Sir Archibald Sinclair to Winston S. Churchill
Dalnawillan,
Altnabreac,
Caithness
22nd September 1922

My dear Winston,

Many thanks for your telegram, it is nice of you to say you want to have a talk with me & I am just longing to listen & to see a little below the surface of these tremendous events. We have travelled a long way since the defeat of Denikin was gloated over in the same quarters as had heralded the Greek landing in Smyrna with a flourish of trumpets and it is amusing to recollect the arguments that were adorned to prove that the Bols would never ever over-run the Trans-Caucasian republics[295] – and the absurdity of supposing that they could powerfully influence events to the detriment of British interests in Persia or Anatolia. I suppose the effect of the crisis on home politics will hardly become clear for another few weeks until the foreign situation is established. Your watchword of "stability" sounds almost like an echo of pre-war days!! Little enough sign of it yet.

As for me, I must stay here till the second week in October as I have to unveil two more War Memorials – the work of the second being rushed on in order to have it ready in time for me to unveil one day in the second week of next month. I can assure you I don't enjoy these ceremonies, but I think I ought to stay & perform them unless you really want me and telegraph for me urgently. Incidentally we have got people staying here – Violet Bonham-Carter[296] & Rosemary & Eric arrive to-morrow but I would willingly return if you seriously want me. I wish you could spare a week to join us. With love to Clemmie,

Yours,
Archie

The Chanak crisis continued to boil to a head.

---

295 Which the Bolsheviks had invaded in early 1920 and subsequently incorporated into the Soviet Union as Soviet Republics.

296 Violet Bonham Carter, Baroness Asquith of Yarnbury (1887–1969): eldest daughter of H.H. Asquith, Liberal leader and Prime Minister; married Maurice Bonham Carter, Asquith's principal private secretary, in 1915; President, Women's Liberal Federation 1923–25; President, Liberal Party Organisation 1945–47 (the first woman to hold the post); member of the Board of Governors of the BBC, 1940–46; awarded life peerage in 1964; her maiden speech in the House of Lords, on 25 January 1965, took the form of a eulogy on her friend Churchill, who had died the previous day.

Winston S. Churchill to Sir Archibald Sinclair
25th September 1922
Private

The matter about which I wished to talk with you has become less urgent for the moment. It concerns Perth and your political prospects generally. It may become more urgent in the course of the week, and if I telegraph to you again I hope you will be able to come down without delay. I am so glad you are enjoying yourself.

Thank God that awful pro-Greek policy against which we have so long inveighed has come to an end. We have paid an enormously heavy price for nothing. However, at the very end I have had to throw in my lot with L.G. in order to try to make some sort of front against what would otherwise have been a complete Turkish walk-over and the total loss of all the fruits of the Great War in this quarter. They make a great deal of fuss about the communiqué which I drafted for the P.M. at his request and which he issued. All the same, I am convinced that if we had not got a move on there would be no question of the Turks accepting the terms we have now offered, and even now it is possible that he will prove uncontrollable.

Mind you do not fail to come quickly when I telegraph.

WSC

Churchill was laid low by appendicitis for most of the 1922 election campaign and had to rely on his wife, Clementine, to speak at his rallies and undertake constituency tours across Dundee; he lost badly in what he had once referred to as his 'seat for life'. He was also to fail to be elected for the Liberal Party in the 1923 election and in a by-election in 1924 when he stood as a 'constitutionalist'. He completed his drift from Liberal back to Conservative politics in time for the 1924 general election. Sinclair successfully contested the Caithness & Sutherland seat in 1922 for the Lloyd George Liberals, a seat he was to retain until 1945.

No letters have been found for 1923.

Part 3

Separate Paths
1924–1939

Introduction

The period from 1924 to 1939 saw Sinclair's and Churchill's careers diverge significantly. Over this fifteen-year period Sinclair emerged as a national politician in his own right, remaining true to the colours of the Liberal Party, while Churchill returned to the Conservatives and, after 1929, entered what has been referred to as his 'wilderness period', in which he remained excluded from office until the opening of the Second World War.

Churchill was out of parliament from November 1922 until October 1924, when he was returned as a 'Constitutionalist' MP for Epping – in reality a Conservative in all but name. Much to everyone's surprise, including Churchill's, he was appointed Chancellor of the Exchequer by Baldwin in the new Conservative Government.

He proved an ebullient, if not entirely convincing, figure at the Treasury. Although not particularly well versed in financial matters, he worked hard – as usual – and produced a series of well-received Budget speeches. His most contentious decision, taken with almost unanimous support from official Treasury advisors, was to return Britain to the Gold Standard in 1925 at the pre-war parity. In retrospect this was almost certainly the wrong decision, given the state of the economy, and attracted substantial contemporary criticism – not least from John Maynard Keynes, who published his famous critical pamphlet *The Economic Consequences of Mr Churchill*.

In 1926 Churchill took an aggressive part in opposing the General Strike, typified not least by his hands-on editorship of the government's official strike-breaking newspaper, the *British Gazette*. The failings of the 1924–29 government and the disappointment of the 1929 election cannot be laid solely at Churchill's door, though many Tory supporters felt that his economic stewardship, and the decision to return to the Gold Standard in particular, were partly at fault.

After the Tories were defeated in 1929, Churchill fell out with Baldwin over the question of giving India further self-government and was excluded from involvement in MacDonald's, Baldwin's and Chamberlain's National Governments during the 1930s. He became more and more politically isolated, and found the experience of perpetual opposition deeply frustrating. He further alienated himself from many in the Conservative Party by his pursuit of leading Tory politicians Hoare and Derby with regard to the Committee of Privileges where Churchill alleged that both senior Conservatives had breached parliamentary privilege to exert improper pressure on the representatives of the Manchester Chamber of Commerce to change their evidence to the Joint

Select Committee investigating the feasibility of dominion status for India. Churchill lost further Tory support over his refusal to abandon support for King Edward VIII during the abdication crisis of 1936. Largely as a consequence of such errors, very few heeded his warning of the rise of Hitler and the hopelessness of the government's appeasement policy. After the Munich crisis in 1938, however, his prophecies were seen by many to be coming true and when war broke out in September 1939 Prime Minister Neville Chamberlain appointed him First Lord of the Admiralty. Nearly twenty-five years after he had left the Admiralty in despair and anger, the Navy sent out a signal to the fleet: 'Winston is back'.

The 1922 general election proved a very different experience for Sinclair. While Churchill, standing as a Lloyd George-supporting National Liberal, lost his Dundee seat by more than 10,000 votes, Sinclair, standing under the same flag, was elected for the first time to Parliament as MP for Caithness & Sutherland. He defeated the official (Asquithian) Liberal Party candidate, Sir R. L. Harmsworth, by 7,715 votes to 5,809.[297] T. E. Lawrence ('Lawrence of Arabia'), a friend of Sinclair's since the latter's service at the Colonial Office, declared the result 'magnificent'. Although the election was a personal victory for Sinclair, it was a huge setback for Lloyd George's National Liberals, who saw their parliamentary strength fall from 133 to 62.[298]

Sinclair soon built up a reputation as a skilful Parliamentary speaker. His maiden speech, on 21 March 1923, dealt with his concerns over the Air Estimates contained in the budget; he warned of the growing significance of air power in war and of the threat of possible 'aerial attack from East of the Rhine or even East of the Vistula'.[299] He was re-elected in Caithness & Sutherland unopposed in the 1923 and 1924 general elections, and from 1925 to 1930 served as Temporary Chairman of Committees in the House of Commons, managing the committee structure set up to undertake the detailed study of proposed legislation and the scrutiny of government policy and programmes. In 1927 he was nominated by Lloyd George for membership of the Empire Marketing Board (the British government's first attempt to run a large-scale commercial advertising campaign, promoting Empire produce and goods), and served on the Board until 1930.

The 1923 election, called by Conservative Prime Minister Baldwin in an attempt to win a mandate for his conversion to protectionism, led to a reunification of the Asquithian and Lloyd George Liberals, and the combined party ended up holding the balance of power in the House of Commons. Asquith's decision to support a minority Labour Government under Ramsay MacDonald, although probably inevitable, was in retrospect disastrous for the Liberals, who lost three-quarters of their seats in the 1924 election, as the electorate increasingly opted for a straight choice between Conservatives and Labour. Asquith himself was defeated and accepted a seat in the House of Lords; in 1926, he resigned the leadership after divisions with Lloyd George

[297] The seat returned to the Sinclair family when his grandson, John Thurso, was elected as Liberal Democrat MP for Caithness & Sutherland in the 2001 general election.

[298] The Conservatives won 345 seats, Labour 142 and the Asquithian Liberals 54.

[299] *Hansard* (House of Commons debates), 21 March 1923.

over the General Strike. Lloyd George was elected in his place, and Sinclair worked closely with him in a comprehensive overhaul of Liberal policy. Sinclair was always a strong supporter of home rule for Scotland, and for the 1929 election he wrote much of the Liberal 'Tartan Book', proposing devolution for Scotland on the lines of the Stormont system in Northern Ireland.

The 1929 election saw Sinclair triumph in a three-way fight in Caithness & Sutherland, winning 13,462 votes compared to the Tory candidate's 3,041, and 1,711 for the Independent Labour Party. Overall, however the 1929 election was a huge disappointment for the Liberal Party. Lloyd George's money and revamp of policies delivered a significant rise in the party's vote, but Liberal support was too evenly spread across the country for this to translate into many seats. The Liberals ended up with a total of 59 MPs and the balance of power in the House of Commons, but the real victor was the Labour Party which, with 288 seats, against 260 for the Conservatives, emerged, for the first time, as the largest party. MacDonald's second government, however, quickly found itself facing the onset of the economic of the Great Depression. Lloyd George offered Liberal support to MacDonald in return for electoral reform, but before the bill could complete its passage through Parliament the Labour Cabinet split over the proposal to reduce unemployment benefits to balance the budget. The Labour Government fell on 24 August 1931, and by the end of the month Ramsay MacDonald formed the first National Government with Conservative and Liberal support.

The 1929–31 period provoked further Liberal splits. Many on the right of the party, led mainly by Sir John Simon, felt they had more in common with the firmly anti-socialist stance of the Conservatives and were profoundly uncomfortable with what they saw as Lloyd George's attempts to outmanoeuvre Labour from the left. They also began to question the historic Liberal attachment to free trade, which seemed to make less sense in the face of the protectionist barriers erected by other countries.

It was also during this period that Sinclair and Churchill's desire to work together again, as articulated in their letters, almost came to fruition. On 21 July 1931, Lloyd George, Churchill and Oswald Mosley[300] met at Sinclair's Kingston Vale home to discuss the formation of a new centre party that could form a national opposition to any national government that might be formed under MacDonald's and Baldwin's leadership. However, although a dream of a new party had been under consideration by Churchill and Lloyd George since the days of the 1918–22 coalition, events overtook these discussions, as the letters show clearly, not least because of the issue of India which set Churchill and Lloyd George on different paths.

Sinclair, who had been appointed Liberal Chief Whip in 1930, accepted office in the National Government, as Secretary of State for Scotland (a cabinet position from

[300] Sir Oswald Ernest Mosley (1896–1980): Conservative, Independent, and Labour MP for Harrow 1918–24, Labour then New Party MP for Smethwick 1928–31; in the 1920s seen as one of the rising stars at Westminster; Chancellor of Duchy of Lancaster 1929–30, resigned over government's failure to adopt his radical proposals to deal with unemployment; left Labour and founded New Party in 1931; founded British Union of Fascists in 1932. At the time of this meeting, he was not yet the hate figure that he was to become after the BUF became viciously anti-Semitic and pro-Nazi.

November 1931), along with other prominent Liberals such as Herbert Samuel, who became Home Secretary (Lloyd George was out of action at the time after a prostate operation). In October Sinclair and Samuel, who feared that any election would simply reinforce the strength of the Conservatives, the main supporters of the National Government, reluctantly agreed to fight an election under the National Government's banner. This decision triggered Lloyd George's resignation as Liberal leader and his replacement by Samuel, and the Liberals fought the election in three groups, Samuel's official Liberals, Simon's fervently pro-National Government Liberal Nationals, and a small group of Lloyd George Liberals, mainly relatives of the former leader. The general election of 1931 produced a massive landslide for the National Government, and Labour's biggest defeat in its history.

The new government was even more heavily dominated by the Conservatives, and in January 1932 the Cabinet decided in favour of introducing protectionism through a system of 'Imperial Preference' tariff barriers more favourable to countries within the British Empire. This struck at the heart of the long-held Liberal belief in free trade; Samuel and his colleagues opposed the move but remained in the Government under an 'agreement to differ'. Inevitably, however, their position became untenable, and in September 1932 the Samuelite ministers left the government after tariffs were introduced, joining the Lloyd George group in opposition in 1933. Simon and his colleagues remained in the Government, and were gradually absorbed into the Conservative Party, disappearing completely in the 1960s.

The election of 1935 further reduced Liberal strength to 21 MPs, and Samuel himself lost his seat. With the leadership of the party vacant and Lloyd George refusing to be considered, Sinclair was, at Lloyd George's suggestion, elected leader. He inherited a deeply demoralised party, which had lost its sense of purpose and had been driven to the edge of extinction as an independent political force. He had few cards to play, but his performance as leader over the following five years was impressive. By sheer hard work, highly focused campaigning and a carefully managed internal reorganisation he built a national reputation as a capable and principled opposition leader.

Sinclair's most significant campaign was as one of the early voices opposing the National Government's policy of piecemeal concessions to Mussolini and Hitler. Although before 1935 Sinclair had been critical of proposed increases in defence spending he was quicker than most senior parliamentarians to realise the dangers that political extremism raised in continental Europe. Under Sinclair the Liberals combined support for collective security through the League of Nations with pressure for targeted expenditure in building a first-rate Royal Air Force and secure naval defences. In this policy the Liberals offered a genuine alternative to Chamberlain's approach of appeasing the European dictatorships, and were quicker than the Labour leadership, which argued against any increase in Britain's spending on arms, to realise that Hitler must be stopped.

In the House of Commons Sinclair and Churchill found themselves working closely together during 1938 in condemning the Munich agreement, urging the formation of a Ministry of Supply (reflecting their experience of the Ministry of Munitions in 1918) and arguing that Britain's foreign policy must focus on isolating and encircling Germany by forging understandings with the Russians in the face of a common threat. However effective Sinclair's arguments were in the Commons, he failed to convince many outside Parliament of the validity of his views and, indeed, some of his own backbenchers remained hostile to his policy of opposing appeasement.

By the end of March 1939, however, the European situation was darkening perceptibly as Hitler abrogated the Munich Agreement and invaded what was left of Czechoslovakia. This was quickly followed by German demands that Danzig, since 1919 a free city under the mandate of the League of Nations, be returned to German control together with other lands of the old East Prussia. In a debate on the international situation on 3 April 1939, Sinclair declared that 'if we are to convince Herr Hitler of our inflexible determination to resist aggression henceforward, there must be no hedging in the policy of His Majesty's Government and no whittling down of their pronouncements'.[301] Sinclair went on to attack the Government's record in maintaining its purpose in the face of the actions of the dictators, reminding the House of every retreat the National Government had presided over.

> Let us be quite clear about this matter. Peace will depend on the ability of His Majesty's Government to convince Herr Hitler that this time they really will be firm. It will not be easy to convince him. He will remember the Government's pledges at the last election about steady and collective resistance to unprovoked aggression and, four or five weeks later, the Hoare–Laval negotiations.[302] He will remember that the independence of Austria was proclaimed by this Government to be an object of British policy ... Tremendous exertions are called for from the Government and this country if we are to live down that record and convince Herr Hitler that in future we will be steadfast.[303]

This speech won Sinclair widespread support from disaffected supporters of the National Government and the national newspapers; Churchill declared in the Commons debate that 'this is a fine hour in the life of the Liberal Party, because from the moment when they realised that rearmament was necessary, they have seemed to seek to bring forward together both the material and moral strength of this country, and I believe that at the moment they represent what is the heart and soul of the British nation'.[304]

The 1920s and 1930s marked a significant switch in the relationship between the two men. Sinclair emerged as a national politician in his own right rather than simply Churchill's assistant. Although he and Churchill walked different political paths from 1924 to 1939, they found themselves being bought back together in their opposition to the continental dictators, and in their concern over the lack of urgency in Britain's preparations to face the possibility of a further European war. The correspondence between

[301] *Hansard*, 3 April 1939, col. 2497.

[302] The agreement in 1935 between British Foreign Secretary Sir Samuel Hoare and French Prime Minister Pierre Laval for the partition of Abyssinia following Mussolini's invasion of the country. The proposal attracted widespread denunciation, forcing Hoare's resignation.

[303] *Hansard*, 3 April 1939, col. 2498.

[304] *Hansard*, 3 April 1939, col. 2497.

them, though lower in volume than in previous years, continues to demonstrate the personal warmth and affection that each felt for the other, linked by their desire to work together again in politics.

1924–1929

1924 proved to be a critical year in the decline of the Liberal Party. The 1923 election had seen 159 Liberal MPs returned (an improvement on the combined total of 117 elected in 1922) as the Asquithian and Lloyd Georgite factions came together to campaign against Baldwin's proposals threatening free trade. However, Asquith's controversial decision to allow the Labour Party to form a minority administration quickly led to a resumption of internal Liberal tensions. For Churchill the Liberals' failure to block Ramsay MacDonald's path to the premiership effectively ended his allegiance to the party he had served since 1904. Sinclair, who had been elected as a Lloyd George Liberal, also took a dim view of the decision to put the Labour Party into office.

The October 1924 election was a disaster for the Liberal Party, with a near halving of their vote and the return of only 40 MPs. Despite losing his seat in the 1924 election, Asquith remained Liberal leader until October 1926 when he resigned due to ill health and was replaced by Lloyd George.

Sir Archibald Sinclair to Winston S. Churchill
Robin Hood Farm, Putney
Kingston Vale, S.W.15
7th May 1924

My Dear Winston,

I spoke to you yesterday about my conversation with Belosselsky[305] but we went on to other things and I came away with a rather indistinct idea of what you wanted me to say to him.

Am I right in supposing that you would wish me to reply that you have lost none of your interest in their affairs but that you are fully occupied with your own at the present time, but that you would be willing to see him later on for a private talk? Would you offer him lunch? If so, I can let you have his address and telephone number.

Yours ever,
Archie

[305] General Prince Belosselsky-Belozersky, former officer in the Russian Cavalry Guard who gave Churchill a portrait of the Duke of Marlborough which hung in Churchill's drawing room – see n206.

Sir Archibald Sinclair to Winston S. Churchill
Dalnawillan,
Altnabreac,
Caithness
23rd September 1924

My dear Winston,

Many thanks for sending me your letters from Reilly.[306] I enclose herewith two letters which I have received from Brunstrom, who is a Finnish financier, a friend of Mannerheim, and was the man who arranged the interview between Savinkoff and Krassin, being a personal friend of both parties, just before the Genoa Conference. He seems to know little about the latest developments, but his comments on Savinkoff's behaviour are more merciful, and, I think, shrewder than Reilly's, whose judgement is no doubt affected by the bitter disappointment he must have felt at the failure of his plans. I suppose you got into touch with Reilly through the Morning Post, and I am sending for the articles which Brunstrom refers.

Do you remember you promised to send me the minutes of evidence taken at the U.S. enquiry into the question of the recognition of the Soviet Government? Of course they were intended for you, but if you do not want to keep them I shall be glad to have them.

I am sorry to see that Craig[307] does not appear to be likely to appoint a commissioner.[308] Surely it was very foolish of JH[309] to go off to South Africa at this crisis. With JH on the ocean, and Ramsay[310] immersed in foreign affairs, and involved in

---

[306] Sidney Reilly wrote to Churchill on 3 September 1924 saying that he could not find any reliable evidence of the fate of Boris Savinkoff but feared that reports that he was now attempting a reconciliation with the Bolsheviks were a plot by the Soviet secret police.

[307] Sir James Craig, 1st Viscount Craigavon of Stormont (1871–1940): Unionist politician, rallied the Protestant opposition to Irish Home Rule in Ulster before the First World War, organising the Ulster Volunteer Force; succeeded Carson as leader of the Northern Unionists in February 1921 and became Prime Minister of Northern Ireland in June, holding the post until his death in 1940.

[308] The Irish Treaty signed in 1921 had left the exact boundary between Ulster and the Irish Free State to be settled by a Boundary Commission consisting of three members, one each to be nominated by the Irish Free State, the British Government and the government of Northern Ireland. The Northern Ireland Government had not been a party to the treaty and was suspicious of its intentions; Craig refused to appoint a Commissioner, requiring the British Government to pass new legislation that enabled them to appoint a representative for Ulster.

[309] James Henry 'Jimmy' Thomas (1874–1949): railway workers' union leader; Labour and National Labour MP for Derby 1910–36; Secretary of State for the Colonies 1924; Lord Privy Seal and Minister for Employment 1929–30; Secretary of State for the Dominions 1930–31; followed MacDonald into the National Government; Secretary of State for the Colonies and Dominions 1931–35; Secretary of State for the Colonies 1935–36.

[310] James Ramsay MacDonald (1866–1937): Secretary, Labour Representation Committee 1900–12 (negotiated MacDonald-Gladstone electoral pact with the Liberals); Labour MP for Leicester 1906–18, Aberavon 1922–29, Labour and National Labour MP for Seaham 1929–37; Leader of the Parliamentary Labour Party 1922–31; Foreign Secretary and Prime Minister 1924; Prime Minister 1931–35; the first Labour MP to be expelled by the party, following his decision to lead the National Government in 1931.

personal explanation of his financial transactions,[311] nobody seems to be making any attempt to handle the Irish question.

With regard to Russia, I wish LG had not been quite so downright.[312] Of course I am delighted that Asquith and Grey[313] have come up to his support, but a good many of the rank and file seem to think he has been trying to snatch the lead, and would be inclined to resort to any expedient to avoid a general election, with which they think LG is threatening them. I am beginning to be doubtful whether we shall get the election on the Russian Treaty after all, but if not we shall at any rate have produced a very uncomfortable situation for the Labour Party.[314]

The Tories are getting busy here, and Novar[315] came and addressed a meeting yesterday. The local Dukes and Harmsworth[316] are lending financial support, and the latter is keeping the old Liberal paper here going, in order to use it against me, and has also promised the full support of the Glasgow Daily Record, which belongs to Rothermere. The solicitor who used to organise in the constituency for Harmsworth, and is still a Liberal, and the solicitor who used to organize in Wick for Sir Arthur Bignold, whose organisation is supposed to have been quite as corrupt as Harmsworth's, are both in the scheme, but my supporters insist that, even if a Socialist candidate comes into the field, our worst danger will be over-confidence. The Duke and Duchess of Atholl have also promised the local Tories to visit the constituency, and it is really flattering to a young Member to have three Dukes, an ex-Cabinet Minister and a Press magnate concentrating their artillery upon him!

We were so grateful to you for our most happy visit to Westerham. I hope all is going well with the dam, and that your work on the lower lake is now finished.

---

[311] Rumours that MacDonald had received a Daimler car and shares in McVitie Biscuits Company in return for a baronetcy for the owner of the firm.

[312] Lloyd George had strongly attacked the two treaties negotiated by the Labour Government with Soviet Russia, dealing with the issues of compensation for British-owned property in Russia nationalised by the Bolsheviks, and the admission of at least some limited liability to repay the war debts contracted by the old regime. In return the British Government undertook to guarantee a loan to Russia when half the bond-holders of the war debt were satisfied. Lloyd George particularly opposed the proposed loan.

[313] Sir Edward Grey, first Viscount Grey of Falloden (1862–1933): Liberal MP for Berwick-on-Tweed 1885–1916; Under-Secretary of State, Foreign Office, 1892–95; Foreign Secretary 1905–16, well known for his utterance on the outbreak of war: 'the lamps are going out all over Europe; we shall not see them lit again in our lifetime'; ennobled in 1916; Liberal leader in the Lords 1923–24; President of the Asquithian 'Liberal Council' 1927–33.

[314] Lloyd George was hoping to use Liberal opposition to the proposed loan to unite the party with the Conservatives in a vote of no confidence in the Government, thereby causing a general election on the issue of Labour's competence in both financial and foreign affairs. Lloyd George was confident that if the election could be fought on these issues the Liberals would look like a credible alternative government-in-waiting.

[315] Sir Ronald Munro-Ferguson, 1st Viscount Novar of Raith (1860–1934): Governor-General of Australia (1914–20); ennobled in 1920; Secretary of State for Scotland 1922–24.

[316] Sir Robert Harmsworth (1870–1937): Liberal MP for Caithness & Sutherland 1900–22; younger brother of newspaper Lords Northcliffe and Rothermere.

The Scotch papers feature your adoption for Epping as the most prominent news of the day. Best wishes for your Edinburgh meeting.

Yours ever,
Archie

PS. My address on & after Tuesday will be Travellers' Club, Pall Mall. S.W.1.

Sir Archibald Sinclair to Winston S. Churchill
Dalnawillan,
Altnabreac,
Caithness
29th September 1924

My dear Winston,

Just a line to offer sincere congratulations on the brilliant success of your speech & the warmth of your reception in Edinburgh.[317] It must have surpassed even your most sanguine expectations.

I am getting more & more unhappy about the Russian Treaty. The political correspondents of the Scottish Tory Press who are as a rule particularly well informed are extremely defeatist & fully antipathetic – and seem to desire an accommodation. I shall make a beeline for L.G. when I get back – if possible before the party meeting – after all he has said & all that the Socialists have said about him, he must stick to his guns.

I shall reach London – The Travellers' Club – Wednesday morning, but hope to return Thursday or at latest Friday night to fulfil several engagements here, at Aberdeen & at Inverness. Do let me know if you are likely to be in London Wed. Thurs. or Friday.

Yours always,
Archie

In the October 1924 election Sinclair, despite much sabre-rattling from local Tories, was again elected unopposed. But for the Liberal Party it was a disaster. Only 40 MPs were elected and the party was relegated to the third-party status from which it has yet to recover. Churchill was elected as a 'Constitutionalist' for the safe Conservative seat of Epping and appointed as Chancellor of the Exchequer under Baldwin.

One of the similarities between Sinclair and Churchill was that both had to overcome stammers when speaking in public. Here Churchill advises Sinclair to try a Harley Street physician who had impressed him.

[317] On the evening of 25 September 1924 Churchill delivered a speech at the Usher Hall in Edinburgh where he declared that there was now no gulf of principle between the Conservatives and Liberals and that the two parties should combine to defeat the Labour Party.

Winston S. Churchill to Sir Archibald Sinclair
21st March 1927

My dear Archie,

I send you these papers which Cortlandt MacMahon[318] sent me. I believe you might find him a help in more ways than one, and anyhow there would be very little expense and no risk. It stands to reason, when one thinks of it, that the internal muscles of the stomach ought to be as fit as the external, and only exercise can develop them. He has been wonderfully successful in curing stammer; and though yours is so slight as not to be a barrier to successful speaking, it is an impediment. Anyhow he has done me so much good that I am anxious to spread the good tidings to my friends.

Yours,
W

Sinclair kept closely informed on foreign affairs and wrote to Churchill to update him on events in China, where the civil war between the Nationalists and Communists was reaching a critical stage. Two days later Churchill forwarded the letter to Baldwin, noting on the top: 'Prime Minster, You may perhaps care to see. WSC'

Sir Archibald Sinclair to Winston S. Churchill
Robin Hood Farm,
Kingston Vale, S.W.15
2nd April 1927
Personal & Confidential

My dear Winston,

I hope you found Myers on China interesting. It was very kind of you to ask me to join you at your interview and I wish it had been possible.

Meanwhile I have received some more information, which I think you ought to have, from a very important and reliable source. It appears that the efforts which have been made to reach an understanding between Chang Kai Shek[319] and Chang Tso Lin[320] are likely to come to a head next week.

[318] A well-known speech therapist during the 1920s and 1930s; based in Harley Street.

[319] Chiang Kai-shek (1887–1975): Chinese Nationalist leader; during 1926–28 defeated the provincial warlords who had emerged after the collapse of the Manchu imperial dynasty, and reunified the country under the Nationalist Republic, of which he was the effective head until 1949; broke with the Chinese Communists in 1927, initiating the long civil war which he eventually lost in 1949; the Nationalists were driven from the mainland to the island of Taiwan, where Chiang established an independent government, remaining President until his death in 1975.

[320] Chang Tso-lin (1873–1928): Chinese soldier and warlord who dominated Manchuria and parts of North China between 1913 and 1928; he maintained his power with the tacit support of the Japanese, and in return granted them concessions in Manchuria; during the early and mid 1920s held control of

Chang Kai Shek who, as you know, has recently been in communication with Chang Tso Lin, had thought of referring the latter's proposals to a Council which had been summoned, I understand, for next Monday at Shanghai, but he was anxious to get, if not a firm offer, at any rate a clear indication of Chang Tso Lin's intentions to put before them. Chang Tso Lin, however, declared that he must consult his friends, including Wellington Koo,[321] the acting Prime Minister in Peking, and would not be ready to take any definite step until Tuesday or Wednesday of next week. Chang Kai Shek, according to my informant, had meantime himself decided against laying these proposals before the Council on Monday. He prefers to obtain the general concurrence of the leading Tupans,[322] and this he feels confident he will be able to do. It is his view – with which, if a Westerner can form any useful judgment of Chinese politics, one would certainly feel inclined to agree – that any agreement must be simply a gentlemen's agreement between the leaders on both sides, and he is emphatic that if an agreement is reached he will employ the whole of his resources to make it effective. He had been a little doubtful of the attitude of one of the most important of his Tupans, Jongg Shai Mon, but he recently received definite information that the latter was prepared to support these proposals: indeed Jongg conveyed to Chang that he himself had sounded Wellington Koo on rather different lines some time ago.

It appears, however, that the Press in China is getting more and more powerful and in particular there is a newspaper in Hangkow, whose name I forget but to which the Nationalists attribute considerable importance; the editor appears to be a rather eminent man who is a Nationalist of long standing and possesses great influence. I understand that he has been requested to come to Shanghai on Monday to discuss matters with Chang Kai Shek.

Of course this information is vague, but at any rate it is evident that Chang Kai Shek is taking every possible step to rally his principal supporters, that the next move between him and Chang Tso Lin rests with the latter, and that important developments may be expected next week.

Yours ever,
Archie

Between 11 and 16 January 1928, Sinclair and his family visited the Churchills at Chartwell.

Beijing and the surrounding Beijing–Tianjin area, until his forces were driven out by Chiang Kai-shek in 1926.

[321] Vi Kuiyuin Wellington Koo (1887–1985): Chinese Nationalist diplomat, and at various times minister of foreign affairs and prime minister; delegate to the Paris Peace Conference in 1919 and then Chinese representative on the Council of the League of Nations.

[322] Possibly 'Taipans', the heads of foreign-owned businesses in China.

Sir Archibald Sinclair to Winston S. Churchill
Robin Hood Farm,
Kingston Vale, S.W.15
22nd January 1928

My dear Winston,

We enjoyed our visit to Chartwell quite inexpressibly – I have never left anywhere except my own home more sadly – but I came away with the firm conviction that if I had stayed another night, the Rignano system[323] would have been incorporated in your very next Budget! I have been trying to get hold of a set of photographs for you to choose from and I enclose the best I can get. The most recent are in the Aberdeen University Liberal Magazines! – but will you please have them sent back to me as I want to put them in my archives.[324]

With love from us both,
Ever yours
Archie

Sir Archibald Sinclair to Winston S. Churchill
24th July 1928

My dear Winston,

I called on you this evening 'pour prendre congé'[325] as I leave to-night for Caithness via Aberdeen – but I found you immersed in speech-preparation; with cabinet-ministers and officials, rate-reformers and safe-guarders, protectionists and free-traders jostling each other in the door-way and your faithful servants shooed me away.

I returned your Washington[326] to Fergusson[327] with many thanks for the loan of a book which is most entertaining even apart from the dissertation on the art of building!

Don't forget that Oswald Birley[328] wants to paint you. He is a very nice fellow to deal with and an ardent admirer of yours and the P.M.'s.

[323] Eugenio Rignano (1870–1930): Italian economist, built an international reputation on his proposal to make inheritance tax more progressive so that the tax rate on inherited property would be higher than the rate on self-created wealth; influential amongst Liberals like Sinclair because he argued that his proposals did not affect the incentives to work and save and would lead to gradual nationalisation of wealth, and hoped that his thinking would help bring about the reconciliation of socialism and liberalism.

[324] The pictures have not survived in the archives.

[325] 'To take my leave.'

[326] Possibly *George Washington's Diaries 1748–1799*, which had just been published in 1928.

[327] John Donald Fergusson (1891–1963): Churchill's Private Secretary during his tenure as Chancellor of the Exchequer.

[328] Sir Oswald Birley, MC, RA (1880–1952): famous British portrait painter, much favoured by the Royal Family; painted Churchill on three occasions (1928, 1946 and 1951) and in the last years of his life was a frequent visitor to the south of France, where he painted with Churchill, to whom he gave valuable lessons.

Lloyd Grissan[329] is in London (Flemmings Hotel), en route for Buchanan Castle which he has taken from Montrose. If you could bear to ask him to lunch, I have no doubt he would be vastly flattered.

Do come up North and put in a few days with us this year. There are more salmon in the River Thurso than in all the rivers of Sutherland! We would all give you a royal welcome.

Yours,
Archie

Between 1923 and 1931 Churchill published his history of the First World War, *The World Crisis*.[330] He was keen to get Sinclair's input into the volume that dealt with the collapse of Russia and the emergence of the Soviet government. Sinclair was happy to oblige, providing a lengthy commentary on what Churchill had written.

Winston S. Churchill to Sir Archibald Sinclair
Chartwell,
Kent
1st November 1928

My dear Archie,

I am sending you two of the chapters about Russia in the new volume. The third, which deals more particularly with your period, will soon be ready. I should be so grateful if you would read them through and suggest any improvements or corrections that occur to you.

I never answered your charming letter about Oswald Birley. But we shall meet so soon, and can have a talk about things.

Yours,
W

Sir Archibald Sinclair to Winston S. Churchill
12th November 1928

My dear Winston,

I have read with excitement and admiration your stirring Russian chapters.[331] You have given to a seething mass of confused events the true perspective and firm out-line of a clear and masterly picture.

---

329 Lloyd Carpenter Griscom (1872–1959): US diplomat. US Minister to Persia, 1901–02, Japan, 1902–06; US Ambassador to Brazil, 1906–07, Italy, 1907–09; US representative to the War Office 1917–19.

330 Provoking a jibe from his friend F. E. Smith that 'Winston has written a huge book about himself and called it the "World Crisis"'.

I have ventured to make a number of short comments and suggested corrections in the margin of your proofs. I am so sorry they are rather dirty when I return them but I had so much to do in the last two or three days at home that I had to read them after all in the train.

Besides these notes, however, the following additional reflections have occurred to me:–

I thoroughly enjoyed your savage indictment of the Bolsheviks. I felt like the man in the crowd who, after one of your vivid denunciations of Liberals or Socialists, bellows through the volley of cheers "Rub it in!" But would not your indictment carry more weight with those who have not been in contact with the actual events which you are describing and who are trying to form impartial judgements if you were to show a little more readiness to allow your readers to understand the difficulties of the Bolsheviks? Your description of Lenin is masterly[332] but, for the rest, the Bolsheviks are utterly inhuman – the nameless beast; baccilli. For example:–

Would it not be advisable for the sake of the general reader to bring out the dominating reason why the Bolsheviks were so anxious to disintegrate the Russian Army, and why there is no inconsistency between their action in this regard and their subsequent creation of the Red Army? It was of course due to the most natural of all instincts, self-preservation, and their memories of 1905 and the revolution nipped in the bud by loyal troops.

The deliberate bad faith of the Bolsheviks, the reasons for it and the consequent impossibly of having dealings with them, especially during the stress of War. The saying "All is fair in love and war" is not true of war between civilised nations because such wars are not in fact à outrance. Even between the nations engaged in the Great War, there was a realisation of ultimate common interest and of the fact that they would eventually have to live together after it was all over. The Bolsheviks, however, challenged the civilised Governments of the world to a fight to the death, and in such a war there can be no possible basis of good faith. There must be many proofs of the fact that the Bolsheviks saw this quite clearly, and in particular I remember an intercept from Bela Kun[333] to Lenin in which he congratulated himself upon having lied grossly in the name of the Hungarian Soviet Government to the representatives of the Big Five – thus showing himself an "apt pupil and faithful disciple" of Lenin. No doubt they felt that if they were to save their own necks, liberate the working

[331] From proofs for the final volume of *The World Crisis – The Aftermath*, published in March 1929.

[332] Churchill described Lenin's character as being rooted in 'implacable vengeance, rising from a frozen pity in a tranquil, sensible, matter-of-fact, good-humoured integument! His weapon logic; his mood opportunistic. His sympathies cold and wide as the Arctic Ocean; his hatreds tight as the hangman's noose. His purpose to save the world; his methods to blow it up.' *The World Crisis*, Vol. 5, p. 74.

[333] Bela Kun (1886–1936): Hungarian revolutionary, responsible for founding the world's second communist government, albeit short-lived, with the disintegration of the Austro-Hungarian Empire at the close of the First World War; forced from power in August 1919 by the right-wing nationalist Admiral Horthy; fled to Moscow, where he remained until purged by Stalin in 1936.

masses from the thraldom of capitalism and secure the triumph of their cause they must oppose to the overwhelming force of militarist Governments the weapons of craft and guile. It is clear, however, that to bridge the gulf between the Allied Governments and the Soviet Government in 1918 it was necessary that there should be a foundation of good faith on both sides. The absence of it on the Bolshevik side was alone sufficient to make bridge building impossible and to compel us to support the loyal Russian Forces.

You say little about Prinkipo.[334] I cannot now remember whether the negotiations for a Conference at Prinkipo broke down quite clearly because the Bolsheviks refused to suspend hostilities or because the Allies refused to refrain from continuing to support the anti-Bolshevik Forces while the Conference was in being.

I have a fairly clear recollection that both these issues were raised at the time. If, however, it can be shown that the Conference clearly broke down on the former issue it is a plain demonstration of the rejection by the Bolsheviks of peaceful advances of the Allies. If on the other hand it broke down on the second issue and if the constant and deliberate bad faith of the Bolsheviks has been clearly established it can equally be shown that it was impossible for the Allies to consent to abandon the loyal Russian Forces unsupported to the mercy of the Bolsheviks while the negotiations were proceeding.

No doubt you have obtained the advice of the proper authorities with regard to the spelling of Russian names, but I remember that in the old days we always spelt "Denikin" with two "i"s and one "e". It is true that the accent is on the middle syllable and that it is pronounced "Deneekin" and you may have adopted your particular method of spelling to suggest this pronunciation, but I doubt its effectiveness. Were not Denikin's "Memoirs" published in English? How is his name spelt in them?

Again the word "Alexiev" as you have spelt it surely suggests to English people that the "i" is short, whereas my recollection is that the Russians pronounce it "Alexaeff" which was generally rendered in English spelling "Alexeiev".

These, however, are very small points. I am most grateful to you for letting me see these chapters and I shall greatly look forward to the next instalment.

Yours ever,
Archie

Christmas 1928 did not find Sinclair in the most optimistic frame of mind. By mid-January Churchill was again circulating proofs of his final volume of *The World Crisis* to Sinclair for comment.

[334] The proposal for a conference involving the Red and White Russian forces in 1919; see n194.

Sir Archibald Sinclair to Winston S. Churchill
Apperley Court,
Tewkesbury
29th December 1928

My dear Winston,

The telegram from you and Clemmie was a ray of sunlight in the gloomiest Christmas it has ever been my misfortune to experience! We came down here – the whole family – just a week ago and Angus John,[335] aged 3½, immediately developed acidosis with every alarming symptom – high fever, rigor, delirium etc. The day before yesterday for example – the sixth day of his illness – his temperature started at 99° in the morning, soared to 106° at midday and by yesterday evening – just over 24 hours later – had swooped to 96°! To-day, however, he is continuing to improve and as this is his second day without a high temperature and as all external & visible signs & tests are satisfactory, we are feeling much more confident and are hoping to get home next week.

You told me I might propose myself to come to Chartwell for a night or two. Would you have me next week – say Wednesday & Thursday – if all goes well with Angus John?

With love and all good wishes for the New Year to you all from Marigold, Robin[336] & me.

Yours
Archie

Sir Archibald Sinclair to Winston S. Churchill
Robin Hood Farm,
Kingston Vale, S.W. 15
21st January 1929

My dear Winston,

I received by hand on Saturday a letter from Ferguson enclosing two sections of page proof of your book[337] and by post the same evening I received two more sections. I have read all four and now return them with notes on pages 169, 175, 176, 179, 217, 219 and 221. I think they sufficiently explain themselves.

---

335 Sinclair's second son, Angus John Sinclair (1924–2003): educated at Eton and Oxford; worked in the City as a fund manager, then enjoyed a career in the BBC including time as a studio production manager; never a political animal, he remained outside party politics.

336 Sinclair's elder son, Robin Macdonald Sinclair, 2nd Viscount Thurso (1922–95): educated at Eton, New College, Oxford and Edinburgh; RAF flight lieutenant during the Second World War, undertaking photo-reconnaissance missions in the Far East; Liberal county councillor (Caithness), town councillor (Thurso) and unsuccessful parliamentary candidate for East Aberdeenshire 1966; Lord Lieutenant of Caithness 1973–95; President of the Boys' Brigade 1985–93; close friend of the Queen Mother.

337 Further proof chapters from *The Aftermath*, the final volume of *The World Crisis*.

Two other points, however, connected with the chapters have occurred to me.

First of all with regard to the blockade, Prince Max of Barden's[338] book happened to be the subject of discussion at a luncheon table at which I was present the other day, and it was mentioned that Hoover had a number of food ships ready in the United States to take to Germany and that Americans generally and Hoover in particular were clamouring all during the winter and early spring of 1919 for the blockade to be raised and were furiously indignant of their comments on the attitude of the European statesmen.[339] If in fact some such episode, of which I have some vague recollection, occurred would it not be in the interests of historical completeness that you should mention it in the book, and would it not also provide you with the opportunity of amplifying the tributes you have already paid to the next President of the United States of America?[340]

The next point is one which I had intended to make a note on when I was reading the Turkish chapters and somehow it went out of my mind. Surely one of the strongest reasons which impelled you, at any rate after the beginning of 1921, to urge the importance of a satisfactory peace with Turkey was the importance of giving the Middle East, and especially Iraq, a chance of settling down and to avert the danger of an effort by Turkey to recover her lost possessions in Mesopotamia and Arabia? I have not seen much about the Middle East or the Arabs in the book but I suppose you are dealing with them in a chapter which I have not yet read.[341]

Yours ever,
Archie

Winston S. Churchill to Sir Archibald Sinclair
14th January 1929

Archie,

Thank you so much for your letter. Your comments are always so pregnant and instructive, and also appreciative that I venture to send you a few more chapters. If

---

[338] Mis-spelling of Baden.

[339] The wartime blockade of imports to Germany was only raised in the spring of 1919. The British and French politicians at the Peace Conference were reluctant to raise the naval blockade until the Germans had signed the Peace Treaty. During June and July 1919 the blockage was reimposed by the Royal Navy (much to the anger of President Wilson), when it seemed that the German peace delegates were about to advise their government that the Treaty should not be signed.

[340] Herbert Hoover (1874–1964): Head of the American Relief Administration 1918–21, organising shipments of food to central Europe: it was a violent outburst of anger on Hoover's part that persuaded Lloyd George that a drastic change in the Allied policy of maintaining the blockade was urgently needed, and it was raised in March 1919; Secretary of Commerce 1921–28; US President 1929–33. Churchill does not mention Hoover in *The Aftermath* though he does (on pages 66–67) refer to the suffering caused by the prolonged blockade.

[341] Interestingly the Middle East is given very scanty treatment in *The World Crisis.* Perhaps as a result of this prompt from Sinclair, Churchill added a small appendix to the final volume, headed 'A memorandum upon the pacification of the Middle East'.

they reach me in the next five or six days there will still be time to incorporate your wisdom in the common stock.

Did you see Lloyd George before he went away, and did you talk to him about the book? I hope so.[342]

W.

Sir Archibald Sinclair to Winston S. Churchill
Robin Hood Farm,
Kingston Vale, S.W.15
16th January 1929
Personal

My dear Winston,

Many thanks for your letters of the 14th and 15th January and for the further chapters which I have started at once to read. In the meantime I return in accordance with your injunctions Chapter IX, in the margin of which I have scribbled a few notes.

There is, however, one question of greater importance that I have yet ventured to raise which I want to put to you in this letter and that is whether the telegrams quoted on pages 8 to 12 should be published.

It seems to me that you have quoted either too much or too little and that if too little your explanations are inadequate for the general reader. My own belief is that the general reader will be confirmed by these quotations in the false and distorted impression which the popular press and your political opponents in this country have created that you were struggling to involve the Allies in general and this country in particular in a fresh war in Russia while Lloyd George was pursuing a course of statesmanlike restraint.

Your first point is that whereas there is no inconsistency between your telegrams to the Prime Minister of the 15th and 16th February, there is marked inconsistency between the Prime Minister's two telegrams of the 16th February, but the whole form of your narrative seems to me most unfortunately – and one might almost say unfairly – to suggest a gradual crescendo of effort on your part.[343] At the bottom of page 7 your proposal is that "to the fifty-eight Commissions there might at least be added a fifty-ninth for Russia". At the top of page 8 this proposal is described in greater detail as "the setting up of an Allied Council for Russian Affairs with political, economic and military sections". On page 9 a telegram is quoted suggesting that "suitable machinery should be set up forthwith to consider

[342] This would not have been the first time that Churchill had tried to involve Lloyd George. During the preparation of one of the earlier volumes of *The World Crisis*, Churchill had insisted, while on a train trip, on reading some of his draft chapters to Lloyd George, who had not enjoyed the experience.
[343] It appears that Churchill acted on Sinclair's comments, as the published volume does not contain the telegrams referred to.

the practical possibilities of a joint military action", etc. At the bottom of page 9 in the quotation from your second telegram this proposal appears to be still further strengthened:– "to set up the Military Commission at once to take stock of the whole situation, to prepare a plan of war against the Bolsheviks." Thus what begins with a Commission of the Peace Conference is next described as a Council with political, economic and military sections, then as "suitable machinery", and finally ends up as a Military Commission; and the functions of the body, having first been described at the top of page 8 as those of "inquiry" become at the top of page 9 "to consider the practical possibility of joint military action" and finally at the bottom of page 9 "to prepare a plan of war".

The general reader and the hostile critic will see in this double crescendo of tone sufficient justification for the "very different tone" upon which you comment as distinguishing Lloyd George's second telegram from his first. They will make no allowances for the pressure of events or for the conditions of which the general reader at any rate is wholly ignorant under which telegrams were drafted at the Paris Conference.

Moreover, whereas your telegrams are obviously unstudied in their phraseology and solely concerned with the practical conduct of affairs, Lloyd George's telegrams might have been written with a view to publication, so full are they of unimpeachable aphorisms of statesmanship. I am afraid, however, that these aphorisms will catch the eye and command the ready assent of many a general reader who is perplexed by the intricacies of the situation both in Russia and at the Peace Conference. Lloyd George's telegrams, and especially his second, will seem to him simple, straight-forward and common sense.

Moreover, I cannot help thinking that it must have been the need of removing this false impression and of justifying your apparent opposition to Lloyd George's copy-book maxims which has led you to denounce with a strength of language which strikes me as perhaps a little excessive the policy which the Allies finally did adopt.

For example, at the bottom of page 12 you say "if they were not prepared to take common action it was wanton to continue a disjointed and half-hearted warfare. It would have been wise and merciful to make peace with the Soviets". Again you say at the top of page 13 "the Allies could neither make peace with the Bolsheviks or plan war against them ... so as a compromise they continued to make war unplanned." The whole drift of these passages is that three alternatives confronted the Allies:– war, peace and unplanned war – that there was much to be said for either of the first two alternatives and most to be said for the first but that the third alternative was wanton and foolish. Surely this is not so? Surely we had then definite hopes that with the amount of help which we were giving the Whites they would be able to defeat the Bolsheviks. In the remaining Russian chapter you have passed strong strictures upon the folly and inefficiency of the Whites, and the reader will certainly gain the impression that if they had been better worth their salt there was quite a good chance that they might have pulled through in spite of the indecision of the Big Four. Surely if there had been a proposal to make peace you would have resigned at once? Whereas in point of fact you were responsible for the policy that was finally adopted not only as a Cabinet Minister but most especially for carrying it out as Secretary of State for War, and indeed your later chapter on Russia and your telegrams and speeches quoted in that chapter make it clear that you threw yourself into the prosecution of this policy whole-heartedly.

The point which you make in the last paragraph of the chapter is amply justified and effective, but if the quotations from your telegrams are included the hostile critic would glance back at those telegrams and would find that, whereas the policy suggested in the Allied Note to Kolchak was to supply him and his associates with "munitions, supplies and food", and whereas you consider that would have been an adequate policy if it had been adopted early enough, you were in February proposing "joint military action by the Associated Powers" and of "preparing a plan of war against the Bolsheviks".

Yours,
Archie

The general election of 30 May 1929 saw Sinclair face his first contested election since 1922. He comfortably beat both Conservative and Independent Labour candidates, winning 74 per cent of the vote. In Epping Churchill was comfortably re-elected with a 5,000 vote majority over his Liberal opponent, with Labour a distant third. Nationally, although the Conservatives won the most votes (8.6 million and 260 seats), the Labour Party won most seats (288 with 8.3 million votes). The Liberals saw a huge surge in their total vote (up from 2.9 million in 1924 to 5.3 million) but the return of only 59 MPs. The Liberal Party held the balance of power but Baldwin resigned immediately and Ramsay MacDonald was asked to form a minority government. Neither the Conservative nor Labour leaders made any attempt to agree a deal with Lloyd George to secure office.

The 1929 election was a deep disappointment for the Liberals. Under Lloyd George's leadership, and supported by his fund, the Liberals had developed some highly credible and original policy positions. In the two years prior to the election a string of Liberal policy documents, including the famous 'Yellow Book', *Britain's Industrial Future* and its popular summary, *We Can Conquer Unemployment*, had given the party a new and distinctive voice. There was a genuine expectation that the Liberals could bounce back from the disaster of 1924; much hope was pinned on the recent enfranchisement of the 'flappers' – women aged between 21 and 30 who the Liberals specifically targeted. However, the Liberal vote was spread too evenly across the country, and was not reflected in the number of seats won.

Churchill, removed from his Treasury position by the electorate, was unknowingly starting on his 'wilderness years', and was not to regain office until September 1939. For Sinclair, however, a cabinet-rank ministerial office was just around the corner.

Sir Archibald Sinclair to Winston S. Churchill
Thurso Castle,
Thurso
4th June 1929

Winston,

Thank you so much for your telegram – it gave us both infinite pleasure.

Bluey & I went fishing on the day that intervenes here between the polling & the declaration[344] and when we returned we heard the excellent news of your substantial majority.[345] In the meantime, however, an absurd rumour had insinuated that you had been defeated & Goonie & Marigold were telephoning desperately to get it contradicted. By the time we returned, however, Jack's telegram had been received and Goonie telegraphed to tell you of our rejoicing.

It is a curious stroke of irony that in the first election under universal franchise, it should be the 5½ million Liberal voters who should turn out to be the virtually disfranchised! The choice before the country is clearly between electoral reform and Socialist rule.

Jimmy Maxton's[346] dictum that the Socialists are digging in & are never coming out again, and that effective political discussions will henceforth take place at Labour Conferences, is not quite so silly as it sounds.

People are too apt to assume quite casually & as a matter of course that the Labour Party in office can never hold together. If you crush the Liberal Party & refuse electoral reform & insist on the two-party system, there can be no split – for where would the dissidents go to? The Left Wing will have the moderates at their mercy. Electoral Reform would not only preserve the 5½ million Liberal voters from falling in the massive majority into the lap of the Socialists but would strengthen the position of the Labour moderates against the Socialist extremists and make possible the split which has occurred in every Continental Country between reformist and revolutionary Socialists. I expect we shall have a slow life in the new parliament but you at any rate will have a gay one! Love from us all to you & Clemmie.

Yours always,
Archie

[344] The 1929 general election was held on 30 May, but Sinclair's result was not announced until 1 June.

[345] Churchill 23,972, Liberal 19,005, Labour 6,472.

[346] James Maxton (1885–1946): one of the 'Red Clydeside' leaders; a pacifist, opposed the First World War and imprisoned in 1916–17 for encouraging munitions workers to strike; Independent Labour Party (ILP) MP for Bridgend 1922–46; consistent critic of the Labour leadership and instrumental in persuading the ILP to break away from Labour after MacDonald formed the National Government in 1931; his pacifism led him to support Chamberlain's appeasement policies in the 1930s.

Winston S. Churchill to Sir Archibald Sinclair
Post Office Telegraph
8th June 1929

Sir Archibald Sinclair – Thurso Castle

I hope you are coming south soon – should like to see you. Winston.

1930–1938

Out of office, Churchill had time to write what many consider his most engaging book, *My Early Life* (published in 1930), his autobiography up to 1904.

Sir Archibald Sinclair to Winston S. Churchill
27th October 1930

My dear Winston,

I am indeed proud of and grateful for my author's copy of your thrilling and enchanting autobiography. It proves conclusively what I had long suspected that of all men I know you have the most enviable and enjoyably adventurous life.

We are all reading it with immense delight and real zest – the children loved the description of Harrow and Robin rocked with laughter at the Amery story![347]

We shall be back on Wednesday and I shall hope to see you then. I hope you have good news of Randolph.

Yours ever,
Archie

The future of India was a key political issue throughout the 1930s. The Labour Government favoured the granting of Dominion status; this was supported by the Viceroy, Lord Irwin,[348] who confirmed this as the ultimate goal of British policy in late

[347] An incident at Harrow, when Churchill pushed Leo Amery into the school pool. Leopold Amery (1873–1955): chief correspondent for *The Times* during the Boer War; Conservative MP 1911–45; First Lord of the Admiralty 1922–24, Colonial Secretary 1924–29; remained out of office throughout the 1930s and emerged as one of the leading critics of the National Government's appeasement policy; instrumental in Chamberlain's removal as Prime Minister in May 1940; Secretary of State for India and Burma 1940–45.

[348] Edward Frederick Lindley Wood, Baron Irwin (1925–34), Viscount Halifax (1934–44), 1st Earl of Halifax (1944–59) (1881–1959): Conservative MP for Ripon 1910–25; President of the Board of Education 1922–24; Minister of Agriculture 1924–25; Viceroy of India 1925–31; President of the Board of Education 1932–35; Lord Privy Seal 1935–37; Leader of the House of Lords 1935–38; Lord President

1930. Dominion status was acceptable to many Conservatives but not to a die-hard group on the right wing of the party with whom Churchill aligned himself following his resignation from the Conservative Business Committee (its shadow cabinet) in January 1931. Churchill was hopeful that Lloyd George would join him in opposing Dominion status and thereby begin the process of winning back some of the Conservatives, such as Lord Birkenhead, who had supported the 1918–22 Coalition. But a speech by the Liberal Lord Reading disillusioned him; Churchill realised that the speech would have been sanctioned by Lloyd George as Liberal leader and that while Lloyd George had indeed chosen to oppose the declaration it was on the basis of India not yet being ready for Dominion status rather than on a platform of complete opposition to the principle.

Winston S. Churchill to Sir Archibald Sinclair
Chartwell,
Westerham,
Kent
8th January 1931
Confidential

My dear Archie,

I am delighted to get your letter and long for a talk. Will you not come down here for a night? I shall be here all next week and almost any day could be arranged on the telephone.

I am deeply distressed by Reading's[349] speech on India. It clearly shows that my last despairing hope that we should see again the great Lloyd George come to the aid of our country in its perils, must now die. India and its fortunes must be flung in to the political stewpan. The Tories have definitely accepted the view that he has fixed up with the left and is adjusting his views on every other topic. I cannot gainsay them. I fear the days when you and I will find ourselves together will never come.[350]

I had a long talk with R. on the lines that India would be a bond of unity between the strong war-time forces and might become the means of joint action leading to a satisfactory adjustment in electoral law.[351] Good-bye to all that! I shall

of the Council 1937–38; Foreign Secretary 1938–40, a key architect, with Chamberlain, of appeasement; British ambassador to the United States 1940–46.

349 Rufus Isaacs, Lord Reading (1860–1935): Liberal MP for Reading 1904–13; Attorney-General 1910–13; Lord Chief Justice 1913–21; Viceroy of India, 1921–26; Foreign Secretary for the first three months of MacDonald's National Government in 1931; Leader of the Liberal peers 1931–35.

350 Many in the Conservative Party had feared that Churchill and Birkenhead were in collusion with Lloyd George after 1929 to form a centre-party alternative to Labour. This letter provides some evidence that this was a real possibility being considered by Churchill.

351 There had been much talk of electoral reform during the 1929–31 Parliament, and Lloyd George had been pushing it as the price of Liberal cooperation. The Labour Government brought in a bill to introduce the alternative vote system, but the government fell before it could become law.

fight my corner on India to the end and have very powerful support guaranteed; but the great support I look for will be events.

Yours always,
W

The following note is undated but was probably written in the immediate aftermath of the general election of 27 October 1931, as Churchill refers to it in a later letter sent in December 1931.[352] Headed 'serious and secret', it is a direct appeal to Sinclair to abandon the remains of the old Liberal Party led by Herbert Samuel and to align himself with the Liberal Nationals or Tories such as himself. It is also one of the few personal letters to Sinclair that Churchill signed with his full formal signature rather than his initials, or first name only, perhaps stressing its importance. It says much for Sinclair's commitment to the principles of Liberalism and his belief in the necessity of maintaining an independent Liberal Party that he never accepted Churchill's advice – it must have been tempting for a young politician in a hurry.

The 1931 election returned a massive majority for the National Government.[353] Churchill, however, was not part of the frontbench team; he and Baldwin had become increasingly suspicious of each other and Churchill had alienated himself from the moderate Conservative MPs over his position on India. During the first half of the 1930s, however, he remained optimistic that he would be called on to serve in a cabinet position and he was eager to ensure that Sinclair, who in August 1931 had been appointed Secretary of State for Scotland in the first National Government, should consider his long-term career. Although the number of Liberal MPs had increased at the election, they were split into three groups – the Liberal Nationals led by Sir John Simon, Samuel's Liberal Party (the remnants of the traditional party) and a Lloyd George family group – and their future did not seem bright.

Winston S. Churchill to Sir Archibald Sinclair
Chartwell Manor,
Westerham,
Kent
Undated but probably late October or early November 1931
Serious and Secret

My dear Archie,

If you are ever to realise the extremely kind wishes you express in your letter,[354] you must carefully but ruthlessly detach yourself from the Samuelite group and

[352] The original of this note is badly burnt, so parts may be missing. The intent is, however, evident.
[353] The results in seats were: National Government – Conservative 473, National Labour 13, Liberal Nationals 35, Liberals 33; Opposition – Labour 52, Independent (Lloyd George) Liberals 4, others 5.
[354] Letter missing, but it is likely that Sinclair was reiterating his desire to work alongside Churchill again.

establish solid Tory or Simonite connections. The Samuelites are wilderness headed and there they will [likely] find their friend L.G. [word missing].

Be warned in good faith by your sincere friend.

Winston S. Churchill

In early November 1931 Sinclair, still Secretary of State for Scotland, was promoted to cabinet rank. One of the first people to offer their congratulations was Churchill.

Winston S. Churchill to Sir Archibald Sinclair
Post Office Telegraph, sent from Salzburg
5th November 1931

Sir Archibald Sinclair – Robin Hood Farm – Kingston Vale
I am delighted all has gone well for you my dear friend – Winston

In December 1931, Churchill went on a lucrative speaking tour of the United States. While crossing Fifth Avenue in New York on 13 December, he was knocked down by a car.

Sir Archibald Sinclair to Winston S. Churchill
Robin Hood Farm,
Kingston Vale, S.W.15
Telephone, Kingston 0151
16th December 1931

Winston,

Just a line of condolence on your accident – and of rejoicing that the results are not worse! The newspapers have been alarmist – the noise of your bump has reverberated through every street in Britain! – but Jack[355] rings us up every evening, tells us that the worst news is all bunkum, and gives us cheerful re-assurances.

I only hope you will take it easy for a good long time and chuck the lecture tour altogether.

People are still talking about your speech on India – I wonder if you ever spoke better or presented to the House so massive a structure of agreement in language so refreshingly clear and caustically and effectively eloquent.[356] At any rate it was the

[355] John Strange Spencer Churchill (1880–1947): Winston's younger brother; stockbroker; served in both the Boer War and First World War, where he fought in France and Gallipoli.

[356] On 3 December 1931, in a debate on government policy on India, Churchill had spoken passionately in opposition to the policy of moving India towards Dominion status and self-governance.

first time I had ever heard a speaker called upon by the applause of the House to continue after an hour and twenty minutes! All your friends are jubilant.

Meanwhile, the National Government continues its majestic, toilsome but exciting progress. Like a charabanc without brakes, we go tearing round awkward corners but we cling patriotically to our seats & none of us has been flung out yet!

With love from us both to you & Clemmie & Diana, and hoping you will soon be safe back home again.

Yours always,
Archie

Winston S. Churchill to Sir Archibald Sinclair
The Waldorf Hotel,
New York
30th December 1931

My dear Archie,

Your letter has just arrived and it is very welcome. I had a terrible bump, and how I was not squashed or shattered I cannot imagine. I was also very lucky in escaping the wheels, which only went over and broke the tips of my toes. I am now quite sound, but very weak, and am off to Nassau in one of those gigantic liners for ten days' sunshine. I hope this will enable me to discharge my lecture tour which now begins on January 14th.

I have two lectures: The Pathway of the English Speaking Peoples,[357] and The Economic Crisis[358] – the latter on the 18th of January, to the New York Economic Club, will make a stir.

The cruel and criminal deflation of commodities and services which has characterized the last two years, and the artificial enhancement of gold, will receive my outspoken condemnation.

There is great bewilderment and depression in this country. The government has largely ceased to function; it merely makes grimaces and gestures, but as for grasping the realities, it shows itself quite incapable. I do hope this disease will not spread

[357] In this lecture Churchill warned that 'England and America are going in the same direction. They have the same outlook and no common discords … remember, I beg you, that, vast as our resources are, there is another power coming into being which makes its appeal to certain classes in all countries and which has its agents in all countries. I mean the force of international communism.' Robert Rhodes James (ed.), *Winston S. Churchill, His Complete Speeches*, Volume 5 (Chelsea House, 1974), pp. 5129–30.

[358] In this second lecture, Churchill asserted that although Germany could not afford to pay reparations now that did not mean that that its debts should be repudiated. He went on to comment on the impacts of deflation, warning that if it continued it would isolate nations as if they were in medieval times and would reduce 'this fair modern world with all its knowledge and science and measureless possibilities to the barbarism and barter of the Dark Ages'. Robert Rhodes James (ed.), *Winston S. Churchill, His Complete Speeches*, Volume 5 (Chelsea House, 1974), pp. 5132–33.

across the Atlantic to the National administration upon which all our hopes are centred.

I do not think I shall be back much before the Budget, when I have a long account to settle with the late financial administration.

I hope you are enjoying your office and taking great pains with your work, and that you will always bear in mind the advice I gave you in the "ruthless letter" I wrote you some time ago,[359] so that when the sheep are parted from the goats you may gambol safely with the righteous.

I rather like the look of things in India. The late Lord Salisbury said, quoting an American, there were two ways of governing men – 'bamboozle or bamboo'. You seem to be trying both at once. I hope that you will be effective.

Yours ever,
W

Winston S. Churchill to Sir Archibald Sinclair
Post Office Telegraph
6th August 1932

Sir Archibald Sinclair – Dalnawillan

Hope you will dine with me at Claridges – 8.15pm August 24th to meet Mr. Bernard Baruch.[360]

Winston Churchill – Chartwell

Sir Archibald Sinclair to Winston S. Churchill
Post Office Telegraph
24th August 1932[361]

Winston Churchill – Chartwell

Have to be in London on Saturday – could I come down Chartwell Sunday?

Sir Archibald Sinclair – Dalnawillan

Winston S. Churchill to Sir Archibald Sinclair
Post Office Telegraph
25th August 1932

Sir Archibald Sinclair – Dalnawillan

359 See letter headed 'Serious and Secret', end October 1931 (page 196).

360 Bernard Mannes Baruch (1870–1965): Wall Street financier and economic advisor to US Presidents Wilson, Roosevelt and Truman.

361 The actual telegram is undated but it is likely that it was sent the day before Churchill's reply on 25th August.

So grieved – we are all going abroad Saturday morning.[362] How nice of you to have suggested coming.

Winston

During the summer of 1932 the position of the Liberal ministers in the National Government became increasingly untenable. With their principled support for free trade at odds with the National Government's policy of protectionism – which was agreed at the Imperial Economic Conference in Ottawa in July – it became inevitable that a break would occur. Senior members of the Liberal parliamentary party met at Sinclair's Scottish estate on 9 September and resolved to quit the government. Churchill was deeply opposed to this action, arguing that swallowing protection was a small price to pay compared to leaving government and losing office after such a short period of service, when a ministerial reputation had not been fully made. Churchill sent this telegram in a desperate bid to halt the inevitable. The Liberal ministers resigned from the government on 28 September.

Winston S. Churchill to Sir Archibald Sinclair
Post Office Telegraph sent from Salzburg
22nd September 1932

Sir Archibald Sinclair – Scottish Office – London
On no account now – Winston.

Winston S. Churchill to Sir Archibald Sinclair
Chartwell,
Westerham,
Kent
September 1932

My dear Archie,

How charming of you to write to me like that![363] Your friendship is very dear to me, and I wish we saw more of each other now-a-days. I am so sorry that you are not now in Government. It would be to me the best justification for its existence. But you have won yourself a very nice dignified position outside, and have established your rank and rights in the House.[364]

[362] The Churchill family left Dover for Calais to tour the battlefields of Flanders and the Low Countries. This tour was part of the research behind the biography that Churchill was writing of his illustrious ancestor, John Churchill, 1st Duke of Marlborough (1650–1722). The party went on to tour Blenheim, where Churchill was taken ill with paratyphoid fever. He had to stay in a sanatorium in Salzburg, Austria, until the end of September 1932.
[363] Letter not found.

I wish I could see prospects of our being together. Still one must always have room for the unexpected.

I send you herewith a copy of Marlborough: it is not published until Oct. 6th so keep it under your control.[365]

With best love,
Yours always,
W

Sir Archibald Sinclair to Winston S. Churchill
Dalnawillan,
Altabreac,
Caithness
15th October 1933

My dear Winston,

I was so grateful to you for your letter and particularly when you said that you were sending 'herewith' a copy of Marlborough. But alas! He never arrived – and here I am like William III down in Devon (or was it Cornwall?) wondering whether he really is coming! I waited because I hated worrying you about the fulfilment of so generous and welcome a promise – but now that the time of publication has passed I feel I must let know lest he has gone astray. I read many – if not all – of the "Sunday Times" extracts and I am longing for the book.

With love from us both to you and Clemmie.
Yours always,
Archie

In spring 1934 Churchill became caught up in controversy over the Committee of Privileges. From March 1934 accusations had spread that Sir Samuel Hoare, the Secretary of State for India, and Lord Derby, the former Secretary of State for War, had abused their position on the Joint Select Committee on Indian Constitutional Reform to persuade the Manchester Chamber of Commerce to change their evidence to the Committee to be more favourable to the government's proposals. The Chamber of Commerce had originally opposed the proposed changes to the Indian constitution, arguing that it would allow the Indian finance minister to impose import duties on cotton goods from Lancashire. At the Select Committee however, the Chamber of Commerce had not objected to the proposals.

[364] Sinclair had been appointed a Privy Counsellor in November 1931, and could therefore expect to be given priority in being called to speak from the opposition benches by the Speaker.
[365] Volume One of *Marlborough* was published in October 1933. Within a week it had sold 8,500 copies and had helped Churchill reduce a bank overdraft of £9,500.

Churchill, who was virulently opposed to the Indian measures, saw this as an opportunity to embarrass the government. He accused Hoare of tampering with evidence, but the report of the Committee of Privileges, published on 6 June, found that there had been no breach of privilege. The House of Commons debated the report on 13 June, and Churchill spoke for an hour with great anger and sarcasm about the work of the committee, claiming that both Derby and Hoare had completely misrepresented the facts. His speech was very badly received and Sinclair felt the necessity to write to Churchill to advise him of what was being said about his intervention.

Sir Archibald Sinclair to Winston S. Churchill
18th June 1934
PERSONAL AND CONFIDENTIAL

My dear Winston,

I am writing in case you may be interested in a few impressions which I have gathered from other people about the debate on the Committee of Privileges.

Nearly everybody I met was talking about it on Thursday and Friday and most people, including Hutchison[366] and Reading strongly condemned your line as ill-advised and mischievous. On Friday night I met Simon[367] at a dinner given by the Belgian Mission and he came and talked to me afterwards, starting on his own account to express regret about the line which you took in the debate. He considered that it could do nothing but harm alike to your own and to the public interest. He then proceeded to make it absolutely clear to me that no new factors had emerged to make the Simon Report[368] obsolete and that he gravely doubted the feasibility of Federation and seemed to regard the prospect of a genuine co-operation from the Princes as illusory. In short, the impression which I gained from my conversation with him was that he regarded your agitation as mischievous in method and premature in time, but a good deal more formidable than he would have cared to admit.

All this was much as I would have expected, and my first surprise was when I called in on your old enemy Snowden[369] on my way back from the country yesterday afternoon. I had been having a long talk with him on other matters when all

[366] Robert Hutchison (1873–1950): Liberal, then Liberal National MP 1922–32; created Baron 1932; Paymaster-General 1935–38 and leading Liberal National in the Lords.

[367] Sir John Simon – see n130.

[368] Sir John Simon's report of 1930 had ruled out parliamentary government for India, because of the fear of discrimination against the Moslem minority by the Hindu majority, but held open the possibility of granting India some measure of independence, which was the essence of Dominion status.

[369] Philip Snowden, 1st Viscount Snowden (1864–1937): originally a Liberal but an early convert to the Independent Labour Party; Labour MP for Blackburn 1906–18, Colne Valley 1922–31; Chancellor of the Exchequer in both the first and second Labour Governments (1924 and 1929–31); followed MacDonald in the National Government where, as Chancellor, he introduced measures including a reduction in unemployment pay; ennobled 1931; Lord Privy Seal, 1931–32.

of a sudden he declared quite of his own accord that he thought that you had had a pretty rough deal from the Committee of Privileges. He made it clear that he was still a convinced supporter of the White Paper[370] but he agreed that the course of the debate had been most unlucky for you and he saw clearly that the House had failed to appreciate the significance of the omissions in the Report of the Committee. He was definitely of the opinion that a breach of privilege had been committed.

Of course I know that you will be receiving much more valuable information than this from a great many sources but I thought it might interest you.

By the bye you seemed to be interested to hear about Bruning[371] the other day. I do not know if he is still in London. Would you care to come and meet him if I can get hold of him? If so give me a choice of dates for lunch.

Yours ever,
Archie

Winston S. Churchill to Sir Archibald Sinclair
Post Office Telegraph
22nd June 1934

Thank you so much for your letter.

Winston
22.6.34

Sir Archibald Sinclair to Winston S. Churchill
1, Thorney Court,
Kensington, W.8
3rd July 1934

My dear Winston,

I knew the Duke of Marlborough, who often showed me kindness and friendship, just well enough to appreciate your noble, moving and truthful tribute to him in today's Times.[372]

[370] The Government's white paper on India suggested that the elected provincial governments should take over all provincial affairs, and that ministerial responsibility for some central government affairs could also be given to elected representatives, but that others (notably defence and foreign affairs) should remain in the hands of the Viceroy.

[371] Probably Heinrich Brüning (1885–1970): German statesman and fiscal expert; Leader of the Catholic Centre Party from 1929; in 1930 appointed Chancellor to put German finances in order, but his drastic deflationary measures were unpopular, and he was forced to resign in 1932 by President Hindenburg; left Germany in 1934 and became a member of the faculty at Harvard 1937–52.

[372] Churchill's cousin, 'Sunny', the 9th Duke of Marlborough, died on 30 June 1934.

I think much of you in your sorrow at losing so suddenly a friend and kinsman who was so dear to you. You are surrounded by devoted friends but none, I know, can replace the two whom you have so recently lost.[373]

Yours always,
Archie

Winston S. Churchill to Sir Archibald Sinclair
Post Office Telegraph
4th July 1934

Thank you so much dear Archie, Winston

On 14 March 1935, a major debate concerning the Naval Supply Estimates took place in the House of Commons. The proposed increase in spending was opposed by both the Labour and Liberal Parties, and Sinclair made a lengthy speech attacking the government's policy, arguing that over £660 million had been spent over the proceeding ten years for little value and uncertain security benefit. Concluding his attack, Sinclair argued that 'in the absence of any clear relation between this country's armament policy and a policy for a collective system, we on these benches will feel bound by speech and vote to do all in our power to deflect the Government's policy from its present dangerous and wasteful course.'[374] The Liberal Party was keen to see the Government move to a defence policy more reliant on the collective security offered by the League of Nations. The day after this debate Churchill passed this note to Sinclair (after they had voted in opposite division lobbies). He was evidently unconvinced by Sinclair's argument, though impressed by its delivery. Churchill himself did not speak in the debate.

Winston S. Churchill to Sir Archibald Sinclair
House of Commons note paper
15th March 1935

Archie,
Manner: Admirable
Argument: False
Purpose: Morbid
Consequences: Fatal

W

[373] The other death alluded to is that of Lord Birkenhead (F. E. Smith) in 1930.
[374] *Hansard*, 14 March 1935, col. 612.

To which Sinclair replied in kind:

Dear Winston,

Any notice from you, however equivocal, is eagerly welcomed by your old disciple and devoted friend but:–

Manner – Rot
Argument – Do think it over – surely better than you admit and not wholly separated from your own
Purpose – Misjudged
Consequence – Kismet[375]

Yours,
A

Sir Archibald Sinclair to Winston S. Churchill
1, Thorney Court,
Kensington, W. 8
29th January 1935

My dear Winston,

Many thanks for your telegram. I am so much looking forward to seeing you to-morrow night.

I hope you have good news from Randolph.[376] There is at least one in the ranks of Tuscany who would not forbear to cheer the success of his audacity!

Yours always,
Archie

Winston S. Churchill to Sir Archibald Sinclair
Post Office Telegraph
16th February 1935

Thank you so much for the lovely salmon you have sent me which has arrived at Chartwell today.

[375] Fate, or destiny (originally 'the will of Allah').

[376] Winston Churchill's son Randolph stood as an anti-India Bill Conservative candidate in the Wavertree by-election on 6 February 1935, even though an official Conservative had already been selected. Churchill was furious with his son for acting without consultation, but did go and speak for him at campaign meetings. Randolph lost, but polled enough votes to let the Labour candidate in.

Sir Archibald Sinclair to Winston S. Churchill
Post Office Telegraph
27th April 1935

Many thanks for telegram. Am sending for paper. Robin has caught his first fish an eighteen pounder. Love from us all – Archie

Winston S. Churchill to Sir Archibald Sinclair
2nd July 1935

My dear Archie,

The death of Geoffrey Howard robs Clemmie and me of one of our two surviving trustees, Jack being the only one left. I should be very grateful if you would step into the vacant place. I do not think you would find the duties very onerous, but I should like it very much if you could assume them, such as they are.[377]

Yours,
Winston

Sir Archibald Sinclair to Winston S. Churchill
1, Thorney Court,
Kensington, W.8
4th July 1935

My dear Winston,

You are my chief creditor and, if I could feel that I was re-paying a tiny fraction of my debt by acting as Trustee to you and Clemmie, I should gladly embrace the opportunity. It is rather because I am grateful for this fresh proof of your trust and friendship that I gladly accept your invitation.

Yours always,
Archie

Churchill replied by telegram: 'Thank you so much – Winston'.

In September and October 1935 Churchill made a series of speeches attacking Britain's lack of preparedness regarding its air and naval defence capabilities. He savaged a recently published Air Ministry paper for minimising German air strength and argued that it would be dangerous to trust its conclusions.

[377] Winston and Clementine Churchill had established a trust fund to provide for their children in the event of either of their deaths. Sinclair was to serve as a trustee of the fund until it was wound up in the 1950s.

Sir Archibald Sinclair to Winston S. Churchill
Dalnawillan,
Altnabreac,
Caithness
13th October 1935

My dear Winston,

Thank you so much for asking me to your dinner party on the 28th but, as Marigold telegraphed to you, I shall have to return here after the big debate[378] next week and fulfil a number of engagements – some arranged long since and others postponed from next week on account of the meeting of Parliament. I am very much vexed and disappointed not to be able to accept.

I have read your speeches not with complete agreement but with immense admiration and with whole-hearted delight at seeing your stock soaring! But a November election would be a rotten trick to play particularly on the Labour Party which has compromised its position as the peace party and shed its leader[379] in order to support the Government's policy. There is something incongruous in the Govt. using the whole power of its machine to secure the re-election of Leo Amery and his fifty supporters who have declared against the Govt's [foreign] policy on the main issue before the country and to defeat Liberal and Labour candidates who are supporting it!

Hoping to see you next week,

Yours,
Archie

The general election of 1935 saw a further fall in the Liberal performance. From a minimal base of 161 candidates, 21 MPs were returned and the party's leader, Sir Herbert Samuel, lost his seat. (The parties supporting the National Government won 432 seats and Labour 154.) In the aftermath Sinclair was elected to the leadership of the Parliamentary Liberal Party, in part because of the recommendation of David Lloyd George.

[378] On 24 October 1935 the House of Commons debated the international situation, and in particular the threat posed by German rearmament and the Italian invasion of Abyssinia earlier that month.
[379] In October 1935 George Lansbury, Labour leader since the debacle of the 1931 election had seen all the other Labour cabinet ministers lose their seats, announced his retirement after mounting dissatisfaction with his pacifist approach to foreign policy (including refusing to support the possibility of military action by the League of Nations against Italy). His successor, Clement Attlee, moved the party towards support for rearmament.

Sir Archibald Sinclair to Winston S. Churchill
Dalnawillan,
Altnabreac,
Caithness
10th October 1937

My dear Winston,

Of all the people to whom you send your books I am probably the least distinguished but, by the same token, the most appreciative. Thank you so much, dear Winston, – and this is a grand book![380]

Of course the thing that pleases me most is to find (to my astonishment!) that you haven't forgotten that morning (7 a.m!) at Shoreham when I introduced you to my round machine – and I can still feel my bitter disappointment there was just too much wind to fly it![381]

Of course, I was delighted, too, that you included Savinkov. Do you remember the story of him following the man in Brussels? He grew more & more certain that it was Azeff[382] – his height, his build, the peculiarity of his walk – and then, just as he was drawing his revolver, the man turned round – a stranger!

You scored a big triumph at Scarborough[383] – but I was glad to observe that one little epigram of criticism "so-called"! An Italian "Spain" would weigh himself in the balance of power against all the ships, guns & aeroplanes which we shall be turning out during the next few months.

Our maternal cousins[384] are waking up. Pittman's[385] support is most re-assuring. Wilson had the Republicans against him & the Senate Foreign Affairs Cttee, but Roosevelt is supported by both Pittman & Stimson.[386] Simon rebuffed Stimson (not indefinitely) over Manchuria; S.B. & Sam Hoare failed to improve the oil sanction in the Abyssinian dispute when Roosevelt was moving in Congress to obtain powers to co-operate; Hull[387] pleads in vain for a commercial treaty; don't let Neville

---

380 *Great Contemporaries*, published in 1937.

381 On page 83 of *Great Contemporaries* (Thornton Butterworth, 1937), Churchill wrote: 'I remember that we [General Sir John French and Churchill] scrambled ashore from a picket-boat before daybreak one morning to watch the first trials of a circular aeroplane upon which a young friend of mine, Sir Archibald Sinclair, had spent a great deal of money.' Sinclair's plane was an early design where the wings formed a circle around the main fuselage; it did not prove popular.

382 Yevno Azeff (1869–1925): Russian Socialist Revolutionary, subsequently discovered to have been a Russian police informer.

383 Where the Conservative Conference was held that year; Churchill's conference speech praised the Foreign Secretary Anthony Eden's achievement in setting up firm Anglo-French resistance to Italian naval piracy.

384 Both Churchill and Sinclair had American mothers.

385 Key Pittman (1872–1940): US politician and Democratic Senator 1913–40.

386 Henry Lewis Stimson (1867–1930): US statesman (Republican), served in the administrations of five US Presidents from 1911 to 1945; Secretary of War 1911–13; Secretary of State 1929–33, when he denounced Japanese aggression in Manchuria (the 'Stimson Doctrine'); Secretary of War 1940–45.

387 Cordell Hull (1871–1955): Democratic member of the House of Representatives 1907–21, 1923–31,

fail to respond to this latest & most important advance from Roosevelt, Pittman & Stimson.

Please give my love to Clemmie & Mary.[388]

Archie

Sir Archibald Sinclair to Winston S. Churchill
1, Thorney Court,
Kensington
30th March 1938

Dear Winston,

I enclose a document which was handed to me by one of the Secretaries of the Spanish Embassy. He assures me that the information which it contains has been carefully checked, and you will see that it indicates that batteries of guns – some of large calibre – have been placed at various places of importance on the coasts of Spain and that some have been placed on that stretch of the Moroccan Coast where fortifications are forbidden by the 1912 Treaty.[389]

Yours ever,
Archie

Winston S. Churchill to Sir Archibald Sinclair
Chartwell
1st April 1938

Dear Archie,

Thank you so much. I have ventured to send your enclosure to the War Office, as I think we ought to hear what they say about it.

W

Senate 1931–33; Secretary of State 1933–44; awarded Nobel Peace Prize in 1945 for his part in establishing the United Nations.

[388] Mary Churchill (Lady Mary Soames) (1922–): the Churchills' youngest child; served in Auxiliary Territorial Service with various anti-aircraft battery units 1941–45, though also travelled extensively with her father from 1943 until the end of the war; married Christopher Soames 1947; Chair of the Trustees of the Winston Churchill Memorial Trust since 1991; author of a number of books, including an award-winning biography of her mother.

[389] Since the fifteenth century the Spanish and French had vied for control and influence along the North African coast. At the end of the nineteenth century, the French occupied Morocco and in 1912, under the Treaty of Fez, the country was put under the control of a French Resident-General; Spanish interests, principally in the form of the enclaves of Ceuta and Melilla, were guaranteed. Morocco achieved independence in 1956, although Spain retained (and still retains) Ceuta and Melilla.

The War Minister, Leslie Hore-Belisha, brushed the report aside, claiming the information in the document did not entirely agree with the information at the disposal of the War Office. He also claimed that the source of the document could not be described as either disinterested or unbiased. Churchill wrote back to Hore-Belisha on 12 April saying that surely the point was not whether the source was disinterested or unbiased but whether the information was true and, if it was true, it raised serious issues which the British Government should deal with as part of its international responsibilities.

Sir Archibald Sinclair to Winston S. Churchill
1, Thorney Court
2nd February 1939

Dear Winston,

I enclose some letters which have passed between Admiral Sir Barry Domvile[390] and me as they refer to you.

Yours ever,
Archie

Winston S. Churchill to Sir Archibald Sinclair
Chartwell
3rd February 1939

Dear Archie,

Many thanks for sending me your correspondence with Domvile, and I am much obliged to you for standing up for me. I have certainly, to the best of my recollection, never referred to Hitler as a gangster, though I think I might easily have done so with great truth. If you think it worth while to use more powder and shot upon him, you should ask him for his references.

L.G., dining with me the other night, said he thought your last speech was the most powerful he had ever heard you deliver. He spoke with deep appreciation of your work. He thought the peroration was a little bit dragged in, instead of arising naturally out of it, but he was remarkably impressed by the cogency and solidity of your argument, and also by its delivery. I thought you would like to know this.

Yours,
W

[390] Admiral Sir Barry Edward Domvile (1878–1971): Director of Naval Intelligence 1927–30; Commander 3 Cruiser Squadron, Mediterranean, 1931–32; President, Royal Naval College Greenwich and commander Royal Naval War College 1932–34; retired 1936.

Sir Archibald Sinclair to Winston S. Churchill
1, Thorney Court
14th February 1939

My dear Winston,

Philip Baker[391] tells me that he has written to you asking you to lunch at the House of Commons on Monday to meet a number of French Deputies, including Paul-Boncour[392] and Grumbach,[393] the Chairman of the Foreign Affairs Committee of the Chamber. He is very anxious that you should come and meet them as he knows that they are particularly hoping to be able to see you. Among the others who are likely to be present are Lord Cecil,[394] Lord Lytton[395] and Harold Nicolson.[396]

Yours ever,
Archie

Sir Archibald Sinclair to Winston S. Churchill
1, Thorney Court
10th July 1939
Personal and Confidential

My dear Winston,

You and I are agreed that Parliament ought not in the present critical situation[397] to rise at the end of this, or at the beginning of next month for a prolonged recess

[391] Philip Noel-Baker, Lord Noel-Baker (1889–1982): commanded Quaker ambulance unit in First World War; Professor of International Relations, London University 1924–29; Labour MP for Coventry 1929–31, Derby 1936–50, Derby South 1950–70; Parliamentary Secretary to the Minister of War Transport 1942–45; Secretary of State for Air 1946–47; entered the cabinet as Secretary of State for Commonwealth Relations 1947–50; demoted to Minister of Fuel and Power 1950–51; awarded Nobel Peace Prize in 1959 for his work on arms control and the regulation of conflict; ennobled 1977; Megan Lloyd George's lover from 1938.

[392] Joseph Paul-Boncour (1873–1972): Prime Minister of France 1932–33; Permanent Delegate to the League of Nations 1932–36; Foreign Minister 1936–38; represented France at the San Francisco Conference which established the United Nations Charter in 1945.

[393] Jacques Grumbach (dates unknown): member Administrative Commission of French Socialist Party; editor of French newspaper *Populaire.*

[394] Lord Hugh Richard Heathcote Gascoyne Cecil (1869–1956): Conservative MP for Greenwich 1895–1906, Oxford University 1910–37; created Baron Quickswood 1941; best man at Churchill's wedding in 1908.

[395] Victor Alexander George Lytton, 2nd Earl of Lytton (1876–1947): Civil Lord of the Admiralty, 1916, 1919–20; Under-Secretary of State for India 1920–22; Governor of Bengal 1922–27; Head of League of Nations Mission to Manchuria 1932.

[396] Sir Harold George Nicolson (1886–1968): diplomat; journalist; active in Mosley's New Party 1931–32; National Labour MP for Leicester West 1935–45; Parliamentary Secretary, Ministry of Information 1940–41; author and biographer; his *Diaries and Letters* (Nigel Nicolson (ed.), Collins, 1971) are an invaluable source of information about political life between the wars.

[397] Following the German occupation of Czechoslovakia on 15 March 1939, on 31 March the Anglo-

unless some means can be devised for maintaining touch between Ministers and members of all parties in the House of Commons. Moreover, if the situation gets worse during the recess, if there is a public demand for the meeting of Parliament, and if members of Parliament who are closely in touch with the situation sympathise with the demand, there ought to be some simple kind of machinery to enable consultations between Ministers and such members to take place.

You asked me to suggest a plan. My proposal is as follows:

(a) All Privy Councillors who have been Cabinet Ministers to be invited by the Prime Minister to hold themselves in readiness for consultation during the Recess.

N.B. 1. No formal appointment of a Committee by the House of Commons.

2. Of the ex-Cabinet Ministers five are Conservative, of whom only one (Sir John Gilmour[398]) was pro-Munich, nine are Socialists (including Attlee who as a matter of fact was never in a Cabinet); and two (Ll.G and me) are Liberals.

3. The total number of ex-Cabinet Ministers is sixteen, so that in the event of a meeting with the Prime Minister and five or six other Ministers responsible for Foreign Affairs and Defence, the number present would be about the same as the membership of the Cabinet.

(b) It would be understood that meetings would be arranged by the Prime Minister either on his own initiative or on that of the Leader of the Opposition or of any three or four of the members of the panel.

(c) If the object of a meeting was to persuade the Prime Minister to ask the Speaker to re-call the House of Commons three things might happen:–

Either (i) The Prime Minister might consent to make the request to the Speaker;

(ii) The Prime Minister might convince those who were present that it would be inadvisable or untimely to recall Parliament;

(iii) The Prime Minister might refuse to make the request to the Speaker, but others might remain convinced that Parliament ought to meet. In such circumstances agreement would probably be reached to meet again within a few days, and meanwhile everybody present, while bound by the obligation of secrecy in regard to everything that had

French guarantee to Poland was announced, followed in April by guarantees to Romania and Greece. In May the 'Pact of Steel' was formed between Germany and Italy. During June and July it became apparent to many British politicians that the country stood on the verge of war and Sinclair argued in Parliament that Britain should agree a pact with the Soviet Union if the commitment to Poland was to be achievable. In August, however, the Nazi–Soviet non-aggression pact was announced; it contained secret clauses agreeing to the partition of Poland.

[398] Sir John Gilmour (1876–1940): Conservative MP for East Renfrewshire 1910–18, Glasgow Pollock 1918–40; Secretary of State for Scotland 1926–29; Minister for Agriculture and Fisheries 1931–32; Home Secretary 1932–35; Minister for Shipping 1939–40.

passed at the meeting, would remain free to say what he thought about recalling Parliament.

N.B. In no case would any vote be taken, and the Prime Minister would of course be free to bring to the meeting as many Ministers and others as he wished.

I attach a list of Privy Councillors in the House of Commons who are not at present members of the Government, distinguishing between those who have, and those who have not, been members of Cabinet.

Do let me know what you think of this proposal. I have framed it on the assumption that if it was pressed upon the Prime Minister by you, Greenwood,[399] Eden,[400] Lloyd George and me, he would accept it. No other assumption seems worth considering because the House would not at present adopt this or any similar proposal if he asked them to reject it. On the other hand, he would probably hesitate to strain the loyalty of his followers by rejecting a practicable plan for removing a probable source of public anxiety in August and September.

Yours ever,
Archie

[399] Arthur Greenwood (1880–1954): Labour MP for Nelson & Colne 1922–31, Wakefield 1932–50; Minister of Health 1929–31; Deputy Leader of the Labour Party 1935–43; Minister without Portfolio, War Cabinet 1940–43; acting leader of the Labour Party in the Commons 1943–45; Lord Privy Seal 1945–46; Paymaster General 1946–47; Minister without Portfolio 1947.

[400] Sir Robert Anthony Eden, 1st Earl of Avon (1897–1977): Conservative MP for Warwick & Leamington 1923–57; Parliamentary Under-Secretary, Foreign Office, 1931–33; Lord Privy Seal 1934–35; Minister for League of Nations Affairs 1935; Foreign Secretary 1935–38; resigned over appeasement; Secretary of State for Dominions 1939–40; Secretary of State for War 1940; Foreign Secretary 1940–45 and 1951–55; Prime Minister 1955-57, resigned after Suez debacle; created Earl of Avon 1961.

Part 4

Winning the Air War 1940–1945

Introduction

At the outbreak of war in September 1939 Neville Chamberlain invited Sinclair to accept office on behalf of the Liberals. Sinclair declined the offer in part because of his mistrust of Chamberlain but also because it did not include a seat in the War Cabinet. Sinclair and Lloyd George both urged Churchill not to accept office under Chamberlain, but their advice was ignored and Churchill returned to the Admiralty, as First Lord, on 3 September 1939.

During the 'Phoney War', from September 1939 to April 1940, Chamberlain claimed that 'Hitler had missed the bus' by hesitating to follow through in the west on his dramatic victory in Poland. This complacent attitude, combined with the military ineptitude shown in the Norway campaign in April 1940, for which Churchill should shoulder significant blame, led to a critical Commons debate on 7–8 May 1940. Sinclair joined with Attlee, Lloyd George, Amery and others in telling Chamberlain to go. There was some gleeful spite in the speeches, although every Opposition speaker professed to be performing a painful public duty. Sinclair told the House of Commons that 'Parliament must speak out today, and tomorrow. It must say that we must have done with half-measures. Let us insist upon and rally to a policy of the more vigorous conduct of the war.' With the Government's majority dramatically cut after more than seventy Tory MPs either abstained or voted with the Opposition, Chamberlain realised that he had lost the confidence of too many in his party and decided to resign as Prime Minister, though he retained the position of Leader of the Conservative Party, hoping (as he admitted in his diaries) to return for a second premiership at a later date.

On 10 May 1940 Churchill became Prime Minister. He appointed Sinclair Secretary of State for Air; other appointments to the defence departments included Anthony Eden (Conservative) as Minister for War and A. V. Alexander (Labour) as First Lord of the Admiralty. Sinclair was left out of the War Cabinet, however, which caused the Parliamentary Liberal Party great concern. As a result, on 11 May Churchill offered Sinclair a partial compromise, proposing that he should join the War Cabinet when matters of major political importance were discussed. In practice Sinclair attended the vast majority of War Cabinet meetings and was also a key member of the important Defence Committee (Supply), where the majority of strategic decisions were taken.

The Liberal Party was also granted two other ministerial positions in the Coalition. Sinclair's and Churchill's friend Harcourt Johnstone[401] was appointed to the position

---

[401] Harcourt 'Crinks' Johnstone (1895–1945): Liberal MP for Willesden East 1923–24, South Shields

of Secretary of Overseas Trade, reporting to both the Foreign Secretary and Minister of Economic Warfare, while Dingle Foot,[402] brother of Michael, was appointed Parliamentary Secretary at the Ministry of Economic Warfare.[403] This was, as Churchill was to point out, 'a lot of sail' for a small ship of twenty-one MPs to carry.

At the start of his appointment Sinclair had little grasp of the technical considerations that governed the management and deployment of a modern air force. However, he was a diligent, hard-working and detail-conscious Secretary of State for Air, who quickly mastered his brief and won the respect of his service chiefs and junior ministers. As Harold Balfour, Under-Secretary of State at the Air Ministry, wrote: 'When Archibald Sinclair was made Secretary of State for Air it turned out to be a very happy day for me. Archie was a grand fellow; the soul of honour, brave, kind and considerate.'[404] Charles Portal, Chief of Air Staff from October 1940 until the end of the war, regarded Sinclair as a very good Minister who combined hard work, considerable ability, personal agreeability and a genuine devotion to the Air Ministry.

Close study of the archives at Churchill College, Cambridge and at the National Archives at Kew provide strong evidence that Sinclair was a more significant influence on strategy and decision-making than he has been given credit for in many histories of the period, including, indeed, Churchill's own war memoirs. There are a number of instances where Sinclair, aided by his senior staff, stood up to Churchill and won the argument – not something that can be said of many members of the Coalition Government between 1940 and 1945.

Following the German attack on the Low Countries and France in May 1940, the choice for the Air Ministry lay between attacking Germany and the German forward armies or retaining strength to defend the United Kingdom. Sinclair and Dowding, Commander-in-Chief of Fighter Command, explained to the War Cabinet on 13 May that sixty squadrons were needed for the defence of Britain: only thirty-nine were in being, and they were therefore opposed to any further dispersal of fighters outside home borders, especially in France. Although this plan was unpopular with Churchill, Sinclair and

---

1931–35, Middlesbrough West 1940–45; member of the Other Club (see n710) and opponent of appeasement; a wealthy bachelor and great friend of both Sinclair and Churchill, he was mainly responsible, along with fellow Liberal MP Jimmy de Rothschild, for keeping the Liberal Party afloat financially during the 1930s; Secretary of Overseas Trade 1940–45 – not a great success as a minister, but in fine Liberal tradition he pushed a post-war free trade agenda during his time in government.

[402] Sir Dingle Mackintosh Foot (1905–78): Liberal MP 1931–45; Parliamentary Secretary, Ministry of Economic Warfare 1940–45; Labour MP 1957–70; Solicitor-General 1964–67; a member of the Foot political dynasty (son of Isaac, brother of Michael), Foot was acknowledged by all parties as a great success at the Ministry of Economic Warfare.

[403] Lloyd George's son Gwilym was also in the government at the Board of Trade but he could only nominally be regarded as a Liberal MP. He operated independently of the formal whip and joined the Government in 1939, when Sinclair refused, and remained in the Government after May 1945, when the other Liberal MPs resigned. He went on to serve as a Conservative Home Secretary in both Churchill's and Eden's administrations in the 1950s.

[404] Harold Balfour, *Wings over Westminster* (Hutchinson, 1973), p. 121.

Sir Cyril Newall, the Chief of the Air Staff, gave full support to Dowding's pleas to stop the dissipation of his valuable fighter squadrons.[405]

With the fall of France in June, Britain stood alone against Nazi Germany. If there was to be any offensive initiatives taken against the enemy it would be the RAF which would provide the means of delivery. Owing to the vulnerability of the RAF's bombers in daylight operations, however, Sinclair argued for the option of night-time bombing. He proposed that the targets should include rail marshalling yards, oil refineries, industry in the Ruhr valley, the oil stores of Leipzig and the docks of Bremen and Hamburg. In this he was enthusiastically supported by Newall, Dowding and Portal, Commander in Chief of Bomber Command. Bombing raids were mounted on these targets, but with lamentable standards of accuracy.

During the height of the Battle of Britain, from July to October 1940, Sinclair was closely involved with Lord Beaverbrook, Minister for Aircraft Production, in trying to mitigate the serious shortage of fighter aircraft. An average of twenty-six fighters were lost each day but the Ministry's figures took no account of damaged aircraft, only of lost ones, and consequently the impact on the numbers of fully operational aircraft available to the RAF was significantly worse than reported. In September 1940 Sinclair was forced by Beaverbrook to admit to the War Cabinet that there were only 288 fighters, eleven days' supply, still in reserve. By the end of the summer the losses had eaten into Britain's reserves to the tune of 45 per cent. If Britain's aircraft factories and storage units had come under concentrated pinpoint attacks by even small groups of enemy bombers, the position would have been desperate.

Beaverbrook and Sinclair had a very stormy relationship during the former's tenure of the Ministry of Aircraft Production from May 1940 to May 1941. Beaverbrook was a charming but duplicitous individual who could play very dirty when he felt the need. Frequently Churchill was called on to intervene and provide an arbitration service to resolve inter-departmental disputes. Generally this was a role that the Prime Minister relished but there were occasions when he lost his temper with both men and urged them to cooperate more fully.

One of Sinclair's most significant contributions as Air Minister was to fight for the allocation of manpower needed to sustain the bomber offensive, which was extremely costly in terms of aircrew's lives. By the end of the war, operational aircrew had sustained losses of more than 55 per cent, with 48,876 out of a total of 89,119 being killed. Their deaths weighed heavily on Sinclair's mind in the post-war years, according to his daughter Catherine.

Nevertheless, Sinclair was proud of the military decisions taken that dictated where the RAF should focus its efforts. He recognised that the strategic bombing campaign could be considered controversial and he actively defended the RAF's actions, both in the press and in parliament. Although he had to rely to a great extent on the professional judgement of the air marshals, he was always ready to champion them in the political

405 Dowding never gave recognition to the support he received at this critical moment from Sinclair, and in his autobiography presented the decision to hold back the fighter planes from going to France as a battle he had to fight on his own.

dog-fights that regularly erupted between the service ministers and in the War Cabinet. For instance, in October 1940, he resisted Admiralty attempts to gain control of RAF Coastal Command. The First Lord, A. V. Alexander, was supported by Lord Beaverbrook and the Prime Minister himself, who was never a great friend of the Air Ministry, but in this instance Sinclair won the argument. He angrily resented the accusations that the Air Ministry had treated Coastal Command as the Cinderella of the Air Force, arguing that its expansion had been hampered by uncontrollable developments, and that his Ministry was prepared to consider any proposals to improve operations in the sector. He was able to produce figures to show that there had been a relatively greater increase in the strength of Coastal Command than in any other command of the RAF.[406]

Further conflict with the Admiralty emerged in March 1942, when Sinclair was prominent in the struggle to prevent the Admiralty diverting bombers from strategic bombing to long-range reconnaissance duties in the Battle of the Atlantic, and obtained Churchill's consent for an extension of the bombing offensive. In a speech to the House of Commons on 4 March 1942, Sinclair emphasised that Bomber Command's primary task was striking at the heart of Germany, and that in 1942, the RAF's bombers were still the only means at Britain's disposal of bringing the war home to the enemy.

Sinclair's strategic views owed much to the experience and thinking of his Chief of Air Staff, Charles Portal, who replaced Newall in October 1940, and who was one of the most influential service chiefs on the Allied side. Portal and Sinclair were joined in early 1942 by Sir Arthur Harris, who was promoted to take control of Bomber Command. Portal and Harris shared the same strategic vision for Britain's bomber force and were responsible for the design and oversight of the delivery of the massive bombing campaign against Germany during 1943–45.

In April 1942 the Prime Minister's scientific adviser, Professor Lindemann (Lord Cherwell) wrote to Churchill suggesting that Bomber Command had attained such a size that it had the capability systematically to destroy the homes of the great majority of the inhabitants of Germany's fifty-eight largest cities. This, he claimed, would destroy the workers' morale and Germany's will to continue fighting. Sinclair commented that he found the argument proposing area bombing rather than precision bombing 'simple, clear and convincing'.[407] Although he did have earlier private misgivings, in his role as political representative of the RAF in the Commons, he was to become a key defender of the area bombing policy.

The strategic bombing campaign produced a degree of moral revulsion, however, from several important public figures who opposed the use of bombing to terrorise and kill civilians. Among them was Bishop Bell of Chichester, who throughout the war was the most persistent and articulate critic of the bomber offensive. Another was the 4th Marquess of Salisbury, head of the famous Cecil family, who wrote to Sinclair expressing fears that by area bombing the Allies were 'losing moral superiority to the Germans'.[408]

[406] There were two Coastal Command stations in his own constituency, one at Wick and its satellite at Skitten.

[407] See Sinclair's letter to Churchill of 6 April 1942 (page 347).

[408] Marquess of Salisbury to Sir Archibald Sinclair, in a letter dated November 23, 1943.

The moral issue did not cause Sinclair any particular difficulty, however, as he believed that the German people should suffer for a war which was their own responsibility – a view which most people accepted at the time. Sinclair thought it wise not to explain the nature of the bombing offensive too frankly in public, however, in case the morale of the bomber crews were affected by any adverse reactions, and publicly emphasised that the goals of area bombing were to destroy mainly military or industrial targets. As he argued in a Commons reply to an opponent of area bombing, 'The targets of Bomber Command are always military, but night bombing of military objectives necessarily involves bombing the area in which they are situated'.[409] An earlier speech by Sinclair produced a reaction from Dr Goebbels,[410] who wrote in his diary on 3 March 1943 that:

> The English Minister for Air delivered a speech that puts into the shade anything ever said. He proclaimed the British intention of causing a German migration ... from the big cities. The cynicism underlying such a statement simply cannot be beaten.[411]

There can be no doubt that area bombing caused a great deal of infrastructural damage, but in fact it accounted for only a very small part of the fall in German industrial production by the spring of 1945, and it was also very costly to the Allies. However, these criticisms were not so apparent at the time and Sinclair had great pride in what the RAF achieved. When he introduced the Air Estimates on 6 March 1945, Sinclair paid tribute to the achievements of the entire RAF, and especially to Bomber Command, pointing out that it was the bombers which had destroyed a third of the U-boats in their dockyards and pens, sunk the powerful battleship *Tirpitz*, and dropped thirty thousand tons of mines in enemy waters, with disastrous results for enemy shipping. He also praised Coastal Command, which had worked in conjunction with the Royal Navy to combat the U-boat menace and to protect Britain's trade routes. Tribute was also paid to the RAF Special Duties units which supplied arms to the resistance movements in occupied Europe and flew out secret agents and members of the resistance.

Sinclair's preoccupation with the Air Ministry during the war years led him to neglect his constituency, and in the general election of July 1945 he lost his seat in the closest fought contest of the election. Each of the three candidates polled roughly a third of the total, and a mere sixty-one votes separated them.[412] This was one of only two Tory gains in the whole of Britain – a harsh reward for Sinclair's service during the war.

Sinclair's contribution as a government minister is best summed up from his own personal viewpoint. He maintained that it was not the job of a politician to take on the role of expert in any particular branch of knowledge; his task was to organise, to persuade, and to coordinate. It was exactly this role that Sir Archibald Sinclair fulfilled so ably as Secretary of State for Air between 1940 and 1945. Although he was not uni-

---

[409] Sinclair, replying to a question from Richard Stokes, Labour MP for Ipswich, in a House of Commons debate on March 31, 1943 (*Hansard* Series 5, Vol 388, col. 502).

[410] Joseph Goebbels (1897–1945): Hitler's Minister of Propaganda.

[411] Louis Lochner (ed.), *The Goebbels Diaries, 1942–1943* (Doubleday, 1948).

[412] The full result was: E. L. Gandar-Dower (Conservative), 5564; R. MacInnes (Labour), 5558; A. H. M. Sinclair (Liberal), 5503.

formly regarded as a success at the Air Ministry, the overall assessment appears to be significantly more positive than negative. Although he could be long-winded and occasionally hesitant, he was remembered by one of his senior civil servants as 'thoroughly competent, completely devoted and highly respected ... a great gentleman'[413] and that probably captures the essence of the man.

The correspondence that follows is not an exhaustive record of all the letters, memorandums, policy papers, telegrams and notes that passed between Churchill and Sinclair during the Second World War. What has been attempted is to include all the personal letters that have survived, as well as much of the key official ministerial correspondence. A selection of the small notes, telegrams and comments that passed between the two has also been recorded. These give the flavour of the style of interaction and the type of issues, from strategic policy to discussions about the day-to-day operation of particular airfields, that engaged the Prime Minister and his Air Secretary over the critical five years they served together.

The correspondence begins with Churchill's offer of the Air Ministry to Sinclair in May 1940. Except where shown, all the letters were addressed either from 10 Downing Street or the Air Ministry.

1940

When Churchill became Prime Minister on 10 May 1940, one of his first appointments was of Sinclair to the post of Air Minister, a senior position but one outside the small War Cabinet; the invitation was issued early in the morning of 11 May. Sinclair was personally delighted by the offer of the Air Ministry, where he had served as Churchill's Private Secretary from 1919–21,[414] but wanted to be included within the small War Cabinet. He was also keen to see many of his small party of followers included in the new government. He wrote to Churchill in the mid-morning of 11 May, outlining his position and suggesting how a way forward might be found if a seat in the War Cabinet was not possible.

Sir Archibald Sinclair to Winston S. Churchill
23, Gayfere Street[415]
London S.W.1
11th May 1940
Personal and Confidential

Dear Prime Minister,

That you should have asked me to undertake so big a task and one so vital to the successful conduct of the war as the Air Ministry is a mark of your confidence which

[413] Sir Maurice Dean, quoted by Richard Overy in *The Battle* (Penguin Books, 2000), p. 31.

[414] At that time the Ministries of War and Air were combined.

[415] The address of the Liberal Party Headquarters. The building was bombed in 1944, destroying much of

I do most gratefully appreciate. It would be a colossal task, but my personal inclination urges me to attempt it under the inspiration of your leadership.

On the other hand I am impressed by the difficulty of leaving the Liberal Party without representation in the War Cabinet. I think this would be a most formidable difficulty in any event, and unfortunately it is emphasised by the fact that I gave this as my reason for refusing the invitation of your predecessor at the beginning of the war – and gave it not only confidentially to him but announced it in a public speech a day or two later.[416] Moreover, the attitude I had adopted has been endorsed by the Liberals in the country. Perhaps you will allow me to add that what I know of your mind in regard to other appointments tends to emphasise the importance of these considerations.

I was particularly grateful to you for suggesting that you would be willing to announce – at any rate if I was outside the War Cabinet – that I should be consulted on major questions of policy. You asked me to draft a formula, and I would suggest something on the following lines:–

"Leaders of the Parties represented in the Government will be consulted on all major questions of policy, on the composition of the Government, and on Patronage."

This is the formula which I propose to discuss with my friends at mid-day to-day, making it clear to them that it is only my own first draft.[417] If you take any strong objection to it I should be grateful if Brendan[418] or somebody would telephone to me before mid-day. At the same time I anticipate that the result of my consultations will be that I shall feel bound to accept the War Cabinet alternative rather than the Air Ministry.

As regards other appointments, you made it clear to me that, while you were willing to receive and consider suggestions from leaders of Parties, you would take the sole responsibility for the selection of members of your Government. Accordingly the names I suggest to you are the following:–

<u>Lord Samuel</u>. It would be absurd for me to emphasise to you his high qualifications, his zeal in support of the national war effort, and his immense powers of work.[419]

<u>Sir Percy Harris</u>. He is our Chief Whip, he is Deputy-Chairman of the Select Committee on War Expenditure, he is a most experienced and popular Member of

the party's archives and the majority of Sinclair's personal and private office papers.

[416] When war broke out on 3 September 1939, Neville Chamberlain offered Sinclair a Cabinet position (but outside the War Cabinet) which Sinclair declined. Churchill wrote twice to Chamberlain suggesting that he bring the Liberals into the Government by offering Sinclair a position in the War Cabinet.

[417] Sinclair met other senior Liberal Parliamentary Party members to discuss whether to enter the Coalition at lunchtime on 11 May 1940.

[418] Brendan Bracken, 1st Viscount Bracken (1901–58): journalist and publisher, managing director of *The Economist* 1928–29; Conservative MP for Paddington 1929–45; strong opponent of appeasement and close associate of Churchill; Parliamentary Private Secretary to Churchill 1940–41; Minister of Information 1941–45; First Lord of the Admiralty 1945; ennobled in 1952.

[419] Churchill did not regard Samuel as decisive enough for a senior appointment and left him out of the coalition government.

Parliament, and, if you were looking for a Minister of Education, he has special qualifications for that office. At any rate I have reason to think that you do not disagree with me that his appointment to the Privy Council would be a suitable recognition of his political services.[420]

Mr. Harcourt Johnstone. He is my closest political friend and, as you know, a man of great political capacity.

Mr. Graham White.[421] He is one of the senior members and Deputy Leader of our Parliamentary Party, and an authority on social and financial questions.

Mr. Dingle Foot. He is a young man of outstanding ability with good political judgment and zealous for service in the war. I stress the last point because I know of sacrifices which he has already made in the national cause and still greater sacrifices which he was willing to make. In the last year or two he has made great strides in the House of Commons and has undoubtedly gained the ear of the House.

Perhaps I ought also to mention to you the name of Mr. Clement Davies, Q.C., because, since he withdrew his support from the last Government, he has accepted our whip. He played an active part in recent events, and I think it only fair to suggest that his claims might be considered.[422]

Yours ever,
Archie

PS. I have just been talking to you on the telephone, and have taken a note of your formula[423] and I will put it to my friends.

Sinclair agreed to join the government as Secretary of State for Air. As well as the position of Prime Minister, Churchill took the role of Minister for Defence, with the service ministers (Sinclair, Eden at the War Office, and Alexander at the Admiralty) reporting to him directly. Sinclair's appointment was announced on 12 May. After a gap of eighteen years, Sinclair and Churchill were back working together in government.

---

[420] Sir Percy Harris (1876–1952): Liberal MP for Market Harborough 1916–18, South West Bethnal Green 1922–45; Liberal Chief Whip 1931–40; Deputy Leader of the Parliamentary Liberal Party 1940–45; a hard-working and principled man, he was neither charismatic nor popular, in spite of what Sinclair claimed, with his fellow MPs (indeed, he was recognised as one of the main bores of the Commons, regularly emptying the Chamber when he spoke).

[421] Henry Graham White (1880–1965): Liberal MP 1922–45; a worthy and dedicated backbencher.

[422] Edward Clement Davies (1884–1962): Liberal and Liberal National MP for Montgomery 1927–62; a key opponent of Chamberlain, when Eden and Churchill joined Chamberlain's administration in September 1939, Davies worked with Leo Amery to organise cross-bench opposition to Chamberlain's premiership and his replacement by Churchill in May 1940; Leader of the Liberal Party 1945–56. Clement Davies became a Liberal National MP in the Liberal split in 1931; this is an interesting statement by Sinclair, as it is commonly held that Davies did not retake the Liberal whip until 1942.

[423] Churchill agreed that although Sinclair was not in the War Cabinet as Leader of the Liberal Party, he would be consulted on all major policy changes.

Winston S. Churchill to Sir Archibald Sinclair and Sir Cyril Newall[424]
2nd June 1940

It is of the utmost importance, in view of the raids on Lyons and Marseilles, that we should be able to strike back with our heavy bombers at Italy the moment she enters the war.[425] I consider therefore that these squadrons should be flown to their aerodromes in Southern France at the earliest moment when French permission can be obtained and when the servicing units are ready for their reception.

Pray let me know at our meeting to-night what you propose.

WSC

In early June 1940, while the Dunkirk evacuation was taking place, a key debate in the War Cabinet was the extent to which Britain could afford to send more fighter squadrons across to France (as requested by French Prime Minister Reynaud) without dangerously weakening British defences. Air Chief Marshal Sir Hugh Dowding, Commander-in-Chief of Fighter Command, and Sinclair vigorously opposed sending any further planes. The War Cabinet eventually decided on caution and kept the squadrons in Britain. Churchill spent much energy probing the Air Ministry about potential bottlenecks preventing the achievement of maximum fighter strength in the face of invasion scares and the likelihood that the Luftwaffe would try to break the RAF over the summer. Churchill was particularly concerned about the perceived shortage of trained pilots and bomber crews.

Winston S. Churchill to Sir Archibald Sinclair
3rd June 1940
Private
SECRET

My dear Archie,

The Cabinet were distressed to hear from you that you were now running short of pilots for fighters, and that they had now become the limiting factor.

This is the first time that this particular admission of failure has been made by the Air Ministry. We know that immense masses of aircraft are devoted to the making of pilots, far beyond the proportion adopted by the Germans. We heard some months ago of many thousands of pilots for whom the Air Ministry declared they

[424] Sir Cyril Louis Norton Newall, 1st Baron Newall (1886–1963): Director of Operations and Intelligence and Deputy Chief of the Air Staff 1926–31; Air Officer Commanding Middle East 1931–35; Air Member for Supply and Organisation 1935–37, where he oversaw the rapid growth of the RAF; Chief of the Air Staff (CAS) 1937–40, where he tried to ensure that the Home Air Force and Bomber Command units at least maintained parity with Germany; seen as hesitant and uninspiring, he was replaced in October 1940; Governor-General of New Zealand 1940–46; ennobled 1946.

[425] On 2nd June the Luftwaffe carried out a series of raids on Lyons and targets in the Rhone valley. Mussolini declared war on Great Britain on 10th June.

had no machines, and who consequently had to be "re-mustered": as many as 7,000 were mentioned, all of whom had done many more hours of flying than those done by German pilots now frequently captured. How then, therefore, is this new shortage to be explained?

Lord Beaverbrook[426] has made a surprising improvement in the supply and repair of aeroplanes, and in clearing up the muddle and scandal of the aircraft production branch. I greatly hope that you will be able to do as much on the Personnel side, for it will indeed be lamentable if we have machines standing idle for want of pilots to fly them.

Yours ever,
Winston Churchill

Sir Archibald Sinclair to Winston S. Churchill
5th June 1940
SECRET

Dear Prime Minister

Thank you for your letter of the 3rd June. I agree that the position in regard to the supply of pilots to the Fighter Squadrons is disquieting and steps have already been taken to deal with it.

You asked me for an explanation of the shortage. I gave a short explanation to the Cabinet but, as you require a fuller explanation and as such an explanation must necessarily relate to a period long before I came into office, I thought it right to let the Air Staff here put the whole case to you, and I enclose their memorandum herewith.

Quite frankly the situation is, for reasons explained in the memorandum, unsatisfactory. A far greater strain has been thrown upon the training system of the Fighter Command than it was designed to bear. The Training Command is short of machines, instructors and flying grounds. It is not very short of machines in relation to its establishment, but an unduly high proportion of them are unserviceable – this in its turn is to some extent the result of a shortage in skilled ground personnel, and especially to a shortage of spare parts. With regard to machines and spare parts, I shall hope to have Lord Beaverbrook's help.

For the rest, as I told you the other day, the capacity of the two existing operational training units of the Fighter Command is being increased by about 50 per

[426] William Maxwell Aitken, 1st Baron Beaverbook (1879–1964): highly successful Canadian stockbroker, moved to Britain in 1909; Conservative MP 1910–18; in 1918 created Lord Beaverbrook; Chancellor Duchy of Lancaster and Minister of Information 1918; Minister for Aircraft Production 1940–41; Minister of Supply 1941–42; Minister of War Production 1942; Lord Privy Seal 1943–45; better known as one of the great newspaper barons: during the First World War he acquired a controlling interest in the *Daily Express*, in 1921 founded the *Sunday Express* and in 1929 purchased the *London Evening Standard*. As Minister of Aircraft Production during 1940 and 1941, he was a significant thorn in Sinclair's side.

cent. and when the new O.T.U.[427] is ready in a fortnight's time, the three O.T.U.s together will have a potential output of 115 pilots a fortnight instead of 39, and we have already turned our attention to remedying the other deficiencies of the training system.

Yours ever,
Archie

The following memorandum was attached:

SECRET
FIGHTER PILOT DEFICIENCIES, JUNE, 1940

The basic deficiency of pilots in Fighter Command on 31st May amounted to 178. This arises partly from the recent formation of new fighter squadrons and partly from the excess of wastage over replacements which is due to general fighting over enemy territory instead of over the United Kingdom as was expected. Moreover in order to relieve fatigue in hardly pressed squadrons it has recently been decided to increase the establishment of pilots from 21 to 26 per squadron. Until this decision can be fully implemented a further deficiency must be recorded which amounted on May 31st to 270 pilots, making a total of 448, or an average of nearly 8 per squadron on the new squadron establishment of 26.

The additional wastage experienced has arisen, as shown above, from a strategical situation which was unforeseeable at the time when our fighter-pilot training policy was formed. As for the formation of new fighter squadrons, it will be recalled that at the outbreak of war we possessed 39 fighter squadrons. To meet the incessant call for increased fighter protection additional squadrons were formed for the Fleet base, for the Component, for trade defence, as well as for strengthening our line at home – and we now have a total of some 60 fighter squadrons, though not all of them are yet in the line. It will be appreciated that the requirement for more fighter squadrons competed with the demand for Fighter Operational Training Units at a time when the flow of fighter aircraft from production was extremely restricted, and the former requirement was given priority because of the expectation of an early attack from the air against this country, the Fleet or our trade routes.

The effect of forming these additional fighter squadrons was thus to increase requirements of pilots and to reduce our ability to create training units. Moreover the Operational Training Unit organisation was designed to meet the expected comparatively small wastage at home plus the wastage of 6 squadrons in France.

Contributory causes to the shortage were the severity of last winter's weather conditions, which reduced the output of pilots by 550, and the requirements of the

[427] Operational Training Unit.

Empire Training Scheme[428] which will become productive at the end of this year, but which has made a heavy demand on our trained personnel in its early stages.

It will be realised that any attempt to accelerate the output by reducing the standard of training for pilots would involve an increase in the wastage rate both of personnel and aircraft which we cannot afford. Training machinery has nevertheless been overhauled with a view to increasing output of pilots, both at the Flying Training School and at the Operational Training Unit stage. Some speeding up is being achieved by means of earlier specialisation at the Flying Training School stage which will have the effect of narrowing the scope of the fighter-pilot's instruction without, it is hoped, rendering it a less through training for fighter duties. Results obtainable by this manner are, however, limited by the availability of modern single-engine training aircraft.

All non-operation units have been combed for trained pilots, and it is intended to make full use of Polish, Norwegian, Belgian and Dutch airmen who are in this country. It is also hoped to obtain volunteers from the United States, and the possibility of launching an appeal is being investigated with the Foreign Office. The Admiralty have also been approached to ascertain whether they have any margin of trained pilots and training facilities which they could make available for the Air Force.

The position of 7,000 pilots to whom the Prime Minister refers is that they were peace-time entrants into the Royal Air Force Volunteer Reserve. At the beginning of the war a few of them were sufficiently advanced to enter operational units, but the great majority required the complete flying training course. They were therefore not "remustered" but had to wait to be absorbed into the flying training scheme.

The number of aircraft devoted to training is necessarily large. Until recently the production programme was based on a maximum development in the third year of war and it was necessary to build up a training organisation designed to correspond. It is now necessary to re-orientate this organisation, but immediate results will not be easily obtained, as the training of a pilot is a comparatively lengthy business which cannot be curtailed without loss of efficiency. The efforts of the training Command are now being directed towards advancing the stage at which specialised fighter training is begun.

[428] The Empire Air Training Scheme was a programme implemented during the war to train Commonwealth aircrew for service with the RAF. Realising it did not have the resources to maintain the RAF at an adequate strength to confront Germany, the UK proposed in September 1939 that 50 elementary flying schools be established in Australia, Canada and New Zealand. The graduates of these schools would then receive advanced training in Canada and proceed to Britain for service with the RAF.

Winston S. Churchill to Sir Archibald Sinclair and Sir Cyril Newall
11th June 1940

This report[429] is most interesting and I shall be glad if you will arrange to use the Squadron you mentioned yesterday for the purpose of infecting the reaches mentioned where the traffic is reported to be so heavy. We do not need to ask the French permission for this, but only for the continuous streaming of the Naval fluvials. This I am doing. Meanwhile you should act as soon as you can on the lower reaches. Kindly report what you will do.

WSC

Winston S. Churchill to Sir Archibald Sinclair
15th June 1940

My dear Secretary of State for Air,

Thank you for your letter of June 5, enclosing the Air Ministry's Memorandum on Fighter Pilots.[430]

The figures which you sent me at the end of May suggest that if we are already short of pilots, the Germans must be suffering from an even worse shortage. You give us 9,000 pilots with recent flying experience but less than 5,000 operational machines, at the same time giving the Germans 12,000 pilots and about 12,000 machines. The fact that the Germans are flying mainly over occupied territory cannot reduce their losses of airmen appreciably. I understand that recent experience shows that only one in ten British airmen lost on operational flights is captured alive, and even if the Germans take to their parachutes somewhat readily it seems unlikely that a much greater fraction survive to fly another day.

Again, either we devote too many machines to the training of each pilot (and should search for economies), or German pilots are inadequately trained. Over the last year our training organisation absorbed 4,000 aircraft and only produced 2,500 pilots. In previous estimates your Department have calculated that the Germans produced roughly one pilot for each aircraft absorbed into the training pool.

The Air Staff complain that they lack modern single-engined training aircraft. I should be glad to see further particulars on the point, for I understand that we have since war began produced more training aircraft than the Germans.

Pray let me have your views on these matters.

WSC

[429] On the mining of the Rhine (Operation Royal Marine).

[430] Reproduced above, pages 226–28.

Winston S. Churchill to Sir Archibald Sinclair
15th June 1940

I notice from the report of June 14 that 355 bombing aircraft are available in Squadrons, and 220 within two or three days, total 575. For these crews available are only 343. This shows a lamentable lag in the pilots, and I should be very glad if you would let me know exactly what you are doing to correct it, and when we may expect an improvement. As long as the Air Ministry is behind production in the pilots it has already trained, it is a serious default.

WSC

Sir Archibald Sinclair to Winston S. Churchill
30th June 1940
SECRET

Prime Minister,

I have now had an opportunity of going carefully into the points raised in your letter of 15th June about the number of pilots in this country and in Germany in relation to the number of aircraft available and to the size of the respective training organisations.

I agree that on the figures you quote, one could make out a case for saying that the German pilot position must be more difficult even than the pilot position in this country. Such a conclusion should, however, I suggest, be treated with great reserve. Our estimate of German pilot strength, although prepared with very great care on the best evidence obtainable, is bound to involve a considerable margin of error. It must also be remembered that it was the R.A.F. policy until quite recently that all flying, staff, Command and technical appointments should be filled from one branch of the Service, the General Duties branch, all entrants to which qualified as pilots. This policy had many advantages but it follows that at the present moment there are, as you know, many officers who are qualified pilots and who are employed in staff and technical appointments. Many of these appointments require staff training and all of them require knowledge of Service methods and requirements. These posts cannot be left unfilled and in consequence the officers filing them can only be released for operational duties as replacements become available from the Volunteer Reserve or from officers who require a rest from operational duties. I am at present engaged in having the employment of pilots analysed, and I should hope that this analysis will show the extent to which we can hope to comb non-operation units for qualified pilots. In the meanwhile, we should, I suggest, be wrong to draw too definite a conclusion from the case on paper. The essential fact is that the pilot position in this country is at present tight to say the least, while there is still no evidence that Germany is short of pilots.

I have gone into the question of the proportion of R.A.F. personnel lost on operational flights who are taken prisoners of war. I understand that the figures given to you were for the period since the 10th May. These figures amounted to 98 prisoners of war as compared with 897 missing. It must be remembered, however, that men who come down on the other side of the enemy's lines may evade capture for some days and also that there is the time lag in the notification of the names of prisoners of war through Geneva. I am told that the figures of missing and prisoners of war since the 10th May (excluding the Middle East) are now 169 confirmed prisoners of war as compared with 850 missing, and I also understand that it is thought that even now there may be still to come quite material additions to the figure of 169.

As regards the size of the training organisation, we still require to allocate proportionately more aircraft to training than the Germans because they had the start of us and have virtually completed their training organisation while we are still engaged in expanding our own. Owing to the time to train a pilot, aircraft allocated to training do not become productive immediately and the number of aircraft absorbed last year in consequence appears high in relation to the number of pilots turned out. This ratio will improve as soon as the training organisation has reached its peak. The expansion of the German training organisation over the same period was proportionately much smaller, and in consequence Germany can show a better ratio of pilots to aircraft for the period. Here again, however, I do not consider that we should be justified in concluding on the evidence available at present either that our organisation is unduly extravagant or that German training is inadequate.

The shortage of advanced single-engine trainers, to which you refer in the last paragraph of your letter, is due to delays and disappointments in the delivery of the Master.[431] As long ago as 1938, when the prospective deficiencies came to light, the Air Ministry placed orders in America for the Harvard to supplement the Master, but out of 2,500 trainers delivered between April 1939 and March 1940, only 430 were of advanced single-engine trainer types. In consequence we have been unable to overtake the serious deficiency in aircraft of this kind which has existed for a considerable time, and shortage of this type is still the limiting factor on the expansion of training. Everything possible is being done to increase the output of trainers and of the Master in particular, and, as you know, these aircraft have been placed in the first priority category.

It is true that the Germans have since the outbreak of war only produced about as many trainer aircraft as we have. They have produced enough, however, to allow them to maintain their training organisation. We have not yet produced enough to overtake our deficiency in advanced trainers as well as to meet wastage and provide for expansion.

Archibald Sinclair

[431] An American single-propeller trainer.

During the summer of 1940 significant tensions developed between the Air Ministry and the Ministry of Aircraft Production, which had been carved out from the Air Ministry in May 1940 and placed under the control of Lord Beaverbrook. Beaverbrook was an enigma to many. He was highly capable, had a reputation for being great company and fun to be with, but was also notoriously unpredictable. He could be wildly generous but also back-stabbing and duplicitous in his dealings with colleagues. Like Sinclair he was part of the small group of politicians who had access to Churchill after midnight, when many of the key decisions and discussions occurred. Sinclair was to experience all sides of Beaverbrook's character during the latter's tenure of the office of Minister of Aircraft Production from May 1940 to May 1941.

Beaverbrook has often been given enormous credit for the boost in aircraft production achieved during the second half of 1940, and in part this is deserved. He burst through the established approach to the manufacturing cycle and by cannibalisation, swifter repairs and the bullying of all and sundry made significant short-term improvements. New aircraft factories did not come into being overnight, however, and the real architect of the increased production, which a close examination of the figures reveals had occurred before Beaverbrook took office, was Wilfrid Freeman who, as head of the Air Ministry's Research and Development function, had been planning new factories and production capabilities since 1938.

Sinclair and Beaverbrook had a rocky relationship, and Beaverbrook was highly critical of Sinclair as a minister. However, Sinclair's patient handling of each successive eruption from the Ministry of Aircraft Production limited the success of Beaverbrook's piratical tendencies, prevented the further transfer of Air Ministry responsibilities to MAP, and ensured that the Air Ministry held its own policy positions in the face of the sustained assault that Beaverbrook launched. Interestingly, Beaverbrook and Sinclair remained friends throughout the war and continued to correspond with each other in the post-war years.

Winston S. Churchill to Sir Archibald Sinclair
27th June 1940
Private and Personal

I should be glad if you would read the enclosed paper[432] which I have received from Lord Halifax[433] before our talk this morning. It is, I am told, written by a highly competent person, who declares he is perfectly ready to be cashiered if necessary, and is evidently in a dangerous mood. The Foreign Secretary was much impressed by his arguments. I have been, as you know, for many months urging something like this policy, and everyone has been astounded at the failure of the Air Ministry to expand the Air Force on the outbreak of war, and recently at the proved failure to provide a proper supply of pilots when they have so long been crying out about the

[432] Not found in the archives.

[433] Then Foreign Secretary – see n348.

plethora of pilots, and 're-mustering' them for other duties. I am hoping that you will be able to make the same kind of practical changes at the Air Ministry as Lord Beaverbrook has made in the production of aircraft, from which we are deriving such inestimable relief in these dark days.

This document attached has nothing to do with Lord Beaverbrook, but you can see how much it confirms his many complaints of being hampered in production.

I note the supply of machines available at 48 hours' notice is growing every day, and also that the Air Ministry have abandoned the 96 hours' notice in preference to the 48. The figures of 96 hours' notice are of course far more impressive in showing the large supply of aeroplanes than the 48 hours' notice recently adopted.

I do hope and pray that you will feel yourself able to effect radical reforms in what is, I am sure, a most cumbersome and ill-working administrative machine. I felt that with your new eye you would have a chance far greater than that enjoyed by persons compromised with the past.

WSC

Winston S. Churchill to Sir Archibald Sinclair
29th June 1940

In your communiqué today you distinguish in several cases between enemy aircraft 'put out of action' or 'destroyed.' Is there any real difference between the two, or is it simply to avoid tautology? If so, this is not in accordance with the best authorities on English. Sense should not be sacrificed to sound.

Will you also report today whether you would like the weather to be clear or cloudy for the operations on the Belgian Coast.

WSC

Winston S. Churchill to Sir Archibald Sinclair
1st July 1940

Archie,

I note that your actual expenditure of bombs in May, 2920 tons, was less than half the monthly estimated expenditure for the second quarter of this year, and that at this rate of expenditure your stock represents thirty months' supply.

The last thing we wish of course is to have any shortage of bombs if and when you are ready to drop them in quantity. But in the light of these figures you might perhaps wish to review your requirements, which seem to be largely attributable to your desire for a six months' reserve.

Unless you are really assured that you will be in a position to make full use of these great quantities, we should consider whether some filling capacity should be transferred to other uses.

WSC

Sir Archibald Sinclair to Winston S. Churchill
1st July 1940
SECRET

You wrote to me about the summarised order of battle (all bomber squadrons) for the 24th June 1940 pointing out that, whereas 355 aircraft were available for operations, only 343 crews were shown as available to man them. These returns fluctuate from day to day. To-day more crews than aircraft are shown as being available. But the figure of "crews available" takes no account of the considerable number who are standing off for a period of rest, and I am assured that there is not the slightest doubt that in the case of urgent need there would be sufficient crews to man the whole of the aircraft now in the squadrons. You mentioned that behind these 355 bombing aircraft were 220 similar aircraft available within 2 days in the A.S.Us.,[434] but of these no fewer than 107 were Battles,[435] and these are the serviceable reserves for the Battle squadrons which are not shown in the return because they are reforming. The remaining 113 aircraft constitute our serviceable reserve and are not a part of the first lines.

As regards pilots in the Fighter Command, I visited several squadrons yesterday and found that their pilot strength was in all cases above the old establishment of 21 per squadron and within 2 or 3 of the new establishment of 26, and we are hoping to complete them up to the full strength of the new establishment quite soon.

At the same time I attach the highest importance to the increase in the production of pilots and crews. It would weary you if I were to detail all the measures which we have taken to bring this about, but the following facts may be of interest to you:–

a) The intake capacity of fighter O.T.Us. has been expanded from 39 at the beginning of May to 90 pilots, and is being further extended to 115.
b) Similarly, the intake of the Bomber Command O.T.Us. is being expanded from 164 to 240 pilots.
c) Pilots, however, in the Bomber Command are of no use without their crews and the most serious factor in the Bomber Command situation is the scarcity of wireless operator air gunners. We have taken several measures to overcome this difficulty and the fortnightly intake of wireless operator air gunners into the O.T.Us. is being raised from 156 to 240.
d) The position in regard to Coastal Command is receiving very special attention because the difficulties there are quite exceptional. On the one hand heavily increased duties have been thrown upon them in connection with attacks upon German ships off Norway and anti-invasion reconnaissance; while, on the other

[434] Aircraft Storage Units.

[435] The Fairey Battle, a light day-bomber that was to prove very easy prey for the German fighters due to its lack of speed and defensive armaments. By the end of 1940 the Battle was phased out of active service by Bomber Command, and became a training workhorse for new pilots attending the Empire Training Scheme.

hand, I found them with a very serious deficiency in pilots and wireless operator air gunners, and progress is now being held up by the removal of their general reconnaissance school from Guernsey.

e) I told you the other day the chief bottle-neck in our training system at the present time is the Service flying training school. As a result of decisions taken at a series of weekly conferences on training, we have been able to increase the amount of actual training done at each school within a given period and thus to reduce the length of courses. The length of the old course was 8 weeks at the intermediate stage and 8 weeks at the advanced stage, and we have reduced the courses to 6 weeks at each stage for Fighter Command pilots and 7 weeks at each stage for Bomber and Coastal Command pilots. The result of this alteration may be seen in the following tables:

	Previous Outputs. 8 + 8 week course all schools	Present Outputs. With courses as above
June	408	612
July	408	408
August	408	646
September	408	442
October	408	578
November	408	510
December	408	578
	2856	3774

These figures assume that shortened courses are maintained for the reminder of 1940 and this may not be possible as the weather deteriorates in the winter months. The variations in output shown in the right-hand column are caused by the varying number of outputs which occur during each month – e.g. during August there are five output dates, whereas in July there are only three. These figures refer only to our schools in the United Kingdom and do not include the output from the Empire Training Scheme.

f) The other day I told you that I thought that the measures we had taken would give an increase of 1/5th that in the output from the Service flying training schools. You will see that the increase will actually amount to almost 1/3rd.

g) We are also expecting to obtain a substantial number of pilots as a result of our comb-out, not only in the Air Ministry but also throughout the Commands, and a few by the release of all operationally fit pilots who are not employed in the ferry pools.

h) We have every reason to believe that there is a substantial amount of excellent material among the foreign pilots in this country – more especially the Poles and the Czechs. We are actively sifting these pilots now.

You sent me the other day a copy of a memorandum which Lord Halifax had given you about the possibility of a large and rapid expansion in the R.A.F. In many respects, which lie within my own knowledge, the statements in the memorandum are inaccurate and out of date. For example, the writer says that "at present few squadrons are up to strength with fully-equipped aircraft though the aircraft exist at M.Us. – (I think he means A.S.Us.). Squadrons should all be fully equipped at once and given aircraft as surplus reserve." I visited several fighter squadrons yesterday and in every case they had their full establishment of 16 machines and they each had in addition 3 machines in what is known as "Command Reserve" – that is to say they are available to each individual squadron if required for any emergency, but that they could be taken away from them, if they were not already being used, by the Command in order to replace losses in other squadrons.

Nevertheless two important suggestions which were already in my mind, emerged from this memorandum – in the first place that excessive staffs and establishments should be rigorously pruned and that is a subject which I am taking up; and, in the second place, that there should be a drastic comb-out not only in the Air Ministry but throughout the Commands – and this is being done.

This is by no means an exhaustive account of all the measures which are being taken by the Air Staff and A.M.P., A.M.S.O.[436] and the Commands in order to increase the flow of pilots and crews; and I hope that the Air Member for Training will be able to speed things up with the help of the new machinery which I outlined to you the other day. Meanwhile I hope the facts which I have mentioned in this letter will give you the assurance that the problem is not being and has not been neglected.

AHMS

With the collapse of resistance in France it was apparent that Britain was in serious danger of an invasion during the three months from July to September, before the autumn tides and weather made an opposed crossing of the English Channel untenable. Churchill was keen that the RAF should use its bombers to disrupt the armadas of barges and landing craft that aerial reconnaissance showed to be building up in Belgian and French ports.

Winston S. Churchill to Sir Archibald Sinclair and Sir Cyril Newall
2nd July 1940
ACTION THIS DAY

I hear from every side of the need for throwing your main emphasis on bombing the ships and barges in all the ports under German control.

WSC

436 Members of the Air Council: Air Member for Personnel (then Sir Philip Babington) and Air Member for Supply and Organisation (then Sir Christopher Courtney).

Winston S. Churchill to Sir Archibald Sinclair, Anthony Eden and A. V. Alexander[437]
5th July 1940

It has been represented to me that our colleagues not in the War Cabinet but above the 'line'[438] are depressed at not knowing more of what is going forward in the military sphere. It would be advantageous if each of the Service Ministers[439] could in rotation have a talk with them, answer questions, and explain the general position. If a weekly meeting were instituted, this would mean that each Service Minister would meet them every three weeks. I trust this would not be too heavy a burden upon you. Nothing must ever be said to anybody about future operations; these must always be kept in the most narrow circles; but explanations of the past and exposition of the present offer a wide field. On the assumption that the above is agreeable to you, I am giving directions through Sir Edward Bridges.

WSC

As well as battles with the Luftwaffe and the Ministry of Aircraft Production, Sinclair was drawn into an internal row within the Air Ministry over the proposals for the retirement of Sir Hugh Dowding, Commander-in-Chief, Fighter Command. Dowding had been leading Fighter Command since 1936 and had been due to retire (after two postponements) on 15 July 1940. Dowding's nickname was 'Stuffy', a reference to his austere personality and his reputation for being difficult to work with; he was regularly at loggerheads with the Air Ministry. Both Newall and Sinclair were keen to move Dowding as soon as was practically possible. Churchill, however, was a supporter of Dowding and wanted him to remain in charge of Fighter Command.

Winston S. Churchill to Sir Archibald Sinclair
10th July 1940
Private and Confidential

My dear Archie,

I was very much taken aback the other night when you told me you had been considering removing Sir Hugh Dowding[440] at the expiration of his present appoint-

[437] Albert Victor Alexander, 1st Earl Alexander of Hillsborough (1885–1965): Labour MP for Sheffield Hillsborough 1922–31, 1935–50; First Lord of the Admiralty 1929–31, 1940–45 1945–46; Minister of Defence 1946–50; Chancellor of the Duchy of Lancaster 1950–51; created Viscount 1950, Earl 1963; leader of the Labour peers 1955–64.

[438] Presumably meaning those senior ministers who in peacetime would have expected a seat around the Cabinet table.

[439] Sinclair, Eden and Alexander.

[440] Hugh Caswell Tremenheere Dowding, Baron Dowding of Bentley Priory (1882–1970): Squadron Commander in World War I, then served in command, staff, and training positions in the new RAF; Commander-in-Chief, Fighter Command 1936–40, where he vigorously promoted the development of radar and the Spitfire and Hurricane fighters that contributed significantly to the defeat of the Luftwaffe

ment, but that you had come to the conclusion that he might be allowed to stay on for another four months. Personally, I think he is one of the very best men you have got, and I say this after having been in contact with him for about two years. I have greatly admired the whole of his work in the Fighter Command, and especially in resisting the clamour for numerous air raid warnings, and the immense pressure to dissipate the Fighter strength during the great French battle. In fact he has my full confidence. I think it is a pity for an officer so gifted and so trusted to be working on such a short tenure as four months, and I hope you will consider whether it is not in the public interest that his appointment should be indefinitely prolonged while the war lasts. This would not of course exclude his being moved to a higher position, if that were thought necessary. I am however much averse from making changes and putting in new men who will have to learn the work all over again, except when there is some proved failure or inadequacy.[441]

WSC

Churchill did not initially win this battle with the Air Ministry. On 13 July, Newall wrote to Dowding offering to defer his retirement for the four months Sinclair proposed until the end of October 1940.

Winston S. Churchill to Sir Archibald Sinclair
11th July 1940

I am concerned at your heavy loss in Blenheims[442] yesterday, and I trust that the inquiry made into the signal of HMS *Dainty*[443] will be accompanied by a drastic re-examination of the liaison at the Admiralty between the two Departments. It is inexcusable that an error of this kind should have been committed in respect of a considerable raid of 12 machines. This should surely have been known beforehand, and all forces concerned taken into consideration by the planning authority.

Generally speaking, the losses in the Bomber force seem unduly heavy, and the Bremen raid, of which only one out of six returned, is most grievous. At the present time a very heavy price may be paid (a) for information by reconnaissance of the conditions in the German ports and German-controlled ports and river-mouths, (b) for the

during the Battle of Britain; replaced by Sholto Douglas; sent on special duty in the US for the Ministry of Aircraft Production, where he made himself unpopular with his outspoken behaviour; retired in November 1942 and ennobled the following year.

441 Despite his success in the Battle of Britain, Dowding had a tense relationship both with the Air Ministry and with senior Group and Sector leaders; he was due to retire in 1940 and pressure was exerted to ensure that he was replaced by someone more flexible and with greater interpersonal skills. Sinclair and Dowding never saw eye to eye, though Sinclair treated him with significantly more respect and patience than Dowding suggested in his memoirs.

442 Bristol Blenheim light bombers.

443 A destroyer, commissioned in 1932, and sunk off Tobruk by enemy aircraft on 24 February 1941.

bombing of barges or assemblies of ships thus detected. Apart from this, the long-range bombing of Germany should be conducted with a desire to save the machines and personnel as much as possible while keeping up a steady attack. It is very important to build up the numbers of the Bomber force, which is very low at the present time.

WSC

Sir Archibald Sinclair to Winston S. Churchill
12th July 1940
SECRET

Dear Prime Minister,

I am sending you herewith a report compiled by the Air Staff on failures of H.E.[444] bombs to explode. The explanation which it offers of the information contained in the telegram from Mr. Kelly (Berne) which you sent to me, seems reasonable and you have doubtless noticed in the intelligence summaries many instances of German bombs dropped in this country failing to explode, no doubt from similar causes. In so far as these causes are preventable, we shall make every effort to prevent them and you will observe that for this purpose Bomber Command is making a complete analysis of all reported failures to date.

AHMS

Note on Reported Failures of H.E. Bombs to Explode under Operational Conditions

1. Every failure of a bomb to explode is investigated by the Armament Staff of the Command concerned, and a Defect Report rendered where applicable. Experience has shown that so far only a small percentage of failures can be attributed to defects in the bomb or fuse, and that the great majority are due to faults on the part of the personnel concerned. These may be roughly divided into:–
   a) Faulty fusing, which is generally due either to fatigue or inexperience on the part of armourers, and
   b) Failure on the part of the bomb aimer to fuse the bomb before dropping, i.e., dropping the bomb 'safe'.
2. With regard to 1a) above, the risk of faulty fusing has on occasions been accentuated by a change of plan necessitating a rapid change of bomb load, giving very little time for the work to be done properly. It has happened that units have had to change the bomb load as many as three times in a day. Senior armament personnel, i.e., those charged with the responsibility of supervising and inspecting the work of armourers, are in general seriously over-worked, on some occasions having been on continuous duty for 36 hours, followed by a six-hours rest before

[444] High explosive.

a further spell of duty. It was noticeable that during the recent battles in France failures of all sorts showed a progressive increase, owing to the tiredness of personnel and the impossibility of providing suitable supervision.

3. The dropping of bombs 'safe' by inexperienced or flustered bomb aimers has occurred on a number of occasions.
4. Reports by crews of aircraft that their bombs have failed to explode may sometimes be due, especially at night, to the fact that bombs have penetrated into buildings or ships or are some distance under water when they explode. In these circumstances the flash would probably not be seen, nor, in the presence of intense A.A.[445] fire, would the sound of the explosion necessarily be noticed. It is very probable that in the case quoted of the dropping of the 2,000 lb. A.P.[446] bomb on the *Scharnhorst* that the bomb either penetrated into the ship or was sufficiently far under water for the flash to be unobserved. This type of bomb has a very thick case and a relatively small amount of explosive which would not cause a very large flash.
5. It is possible that the dropping of a proportion of delay action bombs may give rise to reports from foreign sources that the bombs failed to explode. It may well happen that observers see the bombs fall without any explosion following, and they naturally assume that the bomb has failed.
6. The Armament Staff at H.Q. Bomber Command are preparing a complete analysis of all reported failures to date from which it is hoped that more detailed information will be forthcoming.
7. Finally, a good deal of work has been done since the war by the technical staff to eradicate the causes of failures in our fuses and bombs, and a number of definite causes have been discovered and remedied. It must be borne in mind, however, that we ask a great deal from our bomb fuses. They must be safe to handle, and must detonate the bomb under conditions which may vary from a release at low height on to soft ground to a release from very great heights on to very hard targets. Our existing fuses give a very small proportion of failures under these varying conditions, and it may well be that a fuse capable of 100 per cent. success might be so complicated and expensive that it would prove a very difficult production problem and might easily become a serious 'bottleneck' in the supply of an adequate number of bombs.

Winston S. Churchill to Sir Archibald Sinclair
18th July 1940.

My dear S. of S. for Air,

I am still concerned over the question of the employment of our pilots. According to figures which have recently been furnished by your Department,

[445] Anti-aircraft.
[446] Armour-piercing.

only 3 out of every 10 pilots with Wings[447] are operational. This seems a very low proportion. Of the remaining 7, 2 are pilots with Wings still under instruction, 2 are Instructors and the rest are Air Staff, Administrative, Technical or other non-operational duties. Thus more pilots are employed giving or receiving instruction than are actually serving as operational pilots in the Squadrons.

Our methods of training have produced such good results that we must interfere with them as little as possible, but I do think these figures require some further examination.

I understand, for example, that most of the 2,000 pilots with Wings still undergoing instruction are intended for Bombing Squadrons, also that we habitually send 2 pilots away in each Bomber employed on active operations. Would it not be possible to train some of the newly fledged pilots by employing them as second pilots in the operational Squadrons? Any such adjustment would produce a treble economy. It would release not only pilots under instruction but Instructors, and it would enable some of the machines of operational types now employed for instruction to be added to our operational strength.

I should be grateful if you would give this matter your earnest consideration.

We must increase our numbers available for action.

Yours,
Winston Churchill

Winston S. Churchill to Sir Archibald Sinclair and Sir Cyril Newall
20th July 1940

In case there is a raid on the centre of Government in London, it seems very important to be able to return the compliment the next day upon Berlin. I understand you will have by the end of this month a respectable party of Stirlings[448] ready. Perhaps, however, the nights are not yet long enough. Pray let me know.

WSC

Winston S. Churchill to Sir Archibald Sinclair and Lord Beaverbrook
23rd July 1940

From many quarters come reports of R.A.F. bombs non-exploded. See attached telegram. What is being done about this? It would seem that the officers responsible should be provided with all the references to this in the Intelligence Reports,

[447] Pilots who had completed basic training, who were issued with 'Wings' to be sewn on to their jackets.
[448] The Short Stirling bomber was the RAF's first four-engined bomber of the Second World War, and played a major role in the strategic air offensive until 1943, when it was replaced by the Lancaster. It continued in service but mainly as a transport plane rather than a front-line bomber.

particularly from Switzerland, whence several cases have been mentioned. We ought to make sure of our bombs.

WSC

Sir Archibald Sinclair to Winston S. Churchill
23rd July 1940

Dear Prime Minister,

You sent me a minute on the 20th July about the possibility of bombing reprisals on Berlin and I have had the question examined.

I enclose a detailed analysis of the question by the Commander-in-Chief, Bomber Command, which shows that while we are now only able to operate with Blenheims we shall shortly, during the longer nights, be able to use the heavier types. A Stirling Squadron is in process of formation but I do not think that there will be more than one full squadron of Stirlings available for operation before the 1st September. We should use Blenheims during the moonlight nights but Hampdens, Whitleys and Wellingtons on dark nights.

The figures given by the Commander-in-Chief are, of course, subject to suitable weather conditions.

You will see that, as I mentioned at the Defence Committee this afternoon, our present heavy bombers (and the Blenheims as well with a lighter load) can reach Berlin.

Yours,
Archie

Possibility of bombing Berlin
Result of detailed examination by Bomber Command

a) If less than 24 hours' notice is given between now and 26th July, 8 tons of bombs can be dropped by the Blenheim force each night. This scale of effort can be continued for a week.
b) If 24 hours' notice is given enabling the medium bombing programme to be cancelled the bomb lift will be increased to 15 tons. It could be repeated every second night and the effort could be maintained for a week. This would not interfere with the night bombing programme by the heavies over the same period.
c) Between 26th July and 1st August with less than 24 hours' notice 17 tons of bombs could be dropped on Berlin each night for a week by the heavy Bomber Force.
d) During the same period if 24 hours' notice is given this bomb lift can be increased to 35 tons and can be repeated on alternate nights for a week. There would still be some bombing effort left in the heavy force for other operations.

e) On or after 2nd August the whole of the heavy bomber force can be employed. With 12 hours' notice 65 to 70 tons of bombs could be dropped on Berlin. This scale of effort could be repeated each night for a week.
f) If 24 hours' notice is available this bomb lift could be increased from 130 to 150 tons. This could be repeated every alternate night for a week.
g) If it were desirable to prepare a heavy single blow against Berlin and provided the heavy bomber force were stood off the day before the operation and the day after the operation as much as 200 tons of bombs could be dropped on Berlin, though a more conservative figure would be 150 tons.
h) The Blenheims would operate on moonlight nights but the heavies could operate on dark nights. The Hampdens, Whitleys and Wellingtons would be employed against Berlin.

The first German bombs fell on central London on 24h August 1940. RAF Bomber Command retaliated on 25 August with an eighty-bomber raid on Berlin. From this date onwards the German bomber offensive switched predominantly to hitting Britain's major cities and the attacks on Fighter Command's airfields and radar stations eased, allowing critical repairs to be carried out. This switch of emphasis to the cities was a key blunder by the Luftwaffe, allowing Fighter Command a breathing space ahead of what was to prove to be the pivotal month of the air battle, in September. Sinclair wrote to Churchill later that year that 'in so far as the Germans may have been led away by their theories of the total war into attacking our civilian population instead of concentrating upon our aircraft and air engine factories, it is very lucky for us.'[449]

In early August 1940, Churchill wrote to Sinclair about the threat posed by the Japanese navy in the Far East.

Winston S. Churchill to Sir Archibald Sinclair and Sir Cyril Newall
4th August 1940

Secretary of State for Air and C.A.S.,[450]

The danger of Japanese hostility makes it all the more important that the German capital ships should be put out of action. I understand that the Air Force intend to make heavy attacks on these ships as soon as there is sufficient moon. *Scharnhorst* and the *Gneisenau*, both in floating docks at Kiel, the *Bismarck* at Hamburg, and the *Tirpitz* at Wilhemshaven, are all targets of supreme consequence. Even a few months' delay in *Bismarck* will affect the whole balance of sea-power to a serious degree.

I shall be glad to hear from you.

WSC

[449] See letter dated 31 October 1940.
[450] Chief of the Air Staff.

Winston S. Churchill to Sir Archibald Sinclair
9th August 1940

SECRETARY OF STATE FOR AIR

I do not seem to have had any answer to the minute I sent you on July 18,[451] to which your Secretary replied on July 19 saying that you would look into the question. In view of the fact that the whole question of pilots is now under consideration, I should be glad if I could have an answer by to-morrow.

Surely the fact that 'only 3 out of every 10 pilots with wings are operational' is astonishing.

Exactly 3 weeks have now passed since I ventured to bring this fact to your notice.

WSC

Sir Archibald Sinclair to Winston S. Churchill
9th August 1940
SECRET

My dear Prime Minister,

Since receiving your letter of the 18th July, in which you expressed the concern that you still feel over the employment of pilots, I have been once more into the whole question with a view to seeing if there is any direction in which pilots who are operationally qualified are being mis-employed in posts where they can be relieved either by non-operational pilots or by non-pilot personnel.

Your letter refers to the fact that out of every ten pilots with wings two are still pupil pilots, but it must be remembered that a pupil pilot receives his wings at a comparatively early stage of training, as soon as he is qualified to take other pupils in the air, and that at this stage he has only carried out some 80 to 90 hours flying. In no circumstances can pilots be regarded as operationally qualified at this stage, and before they can be so regarded they must complete something of the order of 200 hours flying and must qualify on service type aircraft.

Two more out of every ten pilots are, as you say, engaged on instructional duties. These instructors are not, however, engaged solely on the instruction of pupil pilots, but on the training of observers, air gunners, etc., and on giving advance training on such courses as the Air Navigation Course and Flying Instructors Course. The ratio of instructors to pupils in flying schools far from being 1–1, is 1–6. Moreover, only a fraction of these instructors, i.e., those at Operational Training Units and some 250 in the whole of the rest of the training organisation, are operationally qualified, and the bulk of our instruction is done by older men or men who are not qualified

[451] Which questioned statistics showing that only three in every ten pilots were engaged in active operational duties. See pages 240–41.

for operational duties. The same is true of the great bulk of the pilots employed on communications, ferrying and miscellaneous flying duties.

The proportion of pilots employed on staff, administration and technical duties is, as you say, not inconsiderable – something like 1,600 in all – though a certain proportion of these officers would not be suitable for operational duties. One reason for this figure is the policy which prevailed in the past of using general duties officers for technical duties, and another is the fact that a larger number of staff posts require recent experience of flying, and a considerable knowledge of the Service. Thus such officers can only be posted to operational duties as, and when, they are relieved by other officers with similar staff and technical qualifications. There has already been a drastic comb-out which has not been subject to any limitation of age, and the number of non-regular personnel employed in staff posts in replacement of regulars is now considerable. We shall, or course, continue to replace operationally qualified pilots or pilots who can be made into operational pilots with non-operational pilots or with non-pilots, to the greatest extent possible.

Another important consideration is that the division between Operational Units, Operational Training Units and other types of employment is by no means hard and fast. There is, in fact, a constant flow of pilots particularly between operational squadrons and Operational Training Units. Indeed the instruction staff in the Operational Training Units represent a trained and experienced reserve available at all times to replace pilots in the line who require to be rested and who, in their turn, are posted to Operational Training Units for a spell of instructional duties. Thus we are, in fact, using for the operational effort a considerably larger number of pilots than those serving at any one time in operational squadrons.

Your letter suggested that we might consider giving bomber pilots their operational training as seconded pilots in actual operations instead of in the Operational Training Units. I am certain, however, that it is very largely the thorough training given in the Operational Training Units which has given us our training advantage over the enemy, and that to adopt this proposal would be to surrender the greatest asset we have. I have discussed it with the Commander-in-Chief, Bomber Command, who fears it would undermine the confidence of each member of the bomber crew in the fitness of every other member for his particular job. The mutual confidence is the mainstay of the bomber crews in carrying out their hazardous enterprises and that is why every effort is made to train and keep crews together.

Archibald Sinclair

Churchill evidently learnt in August that Dowding had only been offered a further four months' employment rather than the indefinite extension Churchill had wanted. He immediately wrote to Sinclair.

Winston S. Churchill to Sir Archibald Sinclair
10th August 1940
Private

My dear Archie,

I certainly understood from our conversation a month ago that you were going to give Dowding an indefinite war-time extension, and were going to do it at once. I cannot understand how any contrary impression could have arisen in your mind about my wishes. Let me however remove it at once, and urge you to take the step I have so long desired. It is entirely wrong to keep an officer in the position of Commander-in-Chief, conducting hazardous operations from day to day, when he is dangling at the end of an expiring appointment. Such a situation is not fair to anyone, least of all to the nation. I can never be a party to it.

I do hope you will be able to set my mind at rest.[452]

Yours ever,
W

Winston S. Churchill to Sir Archibald Sinclair
10th August 1940

My dear Secretary of State for Air,

Thank you for your letter of August 6 about the production of stabilised bombsights.[453]

I have come to the conclusion, after carefully considering your arguments that, in the interests of all concerned, an inquiry should be held into the facts. An informal inquiry by a Judge of the High Court is in my view the best way of achieving this. It is not my intention that there should be any public announcement, and I see no reason why there should be any publicity attaching to it.

There is no need for Counsel to appear on either side; the inquiry would be to ascertain the facts.

There would, of course, be no question of taking disciplinary steps until after the report has been received. If any such steps proved to be necessary, the incriminated parties would have the full protection of the Service regulations.

I propose the following Terms of Reference:–

To examine into the causes of delay in converting the 2,600 A.B.S. Mark II into a stabilised bombsight in accordance with the recommendation of the Conference on

[452] See Sinclair's reply dated 12 August 1940 (page 248).

[453] No copies of this letter from Sinclair have been located; however, a letter to the Lord Chancellor on the same day requesting the release of Mr Justice Singleton for the review indicates that Sinclair had been complaining that the production of stabilised bombsights, which offered a big improvement in performance on those then in operation, had not been progressed since a meeting on 22 December 1939.

Bombsight Design held at the Royal Aircraft Establishment on December 22, 1939: and to report upon whom the responsibility for any avoidable delay rests.

I have in mind Mr. Justice Singleton[454] to undertake the inquiry.

Yours very sincerely,
Winston S Churchill

Winston S. Churchill to Sir Archibald Sinclair
12th August 1940
SECRET

My dear Archie,

1. Yours of August 9.[455] You say the ratio of instructors to pupils in flying schools is 1–6. As there are on May 1, 2,000 instructors, and you have 2,000 pupils, this accounts for 333, leaving 1667 instructors for "the training of observers, air gunners, etc., and on giving advance training on such courses such as the Air Navigation Course and Flying Instructors course." Please let me have the detailed distribution of these instructors.
2. It is not sufficient to say that "The proportion of pilots employed on staff, administration and technical duties is "not inconsiderable" when it amounts to 1,600 as compared with Bomber and Fighter strength of about 2,000. It is difficult to believe that a further comb-out of trained pilots would not yield important results. Will you kindly let me know to-day the exact results of the last comb-out.
3. I should also like to have a statement of the Communication Squadrons, showing numbers of officers and men, numbers of pilots, operational and non-operational, numbers of machines in possession of the Units, serviceable and non-serviceable, number of hours flying per pilot and per machine in June or July, whichever is more convenient.

   I daresay you will not be able to supply these last details in the course of the day.
4. In your paper you mentioned that you impose a limitation on the number of Squadrons in the winter, but you do not give figures. You also speak of an impending reduction in the output in the number of pilots resulting from your proposals, but here again no figures are given. These are essential to any judgment upon your proposals.

Winston Churchill

[454] John Singleton (1885–1957): headed two wartime enquiries, the first on this issue of bombsights, the second on German Air Force strength.

[455] See page 244.

Sir Archibald Sinclair to Winston S. Churchill
12th August 1940
Personal

Dear Winston,

Thank you so much for your private letter of yesterday.[456]

I cannot tell you how sorry I am that there should have been any misunderstanding about our conversation in regard to the length of the Commander-in-Chief's tenure of the Fighter Command.

I have your letter of 10th July in front of me with a note, which I made upon it after our talk at Downing Street, that you agreed that my letter to the Commander-in-Chief should be allowed to stand and that the matter could be considered in about a month's time. I dated my note the 12th July so I hope you will be convinced that I have not deliberately flouted your wishes which, as you must know, is the last thing I should want to do.

As a matter of fact after our talk on Friday I spoke at once to the C.A.S.[457] who has written to the Commander-in-Chief withdrawing the October time limit to the period of his command.

As I think you are aware, Sir Hugh Dowding's tenure of command has been prolonged more than once and I was – deliberately and for the reasons which I explained to you at the time – continuing an existing arrangement, which dates from before the outbreak of war. The effect, however, of what I have now done is to withdraw the time limit and to place him in exactly the same position as the other Commanders-in-Chief.

Yours ever,
Archie

Winston S. Churchill to Sir Archibald Sinclair
17th August 1940

I am very doubtful about the PAC rockets.[458] They are one of many suggestions which we took up at the Admiralty at the time when our small ships were being attacked on the East Coast, and we had nothing to put in them. I do not think they would be suitable for regular use; certainly it would be a great mistake to use up the wire which is needed for the aerial mines. I gathered from the conversation you had with Lord Beaverbrook the other day that your demands are reduced from 60,000 a

---

[456] Churchill's letter of 10 August 1940 (see page 246) which Sinclair would have received on the 11th and replied to on the 12th.

[457] Newall (Chief of the Air Staff) and Sinclair did not work well together and it was a great relief to Sinclair when, at Churchill's insistence, Newall was replaced by Sir Charles Portal on 24 October 1940.

[458] Parachute and Cable rockets. A two-inch rocket device: when fired, a bomb was suspended on a long wire, supported by a parachute. If an aircraft struck the wire then the bomb was dragged up to the wing where it would explode.

month to 8,000, but even this latter figure appears to me to be altogether excessive. We must look to the regular UP[459] weapon, with or without the new fuses, as the future solution of the protection of vulnerable points. Pray let me have a short note on the present position of this supply showing how it could be brought to a close in the course of the next month or six weeks, with a minimum waste of material already assigned to it.

WSC

Winston S. Churchill to Sir Archibald Sinclair
21st August 1940
ACTION THIS DAY

The important thing is to bring the German aircraft down and to win the battle, and the rate at which American correspondents and the American public are convinced that we are winning, and that our figures are true, stands in a much lower plane. They will find out quite soon enough when the German air attack is plainly shown to be repulsed. It would be a pity to tease the Fighter Command at the present time when the battle is going on from hour to hour and continuous decisions have to be taken about air raid warnings, &c. I confess I should be more inclined to let the facts speak for themselves. There is something rather obnoxious in bringing correspondents down to air squadrons in order that they may assure the American public that the Fighter pilots are not bragging and lying about their figures. We can, I think, afford to be a bit cool and calm about all this.

I should like you to see on other papers an inquiry I have been making of my own in order to check up on the particular day when MAP said they picked up no fewer than eighty German machines brought down over the land alone. This gives us a very good line for our own purposes. I must say I am a little impatient about the American scepticism. The event is what will decide all.

WSC

PS. – You were admirable last night. I am so sorry not to have heard you.[460]

[459] Rocket projectiles (officially called UP, unrotated projectile) could carry a heavy high-explosive warhead at sufficient velocity to penetrate armour plating. The first UP was fired on 25 October 1941. Most aircraft carried four under each wing, and either a pair or a salvo could be fired. They were used against tanks and U-boats.

[460] Sinclair had replied for the Government at the end of the adjournment debate on 20 August, following Churchill's review of the war situation where he had made the famous remark about the RAF fighter pilots: 'Never in the field of human conflict was so much owed by so many to so few.' Sinclair's speech was well received, but he would come to regret his statement to the House of Commons that 'We have no quarrel with the peoples of Germany or Italy. We shall never use our powers in the air as an instrument of mass terrorism.' In 1943–45, the strategic air offensive against Germany and Italy was to see massive thousand-bomber raids involving the indiscriminate use of British and American air power against civilian populations.

Winston S. Churchill to Sir Archibald Sinclair
25th August 1940
Secret

I visited Kenley on Thursday,[461] saw the gunner in question and had a rocket fired off. Moreover it was the Admiralty Committee over which I presided early in the year which produced the idea of using these distress rockets. I am therefore well acquainted with the subject. The Air Ministry, not for the first time, spread itself into very large demands and using its priority barged in heavily into other forms of not less important production. I agree that PAC rockets may be a good interim defence against low-flying attack, but they have to take their place in the general scheme. I thought myself about 5,000 a month would be sufficient but I am willing to agree to 1,500 a week or 6,000 a month. This figure could be somewhat extended if the wire recovery projects you mention were further developed, and proved an effective economy. I am sending a copy of this Minute to MAP.

WSC

Winston S. Churchill to Sir Archibald Sinclair
25th August 1940
Private

My dear Archie,

I feel unhappy about your answers on the attached paper.[462] I cannot feel you are justified in maintaining the present scale of communication squadrons when we are fighting so heavily. The sole end should surely be to increase the reserve and operational strength of our fighting squadrons and to meet the problem of trainer aircraft. Surely your dominant idea should be STRENGTH FOR BATTLE. Everything should be keyed on to this, and administrative convenience or local vested interests must be made to give way. In your place I should comb and re-comb. I have been shocked to see the enormous numbers at Hendon, and I would far rather give up flying on inspections altogether for Members of the Government than that this should be made an excuse for keeping these forces out of the fight.

I should have thought that Hendon could provide at least two good squadrons of fighter or bomber aircraft of the reserve category, and that they should have the machines issued to them and practise on them as occasion serves. Then they could be thrown in when an emergency came.

Ought you not every day to call in question in your own mind every non-military aspect of the Air Force? The tendency of every Station Commander is naturally

[461] Churchill visited Kenley aerodrome on Thursday 22 August 1940.

[462] Sinclair had commented, in a letter of 22 August, on a letter from Beaverbrook to Churchill of 15 August, in which Beaverbrook criticised the number of aircraft being used by the Air Ministry solely for training purposes.

to keep as much in his hands as possible. The Admirals do exactly the same. Even when you have had a thorough search if you look around a few weeks later you will see more fat has been gathered.

I hope you will feel able to give some consideration to these views of your old friend.

WSC

Churchill's prime ministerial style is well captured in the following minute which lashes Sinclair, Newall and Ismay[463] for what he perceived as a slow response to repairing the damage caused to aerodromes by enemy action. Churchill's mixture of micro- and macro-management caused much consternation and irritation amongst the civil service and the Chiefs of Staff, but proved an effective way of mobilising resources in the face of national crisis.

Winston S. Churchill to Sir Archibald Sinclair, Sir Cyril Newall and General Ismay
29th August 1940

I was much concerned on visiting Manston Aerodrome yesterday to find that, although more than four clear days have passed since it was last raided, the greater part of the craters on the landing ground remained unfilled, and the aerodrome was barely serviceable. When you remember what the Germans did at the Stavanger aerodrome, and the enormous rapidity with which craters were filled, I must protest emphatically against this feeble method of repairing damage. Altogether there were 150 people available to work, including those that could be provided from the Air Force personnel. These were doing their best. No effective appliances were available, and the whole process appeared disproportionate to the value of maintaining this fighting vantage ground.

All craters should be filled in within 24 hours at most, and every case where a crater is unfilled for a longer period should be reported to higher authorities. In order to secure this better service it will be necessary to form some crater-filling companies. You might begin with, say, two of 250 each for the South of England, which is under this intensive attack. These companies should be equipped with all helpful appliances and be highly mobile, so that in a few hours they can be at work on any site which has been cratered. Meanwhile, at every aerodrome in the attack-area, and later elsewhere, there must be accumulated by local contractors stocks of gravel, rubble and other appropriate materials sufficient to fill without replenishment at least 100 craters. Thus the mobile air-field repair companies would arrive to find all the material all ready on the spot.

[463] Hastings Lionel Ismay, Baron Ismay (1887–1964): served in India and Africa and then on the Committee of Imperial Defence; Chief of Staff to Winston Churchill and later to Clement Attlee 1940–46; Churchill's closest military adviser; participated in many important international conferences, including Moscow, Tehran and Yalta; first Secretary-General of NATO 1952–57.

I saw some time ago that the Germans filled in the shell holes by some process of having the gravel in wooden frameworks. The VCNS[464] drew my attention to it during the Norwegian operation, and they could perhaps put you on to the telegram referred to.

In what department of the Air Ministry does this process now fall?

After the craters had been refilled camouflage effort might be made to pretend they had not been, but this is a refinement.

WSC

Churchill's concern about the allocation of fighters outside the British Isles, first raised in May during the battle for France, resurfaced in September when he wanted to check that any fighters going overseas would be deployed immediately against the enemy.

Winston S. Churchill to Sir Archibald Sinclair and Sir Cyril Newall
1st September 1940

There must be no mistake about this expression 'South African allotment'. All Hurricane aeroplanes allotted to South Africa are allotted on the express condition that they are immediately put into action in East Africa or in the Middle East.

Would it not be well also to enter a caveat that the continued dispatch of operational Fighter aircraft must be reviewed from week to week in the light of the progress of the present grievous battle?

WSC

Winston S. Churchill to Sir Archibald Sinclair
11th September 1940

I understand that you are taking up with the Ministry of Information the possibility of getting additional personnel from the BBC for radio counter-measures. I know that the matter of distribution of scientific personnel is to be considered as a whole in due course, but, in view of the extreme urgency of working these counter-measures to the full immediately, I trust there will be no difficulty in obtaining a few score, or even a hundred, technicians of the £300 – £500 a year class even if only as a temporary measure.

WSC

The picture Churchill painted in his history of World War Two suggested that Sinclair's role was mainly to act as a cipher for Churchill's strategic brilliance. The reality, as the

[464] The Vice-Chief of the Naval Staff, Admiral Phillips.

following letter makes clear, was more complex, and Sinclair played his part in challenging Churchill's thinking and in presenting the Air Ministry's views on which strategic plans should be enacted.

Sir Archibald Sinclair to Winston S. Churchill
11th September 1940
MOST SECRET

Dear Prime Minister,

In Conclusion 1 (i) of the minutes of yesterday's War Cabinet Meeting I am invited "to give instructions that our bombers operating over Germany should not return with their bombs in the event of their failing to locate their targets".

I find that an instruction had already been issued to Bomber Command that pilots should make every effort to avoid bringing their bombs home and I attach a copy of our signal. It does not, however, go so far as the Cabinet Conclusion in that it permits pilots to bring home their bombs in the last resort if they cannot find any military target. I think it would be unwise to go further than this instruction:

a) because our present policy is to bomb only military objectives and this was re-emphasised at this morning's Cabinet
b) because a relaxation of restrictions on bombing indiscriminately might possibly reduce the determination of our pilots to go for their set targets with a consequent loss in military results

and

c) because pilots normally look for their last resort targets in Holland, Belgium or France and if they fail to find them and drop their bombs indiscriminately it would be the Dutch, Belgians and French who would suffer and not the Germans.

I do not propose therefore to issue any further instruction to Bomber Command but I should be glad of your approval.

Yours sincerely,
Archibald Sinclair

Sir Archibald Sinclair to Winston S. Churchill
Air Ministry
15th September 1940
Personal

Winston,

One thing worries me these days – that you stay at Downing Street without a proper shelter. This is sad backsliding since we last made war together, when you insisted on battalion headquarters having the best shelter that was available at Laurence Farm![465] You were right then but you <u>must</u> apply the same principle now and go and live in the War Room or somewhere where reasonable protection exists. You are making us ridiculous if you insist on us living in basements & refuse to do it yourself! Whether the country would agree about the rest of us I am not sure – but I am sure that they would be angry as well as amazed if they knew that you were not sleeping in reasonable safety.

Yours ever,
Archie

Winston S. Churchill to Sir Archibald Sinclair
20th September 1940

Yours of September 18.[466]

1. In your figures on page 3 please distinguish between metropolitan and overseas. It seems to me astonishing that with the supplies now reaching you, you should only produce 74 Squadrons of Fighters by April 1941. You now have 64½, though this includes foreign and Dominions, in the Metropolitan Force alone. You have reduced the additional equipment of the Fighter Squadrons from 16 to 12. It seems incredible that a greater expansion should not be achieved.

2. Even taking the Metropolitan strength for the summer of 1942 in para. 2 of your letter as 270 Squadrons at 12 each, this represents a front line strength of 3,240 aeroplanes. It would be interesting to see how many men, how many machines, and how much money this requires. I am sure an effective policy would secure at least 100 Bomber and 100 Fighter Squadrons by April 1941, and 80 of each by January 1941. Naturally during the fury of the battle expansion is arrested, but we need not expect that these conditions will last throughout the winter. Pray remember that we were supposed to have 125 Squadrons fully ready more than two years before the war in the Metropolitan Air Force alone. I am sure there must be something radically wrong with the organisation, which with its enormous intake of machines, now over 1,700 a month, can only produce this limited and almost stagnant front. If you cannot produce more than 270 Squadrons by the summer of 1942, it will be necessary to examine the relation of all aircraft supplies to this restricted front.

WSC

Winston S. Churchill to Sir Archibald Sinclair
21st September 1940

Secretary of State for Air,

Pray have a look at the Air Ministry communiqué issued in this morning's papers. It includes the following: 'The enemy formations were engaged by our

[465] Churchill's battalion headquarters from January to June 1916 at Ploegsteert (see page 8).
[466] Not found in the archives.

fighters, but cloud conditions made interception difficult. Reports so far received show that four enemy aircraft were shot down. Seven of our fighters have been lost, the pilots of three being safe.' It is very unwise to let the Germans know that their new tactics have been successful and that they resulted in our losing seven fighters as against four.

We do not, of course, want to conceal our losses, at the present time when we are prospering, but surely there is no need to relate them to any particular action.

WSC

One of the key historical debates about the strategic bombing campaign against Germany was the effectiveness of the bombs in achieving the results promised by the service chiefs. Churchill was quick to spot, when studying reconnaissance photographs, that the damage inflicted could often be disappointing – as the letter below shows. The Air Ministry and the RAF were to struggle with problems of accuracy throughout the war. Precision bombing proved to be beyond the technology available and from 1943 onwards both the British and American air forces moved to more indiscriminate bombing policies with very large bomber formations blanket-bombing areas of strategic and military importance, with a consequent impact on local civilian populations.

Winston S. Churchill to Sir Archibald Sinclair
23rd September 1940

What struck me about these photographs was the apparent inability of the Bombers to hit these very large masses of barges. I should have thought that sticks of explosive bombs thrown along these oblongs would have wrought havoc, and it is very disappointing to see that they all remained intact and in order, with just a few apparently damaged at the entrance. Can nothing be done to improve matters?

WSC

Beaverbrook was keen to get the Air Ministry to hand over control of airfield stores of spares to his ministry. This was firmly resisted, but Churchill felt obliged to weigh in on the side of MAP.

Winston S. Churchill to Sir Archibald Sinclair and Sir Cyril Newall
26th September 1940
Private

Considering that everything depends upon Lord Beaverbrook's success in obtaining the supply of aircraft and the heavy blows he is receiving at Bristol, Southampton and elsewhere, I earnestly trust you will see that his wishes are met fully and immediately in the matter of these spares. I really could not endure another bickering over this, considering the gravity of the situation.

WSC

Sinclair's support for his ministry was heartfelt and effective. Churchill recognised that Sinclair was performing a competent job but at times feared that his friend was turning native. During the late 1930s Sinclair had been highly critical of the Air Ministry's approach to rearmament and had publicly attacked the department in the House of Commons for its lethargy and bureaucracy. Churchill was keen to remind Sinclair of his previous stance and to urge him to avoid the trap of complacency.

Winston S. Churchill to Sir Archibald Sinclair
29th September 1940
Private

I am very glad to find that you are as usual completely satisfied. I merely referred the Foreign Office telegram[467] to you in order to test once more that impenetrable armour of departmental confidence which you have donned since you ceased to lead an Opposition to the Government and became one of its pillars. Either you must have been very wrong in the old days, or we must all have improved enormously since the change.

This is, I think, at once the most reasonable and most gratifying conclusion.

I am not by any means convinced that the bombing of marshalling yards is not pushed too far. On the whole I believe the school who think it does very little harm except at moments when great troop movements are in progress, have reason on their side.

WSC

Winston S. Churchill to Sir Archibald Sinclair
30th September 1940

1. In my Minute No. 107 of September 20,[468] I meant 16 instead of 12. I should have said you have reduced the initial equipment of the Fighter Squadrons from the temporary 20 to 16. I am sorry for this slip, but I was dictating from memory. My desiderata figures should therefore be corrected to 1,280 and 1,600 respectively for January and April 1941.

[467] Voicing concerns that the bombing of targets such as railway sidings were not achieving the disruption sought.

[468] See page 254.

2. I see you calculate a wastage of Pilots from between 25–30 per cent first-line strength per month. Actually during these five months of very heavy fighting from May to September inclusive the loss has only been 14 per cent. I should have thought this realised result would be a firm foundation for the summer months, and that two-thirds of this rate might be assumed for the winter months. Will you kindly recalculate your position on this basis, assuming it is found correct, and showing what possibilities of expansion would be open.
3. I do not understand your figures in para. 4 about losses of eight-gun Fighters. My information is that we are definitely stronger in Hurricanes and Spitfires than we were at the beginning of the five months' battle. You have no doubt seen Lord Beaverbrook's tables of loss and gain. For your convenience I attach a copy, which kindly return. You now state that during the heavy fighting of the last seven weeks you have eaten into your Reserves to the tune of 45 per cent. If this refers to the numbers in the A.S.Us., you should consider that these Units were practically empty when the change of Government took place, and that if you look back over the five months' period, which is a truer basis than the arbitrarily selected seven weeks, you are far better off.
4. You also say that you have only 288 eight-gun Fighters in reserve, and that this represents no more than 11 days' supply. This implies that we are losing 26 eight-gun Fighters a day, or roughly 800 a month in this category alone. This, of course, is entirely contrary to any figures you have ever disclosed to the public. Perhaps you will look into this, as I am sure your figures do not represent the facts. The published figures up to date for September amount to no more than 287 Fighter machines, or little more than 10 a day.

WSC

Sir Archibald Sinclair to Winston S. Churchill
7th October 1940
SECRET

Prime Minister

You told me in a recent minute[469] that you were not by any means convinced that the bombing of marshalling yards had not been pushed too far, and I have accordingly been reviewing our policy.

About nine per cent of our total bombing effort was directed against marshalling yards during the month of September. The proportion of the total number of primary targets to marshalling yards was about five to one, but of course they are a convenient last resort target when bad weather makes the location of primary and secondary targets difficult.

[469] 29 September 1940; see page 256.

This scale of attack was somewhat heavier than usual because the primary object of our bombing policy last month was to hinder the transport of supplies from Germany to France, and thus the German preparations for invasion. The Railway Research Service advised us that the best way to cause general dislocation of the railway communications to France was to bomb the marshalling yards in Germany because it is there that the trains are made up.

To dislocate German railway communications is an object of high military and economic importance; but it is very difficult because damage to railway tracks is easily repaired. Their most vulnerable point is marshalling yards because the Germans time all their trains from the marshalling yard and not from the railway terminus as is the custom in England. Moreover, marshalling yards cannot work at night without lights and consequently work at them is easily brought to a standstill by occasional bombing during the hours of darkness. Our object in bombing marshalling yards is therefore not primarily to cause material damage, but to force the railwaymen to dowse their lights and so make the marshalling of traffic impossible. Accordingly we send one or two aircraft to each yard night after night to create cumulative congestion and disorganisation.

Intelligence reports indicate that the Germans have a considerable difficulty in transporting supplies from Germany to bases in Northern France and have been forced to supplement normal ground communication by the use of large numbers of transport aircraft. We also know that the German railways are heavily overloaded. Possibly for example you may have seen the following reports:–

a) A highly placed neutral recently travelling from HOLLAND was routed through BERLIN, MUNICH and CONSTANCE. At the last moment this itinerary was changed and he could not travel either through BERLIN or upon the RHINE route.
(Source: A.I.1.c.)

b) Persons who travelled from BERLIN and COLOGNE to BASLE last week state that in each case they were compelled to change more than 12 times and even then there were delays for long periods outside some stations.
(Source: A.A. Berne.)

In addition, the Ministry of Economic Warfare report that the traffic in perishable foodstuffs from Holland has been practically at a standstill for considerable periods while damage is being repaired; that ships have been held up at Bremen and other ports through a shortage of coal; and that neutral travellers have taken three days for journeys that can normally be completed in a few hours.

Corroboration is given to these reports by our own experience under German bombardment. For example, the Ministry of Home Security report as follows:–

"By the mass use of exploded and unexploded (delay action) bombs, severe dislocation of railway traffic was caused during the earlier part of September. This had the inevitable result of severe congestion in all marshalling and goods yards, thus presenting a set of first-class targets. But the enemy did not take advantage of this situation and no attack has yet been delivered on them. During the past three days repairs to the damaged railway tracks, restoration of signalling apparatus, and the removal of unexploded bombs has enabled the flow of traffic to re-start, but the congestion in the marshalling and goods yards is still proving a difficulty."

I agree, however, that we must be very careful not to dissipate too high a proportion of our heavy bomber effort on purely harassing attacks. We hope in the near future, as the training of our medium bombers improves, to employ a greater proportion of them against these comparatively easily located targets, thus releasing our heavy bombers for the destruction of key objectives in our major plans.

AHMS

With France fallen and Britain standing alone against Germany the RAF provided the only effective weapon for striking back at the enemy. Churchill was also aware of the propaganda and morale-boosting impacts of bomber offensives and was keen for the Air Ministry to plan high-profile retaliation.

Winston S. Churchill to Sir Archibald Sinclair and Sir Cyril Newall
16th October 1940
ACTION THIS DAY

I see it reported that last night a large number of land mines were dropped here, many of which have not yet gone off, and that great harm was done.

Let me have your proposals forthwith for effective retaliation upon Germany.

I am informed that it is quite possible to carry similar mines or large bombs to Germany, and that the Squadrons wish to use them, but that the Air Ministry are refusing permission. I trust that due consideration will be given to my views and wishes. It is now about three weeks since I began pressing for similar treatment of German military objectives to that which they are meting out to us. Who is responsible for paralysing action?

WSC

During October the infighting between the Air Ministry and MAP broke into the open with word reaching Churchill of highly unflattering comments from an Air Vice Marshal about Lord Beaverbrook. Churchill was so indignant at the 'derogatory charge against a member of the War Cabinet' that he sought an apology from the Air Force officer concerned. When Sinclair declined to pursue the matter further, Churchill wrote to him as follows.

Winston S. Churchill to Sir Archibald Sinclair
19th October 1940
Personal and Secret

My dear Archie,

Please refer to [memo] No. 2104 quoting Air Vice-Marshal McKean's[470] telegram 633 of October 9. In this, McKean states that Colonel Bishop made certain statements about Lord Beaverbrook's alleged remarks, and purported to give the "gist of Bishop's conversation on his return". This allegation is now proved, on the evidence of Colonel Bishop, to be quite untrue. Nevertheless, Air Vice-Marshal McKean in his telegram H. 691, in no way withdraws or expresses regret for having made a derogatory charge against a Member of the War Cabinet on grounds now shown to be untrue; nor does he withdraw his own censure upon Lord Beaverbrook to the effect that his "aspersions … are completely unfounded, ungenerous, etc." Do I understand from your Minute of 18.10.40 that you consider that an unfounded charge, accompanied by strictures of this kind, calls for no comment from you to the Officer who had made them, and that no withdrawal or apology should be forthcoming from that Officer? Even in private life, a gentleman who has made a derogatory charge against another and used language of censure about him on the strength of it, would be expected to withdraw and apologise when proved to have been wrongly informed. Am I further to understand that you take responsibility for this behaviour, and thus leave the matter wholly without redress, and the Officer concerned under the impression that you consider that he has only acted "in duty bound to tell his official Chief fully and frankly what was going on"? – by which I suppose you mean also "what was <u>not</u> going on".

I hope indeed I may hear from you that this is not the case.

Yours ever,
Winston S. Churchill

In late October Churchill wrote to Sinclair and Newall with a number of concerns about the preparations being made by Bomber Command. In particular Churchill was concerned about the lack of availability for the RAF of the Lorenz blind-landing set, a landing aid to help bring aircraft back to ground safely at night or in bad weather.

Lorenz, named for its manufacturer, the Lorenz company, had initially been put into service by Lufthansa in 1934, and was adopted in many other countries. It was an elegantly simple scheme, sending out a directional signal with an audio tone on a carrier in a range of wavelengths near 10m/30MHz, using an antenna that switched back and forth to send out two transmission lobes, skewed on alternating sides of the antenna's centre line. The switching was performed by a mechanically driven cam that

470 Lionel Douglas Dalzell McKean (1886–1963): pilot, RFC 1915–18; senior officer in RAF Training Command 1936–40; head of RAF Mission to Canada 1940–43, helping to set up the Commonwealth Air Training Plan.

ensured that the signal was activated for a short time in one lobe and for a long time in the second.

The signal from the first lobe would be received as a series of Morse-code dots, while the signal from the second lobe would be received as a series of dashes. If an aircraft was on the centre line between the two lobes, the receiver would effectively get a continuous tone, with the dots filling in the dashes. If the aircraft drifted off the centre line in the direction of the first lobe, dots would gradually emerge from the continuous tone, and if it drifted off in the other direction, dashes would emerge. Churchill was to become extremely worried that the Luftwaffe's use of such systems would allow the Germans to perform accurate attacks at night, overstraining Britain's air defences.

Winston S. Churchill to Sir Archibald Sinclair and Sir Cyril Newall
20th October 1940
Secret

1. After discussing the whole question of retaliating by parachute land mines on Germany with C-in-C, Bomber Command, I have come to the conclusion that it would at the present time be an improvident use of our bomb-carrying capacity, except as a purely experimental, psychological feature, as proposed by you.
2. The use of the heaviest 1,000-pound and 2,000-pound bombs on Berlin is much to be desired. Would it not be well to save up for this, merely disturbing them meanwhile?
3. I am deeply concerned with the non-expansion, and indeed contraction, of our Bomber Force which must be expected between now and April or May next, according to present policy. Surely an effort should be made to increase our bomb-dropping capacity during this period. In moonlight periods the present arrangements for bombing are the best possible, and the only difficulty is our small numbers compared to the many attractive military targets. On no account should the limited Bomber Force be diverted from accurate bombing of military objectives reaching far into Germany. But is it not possible to organise a Second Line Bomber Force which, especially in the dark of the moon, would discharge bombs from a considerable and safe height upon the nearest large built-up areas of Germany, which contain military targets in abundance. The Ruhr of course is obviously indicated. The object would be to find easy targets, short runs and safe conditions.
4. How is such a Second Line or Auxiliary Bomber Force to be improvised during the winter months? Could not crews from the Training Schools do occasional runs? Are none of the Lysander[471] and Reconnaissance pilots capable of doing

[471] The high-winged Westland Lysander (known to many British pilots as the 'Lizzie') was developed in the early 1930s as a ground support and recon plane. Its first operational use, in France and Belgium in 1940, was disastrous; out of over 170 used, over 80 were destroyed in the air and 30 more on the ground. It was gradually replaced in 1942 and 1943, instead being used as target tugs, in air/sea rescue and, perhaps

some of this simpler bombing, observing that the Army is not likely to be in action unless invasion occurs? I ask that a whole-hearted effort shall be made to cart a large number of bombs into Germany by a Second Line organisation such as I have suggested, and under conditions in which admittedly no special accuracy would be obtained. Pray let me have the best suggestions possible, and we can then see whether they are practical or not.

5. How is it that so few of our Bombers are fitted with blind landing appliances? MAP tells me that a number of Lorenz equipments are available. The grievous losses which occurred one day last week ought not to be repeated. Not only do the Bombers need the blind landing facilities (which have been used in commercial aviation for years) but also if Fighter aircraft are to operate by night, as they must increasingly, such aircraft must also be furnished with the means of making safe landings. Pray let me have your observations.
6. I attach a singularly able paper which has been given to me privately, and which reinforces your paper on the Mine v. Bomb argument, but also contains other suggestive observations. Will you kindly let me have it back.

WSC

Winston S. Churchill to Sir Archibald Sinclair and Chief of Air Staff
20th October 1940

In connection with the plans now being developed for night fighting, not only by individual Aircraft Interception fitted machines, but by eight-gun fighter squadrons, it is worth considering whether in any area where our fighters are operating and the guns have to remain out of action, these guns should not fire blank charges. This would (a) confuse the enemy by the flashing on the ground, and make him less aware of the impending fighter attacks – it would thus have a strictly military reason; (b) it would make a noise to drown the approach of our attacking fighters, and also to avoid discouraging silence for the population. It would not be legitimate to fire blanks merely for the second purpose, but if there is a military reason the objection disappears.

WSC

Churchill returned to the demand for an apology to be issued to Beaverbrook that he had requested from Sinclair on 19 October.[472]

most importantly, covert ops, for example supplying equipment to the French resistance, and carrying agents. Due to a low stall speed, the Lysander could take off from short grass airfields within France.

472 See page 260.

23rd October 1940
Private

My dear Archie,

Yours of October 21, paragraph 2. My reference to 'what was not going on', implied no suggestion that Air Vice-Marshal McKean was deliberately telling an untruth, but only that the facts were different from what he believed them to be. But if a man, however honestly, accepts false facts and on them bases unfounded charges expressed in disrespectful language about his superior, undoubtedly he deserves censure, more especially if he does not mitigate this censure by an apology.

I am sorry that you brush aside what I wrote to you in my letter of the 19th instant. I will not renew my appeal.

I am having all the telegrams printed, and they should be ready by tomorrow. The Cabinet, happily, not I, must pronounce upon the issues which are opened by the very serious and unfounded affront which has been offered to one of their Members. I hope you will not mind my saying that I feel I might have had a little more assistance from you in dealing with this difficult matter.

Yours sincerely,
WSC

On 25 October 1940 Newall was replaced by Sir Charles Portal[473] as Chief of Air Staff. There had been a whispering campaign against Newall, both within the Air Ministry and at the Ministry of Aircraft Production; an anonymous paper attacking him was circulated around the Air Ministry and reached Sinclair's desk in August.[474] It accused Newall of inadequate mental ability, limited practical experience, lack of judgement and a reluctance to remove incompetent officers, including not having the strength of character to deal with personalities like Dowding. All these accusations would have been understood by Sinclair, who never found Newall convivial company or expressed much satisfaction with his abilities.[475] Sinclair enjoyed a very happy working relationship with Portal for the rest of the war.

---

473 Sir Charles Portal, Baron Portal of Hungerford (1893–1971): Lieutenant Colonel, Royal Flying Corps, First World War; remained in RAF where he developed new approaches to improving bombing accuracy; in 1934 appointed Commander, British forces in Aden, where he tried to control the local tribesmen by air power; by 1939 a member of the Air Council and Director of Organisation in the Air Ministry; Commander-in-Chief, Bomber Command April–October 1940; advocated strategic area bombing against German industrial areas instead of bombing specific factories or plants, and gave the first order to bomb Berlin, on 25 August 1940; in response Göring ordered the Luftwaffe to bomb London instead of British airfields; Chief of Air Staff 1940–45; in January 1943, selected to coordinate US and British bomber forces in the bomber offensive against Germany; ennobled 1945; Controller of the Atomic Energy Authority 1946–51.

474 A.J.P. Taylor, Beaverbrook's biographer, has identified Beaverbrook as the likely source of this poisonous letter.

475 Sinclair's views on Newall have been confirmed by Sinclair's two surviving children, Catherine and Angus, who both recall their father's relief when he managed to persuade Churchill that Portal should

During the autumn of 1940 Churchill worked with the Air Ministry to prepare documents for the then still neutral United States Government, along with senior Air Ministry personnel, to help organise production of the aircraft that had been ordered by Britain.

Winston S. Churchill to Sir Archibald Sinclair and Sir Charles Portal
29th October 1940

This paper makes it easy for anyone to understand exactly what we are doing and what we want. It would therefore be of particular value for the purposes of Air Commodore Slessor's mission, as the American Ministers concerned will be able to take it in quickly. The whole movement of the argument leads up to the conclusion that we need the planes from them to carry out a carefully worked out plan, and that we have very nicely adjusted the balance between the pilots and the machines. It may be that some alterations in numbers or phrasing are necessary, but it would be a great pity if the movement and sequence of this orderly argument were in any way deranged. I shall be very glad to go through the paper at 5p.m. to-day at the Central War Room, in order to settle with you the final form which you think it should assume.

It would certainly be a good thing to add to the end something to show how deeply the expansion will rise after June 1941.

WSC

Winston S. Churchill to Sir Archibald Sinclair and Sir Charles Portal
30th October 1940

SECRETARY OF STATE FOR AIR
C.A.S.

I made some general remarks upon this subject[476] at the Cabinet this morning, and you will see the views of the Cabinet recorded in the Summary.

There is no need to make the announcement publicly of any change of policy, but I should like to see the instructions it is proposed to give for this temporary change of objectives to the Bomber Command. Pray see attached and return.

WSC

replace Newall (interviews with the editor, 2002).

[476] Churchill had spoken to the War Cabinet about the need to make preparations to bomb the seat of the Vichy Government should they offer any act of hostility against British forces in North Africa.

Sir Archibald Sinclair to Winston S. Churchill
31st October 1940

PRIME MINISTER

I am grateful to you for letting me see the papers attached to your Minute M.244 of the 30th October, which I now return. I have discussed them with the C.A.S., who tells me that he had sent you, before receiving your Minute, a copy of the new Directions to the Bomber Command. I trust that these are in accordance with your wishes.

C.A.S. has made the following comments on the papers you sent to us, and I agree with them:-

1. The bombing of Italy has been limited not so much by the rival claims of targets in Germany and occupied territory as by:–
   a) The great distance. Only the Whitleys can manage it with a fair bomb load, and they are the smallest of the groups.
   b) The high mountains on the way, which are impassable in "icing" conditions.
2. It has been our belief that our small bomber force could, by accurate bombing, do very great damage to the enemy's war effort, but could not gain a decision against Germany by bombing the civil population. Unless we get a decision we achieve nothing by promiscuous bombing.
3. Except when he uses mines, it is uncertain to what extent the enemy is deliberately choosing to bomb the civil population when he might bomb military targets. When he cannot see to hit the latter he bombs centres of population, and we are now doing the same, though not long ago we were encouraged to bring our bombs home under those conditions.
4. It is agreed that we could probably knock out Italy if we could reach her towns regularly in strength; unfortunately, we cannot, but we will do our best.
5. "Very heavy bombs". The 1,000 lb. bomb cannot be carried by Whitleys, and the 2,000 lb. bomb, when we get it, will go into the Hampden only of our present types.
6. It is most unlikely that as much damage will be done by either of the above bombs when used against towns as by an equivalent weight of 500 lb. bombs. The latter size, with suitable fusing, is considered the optimum for general destruction of buildings and services.

I am returning to the Secretary of State for Foreign Affairs the enclosures attached to your minute from him, and I am sending him a copy of this minute.

In so far as the Germans may have been led away by their theories of the total war into attacking our civilian population instead of concentrating upon our aircraft and air engine factories, it is very lucky for us.

AHMS

Winston S. Churchill to Sir Archibald Sinclair and Sir Charles Portal
1st November 1940

I much regret that no attempt will be made to expand the Bomber Force on the lines indicated in my paragraphs 3 and 4.[477] I must ask for more consideration of this need. I am not at all convinced by the replies given in your minute. It is a scandal that so little use is made of the immense masses of material provided. This discharge of bombs on Germany is pitifully small.

WSC

Winston S. Churchill to Sir Archibald Sinclair
1st November 1940

Archie,

Let me have, on not more than two sheets of paper, an analysis of the German aviators taken prisoner of war since July 1st, showing numbers, ages, amount of training, etc., distinguishing between bomber and fighter prisoners. Any other information about them would be welcome.

WSC

Churchill discussed bombing policy with Sinclair and Portal in early November. He was beginning to be persuaded of the move from precision bombing to the adoption of a campaign that would eventually result, via the enthusiasm of Air Marshal Harris, in the massive and indiscriminate destruction of cities such as Lubeck, Rostock and Dresden.

Winston S. Churchill to Sir Archibald Sinclair and Sir Charles Portal
2nd November 1940

Yours of the 31st.[478] I do not dissent from the general principles and statements which your Minute contains. In view, however, of the consensus of opinion among authorities on German and Italian morale, it is felt that a temporary diversion should be made to less precise objectives, especially in the case of Italy. This diversion is in the nature of an experiment. We have seen what inconvenience the attack on the British civilian population has caused us, and there is no reason why the enemy should be freed from all such embarrassments. Unless the results are seen to be good within a comparatively short time, the emphasis should be thrown again on to the precise objectives.

WSC

[477] Churchill's letter of 20 October; see page 261.
[478] Protesting at the diversion of bombing resources from Germany to Italy.

Sinclair returned to his concerns about the safety of the Prime Minister in November when he proposed that Chequers (the Prime Ministerial country retreat) could be more effectively protected by siting Bofors anti-aircraft guns in the vicinity.

Winston S. Churchill to Sir Archibald Sinclair
10th November 1940

Archie,

There is a shelter at Chequers which gives good protection from lateral damage. There is the household to consider. Perhaps you will have the accommodation inspected. The carriage-way is being turfed.[479]

I cannot bear to divert Bofors from the fighting positions. What about trying a few rockets, which are at present only in an experimental stage?

I am trying to vary my movements a little during the moonlight intervals. It is very good of you and your Ministry to concern yourselves with my safety.

WSC

With the Battle of Britain effectively won by the end of September, Sinclair agreed with Churchill that it was now time to bring the debate over the future role of Dowding to a head. It was agreed that Dowding should be appointed to head the mission on war aviation to the US. The note below was Sinclair's summary of his meeting with Dowding in which he persuaded him to accept the new role; it was used by Churchill in preparation for his meeting with Dowding the day after Sinclair's interview.

Sir Archibald Sinclair to Winston S. Churchill
13th November 1940

Note of an interview at the Air Ministry with Sir Hugh Dowding

I told Sir Hugh Dowding that the Government had been increasingly made aware of the need for strengthening our organisation in the United States of America for selecting, modifying and purchasing aircraft and air armament and that it was proposed greatly to enlarge our existing organisation and to send over a considerable number of experts in various departments. At the same time it was realised that unless there was behind this organisation the driving force of a strong personality and unless there was at its head a man whose influence on American production engineers, staff officers and members of the American Government would carry weight, we could not expect to obtain satisfactory results.

There was, moreover, a larger issue. There were, in the United States of America, the finest production engineers in the world with huge resources at their disposal;

[479] Presumably to make the target less obvious from the air.

but they lacked war experience and needed to be told what to do. So it was with the Government and the military staffs. We believed that they would be willing to accept the guidance of a man whose opinion and personality would command their respect. We believed that, with the help of such a man, we could not only obtain the kind of aircraft we need ourselves, but we could go far to shape the American Air Force of the future. So much importance was attached to this appointment by our friends in the United States of America, including Mr. Morgenthau,[480] that they had asked for Air Marshal Portal to come over, but I felt bound to refuse to let him go.

Naturally, this project was primarily the concern of Lord Beaverbrook and he had told me that he desired for the purpose, the services of Sir Hugh Dowding; and I, for my part, had formed the opinion that to make Sir Hugh Dowding available for this undertaking would be the best disposition of our resources.

Before reaching this conclusion I had weighed very carefully all the factors in the problem. I wished to express to him, in no perfunctory way, my appreciation of his great services as Commander in Chief of the Fighter Command. Nevertheless, I had come to the conclusion that it was right to make the change which this new project would involve and I had therefore told Lord Beaverbrook that I would make Sir Hugh Dowding's services available to him.

Sir Hugh Dowding replied that he did not suppose that I would wish him to give an answer straightaway. I said that I feared that I might not sufficiently have impressed upon him the high importance of the mission which we were asking him to undertake and I hoped very much that he would not refuse it.

He said that it would be one thing if it was only a temporary mission which he was being asked to undertake and that he would be returning, at its conclusion, to his Command.

I replied that I must tell him that that was not in my mind and that I was proposing to appoint Air Vice-Marshal Sholto Douglas[481] to Fighter Command.[482]

He said that he quite understood but that he would want a night to think it over and that he would want to see the Prime Minister.

---

480 President Roosevelt's Treasury Secretary, Henry R. Morgenthau.

481 Sir W. Sholto Douglas, 1st Baron Douglas of Kirtleside (1893–1969): ended the First World War as a major in the Royal Flying Corps; made Air Vice-Marshal in 1938; Deputy Chief of the Air Staff 1940; succeeded Dowding in November 1940 as Commander-in-Chief, Fighter Command; Commander RAF Middle East Command 1943–45; Commander-in-Chief British Air Forces of Occupation in Germany 1945–48; ennobled in 1948, and sat on the Labour benches.

482 During the Battle of Britain Douglas was highly critical of Dowding's strategy, arguing that RAF fighters should be sent out to meet the German planes before they reached Britain; Dowding rejected this approach as too dangerous, believing it would increase the number of pilots killed. Sinclair and Portal agreed with Douglas and in November 1940 he replaced Dowding as head of Fighter Command and developed the 'Big Wing' strategy, involving large formations of fighter aircraft deployed in mass sweeps against the Luftwaffe over the English Channel and northern Europe; although RAF pilots were able to bring down a large number of German planes, critics claimed that they were not always available during emergencies and prime targets became more vulnerable to bombing attacks.

I answered that, of course, I would not press him and that he should have time to think it over. I had no doubt that the Prime Minister would be most willing to see him; at the same time it was possible that after thinking it over he might not think it necessary to see the Prime Minister.

He answered that he would certainly wish to see the Prime Minister – and so we parted.

AHMS

Winston S. Churchill to Sir Archibald Sinclair
14th November 1940

<u>SECRET</u>
<u>SECRETARY OF STATE FOR AIR</u>

I saw Sir Hugh Dowding this morning, and explained to him the importance of getting American war aviation developed on right lines, and lines parallel with ours. He expressed great doubts of his ability to fulfil this mission, but on my telling him I wished him to undertake it in the public interest, of which I was the judge, he accepted the task subject to the condition that if he wrote to me saying he was not getting on with it over there, he should be allowed to come home.

Personally I think he will perform the task very well,[483] and I will give him a letter to the President. I have a very great regard for this Officer, and admiration for his qualities and achievements.

Let me see his instructions please in draft form.

WSC

One of Sinclair's key roles as Air Minister was as the RAF's unofficial Chief Personnel Officer. In mid-November Sinclair found himself defending one of his (unidentified) officers from the Prime Minister's wrath.

Sir Archibald Sinclair to Winston S. Churchill
15th November 1940
Personal and Secret

My dear Winston,

You told me this morning that it has been reported to you that a certain officer had been talking loosely in a defeatist way at a dinner party and you asked

[483] Unfortunately this prediction was to prove inaccurate. Dowding's interpersonal skills were not up to the diplomatic tasks that his US posting was to require and he proved neither popular nor influential with the Americans. Furthermore, he found it difficult to toe the party line and often argued with the local British diplomats and the team sent to the US from the MAP. He was recalled to the UK in June 1941.

me to make enquiries from a certain friend of mine who had been present at the conversation.

I got through to his house on the telephone but he is ill in bed and without a telephone in his room. His wife offered to take a message but obviously it was impossible to make enquiries on so delicate a subject in that way.

I know this officer well as I have been working with him very closely for six months. I do not pretend to know every facet of his character and some questions might arise about his conduct which I would be unable to answer. I am, however, quite certain that there is no defeatist weakness in him. He is tough, cool, not at all temperamental, and resolute. Phlegm was his characteristic in the critical times we have been through – not jumpiness.

As it is impossible for me to make the enquiries which you asked me to make I hope you will trust my judgement. If you want another opinion I would suggest that you should ask Portal or Newall. I have no doubt at all what their answer will be. As I told you this morning I have already given this officer, after more than one consultation with you, an appointment. It has been approved by the King and will be announced on Monday.

Yours always,
Archie

Winston S. Churchill to Sir Archibald Sinclair and Chief of Air Staff
15th November 1940

This amounts to a loss of eleven of our bombers in one night.[484] I said the other day by Minute that the operations were not to be pressed unduly during these very adverse weather conditions. We cannot afford to have losses of this kind in view of your very slow replacements. If you go on like this, you will break the bomber force down to below a minimum for grave emergencies. No results have been achieved which would in any way justify or compensate for these losses. I consider the loss of eleven aircraft out of one hundred and thirty-nine – i.e., about eight per cent – a very grievous disaster at this stage of our bomber development.

Let me have the losses during the first half of November.

WSC

Winston S. Churchill to Sir Archibald Sinclair
18th November 1940

Please report on progress with operational use of LAM.[485]

[484] Churchill was responding to one of the routine reports of operations that were circulated around the Defence Committee.

[485] Land Arm Mode – an automatic landing device.

I understand that the first experiment was very promising, though marred by a hitch in the release mechanism. It would be a great pity if this operation were held up by this when the need of some counter to the night bomber is so patent.

Operational experiments should surely continue whilst improvements are being made, to avoid a recurrence of the trouble.

WSC

Churchill was anxious that the Air Ministry should consider using aerial mines[486] ('egg-layers') to combat the use of the Lorenz beams to navigate to the bomb targets in Britain.[487] Churchill argued that as the RAF was able to track the direction of the beams then aerial mines could be laid in their path to bring down the bombers as they tracked towards their targets.

Winston S. Churchill to Sir Archibald Sinclair
19th November 1940
ACTION THIS DAY
Secret

1 It is now, I think, more than three weeks since you very kindly promised to give me your new forecast of expansion, based on the adoption of the ascertained wastage during the five battle months. I cannot understand why it should be such a complicated business. It only means carrying different basic figures through whatever is the variety of calculations on which you depend.

2 I was very glad to read in your minute to me yesterday about appointments that you are pressing forward with the Egglayer proposal. I have so long and repeatedly urged this method, and have been so consistently baffled by delays and obstructions, that I almost despair of action. The paltry assignment of three Harrows[488] to this vital task is characteristic of the process which has paralysed us. The fact that the enemy rely upon the Beam, and that we can ascertain beforehand the probable direction of his main attack, and to a very great extent can measure his altitude, should make this obvious method of interpreting and deterring him our first endeavour. But even now only 100,000 aerial mines have been ordered, and every kind of difficulty is made about the wires, &c. Everyone on the route heard the stream of enemy Bombers passing continuously for hours to and fro to bomb Coventry. There was plenty of time to put up 20 Egglayers in releases of 5, making a curtain of death through which these enemy machines would have had to pass coming and going. You might easily have had 20 or

[486] A mine suspended from a parachute with a trailing wire so that if an aircraft struck the wire then the bomb was dragged up to the wing where it would explode.

[487] See page 310.

[488] The Handley Page Harrow bomber.

30 brought down, with all the resulting deterrent in the future. Moreover, the enemy could not retaliate in the same way on our Bombers, which do not work on the Beam, but by navigational skill. If the enemy is driven off his Beam, he must go through a long process of training to reach a particular objective.

Pray let me have a report every three days on the progress you are making.

WSC

Sir Archibald Sinclair to Winston S. Churchill
25th November 1940
SECRET

Prime Minister

You asked for my comments on the attached telegram from Berne.

Our attacks have, of course, been more widely dispersed than the Germans and we have directed them, accurately we hope, on to carefully selected targets, principally harbours, oil installations, power plants, aluminium and aircraft assembly factories. Many of these are sited well out in the country and even in towns the Germans are notoriously expert at preventing the public from seeing the damage that has been done.

We have a mass of reports from various sources confirming the damage done to specified objectives which we selected for attack.

Reports such as those submitted by Mr. Kelly are, of course, relatively valueless unless they give some indication of the districts which the informant visited. It would be quite possible to travel widely in England without seeing more than minor damage. Recent visitors to this country – like M. Rougier of the Spanish Officers – have expressed their astonishment at the "small" amount of damage done to London.

AHMS

Churchill celebrated his 66th birthday in November 1940.

Sir Archibald Sinclair to Winston S. Churchill
Air Ministry
30th November 1940

Dear Winston,

With all my heart I wish you a happy and victorious return of your birthday. Amid all your anxieties, you have much to gladden your heart this birthday – the successes against Italy,[489] for example, which owe so much to your own judgement and action, and Randolph's brilliant start in the House of Commons.[490]

[489] The British armies in North Africa had pushed the Italians into retreat and were on the verge of taking

So good luck to you in the coming year – and take care of yourself, for you carry in your hands the destinies of us all.

Yours always,
Archie

PS. Alas! No Stiltons this year – so I hope you will like these cigars!

Winston S. Churchill to Sir Archibald Sinclair and Sir Charles Portal
2nd December 1940
ACTION THIS DAY
Secret

One cannot doubt that the Germans will be making tremendous efforts to increase their Air Force this winter, and that a far more serious attempt must be expected against us in the Spring. It is most necessary to form the best opinion possible about the potential scale of the German increase (a) by March 31, (b) by June 30 – these dates not being arbitrary if other dates are more convenient and equally illustrative. It is important not to exaggerate the German capacity, and therefore the limiting factors, e.g., engines, special raw materials, pilot training, effect of our bombing, are of special interest. On the other hand, full weight should be given to the German use of factories in the captive countries.

I should be glad if your Intelligence Branch would let me have a paper (not more than two or three sheets) upon this vital matter, and it would be convenient if they could keep in touch with Professor Lindemann[491] while they are preparing this, so that we do not have to argue about the various bases of calculations adopted. While I want the report to be short, I want to be cognisant of the data and reasoning processes on which it has been built up. I am not sure to what extent MAP comes into this. It would be a comfort if an agreed view could be presented by the two Departments. Let me know how you will set about this. One week is all that can be spared.

WSC

Tobruk and throwing Mussolini's forces out of Egypt.

[490] Randolph had been returned unopposed for Preston under the wartime truce between the coalition parties. He was introduced to the House by his father and made his maiden speech on 8 October. Randolph made a series of speeches that were warmly received although Sinclair is exaggerating to refer to them as 'brilliant'.

[491] Frederick Alexander Lindemann, Viscount Cherwell (1886–1957): physicist and Fellow of Christ Church, Oxford; during World War I, was the first to develop the mathematical theory of aircraft spin, put into practice in air combat; Churchill's scientific advisor; firm advocate of the policy of area bombing; Paymaster-General 1942–45, 1951–53; established the Atomic Energy Authority.

Winston S. Churchill to Sir Archibald Sinclair
8th December 1940

I regret to have to draw your attention to the article by Sir Philip Joubert de la Ferte[492] appearing in to-day's Sunday Express.[493] What are the regulations governing the publication of articles by newspapers by Officers serving in the Air Force? Was he paid for this article? Who decided that he should write for any one particular paper? Disciplinary action in regard to this Officer is long overdue. The very important, nay vital work with which he is charged is not prospering, and he is unsatisfactory as is the air action upon the North-Western approaches in respect of which he has most important liaison duties, I wonder if it would not be better if he confined himself more precisely to these professional duties upon which our safety so largely depends.

WSC

Winston S. Churchill to Sir Archibald Sinclair
8th December 1940

There is no doubt we have been much vexed by the German land mines, which have done grievous damage and much impressed the public with their power. If you cannot carry them over the Alps, why not make deliveries from Malta and also from the new aerodromes we are establishing in Greece?

WSC

Sir Archibald Sinclair to Winston S. Churchill
9th December 1940

Dear Prime Minister,

My own opinion is that the difference in morale effect between the heavy bombs we are now dropping on Italy and the land mine is not sufficient to justify sending Hampdens out to Malta, and so introducing a new type of heavy bomber (with the necessary personnel, equipment, spares, etc.) to the Middle East. Nevertheless, it can be done if you so wish.[494]

AHMS

[492] Air Chief Marshal Sir Philip Bennet Joubert de la Ferte (1887–1965): served in RFC and then RAF, from 1914; Air Adviser on Combined Operations, 1940; Assistant Chief of the Air Staff (Radio) 1940–41; Air Officer Commander-in-Chief, Coastal Command, 1941–43; well known for his commentaries on the progress of the war on the BBC and in national newspapers.

[493] In this article, headed 'Will this winter weather stop the bomber', Joubert de la Ferte had dismissed claims that bad weather would impede the Luftwaffe's ability to reach England.

[494] To which Churchill noted in reply on the letter, 'Not in view of your opinion'.

Churchill wrote to Sinclair and Portal requesting their views on how to make best use of the British ability to receive and decrypt German secret radio signals which had recently been achieved thanks to the recovery of an Enigma code machine and code books from a captured German submarine.

Winston S. Churchill to Sir Archibald Sinclair and Sir Charles Portal
9th December 1940

I spent four hours on Saturday[495] with the Officers of the Air Ministry Intelligence Branch and those of MEW.[496] I have not been able to reach a conclusion as to which are right. Probably the truth lies mid-way between them. The subject is of capital importance to the whole future picture we make to ourselves of the war. It also would influence the use we make of our forces in the meanwhile. I am most anxious that the two Branches mentioned, whose Officers are in the most friendly relations, should sit together in an inquiry, to sift the evidence and ascertain the facts. There should be an impartial Chairman accustomed to weigh evidence and to cross-examine, and I wonder whether for this purpose Mr. Justice Singleton, who had war experience as a Gunner and recently conducted an inquiry for me into bomb sights, would not be able to guide the discussions and throw a valuable light on the obscurities of this all-important scene. He would, of course, have to be told about the secret information.[497]

Before taking any decision, I would like to have your views.

Meanwhile, I have set out a statement of what I learned in our discussion on Saturday, as something for the Department to bite on. Every fact in it is open to question, modification or offset. I have sent a copy to each Branch, and it would form the staple of the investigations I contemplate.

WSC

The Air Ministry and the MAP were at loggerheads over the need for training aircraft: the Air Ministry felt that far more were required to maintain the stream of pilots and crew than MAP believed appropriate.

[495] 7th December 1940.
[496] Ministry of Economic Warfare.
[497] That the top-secret German messages could be read by the British.

Sir Archibald Sinclair to Winston S. Churchill
11th December 1940
SECRET

PRIME MINISTER

The Minister of Aircraft Production sent me a copy of his minute to you dated 2nd December, and I have had occasion today to refer to it in a letter which I have written to him, so I send you a copy of my comments on it.[498]

You will see that I have denounced his assertion that we have "too many trainers!" The need of advanced trainers is now the limiting factor in our expansion. We are doing all we can to make every suitable machine available from our own resources. I assure you that we are fully alive to Lord Beaverbrook's difficulties and, for this reason, we are not leaving undone anything that it is possible for us to do to help him.

He must give us these advanced trainers or we shall not be able to man his aircraft.

AHMS

Winston S. Churchill to Sir Archibald Sinclair
11th December 1940
ACTION THIS DAY

Pray see attached.[499] What are we to do about para. 14?[500] What is the truth? Are you really going to use 7,000 brand-new combat airplanes in the training units? Considering that you put these words in my mouth and I cabled them accordingly, I hope you will be able to explain Air Commodore Slessor's[501] amendments. Please return urgent.[502]

WSC

---

498 Beaverbrook was objecting to the number of planes that he felt were being diverted from frontline duty to serve as trainers for new pilots – part of a wider campaign he was fighting about the Air Ministry not protecting his factories sufficiently from German bombers.

499 Telegram from Lord Lothian, British Ambassador to Washington.

500 Paragraph 14 of Churchill's telegram to Roosevelt of 8th December 1940, which had requested that the US agree to manufacture for Britain 2,000 combat aircraft a month, principally heavy bombers, to help increase the frontline strength to 7,000 planes.

501 Air Marshal Sir John Cotesworth Slessor (1897–1979): commanded No 5 Group, Bomber Command 1941; Assistant Chief of the Air Staff (Policy) 1942–43; Air Officer Commander-in-Chief Coastal Command 1943; Deputy Air Commander, Mediterranean Allied Air Forces, 1945; Air Member for Personnel 1945–47; Chief of the Air Staff 1950–53.

502 Churchill was concerned that he had explicitly requested from Roosevelt his support for orders of combat planes for frontline action. Subsequent clarifications from Slessor had implied that many of the planes would actually be for training purposes, which Churchill feared would not be given equal priority in the US.

1 Top left: Sinclair in 1904 – aged 14, at Eton

2 Top right: Sinclair in 1918, as a major in the Household Cavalry

3 Left: Portrait of Sinclair by Augustus John, c.1920–24 (in the early 1990s the family sold this picture, which none of them liked, to the Scottish National Portrait Gallery to fund the biography by Gerard DeGroot)

4 Sinclair and Churchill at Armentières, 11 February 1916

5 Top: the officers of the 6th battalion, Royal Scots Fusiliers, spring 1916 (Sinclair and Churchill, seated centre)

6 Left: Churchill and Sinclair, Cologne, August 1919

7 Top: Sinclair, c. 1936

8 Right: portrait of Sinclair by

9 'All behind you, Winston' (*Evening Standard*, 14 May 1940) (Sinclair is in the middle of the second row, wearing a wing collar)

10 The Cabinet, c. 1941 (Churchill seated, centre; Sinclair standing, left)

11 Sinclair and Churchill watching a flying demonstration, June 1943

12 Sinclair meets Flight Sergeant K. W. Brown, one of the crew members from the Dambusters raid, 10 June 1943

13 The Sinclair family out walking near Thurso Castle, c. 1939 (left to right: Sinclair, Elizabeth, Robin, Marigold, Angus, Catherine)

14 Churchill, Marigold and Archie Sinclair outside Sinclair's home in Twickenham, c. 1955

Winston S. Churchill to Sir Archibald Sinclair
13th December 1940

Your letter to Lord Beaverbrook of the 11th December.[503] Out of 1,800 estimated monthly German aircraft production, the Intelligence Branch of the Air Ministry consider that only 400 airplanes are provided for training. This seems very few considering that the Air Ministry's view is that the Germans are maintaining about 2½ times our strength in the front lines. Alternatively, if the Air Ministry's requirements of Trainers is warranted, and if our Trainers are not profusely and unthriftily used, and large numbers kept about the aerodromes in an unserviceable state, the German front-line strength cannot well be maintained on such a small proportion of Trainers.

Mr. Justice Singleton is coming to lunch with me on Sunday, and I will set him to work on the enquiry on which we are agreed.

WSC

Churchill watched with interest the continuing battles between the Air Ministry and the Ministry of Aircraft Production.

Winston S. Churchill to Sir Archibald Sinclair
PRIME MINISTER'S PERSONAL MINUTE
Serial No. M. 409
14th December 1940
(Action this day)

SECRETARY OF STATE FOR AIR.

There is one thing about the warfare between A.M. and M.A.P.[504] which is helpful to the public interest, namely that I get a fine view of what is going on and hear both sides of the case argued with spirit. Will you very kindly address yourself to the various statements made in his letter attached, and especially to the one marked A, that on September 1 you had over 1,000 unserviceable Trainer aircraft. I have long suspected that the inefficiency which formerly ruled in the A.S.U.s and left us with only 45 aeroplanes, when the new Government was formed, as against about 1,200 now, was reproduced in all the trainer establishments and communication flights, and that a great mass of aeroplanes were kept in an unserviceable state, and I remember particularly the statement of one of your high officers that the Training Command worked on a basis of 50 per cent unserviceable. Who is responsible for Repair and Training Establishments? If I were you I should throw the whole business of repair on to M.A.P., and then you would be able to criticise them, as you would readily do, for any short-comings.

[503] In which Sinclair had argued his case again for more trainer aircraft.

[504] Air Ministry and Ministry of Aircraft Production.

See also the figures of how repaired aircraft and engines have increased since the change was made.

I recur to the point I made to you yesterday when you sent me your letter to M.A.P. The Air Ministry's view is that the Germans have nearly 6,000 airplanes in front line action, and we have about 2,000. Air Ministry also believe that the German output is 1,800 a month, out of which they provide only 400 for Training Establishments, while we, out of 1,400 output, provide also 400. How do you then explain that the Germans are able to keep three times our establishment in front line action with only an equal monthly subscription of Trainer aircraft? Apparently on your figures, which I may say I do not accept, (except for controversial purposes) the Germans can keep three times as large a force in action as you can for the same number of Trainer planes. I know that you will rightly say you are preparing for the expansion of the future, but they have to keep going on a 3 fold scale, and expand as well.

I await with keen interest further developments of your controversy.[505]

WSC

Sinclair replied to Churchill defending the efforts made by the Air Ministry and urging that the Ministry of Aircraft Production should not have its remit widened (Beaverbrook was keen to carve more chunks from the Air Ministry), but should focus on doing what it currently did better.

Sir Archibald Sinclair to Winston S. Churchill
18th December 1940

PRIME MINISTER

We have examined the comparative British and German figures which you quote, and we have set against the German first line strength of 5,700, the Metropolitan and Overseas strength of the R.A.F., together with the Fleet Air Arm, since the flying training of the Fleet Air Arm is carried out by the R.A.F. This gives a figure of some 3,000. Since June our average production of aircraft of all types has been 1520 and of trainers 450. The Air Staff estimate of German production is 1800 of which 500 are trainers. The figure of 400 trainers related to a total of 1600 for the German Air Force. And they estimate also that the German Air Force may expand over the next six months at the rate of six squadrons a month. Our rate of expansion is sixteen squadrons a month during the next six months. So it is not to a force

[505] Interestingly, the next day Churchill wrote to Beaverbrook that the Air Ministry 'regard you as a merciless critic, and even enemy. They resent having had the M.A.P. functions carved out of their show, and I have no doubt they pour out their detraction by every channel open. I am definitely of opinion that it is more in the public interest that there should be sharp criticism and counter-criticism between the two departments than that they should be handing each other out ceremonious bouquets. One must therefore accept the stimulating but disagreeable conditions of war.'

of 3,400 aircraft that our training reorganisation is directed but to a force which by next June alone will be greater than its present strength by 100 squadrons.

I attach a copy of a reply to Lord Beaverbrook's letter of the 12th December in which I have repeated that the efficiency of the trainer aircraft is retarding our expansion and I have explained also to the Minister of Aircraft Production that the unserviceability in Training Command is due to a large extent to causes which you have placed within his control and are no longer within mine.

The Training Command basis of 50% unserviceability was abandoned some six months ago, when we began to accelerate and increase the output from the schools. At the present time the unserviceability is 33%, and the aircraft are being worked far harder than they used to be. In November, 1940, the average number of hours flown per aircraft on the initial equipment at elementary and service flying training schools was 49, as compared with 26 at elementary flying training schools and 35 at service flying training schools a year ago. And a year ago, there were none of the difficult maintenance problems arising out of the dispersal of the aircraft out of doors in bad weather round the aerodrome. But of the aircraft now unserviceable, some 40% lack spares.

I am responsible for training in the R.A.F. and I am responsible for repairs carried out at units. In this, the Air Ministry has received valuable help from the servicing parties provided by the Minister of Aircraft Production. Certainly I am not satisfied with the present rate of unserviceability, but I do not think it would be a good plan to transfer the responsibility for repair at units to the Ministry of Aircraft Production. I am not anxious to criticise the Ministry of Aircraft Production, but I am anxious to increase the number of serviceable aeroplanes in the Flying Training Command. Accordingly, it seems to me that the Ministry of Aircraft Production should instead of taking over fresh responsibility concentrate upon the production of spares and of advanced training aircraft.

AHMS

Winston S. Churchill to Sir Archibald Sinclair
19th December 1940
PERSONAL AND SECRET

Dear Archie,

The time has come to make a selection here in succession to Sir Wilfrid Freeman.[506]

[506] Wilfrid Rhodes Freeman (1888–1953): in charge of RAF research and development 1938–40, responsible for pushing through the development of key equipment such as the four-engined heavy bombers (Halifaxes and Manchesters), the Mosquito reconnaissance and pathfinder plane, and the testing of the radar early warning system; also, crucially, involved in the development of the eight-gun fighters (Hurricanes and Spitfires); served in MAP from November 1940 to the end of the war; his relationship with Portal, who replaced Newall as Chief of Air Staff in October 1940, was one of the key relationships of the war and ensured that the relations between the Air Ministry and MAP never reached breaking point – even when Beaverbrook was in charge.

Will you make a suggestion, please?

Yours ever,
W

Winston S. Churchill to Sir Archibald Sinclair and Sir Charles Portal
22nd December 1940

BRITISH AERODROMES IN GREECE[507]

The Foreign Office must be asked to take this matter up with the Greek Government. It is not our interest to draw down German vengeance upon Greece. In any case, the Greeks would have to be the final authority as to the use made of their Aerodromes. They must be asked to allow us to develop at once all the Airfields which are effective against Italy, and we must let them know that the sending of any further Squadrons is dependent upon this.

With regard to the Aerodromes which would be effective against the Roumanian oilfields, &c., they should be told we should not use these without their permission for that purpose, but in case they are attacked by Germany in the Spring, we must know about them. Perhaps, in the first instance, our Officers could reconnoitre them in plain clothes and report exactly what had to be done to fit them for the latest Fighters and Bombers. If you raise these matters with the Foreign Office, and mention them in the Cabinet, I shall be obliged, and will advise the Cabinet in this sense.

What is being done in Turkey? There surely a number of Aerodromes can be made of proper size, from which we could aid the Turkish defence if they are attacked.

WSC

Winston S. Churchill to Sir Archibald Sinclair, Chief of Air Staff and Lord Beaverbrook
30th December 1940
Secret – Action this day

1. I am deeply concerned at the stagnant condition of our bomber force. The fighters are going ahead well, but the bomber force, particularly crews, is not making the progress hoped for. I consider the rapid expansion of the bomber force one of the greatest military objectives now before us. We are of course drawing upon the bomber force for the coastal command and for the Middle East. If the bottleneck is, as I am told, crews, we must either have the pilots and personnel we are sending out to the Middle East returned to us after they have delivered

[507] Greece had been invaded by Italy from occupied Albania in October 1940 but had, much to most people's surprise, repelled the Italians and in early December 1940, pushed on into Albania; in due course this triggered German invasion and occupation of Greece in April 1941.

their machines, or, what would be less injurious to formed squadrons, have other pilots and personnel sent back from the Middle East in their place. The policy is to remount the Middle East, and this must be achieved before reinforcements of a permanent character can be indulged in. Even before the recent reinforcements there were one thousand pilots in the Middle East. Air Marshal Longmore[508] must be told to send back an equal number of good men of the various classes, and not add to his already grossly distended personnel.

2. In order to increase the number of crews available, the training must be speeded up and a certain measure of dilution accepted.
3. The figures placed before me each day are deplorable. Moreover, I have been told on high authority that a substantial increase in numbers available for operations against Germany must not be expected for many months. I cannot agree to this without far greater assurance than I have now that everything in human wit and power has been done to avert such a complete failure in our air expansion programme.
4. So far as aircraft are concerned, the question arises, from constant study of the returns, whether sufficient emphasis is put upon bomber production. The fighters are streaking ahead, and it is a great comfort that we have so good a position in them. We must however, increase our bomb deliveries on Germany, and it appears some of the types and patterns most adapted to this are not coming forward as we had hoped. I am well aware of the damage done by enemy action, but I ask whether it cannot be remedied, and what further steps are possible.
5. I wish to receive a programme of expansion week by week, and also a plan set forth showing what measures can be taken to improve the position, which at present is most distressing and black.

WSC

Winston S. Churchill to Sir Archibald Sinclair
31st December 1940

This is the most serious and precise of the many melancholy reports we are having of our Air bombing.[509] I hope you will address yourself further to the matter, which causes me a great deal of anxiety, and also the Cabinet.

WSC

508 Air Chief Marshal Sir Arthur Murray Longmore (1885–1970): Air Officer Commander-in-Chief, Middle East Command, until June 1941; his vociferous complaints about the failure to replace RAF units he had sent to support the Greeks cost him Churchill's confidence (even though Churchill had supported his actions); recalled to London in May 1941 to discuss the supply problem and relieved of his command (his deputy, Arthur Tedder, being appointed in his place).

509 This refers to a telegram received from the British Embassy in Budapest passing on comments from the US Naval Attaché in Berlin that British air raids on Berlin had achieved little damage.

1941

During 1941, with the threat of invasion much reduced, the attention of the Air Ministry turned to the creation of a strategic bomber force capable of delivering massive destruction to Germany. Sinclair and Portal had to argue constantly with the Chiefs of Staff and the War Cabinet to be allocated the resources necessary to complete the bomber programme.

Winston S. Churchill to Sir Archibald Sinclair and Air Chief Marshal Sir Charles Portal
4th January 1941

I note also that the current returns show 100 more Bomber aircraft serviceable than there are crews. Evidently it is the crews which are the limiting factor at the moment.[510]

Sir Archibald Sinclair to Winston S. Churchill
8th January 1941
SECRET

PRIME MINISTER
Your Minute M.487.[511]

I attach a dossier (A) showing the history of our bomb raids on Berlin with reports, both favourable and unfavourable, which have been received. I also attach a list (B) of the types and numbers of bombs dropped on Berlin for 5 months August to December and a list (C) of the numbers dropped on London from the beginning of hostilities to the end of December.

Even allowing for the fact that Greater London is approximately double the size of Berlin it is apparent that the density of the German attack on London has been far greater than that of our raids on Berlin.

Captain Schrader's account of the results of our raids is perhaps not surprising, in view of the very moderate tonnage of bombs dropped. If he is known to be strongly pro-British it may be that he is discouraged from viewing serious damage. There is a tendency, too, for sources living in Germany to compare the damage to Berlin with that inflicted on Warsaw and Rotterdam.

A number of reports refer to the small size of our bombs. You will see from the statement that we have been increasing the number of 500 lb and decreasing the number of 250 lb bombs recently.

[510] Beaverbrook had persistently argued that his actions at MAP had removed any production bottlenecks and that the Air Ministry, which was responsible for the recruitment and training of pilots and crew, had not sufficiently addressed their challenges.
[511] See letter dated 31 December 1940.

Although the date 17th December is given, Captain Schrader is undoubtedly referring to our heavy raid on the 15th/16th, during which 43½ tons of bombs were dropped. We have already received a report from A.A. Belgrade which confirms his remarks concerning the effectiveness of this raid.

NUMBERS OF BOMBS DROPPED ON LONDON

	H.E.	Oil Bombs
October 7th – 31st	8935	792
November 1st – 30th	7637	135
December 1st – 28th	1105	14
	17,677	941

For the period from beginning of hostilities up to 7th October 1940, 27 Boroughs have so far reported, as follows:–

H.E.	Oil Bombs
4029	233

There are 95 Boroughs in London so that a figure of 10,000 H.E. bombs would probably be a safe estimate for period up to 7th October for whole of London.

This brings the total number of H.E. bombs dropped on London to the neighbourhood of 30,000 and of oil bombs say 1400.

In addition at least 190 land mines have been dropped.

No incendiary bombs are included.

MOST SECRET
TYPES OF BOMBS DROPPED IN BERLIN

Date	Mines 1500 lb.	1000 lb.	500 lb.	250 lb	20 lb	25 lb. in.	4 lb. in.	Total tonnage including incendiaries
AUG.			157	379			3,652	84
SEPT.	6	2	396	623	20	8	5,573	170
OCT.		11	197	338	4		3,230	92
NOV.		5	258	59			9,280	87
DEC.		8	185	87			6,080	65
TOTALS	6	26	1,193	1,486	24	8	27,905	498

Sir Archibald Sinclair to Winston S. Churchill
8th January 1941
SECRET

PRIME MINISTER

On several occasions you have drawn my attention to reports which have reached the Foreign Office that the bombs which we drop in Germany and Italy fail to explode.

At your request I have tested these reports against the results during training in the U.K. with the following results:–

Command	Total Dropped	Total Failures	Percentage
Bomber	1,012	24	2.4
Army Co-op	802	38	4.7
R.A.F.N.I.[512]	)		
R.T.C.[513]	) Nil failures		
Coastal	)		
	1,814	62	3.4

None of the small numbers of failures was due to defective bombs. The cause was either an omission on the part of an airman undergoing training or of maintenance personnel. The former are only to be expected and we should hope that training would eliminate them. The latter may, however, possibly be the cause of some failures in the bombs dropped on Germany and the C.A.S. has personally written to the Cs-in-C., Bomber and Coastal Commands calling their particular attention to these points and impressing upon them the importance of efficient armament organisation in units.

A proportion of our bombs, which varies according to the type of target but which, overall, can be taken as 25%, consists of delay action bombs. It is possible that some confusion in the minds of observers may have arisen from this cause.

We have, I find, very little information about the effects of our delay action bombs in Germany. We think the Germans find them as difficult to deal with as we do and that they are particularly effective in dislocating railway communications. Only two specific reports have been received. One stated a bomb which fell on the Badische Anilinwerke on 16th/17th June exploded 4 hours after the raid causing great damage. The other stated that the two main streets of Hamburg were threatened by delay action bombs which were causing serious dislocation of traffic.

As I said in my recent Cabinet paper, individual adverse reports on our bombing can be very misleading and must always be considered with such factors as the actual weight of attack, the location of the actual target, the speed with which the damage

[512] RAF Northern Ireland.

[513] (Possibly) RAF (or Royal) Training Command.

is covered up, etc. Moreover there are just as many favourable as adverse reports. You can be sure that we are doing everything possible to eliminate causes of failure.

AHMS

Winston S. Churchill to Sir Archibald Sinclair and Charles Portal
12th January 1941

Must the operational reports from the Middle East be of their present inordinate length and detail? It surely is not necessary to describe minutely what happened in every individual raid of a dozen aircraft over the enemy's lines and encipher and decipher all this at each end, and cable it, thus congesting the lines.

I suggest that the average weekly wordage of these routine telegrams should be calculated for the last two months and Air Marshal Longmore asked to reduce them to, say, one-third their present length. The Foreign Office is also asking for condensation of their messages.

WSC

In late January Churchill had to intervene in the relationship between MAP and the Air Ministry.

Winston S. Churchill to Sir Archibald Sinclair and Lord Beaverbrook
25th January 1941

Rank of RAF Officers Serving in the Ministry of Aircraft Production

This difficulty arises when Army officers are required for position in the Ministry of Supply, and it has usually been settled amicably between sister Departments. Positions of certain consequence in the Ministry of Supply have carried with them a certain rank, and this rank has been conferred temporarily, locally, and for the purpose of the appointment, upon the officers selected. This rank, of course, is not a substantive rank but only a kind of brevet or acting rank. Therefore it in no way interferes with the permanent flow of promotion in the Regular Army. It lapses with the appointment, not even persisting as Brevets do. The War Office made no objection when I asked that Lt-Colonel Asquith should be appointed Brigadier on becoming Director of Trench Warfare in 1918, in fact, they tried all they could to help me in my work, which was supplying them with all they needed. All the arguments on page 2 of the Secretary of State for Air's letter completely ignore the temporary and *ex officio* character of the rank, which I thought was very clearly recognised in our conversation.

Naturally there should be friendly consultations between the Departments, but it is the duty of the Air Ministry to try to meet the legitimate needs of the Minister of Aircraft Production in regard to the ranks held by officers definitely seconded to his side of the Service. On the other hand, it would never do for MAP to lay down, for instance, the rule that posts with ranks assigned to them could be created ad lib. without any regard to the character of the post or of the effects produced in the Air Force Service.

None of these matters would raise difficulties if they were dealt with in the spirit of goodwill and co-operation. I could not give an unlimited right to the Minister of Aircraft Production such as is suggested in his letter. On the other hand, it would be a very serious thing for the Air Ministry to refuse a reasonable request made in any specific case. All disputed cases are to be referred to me as Minister of Defence.

WSC

Winston S. Churchill to Sir Archibald Sinclair and Hugh Dalton[514]
26th January 1941

There must be a very great deal of railway traffic from Germany to Italy; coal alone should account for nearly 200,000 tons a week averaged over the year. It is obviously most important that this should be impeded in every way. In view of the mountainous nature of the country through which the railways run, this should be feasible. Please let me have a report on what has been done and is being done.

WSC

Further battles over the roles and responsibilities of the Air Ministry versus MAP broke out in late January. The issues in dispute in this case were over who controlled spares and maintenance equipment at the airfields, and the pool of ferry pilots who moved planes nationally and internationally (mainly from Canada and the US).

Winston S. Churchill to Sir Archibald Sinclair
28th January 1941

The understanding which I hoped would be reached the other night was that you would make your concessions on the equipment side in return for receiving back Ferry organisations. Without the slightest reference to what you were to give, you proceed to claim all you were to get. I do not wonder, therefore, that misunderstanding and friction has arisen.

[514] Edward Hugh John Neale Dalton, Baron Dalton of Forest and Frith (1887–1962): academic economist; Labour MP for Peckham 1924–29, Bishop Auckland 1929–31, 1935–59; Minister of Economic Warfare 1940–42, established the covert operations organisation, the Special Operations Executive (SOE); President of the Board of Trade 1942–45; Chancellor of the Exchequer 1945–47, resigned in 1947 after inadvertently leaking Budget details to a journalist; Chancellor of the Duchy of Lancaster 1948–50; Minister of Town and Country Planning 1950–51; ennobled 1960.

I do not wish this matter to be discussed in the Cabinet at the present time, or until I have first made a further effort to adjust the unhappy differences between you and MAP by which my labours are greatly increased.

It is for me to decide the division of functions between the Air Ministry and MAP, and I propose to do this in the next few days.[515]

WSC

In late winter, British attention turned to Italy, which had entered the war in June 1940.

Sir Archibald Sinclair to Winston S. Churchill
31st January 1941
SECRET

PRIME MINISTER

Your minute 92/1 of the 27th January about interfering with railway traffic from Germany to Italy.

We estimate the Italian coal requirements at 12,000,000 tons per annum and according to our information the main lines of supply are:–

a) Ruhr
Via St. Gotthard)
Via Simplon) 50%
Via Brenner)

b) Saar
Via Bourg–Mont Cenis–Modane 20%

c) Silesia
Via Mahrisch Ostrau–Vienna–Villach–)
Tarvisio–Udine–Mestre)
Via Vienna–Semmering–Maribor–) 30%
Postumia–Trieste)

'c)' is beyond our reach with our existing types of heavy bombers .

I have consulted the Air Staff and the Minister of Economic Warfare about possible points of attack by air with the following results:–

a) Marshalling yards and junctions in Northern Italy

Persistence and continuity are the essence of our policy for attacking marshalling yards. Traffic congestion that cannot be cleared in a few days tends to pile up and the problem of its clearance becomes progressively more serious. Recent reports from the Railway Research Organisation confirm that the repeated bombing of Hamm has caused considerable dislocation of traffic whereas occasional small-scale attacks on railways are quickly repaired and have caused little dislocation.

[515] See letters dated 1 March 1941.

This has been borne out by our experience of German attacks on our own railways. Therefore, marshalling yards and junctions in Northern Italy are considered too far away to be good targets because operations would have to be carried out at extreme range and only at infrequent intervals because of weather conditions. Moreover at such a range the aircraft would only carry a comparatively small load of bombs and would have little time for searching for their targets.

b) Electric railway power stations in Italy
These are thoroughly bad targets. We should have to send a great many aircraft to attack a power station before we could be sure of knocking it out, and then we should not by any means be certain that our object had been accomplished because we should probably have to knock out several power stations before we seriously weakened the Swiss and Italian grid system.

c) Bombing of a line at points likely to cause a landslide
This is a most attractive idea and we have considered it very carefully. It has not, however, been accepted as a suitable objective owing to the difficulty of finding the right place by night, even in moonlight. The very fact that these objectives are located in mountainous country increases the difficulty of finding and bombing them accurately without undue risk to the attacking aircraft.

d) Marshalling yards and junctions between the Ruhr and the Swiss Frontier
This is the way in which the Royal Air Force can most effectively interrupt the communications between Germany and Italy. We can maintain – and indeed are maintaining, when weather permits – a fairly regular and continuous scale of attack on these communications. Cologne, Duisberg and Mannheim are important junctions; I understand that much of the coal from the Ruhr is brought up the Rhine as far as Mannheim and there transferred to the railway. Accordingly we are now applying our policy of cumulative dislocation of railway communications to those between Ruhr and Southern Germany and Italy by means of attacks on Mannheim and the inland port of Duisberg. By making these alternative targets in the moon period and allotting them fairly frequently as primary targets in the dark period it should be possible to create a good deal of dislocation and I will see that the Commander-in-Chief, Bomber Command is made aware of your interest in the interruption of these communications.

There remains only the question of helping the Minister of Economic Warfare in his Swiss operations. Without present commitments I think you will agree that it would be impossible for us to contemplate running a regular service of civil aircraft to Switzerland. I understand from him, however, that all that he would ask would be two or three experimental flights. I will look into ways and means if, in your opinion it would serve a useful military purpose, and if you will let me know that you wish it done.

AHMS

In response to a query from Churchill over the preparedness of Bomber Command to strike at Rome, Sinclair urged that the centre of the city should be bombed.

Sir Archibald Sinclair to Winston S. Churchill
24th February 1941
SECRET

PRIME MINISTER

We can at any time order the bombing of Rome – but we should have to consider in consultation with the A.O.C.-in-C.[516] whether it would be wise to divert the Wellingtons at Malta – now 11 in number – from their present targets. Among these targets are the aerodromes in Sicily, the bombing of which is necessary for the protection of Malta, and the ports where the sea-borne traffic between Italy and Libya can be hammered.

It was not, of course, to protect Salonika but Athens that we refrained from bombing Rome.

Salonika has already been frequently bombed, but Athens has so far been immune. In view of the decision at the Cabinet tonight you may think it untimely to authorise any action which might draw Italian or even German squadrons to Athens and the Piraeus.

There would be two alternative ways of carrying out the operation:–

a) To go straight for the Palazzo Venezia and other targets in the centre of the city – taking the risk that some bombs might hit the Vatican and with the certain knowledge that a number of historic and beautiful churches would be damaged or destroyed; or
b) To bomb the ports at Ostia and Civita Vecchia, the civil airport at Rome and the military aerodrome at Littorio, all on the outskirts of the city.

Whether to bomb Rome at all and, if so, which of these alternatives to choose are questions on which you would probably wish to consult, in addition to the A.O.C.-in-C., Middle East, the Foreign Office, (and, through them, the Greek Government) and, perhaps, also representative Roman Catholics.

My own inclination, therefore, would be to bomb Rome when, but not before, we have reason to believe that such action will decisively influence public opinion in Italy. For that reason I do not like course b) above although I believe it is favoured by the Foreign Office. The targets are too far from Rome to have any real political value. So I should prefer a) to be carried out after the next important Italian reverse in East Africa, Albania or operation M. and if possible to be synchronised with another Genoa.

---

[516] Air Officer Commander-in-Chief.

Winston S. Churchill to Sir Archibald Sinclair
28th February 1941
Secret

BOMBING OF ROME

This matter is not pressing at the present time. If we should decide later on to do it, I hope we shall not confine ourselves to the targets shown in (b), but let them have a good dose where it will hurt them most.

WSC

Winston S. Churchill to Sir Archibald Sinclair, Air Chief Marshal Sir Charles Portal and Lord Beaverbrook
1st March 1941

MAP will continue to be responsible for the Atlantic Ferry Service. The Air Ministry is to supply the desired personnel or their equipment.

By the end of the first week in March, I wish to receive a report that this has been done in such a manner as to render the Ferry Service effective.

WSC

Winston S. Churchill to Sir Archibald Sinclair and Lord Beaverbrook
1st March 1941

1. All promotions of RAF Officers rest in the domain of the Air Ministry.
2. All appointments inside MAP including No. 41 Group and kindred establishments, belong to the Minister of Aircraft Production. If the Minister wishes to fill a vacancy with an RAF officer, but has no suitable officer available under his own control, he will ask the Air Ministry to submit a succession of names of suitable officers whom they can make available.
3. Where RAF personnel is serving in MAP, the Air Ministry, before making any promotions, even by routine, will consult the Minister of Aircraft Production.
4. Seeing that certain specified posts in MAP carry with them a definite rank in the RAF, the Minister of Aircraft Production will consult the Air Ministry before making such appointments in order to avoid inconvenience in the Service.
5. The Air Ministry will consider it their duty as a general rule to meet the wishes of the Minister of Aircraft Production in the above matters, even though they may not agree with the course proposed.
6. In the event of disagreement arising in any particular case under paras. 3, 4 and 5, the matter is to be referred to me as Minister of Defence for decision.
7. A Branch will be established in the Office of the Minister of Defence in order to advise me upon the details of such disputed cases. General Ismay will make proposals to this end.

8. All superior officers of the Air Ministry and all high officials of MAP are hereby reminded that it is their duty to meet the wishes of the sister Department to the utmost possible extent. Failure to comply with this instruction will be regarded as disservice to the public in time of danger.
9. The above paragraphs will be brought to the notice of those concerned by the Secretary of State for Air and the Minister of Aircraft Production in their respective Departments.

WSC

Sir Archibald Sinclair to Winston S. Churchill
6th March 1941
SECRET

PRIME MINISTER

Your Minute M. 229/1.

1. The broad basis upon which the programme set out in W.P. (41) 18 was planned was the forecast of pilot output. This, at the time, seemed likely to prove the dominant factor in expansion.
2. Since the programme was planned, training has suggested two setbacks – first, the bad weather (we had made an allowance for bad weather slowing down the training machinery but we have had to prolong courses by periods of weeks in order to give the pupils the necessary flying hours; and, secondly, the shortage of advanced trainers. Broadly, the situation as regards pilots is that training delays, Middle East reinforcement and demands from the Ministry of Aircraft Production for help in ferrying have reduced the strength in all Commands below establishment. We hope to overtake these shortages within the next month or two but this depends upon the size of the demands for Atfero.[517] Thereafter, when the curve of expansion begins to rise steeply in July and August we shall again be short of pilots but this shortage should be overtaken soon after the end of the year.
3. You asked about production. The only data we have had to work upon was the M.A.P. forecast of 2nd October 1940. The Minister advises us to assume, for planning purposes, that we should receive 80% of the deliveries promised in this forecast. On this basis the requirements described in W.P. (41) 18 could, approximately be met, though shortages were foreseen in flying boats, medium bombers and advanced trainers. I am in correspondence with the Minister of Aircraft Production about this lack of balance as between fighters and other types.
4. As Professor Lindemann points out the fulfilment of our programme depends on the accuracy of the estimates of wastage and production. You will remember that in preparing it at the time when Air Vice Marshal Slessor went to the U.S.A.

[517] The Atlantic Ferry Organisation.

we cut the margin of safety in our postulated rate of wastage to the minimum. Nevertheless, during the winter fighting our actual casualties have fallen below the estimate for the winter; it is by no means certain that the estimate for the summer will prove to be on the low side.

5. No doubt you will obtain the information you require about aircraft production from the Minister of Aircraft Production. I am a waiting the new programme which Lord Beaverbrook has promised to send us before attempting to assess how seriously the new forecast will affect our plan.
6. The circulation of paper W.P. (41) 18 was intended to comply with your suggestion that we should circulate to the Cabinet a short and simple account of our expansion plan. Nevertheless, I entirely agree that drastic restriction would in any event be necessary on grounds of secrecy and do not at all wish to press for circulation as you think it better not to do so.

AHMS

Winston S. Churchill to Sir Archibald Sinclair
7th March 1941

RESEARCH AND DEVELOPMENT OF AIRCRAFT ENGINES

MAP has also asked to circulate a paper which contains a lot of secret stuff. I have no objection to this, provided that the circulation is confined to the Defence Committee and the War Cabinet, and that the copies are returned to the issuing Minister after perusal. The number of copies printed should be kept to a minimum, each should be numbered, and the issuing Department should be responsible for knowing where every one is.

WSC

In December 1940 Lord Halifax, who was too strongly associated with Chamberlain for Churchill to tolerate in the War Cabinet following Chamberlain's death in November, was transferred from the Foreign Office to the post of British ambassador in Washington. He replaced the popular and genial Liberal peer Lord Lothian, who had died of a sudden illness. Halifax was never greatly at ease with American political culture but he was to see the lend-lease agreements to a successful conclusion and remained at the Washington Embassy for the remainder of the war. He provided regular intelligence updates of the information that he acquired during his discussions with the American administration and Congress. In March 1941 Halifax provided confidential information to Churchill about the state of German oil supplies, one of Bomber Command's principal targets.

Sir Archibald Sinclair to Winston S. Churchill
9th March 1941

Prime Minister

Lord Halifax's telegram 1020 of the 5th March is to some extent inconsistent with his telegram No. 840 of the 21st February, and we shall have to wait the arrival of the full report to clear this up.

According to the earlier telegram the report showed that the Germans were getting into great difficulties over raw materials and especially oil, and that this would become acute in the Autumn of 1941 and earlier if Anglo-American air action, as the German Staff feared, was in a position to do serious damage.

This version of the report seems to bear out the estimate of the Ministry of Economic Warfare that in the last six months of 1940 the synthetic oil output of the plants attacked in Germany was reduced by not less than 15%.

In any case, it will not be until we receive the report that we can determine the degree of authenticity which we attach to it.

When we have had an opportunity to examine the report in all its implications we propose to reconsider fully whether oil targets are still the most suitable primary targets for Bomber Command.

Since the Defence Committee approved our Oil Policy we have unfortunately been able to do very little damage to any of the principal oil targets. This has been due to the exceptionally bad weather of the last two months, which confined the great majority of our attacks to targets near the coast. We hope for better luck during the present moon.

AHMS

Winston S. Churchill to Sir Archibald Sinclair
14th March 1941

Your programme [of RAF expansion] assumed for these four months a loss [in pilots] of 1550, whereas actually 1229 was the figure. You have therefore saved 321 pilots, and your original estimate was 26 per cent on the safe side. This is satisfactory.

I always expected and repeatedly told you that there would be a marked falling-off in war activity during winter months. This has always been so. Let me know what are your forecasts for the next four or six months, including March. The 'postulates', as you like to call them, though 'forecasts' seem more natural, are in any case only of academic interest, because we are making every pilot we can as fast as we can, and our programme is based on capacity, not assignment. None the less, one may just as well see what the possibilities are.

WSC

Sir Archibald Sinclair to Winston S. Churchill
21st March 1941
SECRET

PRIME MINISTER.
Your minute M.318/1 of the 19th March and the attached letter[518] from Sir Walter Citrine.[519]

1. I told the cabinet that only 60% of the German parachute mines go off. Lately, however, there has been a slight improvement and, actually, out of 1,500 mines dropped, 500 have been rendered safe. These 500 mines contained more than the total weight of explosives dropped during the blitz on Coventry. To-day there are 25 unexploded mines in Glasgow, 8 in Liverpool and 8 in London, all of which are being made harmless.
2. Once the enemy get to know that one-third of the mines are duds they can easily remedy the defect. Only a small adjustment to the fuse is required. It does not at all matter that the Germans should read in "Life" that parachute mines fall in this country; all that matters is that they should not know that a large number of them are duds.
3. If the press are allowed to mention land mines at all, nothing can stop discussion and a disclosure of the fact that there is a large proportion of duds, because there is no pre-issue censorship. Some time ago the Germans were dropping a large number of oil bombs of which many were duds and many of their incendiary bombs were inferior. Articles appeared in some of the newspapers – particularly a very well written article in the 'Aeroplane' on a certain date in September – which pointed this out. Recently the number of oil bombs dropped has steadily diminished until now there are very few and the incendiary bombs have greatly improved.
4. Accordingly to allow the press to mention parachute mines would be to run the risk of letting the Germans know that there is a defect in the fuse and of enabling them substantially to increase the devastation which they cause. I cannot see that any compensating advantage would be obtained.
5. Even if you had wished to run this risk it would, I submit, have been injudicious to provoke the press by allowing Sir Walter Citrine to be the first to profit by the raising of the ban.
6. As soon as Air Vice-Marshal Peck[520] heard that there was difficulty with Sir Walter Citrine over his broadcast, he asked to see him. Sir Walter Citrine

[518] The government was keen that Citrine did not disclose in a broadcast that a large number of the parachute mines being used by the Germans were failing to explode due to a problem with their fuse mechanism.

[519] Sir Walter McLennan Citrine, 1st Baron Citrine (1887–1983): General Secretary, Trades Union Congress 1926–46; in 1931 opposed proposals for cuts in unemployment benefits and subsequently led the campaign to have Ramsay MacDonald and Philip Snowden expelled from the Labour Party.

[520] Air Marshal Sir Richard Hallam Peck (1893–1952): Assistant Chief of the Air Staff.

received him with great courtesy and discussed the matter with him at considerable length. He seemed impressed by Peck's arguments but, after thinking quietly for a little time, said that he was going to stand to his guns. Unfortunately it turned out that he had already addressed a press conference on the subject only an hour before he saw Peck.

7. You will have observed that Sir Walter Citrine received little or no support from the press for his protests.
8. I have some reason to believe that Sir Walter Citrine feels that the services which he has rendered to the cause by his series of addresses to large audiences in the United States of America have met with less recognition than is their due. I do not know if it would be possible for you to see him and to express your thanks, and those of the Government, to him for his work in the United States of America; but, if you could, I cannot help thinking that it would be acceptable.

AHMS

Winston S. Churchill to Sir Archibald Sinclair
21st March 1941
Personal

I have lately been putting a great deal of pressure upon the War Office to reduce their intake,[521] and they are making efforts to meet my views. The Air Force, on the other hand, is rapidly expanding. All the more must every effort be made to practise economy in man and woman power. All experience shows that when the Services have a free hand in regard to Establishments, they give very little care to anything except making themselves safe and comfortable. The present ratio of Ground Services to First Line Air Strength is deplorable, and getting worse every day.

The suggestion in the enclosed paper seems worth considering. But in addition you should aim at combing off at least 50,000 personnel from the total demanded. I hope you will undertake to do this, and not simply send me long arguments to show that everything is perfect, and all criticism an intrusion. You must remember that there is practically no Treasury control on War Services demands, and that it is my responsibility as Minister of Defence to see that our limited man-power is used to the best advantage. I want proposals for 50,000 men to be combed off the total Establishment, and after this combing has been effected I want a substitution of 50,000 more women if they can be got, or as many as can be got, for the men demanded.

Having been in Office for so many years, I have entirely lost confidence in the Departments where their own interests are concerned unless a policy is enforced upon them by a competent politician at their head. This is what is meant by House of Commons control, of which you used to be the leading champion.

WSC

[521] Of manpower.

Winston S. Churchill to A. V. Alexander and Sir Archibald Sinclair
21st March 1941

The use of aeroplanes not only to attack our ships but also to direct the U-boats on to them is largely responsible for our losses in the North-Western approaches. No effort to destroy the Focke-Wulfs[522] should be spared. If we could employ RDF[523] methods to find their positions and to direct long range fighters or shipborne aircraft to the attack we ought to be able to inflict serous casualties. Might it not be feasible to place a RDF station on Rockall? However inconvenient and unpleasant, the geographical position appears to be so good that it would be worth making a great effort to maintain a station there, at any rate during the summer months. The hills south of Lough Erne would also offer a valuable site. It might be even better if we could find ways and means of establishing stations on Tory Island or on one of the islands off the Kerry coast.[524] These islands might be leased privately by some wealthy American friends. Please let me have a report form the technical point of view on the military results which could be expected if any of these things could be done and upon any other possibilities that have been or might be examined.

We should also study methods of disturbing the aircraft's communications with U-boats. I understand that the system is that the Focke-Wulf signals to Brest, whence directions are sent to the U-boat, the process taking about an hour and a half. Is it not practical either to jam these communications or to confuse all concerned by a series of spurious messages? Presumably apparatus of the usual type for interfering with the Focke-Wulf's radio methods of navigation, which must be vital over the sea in bad weather, has not been neglected.

I assume that we DF[525] the signals he uses. If he uses ASV[526] it should be practicable to locate and home on him with suitable apparatus.

Winston S. Churchill to Sir Archibald Sinclair
23rd March 1941

S. OF S. FOR AIR.

I have already seen Sir Walter Citrine and will take occasion to pay a compliment to him when I am the guest of the T.U.C. at luncheon on Thursday. Meanwhile I think it would be a good thing if you asked him to come to see you, and explained the technical points involved. You should mention that you do this at my desire.

WSC

[522] German fighter-bombers.

[523] Radio Direction Finding.

[524] The county of Kerry, in south-western Ireland.

[525] Direction Finding.

[526] Air to Surface Vessel (a type of radar).

Winston S. Churchill to Sir Archibald Sinclair
31st March 1941

DISCLOSURE OF SECRET INFORMATION TO THE UNITED STATES

I discussed this matter with the United States Ambassador. I told him that I did not like the spreading habit of daily routine returns of secret matters being put into widening lithographic circulation. Not only were daily returns precise and dangerous if they were left lying about or fell into wrong hands, but also that the fact of returns being made every day and circulated led to an immense amount of these papers being extant. Therefore I was not prepared to give the information daily as asked for. On the other hand, I saw less objections to giving the return asked for on a fortnightly basis, which would make it a more valuable and significant paper. In addition, I should be willing to give the President at any time any information on special points. The Ambassador said he would talk to the Naval Attaché. I should greatly prefer to make the return monthly. In any case the most strict engagements must be entered into that the copy furnished is not to be multiplied and sent fooling around to a dozen American Departments. It is already bad enough to do this here.

WSC

In April Sinclair approached Churchill to renew his support for the ambitious bomber programme.

Sir Archibald Sinclair to Winston S. Churchill
2nd April 1941
MOST SECRET

PRIME MINISTER

1. In W.P. (41) 69 dated 26th March you direct that, within the prescribed limits for the import of material and for the programmes of the Navy and Army, British Air power will "continue to be developed to the utmost with the present priorities and assignments". In Annex 1 of the same paper you state that the task of defeating the enemy "can only be done by the staying power of the Navy, and above all of the effect of air predominance".
2. Air Predominance can only be won by the Bomber Force. Lack of fighters or of aircraft to co-operate with the Army or Navy might lose us the war. Only the Bombers can bring victory.
3. How adequate are our plans for winning a decisive margin of hitting power over our enemies? We believe that Germany possesses to-day a striking force of some 1,750 long range bombers. Our own striking force at home and in the Middle East is about half this number, so that ignoring the Italian Air Force altogether, the enemy has a predominance of about 2:1.

4. Our task during the next two years or less must be to reverse the ratio and raise the intensity of our bomber offensive against Germany to an intolerable pitch.
5. During the next twelve months we hope to expand our striking force to a first line strength of 1,750 aircraft. Allowing for the greater capacity of the heavier British types, the achievement of this plan may give us parity of hitting power by the Spring of 1942 unless in the meantime Germany has expanded her force to a greater extent that we consider probable.
6. To achieve predominance in the air, expansion must continue without interruption during 1942. We must aim at a force of not less than 4,000 heavy bombers by the Spring of 1943. Such a force might achieve, on an optimistic basis, a margin of more than two to one. A bolder aim would be desirable but may be impracticable.
7. If we are to achieve our aim, 1942 must be a year of great expansion. The necessary plans must be determined now. Four factors govern the expansion: crews, other man-power, aerodromes and heavy bomber aircraft.
8. The great training organisation we are building up will suffice to supply pilots for a force much in excess of the peak of 1941 expansion. The crews and ground personnel necessary to raise our striking force to the 4,000 mark by the Spring of 1943 can be found if instructions are given now to work up to this figure. The total strength of the Air Force would be about 1½ million men.
9. Aerodromes would present difficulties but no insuperable obstacles. Room would be made for Operational Squadrons by the continued transfer of schools abroad. A proportion of the force would be located in the Middle East.
10. The limiting factor is aircraft. To carry out such a programme 7,000 heavy bomber aircraft would be needed during 1941 and 12,000 during 1942.
11. A great development in heavy bomber production is necessary if these demands are to be met. According to the latest forecast of production, the Royal Air Force is offered only 4,500 heavy bombers during 1941. In 1942 average monthly deliveries may total about 600.
12. On the other hand the production of fighter aircraft is mounting in excess of our probable needs in this class. Towards the end of the present year deliveries will exceed 1,000 per month. We can afford a contraction in fighter output.
13. From my discussions with the Minister of Aircraft Production it has become clear that the difficulty of redressing the balance of the production programme during 1941 is most formidable. Nevertheless the balance must be redressed. Air predominance requires a drastic change in the aircraft production plan in this country, and more especially in America.
14. To obtain an average monthly production in 1942 of 1,000 heavy bombers, two things would be necessary:–

First, to insist that the American programme described in memorandum dated 28th March is unacceptable.

Deliveries now forecast from America from 1st January, 1941 to 30th June, 1942 are 600 heavy bombers against a requirement of 7,000 while our much less important need in the medium bomber class are largely met; and the programme contains 1,500 fighters more than we asked for.

The range and armament of the light and medium bombers must severely limit their operational employment, and although we have asked for large numbers we do not want them at the expense of the heavies.

The performance and armament of the majority of the fighters to be ordered for delivery in 1942 is such that these aircraft might well be considered as obsolescent now.

The Americans themselves continually express anxiety that we should be able to employ usefully the aircraft we get from them. These aircraft are certainly of very limited utility.

The political consequences of failure to use possibly some thousands of aircraft might be very serious.

The Americans must be persuaded to turn over the factories manufacturing these types to the manufacture of heavy bombers. Failing this the raw materials that would have gone into their manufacture should be fabricated in accordance with our needs for embodiment in our heavy bombers, the Halifax and Lancaster. The production of Merlin engines in America should be doubled and might suffice for the suggested heavy bomber programme, provided we select aircraft such as the Halifax and Lancaster which take Rolls Royce engines.

Secondly, it would be necessary to increase production of heavy bombers at home.

I am well aware of the difficulties here, and I understand that the bottleneck is fabricated light alloys; but if further presses were ordered now they should be able to get into production next year – probably, I am informed, within a period of eighteen months.

15. Do you agree that 4,000 heavy bombers in first line should be the target for the Air Ministry and Ministry of Aircraft Production for April 1943?

AHMS

In early April 1941 the Air Ministry issued a booklet, *The Battle of Britain*, that omitted all mention of Dowding, who had been in charge of Fighter Command throughout the battle. Churchill was incensed.

Winston S. Churchill to Sir Archibald Sinclair
12th April 1941
Private

This is not a good story. The jealousies and cliquism which have led to the committing of this offence are a discredit to the Air Ministry, and I do not think any other

Service Department would have been guilty of such a piece of work. What would have been said if the War Office had produced the story of the Battle of Libya and had managed to exclude General Wavell's name, or if the Admiralty had told the tale of Trafalgar and left Lord Nelson out of it. It grieves me very much that you should associate yourself with such behaviour. I am sure you were not consulted beforehand on the point, and your natural loyalty to everything done in your Department can alone have led you to condone what nine out of ten men would unhesitatingly condemn.

WSC

Winston S. Churchill to Sir Archibald Sinclair
15th April 1941

I remain far from satisfied with the state of our preparations for offensive chemical warfare, should this be forced upon us by the actions of the enemy.

I have before me a Report on this matter by the Inter-Service Committee on Chemical Warfare (COS (41) 143), together with a commentary thereon by the Ministry of Supply (COS (41) 200). From these two documents the following special points emerge:

1. The deficiency of gas shell is still serious. Although the production of 6-inch and 5.5-inch gas shell was due to start in February, none has yet been produced. I understand that the shortage of 24-pdr gas-filled shell is due to the lack of empty shell cases.
2. The production of 30-lb. LC bomb,[527] Mark I, will not keep pace with the production of the 5-in UP weapon,[528] the new mobile projector for use with the Army. Indeed, supplies will be insufficient even for training purposes.
3. The production of phosgene gas is inadequate. The output from the plant is now about 65 per cent of capacity, having previously been only 50 per cent, over a period of some months.

I propose to examine the whole position at an early meeting of the Defence Committee (Supply).

In order that this examination may be as complete as possible, I shall be glad to receive from the Minister of Aircraft Production and the Minister of Supply, for circulation in advance of the meeting, brief comprehensive statements of the position so far as each is concerned, showing in respect of each of the main gas weapons and components (including gases):

1. Total requirements notified to them, with dates.
2. Stocks of components in the custody of each on the 1st April.

[527] A special thin-casing bomb which had been used in the Phoney War (through to April 1940) to drop leaflets over Germany. It could also be used to deliver gas.
[528] Unrotated projectile – see n459.

3. Supplies delivered by 1st April to RAF or Army authorities.
4. Estimated output during each of the next six months.

I shall be glad if these statements can be submitted within a week. They should be addressed to Sir Edward Bridges.[529]

I am addressing similar minutes to the Secretary of State for War, the Minister of Supply, and the Minister of Aircraft Production.

WSC

Winston S. Churchill to Admiral Pound,[530] David Margesson,[531] Sir Archibald Sinclair and Ronald Cross[532]
30th April 1941

Further to my Minute of this date on convoy secrecy. Nothing will prevent very large numbers of people knowing that ships are assembled constantly for convoy. Nor can the kind of Cargoes they are carrying be kept secret. There is an immense amount of talk at all the ship owners' offices and at the ports. By all means let every effort be made as proposed by MI5 and in my previous Minute. In such a case, however, where so much is visible and must be known, the continued fabrication and dissemination of false information is necessary to confuse and baffle the truth. Sun helmets or winter clothing should be hawked about and calculated leakages made of false and sometimes true intentions. For this purpose a small group of lively officers should be formed working under the daily Ports Committee or under the MI5 as may be thought desirable. Perhaps FOP[533] could help.

WSC

Sir Archibald Sinclair to Winston S. Churchill
1st May 1941
Secret

Prime Minister

I have not yet heard whether you agree to my proposal for a first line strength of 4,000 Heavy Bombers in April 1943, and I hope that I shall receive your approval of this before long.

---

529 Secretary to the War Cabinet.

530 Admiral Sir Dudley Pound (1877–1943): First Sea Lord 1939–43.

531 Henry David Reginald Margesson, 1st Viscount Margesson of Rugby (1890–1965): Conservative MP for West Ham 1922–23, Rugby 1924–42; Government Chief Whip 1931–40; Secretary of State for War 1940–42, sacked by Churchill following a series of severe military setbacks, including the loss of Singapore; ennobled 1942.

532 Sir Ronald Cross (1896–1968): Minister for Economic Warfare 1939–40; Minister for Shipping 1940–45.

533 Future Operations Planning – a section of the Joint Planning Staff.

Meanwhile, it is important to drive home our demand for heavy bombers up to the hilt now, because during these present weeks the American plans for the creation of new aircraft production capacity are crystallising.

General Arnold[534] has required no converting to our views and he cabled to America while he was here. Mr. Harriman[535] has also cabled Mr. Hopkins,[536] and he has told us that the matter will go to the President for final determination.

Matters are evidently moving in the right direction. Nevertheless I feel, and Lord Beaverbrook agrees with me, that on a matter of such moment as this, it would not be inappropriate that you should yourself address President Roosevelt, and that the magnitude of the issue warrants this exceptional measure.

I attach a draft telegram which I hope will commend itself to you. The requirement of 500 Heavy Bombers a month from America relates to the target of a 4,000 Heavy Bomber first line; but the despatch of the telegram need not await your approval of the target, since the production requirement was put to the British Air Commission in February, and is not a new one.

The difficulty is to get it accepted.

AHMS

Secret

Draft Telegram from Prime Minister to President

I understand Mr. Harriman and General Arnold have already cabled about vital need for great expansion of heavy four-engined bomber production in the United States. May I ask you, Mr. President, to give this requirement your personal attention. Our need is for 1,000 heavy bombers per month during 1942. Still greater numbers will be required during 1943. Maximum output from factories in United Kingdom will be 500 per month. For balance we must look to the United States. It is fully realised here that this demand for heavy bombers cannot be met without sacrifice in other directions. We are immediately instructing our representatives to initiate discussion on reductions in our present planned allocations of fighters and lighter types of bombers. We know from experience that great difficulties must be

[534] General Henry Hartley Arnold (1886–1950): Commander, US Army Air Force from 1940, and a strong supporter of area bombing; the US 8th Air Force, based in southern England, played an important role in this strategic bombing offensive.

[535] Averell W. Harriman (1891–1986): adviser to Democratic Presidents from Franklin D. Roosevelt to Lyndon B. Johnson; lend-lease expediter in London 1941–43, reporting directly to the White House, and bypassing the US ambassador and the State Department; Ambassador to Russia 1943–46; Ambassador to Great Britain 1946; Secretary of Commerce 1947–48; special representative in Europe, administering the Marshall Plan. 1948–50; unsuccessful candidate for the Democratic nomination for the presidency 1952 and 1956; Governor of New York 1954–58; Assistant Secretary of State 1961–63; headed US delegation to Paris peace talks with North Vietnam 1968–69.

[536] Harry L. Hopkins (1890–1946): New Deal administrator; Secretary of Commerce 1938–40; special adviser to Roosevelt and the President's personal envoy to Britain, influential in gaining US aid for Britain prior to Pearl Harbor; headed lend-lease programme from 1941.

faced if the aircraft industry of the United States is to be re-orientated to meet this demand. Believing as we do that air predominance is the key to victory and will be achieved only with the assistance of a greatly increased flow of the heaviest class of bomber from U.S.A. we feel that the inevitable difficulties must be faced and can be overcome. I therefore ask you Mr. President to lend us your help in this great project on the results of which so much depends.

Winston S. Churchill to Sir Archibald Sinclair
4th May 1941

Archie,

This [draft telegram to President Roosevelt about expansion of bomber production in the USA] should surely be put forward through the regular channels. I do not like to send telegrams to the President about the general programme, which ought to be thrashed out by the very elaborate machinery provided for this purpose.

WSC

Sir Archibald Sinclair to Winston S. Churchill
5th May 1941
Secret

Prime Minister
Your M.507/1[537]

Then I will thrash as hard as I can.

There is not a week to be lost if we are to persuade the Americans to switch over in time some of their productive capacity from fighters and medium bombers to heavy bombers; so I do hope you will give me your general approval of the big bomber project.

Yours,
Archie

Winston S. Churchill to Sir Archibald Sinclair
12th May 1941

THE AIR TRAINING SITUATION

I am sorry you do not wish to give me the information on the points of fact mentioned in Lord Beaverbrook's minute to me of the 30th April. I was very tired at the time I wrote my minute of the 3rd May, or I would have embodied the points of fact in Lord Beaverbrook's note in a minute of my own. I hope you will overlook

[537] Dated 4 May – see above.

this lack of ceremony, and make sure the Service does not suffer thereby through my not being able to get the information I seek.

Is it really true, for instance, that no fewer than 1,186 Trainer aircraft, or 31 per cent., were unserviceable on the 18th April? That only one-third of those unserviceable were awaiting spares? That if the Tiger Moths were left out, only 309 machines were grounded for lack of spares? That there are 500 Tiger Moths in store? That in November, when the new programme was laid down, it was planned to turn out 4,008 pilots from the Flying Training Schools, whereas the actual output was 2,731?

It does not seem to me that more than a page would be required to furnish the actual figures, and this was all I asked for.

In suggesting a one-page reply, my only object was to relieve you of the necessity of making lengthy explanations, which I feared might be a burden to you and even, if you will forgive me, to me.[538]

WSC

Sir Hugh Dowding's work in the US was not appreciated by many of his colleagues; even Beaverbrook, who had believed Dowding harshly treated by the Air Ministry, wanted to dispense with his services as his representative in the US. By the end of May 1941 the question of what to do with the Air Chief Marshal was rising up the agenda, and Sinclair hopefully suggested that Dowding could be offered a post in Southern Rhodesia.

Sir Archibald Sinclair to Winston S. Churchill
22nd May 1941
SECRET

PRIME MINISTER

The Minister of Aircraft Production intimated to me some time ago that he no longer required the services of Air Chief Marshal Sir Hugh Dowding and I have been thinking how best to employ them in the Royal Air Force. We were considering the possibility of appointing him as Inspector General to work with Sir Edgar Ludlow-Hewitt[539] in the place of Sir William Mitchell[540] who will shortly be retiring. My idea was that Sir Hugh Dowding should be asked to give special attention

[538] Sinclair was never accused of succinctness. Beaverbrook once wrote to Churchill that 'You must think that this is a letter from Sir Archibald Sinclair, for it is five pages long. But every page is worth reading. And that is the difference.' (National Archives file reference AIR 19/572)

[539] Edgar Ludlow-Hewitt (1886–1973): Commander in Chief, Bomber Command 1937–40; increasingly criticised, in particular for his insistence on the formation of more Operational Training Units at the expense of some front-line aircraft and crews; replaced by Sir Charles Portal in February 1940; Inspector-General of the RAF 1940–45.

[540] Air Chief Marshal Sir William Mitchell (1888–1944): Air Officer Commander-in-Chief, Middle East until May 1940; Inspector-General of the RAF 1940–41; Black Rod, House of Lords 1941–42; asked to return to service in mid-1942, became Commandant, London Command, Air Training Corps, until his death in 1944.

to the problems of maintenance and serviceability in the Royal Air Force – work in which his experience as Air member for Supply and Research a few years ago would have been of particular value.

Now you tell me that there is no chance that Sir Arthur Longmore will accept the Governorship of the Southern Rhodesia it occurs to me that it might be a good plan to offer that Governorship to Sir Hugh Dowding. I am sure he would fill it with distinction and the Secretary of State for the Dominions has promised me to give this suggestion his careful consideration and to let me know in a day or two whether he would be willing to make such an offer to Sir Hugh Dowding.

If Sir Hugh Dowding accepts this post I would suggest that Sir Arthur Longmore should be offered the post of Inspector General. He would divide the work with Sir Edgar Ludlow-Hewitt by mutual agreement as the latter has recently done with Sir William Mitchell.

I should be grateful if you would let me know whether you approve of these projects.[541]

AHMS

Despite victory in the Battle of Britain, the country was still not free from the threat of invasion and as calmer weather arrived with the onset of summer, Churchill warned Sinclair about the need to work closely with the Army.

Winston S. Churchill to Sir Archibald Sinclair
30th May 1941

RE-EQUIPMENT OF ARMY CO-OPERATION SQUADRONS

The Army must be given the modest force they require, and I am satisfied that the 30 Blenheims should be handed over to them, so that some joint training can be achieved before the invasion season. It is not necessary to hand over the whole of the second 30 required for a reserve immediately. Losses up to that amount can be made good as they occur from the A.S.U. reserves.

WSC

At the end of May Beaverbrook resigned from the MAP, being replaced by John Moore-Brabazon. From that date onwards, although there remained the occasional tension between the two ministries, overall relations substantially improved. However, as June arrived a further spat broke out between Sinclair and Churchill over what to do with Dowding.

[541] See exchange of letters on 2 June, pages 306–07.

Winston S. Churchill to Sir Archibald Sinclair and Sir Charles Portal
2nd June 1941
SECRET

S. OF S. FOR AIR and C.A.S.

Sir Hugh Dowding would clearly not be eligible for the United States ferry service.

It seems to me that the best arrangement would be to send Air Marshal Barrett[542] there, and replace him with Sir Hugh Dowding who will give confidence to the Army that they will have their interests fully represented. I hope you will find yourself able to do this, as I am sure nothing but good will come of it.

WSC

Sir Archibald Sinclair to Winston S. Churchill
2nd June 1941
SECRET

PRIME MINISTER

Neither I nor C.A.S. would be prepared to recommend the changes suggested by your minute. Air Marshal Barrett was appointed to the Army Co-operation Command only 6 months ago at the suggestion of the War Office and knows more about Army Co-operation than any other officer of his rank in the R.A.F. He has done his work very well and his knowledge and experience would be wasted in charge of the Ferry Organisation for which he has no special qualifications.

As I have already explained to you the re-employment of Sir Hugh Dowding in an Operational Command would run counter to our recently declared policy and would cause much adverse comment throughout the Service; and I cannot therefore agree to it.

The Ferry Organisation requires a man with very special qualities. Reports which I have received on that service both from British and American sources are extremely bad. There is an immense work of re-organisation to be done.

If you agree, therefore, I propose to offer the post to Air Chief Marshal Sir Frederick Bowhill.[543] He has recent operational experience of the kind which will be most valuable in this post, he has immense prestige with the R.A.F., and he has also the type of personality that would be required to deal with civilian ferry pilots. I should propose to give him as his chief Staff Officer Air Commodore Pirie, now Air

[542] Air Marshal Sir Arthur Barrett (dates unknown): led RAF–Army Cooperation Command December 1941 – March 1943. This was the focus for the interaction of the Army and the RAF, such as close air support; it proved to be a controversial arrangement, with the Chief of the Imperial General Staff, General Sir Alan Brooke, being particularly opposed. Its existence was ended in March 1943, when its assets and responsibilities were transferred to the Second Tactical Air Force.

[543] Air Chief Marshal Sir Frederick William Bowhill (1880–1960): Air Officer Commander-in-Chief, Coastal Command.

Attaché at Washington, whom we were in any case about to relieve on the arrival in Washington of Air Marshal Harris[544] as head of the Air Mission.

AHMS

Winston S. Churchill to Sir Archibald Sinclair
2nd June 1941
Private

My dear Archie,

You have sent me a very serious minute in answer to my request, and I am afraid I must tell you that I do not see how you can expect me to bear my responsibilities if my very clearly and courteously expressed wishes are not treated with proper respect and consideration. As Minister of Defence I am bound to take a direct part in all high appointments in the Fighting Service. No important appointment has been made by either of the other two Services during my tenure without my being consulted, and you yourself have always hitherto followed this practice.

I hope therefore that you will be willing to reconsider your minute, which I now return to you.

WSC

Sinclair and Portal held the line against Churchill, Bowhill being appointed to head Ferry Command on 13 June 1941. Dowding did not return to an operational command, instead accepting an appointment in the Air Ministry involving the scrutiny of RAF establishments to ensure efficiency. This was not a position that either appealed to him or suited his talents, and at his own request he finally retired in July 1942.

Winston S. Churchill to Sir Archibald Sinclair and Air Chief Marshal Sir Charles Portal
18th June 1941
Secret

I saw a statement in the papers the other day that the Air Force were calling for several thousand volunteers to defend their Aerodromes. What is the meaning of this? It was represented that this was part of the application of the lessons of Crete. But many people have wondered why such a petty measure should have been paraded. Perhaps, however, it is all nonsense.

[544] Air Marshal Sir Arthur Travers 'Bomber' Harris (1892–1984): RFC squadron commander in First World War; served in RAF and rose to Air Marshal in 1941 and Commander-in-Chief RAF bomber command 1942–45; a firm believer in mass raids, he developed the 'saturation' technique of mass bombing, though eventually the policy brought him into conflict with Portal and Churchill, when he continued to pursue it even during the last winter of the war.

This gives me the opportunity to say that all Air Force ground personnel at Aerodromes have got to undergo sharp, effective and severe military training in the use of their weapons, and in all manoeuvres necessary for the defence of the Aerodromes. Every single man must be accounted for in the defence, and every effort should be made to reach a high standard of nimbleness and efficiency.

Will you kindly let me have a report on this?

WSC

Winston S. Churchill to Sir Archibald Sinclair and Air Chief Marshal Sir Charles Portal
23rd June 1941
Secret

What is the position about the bombing of the Black Forest this year? It ought to be possible to produce very fine results.[545]

WSC

Winston S. Churchill to Sir Archibald Sinclair
28th June 1941

Archie,

I understand that little or no provision is made for the defence of aerodromes between the date at which they are fit for operational use and the date at which they are actually taken over, and that this interval is often a long one, especially if some minor adjustments have to be made after the main work is completed. This appears to be a serious gap in our defences. Pray let me know what the position is.

WSC

Winston S. Churchill to Sir Archibald Sinclair and Chief of Air Staff
29th June 1941

1. Further to my Minute of 28th June, about the responsibility of the Air Force for the local and static defence of aerodromes. Every man in Air Force uniform ought to be armed with something, a rifle, a tommy gun, a pistol, a pike or a mace; and every one, without exception, should do at least one hour's drill and practice every day. Every airman should have his place in the defence scheme. At least once a week an alarm should be given as an exercise (stated clearly beforehand in the signal that it is an exercise) and every man should be at his post. 90 per cent should be at their fighting stations in five minutes at the most. It must

[545]On 2 July 1941, Portal wrote to Churchill: 'crops will not burn, but forests will'. Bomber Command 'will therefore go for the forests'.

be understood by all ranks that they are expected to fight and die in the defence of their airfields. Every building which fits in with the scheme of defence should be prepared, so that each has to be conquered one by one by the enemy's parachute or glider troops. Each of these posts should have its leader appointed. In two or three hours the troops will arrive; meanwhile, every post should resist them and must be maintained – be it only a cottage or a mess – so that the enemy has to master each one. This is a slow and expensive process for him.

2. The enormous mass of non-combatant personnel who look after the very few heroic pilots, who alone in ordinary circumstances do all the fighting, is an inherent difficulty in the organisation of the Air Force. Here is the chance for this great mass to add a fighting quality to the necessary services they perform. Every airfield should be a stronghold of fighting air-groundmen, and not the abode of uniformed civilians in the prime of life protected by detachments of soldiers.
3. In order that I may study this matter in detail, let me have the exact field state of Northolt aerodrome, showing every class of airman, the work he does, the weapons he has, and his part in the scheme of defence. We simply cannot afford to have the best part of half a million uniformed men, with all the prestige of the Royal Air Force attaching to them, who have not got a definite fighting value quite apart from the indispensable services they perform for the pilots.

WSC

Winston S. Churchill to Sir Archibald Sinclair
1st July 1941

SECRETARY OF STATE FOR AIR

I see that M.A.P. has supplied a new target programme of aircraft output in which the forecast of heavy bomber output is considerably lower than in previous programmes. Moreover I understand from him that a realistic anticipation might well be 15% below the target.

This new programme and the latest figures of prospective deliveries from the U.S.A. must modify the prospects of R.A.F. expansion.

Pray let me know how these new figures affect the programme of R.A.F. expansion over the next twelve months.

I do not desire extreme accuracy in your forecast so much as a realistic picture of how many front line aircraft of the various categories we may expect to have at different dates.

WSC

At the outbreak of the war, the primary equipment of the Royal New Zealand Air Force (RNZAF) was thirty Vickers Wellington bombers, which the New Zealand government promptly offered to the United Kingdom, together with the crews to fly them. The primary role of the RNZAF, however, was to take advantage of New Zealand's distance from the conflict by training aircrew, as part of the Empire Air Training Scheme.

During 1941, however, the perceived threat from Japan in the Pacific grew and both Britain and New Zealand explored options for building up the capability of the RNZAF. Britain proved unable to meet the needs of the RNZAF and following the entry of Japan to the war and her successful conquests throughout the Pacific, it became imperative for New Zealand to start building up its own defence. New Zealand turned to the United States and signed a lend-lease agreement which saw substantial numbers of planes arrive in the country by the middle of 1942.

Winston S. Churchill to Sir Archibald Sinclair
5th July 1941
Secret

REQUEST FROM THE NEW ZEALAND PRIME MINISTER

We cannot afford to send Hudsons away out of this country till the American deliveries reach 100 a month. As soon as they do, the 64 in question may be worked off to New Zealand at 10 a month, provided there is no falling back in the American Supply, in which case 10 per cent can be sent as convenient.

WSC

Winston S. Churchill to Sir Archibald Sinclair
11th July 1941

Archie,

Although radio beam bombing was neutralised last winter by our interference, it seems that the enemy is re-equipping his whole bomber force with improved radio receivers, and hopes to overwhelm our counter-measures next winter by the multiplicity of his beam stations.

No radio methods can of course prevent his finding and bombing targets like Coventry and Birmingham on fine moonlight nights. But it is on these that our normal night defence should be most effective. It is the dark, cloudy nights that will be our main danger, and we should make every preparation to deal with the enemy beams, whose positions and wave-lengths we now know.

I am informed that the equipment needed is not very remote from that used in ordinary commercial practice, so that it should be possible to obtain it from America even if it cannot be manufactured here. Every-thing should be ready by the autumn. Pray let me know what the position is and what measures are in hand to counter enemy developments.

WSC

Winston S. Churchill to Ministry of Aircraft Production, Sir Charles Corven, Sir Archibald Sinclair, Chief of Air Staff and Lord Cherwell[546]
12th July 1941

Minute

1. I was deeply concerned at the new programmes of MAP, which show a static condition for the next twelve or eighteen months in numbers of aircraft. No doubt new production would be bent on the later phase. I asked that these figures should be subjected to the test of man-hours involved in each type of machine. This certainly shows an improvement of about 50 per cent. in the British field by the twelfth month from now. The American figures improve the calculation both from the number of aircraft and the man-hours standpoint, and one might say that the output for July 1942 would be to the present output as 1 to 1.75.
2. I cannot feel that this is enough. Our estimate of German monthly production by numbers is 2,100, which is the numerical level at which we stand up till July 1942, and indeed thereafter, apart from new projects. We must assume that the Germans also would derive comfort from translating their numbers of aircraft into the man-hours. They may or they may not be making a similar expansion in size and quality. Broadly, from the figures put before me, the impression would be one of equality for the next twelve months. So far as British and German construction is concerned, leaving any increase to be supplied by our share of United States production. Moreover this takes no count of MAP's caveat that their estimate may be reduced by 15 per cent.
3. We cannot be content with the above situation, which excludes all possibility of decisive predominance indispensable for victory. I wish, therefore, these programmes to be re-examined, and the following three methods of expansion together with any others suggested, to be explored by the highest authorities concerned. The three methods are:
    1. An improvement in the existing figures by speeding up and working the machine-tools longer, or by any other measures taken in the sphere of MAP production.
    2. By the construction of new factories and assembling plants or by the reoccupation or full occupation of plants vacated for the sake of dispersion. This may well be justified in view of our increasing command of the British air by day and the improvement in night-fighting devices.
    3. By a reclassification of the Bomber programme so as to secure a larger delivery from well-tried types in that period. Fighter aircraft must continually strive for mastery, and rapid changes of design may be imperative. But a large proportion of the Bomber Force will in the next twelve months be employed under steady conditions and within ranges which

[546] Frederick Alexander Lindemann, Viscount Cherwell – see n491.

are moderate. While all Bombers required for long-distance or great heights or daylight action must be the subject of intensive improvement, a large proportion of the Bombing Force will be carrying their nightly load to (say) the Ruhr or other nearby targets. It would seem that the Air Staff could divide their activities into near and far, and that on this basis some good lines of production, which have not yet reached their maximum, could be given longer run at the peak, with every definite addition to numbers. This would, for instance seem to apply to the Blackpool Wellington, which is a new supply, reaching its peak in November, but only running for six months at that level. If it were allowed a twelve months' run at the peak, it may be that a larger delivery would be possible from November on.

4. The criterion of Bomber strength is the weight of bombs deliverable per month on the reasonably foreseeable targets in Germany and Italy. Have the Air Staff plans been applied to the figures of production with this end in view? It may be that a heavier load carried by a new machine would give better results. But a machine which is good enough to carry 2 tons to the Ruhr ought to have a long run in continuous production before it is discarded. There are no doubt other instances. I have asked MAP to review their programmes accordingly, having regard to the grievous loss on too hasty change-overs.
5. The new programme is substantially less that the March figures and far below the October figures. However, many materials have been accumulated on the October basis. A substantial expansion should therefore be possible if all factors are fitted to the optimum. The Air Ministry should show how this latest programme, apart from any expansion, fits in with their pilot production for the next twelve months, having regard, on the one hand, to the reduced scale of losses which has been found operative by experience, and, on the other, to the much more lavish pilot establishment now said to be necessary in proportion to machines. Bombs, explosives, guns and all accessories must be measured in relation both to the existing programme and the necessary expansion. In principle, however, we must aim for nothing less than having an Air Force twice as strong as the German Air Force by the end of 1942. This ought not to be impossible if a renewed vast effort is made now. It is the very least that can be contemplated, since no other way of winning the war has yet been proposed.

Sir Archibald Sinclair to Winston S. Churchill
14th July 1941
SECRET

PRIME MINISTER

You spoke to me the other day about the rate of casualties recently experienced by Fighter Command.

In the last two weeks for which firm figures are available, Fighter Command lost in killed, wounded and missing 29 pilots during the week ending 28th June, and in the week before, 22 pilots. This compares with an average weekly casualty rate in Fighter Command in September of last year of 59 pilots killed and missing; and, of course, these casualties are being borne by a much larger number of squadrons.

You also remarked that the balance of the fighting had not been so much in our favour in recent weeks as it was three or four weeks ago. The reasons for this are:–

a) When these offensive operations started we selected bombing targets to suit the fighter's interests so that the battle could take place under conditions advantageous to us.
b) When the Russians came into the war[547] the aim of these operations was changed; they became primarily bombing operations to destroy important industry and communication centres in North-West France; accordingly, targets were selected primarily to suit the bombers; and fighter operations had to be designed to protect the bombers. We have been penetrating deeper into hostile territory, therefore the close escort has been exposed to more prolonged attack than in the earlier days.
c) Lately, we have been employing heavy bombers in the daylight sweeps. They are not so well accustomed as the Blenheims to formation flying and have been inclined to split up over the target with the result that the escorts had to split up too. Frequent conferences have been held between the fighter and bomber staffs and pilots and, with practice, the co-operation between the heavy bombers and the fighter escorts will improve. The fighters have been remarkably successful in protecting these heavy bombers.
d) For a few glorious days at the beginning of these sweeps, the Germans were increasing their fighter strength on the Western front by using O.T.U. pilots as first line fighters and our fighter pilots ate them up. Now, however, these O.T.U. fighters are getting more experienced and the resistance of German pilots has stiffened. There are signs that the Germans have leavened their fighter forces in the west with experienced men from the Eastern Front – e.g. one crack German pilot was shot down in the air over the sea the other day and another has been forced down on land in this country.
e) Our fighter pilots have been working at very high pressure during this good weather and Fighter Command is devising a number of ways of resting them. The Squadrons in 11 Group have been brought up to their full establishment, and a system of relief of units in 11 Group by others from quieter areas is in operation.

[547] Germany invaded the Soviet Union on 22 June 1941.

You may have noticed that in the last few days the balance has swung back a little in our favour. We are still around the 2 to 1 mark – a remarkable achievement for offensive operations.

AHMS

Winston S. Churchill to Sir Archibald Sinclair
15th July 1941

Investigations by the Ministry of Home Security into the effect of German high explosive bombs has shown that a far greater amount of damage is done by blast, which destroys buildings, &c., than by splinters, which find very few useful targets, especially at night when most people are under cover.

The higher the proportion of high explosive to bomb-case the greater the blast. If the weight of the metal case is increased, we get more splinters.

Our G.P.[548] bombs have a charge-weight ratio of about 30-70. The Germans work with a larger ratio, about 50-50. These are not only more efficient for destroying cities; they are also cheaper.

In these circumstances the charge-weight ratio of our bombs ought to be reconsidered, especially now that the Air Ministry have asked for such a large expansion in output.

Winston S. Churchill to Sir Archibald Sinclair
27th July 1941

Your reply to my Minute No. M.744/1 suggests that my point has not been fully appreciated.

If we rely on blast effect rather than splinters for destroying buildings there is no need for high penetration, more especially as less than one-fifth of the area of most towns is covered with buildings. Hence we should not allow our charge-weight ratio to be reduced by our desire to make a bomb with high penetration.

Small bombs of this type are, of course, useful for destroying services, but it would seem, if the Ministry of Home Security's results are right, that our larger bombs should all aim at a high charge-weight ratio.

Perhaps you could let me have a list showing the tonnage and the charge-weight ratios of the various types of bombs which will be in production six months and twelve months from now.

I am pleased to note that the American bombs have a high charge-weight ratio. Is it really necessary to carry out elaborate tests of their penetrating power before ordering a large number? There seems to be a considerable volume of

[548] General purpose.

evidence that destruction is more widespread if the bomb detonates well above the surface.

WSC

Winston S. Churchill to Admiral Pound, Sir Archibald Sinclair and John Moore-Brabazon[549]
16th August 1941

1. This is a melancholy story. You will see from reading the Minutes that we were promised 'Grummans', with folding wings, at twenty a month beginning in April.[550] We still have none, and are only promised the schedule set out in the First Lord's Minute of July 26.
2. I regard the supply of from 6 to 12 'Grummans' to Victorious and Ark Royal as of first importance; especially is this the case with any carrier operating in the Mediterranean. The surprise which will be effected upon the enemy when these fast Fighters rise to engage them may give considerable easement, almost at once.

   The cutting down of enemy bomber aircraft attack at sea far exceeds in importance and urgency any other duty which can be performed by a Carrier in the Mediterranean; even if they can only work within 40 to 50 miles of the parent ship they can do all that is necessary. The enemy must be made to feel that to go near a ship convoyed by an aircraft carrier is to incur heavy losses from aircraft almost equal to shore-based fighters.
3. We have now no aircraft carriers in the Eastern Mediterranean. Therefore, there is no point in sending folding-wing 'Grummans' there at present. The August, September and October quotas for 'Grummans' now assigned to the United Kingdom (total 22), and the 24 now assigned to the Middle East in the September and October quotas – total 46 – should all be made available in the United Kingdom for the equipping of our aircraft carriers. Deliveries to the Middle East after October should be considered later.

   Let me have a monthly report of the equipment of the aircraft carriers with 'Grummans'.
4. When do we get our new aircraft-carrier Indomitable?
5. Unless there is some reason to the contrary of which I am not aware, the following orders should be given now.

   'The September and October batches of 12 Grummans with folding wings should be sent to the United Kingdom and not (repeat not) to the Middle East.'

WSC

[549] John Moore-Brabazon, 1st Lord Brabazon (1884–1964): first Englishman to pilot a heavier-than-air machine under power in England (1909); served in the Royal Flying Corps during First World War; Parliamentary Private Secretary to Winston Churchill 1919; Conservative MP for Chatham 1919–29, Wallasey 1931–42; Minister of Transport 1940–41; Minister of Aircraft Production 1941–42.

Winston S. Churchill to John Moore-Brabazon and Sir Archibald Sinclair
19th August 1941

NEW AIRCRAFT PRODUCTION PROGRAMME

It is clear that the utmost effort must be made, and that even then results will be short of our requirements. Please report what practical steps you are taking to give effect to my Minute M733/1 of July 12, as modified by your reply of August 2. Let me have a Progress Report before the month is out. Inform me also of any way in which I can assist you. The table of forecasts should be modified, in red ink, to show the somewhat improved target now being aimed at.

WSC

Winston S. Churchill to Sir Archibald Sinclair
20th August 1941

I am glad you are equipping our aerodromes with blind-landing apparatus, which may be most important in the coming winter.

I note that all new bomber and GR[551] aircraft made in England, with the exception of a few Blenheims, have standard equipment, but only 30 per cent. of the aerodromes. We should endeavour to complete the rest before March. No doubt you have explored the possibility of getting standard equipment from America. Perhaps extra pressure could be put on through Harriman and Hopkins to this end.

We should press on also with the night-fighter squadrons. You expect to have 17 ready by the end of this year or early 1942. Cannot we get them completed by the Autumn for the night-bombing season? If the turbin-light[552] proves a success it will be important to be able to use ordinary fighter squadrons to co-operate with the searchlight-carrying aircraft. No doubt you have this in mind.

WSC

Winston S. Churchill to Sir Archibald Sinclair
27th August 1941

Your minute of 6th August shows that the most promising weapon at present in sight for aerial attack on tanks is the Jefferis bomb, and I am pleased to note that you have ordered 50,000 of these.

As I understand these weapons go into the ordinary light bomb container it should be possible to put them into use at once and I should favour postponing

[550] The Grumman Wildcat fighter, with folding wings, was designed for use on aircraft carriers.

[551] General reconnaissance aircraft.

[552] The 'Turbinlight' was a large spotlight mounted on the nose of a Boston Bomber. It was intended to be used to illuminate the stream of enemy bombers so that the accompanying Hurricanes and Spitfires could dart into the stream of light and attack. Needless to say, the plan did not work.

further manufacture of the Sticky Bomb and a part of the Bombard ammunition in order to obtain immediately an adequate supply of these aerial bombs.

It seems likely that when the tactics have been worked out and the pilots have had some practice, considerable improvement in the chance of hitting as shown in the first trials may be expected. We should get immediately a large supply of dummy bombs and give a selected group of pilots plenty of practice against ground targets.

If the expected improvement is achieved we should investigate at once the possibility of sending through the Mediterranean at an early date in a warship an adequate supply with the pilots who have practised with the dummy bombs.

It might also be well to consider whether the Russians might be able to improvise these bombs rapidly, in which case they should be given full details.

General Ismay

General Shearer[553] to be apprised. These might help in ME.[554] Please make proposals for speedy action.

WSC

Sir Archibald Sinclair to Winston S. Churchill
3rd September 1941

PRIME MINISTER

1. The new programme of aircraft production circulated by the Minister under cover of his minute dated 31st August, 1941, shows an advance on its predecessor.
2. In heavy bombers our ultimate expectations have improved by more than 60 aircraft a month, although this is unfortunately accompanied by a slight diminution in the forecast up to the middle of 1942.
3. The medium bombers, 1,600 additional Wellingtons, are promised for the loss of only 440 Warwicks.
4. Fighter production is improved by a larger forecast for the Mosquito and the appearance of the Thunderbolt.
5. These developments are most welcome. Nevertheless, the programme must be studied not only in relation to past expectations but also by reference to our needs.
6. The total production of aircraft forecast for mid-1942, namely some 2200 of all types per month, is roughly identical with that planned in the autumn of 1939. But in the meantime the responsibilities of the Royal Air Force have greatly increased. Early in the war our strategy in co-operation with the French was to maintain relatively large forces on the Continent with the intention ultimately of undertaking land offensive on a large scale. The collapse of France necessitated the abandonment of these ideas and we cannot now expect to operate on the

553 Eric James Shearer (1892–1980): Director of Military Intelligence in the Middle East 1940–42.

554 Middle East.

Continent until Germany has been virtually beaten. The bomber is our prime offensive weapon and it is an essential principle of our strategy that victory can only be won after the German economic life and morale have been subjected to a bombing offensive of vast and sustained intensity.

7. Comparing the requirements of this purpose with the latest M.A.P. programme and with what is known of production in the United States, attention is at once focussed on the heavy and medium bombers which form both the biggest, and the most important, of our needs.
8. Requirements for heavy and medium bombers over the two-year period July 1941 to July 1943 amount to roughly 22,000. Of this number – on the assumption that 85% of the M.A.P. forecast is realised – roughly one half should be available from production in this country. The United States forecast for heavy and medium bomber production over the period amounts to about 11,000, of which possibly one half might reach this country. Even on an optimistic basis of calculation, therefore, and accepting a large number of medium instead of heavy bombers, there is still a gap of more than 5,500 aircraft over the two-year period. This gap can only be bridged by new production.
9. It is for the Minister of Aircraft Production to recommend how this additional capacity should be found and the proportion in which it should be distributed between the United Kingdom and the United States. Clearly there would be great advantages in developing as large a share as possible in the United States, but no opportunities for greater production in this country should be neglected.
10. I notice that in paragraph 11 of the memorandum accompanying his minute the Minister states that the possibility of further production of heavy bombers in this country is still being explored. The main bottle-neck is stated to be engines. I hope the Minister will not hesitate on the grounds of a possible shortage of engines, to employ any additional airframe capacity that can be found. When the bomber offensive has gained momentum, a slackening of fighter production may well be possible, thus releasing engines for the bomber programme.
11. The question of Fleet Air Arm production should also receive consideration. The peak production of 145 Barracudas a month is intended to support not only the requirements of aircraft carriers but also some 10 supernumerary T.B.R.[555] squadrons in addition. It is for consideration whether the requirement for these supernumerary squadrons should not be reduced in view of the desperate need for additional airframe and engine capacity.
12. I hope the Minister will press to the utmost his proposal for producing the Lancaster in Canada. A bigger target than 25 Lancasters per month from this source is eminently desirable.
13. When everything has been done to expand bomber production in this country it is clear that a substantial margin must remain which can only be met by the creation of new capacity in the United States. It is an astonishing fact that

[555] Torpedo bomber reconnaissance.

according to the latest forecast the British production of heavy bombers remains very much ahead of that of the United States throughout the whole of 1942. Remembering the vast resources of the United States, their freedom from enemy action and their virtually untapped manpower, it is all too clear how wide is the gap between American potentialities and American performance and how much remains to be done if they are to redeem their promise to be the arsenal of the democracies and give effect to their determination "to devote their entire industrial effort to the prosecution of the war".

14. No doubt arises as to the ability of the United States to produce the numbers we require. The problem is to induce them to accept that sharp diminution in civilian consumption which is necessary if munitions capacity on the requisite scale is to become possible.
15. The Americans are well aware of our requirements in heavy bomber aircraft and the British Air Commission and the R.A.F. Delegation in Washington have not ceased to urge our case in every possible quarter. There is, however, a limit to what can be achieved on this plane and recent telegrams suggest that this limit has already been reached.
16. A further difficulty is the known reluctance of the United States Chiefs of Staff to contemplate a large expansion of bomber output. Action on decisive lines and on the highest plane is necessary without delay. Would you not think it appropriate to put the proposal personally to Mr. Roosevelt? Great issues depend upon action – or lack of action – in America in the next few months and the utmost pressure must be brought to bear if we are to achieve our purpose.

AHMS

Sir Archibald Sinclair to Winston S. Churchill
9th September 1941
Secret

Prime Minister

While you were away[556] the Lord Privy Seal enquired about the rate of deliveries of aircraft to Bomber Command and the Minister of Aircraft Production and I were instructed to report to the Cabinet on this question.

I asked the Minister to join me in a minute to the Cabinet setting out the position but he preferred to send to the Cabinet his own report, of which I attach a copy.

No criticism can be made of the Minister's Paper except perhaps from one standpoint. It does not seem to me sufficiently to bring home to the Cabinet how serious the position is.

[556] In August 1941 Churchill travelled across the Atlantic to meet Roosevelt and sign the Atlantic Charter.

At the meeting of the Supply Committee last week, you expressed your intention of holding occasional conferences yourself on the lines of the Battle of the Atlantic, Night Air Defence and Tank Conferences.

It seems to me that a full disclosure, for which the Cabinet have asked, of the bomber aircraft delivery position, would be a good preparation for these conferences. I have, therefore, drafted a Paper in which I have set out the facts objectively and avoided any expression of opinion. Do you agree that I should circulate it? I am sending a copy of this minute and of my Paper to the Minister of Aircraft Production.

AHMS

Most Secret

Bomber Production and the Expansion of the Bomber Force

Memorandum by Secretary of State for Air

In W.M. (41) 83rd Conclusions the War Cabinet called for a report on the number of bombers available for service and the present rate of bomber production.

From a variety of causes production throughout the year, both in this country and in the U.S.A., has lagged far behind forecasts, although the forecasts have themselves from time to time been revised downwards. And the development of the operational strength of the Royal Air Force has advanced only at the cost of a steady and serious depletion of the reserves of bombers and G.R. aircraft and of current shortages of aircraft in squadrons, in O.T.U.s and in Flying Training Schools.

The number of bomber aircraft available on the 1st September were as follows:

			A.S.Us.	
	In Bomber & Coastal Command Squadrons formed and forming	In O.T.U.s	Ready in 4 days	In preparation
Heavy Bombers	82	7	1	2
Medium Bombers	807	619	34	269
Light Bombers	198	190	20	94
Totals	1087	816	55	365

This represents a lag of 16 squadrons behind plan.

Taking into account the deficiencies in the establishments of units, the reserves of bombers, including aircraft under preparation but excluding those awaiting repair or modification, on 1st September were:–

Heavy Bombers – Nil.

Medium Bombers – Nil.
Light Bombers – 310
The figures for aircraft deliveries during the first eight months of this year are:–

	United Kingdom			U.S.A.		
	Planned	Actual	Deficit	Planned	Actual	Deficit
Heavy Bombers	502	267	-235 (46%)	91	21	-70 (77%)
Medium & Light Bombers	3428	2896	-532 (15%)	580	344	-236 (49%)

Disturbing news comes from America. The "Slessor Agreement", upon which is based the allocation of aircraft to us from U.S. production, is threatened; the B.26 Medium Bomber, of which we hoped to receive large numbers, looks like being a failure.

The Minister of Aircraft Production has put forward proposals for increasing production at home, and has drawn attention to the need for further action in Canada and in the U.S.A. The Prime Minister has convened a meeting to discuss the problem and has reported to the Cabinet certain action proposed. (W.M. (41) 90th Conclusions).

Sir Archibald Sinclair to Winston S. Churchill
9th September 1941
SECRET

PRIME MINISTER

We have no comments to make on the attached report on the results of our bombing operations against Germany.

The chief lesson to be drawn from it is clear – an increase in the weight of the attack produces a more than corresponding increase in its effectiveness. Therefore as soon as we can double the bomb dropping capacity of Bomber Command we shall much more than double the already considerable effectiveness of its attacks.

AHMS

Winston S. Churchill to Anthony Eden[557] and Sir Archibald Sinclair
20th September 1941

I think that great value might be obtained at the present time by dropping leaflets on Italy referring particularly to the fact that hundreds of thousands of Italians have

[557] Eden replaced Halifax as Foreign Secretary at the end of 1940 – see n400.

been sent from sunny homes to die in the frozen mud of the Ukraine. Pray have this matter considered by the Political Warfare Executive.

I am sending a copy of this minute to the Secretary of State for Air, in order that the operational aspect also may be considered.

WSC

Winston S. Churchill to Sir Archibald Sinclair and Brendan Bracken
27th September 1941

What is the reason for giving so much publicity to the discreditable behaviour of the six American airman published in all the newspapers today?[558] The story is one which will be meat and drink to our enemies over there. Surely the matter could have been handled as one of internal discipline?

Who is responsible?

WSC

In early October Sinclair was due to make a speech at Middlesbrough concerning German aircraft shortages, which Churchill himself had mentioned in a speech on 30 September. Sinclair sent his draft to the Prime Minister for approval and comment.

Winston S. Churchill to Sir Archibald Sinclair
1st October 1941

I really do not think you need refer to my statements, especially as you agree with them, or go worrying about headlines or anything silly like that. I do not like the passage you propose to use, at all. The plans I mentioned are not 'grandiose' plans. There would be nothing 'grandiose' in Hitler using seventy-five divisions against Russia, using twenty-five towards the Middle East, sending half a dozen through Spain to stir up trouble at Gibraltar or in Morocco and keeping fifty divisions available for invasion. He would still have one hundred to spare. His difficulty would be shortage in aircraft, for all these campaigns at once, which is what I said. The sentence marked (A) implies that their current production equals their losses; this is certainly not true when you consider all the crashes and wastage. With far less losses we make very slow headway, in fact our A.S.Us. are drained for the petty expansions made. The striking power of the German long-range bomber force is affected not only by its losses, but by large numbers employed in Russia. I do not therefore think your statement is sound, it certainly would cause lively controversy and force me to make a pretty sharp answer. See also my other notes.

558 Six American airmen had returned to the US in protest at being paid a lower rate by the RAF than they believed they had been offered. They were asked to resign their commissions in the RAF.

I should have thought it was sufficient to say at this moment that while the German air force was engaged so deeply in Russia it was doubtful whether they could maintain the same continuity of attack as last winter, but that they still had a substantial bomber force in the west, and by saving up could make attacks which, though not so continuous, might be as bad as, or worse than, last year. You might mention that tip-and-run attacks on the coast towns were a temptation to them.

WSC

Sir Archibald Sinclair to Winston S. Churchill
4th October 1941

Prime Minister

I think you will be interested in these two telegrams which I have received from Balfour.[559] The main points are:–

1. Strong resistance from U.S. Air Corps to release of 500 heavy bombers between now and the end of June (as proposed to Mr. Harriman by Lord Beaverbrook) on following grounds:–
   a) Heavy bombers required for Philippines against Japan
   b) U.S. Army wants to train squadrons which could be flown to any part of the world and in particular to Russian aerodromes near Vladivostok.
   c) Air Corps require heavy bombers to train crews.
2. Stimson[560] thinks America will soon be in the war and therefore agrees with these arguments.
3. Mr. Hopkins does not consider position hopeless but is doubtful whether President will over-ride Stimson.
4. Hopkins advises against an approach from you to the President at this juncture. I do not myself think that we ought to ask your help to obtain these 500 bombers. We shall need it to obtain the American contribution of 5,500 heavy bombers to our big programme.
5. Hopkins strongly advises that Balfour should see Arnold and perhaps the President. My opinion is that we should follow the advice of Hopkins and instruct Balfour accordingly.

I therefore attach a signal which I propose to send to Balfour.

Draft Telegram to Captain Balfour

1. Your 471 22/10/ Personal and Secret. Glad to know that Americans are still firm against diversion of heavy bombers to Russia.

---

[559] Harold Harrington Balfour, Baron Balfour of Inchrye (1897–1988): served in RFC during First World War; Conservative MP for Isle of Thanet 1929–45; Parliamentary Secretary for Air 1938–44; Minister Resident for West Africa 1944–45; ennobled July 1945.

[560] US Secretary of War; see n386.

2. You should certainly take Hopkins' advice and renew the proposal made by Beaverbrook to Harriman that we should receive 500 heavy bombers out of the forecast production of 770 between now and the end of June. I think you should take Harris[561] with you but in this and all else consult Hopkins. If he advises you to see the President you should certainly do so. If you cannot get the 500 do not commit us to acceptance of any smaller number. If we fail to get what we want this time, we must be free to ask again later on.

Beaverbrook is seeing Russians about Airacobras.[562]

Winston S. Churchill to Sir David Margesson and Sir Archibald Sinclair
8th October 1941

I think now the time is ripe to form an Irish Brigade, also an Irish Wing or Squadron of the RAF. If these were taken in hand they would have to be made a great success of. The pilot Finucane[563] might be a great figure.

Pray let me have proposals. The movement might have important political reactions later on.

WSC

Winston S. Churchill to Sir Archibald Sinclair
11th October 1941
(Action this day)

Prime Minister to Secretary of State for Air, Minister of Supply, and M.A.P.

I have re-read the report of the Select Committee to the Albemarles,[564] and I think it requires a far more definite and categorical reply than those which have hitherto been presented to me. I shall be glad to know what is the evidence which the two Supply Ministers will give, especially on the financial side; and from the Secretary of State for Air I desire to learn (a) what real use this machine will be when the first five hundred are completed. Can he tell me that it will be a bona-fide useful machine in the summer of next year? What parts of Germany could it bomb, or is it only of use on the French invasion ports? (b) What are the reasons, shortly,

[561] Air Marshal Harris – see n544.

[562] A fighter plane designed and manufactured in the US.

[563] Wing Commander 'Paddy' Finucane was to be killed on 15 July 1942, at the age of 22. He ditched his damaged fighter in the sea and drowned rather than crash-land in enemy territory and risk being taken prisoner.

[564] A light twin-engine reconnaissance bomber built from wood and steel instead of aluminium alloys, and suitable for construction in dispersed factories. It was introduced in 1940 but proved to be a major disappointment, with neither the defences or bomb delivery capability to be useful. It was eventually used mainly as a glider tug and transport plane; on D-Day, Albemarles dropped pathfinding troops for the 6th Airborne Division.

for refusing to publish the report? What information in particular is contained in it which would be of value to the enemy?

As this matter will be debated on Wednesday and I shall have to watch over it myself in all probability, I want to be sure of my ground. The matter is urgent.

WSC

The final phase of Sir Hugh Dowding's career engaged Sinclair and Churchill again.

Sir Archibald Sinclair to Winston S. Churchill
29th October 1941

PRIME MINISTER

Sir Hugh Dowding came to see me yesterday.

I explained to him the nature of the task which I invited him to undertake[565] and pointed out that the problem of man power had become one of extreme delicacy, as well as urgency, for us because, on the one hand, of the efforts which we had already made to reduce our establishments and, on the other hand, of the big demand which our plan of expansion was compelling us to make on a narrowing labour market. I made it clear that it was only within recent weeks that the problem had entered so acute a stage that you had even suggested to the Chief of the Air Staff that he should personally spend a week or two visiting units and attempt to solve it. Apart from that the only mention which I made of your name was that you cordially approved of the invitation which I was giving him.

Sir Hugh Dowding was most agreeable and even friendly. He mentioned two doubts in his mind. The first was whether he was the right man for the job.

I said that we required a man of his great experience, with knowledge of the Royal Air Force and high rank to undertake it effectively. I said that the Chief of the Air Staff and I were satisfied that he possessed unique qualifications for undertaking it because of his experience not only in operations but also in administration and on the research, developing and engineering sides of the work of the Royal Air Force. His second objection was that he was writing a book. He wanted to get it published and it was not the kind of book which could be published while he was employed in the R.A.F. My reply to this was that it was certainly a matter that required consideration but I felt sure that it ought not to constitute an obstacle to his undertaking this important work.

We then had a short and friendly discussion on possible methods and procedure.

I then told Sir Hugh Dowding that, while the normal procedure would be that he would be recalled to serve as an Air Chief Marshal while undertaking this duty, I should be quite prepared to cancel the Gazette[566] which had so recently appeared

[565] Dowding was asked to lead a review of RAF Establishments.

[566] The *London Gazette*, first published in 1665, is the oldest continuously published newspaper in Britain. It contains a wide range of official notices, including state, parliamentary and ecclesiastical notices;

if he preferred that course. He said that he would like to think that over and would give me his answer on that point when he was writing to me about his acceptance or refusal of the task which I had asked him to undertake.

I have now received from him the letter which I enclose. You will see that he refuses my invitation. He tells me that he has readjusted his whole life and outlook, that he has taken and furnished a house, brought his sister up from the country to keep house for him and has written a small book. He says "I have in fact been completely happy as my own master for the first time in my life".

There does not seem to be any course open for me, but to accept this decision and in the course of a day or two I will make other proposals to you for the accomplishment of the task which I had hoped Sir Hugh Dowding would undertake.

Archie

Winston S. Churchill to Sir Archibald Sinclair and Air Chief Marshal Sir Charles Portal
31st October 1941

I saw Sir Hugh Dowding this afternoon and he accepted your proposal for reinstatement on the active list and for his taking charge of the Committee on Establishments. He asked for a fortnight in which to complete the small book he has written during his unemployment. I have undertaken to read the book myself at the week-end. I cannot think it will affect technical matters in any way.

In the meanwhile he will read up any papers on the subject and prepare his mind for his new duties. Pray let me have your other names for the Committee, which should not exceed three. There is no need to publish his reinstatement in the Gazette until this book trouble is cleared up, but let me see the form which the announcement will take.

WSC

Sir Archibald Sinclair to Winston S. Churchill
1st November 1941
SECRET

PRIME MINISTER

Your Minute M.1023/1.

1. The proposal which I made to Sir Hugh Dowding was not that he should take charge of the Committee on Establishments. That Committee is at present in the Middle East and I want Sir Hugh Dowding to get to work at once. On its return the Committee will of course be expected to give Sir Hugh Dowding any help or information for which he may ask and meanwhile he will of course be free

supplements announce the granting of honours and awards as well as promotions and regradings in the Armed Forces.

to consult them by signal if he so wishes. My idea, however, was that he should work and report on his own with such staff as he may require.

2. Meanwhile, however, the Chief of the Air Staff has suggested to me – and I believe he has made the same suggestion to you – that, as all the Services are engaged on the same task of cutting down establishments to the lowest limit compatible with operational efficiency, they should work together. One Service, for example, may have dispensed almost entirely with batmen and may be able to suggest to other Services that they should follow the same example; and, in return, that Service may be able to profit from suggestions made by the sister Services in regard to economies which they have found possible without loss of efficiency. This seems to me to be an attractive suggestion and, if it appeals to you, you may possibly decide to appoint Sir Hugh Dowding as Chairman of the Inter-Service Committee. Such an appointment, however, would obviously not be within my competency.
3. Am I right in supposing that you would wish to receive a statement of the Air Staff's objections on security grounds to a number of passages in Sir Hugh Dowding's book before you come to a decision on its publication? You have often expressed to the Cabinet your dislike of the obligations, which Parliament throws upon Ministers, of making speeches which reveal the drift of our thoughts. This book, by so eminent an author, will be subject to the detailed scrutiny of the enemy, and it contains many indications, which would be by no means misleading, of the lines of development on which we are now proceeding.
4. Incidentally, I think you will agree that publication of the book, which is bound to excite a great deal of attention, will make it impossible to cancel notification in the Gazette of Sir Hugh Dowding's retirement. It is a book which, as the author himself says in the text, could only be published by an officer on the retired list, though it is doubtful whether even a retired officer would be allowed, in the ordinary way, to publish such a book in time of war. If the Gazette were cancelled, the position would be that Sir Hugh Dowding would never have been a retired officer and, therefore, the book should certainly never have been published. This would be quickly asserted in some quarters. In others it would be said that we had made a pretence of putting him on the retired list in order to enable him to publish his book. Altogether, it would be impossible to give satisfactory explanations.
5. In these circumstances, I hope you will agree that the proper course would be to recall Sir Hugh Dowding from the retired list immediately after the book was published. This would avoid publicity which would put me in particular, and the Government in general, in an awkward position; it would entail no disadvantage for Sir Hugh Dowding and would, indeed, inure financially to his benefit.[567]

AHMS

[567] Dowding's book, *Twelve Legions of Angels*, was eventually published in 1946. See letter of 9 November 1941, page 332.

Winston S. Churchill to Sir Archibald Sinclair
5th November 1941

Prime Minister to Secretary of State for Air
Your reply to my minute (1024/1).

I do not think you should dismiss a matter like this (whereby mechanics and fitters worked for certificates of competence in each different make of engine) so lightly. I am told it is the explanation of the far higher economy reached by the Germans in maintaining their air force.

I must beg you to have the matter more searchingly examined.

W

Sir Archibald Sinclair to Winston S. Churchill
8th November 1941
Secret

Prime Minister

The Defence Committee (Supply) at their meeting on 31st October agreed that a report should be prepared dealing with the steps to be taken to ensure a reasonable allocation of United States bomber production. That report is attached to this Minute.

To the diversion of aircraft to Russia and the delays in production at home is now added the disappointment of our American expectations as a serious impediment to the expansion of the Royal Air Force.

Now instead of expanding our day bomber squadrons, we are forced to contemplate the possibility of rolling up squadrons in No. 2 Group because the Americans have allocated the whole of the Defence Aid Bostons to Russia.

Heavy bomber deliveries are our main source of anxiety. Under the Slessor Agreement we hoped to receive up to 80% of the ultimate heavy bomber output. By August General Arnold was talking of 50/50 division. In the same month Lord Beaverbrook obtained from the President an assurance that the Slessor Agreement would govern heavy bomber allocations at least till next April and perhaps longer. Nevertheless, the Supply Council in Washington has now been officially informed that we are to expect only 238 heavy bombers up to mid 1942, or little more than a quarter of the total forecast production up to that date. Of long-term expectations in this class of aircraft we have no indication whatever.

I need not remind you of the grave effects of this uncertainty on future planning. An important part of the large bomber force we are planning depends upon the supply of heavy bombers from the United States. Failing a long-term and reliable forecast of deliveries there is every chance that we shall either plan too ambitiously and so waste resources, or underestimate the numbers of aircraft we are to receive and so fail to make the essential preparations to use them.

Accordingly I suggest for your consideration that a telegram should be sent to Mr. Roosevelt:–

Informing him of the steps we are taking to expand bomber production in the United Kingdom and of the gaps which still remain;

Urging him to give directions for a further expansion of American production; and

(Above all) asking that we should be given an authoritative estimate of the deliveries upon which we can depend over the next two years in order that we may have a firm basis for planning expansion of the Royal Air Force.

I would also suggest that this telegram should be followed up by personal representations in Washington by the most influential figure we can afford to send.

The Minister of Aircraft Production and the Minister of Supply are in general agreement with this minute.

AHMS

Secret

Allocation of U.S. Production

Up to the Beaverbrook/Harriman discussions in September this year British expectations regarding the allocation of aircraft from United States production were based upon the so-called "Slessor Agreement".

The "Slessor Agreement" is a Report on Air Policy drawn up by a Sub-committee of the United States Staff Committee and the United Kingdom Delegation during the Staff Conversations held in Washington in the early months of this year.

The Report accompanied the Main Report on the Staff Conversations (A.B.C.1). So much importance was attached to it on the British side that the British Air Representative made his signature of the main Report contingent upon the joint signature of the Air Report. The Air Report was later given the general approval of the British Government. No specific approval has ever been forthcoming from the American side beyond the original signatures appended by the American representatives.

The Slessor Agreement laid down both a provisional allocation of United States production and a machinery of consultation by means for which this provisional allocation could be varied from time to time in accordance with strategic requirements. The Agreement was exceptionally favourable to the British interest, as it provided not only for the allocation to Great Britain of a major share of American production then existing or approved, but also that until the United States entered the war Great Britain should receive the entire output from new capacity. If the United States entered the war the output from new capacity would, in principle, be divided equally between Great Britain and the United States.

Doubts as to the intention of the United States to fulfil the Slessor Agreement first arose in July. The "Riviera" talks showed that the American Staff were anxious to amend the Agreement particularly in its application to heavy bomber output. On the latter point, General Arnold in conversation with Lord Beaverbrook in

Washington stated that he had in mind a 50/50 division of heavy bomber output during the first half of 1942. The question of heavy bomber output also arose in conversation between the President of the United States and Lord Beaverbrook when the former stated that the Slessor Agreement as affecting heavy bombers would operate until April 1942. Lord Beaverbrook formed the impression that it should be possible to obtain a renewal thereafter.

In September the Beaverbrook/Harriman talks took place in London. The Americans tabled a complete set of proposals showing what share of United States production they proposed to "make available for export" and how they proposed to allocate it between the United Kingdom, Russia, China, and other countries. The British share consisted of:–

British order, plus

50% of Defence Aid Orders, plus

7½% of Army Air Corps orders,

and amounted to 7,500 aircraft of operational type over the period September 1941 to June 1942, inclusive. This proposal represented a loss to the United Kingdom of at least 1,800 combat aircraft over the period.

So far as heavy bombers were concerned the British share (including deliveries from British financed contracts) amounted to 188, or roughly 25% of the total production then forecast of 770 to 30th June 1941.

The protests of Lord Beaverbrook and of the Air Staff made no impression on Mr. Harriman, and Lord Beaverbrook was compelled reluctantly to acquiesce in the American proposals. It was, understood, however, that the question of heavy bombers would be treated as a separate issue and raised again at a later date.

Towards the end of the Beaverbrook/Harriman talks Mr. Harriman intimated that the allocation described above had not been formally approved in Washington. This warning has proved to be well founded, as the latest telegrams from Washington show that a quite different method of allocation has now been decided upon. Full details are not yet available but the broad outline of the position seems to be:–

Heavy Bombers

We are promised 99 heavy bombers, plus 139 off British contracts, out of a total forecast production of 856, up to June, 1942.

Other types

Except in types affected by diversions to Russia (namely Kittyhawks and Bostons) we shall receive 100% of Defence Aid orders up to June 1942. There are to be no releases from Army orders. In Bostons the entire Defence Aid orders will be diverted to Russia. In Kittyhawks the main bulk of Defence Aid orders are earmarked for the Royal Air Force, only some 350 being diverted to Russia.

We have thus at last received official notification of the abrogation of the Slessor Agreement. The main consequences may be summarised as follows:–

a) Generally, there will be a grave drop in our expectations, arising partly from diversions to Russia but mainly from the fact that, broadly speaking, there are to be no releases from U.S. Army contracts.
b) In heavy bombers our expectation for the period up to mid-1942 has receded from the minimum of 400 expected under the Slessor Agreement to 238.
c) After mid-1942 we have no forecast whatever of the number of aircraft we are to receive from the United States. Whereas, under the Slessor formula we hoped to receive some 400 heavy bombers out of a monthly planned production of 500, we now have no picture whatever of the numbers we are likely to receive.

The effect of this state of affairs on long-term planning is serious. It is impossible to plan effectively and economically while such a major uncertainty persists. So long as we are without knowledge of what the American contribution will be we are bound either to over-estimate our expectations and therefore to over-produce aircrews, aerodromes and equipment of all kinds, or to under-estimate it and so give substance to the familiar American criticism that we cannot effectively employ the aircraft they send us.

It is a matter for little surprise that the Americans have found it necessary to revise the provisional allocations laid down in the Slessor Agreement. The Agreement itself contemplated such revision. Russian requirements and the growing tension in the Far East would have provided ample grounds for drawing up a revised allocation. But the Americans have preferred to keep their own counsel, to ignore the machinery for revision provided in the Agreement and to present their decisions in the form of accomplished facts.

At the root of the matter lies the hard fact that American production has not yet faced up to American policy. America has promised to be the arsenal of democracy and to send a vast flow of armaments to Great Britain, China and the other countries resisting aggression. America has decided to send help on a large scale to Russia. America is also resolved to have powerful well-equipped forces of her own. These commitments cannot be faced with the capacity yet created in America, and no system of allocations will resolve a dilemma which springs from inadequate supply. America has stood for long on the brink of changing to a war economy but she has yet to make the plunge. No permanent solution is possible until this difficulty is faced.

To sum up. Immediate action is necessary on the following lines:

a) To persuade the United States to face up to the commitments they have undertaken and to create new capacity as a matter of urgency; and
b) To persuade the United States that, irrespective of whether they undertake a., it is of prime importance that they should give us an accurate picture of the aircraft they are intending to send us so that we may make realistic plans.

Action to achieve a. and b. should if possible be coupled with an attempt to bring British and American strategy into closer touch than is maintained at the moment.

Sir Archibald Sinclair to Winston S. Churchill
9th November 1941

PRIME MINSTER

I understand that Sir Hugh Dowding has consented, at your request, both to accept my invitation to review the establishment of the Royal Air Force and to postpone the publication of his book.[568]

Accordingly the way is now clear for the cancellation of the Gazette notice concerning his retirement and for the issue of a statement about the work which he is undertaking. As you requested in your Minute 1023/1 of the 31st October, I attach to this Minute the proposed announcement and Gazette notice.

The only question which remains is whether you want us to work alone or whether you like the idea, which Portal and I have put forward, of an Inter-Service Committee; and whether, in the latter case, you would wish to make Sir Hugh Dowding Chairman of the Committee.

AHMS

Winston S. Churchill to Sir Archibald Sinclair and Air Chief Marshal Sir Charles Portal
11th November 1941
(Action this day)

The losses sustained both by the night bombers and the day fighters have lately been very heavy. There is no need to press unduly the offensive by the fighters over France; about two sweeps a month instead of four should be sufficient, combined with a continuance of the attacks on shipping. While the degree of attack may be lightened, the impression of its continuance should be sustained.

I have several times in Cabinet deprecated forcing the night bombing of Germany without due regard to weather conditions. There is no particular point at this time in bombing Berlin. The losses sustained last week were most grievous. We cannot afford losses on that scale in view of the shortfall of the American bomber programme. Losses which are acceptable in a battle or for some decisive military objective ought not to be incurred merely as a matter of routine. There is no need to fight the weather and the enemy at the same time.

It is now the duty of both Fighter and Bomber Command to re-gather their strength for the spring.

Let me have a full report about the heavy losses of bombers on the night of the last heavy raid on Berlin.

WSC

568 See letter of 1 November 1941, page 326.

In November 1941, Sinclair's Parliamentary Personal Secretary, Wilfrid Roberts, caused great offence to Churchill. As reported in the *Daily Mirror* of 17 November, under the headline 'Criticism of Govt. essential says Minister's M.P.-secretary', in a speech in Carlisle, Roberts claimed that 'Criticism of the war's conduct is essential ... Yet the Prime Minister, though welcoming debates in the House of Commons, shows a certain sensitiveness about criticism. I think that is a mistake.'

Later that day, Roberts wrote to one of Churchill's PPSs that 'Archie Sinclair tells me that the Prime Minister has spoken to him about a speech I made on Saturday, parts of which have had considerable prominence in the press. I would be grateful if you would assure the P.M. that the subject of my speech was to urge my constituents to make the greater efforts which are necessary, and those who heard it as a whole could not have got the impression that I wished to criticise the Prime Minister.'

Winston S. Churchill to Sir Archibald Sinclair
18th November 1941

Secretary of State for Air

Please see attached.[569] It is astonishing that Mr. Roberts should have formed the impression described at A[570] as a result of working under you in the Air Ministry and also that while enjoying confidential views of our affairs in his relations with you he should make such statements in public. I do not think such behaviour is compatible with his position as your P.P.S. No sort of apology is contained in his letter. There would be no objection to his making criticisms of this kind from a independent position and I do not think he should be hampered by being retained in quasi confidential circles. By all means let him go outside and abuse us to his heart's content, so long as he does not reveal any of the secret matters which he has picked up in your office.

It would do him no harm to improve his spelling.

WSC

Sir Archibald Sinclair to Winston S. Churchill
19th November 1941
Personal

Prime Minister

Your Minute 1056/1

Naturally you resent the speech of Wilfrid Roberts – but you cannot possibly resent it as much as I do. He gave me to understand on Monday night that he was going to send your P.P.S. a letter of apology. The letter which you enclose is not a

569 Press clipping from the *Daily Mirror*, 17 November 1941.

570 Part of the press cutting.

letter of apology. Therefore I ask you to accept from me my profound apologies for a very foolish and deplorable speech by my Parliamentary Private Secretary.

Roberts offered his resignation on Monday but I told him that I expected him to stay on until Christmas. To dismiss him out of hand would be to play straight into the hands of our enemies who are gleefully expecting that to happen. In the Liberal Party his fate would be contrasted with the more fortunate fate of members of the Government – and Roberts is not a member of the Government – who have made even more indiscreet speeches. No Liberal member would consent to succeed him in such circumstances.

I have no right to ask favours of you. I am bound to accept responsibility for the folly and obtuseness displayed by Roberts. I can only hope that you have sufficient confidence in me to allow me to handle the situation in the way which is likely to dispose of the incident with the least damage to the Government and to one of the political parties which support it.

Archie

PS. I have shown this minute to Wilfrid Roberts. A.

The following note was attached to the letter:

22nd November 1941
Personal

Sir Archibald Sinclair

The Prime Minister has seen your minute of November 19 about the recent speech by Mr. Wilfrid Roberts and has minuted on it:–

"Keep him and teach him to spell"

On 7 December 1941, Japanese planes attacked the American fleet in Pearl Harbor. Honouring the Tripartite Treaty, Japan's allies, Germany and Italy, declared war on the United States on 11 December. The following day Churchill embarked for Washington, with the aim of discussing with Roosevelt joint tactics for making war in the Far East, Europe and the Mediterranean.

Sir Archibald Sinclair to Winston S. Churchill
20th December 1941
Strictly Personal

Prime Minister

We are anxiously following your progress and I hope all goes well with you. I am afraid you have had rather a rough passage.

It was a bit rough too in the House of Commons yesterday, but not as bad as I had been led to expect.[571] Roger Keyes made a very emotional and largely irrelevant speech (including a long account of his failure to persuade you to abandon the Weygand plan for closing the gap between the French and British Armies), but it caught the mood of the House and must be rated a success. Alexander made a good speech in winding up, but, although the debate had been quiet up till then (as I had observed to Kingsley Wood, who agreed with me), the House did not give him a very good hearing. Nobody complained of your absence – indeed, I am sure that everybody approved the reason for it. Nevertheless, it seemed to me that the House could not get over their disappointment that you were not there to hear their complaints and answer them with your unique authority. David[572] said a few sentences at the end on the defence of aerodromes, and that went well. They are restive and anxious and it is important that you should be there before we have another debate.

The daylight attack on Brest was successful yesterday. The telegrams will give you the main facts. Let me only add that Peirse[573] tells me that the squadrons who took part in the attack are very pleased with the result. The operation was well planned and for once we were favoured by the weather. The defence of the heavy bombers proved remarkably effective. One Stirling, indeed, on the way back had the insolence to break formation and dive after four Messerschmitts, shooting down one. The latest figures of casualties suffered and inflicted are:–

Casualties suffered:
4 Stirlings and 1 Manchester missing.
1 Manchester crashed, crew killed.
1 Halifax down in the sea, crew rescued.
1 Long Range Hurricane missing.
Enemy casualties claimed:
10 Me.109s certain.
3 Me.109s probable.
6 Me.109s damaged.

The Stirlings alone claim six Messerschmitts. One Stirling claims to have beaten off an attack by nine of them. It always takes some time thoroughly to sift the reports, and these figures may be later and more accurate than those which you will have received in your signals. The photographs which I have seen show that both battle cruisers were damaged but that the Prince Eugen[574] was not hit.

---

[571] It is often forgotten that during 1941 and 1942 there were increased rumblings of dissatisfaction with Churchill's leadership, as military setback followed military setback. Indeed, Churchill faced two votes of no confidence in the Commons, though he won both with massive majorities.

[572] David Margesson – see n531.

[573] Richard Peirse (1892–1970): Deputy Director of Operations and Intelligence, Air Ministry 1930–33; commanded British Forces in Palestine and Transjordan 1933–36; Deputy Chief of Air Staff 1937–40; Commander-in-Chief Bomber Command 1940–42; Allied Air Commander-in-Chief, South East Asia Command 1943–44.

[574] The German heavy cruiser *Prinz Eugen*, which had accompanied the *Bismarck* on its Atlantic sortie in May 1941, in which the British battle cruiser *Hood* was sunk and the battleship *Prince of Wales* damaged.

Good luck to you in the conversations in America, on which so much depends for all of us and especially for the Royal Air Force.

Archie

1942

Preparing for the strategic bombing offensive and building new relationships with the Russians and Americans were Sinclair's priorities for the first half of 1942. With the entry of the Americans into the war in December 1941 and the German attack on the Soviet Union in June 1941 Britain no longer faced Germany without allies. The Battle of the Atlantic, where British aircraft hunted U-boats and provided protection to convoys, was a critical area for the RAF throughout 1942. The year ended with the first large-scale joint venture, Operation Torch, where British and American troops landed in Algeria and Morocco in November 1942.

In December 1941, Churchill travelled to the US for the Arcadia conference, which restated the US commitment to a 'Europe first' strategy, created a Combined Chiefs of Staff, and agreed the Declaration of the United Nations. During his return journey from the US, in mid-January, Churchill telegraphed Sinclair. Under pressure from Stalin to demonstrate that Britain was doing all it could to support the Soviet Union, Churchill was keen to ensure that there should be no difficulties in supplying Russia with the aircraft that had been promised.

Winston S. Churchill to Sir Archibald Sinclair
18th January 1942

Secretary of State for Air,

I hear you are in default of 45 aircraft for December for Russia, and that this will not be rectified until 25th January, and that the January quota will not be cleared until February.

It seems a great pity to fall short in Russian deliveries by these comparatively small quantities which cannot effect your main problem here.

I must emphasise that exact and punctual deliveries to Russia are of the utmost importance, as this is all we can do to help them.

WSC

See also n587.

Sir Archibald Sinclair to Winston S. Churchill
21st January 1942
SECRET

PRIME MINISTER

You have wished us to try and develop a Radio Marker Beacon for the guidance of our light bombers and, in co-operation with the Ministry of Aircraft Production, we have been pressing forward with the necessary research. The results show that it can be done, but it is apparent that success will demand a great deal of effort from our limited number of skilled workers, and, when attained, will involve an additional drain upon the limited and strained capacity of the Radio Industry. Moreover, even when the technical problem was solved, the operational use of the beacon would be strictly limited.

On the other hand, GEE,[575] and a still newer and most secret device which we call H2S,[576] offer us more practical means of attaining the same object. If you agree, therefore, I propose to stop further developments of the Radio Marker Beacon. Lord Cherwell, to whom I am sending a copy of this minute, is in agreement with this proposal. GEE and H2S will be pressed forward with all urgency.

AHMS

Sir Archibald Sinclair to Winston S. Churchill
27th January 1942
MOST SECRET

PRIME MINISTER

On the 8th January, 1942 the War Cabinet again considered my Memorandum W.P. (41) 260 asking for authority to bomb certain factories in Occupied France, known to be engaged in the manufacture of munitions supplies for the enemy. The War Cabinet concurred in the views set out in the Memorandum that steps should now be taken to bomb these factories, subject to your agreement that this would be consistent with Super Gymnast.[577]

---

575 GEE was a navigational aid, although there were some attempts to use it as a bombing device. In England three widely separated stations transmitted pulse signals which were received in the bomber by a 'Gee Box'. GEE computed the difference between the receipts of these signals, thus enabling the navigator to fix his position. GEE was a 'line-of-sight' device and as such was limited by the aircraft's height and range. An aircraft flying below 20,000 feet and further than 400 miles from England lost the GEE signals due to the curvature of the earth. The major benefit of GEE was to enable crews to reach the general target area and return to England, especially when adverse weather conditions may have taken the aircraft off course. It was first trialed in August 1941, and first used operationally in March 1942.

576 H2S was the forerunner of ground-scanning radar that modern aircraft now take for granted. In 1942 and 1943, however, the faint and flickering image could just about determine coastlines, wide rivers and city outlines at a push. In the hands of a skilled operator, H2S could be an invaluable navigational aid, especially when the Germans began jamming GEE.

577 Super Gymnast was the code name given to a projected US–British joint operation in North Africa

The Lord Privy Seal, in his Taut[578] No. 431, informed you of this conclusion and asked whether you agreed.

I understand that it was then felt in Washington that careful consideration must be given to the possible repercussions on Super Gymnast and that in any case a decision was not a matter of urgency, as operations could not take place until the next suitable moon period.

Super Gymnast is now more remote. Weather conditions which at this time of year are often unfavourable for long-range operations may well be suitable for operations against Occupied France. Moreover, we should like, before Gee is introduced, to try new tactical methods which are to be used in conjunction with it and which could, with advantage, be tested on short-range operations in not too strongly defended areas.

I hope, therefore, that you will now concur in the proposals put forward in my Memorandum.

AHMS

At the end of January 1942 Churchill decided that he should call a full three-day vote of confidence debate in order to face down parliamentary criticisms of his leadership during the second half of 1941, when military success had been evasive. Churchill produced a masterful performance, speaking for two hours at the start of the debate and winding up with another speech of forty-two minutes. He then insisted on a division and won the vote 466–3, with only James Maxton and two other members of the Independent Labour Party voting against. Even with this commanding majority Churchill was not best pleased with the level of support he received from the Liberal Party.

Winston S. Churchill to Sir Archibald Sinclair
31st January 1942

I must draw your attention to the voting of the Liberal Party in the House on the Vote of Confidence. Out of a total of twenty, six abstained or were absent, leaving fourteen to represent the party. Of these fourteen, three were Ministers, viz., yourself, Johnstone, and Foot. You also have an Under-Secretaryship in the Lords. This is a lot of sail to carry on so small a hull, and I fear that the Conservative Party, which in the three divisions during the life of the present Government has voted 252, 281, and 309 respectively, will become critical of the lack of support given to the Government.

that would combine an American landing at Casablanca with a British landing further eastward on the Mediterranean coast.

578 Memo.

At the same time, the News Chronicle has become one of the most critical and often hostile newspapers, and fallen sadly below the splendid but instructed independence of the Manchester Guardian.[579]

I suggest to you that these matters require your very earnest attention. As you know, I have never measured the strength of the Liberal Party by its Parliamentary representation. Nevertheless, when its numbers are so small it seems to me all the more necessary to have unity of action on occasions of confidence in the Government, which the party has formally and officially decided to join and support.[580]

Winston S. Churchill

Sir Archibald Sinclair to Winston S. Churchill
2nd February 1942
Private and Confidential

Dear Prime Minister,

Let me say at once in answer to your letter of the 31st January that I am certainly not satisfied with anything less than 100% support for the Government from the Liberal Party. Such support on the issue of confidence in the Government was given by the spokesmen of the Liberal Party in the debate – by Mander[581] on the first day with his effective retort to Herbert Williams,[582] by Percy Harris, and by Graham White.

In the lobby, it is true, only fourteen members out of twenty supported the Government or 70%. This was better than the Labour Party which, with three representatives in the War Cabinet, but only 101 members into the Lobby, or 62% of its voting strength.

It is true that the News Chronicle is critical of the Government, but it is no more a Liberal paper than the Evening Standard, Sunday Express, Daily Mirror and Sunday Pictorial are Conservative papers – I should say rather less so – and you may have noticed that it does not spare the Air Ministry in its chastisements! I will, however, tackle Walter Layton again.

The Manchester Guardian is splendid, as you say. As you refer to the greater strength of the Liberal Party in the Country than in London, let me say that recent meetings at Newcastle and in Manchester have demonstrated to me the warmth of its support for the Government. The luncheon at the Manchester Reform Club at which I delivered my Presidential address ten days ago was packed and enthusiastic, especially at any mention of your name and work.

---

[579] Both these newspapers traditionally supported the Liberal Party.

[580] See Sinclair's reply on 2 February 1942.

[581] Geoffrey Le Mesurier Mander (1882–1962): Liberal MP for Wolverhampton East 1929–45; Parliamentary Private Secretary to Sir Archibald Sinclair 1942–45.

[582] Herbert G. Williams (dates unknown): Conservative MP for Croydon South 1931–45.

As for the Parliamentary Party, if Mr. Lloyd George and Megan[583] won't support the Government for Gwilym's[584] sake, you cannot expect them to do it for mine.[585] You can rely on Percy Harris, who has been splendid, and me to do all we can to keep a notoriously fractious team pulling with the Government towards victory.

Yours sincerely,
Archibald Sinclair

PS. One of the six absentees was Jimmie[586] on Government business in America. He would certainly have voted.

Winston S. Churchill to Sir Archibald Sinclair
14th February 1942

Prime Minister to Secretary of State for Air

We are placing great hopes on our bomber offensive against Germany next winter, and we must spare no pains to justify the high proportion of the national effort devoted to it. The Air Ministry's responsibility is to make sure that the maximum weight of the best type of bombs is dropped on the German cities by the aircraft placed at their disposal. Unless we can ensure that most of our bombs really do some damage it will be difficult to justify the pre-eminence we are according to this form of attack. The following seem to be needful for success: (i) To make sure that crews are practised in the use of blind bombing apparatus, which should be installed by this autumn in most of our night bombers. (ii) To discover any difficulties which navigators may find in the use of sextants for astro-navigation, overcome them, and make sure they employ this method to get them within twelve to fifteen miles of the target, after which the blind bombing equipment comes into play. (iii) To make certain that the large number of bombers we expect to get will not be immobilised by bad weather. This will entail preparing adequate runways, homing devices, and

[583] Megan Lloyd George (1902–66): daughter of David Lloyd George; Liberal and Independent Liberal MP for Anglesey 1929–51; Deputy Leader of the Liberal Party 1949–51; joined the Labour Party in 1955, Labour MP for Carmarthenshire 1957–66.

[584] Gwilym Lloyd-George, 1st Viscount Tenby (1894–1967): second son of David Lloyd George; Liberal MP for Pembrokeshire 1922–24, 1929–50; the only Liberal MP to join the Chamberlain Government (as a junior minister) at the outbreak of war in September 1939; Minister of Fuel and Power 1942–45; Liberal and Conservative MP for Newcastle-on-Tyne North 1951–57; Minister of Food 1951–54; Home Secretary and Minister for Welsh Affairs 1954–57; ennobled 1957.

[585] David (see n27) and Megan (but not Gwilym) Lloyd George were members of the four-strong 'Lloyd George family group' of MPs who, unlike the rest of the Liberal Party, had opposed the formation of the National Government in 1931. They took the Liberal whip again after Sinclair's election as leader in 1935 but remained an unpredictable group who were frequently given greater freedom than would be typical for party backbenchers.

[586] James de Rothschild (1878–1957): Liberal MP for Isle of Ely 1929–45; Parliamentary Secretary, Ministry of Supply March – May 1945; leading Zionist; a close friend of Sinclair's, he used his personal wealth to fund Liberal parliamentary activities during the period 1931–45. It is unclear what government business he was on in the States during the vote of confidence.

possibly providing clearing gear on the aerodromes, and de-icing and blind-landing equipment, etc., on the planes. (iv) To insist that a sufficient supply of incendiary and high-charge-weight-ratio bombs is available, even if this implies relaxing the penetration specifications. I raised this matter last July, and was assured there would be no shortage, but I gather that the 1000-lb. and 500-lb. bombs which form the bulk of our loads are still of the old inefficient type.

We must expect that the enemy will improve his defences, both ground and air. Various counter-measures are, I understand, in sight, which we are quite properly holding up for the time being. No doubt you will see that everything is concerted so that we can install and use each of them immediately it is deemed desirable.

Winston S. Churchill to Sir Archibald Sinclair and Chief of Air Staff
14th February 1942
(Secret)

1. The Brest question has settled itself by the escape of the enemy.[587]
2. I am entirely in favour of the resumption of full bombing of Germany, subject always, of course, to our not incurring heavy losses owing to bad weather and enemy resistance combined. It is to be expected that better weather is at hand.

WSC

Winston S. Churchill to Sir Archibald Sinclair and Sir Charles Portal
26th February 1942

SECRETARY OF STATE FOR AIR
C.A.S.

I am informed that many air accidents and failures to reach targets in bombing may be attributed to delay in obtaining the latest form of oxygen mask, for which orders were placed many months ago. Pray let me know the facts. If they are as stated, the question of expediting supplies should be taken up immediately.

WSC

On top of his other burdensome duties Churchill found time to offer advice on how the Air Ministry should best present itself to the news media and to the War Cabinet.

[587] In February 1942, after a period spent in the port of Brest, the German heavy cruiser *Prinz Eugen*, together with the battleships *Scharnhorst* and *Gneisenau*, successfully passed through the English Channel on their way back to Germany. The failure of the British Navy and RAF to impede their passage caused much critical comment in the press and parliament.

Winston S. Churchill to Sir Archibald Sinclair and Sir Charles Portal
26th February 1942
(Secret)

SECRETARY OF STATE FOR AIR
C.A.S.

1. It is thought in many quarters that the Air news and propaganda defeats itself by the excessive recording of ordinary routine fighting. Many people turn off the wireless when the air news is reached. There is perhaps an inevitable sameness about it, and one cannot see the wood for the trees. It is a pity, because fine exploits and exceptional occurrences do not always receive the distinction and attention which they deserve.
2. You would be well advised to adopt a much more highly selective process not only in the communiqués and on the broadcast, but in the reports made to the Cabinet. It has never been thought necessary to give an exact list of ordinary trench raids or skirmishes on the fronts of large armies. Fighting of a normal character in the different theatres should surely be summarised once a week, e.g., Malta has had a hard week (or a busy week) in the Air, so many sorties have been made, and so many enemy shot down, &c., instead of a daily laborious catalogue. If this were done, any event like 20 or 30 enemy aircraft being bowled over would make the right impression on the public. As it is, the Air Ministry's fine tale runs the risk of becoming a bore instead of an inspiration. Monotonous repetition should at all costs be avoided.

WSC

Winston S. Churchill to Sir Archibald Sinclair
28th February 1942

SECRETARY OF STATE FOR AIR

I have had prepared for me the following table showing the numbers of aircraft wrecked or damaged by enemy action and in flying accidents in 1941:–

	Enemy Action	Flying Accidents	
	Operational Machines	Operational Machines	Trainers
Wrecked beyond repair	1,900	2,500	1,100
Repairable –			
Only at Contractor's Works	300	2,900	1,500
By working party from Contractor's works	–	3,300	1,300
By ground staff of unit	–	1,800	1,900

It is true that nearly all the damaged aeroplanes are repaired and ultimately come back to service, but this all means many man-hours of skilled labour. Even without exact figures, there seems to be little doubt that by far the greater part of the efforts of M.A.P. are squandered in making or repairing machines which are destroyed or damaged not by enemy action, but in flying accidents.

Pray let me know what steps you propose to take to remedy this very unsatisfactory position.

WSC

Winston S. Churchill to Sir Archibald Sinclair and Sir Charles Portal
10th March 1942

SECRETARY OF STATE FOR AIR
C.A.S.

I am not at all convinced by Fighter Command's defence of their accident rate, and am not prepared to remain satisfied with it. Considering the great plethora of pilots, the training can be extended, and properly trained pilots coming from long courses of instruction ought not to be represented as undisciplined boys.

I must request a continuance of severe pressure from the Air Ministry upon all Commands.

Let me have a weekly return by Groups from Fighter Command of the accidents, together with the sorties.

I should be glad to receive proposals for increasing the length of the runways with a view to assigning a higher priority for the supply of materials. &c.

WSC

Sir Archibald Sinclair to Winston S. Churchill
11th March 1942
SECRET

PRIME MINISTER

You may be interested in one or two tactical features of the attack on the Renault Works.

An intensified system of flare illumination was used. Some 15 Wellingtons carried maximum loads of flares apart from those normally carried in the individual attacking aircraft. The degree of illumination achieved was remarkable.

Owing to the weather one attack had to be concentrated in time to an extent hitherto not attempted. The whole of the 22 aircraft completed their attack within 1½ hours.

The attack was carried out between 1,000 and 4,000 feet, except for the final phase when the 4,000 lb. bombs were dropped between 4,000 and 6,000 ft., so that the aircraft should be clear of blast. 461 tons of bombs were dropped. This compares with the German attack on London on the 16/17th April when 446 tons of bombs (including incendiaries) were dropped in the heaviest raid on this country. In the Coventry raid on 14/15th November, 1940, 185 tons (excluding incendiaries) were dropped.

There was no opposition from either guns or searchlights.

AHMS

Winston S. Churchill to Sir Archibald Sinclair and Sir Charles Portal
13th March 1942
(Secret and Private)

SECRETARY OF STATE FOR AIR
C.A.S.

1. The attached papers[588] represent opinions which I hear repeated from all quarters. Pray let me have your answer to the principal points raised, not for communication in that form to my correspondent, but in order that the position shall be made clear. Afterwards it will have to come before the Defence Committee.
2. You will not argue the value of bombing Germany, because I have my own opinion about that, namely, that it is not decisive, but better than doing nothing, and indeed is a formidable method of injuring the enemy. I am aware also that a considerable conversion into torpedo-bombers has taken place, and that torpedoes are perhaps a bottle-neck: also that many have been sent to the Eastern Mediterranean: others will be needed in the Bay of Bengal, &c. Let me, however, have all the figures of what has been done and what is now planned. I certainly

[588] Letter from Major G. Owen, M.P., enclosing a memorandum by a friend on torpedo-carrying aircraft.

consider that shore-based torpedo-bombers should have priority over high-level bombers. Evidently they are a great defence against invasion.

3. I hope you realise how very widely the existing policy of the Air Ministry is challenged by opinion. For instance, the Archbishop of Canterbury yesterday spoke to me for half an hour at luncheon on the failure of high-level bombing. He seemed to know a great deal about it, and said these were the opinions he heard on every side in the elevated circles in which he moves.
4. There are also great complaints that the Navy has not been given a fair share of the aircraft it needs, both fighters and torpedo-bombers, and that it has been overlain by the Air Ministry. I do not want lengthy explanations, but the dominant facts.
5. The question of putting the Coastal Command under the Admiralty is one which will have to be faced in the near future.

WSC

Sir Archibald Sinclair to Winston S. Churchill
15th March 1942

PRIME MINISTER

I think you may be interested in the attached letter which I have received from the Counsellor of the American Embassy about the bombing of the Renault factory. You probably know that Mr. Matthews[589] has just been posted here from Vichy where he has been since the collapse of France.[590]

COPY
EMBASSY OF THE UNITED STATES OF AMERICA
London, March 13, 1942

Dear Sir Archibald,

You may recall that during our conversation at Mr. Harriman's very enjoyable dinner the other evening we discussed the question of possible public reaction (as distinct from that of the Vichy Government!) in France to the bombing of the Renault works near Paris. We have to-day received a copy of a telegram on that general subject from our Embassy at Vichy to the Department of State.

I believe that you may find its contents of some interest, and I therefore take pleasure in enclosing a copy in paraphrase, with the understanding of course that it be kept confidential. I have naturally likewise shown a copy to the Foreign Office.

[589] Harrison Freeman Matthews (1899–1986): US Foreign Service officer, London Embassy 1941–45; Ambassador to Sweden 1947–50, Netherlands 1953–57, Austria 1957–62.

[590] The letter made it clear that the reaction of the public (as distinct from that of the Vichy Government) in France to the bombing of the Renault works near Paris was generally supportive of the British effort.

With all good wishes,
Yours sincerely,
(Sgd.) H. FREEMAN MATTHEWS

Encloses:
As stated.

Sir Archibald Sinclair to Winston S. Churchill
19th March 1942

Prime Minister,

We have now carried out tests in order to compare the effects of German and British bombs. The experts have warned me that it is extremely difficult to devise satisfactory tests. So much depends upon a number of factors which it is difficult accurately to regulate, e.g., the exact angle at which the bomb strikes the target.

It seems that the Germans generally use a light case bomb weighing 250 Kilogram, which is intended to give the maximum effect. Its characteristics when exploded are almost identical with those of the British 500 lb. anti-submarine bomb. The chief difference being that the British bomb has a proportionately lighter case and, therefore, breaks into a smaller number of fragments of the same average weight, namely 1/20th ounces, but with greater blast pressure.

The British General Purpose 500 lb. bomb was designed with a heavy case so as to cause the maximum damage to industrial targets by breaking into large fragments with an average weight of 2 ounces. These fragments have only 58% of the initial velocity of those of the German bomb tested and there are less than 3,000 of them compared with 80,000 in the German bomb. The pressure created by blast at 40 feet is only 7 lbs. per square inch, compared with 25 lbs. for the German bomb and the charge constitutes only 24% of the total weight compared with 54%.

A medium case 500 lb. British bomb is being produced in recognition of the fact that the blast has a more destructive effect against small houses and other lightly built structures than do bomb fragments. On the other hand, the destructive force of the large fragments of the present British 500 lb. bomb is greater that that of the German blast bomb against more strongly built structures and against machinery and pipes. You may have noticed a recent speech by Field Marshal Milch[591] in which he declared that "British bombs have a terrific explosive force and defective or unsupported walls are just as useless against their splinters as are sandbags".

The Middle East have been asked for a report on the effectiveness of British bombs and experts have been sent to examine the results of our bombing in Libya.

AHMS

[591] Field Marshal Erhard Milch (1892–1972): State Secretary, Reich Aviation Ministry; oversaw the development of the Luftwaffe as part of the rearmament of Germany after 1933; Air Inspector General 1940–44, forced out by Göring after joining Goebbels and Himmler in attempting to convince Hitler to remove Göring from command of the Luftwaffe; found guilty of war crimes at Nuremberg, sentenced to life imprisonment but released in June 1954.

During April 1942 bombing strategy became the focus of discussions between Portal, Sinclair and the Prime Minister. Portal and Sinclair were pushing for the maximum possible allocation of people and resources to build up the heavy bomber wing of Bomber Command and were convinced that the strategic bombing of Germany could bring an early end to the war through the destruction of German morale, infrastructure and industry.

Sir Archibald Sinclair to Winston S. Churchill
6th April 1942

Prime Minister,

C.A.S. and I have read with great interest Lord Cherwell's minute to you dated 30th March estimating what we can expect to achieve by the bombing of Germany during the next eighteen months.[592]

We both find Lord Cherwell's calculations simple, clear and convincing, and we suggest that they might be of general interest to the Defence Committee.

There are, of course, certain very important conditions which must be fulfilled before bomber production is converted into the necessary scale of destruction in Germany.

a) We must not only get the bombers, but we must also be able to employ them to the full, i.e. we must develop a broad enough front of first line squadrons. We expect to be able to achieve this.
b) We must continue to get at least 13 or 14 sorties out of each bomber produced. To do so we must keep down wastage, both 'battle' and 'accident'. We hope to do this. The struggle with the German defences will be a hard one, but recent experience is encouraging.
c) We must ensure that not less than half the bomb lift from our bases reach the built up areas of Germany. This depends on unremitting effort in the development of and perfection of all modern aids to target finding and in the training of crews in their use. This is in hand, and we think we did better than 50% on the targets at Cologne and Lubeck last month.
d) We must resist to the utmost any avoidable diversion of bombing effort away from Germany. Some will, of course, be unavoidable.

I think, and C.A.S. agrees, that the start that has been made in the recent attacks on the Ruhr, Cologne and Lubeck is a promising one, and we see no reason to doubt that within eighteen months and with American help the degree of destruction which Lord Cherwell suggests is possible can in fact be achieved.

AHMS

[592] Lord Cherwell had written to Churchill on 30 March 1942, observing that 'one ton of bombs dropped on a built-up area demolishes 20–40 dwellings and turns 100–200 people out of house and home'.

Winston S. Churchill to Sir Archibald Sinclair
14th April 1942
(Secret)

SECRETARY OF STATE FOR AIR

We are placing great hopes on our bomber offensive against Germany next winter, and we must spare no pains to justify the large proportion of the national effort devoted to it. The Air Ministry's responsibility is to make sure that the maximum weight of the best type of bombs is dropped on the German cities by the aircraft placed at their disposal. Unless we can ensure that most of our bombs really do some damage, it will be difficult to justify the pre-eminence we are according to this form of attack. The following seem to be needful for success:–

1. To make sure that crews are practised in the use of blind bombing apparatus,[593] which should be installed by this autumn in most of our night bombers.
2. To discover any difficulties which navigators may find in the use of sextants for astro-navigation, overcome them, and make sure they employ this method to get them within 12 to 15 miles of the target, after which the blind bombing equipment comes into play.
3. To make certain that the large number of bombers we expect to get will not be immobilised by bad weather. This will entail preparing adequate runways, homing devices and possibly fog clearing gear on the aerodromes, and de-icing and blind landing equipment, &c., on the planes.
4. To insist that a sufficient supply of incendiary and high charge–weight ratio bombs is available, even if this implies relaxing the penetration specifications. I raised this matter last July and was assured there would be no shortage, but I gather that the 1,000-lb. and 500-lb. bombs, which form the bulk of our loads, are still of the old inefficient type.

We must expect that the enemy will improve his defences, both ground and air. Various counter-measures are, I understand, in sight, which we are quite properly holding up for the time being. No doubt you will see that everything is concerted so that we can install and use each of them immediately it is deemed desirable.

WSC

Sir Archibald Sinclair to Winston S. Churchill
23rd April 1942
SECRET

PRIME MINISTER

I have examined the questions raised in your Minute No. M.138/2,[594] and the following is a brief summary of the information available:

---

[593] Blind-bombing devices allowed pilots to seek out their targets in all weathers; they usually relied on the pilot tracking a radio beam.
[594] Churchill's letter of 14 April 1942 (above).

a) Blind Bombing Apparatus

a. H.2.S. Two experimental sets have been fitted in Halifaxes, and airborne trials have already been carried out. They are proceeding satisfactorily. In anticipation of success, an order has been given for 200 sets of which 50 made by hand might be ready by October. This equipment has Priority A.1. and we are putting all possible pressures on M.A.P. to ensure that nothing is allowed to delay its delivery.

b. Oboe.[595] This is the only aid to blind precision bombing which we have in prospect. With the assistance of a relaying aircraft, its range extends up to 600 miles. Trials are being pushed ahead on a high priority with experimental sets. They are not, however, allowed to interfere with H.2.S.

b) Astro-navigation

A year ago, astro-navigation was not in the basic training syllabus on account of the shortage of equipment and instructors. The introduction of the astrograph and the wider distribution of sextants and similar instruments has resulted in an improvement in astro-navigational training and in its more extensive use in the squadrons during recent months. A further improvement should be seen in the standard of astro-navigation from about the beginning of July, as a result of the reform in the system of training in November last.

The accuracy of astro-navigation depends on the stability of the aircraft, and the present need is for a stabilised periscopic sextant. An American model is undergoing trials in U.S.A., but it is unlikely to be in service by the end of this year.

The training organisation hope, however, that in six months' time the average navigator will have achieved a standard of accuracy which will enable him to approach with certainty to within 14 miles of his target.

We are considering a proposal for setting up a Bomber Development Unit attached to a Target Finding Force which would analyse the results achieved by astro-navigation and other navigational aids.

c) Bad Weather

a. Runways. Our policy is to provide one runway of 2,000 yards, and two of 1,600 yards on each bomber aerodrome. 23 aerodromes already have runways of 2,000 yards, and 86 more will be completed by the end of

[595] Oboe was a blind-bombing device installed into an aircraft but controlled from ground stations in England. Two stations transmitted pulses which were picked up by aircraft and then retransmitted to the ground stations. The aircraft receiving the Oboe signals used the pulses to keep itself on the correct path in order to pass over the target; the stations in England, by measuring the time taken to receive the pulses back again, calculated the aircraft's exact position and sent a short signal at the moment when the bombs should be released. Oboe had several limitations; it was – like Gee – a 'line-of-sight' device and thus limited by the curvature of the earth. Also each of the three base stations in England could only control six aircraft per hour, and those aircraft had the highly dangerous task of flying straight and level for several minutes.

October 1942. We are also constructing 3 emergency runways, each 4,500 yards in length, as near as possible to the East Coast.

b. Homing and Beam Landing Devices. Beam approach training is started at Advanced Flying Units and carried on at O.T.U.s. More and more time is being devoted to it and all pilots now undergo a course covering a 10 hours' syllabus which involves up to 12 landings. In March, 1941, there were 202 trained pilots in Bomber Command; in April, 1942, the number had risen to 1,910. No officer is eligible to command a squadron or flight until he has completed a Beam Approach Course. Operational Pilots in Bomber Command, whose original training did not include this technique, are being trained retrospectively; 8 Beam Approach Training Flights are employed for the purpose. Standard beam approach equipment will be available at 56 aerodromes by August. A further 64 have been surveyed, but installation is held up pending supply of equipment and construction of runways.
A valuable aid to Homing has been the installation of two long-range track-guide beams covering North West Germany. Two more are being laid over North West France. Thus a pilot can track out and in on the same beam, and then on return, at a suitable point over the U.K. pick up his local station beam.

c. Fog Clearance. We under-rate neither the extreme value nor the extreme difficulties of this project, and although previous experiments have cast doubts on its practicability, we should like study of the problem and experiments to continue. I will inform M.A.P. accordingly, and at the same time ask them to send you a full brief on previous investigations.

d. De-icing. For propellers, we employ paste on two-engine bombers, and slinger-rings on four-engined types.
All engine intakes are fitted with snow-guards. All carburettors, except those so designed as to be immune from icing are fitted with adequate de-icing equipment.
Protection of the oiling system is satisfactory.
For wings, we have hitherto relied on paste and the Goodrich system, which is unsatisfactory. Bomber Command are not without confidence in paste, but I am not prepared to rely on it indefinitely. M.A.P. are being asked to fit the Dunlop system, which has given good results in trials. A system of wing heating is under consideration, and will be tested on a Halifax in May. This method, however, involves such drastic modifications – generally an entirely new wing – that production would be seriously affected.

e. Radio Altimeter. I have great hopes of this device for countering bad weather. It is capable of following the contours of the ground within 5 feet. Trials which are still proceeding have so far been extremely successful. We hope that deliveries (100–200) will begin in September, but the first deliveries will go to Coastal Command. Moreover, there may be some delay since the instrument has to be varied according to the type of aircraft to which it is fitted.

The Glide Path Indicator is promising and with the radio altimeter may well prove the final answer to landing under fully blind conditions.

d) Bombs

a. Incendiary. The supply is satisfactory. Details of stocks are given in Appendix 'A'.

b. M.C. Bombs.[596] The superiority of the M.C. Bomb over the G.P. is universally admitted. 500 welded 500 lb. M.C. Bombs are now in production. It is, however, intended to introduce this type of bomb in a case instead of a welded form, and the placing of an order awaits the completion of trials. If hammer tests prove satisfactory, we shall ask M.A.P. to commence production without waiting for dropping trials. The 1,000 lb. Cast M.C. Bomb is a new design. M.A.P. realise the urgency of this requirement, but it is not likely that any will be ready for operational use by the end of this year.

c. American M.44 1,000 lb. Bomb. We are pressing for supplies from U.S.A.. but have not yet received any firm programme for deliveries. Our estimated requirements are set out in Appendix 'B'.

e) COUNTER MEASURES AGAINST ENEMY DEFENCES

a. Metallised Leaflets and Rods. We propose to employ these to dislocate enemy R.D.F. 5 million leaflets are in stock. It is, however, necessary to take into account the effect on our own R.D.F. system. Certain objections have been raised by Anti-Aircraft Command, who are afraid that there will be interference with the 10 c.m. G.L.[597] which they are shortly introducing.

b. Airborne Jammers. Small airborne sets are under development. They present, however, many difficulties since they must be designed to cover four or five enemy wavelengths and would have to be installed in very large numbers of aircraft in order to give substantial protection to a raiding force. The outlook is not very promising.

c. Monica. This is a radio detection system which warns a bomber of the approach of fighters. M.A.P. are carrying out trials on all heavy bombers and the results have been extremely promising. An order has been placed for 2,000 equipments, but it is not yet possible to say when they will be forthcoming.

I accept the responsibility and will spare no pains to ensure that Bomber Command will strike at Germany next winter as a fully trained force, armed with the best and most modern equipment so far devised.

---

[596] Medium-capacity bombs.

[597] Gun-laying radar, used to detect low-flying aircraft.

APPENDIX 'A'
STOCKS OF INCENDIARY BOMBS

Bomb	Stock in U.K.	Stock required for 6 months holding	Total Production
4 lb Incendiary	3,244,521	6,030,493	Approx. 800,000 per month
30 lb Incendiary	101,315	234,383	68,000 per month
250 lb Incendiary	8,860	12,927	14,909 filled but require fuses. Production suspended six months, as stocks are adequate

APPENDIX 'B'
REQUIREMENTS OF AMERICAN M.44 1,000 LB. BOMBS

1942

2nd Quarter	3rd Quarter	4th Quarter
11,500	15,500	18,000

1943

1st Quarter	2nd Quarter
23,000	20,500

Winston S. Churchill to Sir Archibald Sinclair
6th May 1942

Prime Minister to Secretary of State for Air

I am glad to learn that the numerous matters raised in my minute of April 14th are in hand.

I hope that a really large order for H2S has been placed, and that nothing will be allowed to stand in the way of getting this apparatus punctually. If it fulfils expectations it should make a big difference in the coming winter.

Your statement that the Ministry of Aircraft Production cannot supply medium capacity bombs in quantity before the end of this year is most surprising. Last July I wrote to you on this subject, and you replied that they had been promised at an early date. Now it seems that they are still awaiting hammer tests, etc. Surely it would be better to drop plenty of high explosive in any thin-walled container than to waste so large a proportion of our bombing effort.

Although all the essential matters are being dealt with, there are so many facets of the task which have to be completed at the proper time that it might be a good thing to appoint some one man to be responsible for taking the necessary action of the proper dates and rendering a monthly report. I have heard Sir Robert Renwick[598] mentioned as a man of drive and business experience who has already rendered valuable service in connection with "Gee". Perhaps you might think he is a good man for this purpose. It would be most unfortunate if we found later on that the bombing programme was held up because one or other of the items was lagging behind.

WSC

Sir Archibald Sinclair to Winston S. Churchill
6th May 1942
PERSONAL AND SECRET

PRIME MINISTER

You asked for the Digest of Bomber Operations which the Commander-in-Chief, Bomber Command, prepares weekly, to be circulated to the Cabinet. I am very glad that the Cabinet should receive a weekly report of these operations.

At the same time, the Commander-in-Chief's Digest is not prepared for the Cabinet. It does not pretend to present a balanced picture of the results achieved by Bomber Command. It needs to be corrected in the light of the information which is available to us in the Air Ministry; and it contains a certain amount of information from most secret sources which, in the opinion of C.A.S., and I agree with him, ought not to be included in any Papers, even for Cabinet circulation. Moreover, the Report would not lose anything – and might be more likely to be read by the Cabinet – if it were shortened. Accordingly, as I feel that I should be called upon in Cabinet to defend the statement or implications of a weekly report on bombing operations, I should be grateful if you would allow me to circulate myself to the Cabinet every week, a report compiled from information supplied by Bomber Command and Air Ministry Intelligence.

AHMS

Sir Archibald Sinclair to Winston S. Churchill
2nd June 1942
SECRET

PRIME MINISTER

Your M.211/2.

[598] Robert Burnham Renwick (1904–73): businessman who operated a number of factories in the Midlands producing equipment for the Ministry of Aircraft Production.

1. Spitfires.
   Half the deficiency of 154 junction boxes has now been put right.
   Six out of the thirteen short of propellers have now been provided with them.
2. Bisleys.
   The 83 turrets are now available and are being put on.
3. Beaufighters.
   134 were in the "unready" state when I wrote the minute of May 15th to which you refer. 114 of these have now been got ready.
4. Electric Propellers are still short; these are difficult to make. We are replacing them on Wellingtons by hydraulic ones. It is of these simpler ones that I am boosting up the production. We are not increasing the capacity for electric ones, but as soon as the new Wellingtons are equipped with hydraulics, the present capacity will become available to make propellers for those now in A.S.Us. The hydraulics should come on to the machines in the production line during the course of this month.
5. On Sunday there were 831 aircraft "ready" or "ready within four days".
   I appreciate to the full that it is important to keep this proportion of our stock as high as possible. Everything possible will be done to achieve this.

AHMS

Winston S. Churchill to Sir Archibald Sinclair
7th June 1942

I have learnt with pleasure that the preliminary trials of H2S have been extremely satisfactory. But I am deeply disturbed at the very slow rate of progress promised for its production. Three sets in August and twelve in November is not even beginning to touch the problem. We must insist on getting, at any rate, a sufficient number to light up the target by the autumn, even if we cannot get them into all the bombers, and nothing should be allowed to stand in the way of this.

I propose to hold a meeting to discuss this next week and to see what can be done. The relatively disappointing results of our second big raid make it doubly urgent.

I am glad you have arranged with the Minister of Aircraft Production for Sir Robert Renwick to make a personal effort to accelerate production of the needed radio equipment. But I hope you will not let him disperse his efforts on too many bits of apparatus. The main thing is to hit the target, and this we can do with H2S. All the other items are of course useful, but nothing like so urgent.

It is most necessary that training, aerodromes, runways, and bombs should all be synchronised, and it was for this reason that I suggested it might be well to put Sir Robert Renwick in charge of the whole thing. The difficulty of co-ordinating all these matters is obvious, but the urgent need is clear. If you do not wish Sir Robert Renwick to undertake it, I trust you will appoint some other individual to be responsible for ensuring that everything marches in step, so that we are not faced at the end with some missing item. I do not think it is sufficient to leave this matter to the ordinary processes of departmental organisation.

As to the bombs, you told me in your minute of July 19, 1941, that a production order had been placed for 500-lb. special bombs, and that you were proceeding with the design of a larger one. It has been stated at several meetings that you entirely agreed that they were superior to the General Purpose bomb, and I am disappointed that such a large proportion of our effort should still be applied to carry bombs with only half the blasting power they might have.

WSC

At the end of May 1942 the first thousand-bomber raid took place over Cologne, dropping 1,455 tons of explosives, two-thirds of which were incendiaries. The city suffered severe damage: 469 people were killed, and about 250 factories and 18,400 houses were destroyed or damaged. Half of the city's power supply was put out of action, and some 12,000 fires started, many of which burned for days. Although forty-one aircraft were lost, the results of the raid were judged worthy of the loss of crew and planes and further mass raids took place in June over Essen and the Ruhr valley, though with more mixed results than the Cologne raid.

Sir Archibald Sinclair to Winston S. Churchill
7th June 1942
SECRET

PRIME MINISTER

We are proposing to bomb by night certain targets, a list of which I attach, in Norway, Holland, Belgium and Denmark, which will be in addition to those already approved for night bombing in France. They are important targets, chiefly factories engaged on producing substantial quantities of munitions for Germany.

The Governments of the three countries have agreed. The Dutch Government are fully in agreement with our proposals, and they have already broadcast to Holland a warning explicitly addressed to workpeople in factories engaged in production for Germany, telling them that they are liable to be attacked at night by the Royal Air Force. The Norwegian and Belgian Governments have told us that they have no objection to raise.

The Political Warfare Executive is pressing us to undertake these operations.

During the short nights of June and July, when there is practically no darkness at 10,000 or 15,000 feet, tactical conditions may make attacks on these closer and less heavily defended targets more profitable in hastening the rate of decline in German war production than attacks on factories within the Reich itself.

We are stipulating that no freshmen are to be employed on these raids, that they are only to be undertaken in the most favourable conditions, and that bombs are to be brought back if the crews cannot accurately identify their targets.

The Foreign Secretary, to whom I am sending a copy of this minute, does not object to these proposals, but thought that you should be warned before we attack these targets.

1.	NORWAY	HEROYA	Norsk Hydro Aluminium and Magnesium Plant
2.	DENMARK	COPENHAGEN	Burmeister & Wain, Diesel Engines
3	HOLLAND	ROTTERDAM	Port area and Shipyards
4.	HOLLAND	EINDHOVEN	Phillips Valve and Radio Works
5.	BELGIUM	LIEGE	Heavy Engineering Works
6.	BELGIUM	TERTRE	Coke Ovens and Chemical Plant
7.	BELGIUM	GAND-TERNEUZEN	Canal and paths alongside
8.	BELGIUM	ANTWERP	Ford and General Motors Works

Sir Archibald Sinclair to Winston S. Churchill
12th June 1942
MOST SECRET

PRIME MINISTER

Your minute M.238/2 (7th June 1942).

1. The Minister of Aircraft Production and I are fully persuaded that the work on H2S is of extreme urgency. We are grateful to you for giving the time next week to holding a meeting about it.
2. Sir Robert Renwick thoroughly understands that H2S is the most important piece of work he has to undertake. Some of the other gadgets, however, which I mentioned to you are also of extreme urgency. To take one example, Bomber Command are clamouring for 'Monica', which in no way competes with H2S.
3. Phasing the production of bombs, runways, aerodromes and crews have long been among my chief preoccupations. So far, we have kept abreast of production of aircraft and aircraft equipment. The important decisions which, but for adverse circumstances, would have kept us well ahead in training and aerodromes were mostly taken last winter, and some in the early months of this year.
4. The Minister of Aircraft Production and I are fully alive to the importance of the M.C. bomb. Strenuous efforts are being made to produce it at the earliest possible moment. The latest production forecasts are:–

500 lb. M.C. Fabricated

1942							1943
June	July	Aug	Sept	Oct	Nov	Dec	Jan
100	1,000	2,000	3,000	5,000	7,000	9,000	9,000

500 lb. M.C. Cast

1942				1943
Sept	Oct	Nov	Dec	Jan
4,000	8,000	8,000	8,000	8,000

5. My chief anxiety has been in regard to aerodromes, because of shortage of labour. Now, the accelerated arrival of the Americans and the requirements of 'Round-up'[599] are throwing a heavy additional burden on our Works Organisation. We are therefore being compelled to make urgent demands for additional labour.
6. The Minister of Aircraft Production is also concerned with the short supply of labour to complete extensions to some of his factories which are vital if the full bomber programme is to be achieved; and with the short-fall of labour with which to man his factories for the extended programme.
7. The training organisation will meet all requirements up to the O.T.U. stage. The bomber O.T.Us., however, are now suffering under the heavy handicap of shortage of aircraft, aggravated by the diversion of Whitleys to Coastal Command and to the Airborne Division. The big raids, too, cost us 58 O.T.U. aircraft (of which 32 were missing or written off) and 59 instructors. The Commander-in-Chief has a difficult balance to strike between the demands of operations and those of his O.T.Us.

You make it clear that you wish one man to synchronise the production of aerodromes, runways, bombs, scientific gadgets and crews, and in a previous minute you express a wish to be informed at regular intervals – you suggested monthly intervals – of the progress made. In this Department, the only man who can co-ordinate the work of all the Members of Council concerned is the Secretary of State, and for his part, the Minister of Aircraft Production has consented to co-operate with me in this task. I propose to render you my first report as soon as possible after the conclusion of the conversations in Washington, and further reports on the first day of every month.

[599] The initial codeword used for the planned Allied invasion of the European continent.

Winston S. Churchill to Sir Archibald Sinclair
15th June 1942

It was very good of you to undertake this work yourself. Will you please however keep in touch with Lord Cherwell, so that he can keep you apprised of my point of view?

I hope to have a H2S meeting on Wednesday at 11 a.m.

Sir Archibald Sinclair to Winston S. Churchill
24th June 1942

PRIME MINISTER

You asked for my comments on the Minister of Aircraft Production's minute to you of the 2nd June.

1. Spitfires.
   I am very glad to see that the shortage of junction box assemblies is being tackled. It is, of course, of the highest importance that the maximum number of operationally complete Spitfires should be available in the coming months, and the solving of the junction box difficulty will be of material assistance in meeting this need. I understand that there are still 157 Spitfires deficient of junction box assemblies.
2. Blenheim Vs.
   The news that the 83 turrets are now available and are being put on is most welcome, as these aircraft are badly needed for despatch to the Middle East. These aircraft also require modification, and we do not anticipate that they will have been completed operationally until August.
3. Beaufighters.
   The recent drive that the Minister has made for the more rapid preparation of these aircraft in A.S.U.s has yielded good results, and as far as tropicalised types are concerned all arrears of both fighter and coastal types have now been cleared up to, and including, the May overseas quotas.
   However, there still remain some 120 aircraft deficient of such equipment as A.I.[600] and constant speed units, which are badly needed in Squadrons.
4. Propellers.
   The shortage of propellers and constant speed units continues to be the most serious limiting factor on the expansion of our striking forces. The Minister of Aircraft Production is fully seized of the vital need for these items of equipment, and I am grateful for all that he is doing to boost up production.
   At the moment, however, the situation is still showing little signs of improvement, as on the 18th June out of 303 Wellington IIs in A.S.Us, 283 were deficient of propellers, and/or constant speed units, while of 146 Whitley Vs, 120 were in the same state.

[600] Aerial interception (airborne radar).

C.A.S., whom you also asked to comment has seen this minute, and agrees with it. I am sending a copy to the Minister of Aircraft Production.

AHMS

Sir Hugh Dowding's career continued to occupy the time of the senior levels of the Government – but this time his effective retirement was to be agreed.

Sir Archibald Sinclair to Winston S. Churchill
27th June 1942
SECRET

Prime Minister

I regret to inform you that Air Chief Marshal Sir Hugh Dowding has intimated to me the resignation of his present appointment and has asked to be permitted to retire. He gives as his reasons:–

(a) The obstruction, inertia and the supply of incorrect information, by which he alleges his work has been hindered;
(b) The gratuitous impertinence of an officer junior to himself – a reference to a minute by the Vice Chief of the Air Staff dated 15th April, a copy of which was sent to General Ismay at the time.

I saw Sir Hugh Dowding on Tuesday and asked him to complete his task. He had previously reported that it was nearly finished. I reminded him that on the one or two occasions when he had come to tell me of his difficulties I had been able to overcome them but that on this occasion he had not given me a chance to investigate the matter of which he was making complaint.

I told him that from my personal knowledge the Vice Chief of the Air Staff had exerted himself to secure the adoption of Sir Hugh Dowding's recommendations. In some cases, when his recommendations had involved departures in policy which, in the opinion of our expert advisers, would be detrimental to operational efficiency, we had deferred to Sir Hugh Dowding's judgement on the policy issue.

He told me in reply that he was convinced that to give a senior officer a task involving criticism without responsibility of the work of the Commands and staff of the Royal Air Force was unsound in principle. In reply to my reproach for not giving me an opportunity of considering his complaints before submitting his resignation, he answered quite frankly that he had seized upon these recent difficulties as an opportunity for claiming his release from an invidious position. I asked him to think it over for a few days before deciding finally to resign, and offered him my close co-operation if he was willing to remain. He has since written again adhering to his decision to resign. He encloses a list of matters in which his recommendations have either not been accepted or, having been accepted, have not yet been put into effect. I propose to examine these cases. I shall see that any recommendations which do not involve departures in policy affecting operational efficiency are put promptly into effect. Those that do raise important and difficult questions of policy, a wrong decision upon which might injuriously affect the efficiency of the Royal Air Force, I shall ask the Inspector General to examine and furnish me with a report.

Sir Hugh Dowding achieved a sufficient measure of success to refute his argument that his appointment was unsound in principle. Not even a man endowed with exceptional tact and good humour could have found the task easy, but Sir Hugh Dowding had great qualifications for it. He worked hard, and I have thanked him for his services. His mind is made up and I hope you will agree that I have no option but to accept his resignation.

AHMS

Winston S. Churchill to A. V. Alexander and Sir Archibald Sinclair
14th July 1942

FIRST LORD
SECRETARY OF STATE FOR AIR

I understand that Coastal Command squadrons, with an initial establishment of 20 machines, are flying only about thirty hours a day, and that a substantial increase in the number of sorties per squadron could be obtained if the maintenance organisation were expanded and improved. Until everything possible has been done in this direction there can be no case for transferring additional squadrons from Bomber to Coastal Command.

It is true that the standard of serviceability in Costal Command will fall off if the aircraft make more frequent sorties. But could not this be permitted without anxiety if a clear understanding were reached that Coastal Command could call on Bomber Command for help in case of sudden emergency?

WSC

Sir Archibald Sinclair to Winston S. Churchill
16th July 1942
MOST SECRET

PRIME MINISTER

I am anxious that we should have authority before the coming July moon period to attack two further targets in Occupied France – the Schneider Works at Le Creusot and the Citroen Plant at Quai de Javel in Paris.

When I mentioned the Le Creusot project to you at the beginning of June you felt that the time was not ripe for a night attack, although you would agree to one being delivered in daylight. I told you then that the Commander-in-Chief did not wish to risk his Lancasters, which were the only suitable aircraft, except as part of an operation which would be continued that night and which would have a real chance of knocking the Schneider factory out. You agreed with this point of view.

The importance of this plant I need not stress. It warrants attack on the heaviest scale and the weight of attack which can be applied by day would not be enough to do decisive damage and would undoubtedly result in a strengthening of the defences. In good weather conditions – and an attack would be made only in such conditions – an accurate attack can be made by night, though not, of course, without causing some loss of life among the French population.

The Citroen plant is one of the most important in the M.T.[601] industry in Occupied territories. The Ministry of Economic Warfare consider, in the light of our previous successful operations, that we should concentrate on the motor transport industry. We intend, therefore, if authority is given, to associate an attack on this plant with attacks on the Ford General Motor Works in Antwerp and on the Gien Ordnance Depot, authority for which has already been given. The target is closely surrounded by a built-up area, but given the necessary good weather, selected crews should be able to achieve accurate results.

I ask, therefore, for authority to attack these two targets by night on the condition that only experienced crews be employed, that the targets are attacked only in really favourable weather conditions, and the crews bring back their bombs if they cannot identify the target with a reasonable degree of certainty.

I am sending a copy of this minute to the Foreign Secretary.

AHMS

Sir Archibald Sinclair to Winston S. Churchill
25th July 1942
SECRET

PRIME MINISTER

The Germans are suffering from an increasing shortage of railway engines and rolling stock. The production of locomotives has been placed on equal priority with that of tanks and aircraft. We are, therefore, attacking trains and railway engines as hard as we can within the limits of the present Cabinet decision, i.e. that bombers may only attack trains in occupied France by day and when they are stationary (when they can be identified as goods trains) and that fighters may do the same and, in addition, may attack goods trains when they are moving. Passenger trains must not be attacked, nor moving trains at night. We have been encouraged by the reports of the damage done to locomotives by low-flying fighters in daylight.

I now ask for authority to attack moving trains at night, either with cannon or with bombs. It would not be practicable to discriminate between passenger and goods trains, but the attacks may be justified on the following grounds:–

a) They would increase the disorganisation of the enemy's transport system.

[601] Motor transport.

b) Nearly nine-tenths of the traffic at night is goods traffic and the number of passenger trains likely to be attacked is, therefore, small.
c) French civilians are not allowed to travel at night during the curfew hours, which are at present 11 p.m. to 4 a.m., except with special permission. The few Frenchmen, therefore, who might be travelling on a train we attacked would, in all probability, be collaborationists.

I am sending a copy of this minute to the Secretary of State for Foreign Affairs. Do you consider that I should bring this matter before the Cabinet?

Sir Archibald Sinclair to Winston S. Churchill
31st August 1942
SECRET

PRIME MINISTER

Your Minute M.1623/2 about preparations for the bomber offensive in the autumn.

1. The Minister of Aircraft Production and I are fully persuaded of the importance of getting H.2.S. into the squadrons as rapidly as possible. Three handmade sets are expected to be ready by the end of August and a further twelve in November. At present no definite date can be given as to when main production will begin. It is still in the early development stage; but work on it is receiving the highest priority.
2. I cannot remember or trace giving you any assurance about the production of M.C. bombs last July. The Minister of Aircraft Production and I have been invited to furnish the Defence Committee (Supply) with a programme for the maximum production of M.C. bombs. This will be ready very shortly and I will send you a copy. Certainly we must press ahead with these bombs with all speed. The facets of the task are, as you say, numerous. They fall into four main groups:–
   a) Training
   b) Aerodromes and runways
   c) Bombs
   d) Scientific gadgets
      The last category falls into the following sub-divisions:–
      Gee (Mark II should be coming off production in the autumn)
      Air Position Indicator
      H.2.S.
      Oboe
      Monica
      Airborne Jammers
      Long Range Track Guide Beams
      Beam Approach Equipment
      Radio Air Altimeter
      Glide Path Indicators
      De-icing Equipment

3. Sir Robert Renwick is already doing important work for the Minister of Aircraft Production and me on the:–
   Equipment of the Airborne Division
   R.D.F. Chain
   Gee
   We must not overload him, nor should we ask him to undertake the supervision of pure development work (e.g. on Oboe) which is being carried on under the supervision of the Minister of Aircraft Production by his responsible officers. It is in the field of Production that Sir Robert Renwick's qualities of drive and tact and his engineering skill and resources are of especial value.
4. The Minister of Aircraft Production and I are, therefore, inviting Sir Robert Renwick to add to the work which he is now doing on the R.D.F. Chain and on Gee, the task of accelerating the production of and rendering monthly reports on:
   The Air Position Indicator
   H.2.S.
   Beam Approach Equipment
   Long Range Track Guide Beams
   Radio Air Altimeter
   Monica

Winston S. Churchill to Sir Archibald Sinclair
13th September 1942
(Most Secret)

SECRETARY OF STATE FOR AIR

1. Many thanks for your paper on expansion of Bomber Command. I am glad to see the great efforts which you and the Air Staff are making to improve the position. Will you please let me have your programme of expansion by squadrons?
2. Will you also let me know:–
   a) How many bombers we have sent to the Middle East since 1st May, 1942 and
   b) How many crews of these bombers have been returned?

Tedder[602] has got into the habit of keeping all, or nearly all, of the crews used for ferry purposes. This cannot be allowed. I had thought of sending him a telegram myself, but I await your reply to this.

WSC

[602] Arthur William Tedder, 1st Baron Tedder (1890–1967): Commander, RAF Far East Command 1936–38; Director, Research and Development 1938–40; Commander, RAF Middle East Command 1940–43; Deputy Supreme Allied Commander 1943–45, under Eisenhower – the two men worked closely together in planning the D-Day landings in June 1944; responsible for providing tactical air support and a strong advocate of destroying the German communication system during the invasion; ennobled and became Chief of the Air Staff in 1946.

Winston S. Churchill to Sir Archibald Sinclair and Sir Charles Portal
17th September 1942
(Secret)
(Action this Day)

SECRETARY OF STATE FOR AIR
C.A.S.

1. It is necessary that the Bomber Command at home should be raised from 32 operating squadrons, which it now has, to 50 squadrons fully operative, by the end of the year. The expansion should be progressive. No American squadrons should be counted. Let me have the best plan that you can make for achieving this prime military object. For this purpose you should bring under new and close scrutiny all the following spheres, so as to obtain:–

	Squadrons
From the Coastal Command	2
From the Air-borne division	1
By restricting the flow of heavy bombers to the Middle East and India	2
By improving the working-up arrangements of the Bomber Command itself so as to make operational additional	2
By present promised increase from M.A.P.	9
By further exertions of M.A.P. additional	2
Total	18

2. You should, of course, vary these apportionments if the same result can be produced more conveniently. When the resulting plan has been shaped, I will bring it before the War Cabinet and ask for discussion and approval. It will then become binding and will have, within the above limits and for the above period, priority over every other competing claim.

WSC

Winston S. Churchill to Sir Archibald Sinclair
25th September 1942

SECRETARY OF STATE FOR AIR

I am very much surprised to receive your minute,[603] to which I am not at all prepared to agree. You seek a reversal of a Cabinet decision to which you and the Chief of the Air Staff were parties. If the matter is raised again it must come before the War Cabinet alone. It will be necessary to have an unbiased report from the Commander-in-Chief, Bomber Command, who, after all, is principally concerned. There is no reason why the Dominions and the Americans should be consulted, or still less that they should have a veto on our procedure. Meanwhile, let me know

[603] Concerning the publication of aircraft losses.

Air Marshal Harris's considered and unprejudiced opinion. It is clearly understood that the figures would be circulated in Bomber Command. I propose to make the announcement myself and will take the fullest responsibility with the press. The figures are grossly misleading without the number of sorties.

WSC

Winston S. Churchill to Sir Archibald Sinclair and Ernest Bevin[604]
8th October 1942

SECRETARY OF STATE FOR AIR
MINISTER OF LABOUR

1. I cannot agree that men under 25 should be employed on these highly localised duties.[605] No more should be recruited at present. With regard to those now there, I am not certain under what tenure they are serving. Have we the power to transfer them to Army units? Please advise me. The transference should be made gradually, so as to avoid any shock to the formations. A period of four months would not be excessive for this.
2. The replacement of the under 25s would, of course, come from the older categories called up, and these should be supplied sufficiently to maintain the approved strength of the Royal Air Force Regiment. I shall be content if the total strength is allowed to run down from 79,000 to, say, 70,000.
3. Is it not very absurd that the officers of the ground service should be called pilot officers, flight-lieutenants, &c., when they have never flown and are never going to fly. No one ought to be called a pilot officer who has not flown or does not fly. Most people would be ashamed to call themselves pilots of the Royal Air Force when, in fact, they are never going to get off the ground. I wonder the pilots themselves do not feel rather scornful about this multiplication of borrowed plumes.

WSC

[604] Ernest Bevin (1881–1951): Secretary-General, Transport & General Workers' Union 1921–40; Labour MP for Wandsworth Central 1940–50, East Woolwich 1950–51; Minister of Labour and National Service 1940–45, where he achieved the mobilisation of Britain's workforce and became one of the most significant members of the coalition government; Secretary of State for Foreign Affairs 1945–51, where he played an important role in the acceptance of the Marshall Plan, the creation of NATO and Britain's decision to develop nuclear weapons (he held strong anti-communist views); Lord Privy Seal 1951.
[605] Mainly the manning of airfield perimeter defences.

Sir Archibald Sinclair to Winston S. Churchill
23rd October 1942
COPY
MOST SECRET

PRIME MINISTER

The Chief of the Air Staff and I will send you our considered answer to your minute of yesterday, on future strategy within the course of a day or two.

Meanwhile, I hope you will allow me to make one or two comments on it.

1) I welcome your ruling that the 50 bomber squadron plan is to be put into effect forthwith – the more so as I have already had to make one or two decisions in anticipation of Cabinet approval.
2) With 4,000 to 6,000 bombers operating from this country we can pulverise German war industry and transport and bring the harvest of victory within the compass of such land forces as we shall have available in 1944. Such a force of heavy and medium bombers could be operating from the country by middle – or certainly by the third quarter – of 1944 if:–
    a) You now declare unequivocally for the heavy bomber as the main instrument of victory.
    b) The necessary priorities are given within the present aircraft and air force target programmes of the U.S.

   According to our information your pronouncement would be decisive in its influence upon American deliberations at this critical juncture.
3) American opinion is divided; some want to concentrate on the Pacific; others against Germany; some want an Air Force which would be mainly ancillary to the Army, equipped with Army support aircraft and employed (no doubt in extravagant numbers) in the theatres of land operations; others want to build up a big bomber force to attack the centre of German power. It is in your power to crystallise American opinion and to unite it behind those schools of thought which want to attack Germany and want to do it by building up an overwhelming force of bombers in this country.
4) Instead, however, of uniting those schools of thought which want to build up a big bomber force and want to use American power for a decisive attack upon Germany in 1943 and 1944, you will throw these forces into confusion and impotency if you set yourself against their cherished policy of daylight penetration.
5) In the opinion of the Air Staff, and in my own inexpert opinion, this policy of daylight penetration has a chance of success, if only they can get the numbers and if only they are not rushed by impatience into taking on heavy opposition with half-trained gunners. The Americans are prepared to pursue it ruthlessly and to pay the high cost in casualties which it will entail.

   If it succeeds, it will be possible in the earliest months of next year for us to send a thousand bombers over Hamburg one night, for the Americans to follow up with 5 or 600 bombers the following day and, if the weather is kind, for us to follow up with a large force of heavy bombers in the next night – and then to go on bombing one city after another in Germany on that scale. If it succeeds, the Fortresses will be able to pinpoint vital aircraft factories and to knock them out in a series of daylight attacks. Making every allowance for great exaggeration in the figure of aircraft hitherto destroyed by the Fortresses in daylight attacks, it remains true that in a series of attacks upon Germany the Fortresses would shoot down a large – perhaps a crippling – number of German fighters.

If it succeeds, we shall probably go a long way toward winning the war before the great force of 4,000 to 6,000 heavy bombers is ever deployed.

If it fails, it will at least do a lot of damage to Germany and to the German fighter force in the process. Nor is encouragement in its pursuit inconsistent with advice to re-insure by preparation for night bombing.

6) The American Air Force in this country are determined to try out this theory. They are not irresolute; they are being hampered by diversions of their best trained crews for "Torch"[606] and by the slow arrival of their bomber squadrons. Already, however, they have got as far as the Lorient outside the shelter of our fighter cover, and bombed their target with astonishing accuracy. They are proceeding phase by phase. If they are not asked to divert too much to other tasks, it is their firm intention to drop bombs on Germany in daylight next month. It would be a tragedy if we were to frustrate them on the eve of this great experiment.

7) To ally ourselves with the American Navy against General Spaatz[607] and General Eaker[608] and the United States Air Force in this country, and to force them into diverting their highly trained crews to scaring U-Boats instead of to the bombing of Germany would be disastrous. It would waken and alienate the very forces in the United States on which we depend for support in a European as distinct from a Pacific strategy and for the production of heavy bombers as distinct from the types which it is so much more easy to produce in quantity.

8) I would therefore strongly urge that we should give our whole-hearted support to General Spaatz and General Eaker in the prosecution of their plans for daylight penetration into Germany and ally ourselves with them in pressing the Americans to adopt a highly selective attitude and to think less of target numbers than of producing the right designs of aircraft.

AHMS

---

[606] Operation Torch was the codeword for the allied invasion of the North African French Colonies.

[607] Carl A. Spaatz (1891–1974): General, US Air Force; Chief of the Air Force Combat Command 1941, began planning of the American air effort in Europe; Commander Allied Northwest African Air Forces 1943–44; Commander Strategic Air Force in Europe 1944–45, responsible for all deep bombing missions against Germany; Commander US Strategic Air Force in the Pacific 1945–46 – the atomic bombing of Hiroshima and Nagasaki took place under his command.

[608] Ira C. Eaker (1896–1987): Lt.-General US Air Force; in January 1942, assigned task of organising Eighth Air Force Bomber Command, which was to be the backbone of US airpower in Europe; in August, he personally led the first strike on continental Europe; Commander Allied Air Forces in the Mediterranean 1944–45.

Sir Archibald Sinclair to Winston S. Churchill
23rd October 1942
SECRET

PRIME MINISTER

GIEN

The Gien Tank Repair and Fitting Depot is situated some 10 miles south of Paris. In September 1941 photographic reconnaissance showed a concentration of some 2000 vehicles there, probably A.F.V.s[609] Confirmation that a large proportion were in fact tanks was not obtained until better photographs were taken in December. These tanks were mainly French and British which were being repaired and armed, or newly made tanks being fitted with German guns, wireless etc.

This target was considered by the Air Ministry Targets Committee. At the time the Air Ministry had no authority to attack targets in Occupied France by night and authority was not given by the War Cabinet until February 2nd, 1942. Gien would not, however, have been attacked and when authority was given for a list of targets in Occupied France Gien was placed low on the list for the following reasons:–

a) Attacks on tank factories were considered more effective than an attack on a depot where the number of tanks present would fluctuate.
b) The psychological effect of an attack would be greater if directed against factories in a thickly populated area where the destruction could be seen by a large number of people.
c) Gien is a small target and extremely difficult to find and an effective attack could be made only by highly skilled crews in exceptionally favourable weather conditions.

The target was attacked in July 1942 by a small number of special aircraft. Considerable damage was done to the buildings which were a more profitable target than the tanks themselves.

The Air Ministry has been criticised for two reasons.

1) Originally for not attacking the target.
2) For not attacking the target until most of the tanks had left for one or other of the German war fronts.

The answers to criticism 1) have already been given.

Criticism 2) arose from the publication of photographs of Gien before and after bombing, the "before" photographs being taken some months earlier when a large number of tanks were present, the "after" photographs being taken at a time when the tank population was considerably smaller. The selection of the "before" photograph was made by the C.I.U.[610] on purely technical ground that it was the best available photograph for reproduction in newspapers.

The answer to criticism 2) is similarly that Gien was attacked as soon as strategic and tactical factors warranted its elevation to a high place on the list of priority

[609] Armoured fighting vehicles.

[610] Central Information Unit.

targets in Occupied France (the more important targets like the Renault works having being disposed of).

I have not informed the critics – nor do I think it necessary to inform them – that there was a War Cabinet ban on the bombing of France by night until February of this year.

Balfour snatched a chance of introducing Mr. Purbrick[611] to the C. in C. Bomber Command who told him the facts in very direct language. An hour or two later Mr. Purbrick was denouncing the inaction of the Air Ministry to the 1922 Committee, never mentioning that he had received from the man responsible for these operations, a clear explanation of the facts!

AHMS

Winston S. Churchill to Sir Archibald Sinclair
24th October 1942
(Secret)

SECRETARY OF STATE FOR AIR

1. I do not feel this is a very convincing answer. You make a lot of the War Cabinet decision not being repealed till 2nd February, 1942, but you had only to ask at any time to have it reconsidered. You have always asked me when you wanted anything in particular. I am sure that if I or the War Cabinet had known that there was a concentration of some 2,000 A.F.V.s parked at this place, they would have urged you to go for them.
2. Nor is the argument that "Gien is a small target and extremely difficult to find" very valid, because when you did go, you found it all right. The Target Committee seem to have been at fault in this matter. I am not at all surprised that it has caused unfavourable comment. I wish you had consulted me.

Sir Archibald Sinclair to Winston S. Churchill
24th October 1942
SECRET

PRIME MINISTER

Your minute M.482/2. You have put quite a different construction on my minute about Gien from what I intended.

I do not at all wish to shelter behind the fact that the Cabinet did not approve of night bombing of France until February of this year. I take full responsibility for the delay in bombing Gien.

611 Reginald Purbrick (dates unknown): Conservative MP for Walton, Cheshire 1929–45.

It is true that in my Minute I twice referred, in passing, to the lifting of the Cabinet ban on night bombing of France – the first time as an incident in the chronological story, and the second time to warn you that I had not told the critics about the Cabinet ban. I mentioned this in the hope that you would not break fresh controversial ground by mentioning it in any reply that you might send to the critics.

At the same time, I made it clear on the first page of my minute, that "Gien would not, however, have been attacked even if there had been no ban on night bombing in France".

I am sorry that you were not convinced by the selection which I have sent you in a condensed Minute from the array of arguments which I might have used against the earlier bombing of Gien.

Dry tanks with no petrol in them are thoroughly bad targets. The place was difficult to find. Without "GEE" success would have been improbable. As it was, our success consisted in destroying the buildings, and it is unlikely that we did much harm to the tanks. Compare that with the results of the attack on the Renault factory which amounted to denying to the Germans the equipment of three armoured divisions until the end of the war.

You are very kind, and you are quite right, in saying that I should not hesitate to come to you if I wanted anything in particular; but I did not require any special authority from you for the bombing of Gien, and I am in complete accord with the assessment of its value as a target and of the difficulties of attacking it, on which the Commander-in-Chief, Bomber Command, the Air Staff, and the Target Committee, agree.

Archibald Sinclair

Winston S. Churchill to Sir Archibald Sinclair and Sir Charles Portal
26th October 1942
MOST SECRET

PRIME MINISTER'S PERSONAL MINUTE
SECRETARY OF STATE FOR AIR, CHIEF OF THE AIR STAFF
(Copy to: Air Marshal Harris)

1) The Secretary of State's minute of October 23.[612] It is much better at the present time to persuade the Americans to use Flying Fortresses and Liberators to give additional protection to convoys for "TORCH" (assuming of course that they can make the distances), though this may be at the expense of their daylight raiding of France. I hope that, having got them up to the trade routes for this purposes, they will remain there and help to control the Bay of Biscay, both against U-boats and enemy blockade runners. The alternative would be to take more Lancaster squadrons from Bomber Command, which I have been trying my best

[612] See page 366.

to prevent for a long time past. It is in this sense that I have spoken to General Eisenhower[613] and Admiral Cunningham.[614]

2) I have not raised with any American authority the question of whether the "daylight penetration" of Germany is a sound operation. The position remains as stated in my telegram to the President, which C.A.S. saw and approved.
3) I am not at all convinced of the soundness of the Secretary of State's minute of October 23, either on the merits of "daylight penetration" policy or on the tactics we should pursue towards the Americans. There is no need however to discuss that now.

WSC

Sinclair wrote to Churchill asking his advice concerning a proposed series of morale-boosting lectures at RAF Yatesbury. He received a caustic reply.

Winston S. Churchill to Sir Archibald Sinclair
26th October 1942

Secretary of State for Air

It seems to me essential that we should see beforehand what is going to be said to the troops. This rule might be waived in the case of the Archbishop of Canterbury and Sir Stafford Cripps.[615] In all other cases it should be enforced, and most particularly in the case of Sir Richard Acland,[616] who, I should have thought, is utterly unfit to speak to soldiers.

---

[613] Dwight David Eisenhower (1890–1969): US general, with a talent for organisation, persuasion and coordination; Commander, Allied forces, Operation Torch (the invasion of French North Africa) 1942–43; directed invasions of Sicily and Italy, 1943–44; Supreme Commander Allied Expeditionary Forces, Operation Overlord (the cross-Channel invasion of Europe), 1944–45; US Army Chief of Staff 1945–48; Supreme Commander, NATO 1950–52; President of the United States 1953–61.

[614] Admiral Andrew Cunningham, Viscount Hyndhope (1883–1963): Commander-in-Chief Mediterranean Fleet 1939–42, 1943, oversaw landings in North Africa and Sicily 1942–43; First Sea Lord 1943–46.

[615] Sir Richard Stafford Cripps (1889–1952): barrister; Labour and independent MP for Bristol East 1931–50; Solicitor-General, 1931; led the Socialist League, and founded *Tribune*; expelled from Labour Party in 1939 for urging a popular front; Ambassador to the Soviet Union 1940–42; member of War Cabinet as Lord Privy Seal, February – November 1942; Minister of Aircraft Production November 1942–45; readmitted to Labour Party 1945; President of the Board of Trade 1945–47; Minister of Economic Affairs and Chancellor of the Exchequer 1947–50.

[616] Sir Richard Acland (1906–90): MP for Barnstaple 1935-45 (Liberal 1935–42, Common Wealth 1942–45); founded Common Wealth Party in 1942, arguing for common ownership of land and industry; constant thorn in Churchill's side, both in and out of parliament; joined the Labour Party after electoral defeat in 1945; Labour MP for Gravesend 1947–55; resigned from Labour over the leadership's unwillingness to oppose the development of the hydrogen bomb.

Sir Archibald Sinclair to Winston S. Churchill
27th October 1942

PRIME MINISTER

1) You have asked for the comments of C.A.S. and myself on your note on Air Policy. As you know, we are in cordial agreement with your first paragraph.
2) The American air authorities, both in London and in Washington, have been most co-operative and helpful in respect of the TORCH convoys. They are providing two squadrons (24) of amphibian Catalinas which are to go to GIBRALTAR and DUNKIRK (T)[617] respectively as soon as aerodrome space is available; General Arnold has offered another squadron of 16 Liberators and Fortresses from America for TORCH convoy protection; and General Spaatz is providing all we ask for in the way of antisubmarine patrol and bombing of the Biscay Ports during the passage of the TORCH convoys. No further pressure is necessary either here or in America to enlist their full support in this respect.
3) With regard to your paragraph 3, we feel bound to warn you most seriously against decrying the American plan for daylight attack of Germany. We cannot reconcile the opening sentence of your note, nor your telegram to the President of the 16th September (T.1229/2) with your suggestion that we should now try to persuade the United States Army Air Force to divert their energies to sea work. Their present attitude shows that on special occasions when help is required at sea they will not hesitate to give it. But we are convinced that it would be fatal to suggest to them at this of all times that the great bomber force they are planning to build up is no good except for coastal work and perhaps ultimately for night bombing. They are convinced that they will be able to bomb GERMANY by day and they are determined to do so. They may be wrong – indeed we think they are unduly optimistic on the subject. But on three different occasions their Heavy Bombers have encountered strong enemy fighter opposition without any fighter escort of their own, and they have given good account of themselves without disproportionate loss. On the last occasion their bombing was remarkably accurate.
4) We fully agree that we should advise them to address themselves to the difficult problem of night-adapting their bombers and adjusting their training programme in case they find the daylight policy too costly. But if we go any further at this stage we may find ourselves confronted with an abandonment of the policy of an all-out air offensive against Germany, and a swing to the PACIFIC where their Heavy Bombers have already shown themselves capable of taking on the Japanese by day.
5) We are not sure whether you realise the extent to which General Spaatz has suffered setbacks in fitting his bombers for their true role against GERMANY. Squadrons which were scheduled to come to his Command have been diverted

[617] The destinations of the Catalinas are unclear: Gibraltar and Dunkirk were both codenames for radar stations, but neither had an airfield.

to HAWAII and to the South-West PACIFIC; the first squadrons to be operationally fit, on which he was depending to leaven those that came after, are being diverted to TORCH and he has had to conserve their energies and keep down their wastage. Are we now to press him to divert them to the anti-submarine work in the Atlantic? General Spaatz is determined to attack GERMANY as soon as he has the trained personnel to do it with; but he is equally – and rightly – determined not to do so prematurely with half-trained crews and inadequate numbers.

6) We fully agree that our best endeavours will be required to combat the quantitative obsession in the American outlook on aircraft production. It may be found, however, that the immediate American programme is not so flexible as we could wish, and that really drastic changes in its pattern could only take full effect in 1944 and later. We are now examining, in conjunction with the Ministry of Aircraft Production, various possibilities including the introduction of the Lancaster into American or Canadian production and a largely increased production of the Mustang with the Merlin 61 engine by assembly both in America and in this country.
7) We are also examining the possibility of expanding Lancaster production in this country at the expense of other types. The Air Staff are acutely aware of the need for a constant rise in the curve of bomb deliveries upon Germany, and the Wellington will certainly not be prematurely discarded. We must warn you, nevertheless, that the older types of bomber cannot, in the face of modern defences, continue indefinitely in service. Deliveries are essential, but leadership and performance count for as much in bombers as in fighters. Bomb delivery is not dependent only on production; it depends also directly on the casualty rate, which also vitally affects the quality of the bombing, i.e. the ability of our crews to reach their target. All bombers have to penetrate the same defences to get into Germany at all. We could not make a greater mistake than to imagine that it would pay us to go on producing obsolete bombers for the purpose of attacking the nearer targets. It must be our aim to use U.S. production, in conjunction with our own, to ensure the maintenance of quality without any interruption of the rising curve of bomb-delivery, and we are sure that this is possible.
8) We are pressing on with this investigation as a basis for the negotiations by the Minister of Production and the Air Ministry representative in Washington next month and we shall report to you our conclusions as soon as they are crystallised.
9) I attach a note on the American 1943 programme and a comparison of their new types with our own.

We agree as to the importance of a high proportion of fighters in the carriers of the Royal Navy. The source of production of the substantial numbers concerned will need careful investigation by the Chief of Naval Air Services and A.M.S.O.[618] in

[618] Air Member for Supply and Organisation on the Air Council – then Sir Christopher Courtney.

conjunction with the M.A.P. Our Spitfire production is already very fully mortgaged and not all the later types coming on are suitable for operation from carriers. The American production programme includes numbers of Naval fighters which appear in excess of anything that could be absorbed by the U.S. Navy, and during the forthcoming discussions in Washington we must endeavour to obtain some allocations from America, in the common interest of the sea security which is so vital to us both.

AHMS

Winston S. Churchill to Sir Archibald Sinclair and Sir Charles Portal
3rd December 1942

SECRETARY OF STATE FOR AIR
C.A.S.

1. Is 3,000 tons a month the maximum you can discharge in the next few months? I thought you were aiming at bigger figures than that.
2. The heat should be turned on Italy in the manner proposed by you at present, but Germany should not be entirely neglected. I am looking forward to a big raid on Berlin this month if conditions are favourable.
3. Our policy can be reviewed and changed from time to time as may be desired.
4. The Secretary of State might, if he felt inclined, supply the War Cabinet with a short statement, as the matter was mentioned to them.

WSC

Winston S. Churchill to Sir Percy Grigg[619] and Sir Archibald Sinclair
3rd December 1942

SECRETARY OF STATE FOR WAR
SECRETARY OF STATE FOR AIR

1. Now that the application to France of the Western Desert system of co-operation between the Army and the Royal Air Force has been agreed, except for the point mentioned in the Secretary of State for War's Minute of the 14th November, we should proceed with the second stage in the investigation. I should like to see a statement similar to that attached to the Secretary of State for War's minute, but covering the phase of the operation during which the Army moved from England to France.
2. The organisation in this second phase must be such as can merge smoothly into that which you have worked out together for the third phase. I consider that the difference of opinion on the responsibilities of the Air Officer

[619] Sir Percy James Grigg (1890–1964): civil servant and politician; Principal Private Secretary to successive Chancellors of the Exchequer, 1921–30; National MP 1942–45; Secretary of State for War 1942–45.

Commanding-in-Chief will solve itself when phases two and three are considered together. In the second phase, the Air Officer Commanding-in-Chief cannot disinterest himself in the protection of his base, which will be in the United Kingdom. Later, when the invasion has made considerable progress on the Continent, it may well be that the Air Officer Commanding-in-Chief will not need to concern himself with anything further to the rear than the French Channel ports. I see no difficulty in the transition.

3. When you have agreed upon the organisation for the second phase, we can then proceed to the final step, which is the organisation of the preparatory training period, or first phase.

WSC

In December 1942 the debate between the Air Ministry and the Prime Minister focused on the options for stepping up Bomber Command attacks on Italy and Rome.

Sir Archibald Sinclair to Winston S. Churchill.
4th December 1942
MOST SECRET

PRIME MINISTER

The C.A.S. has sent me the attached minute about bombing Rome. I am for bombing Rome at the convenient time, but we must face the serious risks and disadvantages of the project and choose the time well.

The bombing of Rome is bound to have unfavourable repercussions in two directions:

a) On Roman Catholic opinion, in this country, in North and South America, and in Spain and Portugal. This would be so even if it were only famous and beautiful old churches and religious seminaries in the City of Rome which we hit by our bombs. There could, however, be no guarantee that, if we aimed at some target near the centre of Rome, our bombs would not hit the Vatican City.

b) On liberal opinion which regards Rome as one of the shrines of European civilisation. This liberal opinion is a bit sticky about bombing. You were quoting the Archbishop of Canterbury against me at the beginning of the year. Success is enabling us to carry them with us; but they might come out against bombing rather than acquiesce in the bombing of Rome, as a mere incident in the air war against Italy.

The risk of destroying churches, works of art, Cardinals, priests and students are great, and I think you will agree that we could not afford to run them more than once or twice – or at the most three times. We ought not, therefore, I suggest, to run them until we have thoroughly shaken the structure of the Fascist State by repeated bombings of the main centres of Italian war industry and transport and by close military approach to the heart of the country.

I cannot believe that an early attack on Rome would precipitate the downfall of Mussolini, or that it would facilitate our operations on land, on the sea or in the air. The risks, therefore, do not now seem to me to be justified by any hope of a decisive advantage. If, on the other hand, we had heavily bombed important Italian cities, had seized Sardinia and were in a position from which we appeared to threaten a descent by sea on the mainland of Italy, a stroke from the air at the heart of Rome might bring the Fascist State toppling down and would, therefore, be worth all risks.

It is no use fiddling with the bombing of Rome and attacking the outskirts, as was at one time suggested. The blow when it comes should be aimed at the Palazzo Venezia – although it must be realised that it is only about 2,000 yards from the Vatican City. If it is clearly seen to be part of a comprehensive design of land, sea and air attack upon Italy and intended as a decisive stroke at the heart of the Fascist State, few will condemn it. In short, the question of attacking Rome is, I suggest, essentially one of timing.

I am sending a copy of this minute to the Foreign Secretary.

AHMS

Sir Archibald Sinclair to Winston S. Churchill
15th December 1942
MOST SECRET

PRIME MINISTER

1) With reference to your personal minute M.580/2 of 5th December, 1942, I attach a short paper on the subject of the bombing of Italy which I would propose to circulate to the War Cabinet.
2) With regard to para. 1 of your minute, the actual dropping capacity of Bomber Command at the present time is about 6,000 tons per month but large scale operations are severely limited by winter weather and we cannot count on more than four or five nights a month being suitable for them during the winter months. The reduction of our bombing effort on Germany, which will result from the plan to bomb Italy, is dealt with in para. 5 of the attached paper.
3) With regard to an attack on Berlin, the Commander-in-Chief considers that he requires a minimum of 300 heavy aircraft to undertake this operation. An attack in fewer numbers would be likely to result in disproportionate losses which would cripple his expansion for a long time. Largely owing to various recent withdrawals from his Command he doubts the possibility of having 300 operational heavy aircraft and crews on any one night before the end of this year. We are keen to do it in January, weather permitting.

THE BOMBING OF ITALY
NOTE BY THE SECRETARY OF STATE FOR AIR

1) The War Cabinet will wish to be informed of the plans that are being made for conducting the bombing offensive on Italy from this country and from Mediterranean bases.
2) It is necessary to maintain the flexibility of our bomber force so that it can be switched at any time to targets in Germany. As much as possible of the bombing of Italy must therefore be conducted from bases in this country. Home based bombers can only cover the northern part of the country; their efforts must therefore be supplemented by aircraft based in North Africa.
3) The proposed plan, to which complete effect cannot be given until the enemy bridgehead in Tunisia has been seized, is as follows:–
    a) The heavy bombers of Bomber Command based in this country will usually operate against targets in Northern Italy whenever weather permits; but no opportunity of attacking important German targets in favourable weather conditions will be missed.
    b) The heavy and medium bomber squadrons at present in the Middle East will concentrate against targets in Southern Italy from bases in the Benghazi area, using Malta as an advanced base to the extent that the supply position and the primary needs of the local fighter defences allow.
    c) The effort of the American heavy and medium bomber groups in North Africa which will be available for the attack on targets in Italy may be supplemented by Wellington squadrons of Bomber Command detached periodically to North Africa to the extent that airfield capacity and maintenance facilities allow. It is unlikely that at first more than two Squadrons could be accommodated in North Africa for this purpose but the number might later be built up to four.
4) With these dispositions, all important Italian towns will have been brought within the range of effective attack. It is estimated that it will be possible to drop some 4,000 tons of bombs a month, an amount comparable with the average weight of attack delivered on Germany in the months before North Italy was made the main target of our heavy bombers. Of the total of 4,000 tons a month, about 2,000 would be delivered by aircraft of Bomber Command.
5) During the winter, large-scale operations are severely limited by weather both at the bases and over the target. Except during spells of unusually good winter weather, it would be imprudent to count upon more than four or five nights a month as suitable for large scale raids. Since the weather is more likely to be suitable in Northern Italy than in Germany, the great majority of the good nights will be taken up with operations against Italian targets and comparatively few will be available for bombing Germany. It seems possible therefore that the effort on Germany may not be more than between 500 and 1,000 tons a month. Every advantage will be taken of good weather to improve on these figures. On the other hand, the important sea mining effort of Bomber Command would

be unaffected and it should be possible to continue to lay mines at the rate of about 1,000 a month. So long as Italy remains the main target, the monthly effort of Bomber Command, leaving out of account the U.S.A.A.C.[620] and British Bombers based in Africa, will be of the order of:–

Italy:	2,000 tons.
Germany:	500/1,000 tons.
Sea Mining:	1,000 mines.

The weight of attack should increase towards the Spring as the strength of Bomber Command increases and the weather improves.

Churchill frequently passed on suggestions he received about possible targets for the RAF. An example is the suggestion by David Robertson MP, about the attractions of the Burmeister and Wain Works at Copenhagen as a target.

Winston S. Churchill to Sir Archibald Sinclair
17th December 1942

SECRETARY OF STATE FOR AIR

You should yourself I think see this M.P. and impart to him verbally and in strict confidence the substance of the reply drafted by C.A.S. marked by me 'A'. I am telling him that you will speak to him on the subject – presuming thus far on your good nature.

WSC

15th December 1942

DRAFT LETTER FROM THE PRIME MINISTER TO MR. DAVID ROBERTSON, M.P.

At this time when we must do all we can to fight the U-boat menace, I am grateful to you for drawing my attention to the importance of the Burmeister and Wain Works at Copenhagen. My information does not suggest however that we ought to put these works very high on our list of targets. The ship building yards are engaged mainly in repair work and make but little contribution to U-boat construction. The Diesel engine works, although among the first dozen in Germany, are far less important than the M.A.N.[621] works at Augsburg and the Humbolt-Deutz factory at Cologne which we have already attacked. Further, there is no doubt that at present the attack on the leading construction yards pays far better dividends than

[620] US Army Air Corps – renamed US Army Air Force in March 1942, so Sinclair was out of date.
[621] MAN was, and still is, a manufacturer of large industrial diesel engines.

the attack on Diesel engine works and is likely to have a much greater effect on U-boat construction in proportion to the effort expended.

Sir Archibald Sinclair to Winston S. Churchill
24th December 1942
MOST SECRET

PRIME MINISTER

I was arranging to see Mr. Robertson as you asked me to do in your Minute 616/2 when my attention was drawn to the fact that, in his letter to you, which I enclose herewith, he had informed you:–

a) That he had met me with a Deputation from the 1922 Committee to protest against our failure to bomb Gien;
b) That he had expressed to me his dis-satisfaction with my explanation.
c) That he "understands" that you felt that the Deputation had just cause for dis-satisfaction.

Please do not suppose that I think you said anything of the kind but if I see Mr. Robertson, I must of course tell him that he has been mis-informed and I should be grateful for your authority to do so.

Of course it is only right that I should see him. It is monstrous that he should take up your time discussing bombing targets. Moreover, I must confess that he is a Caithness man. At the same time, I must warn you, from my previous knowledge and experience of him, that I shall fail utterly to convince him that the Burmeister and Wain Works are not in his words "the most juicy target in Europe".

AHMS

1943

1943 saw the realisation of Portal, Harris and Sinclair's vision of Bomber Command's real potential, as strategic air power came of age. The offensive against Germany took the form of three distinct battles: the Battle of the Ruhr (a major industrial region), from early March to July, the Battle of Hamburg, from July to August, and the Battle of Berlin which began in November and lasted until March 1944. Massive thousand-bomber raids became the norm, with the RAF working alongside the American Air Force (USAAF).

The primary goal of the RAF was the progressive destruction of the German military, industrial and economic system, and the undermining of the morale of the German people – though it also remained engaged with the anti-U-boat war through its Coastal Command and Bomber Command wings. During 1943 the effectiveness of the Allied air offensive was assisted by the introduction of four new bombing aids: OBOE, H2S, target-indicator bombs dropped by Pathfinder aircraft ahead of the main bomber force and, finally, WINDOW, short metal strips which disrupted German radar interception. These four technological innovations transformed the operational capacities of Bomber Command.

At the start of January Sinclair had to inform Churchill that the RAF was behind in its programme of expanding Bomber Command to provide the ability to fly regular thousand-plus-bomber waves over Germany and occupied Europe.

Winston S. Churchill to Sir Archibald Sinclair
4th January 1943

SECRETARY OF STATE FOR AIR

The failure to carry out the bomber expansion programme is a disappointment to me, and I think I should have been warned beforehand.

I note that the Americans have not yet succeeded in dropping a single bomb on Germany.

WSC

Winston S. Churchill to Sir Archibald Sinclair and Sir Charles Portal
7th January 1943

SECRETARY OF STATE FOR AIR AND CHIEF OF THE AIR STAFF

Considering that Bomber Command have done hardly any flying in the last month worth speaking of, it is astonishing that only 547 aircraft should be serviceable and fit for operations out of an establishment of 808. And why are only 557 crews available out of 1010 establishment and 909 effective strength?

I quite understand not going out in impossible weather, but then the result should be a strong accumulation, whereas an increasingly low standard of readiness prevails.

Winston S. Churchill to Sir Archibald Sinclair and Anthony Eden
Telegram from H.M.S. BULOLO
18th January 1943
IMMEDIATE

Prime Minister to Foreign Secretary and Secretary of State for Air. Most Secret and Personal.

If second night's attack on Berlin was on an appreciable scale you should send another telegram to Stalin from me with the new total of bombs dropped.

WSC

Winston S. Churchill to Sir Archibald Sinclair
Telegram
27th January 1943

Following from Prime Minister to Secretary of State for Air.

It seems to me most important to keep on at the big city[622] whenever the weather allows lest it be thought their feeble but vaunted reprisals have damped our ardour.

Winston S. Churchill to Sir Percy Grigg, Sir Archibald Sinclair and Herbert Morrison
6th March 1943

SECRETARY OF STATE FOR WAR, SECRETARY OF STATE FOR AIR, AND MINISTER OF HOME SECURITY

I am told by the Minister of Home Security that there is some talk of reducing smoke-screens in this country in order to save man-power. So long as we maintain a large force in A.D.G.B.[623] for protection against the night bomber, it seems a pity to reduce this comparatively economical form of defence.

I should have thought that, as all the installation is available, it is possible to run smoke-screens without much cost in manpower. At present, according to War Office returns, 9000 men are employed full time. I understand that smoke-screens operate on the average only about six nights a month. Surely it should be possible for all but a nucleus of the men engaged on this work to combine it with other duties, rather than having thousands set aside for this purpose alone. Pray let me have proposals.

WSC

Sir Archibald Sinclair to Winston S. Churchill
15th February 1943

MOST SECRET
PRIME MINISTER

As you have taken a personal interest in H.2.S. I think you will be interested to see the attached Bomber Command Memorandum on its Operational Use. The meat of it is in the conclusions on the last page.

I visited the Pathfinder Force last Saturday. They are enthusiastic about H.2.S.

Naturally, at this early stage, their chief difficulty is to keep the equipment serviceable. So far they have achieved a satisfactory degree of success but only by maintaining at the Central Pathfinder Station all the available experts and serviceability must almost inevitably decline when fitting becomes general. Every effort must,

622 Berlin.

623 Air Defence of Great Britain.

therefore, be made to make the equipment inherently reliable between now and the time when its use will be extended throughout Bomber Command.

It is doing very well and we want as much as we can get.

In the last three nights Bomber Command has attacked Cologne, Milan and Lorient – over 1,000 sorties – 25 bombers missing – 2.5%. Blind bombing with H.2.S. puts searchlights, guns and fighters at a disadvantage and therefore substantially reduces casualties.

I have asked C.A.S. to send you the evidence, which I mentioned to you this morning, of its efficiency.

Winston S. Churchill to Sir Archibald Sinclair and Sir Charles Portal
13th March 1943

SECRETARY OF STATE FOR AIR AND CHIEF OF AIR STAFF

I arranged with General Eisenhower at Algiers that the code numbers of American aircraft should always be followed by their names, the idea of being that the names would eventually in practical working supersede the inconvenient code numbers, which are difficult to remember and confusing when mixed up with other figures in a telegram. General Eisenhower immediately issued orders to this effect, and you will see how strictly they are being fulfilled in all American communications.

I have also asked that a similar practice should be followed here. Pray note these two omissions, and take steps to prevent any such recurrence. Meanwhile kindly inform me what are B.25s and what are P.40s.

WSC

Winston S. Churchill to Sir Archibald Sinclair and Sir Charles Portal
15th March 1943

SECRETARY OF STATE FOR AIR AND CHIEF OF AIR STAFF

This week a record number, viz., ninety-five, of heavy bombers, Stirlings, Halifaxes, and Lancasters, were delivered by M.A.P. Would you please let me know exactly what will happen to these ninety-five aircraft? Where will they be sent?

In taking a concrete example like this one may be able to find out why it is that a more rapid increase in our Bombing Squadrons does not follow from the output.

WSC

Sir Archibald Sinclair to Winston S. Churchill
8th April 1943

MOST SECRET
PRIME MINISTER

You may be interested to see this latest assessment report of the raid on Berlin on March 1st/2nd.

"A final interpretation of photographs taken subsequent to the attack on 1st/2nd March shows good reason why ground sources have reported this attack as outstanding. As one source stated, the Berlin fire services had been organised in the true Prussian manner on the assumption that there would never be more than a certain number of fires at the same time, and each official had received orders as to what he was to do according to the number of fires. In this attack the number of fires exceeded that permitted by the Prussian drill orders, and organisation and discipline completely collapsed. Assistance was received from the fire brigades of Leipzig and other centres. Berlin, to a far greater extent than London, relies upon trams for municipal transport, and the dislocation caused to the tramway system accentuated the effect of the attack.

The photographs show some 30 factories to have been damaged. The principal feature is probably the destruction of the railway repair shops adjoining the Tempelhof Marshalling Yards where workshops have been destroyed over an area of 22 acres. Two large manufacturers of wireless sets, Telefunken and Blaupunktwerke, have been severely damaged, also two branches of Askania Werke, makers of optical and precision instruments. Among other works whose premises have suffered severe damage, are makers of telephone equipment, roller bearings and fire control apparatus. Warehouses in the inland docks or military barracks were burnt out or destroyed by H.E. and at a conservative estimate at least 4,800 flats or houses and 600 detached or semi-detached houses were destroyed or very severely damaged.

It is of interest that the damage reported by ground sources to the Air Ministry and the Foreign Office is not seen on the photographs. The damage to the Air Ministry was caused by a bomb which fell in one of the inner courtyards and between 200 and 300 rooms were destroyed or severely damaged, coupled with the loss of important records.

Two factors seem to have caused the greatest effect:–

a) The phosphorous incendiary bomb, which apart from its destructive effect, caused numerous casualties through burns to persons who attempted to deal with it, and
b) The effect of heavy bombs, which apart from completely destroying all buildings in the immediate neighbourhood of impact would blow out all windows within 500 yards."

AHMS

Winston S. Churchill to Sir Archibald Sinclair and Sir Charles Portal
Prime Minister to Secretary of State for Air and Chief of the Air Staff
10th April 1943

1. These are impressive photographs, given to me by Mr. Geoffrey Lloyd. I should have thought it would be well to have half a dozen installations at different parts of the country, so as to avoid a disaster if a sudden fog comes down upon our returning bombers.[624] Also this would give greater freedom to act on doubtful nights. Will you consult the Chief Bomber,[625] and let me know what he thinks.
2. How are you getting on with your infra-red approach methods?

Winston S. Churchill to Sir Archibald Sinclair and Herbert Morrison
8th June 1943

PRIME MINISTER TO SECRETARY OF STATE FOR AIR AND MINISTER OF HOME SECURITY

Please let me have a report setting out what is being done to protect our reservoirs from attacks like those we have made recently in Germany. (On the Mohne Dam.)[626]

Winston S. Churchill to Sir Archibald Sinclair and Sir Charles Portal
5th July 1943

Prime Minister to Secretary of State for Air and Chief of the Air Staff

In view of all the assurances given about the comparative impotence of enemy bombing, I am of the opinion that the time has come to review the question of the black-out so far as night work in industrial establishments is concerned.

The need for saving labour in every direction in order to speed up the aircraft programme makes it indispensable that night work is not hampered by black-out restrictions.

I should like an assurance that the Air Ministry is not insisting on any restrictions of this character which hamper production.

Winston S. Churchill to Sir Archibald Sinclair and Sir Charles Portal
12th July 1943
Secret

SECRETARY OF STATE FOR AIR
CHIEF OF THE AIR STAFF

[624] The RAF were testing apparatus that assisted crews in landing in poor weather conditions.

[625] Sir Arthur Harris, Commander-in-Chief Bomber Command; see n544.

[626] RAF Bomber Command's Squadron 617 'dambuster' raid on the Möhne, Eder and Sorpe Dams in the Ruhr on the night of 16–17 May 1943.

C.A.S.'s minute of the 6th July[627]

1. It is of high importance for the future of the British Commonwealth and Empire that we should be represented in the defence of Australia and the war in the Pacific. From this point of view, the single squadron of the Royal Air Force which we have sent has played a part out of all proportion to the size of the unit. The fact that they have over here 8,100 Australian air crew, including some of their very best airmen, and the share they have taken in the Empire Training Scheme, certainly leaves us heavily in their debt so far as the air is concerned.
2. It is not merely a question of Spitfires or other fighter aircraft, but of British squadrons capable of doing full justice to the Royal Air Force. I should therefore like to send three Spitfire fighter squadrons to Australia during the present year and persuade the Americans to give us the fighter aircraft they would otherwise have sent to Australia. I have little doubt that I can explain all this quite satisfactorily to the President. You will note, however, that I am not proposing to mount Australian airmen on British machines, but to send complete British units. I note from my last return (W.O.7 of the 7th July) that you have 945 more fighter pilots on effective strength than fighter machines serviceable and therefore it seems to me that 40 or 50 could easily be spared out of these. It is my duty to preserve goodwill between the Mother Country and the vast continent of Australia, inhabited by 6 million people of our race and tongue.
3. Pray let me have your comments and proposals.

WSC

Sinclair's rugged defence of the Air Ministry sometimes led him into direct conflict with Churchill. A proposal that a War Cabinet committee should review the use of manpower in the RAF produced a strong note of dissent from Sinclair. The need to raise a large land army, together with the demands of industry for workers to operate factories and production facilities, meant that the RAF came under pressure to release some of the massive resources tied up in servicing and maintaining its squadrons and airfields. Sinclair took the proposed review as a sign of no confidence in his abilities, and considered resigning in protest.

Winston S. Churchill to Sir Archibald Sinclair
20th July 1943
Secret

My dear Archie,

I hope I am not to take your Minute as a refusal to allow the War Cabinet to inquire into the use of Manpower in the Royal Air Force. A similar Committee made

[627] Referring to plans for aircraft for Australia.

an examination on the use of Manpower by the War Office about eight months ago – see W.P. (42)496 – and I have a letter to hand from the First Lord saying that the Admiralty would welcome an inquiry into their treatment of the question. I should not be able to agree to the Air Ministry adopting an exceptional attitude.

There is no question of "asking the Committee to do your job for you". The Committee is only asked to report to the War Cabinet, who have every right and duty to satisfy themselves on the subject.

I thought it was clearly the view of the War Cabinet that there should be an inquiry of this character but, if you wish, I can bring the matter before them as a definite issue.

There is not question of my "having lost confidence in your ability to administer your Department". But the needs of other Departments have to be considered too in this acute Manpower crisis.

Yours sincerely,
Winston S Churchill

PS. If you would prefer not to be a member of the Committee that can be arranged. But I thought my proposal would be more agreeable to you.

Churchill persuaded Sinclair that he should allow the review to go ahead.

Winston S. Churchill to Sir Archibald Sinclair
22nd July 1943
Secret

My dear Archie,

Thank you very much for your letter. I will have the reference amended by the substitution for the previous form of the words "to enquire into". I will add the Paymaster-General[628] to the Committee and leave you free to state the Departmental case. I hope however that you will think of us all as well.

I may add that the War Office and the Admiralty are at this moment equally liable to Cabinet enquiries of this character and there is nothing derogatory or invidious in the Air Ministry occupying our prior attention.

Yours very sincerely,
WSC

Winston S. Churchill to Sir Archibald Sinclair
23rd July 1943

SECRETARY OF STATE FOR AIR

[628] Lord Cherwell – see n491.

1. Your minute to me of 19th July about squadrons for Australia: I am, of course, aware of all the military objections. I cannot agree, however, that the despatch of a Spitfire squadron or two would not have an important effect on the relations of the Mother Country and the Commonwealth, or that apart from this such a movement would, militarily, be "quite indefensible."
2. Of course, we shall want air superiority for "Starkey,"[629] "Priceless,"[630] "Overlord,"[631] and for all other operations we undertake. I am convinced however that we must send at least one squadron in addition to the increase of ten Spitfires a month from November onwards. I do not see the point of the offer of 75 Spitfire pilots when Spitfire machines are so short.
3. I cannot undertake that this should be conditional on the Americans agreeing to give us equivalent aircraft to replace those sent to Australia. We can, of course, ask them.
4. In the above arrangement we are going less than half-way towards meeting the Australian requests. I am prepared however to agree that we cannot send Lancasters and Sunderlands, and to wait till November before commencing the increased flow. The Spitfire squadron ought to go out as soon as possible.
5. When this is settled I will draft a telegram to Dr. Evatt,[632] and will explain matters to the President.

WSC

Winston S. Churchill to Sir Archibald Sinclair and Sir Charles Portal
1st August 1943
Secret

SECRETARY OF STATE FOR AIR
CHIEF OF THE AIR STAFF

I do not see what is the point of sending 10 extra Spitfires a month to Australia and 75 Spitfire pilots and declining to send two squadrons. The latter seems to be a more attractive way of using the force. I should therefore like to offer Dr. Evatt 2 squadrons of 20 machines and 25 pilots each (total 40 machines and 50 pilots) provided that the ground personnel can be found in Australia, and to make the above 2 squadrons the first charge on the monthly additional increments of Spitfires and Spitfire pilots which you are prepared to offer.

---

[629] 'Starkey' was the codeword for an attack by fourteen British and Canadian divisions to establish a bridgehead on either side of Boulogne between 8 and 14 September 1943; the operation was planned in order to contain enemy forces in the west to prevent their transfer to the Eastern Front, and to serve as a dress rehearsal in the Pas de Calais area for the invasion of Western Europe. It was never carried out.

[630] 'Priceless' was the codeword for Allied support activities planned after the invasion of Sicily.

[631] 'Overlord' was the codeword for the Allied invasion of Normandy.

[632] Herbert Vere Evatt (1894–1965): Australian Labor Party politician; Attorney-General and Minister for External Affairs 1941–45; Deputy Prime Minister 1946–49.

Far better sentimental results will be produced in this by the recognisable arrival of 2 British squadrons than by giving even a larger quantity of Spitfires and pilots without the squadron personality.

I shall delay the actual offer till the election[633] is over.

WSC

In 1943 there was great debate about who should be the new Viceroy in New Delhi. Sinclair was seriously considered for this prestigious appointment but Churchill was reluctant to lose his services at the Air Ministry. He was also worried that if Sinclair left for India, he would be replaced as Liberal leader – with, necessarily, a senior position in the Government – by Lord Samuel. Samuel, Sinclair's predecessor as Liberal leader (1931–35), had served in Asquith's Cabinet alongside Churchill, but the two men had little in common; worthy, but dull, he lacked most of the attributes Churchill sought in his ministers. Consequently Sinclair remained in office and Lord Wavell was appointed Viceroy. Sinclair was asked to coordinate the arrangements for flying the new Viceroy to India and bringing the old one back.

Sir Archibald Sinclair to Winston S. Churchill
15th September 1943
SECRET

PRIME MINISTER

Your Minute of August 5th, M.576/3, about Lord and Lady Linlithgow's[634] journey home.

Your offer to send your York for them has been carefully considered, but there are drawbacks.

One York, for instance, could not accommodate the full party and luggage, and a second York, which could ill be spared, would be required, or a Liberator would have to be diverted from our war-time services.

All things considered, the best solution seemed to be to lay on two civil Sunderlands[635] operated by B.O.A.C.,[636] and we have planned accordingly. These will take Lord Wavell's[637] party to India and bring Lord Linlithgow's party home. One of

[633] 1943 Australian general election.

[634] Victor Alexander John Hope Linlithgow, 2nd Marquess of Linlithgow (1887–1952): Civil Lord of the Admiralty 1922–24; Chairman of the joint select committee on Indian constitutional reform on whose report was based the Government of India Act of 1935; Viceroy of India 1936–43; Chairman of Midland Bank 1943–52.

[635] The Short Sunderland flying boat. From the outbreak of war in 1939 the Sunderland was used in military service hunting and destroying U-boats, rescuing seamen and engaging so effectively with enemy aircraft that the Luftwaffe nicknamed it 'the flying porcupine'.

[636] British Overseas Airways Corporation, the British state airline from 1939 to 1974, when it merged with British European Airways to form British Airways.

the boats is now being fitted up to V.I.P. standard of comfort and will accommodate the main party. The second will take the luggage and any additional passengers.

B.O.A.C. have much experience of Sunderlands on the India route. Moreover, these boats are convertible into really comfortable passenger aircraft and they can be spared with less difficulty than, say, Liberators. In any case, it is important that British-built aircraft should be used.

You asked for a schedule for Lord Linlithgow's flight from Karachi to this country. Here it is:–

Route

Karachi–Bahrain–Cairo–Djerba–Gibraltar–Poole.

Schedule

20th October	Dep. Karachi	Morning	(07.30 L.S.T.[638])
	Arr. Bahrain	Afternoon	)
	Dep. "	"	) 1½ hrs. stop
	Arr. Cairo	Night	(22.50 L.S.T.)
21st October	AT CAIRO		
22nd October	Dep. Cairo	Morning	(08.00 L.S.T.)
	Arr. Djerba	Evening	)
	Dep. "	Night	) 7 hrs. stop
23rd October	Arr. Gibraltar	Morning	)
	Dep. "	Evening	) 11½ hrs. stop
24th October	Arr. Poole	Morning	(08.30 L.S.T.)

The actual change-over of Viceroys will take place at Delhi, the sector from Delhi to Karachi being flown by the Royal Air Force.

AHMS

In September 1943 Churchill reshuffled his government. Sinclair asked him to consider promoting Harold Balfour, junior minister at the Air Ministry, and Harcourt (Crinks) Johnstone, Secretary of Overseas Trade and one of the other two Liberal ministers in the government.

Sir Archibald Sinclair to Winston S. Churchill
24th September 1943

Dear Prime Minister,

[637] Archibald Percival Wavell, 1st Earl Wavell (1883–1950): British field marshal; Commander-in-Chief Middle East 1939–41, where he destroyed the numerically vastly superior Italian armies in North Africa but could not contain Rommel's Afrika Korps; Commander-in-Chief Southeast Asia 1941–43, defeated by Japanese in Malaya, Singapore and Burma; Viceroy of India 1943–47.

[638] Probably Local Standard Time.

Thank you for giving me a share in your discussions on the proposed reconstruction of the Government. You asked me for my opinion and I gave it you; but of course I shall support whatever you decide – vigorously if need be!

I would only ask you, when you consider changes, which will be consequential on the larger ones, to remember:–

(A.) Crinks

(B.) Harold Balfour

AHMS

Winston S. Churchill to Sir Archibald Sinclair
25th September 1943

My dear Archie,

Thank you very much for your letter.

I have both the men you mention in mind. As you will see I did not go beyond the upper circle.

You ought to know that I have been told that Crinks made an extremely poor Parliamentary performance on his last public appearance. On no account show him this, but find out for yourself.[639]

Yours always,
W

Winston S. Churchill to Sir Archibald Sinclair
13th October 1943
Secret

SECRETARY OF STATE FOR AIR

I am strongly convinced that Air Chief Marshal Sholto Douglas would be an accession to our strength at the top, and would make the best Vice-Chief of the Air Staff available.

I hope this may be arranged as soon as possible.

WSC

The war in North Africa came to an end in May 1943, and in July Sicily was invaded. Anxious to avoid further loss of life, the Italian Fascist Grand Council revolted against Mussolini; he resigned and was arrested on the orders of King Victor Emmanuel, who then entered into secret peace negotiations with the Allies. The Allies invaded the Italian mainland in September and Italy capitulated on the 8th.

[639] Johnstone was never in command of the House of Commons when he spoke, and many Tory MPs took delight in asking obscure questions in attempts to trip him up.

Winston S. Churchill to Sir Archibald Sinclair
22nd October 1943
Most Secret

SECRETARY OF STATE FOR AIR

1. No alteration should be made in the Air Commands in the Mediterranean pending the changes which may soon take place in the highest stations. Should General Alexander[640] succeed to the Supreme Command, I contemplate a unification of the whole Mediterranean, and I doubt whether a separate set of Commanders-in-Chief will be required at Cairo. General Wilson[641] may exercise a wide authority over the rear, leaving Alexander free to direct the Italian campaign personally although Commander-in-Chief. I understand that Marshall[642] wants Tedder as his Deputy here for "Overlord". I am not yet convinced that this is the best plan. If Tedder is moved from the Mediterranean for any reason, especially after Alexander has succeeded to the Supreme Command, the Americans will insist on having Spaatz, and for us it will be a question of finding someone good to sustain him.
2. The movement of Air Marshal Coningham[643] to "Overlord" cannot even be considered before Rome is taken. I am, however, not at all inclined to move him from the Mediterranean theatre since he is so closely linked with Alexander, who will need him: and all the more if Spaatz became Chief of the Air.
3. There really is no need for Sholto Douglas to return to the Middle East. Linnell[644] is quite capable of doing what is necessary in the intervening period, now I hope a short one. There is only one place for Douglas, namely, that of Vice-Chief of the Air Staff. This post I wish him to have, and the sooner the better. I trust you will meet my strong views in this matter.

WSC

You should discuss the above with C.A.S.

---

[640] Sir Harold Rupert Leofric George Alexander, 1st Earl Alexander of Tunis (1891–1969): fought on the Western Front 1914–18; led the Baltic Landwehr, a brigade of ethnic Germans, against the Red Army during the Russian Civil War; commanded 1st Division British Expeditionary Force 1939–40; Head of Southern Command 1940–41; Commander-in-Chief, Burma, 1942; Commander-in-Chief, Middle East 1942–43, instrumental in defeat of Rommel at El Alamein in November 1942; Supreme Allied Commander in Italy 1943–45; Governor-General of Canada 1946–52; Minister of Defence 1952–54.

[641] Henry Maitland Wilson, 1st Baron Wilson (1881–1964): Commander-in-Chief, Middle East, 1943; Supreme Allied Commander in the Mediterranean, 1944; popularly known as 'Jumbo' because of his great height and bulk.

[642] George Catlett Marshall (1880–1959): US Army Chief of Staff 1939–45; Secretary of State 1947–49; proposed European Recovery Programme in 1947, later known as the Marshall Plan; Secretary of Defense 1950–51; received the Nobel Peace Prize in 1953.

[643] Sir Arthur Coningham (1895–1948): commander 4 Group, Bomber Command (based at York), 1939–41; 204 group (Cairo), 1941–43; commander British and American tactical air forces in Tunisia, under General Spaatz, 1943–44; commander 2nd Tactical Air Force (UK), 1944–45.

[644] Sir Francis John Linnell (1892–1944): Controller of Research and Development, MAP, 1941–43: Deputy Air Officer Commander-in-Chief, RAF Middle East/Middle East Command 1943–44; killed in a road accident in 1944.

On 25 October 1943 Churchill telegraphed to Eden: 'Archie says that weather has almost always frustrated Bomber Command's wish to bomb German targets immediately after a Fortress attack. This happens even when the two Commands are sitting side by side. He does not think the shuttle-bombing of industrial Germany would pay because of the substantial salvage and repair organisation which would be required and parks of stores and spares, which means filling a new pipeline with men and stores from America to Russia. He says, "Let the Russians bomb the good targets in the East of Germany and let the British and Americans continue to bomb in the West and South of Germany from Britain and Italy". He asks that you consult the Air Attaché before encouraging Stalin to believe that a close concert is possible at the present time in the teeth of weather and distance.'

Winston S. Churchill to Sir Archibald Sinclair
27th October 1943

SECRETARY OF STATE FOR AIR

1. I cannot form any opinion about the Mediterranean air until the High Commands are settled. I share your high esteem of Park.[645] I do not think the settlement will be long delayed, and it will then be possible to make the whole series of changes involved.
2. I remain of opinion that Sholto Douglas should be made V.C.A.S.[646] This matter affects me very directly as Minister of Defence because of the contacts with the high Cabinet work, especially when C.A.S. is away for conferences. I hope therefore you will meet my wishes in the same way that the other Service Departments do.

WSC

Winston S. Churchill to Sir Archibald Sinclair
30th October 1943
Secret

My dear Archie,

I very much regret to receive your letter,[647] and I still hope you will be willing to meet my wishes. The responsibility for these high appointments falls ultimately upon the Minister of Defence who is of course himself responsible to the War Cabinet, by whom if need be a decision must be taken.

[645] Sir Keith Rodney Park (1892–1975): Air Officer Commanding No 11 (Fighter) Group, 1940; commander RAF in Egypt 1941–42; Malta 1942–43; Air Officer Commander-in-Chief, Middle East Command, 1944; Allied Air Officer Commander-in-Chief, Air Command South East Asia, 1945.

[646] Vice Chief of the Air Staff.

[647] Not found in the archives.

I may add that there is no possibility of Sholto Douglas becoming Allied Air Commander in the Mediterranean. If Tedder is moved, the Command would have to go to an American officer, almost certainly Spaatz. Considering the unfair prejudice the Americans have expressed about Sholto Douglas, it would indeed be foolish to bring him forward there.

Your second suggestion is almost equally inadmissible. That Peirse should go at the beginning of the campaign for which he has been preparing because he has completed two years' service is not a proposal which does justice to the impending operation. Here also, in this Combined Command, we might meet again the American prejudice and have further difficulties. Besides, it does not seem appropriate to invite Douglas to take the secondary Command in the theatre for which he knows he was our first selection for the Supreme Commander. It would be embarrassing from every point of view, and the Americans would certainly resent it.

I think it most important to find for Douglas a purely British position which will assert in a decisive manner our confidence in him and at the same time offer no foothold for American objections. Quite apart from this, I consider Douglas is by far the most highly qualified officer for the post of V.C.A.S., and I desire to have his advice at the centre, especially when the C.A.S. may be abroad. You told me yourself that you regard him as beyond question Portal's successor should a vacancy occur. It should be quite possible to find high employment for Evill.[648] I think you mentioned to me that the post of Director of Personnel would soon be vacant.

Finally, it was my thought to make all these appointments at the time when the changes in the high Command of the Mediterranean and OVERLORD theatres are announced, which will probably not be till after Operation SEXTANT.[649]

Yours ever,
Winston S. Churchill

In late November Churchill and Portal travelled to meet Roosevelt in Cairo. From there Churchill and Roosevelt flew to Tehran to meet Stalin. Sinclair kept Churchill and Portal up to date with the latest bombing figures.

[648] Sir Douglas Claude Strathern Evill (1892–1971): senior air staff officer to Air Chief Marshal Sir Hugh Dowding, 1940; led RAF delegation in Washington 1942–43; Vice-Chief of the Air Staff 1943–45.

[649] Sextant was the Cairo-Tehran conferences, 22 November – 7 December 1943, attended by Roosevelt, Churchill, Stalin and Chiang Kai-Shek. Stalin was reassured that the Allies would invade Western Europe in 1944. The timetable for operations in the Central and South-western Pacific areas was established and it was agreed to continue the war against Japan after Germany was defeated. It was also agreed that former Chinese territories would be returned to China after the war and 'that in due course Korea shall become free and independent'.

Sir Archibald Sinclair to Winston S. Churchill and Sir Charles Portal
MOST SECRET CYPHER TELEGRAM
27th November 1943
IMMEDIATE

Following for Prime Minister and C.A.S. from Secretary of State for Air:–

Many thanks for your FROZEN[650] No. 107.

On Thursday night 224 aircraft of which 200 were Halifaxes dropped 612 tons through nearly ten tenths cloud on Frankfurt. Bombing not well concentrated but fires and heavy explosions were observed. Twelve aircraft missing plus one crashed. In addition one Stirling lost mining.

Yesterday the Americans carried out their biggest operation yet – 508 Fortresses and Liberators on Bremen and 128 on ball bearing factories in Paris. Unfortunately, cloud forced the Paris party to return without bombing but the other party dropped over eleven hundred tons on Bremen. American bombers and fighter escort claim for loss of 29 bombers and four fighters.

Last night 443 Lancasters and seven Mosquitoes dropped 1352 tons on Berlin for the loss of 27 Lancasters plus seven crashed at home. Several fires were found still burning in Berlin from previous attacks. Weather was clear and exceptionally good concentration was achieved in West Central district of Berlin. Fighters thrown off the scent by feints appeared only at end of attack. Casualties were mostly due to flak working with searchlights.

In addition 157 Halifaxes and 21 Lancasters dropped 422 tons on Stuttgart five missing plus two crashed. Good fires were seen in two concentrations one each side of river.

Fires and smoke to 7,000 feet reported Frankfurt from previous night's attack.

Total aircraft despatch last night including mining and leaflets 666 of which 31 are missing and ten crashed.

Conditions at base were very bad, low cloud and rain shifting from airfield to airfield. Fog clearance and the special long runway proved valuable and we are pushing on with fog clearance equipment on airfields in all Group areas.

Still impossible to photograph recent German targets. P.R.U.[651] tried yesterday.

Sir Archibald Sinclair to Winston S. Churchill and Sir Charles Portal
MOST SECRET CYPHER TELEGRAM
3rd December 1943

Following for Prime Minister and C.A.S. From Secretary of State for Air.

Last night 425 Lancasters of which 37 are missing, 15 Halifaxes of which 2 are missing, and 18 Mosquitoes of which 1 is missing dropped 1500 tons mainly on

[650] Codeword for a secret telegram.

[651] Photographic reconnaissance unit.

Southern and South Eastern districts of Berlin. Total 458 aircraft despatched to Berlin of which 40 are missing plus 5 crashed. Good fires visible from 200 miles and smoke up to 15,000 feet. Weather conditions were generally cloudy en route as forecast but thin and broken at target, enabling markers to be seen. Wind strengthened from north so some bombers got south of track on return thus reducing protection from Window. Low cloud and rain at base.

Cloud is still thwarting all attempts to photograph Berlin. Reports from ground sources on results of four recent big attacks indicate that main weight of attacks has fallen on Central, Western and North Western districts. All embassies and legations with exception of Spanish Embassy, also the Ministry of Foreign Affairs, Home Office, Propaganda Ministry and several other government departments are damaged or destroyed. Potsdammer station wholly burnt out and five other stations hit, some severely damaged. Public transport and main line railway traffic in and from the centre of city was wholly suspended. Electricity, gas and water were cut off. No confirmation yet from our sources of Press stories of important industrial damage but evidence of closing down and evacuation of businesses is beginning to come in. It indicates that there is hardly any quarter in the City unaffected. Minimum figure of those bombed out as a result of these four attacks is 800,000.

Sir Archibald Sinclair to Winston S. Churchill
MOST SECRET CYPHER TELEGRAM
17th December 1943

For Prime Minister from Secretary of State for Air.

Last night 482 Lancasters and 15 Mosquitoes on Berlin. Germans refused to be spoofed and Pathfinder Force consisting of the Mosquitoes and 90 Lancasters found fighter flare path already lit over approaches to city. As a result 6 Pathfinder Lancasters were lost.

Losses from main force of 392 Lancasters were 19 but exceptionally bad weather conditions with drifting masses of very low cloud developed at base some 20 minutes before bombers returned resulting in 34 crashes. From these 16 entire crews are safe, and a number of other individuals are known to be safe.

Group Commanders are optimistic about results of attack which appears to have fallen along a line running from S.W. to N.E. across centre of city with main weight in N.E.

Winston S. Churchill to Sir Archibald Sinclair
MOST SECRET CYPHER TELEGRAM
18th December 1943

Prime Minister to Secretary of State for Air.

Thank you for your GRAND 641.[652] I hope the fog clearing apparatus saved some lives. Compliment officers and crews from me on all this series of great attacks.

Sir Archibald Sinclair to Winston S. Churchill
MOST SECRET CYPHER TELEGRAM
19th December 1943

For Prime Minister from Secretary of State for Air.

Thank you for your FROZEN 722. I have conveyed your message to Bomber Command.

Fog clearing apparatus was not used because although cloud was drifting about very low, visibility at ground level was good.

This apparatus is now practically complete at eight airfields, and we are now installing it at seven more, all in Bomber Command. Transport and Coastal Commands will get it later.

On night of 26/27th November eleven Lancasters with crews not specially trained made visual landings at Fiskerton on returning from operations. Apparatus cleared visibility from 450 to 3,000 yards. Rate of landing was one aircraft per three minutes.

P.R. on Berlin still unsuccessful.[653]

Sir Archibald Sinclair to Winston S. Churchill
MOST SECRET CYPHER TELEGRAM
20th December 1943

For Prime Minister from Secretary of State for Air.

Commander-in-Chief[654] sends the following reply.

"Please convey to the Prime Minister our gratitude for his message and our heartfelt wishes for his speedy convalescence[655] and return. His support, advice and unfailing encouragement through four dark and strenuous years have been the mainspring of our effort".

About 20 buildings and other structures have been destroyed or damaged.[656]

---

[652] Telegram dated 17 December 1943.

[653] Photo-reconnaissance, used to update damage estimates following air-raids.

[654] Arthur Harris, Commander-in-Chief Bomber Command.

[655] Churchill suffered from pneumonia during the last two weeks of December. His doctor, Lord Moran, insisted on a three-week convalescence and he rested at Marrakech from the end of December 1943 to mid-January 1944.

[656] Presumably the progress report on Berlin referred to in the previous telegram.

1944

1944 saw the Air Ministry working to continue the air assault on Germany and make detailed preparations for the Normandy landings (Operation Overlord) planned for the early summer. The issue of the leadership structure of RAF/USAAF combined operations was a subject on which Sinclair and Churchill spent much energy in trying to reach agreement with Roosevelt.

Winston S. Churchill to Sir Archibald Sinclair
6th January 1944
MOST IMMEDIATE

Prime Minister to Secretary of State for Air and C.O.S.[657]

1. You may announce that Slessor will be deputy to Eaker and that Sholto Douglas will succeed to Coastal Command.
2. Both Eisenhower and Bedell Smith[658] have spoken to me in anxiety about the air set-out for OVERLORD. They do not like the plan of two tactical air forces under Leigh-Mallory,[659] who also presumably would have some relation to Spaatz, and to Harris and who has apparently let it be known he intends to be a real Commander-in-Chief of the Air. But this is not what was meant at all. I do not consider Leigh Mallory is the equal of Sholto Douglas who so unfortunately got side-tracked, and in any case Tedder with his unique experience and close relation as Deputy to the Supreme Commander ought to be in fact and in form the complete master of all air operations. Everything is then quite simple. There need only be one Tactical Air Force which Leigh Mallory can command. Spaatz will come directly under Eisenhower as his senior officer and can be told to obey Tedder. There will be no difficulty in arranging between Tedder and Harris. I do not like the idea of Tedder being an Officer without Portfolio. We deliberately gave this post to an airman because of the vast part the air is to play in this Battle and he must have all the powers necessary. Pray let me have your views.

WSC

---

[657] Chiefs of Staff.

[658] Walter Bedell Smith (1896–1961): Eisenhower's Chief of Staff; US Ambassador to the Soviet Union 1946–48; Director of the Central Intelligence Agency (CIA) 1950–53; Under-Secretary of State 1954–56.

[659] Sir Trafford Leigh-Mallory (1892–1944): commanded fighter groups 1937–42; Commander-in-Chief Fighter Command 1942–44, commanded Allied expeditionary air forces for the Normandy invasion; appointed Commander-in-Chief Allied air forces in Southeast Asia, but was killed flying out to Burma in November 1944 to take up the post. During the Battle of Britain Leigh-Mallory, who sent his fighters out to meet the German planes before they reached Britain, came into conflict with Park and Dowding, who argued that they would be better deployed defending the airfields. Portal and Sinclair agreed with Leigh-Mallory and, in November 1941, removed Park and Dowding from their posts.

Sir Archibald Sinclair to Winston S. Churchill
MOST SECRET CYPHER TELEGRAM
Grand 1220
7th January 1944

To Prime Minister from Secretary of State for Air
Your Frozen 1134

1. The Slessor and Douglas appointments will be announced on Sunday.
2. C.O.S. are sending you their views on your paragraph 2. What follows are mine.
3. The formations comprised in Allied Air Expeditionary Forces are larger and more complex than your signal suggests. Most important indeed are the British tactical force which Coningham will command and which will work with Montgomery's[660] group of Armies and the American Tactical Air Force under Brereton,[661] one of the best of the American Air Generals, which will ultimately work mainly with the American Group of armies. Leigh-Mallory however as Commander in Chief will be able to reinforce the one from the other as the situation demands and in the meantime is in active command of both British and American Tactical Air Forces.
4. Moreover, Leigh-Mallory is responsible for the Air Defence of Great Britain and in the opening stages of Overlord his responsibility for the allocation of forces between ADGB (including the defence of Overlord bases and communications) and the land battle will be important and will require prompt decisions. In addition Leigh-Mallory commands the British and American Airborne groups and must be the officer who will integrate with the operation of the Tactical Air Forces, those of such heavy bombers from the commands of Harris and Spaatz as are placed at his disposal from time to time by the Chiefs of Staff. He will also have the photographic reconnaissance wing besides a number of miscellaneous units as well as all the administrative supply and operational training units of the British forces under his command. The command of all these forces is believed indispensable to the effective discharge of his responsibilities by the Commander in Chief of the allied air forces under Eisenhower. Leigh-Mallory has been appointed to that post by you and the President at the insistence of the Combined Chiefs of Staff at Quadrant. He is a thoroughly competent officer.

[660] Bernard Law Montgomery, 1st Viscount Montgomery of Alamein (1887–1976): arguably the best British field commander since Wellington; commanded 3rd Division in France, 1939–40; commanded 8th Army in Africa and Italy, 1942–43, under Alexander; won crucial battle of El Alamein, 1942; helped formulate the invasion plan for France, and in the Normandy campaign acted as field commander of all ground forces until August 1944, then led the 21st Army Group; commander British occupation forces in Germany 1945–46; Chief of the Imperial General Staff 1946–48; Deputy Supreme Commander of NATO forces in Europe 1951–58.

[661] General Lewis H. Brereton (1890–1967): commander US Far East Air Force in the Philippines, 1940–42; Deputy Air Commander-in-Chief, Allied Air Forces, Java, 1942; Commander, Middle East Air Forces 1942–43; Commander Ninth Air Force, European theatre, 1943–44; Commander First Allied Airborne Army 1944–45.

He has been called upon to carry these closely articulated responsibilities as one whole. I am sure it would be a mistake to derogate from them or to blur the line of definition between them and the responsibilities of the Supreme and Deputy Supreme Commander.

5. Eisenhower will dictate strategy and policy. Tedder will be there to share his responsibility over the whole field of land, sea and air. We may be fairly confident that more will not be asked of Leigh-Mallory than he will be able to perform. Tedder's experience and the confidence which the Air Staff feel in his judgement will also ensure that the liaison between the Supreme Command, the Air Staff Bomber Command, and I hope Spaatz, will work and that difference of opinion will be resolved with the greatest possible good will and understanding.
6. C.O.S. gave you some weeks ago their general ideas about the contribution which Bomber Command ought to be called upon to make to Overlord – an increasing amount from some weeks before Overlord is launched rising to 100 percent on 'D' Day and for some time after. The Americans want to put Spaatz and Harris directly under Eisenhower. I am convinced that would be a mistake. Not even Tedder has experience of conducting the Bomber Offensive, nor if he is to be an effective deputy over the whole range of land, sea and air should he concentrate exclusively on air problems. Harris should remain under Portal's direction and that of the Chiefs of Staff. The time may come when you will be glad to have him there. Spaatz should, if possible, remain as now under Portal representing the combined Chiefs of Staff.
7. I have seen a good deal of Spaatz and Eaker during the past week. They are in entire agreement with each other and with us that the American Army's idea that Spaatz should control Bomber operations from Italy as well as from here is impracticable. They have decided to make practically no change in the present arrangements, i.e. Spaatz will give Eaker a directive for the use of his heavy bombers which Eaker will carry out as the weather and the operational requirements of Shingle[662] and Anvil[663] may dictate.
8. Harris tells me that the weather over Stettin on Wednesday night was clear and that excellent night photographs were obtained. These show the attack to have been an outstanding success. Hope to get day photographs today.

Churchill wrote at the bottom of this telegram that: 'all these arrangements will have to be reviewed when General Eisenhower assumes effective command. I certainly do not subscribe to them as at present informed. WSC 8.1.44'

[662] Shingle was the name given to the amphibious operation at Anzio, Italy in 1944.

[663] Anvil was the planned 1944 Allied invasion of southern France in the Toulon-Marseille area.

Sir Archibald Sinclair to Winston S. Churchill
19th January 1944

MOST SECRET
PRIME MINISTER

The Cabinet approved the man-power allocations in the Report of the Official Committee. It was there estimated that the effect of the R.A.F. allocation would be that we should reduce the aircrew intake from the Spring of 1944 and squadron strength would fall off from Autumn of 1945; i.e. after that date, aircrews completing their training would only be enough to maintain a front line for the war against Japan, plus the occupation of Europe.

We cannot put this proposal into effect without discussing it with the Dominion Governments, who are partners in our aircrew training plan. We want, therefore, to open discussion with them as soon as possible as to where and how the reductions shall be made.

The Dominions are proud of their training schemes, and from some points of view they will be very sorry to close down any of their schools. It may involve them in political difficulties of their own. Negotiations for the reductions will, therefore, need to be very carefully managed, and we cannot hide from them the fact that we are planning in the expectation that the war with Germany will be over, although the war with Japan will be continuing, in the autumn of 1945.

Lord Cranborne agrees.

Do you object to this course?

Archibald Sinclair

Sir Archibald Sinclair to Winston S. Churchill
16th February 1944

Secret
Prime Minister

You may be interested in this Analysis of our losses in last night's attack on Berlin. It would, of course, be a mistake to draw definite conclusions from the results of one attack even on the scale of last night; but you will observe that the experience of the Halifax III was encouraging.

The Commander-in-Chief is particularly pleased with its flame damping, which is even better than that of the Lancaster.

AHMS

SECRET
BERLIN RAID – 15TH/16TH FEBRUARY

	Despatched		Missing		%	
Main Force		780		35		4.5
P.F.F.[664]		111*		7		6.3
Main Force Halifaxes		295		15		5.1
P.F.F. Halifaxes		19		1		5.3
Halifax IIIs		174		7		4.0
Halifax II/V		140		9		6.4
Lancasters Main Force	485)		20)		4.1)	
Lancasters P.F.F.	76)	561	6)	26	7.9)	4.6

* Includes 16 Mosquitoes – none lost.

Sir Archibald Sinclair to Winston S. Churchill
26th February 1944

PRIME MINISTER

On the 28th January you approved my proposal that Captain Balfour[665] should proceed to Ottawa for the purpose of discussing with the Canadian Minister of National Defence (Air), Mr. Power,[666] the arrangements for reducing the scale of training under the British Commonwealth Joint Air Training Plan and for extending the operation of the Plan beyond 31st March, 1945.

Captain Balfour has now returned, having reached agreement with Mr. Power on both phases of the question.

Mr. Power took advantage of Captain Balfour's visit to hand to him an Aide Memoire approved by the Canadian Government War Committee about the position which will arise if Germany is defeated before Japan, and about the contribution to be made in that event by Canada to the United Nations forces in the war against Japan and in the occupation of enemy territories in Europe.

I attach a copy of this Aide Memoire and of the covering letter from Mr. Power which accompanied it.[667]

664 Pathfinder force.
665 Harold Balfour – see n559.
666 Charles Gavan Power (1888–1968): Canadian MP 1917–55; Minister for National Defense for Air 1940–44, where he promoted the interests of Canadian air forces serving under British command and created Canadian squadrons in Europe; responsible for the local administration of the British Commonwealth Joint Air Training Plan which ran from April 1940 until March 1945 and turned out 131,553 pilots, navigators, bomb-aimers, wireless operators, air gunners and flight engineers.
667 Not available.

Under the original agreement for the establishment of the Joint Air Training Plan very large numbers of Canadian graduates (as well, of course, as Australian and New Zealand graduates) were placed almost unreservedly at the disposal of the R.A.F. on the completion of their training and were posted freely to R.A.F. squadrons although provision was made for the establishment of a certain number of Dominion squadrons to which a minority of the Dominion graduates were to be posted.

When, however, it became necessary in 1942 to negotiate for the extension of the period of operation of the Plan for another two years, i.e. till the 31st March, 1945, the Canadian Government took the opportunity of assuming considerably more control over the Canadian aircrews placed at the disposal of the R.A.F. and in the negotiations which Captain Balfour has just concluded the Canadian Government have stipulated that they shall henceforth have still more control over them.

The Aide Memoire marks a further step in the same direction and indicates that the Canadian Government have made up their minds that in the post-German phase of the war all R.C.A.F.[668] personnel attached to the R.A.F. shall be at the disposal of their own Government.

Since these developments mean that we shall not be able to use the R.C.A.F. personnel attached to the Royal Air Force as freely and as effectively as we should otherwise have been able to do, I cannot profess to welcome them, but we have no alternative but to accept them and we shall of course do our very best to minimise any ill effects which may result.

In forwarding the Aide Memoire to me Captain Balfour stated that, whilst it confirmed Canada's determination in the post-German phase of the war to assume much greater control over all R.C.A.F. personnel, he was assured by Mr. Power that the change-over to complete Canadian control would not be begun until after the defeat of Germany and that there was no question of Canada's not being willing in the post-German phase to place her Air Force under the strategical direction of the Royal Air Force. Mr. Power had remarked to him that when that phase of the war was reached the R.C.A.F. would have the alternative of working with the United States Air Force or with the Royal Air Force, and that undoubtedly they would choose the latter alternative. In Mr. Power's words "They would prefer to be in the family; the devil you know rather than the devil you do not know."

Captain Balfour states that Mr. MacKenzie King[669] desires that the issues raised in the Aide Memoire should be discussed between the two Governments as soon as possible. Meanwhile I am arranging for the air aspects of the policy laid down in the Aide Memoire to be examined in the Air Ministry and a report prepared.

Archibald Sinclair

---

668 Royal Canadian Air Force.

669 William Lyon Mackenzie King (1874–1950): Leader of the Canadian Liberal Party 1919–48; Prime Minister of Canada 1921–26, 1926–30, 1935–48.

Winston S. Churchill to Sir Archibald Sinclair
7th March 1944

I understand that you are considering the best means of making minor improvements in the allowances of the forces. I am quite firm about changes in basic pay. But the war has now been going on a long time, and this, together with the arrival of large numbers of better-paid American Service personnel, does justify some concession to our own forces. Without having gone into the matter deeply, I consider that it would not be unreasonable if the concessions made involved an additional expenditure at the rate of £20,000,000 per annum. Furthermore, I think that special consideration should be given to married personnel, and in this category especially to the lowest-paid classes.

I should be glad if you would take the above into account in framing your proposals, which you will no doubt submit to me.

While during 1940–43 the requirement had been to train as many pilots and support crew as possible to build up fighter and bomber squadrons, by 1944, so successful had this policy been that experienced pilots were being placed on the retired list to make way for younger men.

Winston S. Churchill to Sir Archibald Sinclair and Sir Charles Portal
13th April 1944

SECRETARY OF STATE FOR AIR
CHIEF OF THE AIR STAFF

Surely you can find employment for a D.S.O.,[670] M.C.[671] and D.F.C.[672] of 50 who commanded No. 10 (F) Group during the Battle of Britain and flew a Hurricane himself by day and by night. I wish more of our senior officers adopted this practice, at any rate in bombers, for which the Americans have gained so much distinction. I hope you will look into this again.

WSC

Sir Archibald Sinclair to Winston S. Churchill
26th April 1944

PRIME MINISTER

1. I am very sorry that we have no employment to offer to that gallant and experienced officer, Air Vice-Marshal Brand. Indeed, there are a number of officers,

[670] Distinguished Service Order.
[671] Military Cross.
[672] Distinguished Flying Cross.

equally good, who have reached their ceiling and whom we are being compelled to place on the retired list to make room for younger men. It is our definite policy to maintain a flow of promotion through the Service and we have already had to place a number of distinguished officers of the highest rank on the retired list: others must follow shortly. I know you are as keen as I am that room should be made at the top for younger men with first-hand experience of operations in this war, but this necessarily involves dispensing with older men with fine records.

2. We encourage officers up to Station Commander, i.e. up to the rank of Group Captain, to take part personally in operations. Above that rank the other duties of a Commander prevent his keeping himself sufficiently in practice for flying on operations. Most of such higher Commanders have been on operations when in command of lower formations and some have done complete operational tours with squadrons. There is only one pilot in a heavy bomber; he is the captain of the aircraft. A Group Commander would be ill qualified to act in that or any other capacity in a heavy bomber, and there is no room for a passenger. Moreover, we cannot afford the loss of Commanders who by long experience have become expert in planning and control of operations and have rightly gained the confidence of their units.
3. On the other hand, our policy is to bring on into the Air Rank Commands our best young officers who have themselves been through operational tours in this war in more junior rank. It is this aim, tempered by consideration of other qualifications and experience, that guides promotion and necessitates retirements even though these on occasions involve officers with some admirable qualities.
4. I have much sympathy with Air Vice-Marshal Brand's complaint that on retirement he is entitled only to the pay of his substantive rank of Air Commodore, but our rules are the same as those for the Navy and Army, and the Admiralty and the War Office have hitherto been content with them. My efforts to get them altered have so far been unsuccessful. I have, however, recently raised the matter again and it is now on the point of being reviewed once more by all the Departments concerned.

AHMS

Operation Overlord, the Allies' long-awaited invasion of northern France, finally took place on 6 June 1944, when 156,000 men were landed on the beaches of Normandy in what remains the largest ever combined military operation. Sinclair visited Normandy shortly after the D-Day landings.

Sir Archibald Sinclair to Winston S. Churchill
8th July 1944
Personal

Dear Winston,

Just a line to say how grateful I am to you for letting me and Portal go over to Normandy yesterday.

I won't bother you with a description of our visit, but the keen-ness of the officers and men and their confidence in themselves, their equipment and their mastery over the enemy was impressive.

I saw Jock.[673] His squadron is still on the mark IV[674] which has the American engine. I hope we shall get it re-equipped soon. Nevertheless, he seemed very happy, extremely fit and keen to stay with his squadron.

They all seemed glad to see us. Quite junior officers and sergeants said how "kind" it was of me to come out! I remembered then how welcome visitors were in the last war – not, perhaps, to high commanders and staff but to the troops in or near the line.

A visit from you would give them unbounded pleasure – and to me too if you would take me in your train!

Yours ever,
Archie

Sir Archibald Sinclair to Winston S. Churchill
17th August 1944

Dear Winston,

You will remember the interest which you took – and the opposition which you encountered – in securing the continued existence of the 6th Guards Tank Brigade. It has covered itself with glory in the recent fighting. I am told that General Dempsey[675] sent them a letter of high commendation on their exploits and General Verney (Ralph Verney's nephew) who commanded them has now been given command of the famous 7th Armoured Division.

I think you may be interested in a letter which Verney[676] has sent me. It is mainly about George Grey[677] who served in that Brigade, but I have marked a passage in which Verney pays a glowing tribute to the Churchill tank.[678]

---

[673] Probably John Colville – one of Churchill's principal private secretaries from 1940 to 1944. Wrote *The Fringes of Power, Downing Street Diaries 1939–1955* (W.W. Norton & Company, 1984).

[674] The Mark IV Spitfire.

[675] Miles Dempsey (1896–1969): commanded British 2nd Army during the D-Day landings in June 1944.

[676] Gerald Lloyd Verney (1900–57): commander 2nd Battalion Irish Guards 1940–42, 6th Guards Armoured Brigade 1942–44, 7th Armoured Division 1944, 1st Brigade, Italy – Austria, 1945.

[677] George Charles Grey (1918–44): Liberal MP for Berwick-on-Tweed 1941–44; Captain, 4th Battalion Grenadier Guards; commanded part of the 6th Guards Tanks Brigade, equipped with Churchill VII tanks,

Yours ever,
Archie

Sir Archibald Sinclair to Winston S. Churchill
18th August 1944

Prime Minister

I understand that Eisenhower is thinking of taking over direct command of the land operations in North Western France within the next 3 or 4 weeks. As a consequence of this, he wants to make some alteration in the 'set up' of the Air Command. His idea is that there should be one Tactical Air Force under an American Commander working with Bradley[679] and one under a British Commander working with Montgomery. Above them would be a Commander of the two Tactical Air Forces – I understand he wants Coningham – directly under his own Headquarters. Tedder, under this arrangement, would include among his functions as Deputy Supreme Commander the co-ordination of the Allied Strategic and Tactical Air Forces.

Eisenhower has not yet produced his plan in detail for this organisation, but I imagine that Coningham as the Tactical Air Force Commander would have administrative command of his rearward services and of his operational training organisation, while A.D.G.B. would hive off and come directly under Portal. If this happens, Leigh-Mallory's occupation would be gone. He has done well as Air Commander-in-Chief. Eisenhower, before these changes were being considered, wrote to Portal in terms of the highest commendation of Leigh-Mallory's work.

Now it so happens that Mountbatten[680] is very anxious to get Leigh-Mallory as the Air Commander-in-Chief in South East Asia. He told Portal this when he was first appointed Supreme Commander and he reverted to the subject when he came over here the other day. On his own initiative, but with Portal's permission, he asked

during the advance through Normandy following D-Day; killed in action; a rising star in the Liberal Party, his death at the age of twenty-five was deeply mourned within the Parliamentary party. In the subsequent by-election, Sir William Beveridge was elected Liberal MP in Grey's place, but lost the seat in the 1945 general election.

[678] Verney wrote with great pride about the 'magnificent' Churchill tank's ability to cross very rough terrain with 100% reliability.

[679] Omar Nelson Bradley (1893–1981): Assistant Secretary, US General Staff 1940–41; Commandant, Infantry School 1941–42; Commander, 82nd and 28th Infantry Divisions 1942–43, II Corps, North Africa and Sicily, 1943, and First Army and 12th Army Group in Normandy invasion and European campaign 1944–45; Chief of Staff, US Army 1948–49; first Chairman, NATO Military Staff Committee 1949–50.

[680] Louis Francis Albert Victor Nicholas Battenberg, 1st Earl Mountbatten of Burma (1900–79): great-grandson of Queen Victoria; naval commander; chief of Combined Operations Command 1942–43; Supreme Allied Commander, South-East Asia, 1943–46; Viceroy of India 1947 (the last Viceroy), Governor-General 1947–48; First Sea Lord 1955–59; Chief of the Defence Staff 1959–65; killed by an IRA bomb on his boat at his holiday home in Ireland in 1979.

Leigh-Mallory whether he would like to join him and Leigh-Mallory welcomed the proposal. Mountbatten told me himself that he was keen to get him.

Peirse himself has been commanding in the South Eastern Asia theatre for nearly 3 years and it would be unreasonable to expect him to carry on until the end of the Japanese war. If, however, we are going to make a change, now is the time to do it, so that a new Commander-in-Chief will have the time to get comfortably into the saddle before the big operations start.

It is difficult to take definite decisions until we know precisely what Eisenhower wants. We understand, however, that he would be willing to release Leigh-Mallory on the 1st October; so I feel that I should like to consult you at this stage. Portal and Tedder and I have had several talks on this subject and I should be grateful if you would let him discuss it with you.

I hope all is going well with you and that you are having a restful as well as an interesting time. The battle in Normandy is in an exhilarating phase. The only black spot in the whole war is Warsaw.[681]

AHMS

In August 1944 Churchill travelled to Italy to review the progress of the war on the Southern European front. He returned to Britain in early September and almost immediately left to meet Roosevelt in Quebec.

Winston S. Churchill to Sir Archibald Sinclair
TOP SECRET CYPHER TELEGRAM
21st August 1944

Prime Minister to Secretary of State for Air.

Your minute of August 18th regarding set-up of the Air Command. I entirely approve of your proposals which I have discussed with CAS. They constitute a great improvement on the present double storeyed arrangements. Please take action at once accordingly.

All good wishes. I am having a very easy time and have felt ever so much better through moving about in the sun-shine.

[681] By the late summer of 1944 forward units of the Red Army had reached the suburbs of Warsaw. On 1 August the Polish Home Army, loyal to the Polish Government in exile in London, rose in revolt against the Germans and briefly gained control of the city. But three SS armoured divisions arrived to suppress the revolt, and the Soviets stood by across the Vistula. The rising lasted for sixty-six days, but by October, German artillery and aircraft had destroyed most of the city, and 55,000 Poles had been killed. Stalin, planning for the post-war world, clearly wanted the pro-Western Polish forces destroyed and let the Germans do it for him.

In late 1944 Churchill was again considering a minor government reshuffle. Sinclair lobbied for his fellow Liberal MP, Dingle Foot, to be given a new challenge.

Sir Archibald Sinclair to Winston S. Churchill
PERSONAL & SECRET
28th October 1944

Dear Prime Minister,

Harold Balfour tells me that he wants to stay here.[682] In these circumstances, would you consider Dingle Foot for the post[683] for which you had provisionally designated Balfour?

I do not know if you have followed Foot's work at the Ministry of Economic Warfare, but I am sure that Selborne[684] will tell you that he has done conspicuously well. He has handled important negotiations in Washington and with the Swedes and the Swiss successfully. He makes a good speech in the House of Commons and I should be grateful if you would consider his claim.

Yours ever,
Archie

Winston S. Churchill to Sir Archibald Sinclair
29th October 1944

PERSONAL AND SECRET
SECRETARY OF STATE FOR AIR

The appointment is a Conservative one, and I have already appointed Osbert Peake.[685]

I hope to find a place for Foot when his present office is abolished.[686]

WSC

[682] Balfour was actually offered the position of Resident Minister, West Africa, together with a peerage in the next Dissolution Honours List. He accepted and left the Air Ministry in November 1944.
[683] Financial Secretary to the Treasury.
[684] Cecil Roundell Palmer, 3rd Earl of Selborne (1887–1971): Conservative MP for Newtown, Lancashire, 1910–18, Aldershot 1918–40; ally of Churchill in the struggle against the India Act of 1935; Director of Cement, Ministry of Works, 1940–42, responsible for the construction of anti-invasion pillboxes all over southern England; Minister of Economic Warfare 1942–45.
[685] Osbert Peake, 1st Viscount Ingleby (1897–1966): Conservative MP for Leeds North 1929–56; Parliamentary Under-Secretary of State to the Home Office 1939–44; Financial Secretary at the Treasury 1944–45; Minister of National Insurance 1951–53, for Pensions and National Insurance 1953–55.
[686] With the war in Europe practically won the need for a large Ministry of Economic Warfare had passed. Foot remained at the Ministry, however, until the end of the Coalition Government in May 1945. In April 1945 he was part of the British delegation to the San Francisco Conference which helped frame the United Nations charter.

In early November Churchill arranged for his doctor, Moran, to treat Sinclair (it is not known for what).

Sir Archibald Sinclair to Winston S. Churchill
2nd November 1944

My dear Winston,

Lord Moran was kind enough to come with Dr.Young this morning and your secret weapon was at once brought to bear on the enemy who is already in full retreat!

It was most awfully kind of you to think of it. I hate causing so much trouble but I am sure that this stuff of yours will quickly put me right.

Randolph had a merciful escape. He must be gaining credit and friends for Britain in the Balkans.[687]

Your two cocks, Alexander and Montgomery, are fighting well. The "Crowbar" principle takes time but it looks as if it works if you give it time.

Thank you again for your unfailing help in time of trouble.

Archie

1945

1945 brought final victory in Europe. From January to April Bomber Command kept up a steady bombardment of German cities – including Dresden, where a massive use of bombs and incendiaries created a firestorm leading to substantial loss of life. The ferocity of this attack at such a late stage in the war, when it was evident that Germany would soon be defeated, has been a matter of continuing historical controversy. Although Sinclair had assured the House of Commons in August 1940 that Britain would not use its air power to rain terror down on the German people, it was far from clear whether the policy that he, Harris, Portal and Churchill had agreed had lived up to this ambition.

1945 also bought a return to party politics, and the breakup of the Coalition Government at the end of May.

Winston S. Churchill to Sir Archibald Sinclair
1st January 1945

SECRETARY OF STATE FOR AIR

[687] Churchill's son Randolph had been parachuted into the Balkans to work alongside Tito's rebels.

1. I cannot think of a better Commander for S.E.A.C.[688] than Air Marshal Sir Keith Park. I am not acquainted with Air Vice-Marshal Cochrane[689] and I am sorry to hear that Air Chief Marshal Sir Frederick Bowhill's period has expired. However I am glad to give my approval to your choice.
2. I think it wrong to move Air Marshal Slessor from his war command in the Mediterranean. He has been there less than a year and just as he is beginning to get a grip of all the complications of this theatre, he is to be moved out to a home appointment. I think he should stay where he is at any rate until the end of the German war. This habit of moving people from vital war positions just as they have mastered the detail of their work, because of the routine of the service, is not beneficial to His Majesty's affairs.

WSC

Sir Archibald Sinclair to Winston S. Churchill
26th January 1945
TOP SECRET

PRIME MINISTER

You asked me last night whether we had any plan for harrying the German retreat from Breslau.

The target which the enemy may offer in a large scale retreat Westward to Dresden and Berlin is best suited to Tactical Air Forces. This is impossible to bomb from high level.

The Russians, as they swing round on lines parallel to the retreating Germans, should have excellent opportunities for ground strafing with their fighters.

It would be extremely difficult for our heavy bombers to interfere with these enemy movements by direct attack on their lines of retreat. The targets are at extreme range from U.K. and Mediterranean bases; precise Intelligence as to movements is not available; and it would be inadvisable to make attacks within the Russians' tactical area without prior consultation and co-ordination.

I feel strongly that the best use of our heavy bombers at the present time lies in maintaining the attack upon German oil plants whenever the weather permits. The benefits of these attacks are felt equally by the Russians and by ourselves and nothing should be allowed to interfere with them. There may, however, be occasions when the weather is unsuitable for attacks on the comparatively small targets presented by the oil plants but yet would permit area attacks on Eastern Germany. These opportunities might be used to exploit the present situation by the bombing

---

[688] South East Asia Command.

[689] Sir Ralph Alexander Cochrane (1895–1977): Air Officer Commanding 7 Group, RAF, 1940; Director, Flying Training, Air Ministry 1940–42; Air Officer Commanding 3 and 5 Group, RAF Bomber Command 1942–45; Vice Chief of the Air Staff, Air Ministry 1950–52; Managing Director Rolls Royce Ltd 1956–61.

of Berlin and other large cities in Eastern Germany such as Leipzig, Dresden and Chemnitz, which are not only the administrative centres controlling the military and civilian movements but are also the main communications centres through which the bulk of the traffic moves.

To achieve results of real value, a series of heavy attacks would probably be required, and weather conditions at this time of the year would certainly prevent these being delivered in quick succession. The possibility of these attacks being delivered on the scale necessary to have a critical effect on the situation in Eastern Germany is now under examination.

Winston S. Churchill to Sir Archibald Sinclair
26th January 1945

SECRETARY OF STATE FOR AIR

I did not ask you last night about plans for harrying the German retreat from Breslau. On the contrary, I asked whether Berlin, and no doubt other large cities in East Germany, should not now be considered especially attractive targets. I am glad that this is "under examination". Pray report to me tomorrow what is going to be done.

WSC

Sir Archibald Sinclair to Winston S. Churchill
27th January 1945
TOP SECRET

PRIME MINISTER

Your minute M.115/5. The Air Staff have now arranged that, subject to the overriding claims of attacks on enemy oil production and other approved target systems within the current directive, available effort should be directed against Berlin, Dresden, Chemnitz and Leipzig or against other cities where severe bombing would not only destroy communications vital to the evacuation from the East but would also hamper the movement of troops from the West.

The use of the night bomber force offers the best prospects of destroying these industrial cities without detracting from our offensive on oil targets, which is now in a critical phase. The Air Officer Commanding-in-Chief, Bomber Command, has undertaken to attempt this task as soon as the present moon has waned and favourable weather conditions allow. This is unlikely to be before 4th February.

AHMS

Winston S. Churchill to Sir Archibald Sinclair
21st February 1945

SECRETARY OF STATE FOR AIR

Pray convey my warm thanks to all concerned for the excellent arrangements made in connection with the air courier service during my visit to the Crimea and on the return journey.[690] The service was maintained with impressive efficiency and regularity and I need not tell you how much it helps me when away to have this close link with London headquarters. I wish I could have seen the officers personally.

WSC

In early March 1945, 'Crinks' Johnstone, Liberal Minister for Overseas Trade, died at his desk in Whitehall at the age of forty-nine. In a letter to his Chief Whip, which shows how the focus of attention was shifting to the pending general election and a return to politics as usual, Churchill wrote: 'I notice you do not propose to give the Liberals any representation in place of Crinks Johnstone. While the Coalition lasts they are entitled to keep their present proportion unless you advocate an immediate declaration of war. I have, in my contacts with Archie, assumed that he would have another Liberal in, and this is still my position. However it would be a good moment to put to him the extremely shabby position which he and his Liberals are adopting at the present time, having three, if not four, Ministers[691] with only about 17 members; preparing to run large numbers of candidates to defeat our people in election; and thirdly, obviously holding themselves up to auction on the morrow of the polls. Moreover there is no real difference of principles between them and us on practical issues such as exists between Socialists and anti-Socialists.'[692] In the end, the Liberal MP James de Rothschild was appointed to a Parliamentary Secretary position in place of Johnstone.

At the end of March Churchill wrote to Sinclair requesting the release of his daughter Sarah from the RAF to help him while his wife travelled to Russia.

Winston S. Churchill to Sir Archibald Sinclair
28th March 1945

SECRETARY OF STATE FOR AIR

During Mrs. Churchill's absence on public work from this country, which may last about seven weeks, I require the assistance of my daughter, Section Officer Oliver, at week-ends, Friday to Monday, when I constantly have official visitors to entertain.

[690] Churchill's visit to the Yalta summit with Roosevelt and Stalin.

[691] As well as Sinclair, Foot and Johnstone, the Liberal Lord Sherwood was Parliamentary Secretary at the Air Ministry 1941–45.

[692] National Archives: PREM 4/65/2.

Pray see that she is instructed as a matter of duty to be at my disposal at these times, and for these purposes.

WSC

In a speech to the Commons on 26 March Sinclair laid claim on behalf of the RAF to a major share of the credit for defeating the V1 'doodle-bug' flying bombs and V2 rocket attacks. This claim provoked a stiff response from Churchill.

Winston S. Churchill to Sir Archibald Sinclair
28th March 1945

SIR ARCHIBALD SINCLAIR

You have no grounds to claim that the R.A.F. frustrated the attacks by the V weapons. The R.A.F. took their part but, in my opinion, their effort ranks definitely below that of the A.A. artillery, and still farther below the achievements of the Army in cleaning out all the establishments in the Pas de Calais which so soon would have opened a new devastating attack upon us in spite of all the Air Force could do.

As to V2, nothing has been done or can be done by the R.A.F.

I thought it a pity to mar the glories of the Battle of Britain by trying to claim overweening credit in this business of the V weapons. It only leads to scoffing comments by very large bodies of people.

WSC

With the end of the war rapidly approaching, Sinclair decided that the British Commonwealth Air Training Plan should be wound up; there was no longer any need for training large numbers of aircrew, and the training needs that remained could be met within mainland UK facilities. Churchill, however, proved reluctant to acquiesce.

Winston S. Churchill to Sir Archibald Sinclair and Sir Charles Portal
16th April 1945

SECRETARY OF STATE FOR AIR
C.A.S.

I never understood why all this thing was broken up so abruptly. Many people have been distressed thereby. The nucleus should have been preserved. I have however agreed to your various telegrams, but please press me no further.

WSC

Winston S. Churchill to Sir Archibald Sinclair
18th April 1945

SECRETARY OF STATE FOR AIR

Why is it necessary to fly aircraft in such great numbers over London during the night? Has this any war value at all? It is a great nuisance.

WSC

On the night of the 14/15 April 1945, 500 Lancasters and 12 Mosquitoes attacked Potsdam. This was the first time that Bomber Command heavy bombers had entered the Berlin defence zone since March 1944 but the approach, across parts of Germany recently captured by Allied troops, led to only one Lancaster being lost; it was shot down by a night fighter. The aiming point was the centre of Potsdam and the intention was to destroy the local barracks (the depot of the old German Guards regiments) and the railway facilities. The attack was reasonably successful and severe damage was caused in Potsdam, but bombs also fell in the nearby northern and eastern districts of Berlin.

At this late stage of the war Churchill's concerns about the strategic value and moral acceptability of such raids led him to write a curt questioning note to Sinclair. In fact this was the last raid of the war by a major Bomber Command force on a German city.

Winston S. Churchill to Sir Archibald Sinclair and Sir Charles Portal
19th April 1945

SECRETARY OF STATE FOR AIR
C.A.S.

What was the point of going and blowing down Potsdam?

WSC

Sir Archibald Sinclair to Winston S. Churchill
20th April 1945

PRIME MINISTER

Your M.353/5.[693] The bombers on Monday night were going to Pilsen, in Czechoslovakia – about the limit of their range. They were routed over London as it was the shortest cut to the target and left the biggest margin of safety. The course to the East of London is barred by the gun belt on the East Coast over which our bombers would be obliged to pass at height and risk detection by enemy radar on the Dutch Islands and consequent attack by night fighters. It is open to question whether it would have made very much difference if they had been routed a little

[693] See letter dated 18 April 1945.

further to the West. The Commander-in-Chief will avoid London at night unless it is absolutely essential to pass over it.

It so happens that there was also an exercise going on that night and the newspapers jumped to the conclusion that the aircraft which were flying noisily and low over London were engaged on that exercise. There were not many aircraft engaged on this exercise, and, apart from 4 aircraft which operated at heights between 10,000 and 17,000 feet, all were flying at 17,000 feet and over. The reasons for flying over London are that it is necessary for practising the A.A. defences of London (gun, searchlight and radar crews) and for the training of Bomber Command Crews. A.A. Command attach the greatest importance to these exercises which are essential to maintain the efficiency and morale of the A.A. defence personnel who cannot be moved away from the London static defences for exercises.

AHMS

During March and April Churchill's thoughts increasingly turned to the ending of the Coalition and the pending general election. Although he was keen to delay it until after the defeat of Japan, his Coalition partners in the Labour and Liberal Parties were not prepared to acquiesce. It was nearly ten years since the last general election and Attlee, in particular, felt that the best interests of the country, and the Labour Party, required that a general election be held at the earliest available opportunity now that the war in Europe had been won. Sinclair was also under considerable pressure from his MPs and activists to break with the Conservative-dominated National Government. Vocal backbench Liberals such as Tom Horabin and Clem Davies feared that the Liberal Party would become sucked into a perpetual alliance with the Tories which would ultimately lead them to the same fate as Ernest Brown's Liberal Nationals, who were by then mere appendages to the Conservatives (and effectively merged into the Conservative Party in 1947).

Winston S. Churchill to Sir Archibald Sinclair, Ernest Bevin and Ernest Brown
29th April 1945

MR BEVIN[694]
MR ARCHIBALD SINCLAIR
MR ERNEST BROWN[695]

---

[694] Deputising for Atlee who was attending the San Francisco conference which founded the United Nations.

[695] Alfred Ernest Brown (1881–1962): Liberal MP for Rugby 1923–24, Liberal and Liberal National MP for Leith 1927–45; Minister of Labour 1935–40, Secretary of State for Scotland 1940–41; Minister for Health 1941–43; Chancellor of the Duchy of Lancaster 1943–45; Minister for Aircraft Production 1945; Chairman of the Liberal Nationals 1940–45. The Liberal Nationals were the former Liberal MPs who, originally led by Sir John Simon, had supported the National Governments of MacDonald, Baldwin and Chamberlain during the 1930s; Sinclair was particularly sensitive about their use of the 'Liberal' brand.

The question of the broadcasts at the impending Election must be the subject of a Conference this week between the Leaders of the Conservative and Labour Parties and the two Liberal Parties. The period during which these arrangements would hold good would be limited to the 38 days between The King's announcement of his intention to dissolve Parliament three weeks later and the date of the poll. A preliminary talk on the subject would be advisable before we meet the B.B.C. authorities.

WSC

Sir Archibald Sinclair to Winston S. Churchill
1st May 1945

PRIME MINISTER

Your 420/5.

Presumably the question of broadcasts at the impending Election would fall to be considered on the basis on which the Government itself was formed in May 1940, when you invited the Leader of the Labour Party, together with me as leader of the Liberal Party, to join you.

I imagine that is what you must have in mind, and I shall be glad to enter these discussions on that footing, from which such successful results and happy relationships have sprung during the last five years.

There is, of course, only one Liberal Party.

Archie

Winston S. Churchill to Sir Archibald Sinclair
3rd May 1945

My dear Archie,

I note the views which you express in your minute of May 1. What I am suggesting is a preliminary talk between four Party Leaders.[696] No one is committed to anything by attending this conversation, but everyone will have an opportunity of expressing his own views. The questions will have to be settled by those who are willing to discuss them.

Yours very sincerely,
Winston S. Churchill

On a personal level Sinclair would willingly have stayed in government serving under his lifelong friend, at least until the war in the Far East had been concluded. The Liberal

[696] Where Churchill tried to gain agreement to continue the Coalition until the autumn of 1945.

Party Assembly, however, had voted in February 1945 not to continue to serve in the Coalition after the fall of Germany.

Sinclair could see the argument for delaying the election until the autumn, when a new electoral register would be available, and in his conversations with Churchill led the Prime Minister optimistically to think that the Coalition could continue in some shape.

Winston S. Churchill to Sir Archibald Sinclair
18th May 1945

My dear Sinclair,

From the talks I have had with you, I have gathered the impression that the Liberal Party, instead of leaving the Government on the defeat of Germany, would be willing to continue the Coalition until the autumn. I have given the most careful and anxious thought to this suggestion, and I regret to say that in its present form I cannot feel it would be in the public interest. A union of Parties like that which now exists should come together and work together not for a particular date without regard to world events, but for the achievement of some great national purpose transcending all Party differences. For the last five or six months our Ministerial and Parliamentary affairs have been increasingly affected by the assumed approach of a General Election at the end of the German War. This has not conduced to the national interest so far as domestic affairs are concerned.

I therefore make you the following proposal, which I earnestly hope you will not readily reject, namely, that we should fix upon another object for our joint endeavours and adjourn the question of our separation until it is gained. The First Lord of the Admiralty has already expressed in his speech in the City of London his regret that a General Election should be held before the Japanese War was finished. It would give me great relief if you and your friends were found resolved to carry on with us until a decisive victory has been gained over Japan. On this basis we could work together with all the energy and comradeship which has marked our long and honourable association.

I am conscious however in the highest degree of our duty to strengthen ourselves by a direct expression of the nation's will. If you should decide to stand on with us, all united together until the Japanese surrender is compelled, let us discuss means of taking the nation's opinion, for example a referendum, on the issue whether in these conditions the life of this Parliament should be further prolonged.

I am sending letters in similar terms to Mr. Attlee, and to Mr. Ernest Brown.

Yours sincerely,
Winston S. Churchill

Winston S. Churchill to Sir Archibald Sinclair
18th May 1945

My dear Sinclair,

Further to my letter of today, I shall be glad if you would insert after the words, 'gained over Japan' in paragraph 2, the following additional sentence:

"In the meanwhile we would together do our utmost to implement the proposals for social security and full employment contained in the White Papers which we have laid before Parliament."[697]

Yours sincerely,
Winston S. Churchill

Sir Archibald Sinclair to Winston S. Churchill
19th May 1945

Dear Prime Minister,

Thank you for your two letters of yesterday. You are right in saying that the Liberal Party is willing to continue the Coalition under your leadership until the autumn.[698] It seems to us that the situation in Europe which the Foreign Secretary described in Parliament on Thursday as urgent, grave and disquieting, and the numerous imperfections of the May Register, would justify that course.

At the same time, both you on behalf of the Government and I on behalf of my Party have declared against a lengthy prolongation of the life of the existing Parliament. Postponement of the Election for an indefinite period, e.g. until the end of the Japanese War, would in these circumstances present a problem of some difficulty. No doubt this is why you propose a referendum.

This would be an innovation in constitutional practice which has more than once been considered in times of political crisis, and rejected for reasons which cannot lightly be set aside. You suggest, however, that other means to taking the nation's opinion might be considered.

Therefore, while the Liberal Party would, I know, prefer that the Election should be held soon after the October Register comes into force, I am of course willing to accept your invitation to discuss with you and Mr. Attlee the possibility of preserving the structure of the National Government under your leadership until the end of the Japanese War.

---

[697] The 1942 white paper *Social Insurance and Allied Services* and the 1944 white paper *Full Employment in a Free Society*. Both written mainly by Sir William Beveridge, a highly regarded economist and expert on unemployment and welfare (and Liberal MP 1944–45), the two papers together provided the blueprint for what became the British welfare state.

[698] Presumably, given the vote of the Liberal Assembly in February 1945 not to continue the Coalition beyond the end of the war in Europe, Sinclair is referring to the Parliamentary Liberal Party here. Even this small group of MPs was far from united in supporting the continuance of the Coalition, however; almost a third supported the end of the Coalition.

Many of those whom I should wish to consult had already scattered to their homes for the Whitsun weekend by the time I received your letters. I shall, however, as soon as possible consult the leading members of my Party on the proposal which you have put to me.

Yours sincerely,
Archibald Sinclair

The refusal of the Labour Party to continue in government with Churchill led to the ending of the Coalition Government – and of Sinclair's ministerial career – on 23 May 1945.

Sir Archibald Sinclair to Winston S. Churchill
24th May 1945

Dear Prime Minister,

My answer to the message which you conveyed to me yesterday is, of course, that my office is at your disposal.

I am proud to have served so close to you and to have occupied the war station which you assigned to me here during these tremendous years.

I part with sadness from you – our tempestuous and lion-hearted leader – and from all the loyal friends with whom I have worked in Cabinet and in this Department.

We have done something together in the past five years. For my part, I can imagine no greater honour than to have served in your war administration, which now passes not ingloriously into history.

Yours sincerely,
Archibald Sinclair

Sir Archibald Sinclair to Winston S. Churchill
26th May 1945

Dear Prime Minister,

I observe, in paragraph 1 (6) of the minutes of our meeting on Friday, that you are recorded as saying that, if it became necessary for you to make a broadcast speech of a non-political nature on the military or international situation, you would be free to do so, and that the Leader of the Labour Party might follow you on the same subject.

If those circumstances arose, I feel bound to ask that the Leader of the Liberal Party should also be allowed to broadcast. To leave the Liberal Party out would be both invidious and contrary to precedent. On the outbreak of war and, if I remember aright, on other occasions, I was invited by Mr. Chamberlain to take part in broadcasts by the Leaders of the three Parties in times of crisis.

Yours sincerely,
Archibald Sinclair

Winston S. Churchill to Sir Archibald Sinclair
26th May 1945

My dear Archie,

I grieve more than I can say that you are separating yourselves from the Government of the country in these months when there is much to gain or lose. Particularly I grieve to separate from you. But alas, we are all the puppets of fate.

I do not wish to embark upon controversy, but I think it will be shown that the Liberal Party have made a crowning mistake in allying themselves with the forces of Socialism and trying to beat down to a minimum those which stand for freedom. The course you are forced to take is the most likely one to lead to political confusion and partisanship which it will not be easy to repair. I do not think the Liberal scheme of doing as much harm as possible to the new Government in the hopes of making a good bargain with the other side will be successful or be greeted with respect. No mercy will be shown you by the Socialists however much harm you may do to the national causes, which I think will draw up in very strong array. We shall do our utmost to carry on the business of the country successfully, and I am strongly of opinion that its confidence will be given to us.

I need scarcely say that however things go, it will make no difference to our life-long friendship. I am happy to think that you have conducted the mighty Air Power through all the course of this 5 years World War.

Yours always,
Winston S. Churchill

Sir Archibald Sinclair to Winston S. Churchill
28th May 1945
PRIVATE

My dear Winston,

Thank you so much for your letter of the 26th May. I will not repeat what I wrote to you the other day about my sorrow in leaving your famous administration.

Neither do I wish to embark upon controversy, but you will be making a mistake if you allow yourself to be convinced that the Liberal Party at this Election is acting from motives of faction. I remember the old days when the Party had money and, like other Parties, richly fertilised the Constituency Associations. Now the movement is all the other way – a genuine and spontaneous movement from Liberals scattered (alas! too widely scattered) all over the country. We may be right or we may be wrong in details of our policy and in our tactics – but there is no doubt that we are responding to a public demand for an organ of Liberal expression.

I cannot expect you to approve our course; but, just as I know perfectly well that when you took the leadership of the Tory Party you were actuated not by personal or Party motives, but by those of strengthening your Administration for the tasks of war, so I feel confident that you, too, will give me and my Liberal friends credit for doing what we honestly believe to be in the public interest.

Again I thank you for entrusting me with this Department and for the privilege which I have now enjoyed for five years of being associated with the Royal Air Force in their glorious achievements.

Yours ever,
Archie

Winston S. Churchill to Sir Archibald Sinclair
29th May 1945
Private and Personal

My dear Archie,

I am sorry but I cannot accept your recommendation of Foot for a Privy Counsellorship on this occasion; but I am aware of his good services at the Ministry of Economic Warfare (of which Selborne has spoken in the highest terms) and I should be prepared to submit his name for the K.B.E.[699] if this would be acceptable to him. Perhaps you would be good enough to let me know as soon as possible.

Yours ever,
Winston S. Churchill

Winston S. Churchill to Sir Archibald Sinclair
Telegram
30th May 1945

From the Prime Minister to Sir Archibald Sinclair.

Thank you so much my dear Archie for your charming letter, Party politics apart.

Winston

Winston S. Churchill to Sir Archibald Sinclair
1st June 1945

My dear Archie,

[699] Knight Commander of the Order of the British Empire.

Yours of May 26th. I quite agree that you should also express your views should such a situation arise. Any speech I make may not however necessitate either a rejoinder or confirmation. Should you wish you would be free.

Yours ever,
Winston S. Churchill

Sir Archibald Sinclair to Winston S. Churchill
23, Gayfere Street,[700]
Westminister, S. W.1.
3rd June 1945

Dear Prime Minister,

Thank you for your letter of 1st June about broadcasting.

If the occasion arises, I shall certainly consult you, and I should not wish to use the privilege unnecessarily.

Archibald Sinclair

[700] Headquarters of the Liberal Central Association – the support organisation for the Parliamentary Liberal Party.

Part 5

Twilight and Dusk 1946–1960

Introduction

The Liberals fought the election of July 1945 in the hope of a breakthrough. They fielded 306 candidates, 2,225,000 votes were won but only twelve Liberal MPs were elected. Sinclair lost his seat by the narrowest of margins, with just 61 votes separating the three candidates in Caithness & Sutherland. It was a bitter blow, reflecting the extent to which Sinclair had focused exclusively on the Air Ministry and winning the war at the expense of maintaining his reputation in the constituency. The Labour landslide also, of course, removed Churchill from the premiership and relegated the Conservative Party to opposition in the Commons.

Sinclair was exhausted from his period in office. He and his family rented out their London home and moved back to Thurso Castle. The Liberal Party elected Clement Davies as Sinclair's replacement as Liberal leader – but this was seen as being very much an interim replacement, as Gandar Dower, the Conservative who had defeated Sinclair, had promised before the election to resign and fight a by-election when the war against Japan was won. Many expected this to result in Sinclair's swift return to Parliament and to the leadership of his party. In the event Gandar Dower reneged on his promise and no by-election occurred.[701]

Sinclair declined all requests from the Liberal Party to remain active in national politics. He exchanged many letters with Clement Davies offering support and advice to the new leader but steadfastly refused to be drawn away from his Thurso base. Even when Churchill tried to tempt him, in November 1946, into being involved in a cross-party 'handling group' to argue for a United Europe, Sinclair refused, saying: 'I am with you in spirit, but cannot be with you in action unless and until I return to Parliament'.[702]

In 1949 he finally returned to national politics with a speaking tour of major cities. The 1950 general election saw a national swing to the Conservative Party and it was a difficult election in which to attempt to take any Tory seat, even one where the MP had been deselected by his local party. Sinclair fought a tough campaign but again suffered the agony of missing election by a whisker – coming second to the new Conservative candidate, Sir David Robertson, by just 269 votes.

The Liberal Leader in the House of Lords, Lord Samuel, was keen to retire and there was significant pressure on Sinclair to accept a peerage and lead the party in the

[701] Gandar Dower was not a successful MP. Many of his own party were appalled at his refusal to honour his commitment to seek re-election when Japan was defeated, and his relations with his constituency party declined to the extent that he was deselected ahead of the 1950 general election.

[702] See letter from Sinclair to Churchill of 18 November 1946, page 430.

Upper House. When Attlee called a surprise election in 1951 Sinclair decided not to stand again for the Commons, and with the return of his old friend Winston Churchill to office, he was offered a peerage, becoming Viscount Thurso of Ulbster in the new Prime Minister's first honours list. In January 1952, however, he suffered the first of a series of strokes that gradually undermined his health throughout the decade. He had been staying over Christmas and New Year at his shooting lodge, Dalnawillan, on the Thurso estates. When he was taken ill the snow around the lodge was so deep that no medical assistance could reach him for more than ten days. In February he was transferred to London and then to Oxford for specialist medical attention. He gradually recovered and by 1954 was able to take his seat in the Lords.

Throughout the 1950s Sinclair and Churchill remained in regular communication. Churchill visited the Sinclairs at their Twickenham home and the Sinclairs visited both Chartwell and 10 Downing Street. Sinclair remained a staunch supporter of the aging Prime Minister and followed debates in the Commons through *Hansard*. He was delighted at Churchill's 'Indian summer' premiership – although he was one of the few confidants to whom Churchill admitted that he suffered a number of strokes – and his letters were full of support and praise for the Prime Minister's handling of the Commons. He became increasingly disillusioned, however, at the level of parliamentary debate and at the new tactics that he felt the Labour Party was deploying to disrupt the Prime Minister, writing to the *Daily Telegraph* in April 1954, for example, to complain about the declining standards of opposition. When Churchill announced his retirement in 1955, Sinclair wrote: 'you leave No.10 at the post-war peak of the country's prosperity at home and of its prestige abroad, dominating the House of Commons and secure in the affection and admiration of your fellow-countrymen. Few think of you as a party leader but rather as the leader of the nation and of the free world.'[703]

Sinclair and Churchill remained close friends for fifty years. Although Sinclair lived his career in Churchill's shadow he was not alone in this, as Churchill's gigantic talents and achievements tower above those of almost any other twentieth-century politician. Sinclair was a talented parliamentarian and a capable minister. He had a successful private and family life and, unlike Churchill, he did not live for politics alone. As the historian Paul Addison wrote, 'Sinclair had two great loyalties which account for his two main contributions to public life. He believed in Liberalism and revived it when it was down; and he believed in Churchill and revived him when he was down.'[704]

After his election defeat in 1945, Sinclair returned to live full-time at the family seat at Thurso Castle. On New Year's Day 1946, it was announced that Churchill had been appointed to the Order of Merit.[705]

---

703 See letter dated 8 April 1955 from Sinclair; page 450.

704 Quoted in the *Dictionary of National Biography, 1961–1970*, p. 950.

705 Order of Merit: British honorary institution founded by Edward VII in 1902 to reward those who provided especially eminent service in the armed forces or particularly distinguished themselves in science, art, literature, or the promotion of culture. The order is limited to only twenty-four members. The order

Sir Archibald Sinclair to Winston S. Churchill
Thurso Castle
1st January 1946

Dear Winston,

A happy new year! The announcement of your O.M. adds happiness to our New Year's Day. Posterity will honour, but neither the King nor Parliament can discharge, the immeasurable debt which we owe you for your leadership in the war; but meanwhile it is fitting that the King should have given you the highest award which it is in his power to bestow.

Lloyd Griscom cables me that he has asked you to stay with him in Florida. You will remember him as Pershing's representative at the War Office when you were Secretary of State. He has a nice house in which I stayed 15 years ago, in North Florida, which might be in a different continent from the country round Miami and Palm Beach – tall, moss-hung – wild and beautiful.

I have told him that I did not imagine that, having reached your destination in South Florida, you would be willing to up-root yourself, till you went on to deliver your University oration; but having enjoyed Lloyd's hospitality both in Florida and on Long Island – most delightful, considerate and warm-hearted hospitality too – I feel bound to commend it to you.

I hope so much that you will have a pleasant and respectful visit to the States and I was delighted to read that you had refused all public engagements except one!

Caithness is rapidly becoming a little corner of Poland! 7,000 troops are coming this month (including an armoured brigade with tanks) and there are two Polish fighter squadrons besides at Wick. This, with 3,000 German prisoners, makes quite a sizable addition to a Scottish population of 27,000. Luckily Marigold and I like Poles but 7,000 idle troops in a strange land with no immediate purpose in view are likely to get a bit restive!

With every good wish from us both to you and Clemmie for 1946,

Archie

Churchill arranged that all ministers who had served in the 1940–45 Coalition Government should receive a commemorative medallion. Sinclair received his in June 1946.

Sir Archibald Sinclair to Winston S. Churchill
Thurso Castle
30th June 1946

My dear Winston,

---

carries no title or knighthood, but a member is entitled to add 'O.M.' after his or her name.

Thank you for the bronze medallion. Your thoughtfulness in designing and sending so stirring a gift evokes countless memories of your kindness and friendship – as well as of the massive achievements of the Coalition (in which the post which you allotted to me was the proudest and happiest which I ever have occupied or even can occupy in the public service) under your mighty leadership.

As bronze is the mirror of the form and wine of the heart[706] – so this medallion will always reflect to me and my family the glory of the Coalition and its chief; and we will drink to your health, happiness and immortal fame.

Yours ever,
Archie

In October 1946 Churchill investigated the feasibility of forming a cross-party group of British politicians and opinion-formers to consider what steps should be taken to advance the cause of a United States of Europe. His relative, Duncan Sandys, spoke to Sinclair to sound him out about whether he would be prepared to join the group. Churchill's enthusiasm for a United States of Europe is not widely known and is certainly rarely referred to by current Conservative politicians, who prefer to use Churchill as a totem of British independence.

Sir Archibald Sinclair to Winston S. Churchill
Thurso Castle
7th November 1946

My dear Winston,

It was grand seeing you the other night and to hear from your own lips about your plans for forcing the growth of the United States of Europe. Philip Lothian used to talk to me about it, as part of his ideas for Federal union, before the War; but then it seemed to me a little remote and not quite consistent – at any rate in the short view, which was then supremely important – with the League of Nations line which I was pursuing. Now it is urgent.

When Duncan Sandys[707] spoke to me about it last week and told me that you were thinking of inviting me to join a re-constituted 'Focus',[708] I told him that I

[706] Quoted from Aeschylus (*Fragments* 384).

[707] Duncan Edwin Sandys, 1st Baron Duncan-Sandys (1908–87): Churchill's son-in-law (married to Diana); Conservative MP for Lambeth 1935–45, Streatham 1950–74; Minister of Works 1944–45; Minister of Supply 1951–54; Minister of Housing 1954–57; Minister of Defence 1957–1960; Secretary of State for the Colonies and Commonwealth Relations 1960–64; sacked from the opposition front bench by Edward Heath in 1966 over his support for Ian Smith's Unilateral Declaration of Independence for Rhodesia; ennobled 1974; a strong supporter of European integration as a means of avoiding future conflict, at the time of this letter he was involved in establishing the United Europe pressure group in the UK.

[708] 'Focus [on Freedom and Peace]' was the name of a group of anti-appeasement politicians who met at luncheons in 1937–38 to encourage support for a foreign policy of peace through strength.

was glad; but I also told him that, unless and until I returned to Parliament, I should be glad to be associated with the work of the 'Focus' and to be kept informed of its proceedings.

I was still more pleased when you confirmed this to me yourself and sketched the outline of your plans. Again, however, I stressed to you, not only that I could not attend meetings, but also that I ought not to be regarded as a representative of the Liberal Party so long as I remain up here and am no longer taking an active part in the councils of the Party. You, on the other hand, implied – unless I misunderstood you – that the new group would not work through private and confidential discussions, like the old 'Focus', but that it would come out into the open and organise national and international conferences.

As I told you that night, Violet[709] had mentioned this project to me before I saw you. Apart from that one conversation with her, I have mentioned it to nobody, because you impressed upon me – and upon the others who were present at the beginning of our talk at the Other Club[710] – the need for secrecy at this stage. I have, however, been thinking about it on my way home; and my conclusion is that, so long as I remain in political exile, I ought not to join a political group which is being designed, not merely for private discussion, like the old 'Focus', but for public action.

Perhaps it is premature for me to write like this; but, as you broached the subject to me yourself, I thought I ought to write before you take the trouble to send me an invitation.

In the meantime, any help I can give – e.g. if you want to get Violet and other representative Liberals to join, I might be able to help – I will give gladly; and perhaps, if and when I return to Parliament, you will give me another chance to join your group. After twenty-three years of public service, however, I know that, until I can regain the confidence of my friends and neighbours here sufficiently to be returned to Parliament, my proper place is not in the forefront of a great political movement.

One thing I forgot when I saw you was this – that, just before I left home to go to London, I received the book of your Secret Session speeches. I am most grateful for it. Some day I must get you to inscribe it for me.

Yours ever,
Archie

Winston S. Churchill to Sir Archibald Sinclair
12th November 1946

My dear Archie,

---

[709] Violet Bonham Carter – see n296.

[710] The dining club founded by Winston Churchill and F. E. Smith in 1911 (and still going strong). It is limited to fifty Parliamentarians of whom no more than twenty-four can be MPs.

Some time ago I was about to send you a letter on the lines of the ones I sent to Citrine. I waited however to receive responses from others and, in the meanwhile, Duncan told me you had had a talk to him and that you were enthusiastic with the project. On this we met, but evidently you were thinking of one thing and I of another. This project has nothing whatever to do with Party, and is concerned solely with world affairs; nor has it anything to do with reviving the 'Focus'. I thought you would like to come in. The invitation is sent you not as Leader of the Liberal Party but as an individual of national standing.

Citrine was very sympathetic and anxious to join, and Attlee entirely approved, but in the end he has come to the conclusion that the Coal Board must claim his undivided attention. Acting on his and Attlee's advice, I have asked Mr. Gibson,[711] the well-known Trade Unionist, and he has accepted.

I now send you herewith a draft statement of Aims and a short communiqué, the second of which I am proposing to publish in the near future, when the list is completed, so that this small Handling-Group will stand out before the world.

I hope you will be among them.

Yours ever,
W.

Sir Archibald Sinclair to Winston S. Churchill
Thurso Castle
18th November 1946

My dear Winston,

Thank you for your letter of the 12th November. Your enterprise is conceived on the grand scale. I share your belief in the importance – indeed grandeur – of its aim, a United Europe. I am with you in spirit, but cannot be with you in action unless and until I return to Parliament. Samson without his hair was not more disabled than I am from participating in national politics without my seat in Parliament.

It is easy to see how a misunderstanding – a slight one – arose. Duncan met me by chance at a party, and cannot have been authorised to make a full disclosure of your plans. So it was that we discussed them on the assumption that you would be working on the lines of the old 'Focus'; and even then I made it plain to Duncan that distance would prevent me from playing much part.

Now, however, I know the full scope of your plans, and realise that your significantly named 'Handling Group' is intended, not for discussion and for the exercise of indirect influence through the political Parties and newspaper Editors and proprietors, but for bold, public and sustained action, not confined to our own country. I am deeply touched and happy that you should have thought of asking me to join you at

[711] George Gibson (1885–1953): Chairman of the Trades Union Congress 1940–41; Director of the Bank of England 1946–48.

the very start of the campaign, but I could not justify your confidence or carry my fair share of the work and responsibility while I am living up here.

I am delighted to hear that you have recruited Gibson. Bevin once impressed upon me that his standing in the Trade Union world is unique.

May your enterprise bring peace, order and happiness to the distraught peoples of Europe.

Yours ever,
Archie

In February 1947 Churchill's brother, Jack, died after a series of heart-related illnesses. Sinclair had known Jack for more than forty years.

Sir Archibald Sinclair to Winston S. Churchill
Thurso Castle
24th February 1947

Dear Winston,

I have just heard about Jack on the wireless – a black day for Marigold and me – a cruel blow for you and Clemmie.

He looked terribly ill when I was last in London – but happy in his new flat with Clarissa not far from him and happy, as always, in his devotion to you and yours to him.

The loss of Jack must be almost the worst thing that has ever happened to you, dear Winston. Jack's friendship was precious and all who held it must share your grief – and Clemmie's – as we do.

Yours ever,
Archie

Churchill replied on 28th February by telegram: 'Thank you both for all your sympathy about Jack. Winston'.

Sir Archibald Sinclair to Winston S. Churchill
Thurso Castle
3rd February 1948

My dear Winston,

Now that Robin is 25 years old, my Children's Trust comes to an end and you will soon be receiving that last batch of papers from my lawyers.

I have often felt that I was asking too much of your kindness and friendship in bothering you with the affairs of this little Trust – especially during the war when I used to say so to dear Jack; but he used to put me off and tell me that he could give you the papers to sign at the least inconvenient times. So, feeling rather ashamed, I continued to trespass!

This Trust has already justified its existence and, although this is only one of many debts of friendship which I owe you, I could not let it pass out of existence without thanking you for your help.

Robin will be entering the Home Farm in May. It is a big undertaking for him – rather like taking over the command of a battalion after a short period in the ranks and several attachments to experience battalion and brigade commands, but with no experience in command of a company or even a platoon; but he is keen and sensible and has the gift of leadership – so I hope he will be successful.

The newspapers were frightening about your illness in Morocco but we gathered later that it didn't put you off your stride for long.

With love from us both to you and Clemmie.

Yours ever,
Archie

Winston S. Churchill to Sir Archibald Sinclair
11th February 1948
Private

My dear Archie,

I am sorry you did not come into our United Europe movement as one of its founders. Great developments have followed. General Marshall said publicly that it was a link in his train of thought, and now Bevin and the whole of HMG are committed to positive action far greater than I had hoped to see in my lifetime. The difficulties about defining the frontiers of United Europe have, for the time being, been settled by the sixteen nations pact,[712] although of course any of the ones inside the Iron Curtain are to join the club as and when they please or dare. Violet, Walter Layton, Lady Rhys Williams[713] are very staunch regular supporters and attend all my committee meetings. Gollancz[714] and our Socialist members have stuck to their guns in spite of a Party ban. I hope this ban will soon be lifted. There is considerable division in the Socialist Party about this.

[712] In 1947 sixteen Western European nations formed the Conference for European Economic Cooperation, a permanent organisation aiming to continue work on the recovery programme for Europe and in particular to supervise the distribution of aid through the Marshall Plan. The Conference became the Organisation for European Economic Cooperation in April 1948 and the Organisation for Economic Cooperation and Development (OECD) in 1961.

[713] Lady Juliet Rhys Williams (1898–1964): Honorary Secretary, Women's Liberal Federation, 1943; joined the Conservative Party, 1945; Honorary Secretary, United Europe Movement, 1947–58, Chairman from 1958; opposed Treaty of Rome and campaigned vigorously against joining the Common Market, which she thought would hand over British sovereignty to Europe and betray the Commonwealth.

[714] Victor Gollancz (1893–1967): publisher; established Victor Gollancz Ltd in 1928, and Left Book Club in 1936; one of the founder members of the Campaign for Nuclear Disarmament in 1958.

Perhaps you will consider whether this all-Party and non-Party movement of a cultural, moral and sentimental character may even now receive your support.

Yours ever,
W.

Sinclair replied to Churchill on 19th February declining his plea to reconsider direct involvement in the United Europe movement, but promising that 'any small influence I can exert will be used on Liberals and others in support of your campaign. Your speeches and action inspired the Marshall Plan and the development of your campaign will facilitate its progress.'

Sir Archibald Sinclair to Winston S. Churchill
Dalnawillan,
Altnabreac,
Caithness
30th October 1948

My dear Winston,

Thank you for your book.[715] As a gift, it is unique – as exciting a gift as a good horse and as lasting as there are descendants of mine to enjoy it and take the same pride as I do in its possession.

I hope Randolph will be very happily married and that his fiancée finds favour in your sight and in Clemmie's! Marigold is good with her son-in-law but a daughter-in-law would be a sterner test of her matriarchal quality!

I read your last speech in the House of Commons. It was splendid! No need to ask if you are feeling well! The silence which greeted your challenging repetition of your tribute to the American possession of the atom bomb as the bulwark of peace was much more than a personal triumph for you.

With love from us both to you and Clemmie,

Yours always,
Archie

In December 1949, Sinclair visited Chartwell for two days. Reporting on his trip in a letter to Lord Beaverbrook dated 19th December, he observed that: 'Clemmie was younger, more active and agile in supervising everything, more exquisitely neat than ever and in excellent queenly looks. Winston was recovering from a very bad cold but he was in grand form – as lively, and incessant, in his conversation as he was in Cabinet in the old days, eating and drinking and smoking as voraciously as ever. He took me round the farms, showed me short-horns, and Jerseys and then a huge brick hen-house which he

[715] *The Gathering Storm*, the first volume of Churchill's *History of the Second World War.*

had built himself – Chickenham Palace. Alongside was a noisome and messy little piece of bare ground – Chickenham Palace Gardens. "What kind of hens?" I asked. "Oh, I don't bother about the details," growled Winston. He seemed hopeful but not, I thought, strongly confident about the result of the General Election.'[716]

The general election took place on 23 February 1950. Sinclair narrowly failed to regain his Caithness constituency. Overall the results were reasonably encouraging for Churchill: the Conservatives won 298 seats, and Labour 315, while the Liberals dropped from twelve to nine. Labour had an overall majority of six.

At the end of the war, Korea, a Japanese protectorate since 1905, had been occupied by Soviet troops in the north and US troops in the south; in 1947 the division effectively became permanent after the failure of negotiations to achieve reunification. In June 1950 North Korean troops invaded South Korea in an attempt at reunification by force; UN (mainly US) troops came to the south's aid, and China to the north's. The war ended in 1953 with the borders of the two Koreas largely the same as they had been in 1947.

Sir Archibald Sinclair to Winston S. Churchill
Dalnawillan,
Altnabreac,
Caithness
27th July 1950

My dear Winston,

I have received an invitation from the General Secretary of the 'New Commonwealth' to sign a statement on the Korean situation.[717] I assume that you have seen it. I enclose a copy of my reply because, while I can't agree to sign it, I should hate to be out of step with you on the big issue of defence.

If MacArthur[718] has gained enough time to make his position impregnable, the Americans have done well, though I feel sorry for the poor South Koreans as one town after another goes up in flames. But how long will this Korean ulcer run and where will Stalin strike next?

I am waiting for the newspapers carrying reports of your debate yesterday.

With love from us both to you and Clemmie.

Yours ever,
Archie

[716] Quoted by Martin Gilbert in *Never Despair: Winston S. Churchill, 1945–1965*, p. 497.

[717] The New Commonwealth was a society for the promotion of international law and order through the creation of an international tribunal and police force. Churchill was its president until 1950.

[718] General Douglas MacArthur (1880–1964): Chief of Staff US Army 1930–35; commanded US forces in Philippines, 1941; Commander Allied forces, Southwest Pacific Theatre 1942–45; Commander, Allied occupation of Japan 1945–51; Commander, UN forces in Korean War 1950–51.

In mid-July 1951 Sinclair wrote to his old leader, asking if Churchill would agree to broadcast an appeal on BBC radio on behalf of the Royal Air Force Benevolent Fund. The BBC made a special concession to Churchill, allowing him to give the broadcast from his home.

Sir Archibald Sinclair to Winston S. Churchill
Dalnawillan,
Altnabreac,
Caithness
14th July 1951

My dear Winston,

You will see my name on a letter which will reach you in a day or two from the Royal Airforce Benevolent Fund. We are not the only people in the Country who need your help but we need it very much. The boon we crave is four and a half minutes of your time for a Broadcast from Chartwell.

We realise that it is a big thing we ask of you because it must be the highest ambition of every suppliant for public benefaction to persuade you to broadcast for them. Our plea for this especial favour rests on the affection and admiration in which you are held by the Service whose uniform you so often wore and still on occasion wear, and on our great need for your help. The Royal Air Force lacks the ancient famous endowments of the older Services and can only look to the Benevolent Fund as its friend in need and, as the men grow older, as their children grow up and their education becomes more expensive, and as the Service enters once more upon a period of expansion, the potential demand for help is constantly increasing. Meanwhile, in times of peace, high prices and heavy taxation, the difficulty of raising funds is also increasing.

This is why this Broadcast, granted to help us by the BBC after four and a half years importunity, is so big a chance to help the airmen whom we exist to serve. Will you seize it for us?

We hope so much that Clemmie is getting well and strong again. Please give her our love.

Yours ever,
Archie

Winston S. Churchill to Sir Archibald Sinclair
26th July 1951

My dear Archie,

Thank you for your letter of July 14th about the broadcast appeal for the Royal Air Force Benevolent Fund. I was going abroad in August but expect to be back about the middle of September and will be very glad to help the Fund in this way.

Yours ever, W

Sir Archibald Sinclair to Winston S. Churchill
Dalnawillan,
Altnabreac,
Caithness
28th July 1951

My dear Winston,

I have looked forward so anxiously to your answer about the broadcast that your acceptance seems almost too good to be true! I doubt if you can realise how grateful everybody connected with the Service will be to you.

Yours ever,
Archie

Sir Archibald Sinclair to Winston S. Churchill
Brooks's Club
17th September 1951

My dear Winston,

It was a moving broadcast that you gave us last night. The final passage was superb. I listened with admiration and thankfulness which everyone connected with the Benevolent Fund must have shared.

Fighter Command flew me up for the Battle of Britain dinner on Saturday. There were more than a hundred (nearer 150 I think) pilots present all of whom had fought between the dates which you fixed for the battle (15th July to the 4th December, I think).[719] Every mention of your name was so warmly cheered as if they were all Conservatives (which they were not! I found myself talking to a man with a particularly plucky record of fighting in that most lethal of aircraft – the fighter Blenheim, who confessed that until the outbreak of war he had been a Blackshirt!)

I hope your visit to France did Clemmie good and that she is as well and strong as you sounded last night. I fly home tomorrow but expect to be returning to London about the beginning of November when I shall hope very much to see you.

Yours ever,
Archie

Winston S. Churchill to Sir Archibald Sinclair
Telegram
19th September 1951

Thank you so much dear Archie.

---

[719] There is no definitive agreement around the formal dates of the Battle of Britain. The Ministry of Defence uses the dates 10 July – 31 October 1940.

In October 1951 Attlee chose to go to the country in an attempt to bolster his slim majority. Labour won just 295 seats, however, while the Conservative won 321 and the Liberals just six. Churchill asked the Liberal leader Clement Davies to join his government, with the offer of a cabinet post at the Ministry of Education. Fortunately for the longer-term survival of the Liberal Party, the offer was declined.

Sinclair did not stand at the general election and in the New Year's honours list of 1952 was given a peerage by Churchill for his public services.

Sinclair was quick to offer the Prime Minister advice on the organisation of the Air Ministry after the election.

Sir Archibald Sinclair to Winston S. Churchill
Dalnawillan,
Altnabreac,
Caithness
27th November 1951
Personal

My dear Winston,

This letter should reach you on Friday and bring you birthday greetings from Marigold and me.

This birthday, at any rate, must be a happy one for you. Clemmie's recovery from her illness and your victory at the General Election are enough to ensure that. Your Government has got swiftly into its stride and commands more support in the House of Commons than seemed likely before parliament met. As I wish for the strength and prosperity of our country and for the happiness of my own children, so I must, and do devoutly, wish for the success of your Government and for a very happy return of your birthday next year.

I have only just come home from London where I saw something of my old war-time friends. I was delighted to hear from them what a strong and stimulating impact the new Secretary of State for Air[720] had already made on the Air Ministry. The backwardness of aircraft production, however, is alarming.

The Chinese (or, if you like, the Russians) have many squadrons of Nene-powered aircraft,[721] capable according to General Vandenberg[722] of trans-sonic speeds, while the R.A.F. has none and Naval Aviation only one (Attacker) squadron.[723] Nor have we got one squadron equipped with jet bombers.

[720] William Philip Sidney, 1st Viscount De L'Isle (1909–91): Conservative MP 1944–45, succeeded to peerage 1945; Secretary of State for Air 1951–55; Governor-General of Australia 1961–66.

[721] 'Nene' was a Rolls-Royce manufactured turbojet engine.

[722] Hoyt Sanford Vandenberg (1899–1954): US Deputy Chief of Air Staff 1943–44; Deputy Air Commander-in-Chief, Allied Expeditionary Forces, 1944; commander US 9th Air Force 1944–45; Director of Central Intelligence 1945–47; Vice Chief of Staff US Air Force 1947–48; Chief of Staff US Air Force 1948–53, succeeding General Spaatz.

[723] The Supermarine Attacker was derived from the Supermarine Spiteful, an intended replacement for

I have no patience with those who demand that Transport and Coastal Command types should be given equal priority with bombers and fighters. For bombers and fighters must gain that air superiority without which Transport Command, Coastal Command and Army Co-operation squadrons cannot effectively function.

Nevertheless, the situation now is quite different from what it was in the last war when we deliberately left the development and production of transport aircraft to the Americans. Then we had very few civil aircraft and none comparable to those which the Americans were already producing. Now our latest types of civil aircraft are superior to American types. Then Lease/Lend enabled us to disregard export production and concentrate on war production. Now export production ranks as *secundus inter pares* with re-armament. Production for export is, however, limited less by the ability of our customers to buy than by shortage of labour and materials. Surely, then, we should concentrate labour and materials on the production for export of goods which will not only be saleable but which will also, by being produced, add to our war potential.

Our new jet civil aircraft and bombers are un-matched. There will be a big market for Comets.[724] Surely there must be on the stocks – or at least on the drawing board – a civil version of our splendid Valiant?[725] I heard (but it may be a false rumour) that Boulton and Paul[726] are producing a remarkable freighter of huge capacity. If labour and materials could be diverted from the manufacture of ordinary consumption goods (a big job for Walter Monckton[727] – an inspired appointment, incidentally!) to the production of these transport aircraft, we might achieve in the world market for civil aircraft the same order of supremacy as we have in shipbuilding. In addition, the tools and equipment could be switched over in war to meet the requirements of the R.A.F.

When you formed your government in 1940 you created M.A.P., a decision which was abundantly justified by events. Towards the end of the war you appointed

the Spitfire; the first production aircraft flew in April 1950. The Attacker was soon out of date and was replaced in front-line service by the Sea Hawk, in 1954.

[724] The de Havilland Comet entered service as the first commercial jet airliner on 2 May 1952; it could carry 36 passengers at a cruising speed of 720 kph (450 mph) over a distance of 4000 km (2500 miles). Within eighteen months two Comets had crashed after fuselage failure, and the Comet was withdrawn as a civil airliner, though a modified military version remained in service until 1967.

[725] The Vickers Valiant, which served through most of the 1950s and into the early 1960s, was the first of the British 'V-bombers', the long-range jet bombers which were the backbone of the UK's nuclear deterrence force; the Valiant was followed by the Victor and the Vulcan.

[726] Boulton Paul Aircraft Ltd was a Norwich-based manufacturing company that started life as an ironmonger's shop and began aircraft production in 1915; during the Second World War it produced such planes as the Defiant fighter and the Fairey Barracuda, a naval dive bomber, torpedo and reconnaissance aircraft. Today it is a part of the TI international engineering group.

[727] Walter Turner Monckton, 1st Viscount Monckton of Brenchley (1891–1965): Conservative MP for Bristol 1951–57; Minister of Labour 1951–55; Minister of Defence 1955–56; the only cabinet minister who disagreed with Eden's policy during the Suez Crisis, he was moved to be Paymaster-General 1956–57.

a Cabinet Committee of which I was a member to consider the organisation of Supply to the Fighting Services. I advocated the resumption of responsibility for research, development and supply by each Service Department. P.J. Grigg took the same line and I distinctly remember that Oliver Lyttelton[728] supported us. We also discussed two other policies, first, the continuation of M.A.P. and of the Ministry of Supply (ancillary to the War Office) and, secondly, the erection of the Ministry of Supply into a department for supplying all the Service Departments; but, unless I am much mistaken, support for this last alternative was confined to our Socialist colleagues. Nobody, however, suggested for one moment that the Ministry of Supply should not only be responsible for supplying all three Service Departments but should also undertake a wide range of responsibility for matters of civil policy and administration including the nationalisation or de-nationalisation of Iron and Steel. The Cabinet, if I remember right, reached no decision on our recommendations. The Ministry of Supply with its present functions and responsibilities is the creation of the Socialist Government and the responsibility for this alarming (but not unforeseen) backwardness of aircraft production is theirs alone.

Surely it is now urgent to make the wheels of aircraft production spin round? I have encountered two main currents of opinion as to how this should be achieved:–

- By creating forthwith a Ministry of Aircraft Production.
- By relieving the Ministry of Supply of all its civil responsibilities (except in the jurisdiction of civil transport aircraft) and bringing it alongside the Service Departments under the Ministry of Defence, with the intention of creating a Ministry of Aircraft Production on the outbreak of war.

The second alternative looks nice and administratively symmetrical but surely the Ministry of Aircraft Production would have a better chance to operate efficiently in war if it had time to run itself in before the war started? Moreover, is not the lag in aircraft production sufficiently serious to justify drastic action now?

I hope you won't think it presumptuous of me to write to you on these matters of grave importance but I rely upon your friendship and on your knowledge of my deep and abiding interest in the strength of our country and the welfare and efficiency of the great Service with which you brought me into association.

We shall surely broach a bottle of Champagne on Friday night and drink to your health and happiness. With love from us both to you and Clemmie.

Yours ever,
Archie

[728] Oliver Lyttelton, 1st Viscount Chandos (1893–1972): Conservative MP for Aldershot 1940–45, 1950–54; President of the Board of Trade 1940–41; Minister of State 1941–42; Minister of State Resident in Cairo 1942; Minister of State for War Production 1942–45; Secretary of State for the Colonies 1951–54; ennobled 1954.

Winston S. Churchill to Sir Archibald Sinclair
Telegram
8th December 1951

Thank you so much for your letter which I am studying and for your and Marigold's good wishes.

Winston

After deciding not to stand again at the 1951 general election, Sinclair was offered a peerage, becoming Viscount Thurso of Ulbster in Churchill's 1952 New Year's honours list.

In January 1952 he suffered a severe stroke while holidaying at his shooting lodge on the Caithness estate. Marigold wrote to Churchill to update him on progress.

Lady Marigold Sinclair to Winston S. Churchill
Dalnawillan,
Altnabreac,
Caithness
7th February 1952

My dear Winston,

It was very kind of you to write to Archie. He is still not at all well but he is improving daily and as soon as his health improves and he can get a bit stronger we will come South.

Our local doctor is sound and he is keeping in touch with Archie's London doctor Sir Alexander McCabe who is satisfied that he is getting the right treatment at present. We cannot move just now because of snow – the road to the nearest station is completely blocked and we can only reach another one 15 miles away in a land rover – it took 3 hours yesterday to do this!

How dreadful it is about the death of the King. It must be a great comfort to his Queen that you are here.

Archie sends you his love and so many thanks for your enquiry – he was touched – and delighted that you thought of him. He is not allowed to write letters yet but he sees them and my answers.

My fond love to Clemmie please.

Yours ever,
Marigold

We have just listened to your broadcast[729] and feel very grateful for its inspiration and comfort.

729 On 7 February 1952 Churchill broadcast to the nation an affectionate and moving tribute to King George VI, who had died the previous day. The passage where Churchill reflected on the King's bravery and courage during the last few months struck a deep chord: 'the King walked with death, as if death were a companion, an acquaintance, whom he recognised and did not fear. In the end death came as a

At the end of March, Jo Grimond, recently elected as Liberal MP for Orkney & Shetland, wrote to Churchill about Sinclair's health, stating that: 'Lady Sinclair tells me that she has spoken to your private secretary so you probably are by now better informed than I am about Sir A. He is now in St Mary's hospital I gather, not well, tired after the journey and suffering from high blood pressure. However, Lady S. seems much relieved that he is now in good hands and out of the isolation of Dalnawillan.'

Lord Thurso to Winston S. Churchill
Fotheringay House
Montpelier Row
Twickenham
9th October 1952

My dear Winston,

Thank you for the latest volume of your book[730] – another possession to be proud of, another source of fascinating entertainment and professional instruction.

I rejoice at the fair winds which are now filling your political sails and giving fresh hope and confidence to us all – Rab's success in balancing our payments,[731] Harold's houses[732] (costly though they may be in the diversion of labour and materials from other desirable enterprises), the cohesion of your tiny minority in Parliament, and the miraculous feat of Parliamentary leadership as part of your continuing dominance of the House of Commons.

Long may these winds blow and bring many other blessings, some Swifts, Hunters, Javelins and Valiants into the squadrons of the R.A.F.!

---

friend.' (Robert Rhodes James, *Churchill: His Complete Speeches*, Vol VIII (Chelsea House Publishers, 1974) p. 8336.

[730] Volume V, *Closing the Ring*, of Churchill's *History of the Second World War.*

[731] Richard Austen 'Rab' Butler, Baron Butler of Saffron Walden (1902–82): Conservative MP for Saffron Walden 1929–65; Minister of Education 1941–45, piloted through Parliament the Education Act of 1944, which provided free primary and secondary education for all; Chancellor of the Exchequer 1951–55; Home Secretary 1957–62; Deputy Prime Minister 1962–63; Foreign Secretary 1963–64; ennobled 1965; Master of Trinity College, Cambridge, 1965–78. As Chancellor of the Exchequer, Butler had presided over a considerable improvement in the balance of trade which had helped bridge the balance of payments gap inherited from the previous Labour administration. The extent to which this was the product of an upswing in the business cycle rather than Butler's economic policy is debatable, as Butler's main proposed solution (the devaluation of the pound by adopting a floating exchange rate) was not adopted at this time.

[732] Maurice Harold Macmillan, 1st Earl of Stockton (1894–1986): Conservative MP for Stockton-on-Tees 1924–29, 1931–64; British representative in the Mediterranean, 1942–45; Minister of Housing 1951–54; Minister of Defence 1954–55; Foreign Secretary 1955; Chancellor of the Exchequer 1955–57; Prime Minister 1957–63; ennobled 1984. Minister of Housing at the time of this letter, Macmillan was implementing the Conservative manifesto commitment to build 300,000 new houses, mainly under the direction of local authorities.

I hope that you and Clemmie are both well and that you enjoyed your visit to Max's villa. He very kindly asked us some time ago but, although I am making progress, I am not yet equal to hopping in and out of trains and customs houses.

With love to you and Clemmie.

From,
Archie

Winston S. Churchill to Viscount Thurso
19th October 1952

My dear Archie,

I cannot tell you how delighted I was to get your vigorous letter and see your well-known handwriting again. I have been deeply anxious and grieved by all I have heard of your long illness. I had hoped that you would have played an important part in the politics of the Liberal Party and in the House of Lords. I still hope that your political career may not be closed. At any rate your letter and the one you wrote before to Clemmie were most cheering signals to your devoted friend,

Winston

In April 1953 Churchill was made a Knight of the Garter. Founded in 1348 by Edward III, the Garter is Britain's highest and most coveted order of chivalry. The Order comprises the sovereign and twenty-five elected Knight Companions, who were only replaced upon death or disgrace.

Viscount Thurso to Sir Winston S. Churchill
Fotheringay House
25th April 1953

My dear Winston,

Not unprepared, we were none the less delighted at the good news which is splashed across this morning's newspapers. Looking back on your life, starting as a cavalry officer, then politics, then your arrival at the Treasury, then the construction of a grander alliance than even your great ancestor contrived, your direction of our powers in the greatest of our wars and now the Garter carrying with it the title of 'Sir Winston', it is as though you had taken your family traditions and combined them in a design of strength and beauty which must appeal to all who are not lacking in a sense of history.

It must also be a source of happiness to our young Queen at the very beginning of her reign thus to fulfil the wishes of her father, to honour her chief minister and to express the feelings of the masses of her people at home and overseas.

I have already thanked you for your wonderfully kind thought about arranging for Marigold and me to see the Coronation; but now that Marigold has heard from Clemmie that the arrangements are actually going forward, I must thank you again for your great kindness.

With love from us both to you and Clemmie.

Yours always,
Archie

In June 1953 Churchill suffered a severe stroke. It was announced publicly that the Prime Minister was suffering from 'overstrain' and needed a period of rest.

Viscount Thurso to Sir Winston S. Churchill
Fotheringay House
28th June 1953

My dear Winston,

It is useless to pretend that we are not miserable – Marigold and I – to know that the superhuman load of responsibility and work, which you have been shouldering with so much advantage to the public interest and to the cause of peace, has overtaxed your strength – but at least we can be thankful that the overstrain has been discovered before you left for Bermuda and that you have promptly accepted your doctors' advice to rest.

That you should rest and go on resting as long as the doctors so desire is, I am sure, the prayer of all who love you and see in your guidance of our Government their chief hope for the future of our country.

I have made up my mind (if spared and well as old Caithness people say) to go to the next dinner of the Other Club in July, if you are well enough to go.

With love to you and Clemmie from us both.

Yours always,
Archie

Sir Winston S. Churchill to Viscount Thurso
2nd July 1953

My dear Archie,

I have had another go of what I told you happened to me four years ago. As I got over that one it is not certain I shall not recover from this.

At present I am physically powerless but not incapable of following public affairs, including the Bye-Elections.[733]

[733] This letter was written on the day of the Birmingham Edgbaston by-election, which the Conservatives

My love to Marigold.

Yours affectionately,
W

Sinclair's recovery from his stroke was a slow one. In July 1953 he fell and broke his leg.

Viscount Thurso to Sir Winston S. Churchill
Fotheringay House
7th July 1953

My dear Winston,

Thank you so much for your letter. I feel that I did not break my leg in vain if it is an effective warning to you against incurring a similar misfortune! May I recommend bars to grip with your good hand in the bathroom and an extra banister on the staircase so that you always have one to grip whether you going up or downstairs?

Also please ask Lord Moran[734] whether it might not be a good thing for you to see Professor Pickering, the head of the Medical Unit at St. Mary's Hospital – a wise and saintly man with a sense of humour and love of wine.

Yours always,
Archie

Mrs Churchill followed up on Sinclair's suggestion and sought Lord Moran's advice. Moran declined the help of Professor Pickering, as he was 'more of a heart specialist than a neurologist'.

Sir Winston S. Churchill to Viscount Thurso
9th July 1953

My dear Archie,

Thank you so much for your letter dated July 7th. I am pondering on your advice, but I gather that the gentleman concerned deals chiefly with a different type of difficulty to mine.

Yours always,
W

won (the Liberals failed to contest it). In the previous month the Conservatives had also won the Abingdon by-election (the Liberals polled 7 per cent).

[734] Churchill's doctor.

Viscount Thurso to Sir Winston S. Churchill
Fotheringay House
13th August 1953

My dear Winston,

Just a line to tell you how delighted we are to see that you were back in the Downing Street saddle yesterday. From your photographs yesterday you look fit to jump any of the big fences – but don't let them bring those tiresome little personal and party wrangles to you. Adopt as your motto your answer to me when I asked you the breed of the hens in Chickenham Palace Gardens – 'I don't bother my head with the details'!

Love from us both to you and Clemmie.

Archie

Viscount Thurso to Sir Winston S. Churchill
Fotheringay House
3rd November 1953

My dear Winston,

I was looking forward to the dinner of the Other Club to-night more keenly than to any other dinner since my first one (during the first war!) and I was most of all looking forward to seeing you again. But Marigold has been on to the Meteorological Department of British European Airways and they prophesy thick fog on the route back here and to be stranded in fog – 'not me in my state of 'ealth'!

We have read your speeches at Margate and in the House with glowing admiration and delight.[735] Your ever-growing domination of a House which might so easily have been ungovernable with a less sure hand on the reins is an astounding phenomenon.

With love to you and Clemmie. From us both.

Archie

Sir Winston S. Churchill to Viscount Thurso
19th November 1953

My dear Archie,

Thank you so much for your extremely kind letter and for what you said about my speech in the House.

We all missed you at the Other Club but I think you were wise to take no risks.

---

[735] In early November Churchill opened the new Parliamentary session with a speech that included a repeated call for a four-power conference to build, in the wake of the death of Stalin, improved East–West relations.

Clemmie sends her love to you both.

Yours always,
W

Sir Winston S. Churchill to Viscount Thurso
21st December 1953

My dear Archie,

I am so glad to know that you will take the Chair at the next dinner of the Other Club, on January 28. If it would be any relief or convenience to you to sleep the night at No. 10, I shall be very happy to accommodate you. Let me know. Everyone was delighted at the idea of your presiding.

Yours ever,
W

Viscount Thurso to Sir Winston S. Churchill
Fotheringay House
4th January 1954

My dear Winston,

Thank you for this volume 'Triumph and Tragedy'.[736] So now this massive and splendid work is complete and, thanks to your generous friendship, becomes my treasured possession. It is a miraculous achievement in the midst of all your political exertions during the last eight years!

It was a terrible shock to hear the news over the wireless the other night that Duff's[737] life had ended so suddenly. It was a crowning mercy for him that Diana was with him.

Yours ever,
Archie

Viscount Thurso to Sir Winston S. Churchill
Fotheringay House
16th February 1954

My dear Winston,

[736] The final volume in the *History of the Second World War*.

[737] A. Duff Cooper, 1st Viscount Norwich (1890–1954): Conservative MP for Oldham 1924–29, St George's (Westminster) 1931–45; Secretary of State for War, 1935–37; First Lord of the Admiralty May 1937–38; disagreed with the appeasement policy of Neville Chamberlain and resigned from office after Munich; Minister of Information 1940–41; Chancellor of Duchy of Lancaster 1941–43; died 1st January, 1954.

Thank you so much for your letter and for the copy of Tudor's letter.[738] I well remember my 'slight alarm and despondency' when a couple of 9.2 shells exploded just behind us and I also remember the more than slight embarrassment shown by the C.R.A.[739] who had so kindly arranged it all for your delectation and perhaps edification.

It is very nice to hear through you from dear Tudor again. He was a good friend to us those days.

Marigold has gone home to Caithness for two or three weeks or she would join me in sending our love to you and Clemmie.

Yours always,
Archie

In April 1954 Sinclair sent Churchill a note which read:

Winston,

An old soldier's cherished memory of his first meeting with you, Archie

Extract from a letter dated 8th April 1954 to Viscount Thurso from Captain G. St. J. Smith, late Volunteer 2 Battn. Cameronians, and Cheshire Regiment 2nd Battn.:–

'One of my cherished memories is seeing a smiling young man in mufti, riding a grey mule, at Flandslaagte (or rather the Sunday River near by) in Natal in 1900. It was the great statesman himself, asking the way to the King's Royal Rifles in our lines.'

On 8 April 1954 Sinclair wrote to the *Daily Telegraph* to express his concern at the decline in standards of parliamentary debate, and in particular how the Opposition was treating the Prime Minister, and how the Tory backbenchers were failing to show sufficient support.

From Viscount Thurso to the Editor of The Daily Telegraph,

Sir, Standards of Parliamentary debate are changing. To drown the voice of the Prime Minister in a debate of perhaps historic importance with irrelevant cries of 'resign' appears to call for little condemnation from any quarter. Even boos are occasionally heard in the House of Commons. Shafts of wit, on the other hand, are often resented.

738 Churchill had forwarded a copy of a letter from one of their old colleagues from the trenches in 1916. It has not been possible to identify who Tudor was.

739 Canadian Royal Artillery.

The deployment by the Prime Minister in Parliamentary language of a massive argument critical of the handling of affairs by a previous Administration produces turmoil in the House of Commons and a torrent of disapproval from the newspapers. Yet the cut and thrust of debate is the lifeblood of Parliamentary government and it ought not to be beyond the power of any member of a deliberative assembly to sit quietly under criticism, comforting himself with the knowledge that either he or one of his colleagues will have the opportunity to reply.

There is also a new development in party tactics. The party is deployed in three echelons. In the vanguard are the glamour boys who attack the public conduct of the Prime Minister with furious and unscrupulous invective and all the tricks of television – the engaging smile, the sly wink – before an audience of their fellow countrymen.

The main body are the ex-Ministers and well-known back benchers, who keep up the attack at large meetings at the week-end, with the co-operation of political correspondents and leader writers in the newspapers.

The supporting echelon comprises the leaders of the party, who make statesmanlike speeches on the same subjects in the House of Commons deprecating partisanship and creating a warm and comfortable 'atmosphere' in which apparently many people consider that it is improper for the Prime Minister to retaliate upon his opponents with hard facts and sharp logic. Let the scribes and orators remain unanswered! Let the Prime Minister's case go by default! Let the public restrain its curiosity to hear it! But on no account allow the 'atmosphere' of a Parliamentary debate to be 'spoiled'.

Meanwhile, the spineless Conservative majority is described in the newspapers as sitting 'silent' and 'glum' upon its benches; and some 'with white faces' slink away, leaving their august leader with the storm of Socialist fury breaking around his head.

Those who fail such a leader in a time of crisis are not worthy of his leadership. But, unless they rally to his support, and that right soon, they will assuredly incur the displeasure of their fellow countrymen of all parties, who realise that Sir Winston Churchill is – and will remain so long as he retains his miraculous power and vision – the greatest personal asset that the free world has to-day.

Yours faithfully,
Thurso

On 9 April Churchill sent Thurso a telegram saying 'Thank you so much dear Archie for your splendid letter. Winston'

Viscount Thurso to Sir Winston S. Churchill
Fotheringay House
9th April 1954

My dear Winston,

Bless you! I don't deserve your thanks. I enjoyed writing it – but I had one serious qualm. I am so much out of the swim, that I was afraid that my little shell might – like Tudor's! – drop on the wrong side of the trench! So it is I who am grateful to you for your telegram which removes that fear.

I have had a number of letters already from staunch friends of yours. Poor Bob[740] writes that the whiteness of his face was due to the loss of blood from his gum which had been operated on at 3.15.

I often miss the House of Commons especially when you have such good laughs as must have had yesterday over Herbert Morrison's[741] memory! To forget something which happened ten or longer years ago and to then to call it to mind after 24 hours for reflection would be quite natural – but the converse is ludicrous.

If ever you feel like looking in here for lunch on your way to or from Chequers or Chartwell, it would be a great treat for Marigold and me.

Yours always,
Archie

In February 1955 Sinclair's son Robin was involved in a plane crash.

Sir Winston S. Churchill to Viscount Thurso
Telegram
23rd February 1955

Thank God your son and his pilot escaped.

Winston

Viscount Thurso to Sir Winston S. Churchill
Fotheringay House
24th February 1955

My dear Winston,

Marigold and I were very grateful to you for your telegram about Robin and he will also be very grateful.

He had two narrow escapes. He was flying in an Auster very low in order to observe animals and distress signals on the ground. The surface of the snow was flat and unbroken and the pilot had just declared that the glare was blinding him when

740 Possibly Sir Robert Boothby, Baron Boothby of Buchan and Rattray Head (1900–86): Conservative MP for East Aberdeenshire 1924–58; Parliamentary Private Secretary to Churchill 1926–29.

741 Herbert Stanley Morrison, Baron Morrison of Lambeth (1888–1965): Labour MP for South Hackney 1923–24, 1929–31, 1935–59; Minister of Transport 1929–31; Leader of London County Council 1933–40; Minister of Supply 1940; Home Secretary 1940–45; Deputy Prime Minister and Leader of the House of Commons 1945–51; Foreign Secretary 1951; ennobled 1959.

they crashed against the side of a low hill. The Auster broke its back and the snow came piling in to the cockpit.

Then they scrambled out, Robin helping the pilot, whose face was cut. The pilot asked where they were and Robin, looking round for a land mark, suddenly realised that he was seeing double – concussion! So there they were, miles from any house, with no landmark in sight on a vast flat boggy moor and not the slightest idea in which direction to start walking while Robin, suffering from shock and concussion was beginning to feel cold! I doubt if he would have had much chance of walking to a house even if they could have found out which way to go!

Then they heard an approaching helicopter, so they opened the petrol cocks and burned the wrecked Auster and the helicopter, seeing the blaze, hovered over them and pulled them in. The pilot reported for duty the next day. Robin has a lot of bruises all over and two stitches in his head – but he is getting over his concussion in hospital. I am hoping to see you at the Other Club this evening.

Love from,
Archie

In April 1955 Churchill resigned as Prime Minister.

Viscount Thurso to Sir Winston S. Churchill
Fotheringay House
8th April 1955

My dear Winston,

I am sure you are right in this as in all your recent great decisions; but your resignation is much more than a wrench, from which, once suffered, the country will gradually recover. The loss of your leadership will be felt increasingly as time passes.

Nevertheless, the moment is well chosen. You leave No. 10 at the post war peak of the country's prosperity at home and of its prestige abroad, dominating the House of Commons and secure in the affection and admiration of your fellow-countrymen. Few think of you as a party leader but rather as the leader of the nation and of the free world. Yet you leave your party in a more advantageous and more honourable position than it has enjoyed for many years. You go out in glory, honoured by your Sovereign and acclaimed by the people.

For my part, I am helpless to express to you my deep gratitude for all the happiness which I owe to you since the day when Maxine[742] made me known to you. The walks and talks on Bushey Heath, the Enchantress, Hendon, the Isle of Grain and Spencer Grey, the Royal Scots Fusiliers, the War Office and the tragic but gallant effort to nip Bolshevism in the bud, the Colonial Office, the Cairo Conference,

[742] Maxine Elliott – see n51.

Dundee, Leicester and the beginning (for me) of politics, your constant and precious friendship at Lullenden[743] and Chartwell with Clemmie and the children, your constant kindness, help and advice even when party controversies swept us apart in politics, Focus and the struggle to rally Britain against Hitler and Mussolini and to crown it all, the Air Ministry.

Now I have to thank you again for the wonderful parties at Downing Street – Clemmie's wonderful birthday party where we not only met a lot of friends with whom Marigold and I had lost touch while I was at home after the war and during my illness and a memorable dinner with the Queen. It was a most enviable honour to be allowed – and kind and generous of you to arrange for me – to talk with the Queen after dinner.

For all this and for much else that I forbear to mention now, fresh as it is in my memory, thank you, dear Winston.

I am sure that you and Clemmie will have a lovely time in Sicily. I see you are going to Syracuse of which I have happy memories. I hope you will let us come and see you at Chartwell when you return. We will propose ourselves one afternoon.

With love to you and Clemmie.

Yours always,
Archie

Viscount Thurso to Sir Winston S. Churchill
Fortheringay House
Early December 1957

My dear Winston,

The Age of Revolution[744] arrived here when I was starting a course of treatment at Oxford, so they kept it for me here till I should return as I did – very much better – for my stay at Oxford. I feel very proud of the splendid volumes. Thank you very much for these precious gifts. I hope that you and Clemmie are well.

Love from,
Archie

From around 1957 onwards, Churchill became less and less able to attend to his correspondence. Anthony Montague Browne, his personal secretary, would frequently compose short responses to his friends on Churchill's behalf, passing each response through Clementine Churchill for her approval when the recipient was a close friend of the former premier. It is likely, therefore, that the following short letters to Sinclair originated from the pen of Montague Browne.

[743] Churchill's Sussex home from 1917.

[744] One of the volumes of Churchill's *History of the English-Speaking Peoples.*

Sir Winston S. Churchill to Viscount Thurso
13th December 1957

My dear Archie,

I am so glad to hear from you again, and above all that you have recovered. Thank you very much for what you say about the three books. I will send you the fourth when it comes out in March.

I dined with the Other Club last night. My salutations to your wife.

Yours always,
W

Sir Winston S. Churchill to Viscount Thurso
16th April 1958

My dear Archie,

Thank you so much for your letter. I am very glad that you have got better. I have had a further setback and am now in bed, but I hope not for long.

I hope to see you at the Other Club, and meanwhile I trust all goes well with you both. Clemmie sends her love.

Yours always,
W

Viscount Thurso to Sir Winston S. Churchill
7th June 1958

My dear Winston,

The splendid news of your recovery and return home fills Marigold and me with delight. I have been having a bad time lately and we were most grateful to Clemmie for her visit just before I went to Oxford for treatment about a month ago. The treatment was a great success and I am now much better and looking forward to seeing you before very long at the Other Club. I have been reading the History with lively interest, and gratitude and much pride in my 'authors copies' which you sent me.

I hope that we shall soon be blessed with sun and warmth and that you will greatly enjoy your summer at Chartwell.

With love to you and Clemmie,

From
Archie

Sir Winston S. Churchill to Viscount Thurso
Telegram
29th October 1960

Belated but affectionate thoughts on your birthday dear Archie.

Winston and Clemmie

A serious second stroke in early 1959 rendered Sinclair unable to play any further part in public life; indeed, for six months he lay in a coma. Although he later recovered partial consciousness he was reduced to the state of a bed-bound invalid requiring twenty-four hour nursing care.

In October 1961 Lord Beaverbrook wrote to Sinclair:

> This is a letter written in anticipation of your next birthday, now a few days off. You are one of the unremembered heroes of the war. No man acted with more balance, with more judgement or greater restraint than yourself.

The following October Beaverbrook wrote again, this time to Marigold Sinclair:

> This is a message for Archie which I would ask you to read to him. He did so much over five years and worried so greatly on account of the boys who lost their lives that it is no wonder that he is now a war casualty.[745]

Tragically Sinclair's condition never really improved, although there were brief moments when he fully recognised his family and visitors and could hold very short conversations. He lived in this state for a further ten years, dying in Twickenham on 15 June 1970. He was buried on a small hill overlooking Dalnawillan, near Thurso – where his wife, Marigold, joined him in 1974.

Churchill's public life was effectively over by 1960; from then on he made only very infrequent appearances in public. He died on 24 January 1965.

745 Both messages from Beaverbrook are quoted in de Groot, *Liberal Crusader*, p. 238.

Appendices

Appendix A
Notes on sources and bibliography

Sources

The original letters from which this collection is drawn are held at either the National Archive (Kew) or the Archives Centre, Churchill College, Cambridge. Sinclair's family passed his surviving personal and private office papers to Churchill College for safe keeping in the 1970s and 1980s. Unfortunately the archive is much diminished, as many of Sinclair's papers were destroyed, first when the Liberal Party's headquarters was bombed in the Second World War and then by a fire in the early 1950s at the Thurso estate in Caithness. Fortunately, the Churchill College Archives contain copies of much of their correspondence spread across the Chartwell Papers (covering the period 1874–1945) and the Churchill Papers (1945–65). There is also a substantial amount held in the National Archive (formerly the Public Record Office) in the PREM 3 and PREM 4 Prime Minister's Office Papers 1940–45 as well as in the records of the Air Ministry (especially classes AIR 19 and AIR 8).

- The Thurso papers held at Churchill College Cambridge, are searchable via http://www.a2a.pro.gov.uk/search/index.asp
- The Churchill papers held at Churchill College Cambridge are searchable via http://www-archives.chu.cam.ac.uk/perl/search

The main source files used for each chapter are summarised below.

Part 1: The First World War 1915–1918
The letters from Churchill to Sinclair written from 1915–18 are held in the Thurso collection at THRS I 1/1-1/28. The letters from Sinclair to Churchill are held within the following files: CHAR 1/117, CHAR 1/118A, CHAR 1/124, CHAR 1/129, CHAR 1/136, CHAR 2/1, CHAR 2/116, CHAR 2/124B and CHAR 2/134/30.

Part 2: Fighting the Bolsheviks 1919–1923

The main source of letters for this period is the extensive collection of files relating to the Russian situation in the Chartwell Papers from 1919–22: CHAR 16/5, CHAR 16/6, CHAR 16/7, CHAR 16/11, CHAR 16/13, CHAR 16/14 CHAR 16/16A–B, CHAR 16/18 A, CHAR 16/22, CHAR 16/23, CHAR 16/24 CHAR 16/25, CHAR 16/26, CHAR 16/27 CHAR 16/28, CHAR 16/32, CHAR 16/33, CHAR 16/40, CHAR 16/43, CHAR 16/48A–B, CHAR 16/50, CHAR 16/52A–B, CHAR 16/55, CHAR 16/56, CHAR 16/57, CHAR 16/64, CHAR 16/70, CHAR 16/71, CHAR 16/72, CHAR 16/73, CHAR 16/76, CHAR 16/77, CHAR 16/241, CHAR 28/140.

Other personal correspondence, mainly about Sinclair's pending political career, can be found at CHAR 1/136, CHAR 1/143, CHAR 1/154, CHAR 1/157, CHAR 1/172, CHAR 1/199, CHAR 2/124B, CHAR 2/122, CHAR 2/134, CHAR 2/151, CHAR 2/177, CHAR 2/164, CHAR 2/214 B, CHAR 8/222, CHAR 28/190.

The few letters that relate to the period from 1921–22 in the Chartwell Papers, when Sinclair and Churchill were at the Colonial Office, can be found at CHAR 17/3, CHAR 17/5, CHAR 17/7, CHAR 17/11, CHAR 17/16, CHAR 17/23.

There are also short notes and file comments between Churchill and Sinclair to be found in the following Colonial Office files at Kew relating to the situation in Mesopotamia (Iraq) and the Middle East: CO 733/3, CO 733/10, CO 733/13, CO 733/14, and CO 733/33.

Part 3: Separate Paths 1924–1939

The following Chartwell Papers files were used:
CHAR 1/194, CHAR 1/200, CHAR 1/346, CHAR 2/212, CHAR 2/134, CHAR 2/151, CHAR 2/164, CHAR 2/177, CHAR 2/224, CHAR 2/237, CHAR 2/357A, CHAR 8/211, CHAR 8/222, CHAR 8/211, CHAR 8/217, CHAR 8/269, and CHAR 8/549.

There is also some scattered correspondence and notes from Churchill to Sinclair within the THRS IV and THRS V sections of the Thurso Papers.

Part 4: Winning the Air War 1940–1945

The vast majority of letters are to be found in the extensive PREM 3 and PREM 4 section covering the 1940–45 period. PREM 3 contains the Prime Minister's Operational papers dealing with defence and operational subjects including the air force and specific military operations. PREM 4 holds the Prime Minister's office papers dealing with civil and political matters. Two other key sources were found in AIR 19 (the Secretary of State for Air's private office papers) and AIR 8 (The office papers for the Chief of Air Staff).

The following files were consulted:

Prime Ministers' Office Papers:
PREM 3/10, PREM 3/11/6, PREM 3/11/7, PREM 3/11/8, PREM 3/11/11A, PREM 3/11/11B, PREM 3/11/12 , PREM 3/12, PREM 3/13/3, PREM 3/13/7, PREM 3/13/8, PREM 3/13/9, PREM 3/13/10, PREM 3/13/11, PREM 3/13/12, PREM 3/13/13, PREM 3/13/14, PREM 3/14/2 , PREM 3/14/3, PREM 3/17, PREM 3/21/1, PREM 3/21/5, PREM 3/334/2, PREM 3/335, PREM 3/336/5, PREM 4/65/1, PREM 4/65/2, PREM 4/65/4, and PREM 5/209.

Air Ministry Papers:
AIR 2/6150, AIR 2/8476, AIR 8/440, AIR 8/480, AIR 8/620, AIR 8/865, AIR 8/919, AIR 8/1015, AIR 8/1354, AIR 14/3507, AIR 14/3512, AIR19/57, AIR19/64, AIR19/74, AIR 19/149, AIR19/150, AIR19/162, AIR19/180, AIR19/235, AIR 19/375, AIR 19/572, AIR 23/1395, and AIR 23/1396.

Churchill Papers:
CHAR 20/2 A, CHAR 20/3, CHAR 20/7, CHAR 20/8, CHAR 20/11, CHAR 20/25, CHAR 20/29A, CHAR 20/67, CHAR 20/94 A–B, CHAR 20/97 A, CHAR 20/103, CHAR 20/127, CHAR 20/129, CHAR 20/146 B, CHAR 20/179, CHAR 20/194A, CHAR 20/207, and CHAR 20/257.

Part 5: Twilight and Dusk 1946–1960
The only surviving correspondence exists in the Churchill Papers at these references: CHUR 1/16, CHUR 1/17 A–B, CHUR 1/19, CHUR 1/39, CHUR 1/43, CHUR 1/53, CHUR 2/23, CHUR 2/67 A–B, CHUR 2/117 A–B, CHUR 2/139, CHUR 2/167, CHUR 2/176 A–B, CHUR 2/200, CHUR 2/201, CHUR 2/324, CHUR 2/342, CHUR 2/390, CHUR 2/406, CHUR 2/423, CHUR 2/492 A–G, CHUR 2/450, CHUR 2/454, CHUR 2/455, CHUR 2/456, CHUR 2/459 A–B, CHURC 2/471 A–G, CHUR 2/483 A–G, CHUR 2/484 A–C, CHUR 2/490 A–G, CHUR 2/495, and CHUR 4/49.

Bibliography

Although there is only one short biography of Sinclair, there are literally hundreds of biographies of Churchill, many of which contain references to Sinclair. The short list below highlights those that were most useful during the editing of this volume together with books that helped provide context to particular periods.

Geoffrey Best, *Churchill* (Hambledon and London Ltd, 2001)
Duncan Brack et al (eds.), *Dictionary of Libveral* Biography (Politico's, 1998)
David Carlton, *Churchill and the Soviet Union* (Manchester University Press 2000)

Randolph S. Churchill (Vols. 1–2) and Sir Martin Gilbert (Vols. 3–8), *The Official Biography of Winston S. Churchill*, with sixteen companion volumes of documents and supporting material (Heinemann, 1966–2002)

Gerard J. De Groot, *Liberal Crusader: The Life of Sir Archibald Sinclair* (Hurst & Co., 1993)

Roy Jenkins, *Churchill* (Macmillan, 2001)

David Stafford, *Churchill and the Secret Service* (Abacus, 2001)

John Terraine, *The Right of the Line* (Wordsworth Military Library, 1998) (an excellent overview of the RAF during the 1930s and 1940s)

Sir Charles Webster and Noble Frankland, *The Strategic Air Offensive against Germany* (Her Majesty's Stationery Office, 1961)

Edgar Trevor Williams and Christine S. Nicholls (eds.), *Dictionary of National Biography, 1961–1970* (Oxford University Press, 1981)

Chris Wrigley, *Winston Churchill: A Biographical Companion* (ABC Clio Press, 2002)

Appendix B

Summary biographies

Sir Winston Spencer Churchill

1874 30 November	Born in Blenheim Palace, eldest son of Rt Hon. Lord Randolph Churchill (third son of 7th Duke of Marlborough), and Jennie Jerome
1888–93	Harrow School
1900	Elected MP for Oldham (Conservative)
1904 31 May	Moves from Conservative to Liberal Party
1906	Elected MP for Manchester N.W. (Liberal)
Dec 1905 – Apr 1908	Under-Secretary of State for the Colonies
1908	Elected MP for Dundee (Liberal)
Apr 1908 – Feb 1910	President of the Board of Trade
1908 12 September	Marries Clementine, daughter of Sir Henry Hozier and Lady Blanche (née Ogilvy)
Feb 1910 – Oct 1911	Home Secretary
Oct 1911 – May 1915	First Lord of the Admiralty
1915 May – Nov	Chancellor of the Duchy of Lancaster
1915–16	Serves on Western Front with Grenadier Guards; appointed Lieutenant–Colonel, commanding 6th Battalion Royal Scots Fusiliers, France
Jul 1917 – Jan 1919	Minister of Munitions
Jan 1919 – Feb 1921	Secretary of State for War (and Air until April 1921)
Feb 1921 – Oct 1922	Secretary of State for the Colonies
November 1922	Loses Dundee seat
October 1924	Elected MP for Epping (initially as a 'Constitutionalist', effectively Conservative)
Nov 1924 – Jun 1929	Chancellor of the Exchequer
Sep 1939 – May 1940	First Lord of the Admiralty

May 1940 – July 1945	Prime Minister, First Lord of the Treasury and Minister of Defence
1945	Elected MP for Woodford (Conservative)
Jul 1945 – Oct 1951	Leader of the Opposition
Oct 1951 – Apr 1955	Prime Minister and First Lord of the Treasury (also Minister of Defence Oct 1951 – Jan 1952)
1953	Awarded Nobel Prize for Literature
1964	Stands down from Commons
1965 24 January	Dies at 28 Hyde Park Gate, London

Archibald Henry Macdonald Sinclair (1st Viscount Thurso)

1890 22 October	Born in London, only son of Clarence Granville Sinclair and Mabel Sands
1900–08	Eton College
1908–10	Military training, Sandhurst
1910	Enters army, serving in the 2nd Life Guards; during 1915 he served in the Canadian Cavalry brigade, and in January 1916 served with Churchill as his second-in-command with the 6th Royal Scots Fusiliers; ended the war as a major in the Guards Machine-Gun Regiment
1918	Marries Marigold Forbes
1919–21	Personal Military Secretary to Secretary of State for War (Churchill)
1921–22	Private Secretary to Secretary of State for Colonies (Churchill)
1922	Elected MP for Caithness & Sutherland (Liberal)
1925–30	Temporary Chairman of Committees, House of Commons
1927–30	Member of Empire Marketing Board
1930–31	Chief Liberal Whip
1931	Privy Councillor
1931–32	Secretary of State for Scotland
1935–45	Leader, Liberal Parliamentary Party
1940–45	Secretary of State for Air
1945	Loses Caithness & Sutherland seat
1942–49	Hon Air Commodore American Air Force
1938–45	Lord Rector of Glasgow University
1952	Created Viscount Thurso
1953–68	President Eighty Club
1956–58	President Air League of the British Empire
1954–61	Political Honours Scrutiny Committee
1970 15 June	Dies in Twickenham, West London

Others

Sir Richard **Acland** (1906–90): MP for Barnstaple 1935-45 (Liberal 1935–42, Common Wealth 1942–45); founded Common Wealth Party in 1942, arguing for common ownership of land and industry; constant thorn in Churchill's side, both in and out of parliament; joined the Labour Party after electoral defeat in 1945; Labour MP for Gravesend 1947–55; resigned from Labour over the leadership's unwillingness to oppose the development of the hydrogen bomb.

William Maxwell **Aitken**: *see* Lord Beaverbrook.

Albert Victor **Alexander**, 1st Earl Alexander of Hillsborough (1885–1965): Labour MP for Sheffield Hillsborough 1922–31, 1935–50; First Lord of the Admiralty 1929–31, 1940–45 1945–46; Minister of Defence 1946–50; Chancellor of the Duchy of Lancaster 1950–51; created Viscount 1950, Earl 1963; leader of the Labour peers 1955–64.

Sir Harold Rupert Leofric George **Alexander**, 1st Earl Alexander of Tunis (1891–1969): fought on the Western Front 1914–18; led the Baltic Landwehr, a brigade of ethnic Germans, against the Red Army during the Russian Civil War; commanded 1st Division British Expeditionary Force 1939–40; Head of Southern Command 1940–41; Commander-in-Chief, Burma, 1942; Commander-in-Chief, Middle East 1942–43, instrumental in defeat of Rommel at El Alamein in November 1942; Supreme Allied Commander in Italy 1943–45; Governor-General of Canada 1946–52; Minister of Defence 1952–54.

Grigorii **Alexinsky** (1879 – ?): Bolshevik deputy to the Second Duma; fell out with Lenin and aligned himself with Plekhanov, the leading Menshevik (the Mensheviks were the more moderate and democratic opponents of the Bolsheviks within the Russian Social Democratic Party); emigrated to France in 1917.

Leopold **Amery** (1873–1955): chief correspondent for *The Times* during the Boer War; Conservative MP 1911–45; First Lord of the Admiralty 1922–24, Colonial Secretary 1924–29; remained out of office throughout the 1930s and emerged as one of the leading critics of the National Government's appeasement policy; instrumental in Chamberlain's removal as Prime Minister in May 1940; Secretary of State for India and Burma 1940–45.

General Henry Hartley **Arnold** (1886–1950): Commander, US Army Air Force from 1940, and a strong supporter of area bombing.

Herbert Henry **Asquith**, Earl of Oxford and Asquith (1874–1928): Liberal MP for East Fife 1886–1918, Paisley 1920–24; Home Secretary 1892–95; Chancellor of the

Exchequer 1905–09; Prime Minister 1909–16; Leader of the Liberal Party 1909–26; created Earl of Oxford and Asquith 1925.

Mustafa Kemal **Atatürk** (1881–1938): commander, Ottoman 19th Division at Gallipoli, prevented Anzac troops from gaining possession of a strategic ridge; emerged as leader of the attempts to retain Turkey's territorial integrity and independence after the war; elected President of the new Republic of Turkey in October 1923; known since 1934 as Atatürk ('Father of Turks').

Nikolai **Avksentiev** (1878–1943): founder member, along with Kerensky, of the Party of Socialist Revolutionaries; served in two senior positions in Kerensky's short-lived government in 1917; opposed the Bolsheviks but also resisted involvement with the Tsarist White Russians; left Russia in 1919 and lived in the émigré community in Paris.

Yevno **Azeffl** (1869–1925): Russian Socialist Revolutionary, subsequently discovered to have been a Russian police informer.

Sir John Picton **Bagge** (1877–1967): civil servant with the Department of Overseas Trade; British Consul-General at Odessa; knowledgeable of economic and political conditions in South Russia.

Arthur James **Balfour**, 1st Earl of Balfour (1848–1930): Conservative MP from 1874 and Leader of the Conservative Party 1902–11; Prime Minister 1902–05; First Lord of the Admiralty 1915-16; Foreign Secretary 1916–19; Lord President of the Council 1919–22 and 1925–29.

Harold Harrington **Balfour**, Baron Balfour of Inchrye (1897–1988): served in RFC during First World War; Conservative MP for Isle of Thanet 1929–45; Parliamentary Secretary for Air 1938–44; Minister Resident for West Africa 1944–45; ennobled July 1945.

Air Marshal Sir Arthur **Barrett** (dates unknown): led RAF–Army Cooperation Command December 1941 – March 1943.

Bernard Mannes **Baruch** (1870–1965): Wall Street financier and economic advisor to US Presidents Wilson, Roosevelt and Truman.

William Maxwell Aitken, 1st Baron **Beaverbook** (1879–1964): highly successful Canadian stockbroker, moved to Britain in 1909; Conservative MP 1910–18; in 1918 created Lord Beaverbrook; Chancellor Duchy of Lancaster and Minister of Information 1918; Minister for Aircraft Production 1940–41; Minister of Supply 1941–42; Minister of War Production 1942; Lord Privy Seal 1943–45; better known as one of the great newspaper barons: during the First World War he acquired a controlling interest in the *Daily Express*, in 1921 founded the *Sunday Express* and in 1929 purchased the *London Evening Standard*.

Walter **Bedell Smith** (1896–1961): Eisenhower's Chief of Staff; US Ambassador to the Soviet Union 1946–48; Director of the Central Intelligence Agency (CIA) 1950–53; Under-Secretary of State 1954–56.

Prince Serge Sergeevitch **Belosselsky-Belozersky** (1895–1978): born in St Petersburg; enjoyed a colourful career including a period in the elite Russian Imperial Horse Guards; fled to Paris via Finland in 1917; became an active organiser of the White Russian forces; migrated to the United States and completed his military career as a Colonel in the US Army Air Force during the Second World War; died in New York in October 1978.

Henri Mathias **Berthelot** (1863–1931): head of the French military mission to Romania in 1917 until the country surrendered to the Central Powers; appointed as Commander-in-Chief of the Danube Army when Romania re-entered the war in October 1918; in February 1919 visited Odessa to meet Denikin; he was not impressed by the White Russian leadership and predicted that Denikin's forces would be defeated; appointed governor of Metz in 1920 and awarded a seat on the French Supreme War Council.

Ernest **Bevin** (1881–1951): Secretary-General, Transport & General Workers' Union 1921–40; Labour MP for Wandsworth Central 1940–50, East Woolwich 1950–51; Minister of Labour and National Service 1940–45, where he achieved the mobilisation of Britain's workforce and became one of the most significant members of the coalition government; Secretary of State for Foreign Affairs 1945–51, where he played an important role in the acceptance of the Marshall Plan, the creation of NATO and Britain's decision to develop nuclear weapons (he held strong anti-communist views); Lord Privy Seal 1951.

Sir Oswald **Birley**, MC, RA (1880–1952): famous British portrait painter, much favoured by the Royal Family; painted Churchill on three occasions (1928, 1946 and 1951) and in the last years of his life was a frequent visitor to the south of France, where he painted with Churchill, to whom he gave valuable lessons.

Tasker **Bliss** (1853–1930): American Military Representative on the Supreme War Council, Versailles 1917–19; American Commissioner, Paris Peace Conference, 1919.

Andrew **Bonar Law** (1858–1923): Leader of the Unionist (Conservative) Party since 1911; Colonial Secretary 1915–16; Chancellor of the Exchequer 1916–18; Lord Privy Seal 1919; Prime Minister 1922–23.

Violet **Bonham Carter**, Baroness Asquith of Yarnbury (1887–1969): eldest daughter of H.H. Asquith, Liberal leader and Prime Minister; married Maurice Bonham Carter, Asquith's principal private secretary, in 1915; President, Women's Liberal Federation 1923–25; President, Liberal Party Organisation 1945–47 (the first woman to hold the post); member of the Board of Governors of the BBC, 1940–46; awarded life peerage in 1964; her maiden speech in the House of Lords, on 25 January 1965, took the form of a eulogy on her friend Churchill, who had died the previous day.

Sir Robert **Boothby**, Baron Boothby of Buchan and Rattray Head (1900–86): Conservative MP for East Aberdeenshire 1924–58; Parliamentary Private Secretary to Churchill 1926–29.

Louis **Botha** (1862–1919): Commandant-General of the Boer armies 1900–02; Prime Minister of South Africa, 1907–19; offered immediate military assistance to Britain in August 1914, and in 1915 launched an invasion of German South West Africa (now Namibia).

Vladimir Lvovitch **Bourtzev** (1862 – ?): Russian revolutionary; exiled to Serbia in 1885 for his revolutionary beliefs and activities; escaped after twelve months, fled to Geneva and then London; after 1917 an equally strong opposition to the Bolsheviks – who he regarded as unpatriotic – replaced his hatred of Tsarism.

Air Chief Marshal Sir Frederick William **Bowhill** (1880–1960): Air Officer Commander-in-Chief, Coastal Command.

Brendan **Bracken**, 1st Viscount Bracken (1901–58): journalist and publisher, managing director of *The Economist* 1928–29; Conservative MP for Paddington 1929–45; strong opponent of appeasement and close associate of Churchill; Parliamentary Private Secretary to Churchill 1940–41; Minister of Information 1941–45; First Lord of the Admiralty 1945; ennobled in 1952.

Omar Nelson **Bradley** (1893–1981): Assistant Secretary, US General Staff 1940–41; Commandant, Infantry School 1941–42; Commander, 82nd and 28th Infantry Divisions 1942–43, II Corps, North Africa and Sicily, 1943, and First Army and 12th Army Group in Normandy invasion and European campaign 1944–45; Chief of Staff, US Army 1948–49; first Chairman, NATO Military Staff Committee 1949–50.

General Lewis H. **Brereton** (1890–1967): commander US Far East Air Force in the Philippines, 1940–42; Deputy Air Commander-in-Chief, Allied Air Forces, Java, 1942; Commander, Middle East Air Forces 1942–43; Commander Ninth Air Force, European theatre, 1943–44; Commander First Allied Airborne Army 1944–45.

Alfred Ernest **Brown** (1881–1962): Liberal MP for Rugby 1923–24, Liberal and Liberal National MP for Leith 1927–45; Minister of Labour 1935–40, Secretary of State for Scotland 1940–41; Minister for Health 1941–43; Chancellor of the Duchy of Lancaster 1943–45; Minister for Aircraft Production 1945; Chairman of the Liberal Nationals 1940–45.

Heinrich **Brüning** (1885–1970): German statesman and fiscal expert; Leader of the Catholic Centre Party from 1929; in 1930 appointed Chancellor to put German finances in order, but his drastic deflationary measures were unpopular, and he was forced to resign in 1932 by President Hindenburg; left Germany in 1934 and became a member of the faculty at Harvard 1937–52.

Henry Pelham **Burn** (1882–1958): Lieutenant-Colonel, Argyll & Sutherland Highlanders during January to April 1916.

Richard Austen 'Rab' **Butler**, Baron Butler of Saffron Walden (1902–82): Conservative MP for Saffron Walden 1929–65; Minister of Education 1941–45, piloted through Parliament the Education Act of 1944, which provided free primary and secondary education for all; Chancellor of the Exchequer 1951–55; Home Secretary 1957–62; Deputy Prime Minister 1962–63; Foreign Secretary 1963–64; ennobled 1965; Master of Trinity College, Cambridge, 1965–78.

Edward Henry **Carson** (1854–1935): Irish Unionist leader; Attorney General, 1915; First Lord of the Admiralty, 1916–17; member of War Cabinet, 1917–18; created Lord of Appeal, 1921.

Sir Joseph Austen **Chamberlain** (1863–1937): son of Birmingham mayor and Liberal Unionist leader Joseph Chamberlain, older half-brother of Neville Chamberlain; elected as Liberal Unionist MP 1892; Chancellor of the Exchequer 1903–05; Secretary of State for India 1915–17, resigned over mismanagement of the Mesopotamia campaign; rejoined War Cabinet 1918; Chancellor of the Exchequer 1919–21; Lord Privy Seal and Leader of the Conservative Parliamentary Party 1921–22, resigned after Carlton Club meeting in October 1922 voted to end the Coalition; Secretary of State for Foreign Affairs 1924–29; First Lord of the Admiralty 1931.

Chang Tso-lin (1873–1928): Chinese soldier and warlord who dominated Manchuria and parts of North China between 1913 and 1928; he maintained his power with the tacit support of the Japanese, and in return granted them concessions in Manchuria; during the early and mid 1920s held control of Beijing and the surrounding Beijing–Tianjin area, until his forces were driven out by Chiang Kai-shek in 1926.

Frederick Alexander Lindemann, Viscount **Cherwell** (1886–1957): physicist and Fellow of Christ Church, Oxford; during World War I, was the first to develop the mathematical theory of aircraft spin, put into practice in air combat; Churchill's scientific advisor; firm advocate of the policy of area bombing; Paymaster-General 1942–45, 1951–53; established the Atomic Energy Authority.

Chiang Kai-shek (1887–1975): Chinese Nationalist leader; during 1926–28 defeated the provincial warlords who had emerged after the collapse of the Manchu imperial dynasty, and reunified the country under the Nationalist Republic, of which he was the effective head until 1949; broke with the Chinese Communists in 1927, initiating the long civil war which he eventually lost in 1949; the Nationalists were driven from the mainland to the island of Taiwan, where Chiang established an independent government, remaining President until his death in 1975.

Georgi Vasilyevich **Chicherin** (1872–1936): member of the Social Democratic Party 1904-14; arrested in London due to his perceived 'enemy associations' after the Russian armistice with Germany following the October 1917 revolution; released in January 1918, returned to Russia as Trotsky's aide and soon succeeded him as foreign commissar; ended the diplomatic isolation of the USSR by gaining formal recognition from European nations.

Clementine Ogilvy **Churchill** (née Hozier), Baroness Spencer-Churchill (1885–1977): married Churchill on 12 September 1908; provided invaluable, though far from uncritical, support to her husband; remained a life-long Liberal even after her husband returned to the Conservative Party in 1924.

Diana Spencer **Churchill** (1909–63); Churchill's first child; married Conservative politician Duncan Sandys in 1935 (divorced 1960); served as an officer in the Women's Royal Navy Service in London 1941–45; suffered declining mental and physical health from 1953, and took her own life by an overdose of sleeping pills in 1963.

John Strange Spencer **Churchill** (1880–1947): Winston's younger brother; stockbroker; served in both the Boer War and First World War, where he fought in France and Gallipoli.

Mary **Churchill** (Lady Mary Soames) (1922–): the Churchills' youngest child; served in Auxiliary Territorial Service with various anti-aircraft battery units 1941–45, though also travelled extensively with her father from 1943 until the end of the war; married Christopher Soames 1947; Chair of the Trustees of the Winston Churchill Memorial Trust since 1991; author of a number of books, including an award-winning biography of her mother.

Randolph Frederick Edward **Churchill** (1911–68); Churchill's only son; Conservative MP, Preston 1940–45; intelligence officer in the Middle East and Yugoslavia during the war; author of several controversial books, including *The Rise and Fall of Sir Anthony Eden* (1959) and *The Fight for the Tory Leadership* (1964); his well-received historical study of Lord Derby (1960) convinced Churchill to give him permission to write his official biography, and by his death he had published two volumes: *Youth, 1874–1900* (1966) and *Young Statesman, 1901–1914* (1967).

Lady Randolph **Churchill**, née Jennie Jerome (1854–1921): Churchill's mother; socialite, magazine editor (*Anglo-Saxon Review*) and journalist; married (1874) Lord Randolph Churchill (died 1895), (1900) Captain George Cornwallis-West (divorced 1913), (1918) Montagu Phippen Porch, colonial administrator.

Sarah Millicent Hermione Spencer **Churchill** (1914–82): the Churchills' third child, nicknamed 'Mule' because of her stubbornness; actress and dancer; served in the Women's Auxiliary Air Force during the Second World War; married three times, and suffered long-term problems with alcohol.

Sir Walter McLennan **Citrine**, 1st Baron Citrine (1887–1983): General Secretary, Trades Union Congress 1926–46; in 1931 opposed proposals for cuts in unemployment benefits and subsequently led the campaign to have Ramsay MacDonald and Philip Snowden expelled from the Labour Party.

Sir Ralph Alexander **Cochrane** (1895–1977): Air Officer Commanding 7 Group, RAF, 1940; Director, Flying Training, Air Ministry 1940–42; Air Officer Commanding 3 and 5 Group, RAF Bomber Command 1942–45; Vice Chief of the Air Staff, Air Ministry 1950–52; Managing Director Rolls Royce Ltd 1956–61.

Sir Arthur **Coningham** (1895–1948): commander 4 Group, Bomber Command (based at York), 1939–41; 204 group (Cairo), 1941–43; commander British and American tactical air forces in Tunisia, under General Spaatz, 1943–44; commander 2nd Tactical Air Force (UK), 1944–45.

King **Constantine** I (1868–1923): King of Greece 1913–17; opposed Prime Minister Venizelos' support for the Allies, but in June 1917, with Venizelos planning to march on Athens with Allied support, handed over the throne to his second son, Alexander, who reigned until dying from a monkey bite in October 1920; a plebiscite in December 1920 voted overwhelmingly for Constantine's return, but his popularity rapidly waned after the Turkish defeat of the Greeks in Anatolia and Smyrna, and in 1922 he was forced to abdicate; died in exile in Sicily in 1923.

A. Duff **Cooper**, 1st Viscount Norwich (1890–1954): Conservative MP for Oldham 1924–29, St George's (Westminster) 1931–45; Secretary of State for War,

1935–37; First Lord of the Admiralty May 1937–38; disagreed with the appeasement policy of Neville Chamberlain and resigned from office after Munich; Minister of Information 1940–41; Chancellor of Duchy of Lancaster 1941–43; died 1st January, 1954.

Percy Zachariah **Cox** (1864–1937): Political Resident in the Persian Gulf 1909–14; Chief Political Officer with the Indian Expeditionary Force to Mesopotamia 1914–17; Acting Minister to Tehran 1918–20; High Commissioner and Commander-in-Chief Mesopotamia 1920–23; plenipotentiary for negotiations with Turkey over the Iraq frontier 1924; Indian representative at Geneva conference on control of arms traffic 1925.

Sir James **Craig**, 1st Viscount Craigavon of Stormont (1871–1940): Unionist politician, rallied the Protestant opposition to Irish Home Rule in Ulster before the First World War, organising the Ulster Volunteer Force; succeeded Carson as leader of the Northern Unionists in February 1921 and became Prime Minister of Northern Ireland in June, holding the post until his death in 1940.

Frederick **Crawley** (1850–1937): Chancellor of the Duchy of Lancaster 1916–18.

Robert Offley Ashburton Crewe-Milnes, 1st Marquess of **Crewe** (1858–1945): Liberal politician; Lord President of the Council 1905–08 and 1915–16; Secretary of State for the Colonies 1908–10; Liberal leader in the Lords 1908–22 and 1936–44; Secretary of State for India 1910–15; President of the Board of Education 1916; Ambassador to France 1922–28; Secretary of State for War 1931.

Frederick **Cripps** (dates unknown): brother of Stafford Cripps; Director of the Russian and English Bank in Petrograd before 1914; served in Gallipoli, Palestine and France in the First World War.

Sir Richard Stafford **Cripps** (1889–1952): barrister; Labour and independent MP for Bristol East 1931–50; Solicitor-General, 1931; led the Socialist League, and founded *Tribune*; expelled from Labour Party in 1939 for urging a popular front; Ambassador to the Soviet Union 1940–42; member of War Cabinet as Lord Privy Seal, February – November 1942; Minister of Aircraft Production November 1942–45; readmitted to Labour Party 1945; President of the Board of Trade 1945–47; Minister of Economic Affairs and Chancellor of the Exchequer 1947–50.

Evelyn Baring, Earl of **Cromer** (1841–1917): Chairman of the Dardanelles Commission of Enquiry 1916–17.

Sir Ronald **Cross** (1896–1968): Minister for Economic Warfare 1939–40; Minister for Shipping 1940–45.

Admiral Andrew **Cunningham**, Viscount Hyndhope (1883–1963): Commander-in-Chief Mediterranean Fleet 1939–42, 1943, oversaw landings in North Africa and Sicily 1942–43; First Sea Lord 1943–46.

George Nathaniel **Curzon**, Marquess Curzon of Kedleston (1859–1925): Conservative MP for Southport 1886–98; Viceroy of India 1898–1905; Lord Privy Seal 1915–18; Foreign Secretary 1919–24.

Edward Hugh John Neale **Dalton,** Baron Dalton of Forest and Frith (1887–1962): academic economist; Labour MP for Peckham 1924–29, Bishop Auckland 1929–31, 1935–59; Minister of Economic Warfare 1940–42, established the covert operations organisation, the Special Operations Executive (SOE); President of the Board of Trade 1942–45; Chancellor of the Exchequer 1945–47, resigned in 1947 after inadvertently leaking Budget details to a journalist; Chancellor of the Duchy of Lancaster 1948–50; Minister of Town and Country Planning 1950–51; ennobled 1960.

Edward Clement **Davies** (1884–1962): Liberal and Liberal National MP for Montgomery 1927–62; a key opponent of Chamberlain, when Eden and Churchill joined Chamberlain's administration in September 1939, Davies worked with Leo Amery to organise cross-bench opposition to Chamberlain's premiership and his replacement by Churchill in May 1940; Leader of the Liberal Party 1945–56.

Miles **Dempsey** (1896–1969): commanded British 2nd Army during the D-Day landings in June 1944.

Anton Ivanovich **Denikin** (1872–1947): Russian soldier, rose to the rank of Lieutenant-General in World War I; Commander of the White Russian forces in Southern Russia 1918–20; escaped to Constantinople and then lived in exile in France and the US.

Admiral Sir Barry Edward **Domvile** (1878–1971): Director of Naval Intelligence 1927–30; Commander 3 Cruiser Squadron, Mediterranean, 1931–32; President, Royal Naval College Greenwich and commander Royal Naval War College 1932–34; retired 1936.

Sir William Sholto **Douglas**, 1st Baron Douglas of Kirtleside (1893–1969): ended the First World War as a major in the Royal Flying Corps; made Air Vice-Marshal in 1938; Deputy Chief of the Air Staff 1940; succeeded Dowding in November 1940 as Commander-in-Chief, Fighter Command; Commander RAF Middle East Command 1943–45; Commander-in-Chief British Air Forces of Occupation in Germany 1945–48; ennobled in 1948, and sat on the Labour benches.

Hugh Caswell Tremenheere **Dowding**, Baron Dowding of Bentley Priory (1882–1970): Squadron Commander in World War I, then served in command, staff, and training positions in the new RAF; Commander-in-Chief, Fighter Command 1936–40, where he vigorously promoted the development of radar and the Spitfire and Hurricane fighters that contributed significantly to the defeat of the Luftwaffe during the Battle of Britain; replaced by Sholto Douglas; sent on special duty in the US for the Ministry of Aircraft Production, where he made himself unpopular with his outspoken behaviour; retired in November 1942 and ennobled the following year.

General Vladimir **Dragomirov** (1862–1920): prominent White Russian general, appointed Military Governor of Kiev by Denikin in October 1919; presumed killed by Polish forces following the fall of Kiev in 1920.

Ira C. **Eaker** (1896–1987): Lt.-General US Air Force; in January 1942, assigned task of organising Eighth Air Force Bomber Command, which was to be the backbone of US airpower in Europe; in August, he personally led the first strike on continental Europe; Commander Allied Air Forces in the Mediterranean 1944–45.

Sir Robert Anthony **Eden**, 1st Earl of Avon (1897–1977): Conservative MP for Warwick & Leamington 1923–57; Parliamentary Under-Secretary, Foreign Office, 1931–33; Lord Privy Seal 1934–35; Minister for League of Nations Affairs 1935; Foreign Secretary 1935–38; resigned over appeasement; Secretary of State for Dominions 1939–40; Secretary of State for War 1940; Foreign Secretary 1940–45 and 1951–55; Prime Minister 1955-57, resigned after Suez debacle; created Earl of Avon 1961.

Dwight David **Eisenhower** (1890–1969): US general, with a talent for organisation, persuasion and coordination; Commander, Allied forces, Operation Torch (the invasion of French North Africa) 1942–43; directed invasions of Sicily and Italy, 1943–44; Supreme Commander Allied Expeditionary Forces, Operation Overlord (the cross-Channel invasion of Europe), 1944–45; US Army Chief of Staff 1945–48; Supreme Commander, NATO 1950–52; President of the United States 1953–61.

Maxine **Elliott** (1868–1940): American actress and grande dame of late Edwardian and inter-war international society; lived at Maidenhead and Chateau de l'Horizon, Golfe Juan; Maxine Elliot was a stage name, although this was what her friends called her – her real name was Jessie Dermot.

Enver Pasha (1881–1922): Turkish War Minister and Commander-in-Chief during World War One, instrumental in bringing Turkey into the war on the side of the Central Powers; fled to Germany after the war; travelled to Moscow in 1919 seeking support for a campaign to overthrow Mustafa Kemal's new government but was met with deep suspicion by the Soviet regime who refused to assist his plans; killed in August 1922 while fighting the Red Army in Turkestan with the Whites.

Herbert Vere **Evatt** (1894–1965): Australian Labor Party politician; Attorney-General and Minister for External Affairs 1941–45; Deputy Prime Minister 1946–49.

Sir Douglas Claude Strathern **Evill** (1892–1971): senior air staff officer to Air Chief Marshal Sir Hugh Dowding, 1940; led RAF delegation in Washington 1942–43; Vice-Chief of the Air Staff 1943–45.

John Donald **Fergusson** (1891–1963): Churchill's Private Secretary during his tenure as Chancellor of the Exchequer.

John Arbuthnot 'Jackie' **Fisher**, Admiral of the Fleet Lord Fisher (1841–1920): entered Royal Navy in 1854, rising to Rear-Admiral in 1890; held a succession of senior positions before becoming First Sea Lord (1904–10); brought out of retirement by Churchill to become First Sea Lord again in 1914, but quarrelled with Churchill over the Dardanelles operation and resigned in May 1915.

Sir Dingle Mackintosh **Foot** (1905–78): Liberal MP 1931–45; Parliamentary Secretary, Ministry of Economic Warfare 1940–45; Labour MP 1957–70; Solicitor-General 1964–67; a member of the Foot political dynasty (son of Isaac, brother of Michael), Foot was acknowledged by all parties as a great success at the Ministry of Economic Warfare.

Wilfrid Rhodes **Freeman** (1888–1953): in charge of RAF research and development 1938–40, responsible for pushing through the development of key equipment such as the four-engined heavy bombers (Halifaxes and Manchesters), the Mosquito reconnaissance and pathfinder plane, and the testing of the radar early warning system; also, crucially, involved in the development of the eight-gun fighters (Hurricanes and Spitfires); served in MAP from November 1940 to the end of the war; his relationship with Portal, who replaced Newall as Chief of Air Staff in October 1940, was one of the key relationships of the war and ensured that the relations between the Air Ministry and MAP never reached breaking point – even when Beaverbrook was in charge.

Field Marshal Sir John Denton Pinkstone **French**, Earl of Ypres (1852–1925): Commander of the British Expeditionary Force deployed to Europe in the opening days of the war; relieved of his command in December 1915; Commander British Home Forces 1915–18 (in which position he dealt with the Easter Rising in Ireland in 1916); Lord Lieutenant of Ireland 1918–21; ennobled 1922.

Bernard **Freyberg** (1890–1963): Lieutenant, Royal Naval Division; awarded the Victoria Cross when commanding the *Hood* battalion in an attack on a German strongpoint on the western front in November 1916.

William **Furse** (1865–1953): Major-General commanding the 9th (Scottish) Division during 1916.

James **Garvin** (1868–1947): Editor of the *Observer & Pall Mall Gazette*; his only son was killed in action.

Sir Auckland **Geddes** (1879–1954): Minister of National Service 1917–19; Minister of Reconstruction 1919; President of the Board of Trade 1919–20; Ambassador to Washington 1920–24.

George **Gibson** (1885–1953): Chairman of the Trades Union Congress 1940–41; Director of the Bank of England 1946–48.

Sir John **Gilmour** (1876–1940): Conservative MP for East Renfrewshire 1910–18, Glasgow Pollock 1918–40; Secretary of State for Scotland 1926–29; Minister for Agriculture and Fisheries 1931–32; Home Secretary, 1932–35; Minister for Shipping 1939–40.

Joseph **Goebbels** (1897–1945): Hitler's Minister of Propaganda.

Victor **Gollancz** (1893–1967): publisher; established Victor Gollancz Ltd in 1928, and Left Book Club in 1936; one of the founder members of the Campaign for Nuclear Disarmament in 1958.

Gustav Adolf Joachim Rüdiger, Count von der **Goltz** (1865–1946): son of Wilhelm von der Goltz, who commanded the Turkish forces in Mesopotamia in the First World War, and defeated the British at Kut; commanded German troops in Latvia (under Article XII of the Armistice, German troops occupying territories of the former Russian Empire were allowed to remain in their positions until ordered to quit; the Allies' intention, obviously, was to use these forces against the Bolsheviks) and hoped to establish a pro-German government in Latvia from which German influence could radiate eastwards; although his troops captured Riga in May 1919, they were defeated by a combined Estonian-Latvian force in June and withdrew to Germany in December.

Hubert de la **Gough** (1870–1963): commanded Fifth Army 1916–18; headed Allied Mission to the Baltic in 1919, retiring in 1922.

Dimitrios **Gounaris** (1866–1922): Prime Minister of Greece March – August 1915 and April 1921 – May 1922.

Alexandre **Goutchkov** or Guchkov (1862–1936): fought in the Boer War against the British; leader of the Octobrist Party in the wake of the abortive Russian Revolution of 1905, a moderate figure arguing in favour of constitutional reform before and during World War One; from 1910–11 President of the State Duma and notable public critic of the Tsar and Tsarina's close advisor Grigory Rasputin; appointed Minister of War by Kerensky in March 1917; sought exile in Paris following the October Revolution.

Arthur **Greenwood** (1880–1954): Labour MP for Nelson & Colne 1922–31, Wakefield 1932–50; Minister of Health 1929–31; Deputy Leader of the Labour Party 1935–43; Minister without Portfolio, War Cabinet 1940–43; acting leader of the Labour Party in the Commons 1943–45; Lord Privy Seal 1945–46; Paymaster General 1946–47; Minister without Portfolio 1947.

Sir Edward **Grey**, first Viscount Grey of Falloden (1862–1933): Liberal MP for Berwick-on-Tweed 1885–1916; Under-Secretary of State, Foreign Office, 1892–95; Foreign Secretary 1905–16, well known for his utterance on the outbreak of war: 'the lamps are going out all over Europe; we shall not see them lit again in our lifetime'; ennobled in 1916; Liberal leader in the Lords 1923–24; President of the Asquithian 'Liberal Council' 1927–33.

George Charles **Grey** (1918–44): Liberal MP for Berwick-on-Tweed 1941–44; Captain, 4th Battalion Grenadier Guards; commanded part of the 6th Guards Tanks Brigade, equipped with Churchill VII tanks, during the advance through Normandy following D-Day; killed in action; a rising star in the Liberal Party, his death at the age of twenty-five was deeply mourned within the Parliamentary party.

Spenser **Grey** (dates unknown): Squadron Commander who at this time was a test pilot for the experimental flights of early versions of flying boats; led the first successful British air attack on Germany in 1915, when two Sopwith Tabloids of the Royal Naval Air Service attacked Zeppelin airship sheds at Dusseldorf, destroying Zeppelin L9.

Edward **Grigg** (1879–1955): served in the Grenadier Guards 1914–18; Churchill served at the front with him.

Sir Percy James **Grigg** (1890–1964): civil servant and politician; Principal Private Secretary to successive Chancellors of the Exchequer, 1921–30; National MP 1942–45; Secretary of State for War 1942–45.

Lloyd Carpenter **Griscom** (1872–1959): US diplomat. US Minister to Persia, 1901–02, Japan, 1902–06; US Ambassador to Brazil, 1906–07, Italy, 1907–09; US representative to the War Office 1917–19.

Hugh **Grosvenor** (1879–1953): 2nd Duke of Westminster.

Jacques **Grumbach** (dates unknown): member Administrative Commission of French Socialist Party; editor of French newspaper *Populaire*.

Frederick Edward **Guest** (1875–1937): cousin of Churchill's and close political friend; Liberal MP, 1910–22, 1923–29; Conservative MP, 1931–37; Chief Whip, Coalition Liberals, 1916–21; during the 1930s Guest was one of the small band of Churchill supporters in the House of Commons.

John William **Gulland** (1864–1920): Liberal Chief Whip 1915–16.

Douglas **Haig**, First Earl Haig (1861–1928): served in Sudan and Boer War; succeeded French as Commander-in-Chief British Expeditionary Force in December 1915; pursued strategy of attrition, at enormous cost in British lives; ennobled 1919.

J. Aylmer Lowthorpe **Haldane** (1862–1950): served in the Boer war and was imprisoned with Churchill in Pretoria; knighted and appointed Lieutenant-General 1918; Commander-in-Chief Mesopotamia 1920–22; appointed General 1925.

Richard Burdon **Haldane**, Viscount Haldane of Cloan (1856–1928): Liberal MP for Haddingtonshire 1885–1911; Secretary of State for War 1905–12; ennobled 1911; Lord Chancellor 1912–15; dismissed by Asquith at Conservative insistence when the coalition government was formed in May 1915, following a press campaign to smear him as pro-German – in large part because of his taste for German philosophers; joined the Labour Party and became Lord Chancellor again in 1924, and leader of the Labour peers until his death in 1928.

Edward Frederick Lindley Wood, Baron Irwin (1925–34), Viscount **Halifax** (1934–44), 1st Earl of Halifax (1944–59) (1881–1959): Conservative MP for Ripon 1910–25; President of the Board of Education 1922–24; Minister of Agriculture 1924–25; Viceroy of India 1925–31; President of the Board of Education 1932–35; Lord Privy Seal 1935–37; Leader of the House of Lords 1935–38; Lord President of the Council 1937–38; Foreign Secretary 1938–40, a key architect, with Chamberlain, of appeasement; British ambassador to the United States 1940–46.

Maurice **Hankey**, 1st Lord Hankey (1877–1963): Secretary to the War Cabinet 1916, Imperial War Cabinet 1917–18 and Cabinet 1919–38; Minister without Portfolio,

War Cabinet 1939–40; Chancellor of the Duchy of Lancaster 1940–41; Paymaster General 1941–42.

Sir Charles 'Tim' **Harington** (1872–1940): Deputy Chief of the Imperial General Staff 1918–20; Lieutenant-General Commanding the Army of the Black Sea 1920; Commanding Officer of the Allied Forces of Occupation in Turkey 1920–23; Governor and Commander-in-Chief Gibraltar 1933–38.

Averell W. **Harriman** (1891–1986): adviser to Democratic Presidents from Franklin D. Roosevelt to Lyndon B. Johnson; lend-lease expediter in London 1941–43, reporting directly to the White House, and bypassing the US ambassador and the State Department; Ambassador to Russia 1943–46; Ambassador to Great Britain 1946; Secretary of Commerce 1947–48; special representative in Europe, administering the Marshall Plan. 1948–50; unsuccessful candidate for the Democratic nomination for the presidency 1952 and 1956; Governor of New York 1954–58; Assistant Secretary of State 1961–63; headed US delegation to Paris peace talks with North Vietnam 1968–69.

Alfred **Harmsworth**: *see* Lord Northcliffe.

Sir Robert **Harmsworth** (1870–1937): Liberal MP for Caithness & Sutherland 1900–22; younger brother of newspaper Lords Northcliffe and Rothermere.

Air Marshal Sir Arthur Travers 'Bomber' **Harris** (1892–1984): RFC squadron commander in First World War; served in RAF and rose to Air Marshal in 1941 and Commander-in-Chief RAF bomber command 1942–45; a firm believer in mass raids, he developed the 'saturation' technique of mass bombing, though eventually the policy brought him into conflict with Portal and Churchill, when he continued to pursue it even during the last winter of the war.

Sir Percy **Harris** (1876–1952): Liberal MP for Market Harborough 1916–18, South West Bethnal Green 1922–45; Liberal Chief Whip 1931–40; Deputy Leader of the Parliamentary Liberal Party 1940–45; a hard-working and principled man, he was neither charismatic nor popular, in spite of what Sinclair claimed, with his fellow MPs (indeed, he was recognised as one of the main bores of the Commons, regularly emptying the Chamber when he spoke).

Arthur **Henderson** (1863–1935): Labour MP for Barnard Castle 1903–18, Widnes 1919–22, Newcastle-upon-Tyne East 1923, Burnley 1924–31, Derbyshire Clay Cross 1933–35; Chairman Parliamentary Labour Party 1908–10, 1914–17; President Board of Education 1915–16; Paymaster-General 1916–17; member of War Cabinet 1916–17; fell out with Lloyd George in 1917 and resigned from government; first Labour Home Secretary 1924; Foreign Secretary 1929–31.

Boris Vladimirovich **Heroys** (dates unknown): chief of the White Russian Military Mission to London.

Paul von **Hindenburg** (1847–1934): Chief of the German General Staff, 1916–18; second President of the Weimar Republic 1925–34; appointed Adolf Hitler as chancellor in 1933.

Herbert Campbell **Holman** (1869–1949): Chief of British Military Mission to South Russia 1919–20, commanding about 500 officers and 2,000 men who trained White Russian forces in the use of artillery and machine guns.

Herbert **Hoover** (1874–1964): Head of the American Relief Administration 1918–21, organising shipments of food to central Europe: it was a violent outburst of anger on Hoover's part that persuaded Lloyd George that a drastic change in the Allied policy of maintaining the blockade was urgently needed, and it was raised in March 1919; Secretary of Commerce 1921–28; US President 1929–33.

Harry L. **Hopkins** (1890–1946): New Deal administrator; Secretary of Commerce 1938–40; special adviser to Roosevelt and the President's personal envoy to Britain, influential in gaining US aid for Britain prior to Pearl Harbor; headed lend-lease programme from 1941.

Sir Robert **Horne** (1871–1940): Chancellor of the Exchequer 1921–22.

Nellie **Hozier** (1888–1957): Clementine Churchill's sister.

Cordell **Hull** (1871–1955): Democratic member of the House of Representatives 1907–21, 1923–31, Senate 1931–33; Secretary of State 1933–44; awarded Nobel Peace Prize in 1945 for his part in establishing the United Nations.

Robert **Hutchison** (1873–1950): Liberal, then Liberal National MP 1922–32; created Baron 1932; Paymaster-General 1935–38 and leading Liberal National in the Lords.

William Edmund **Ironside** (1880–1959): Major-General commanding Allied troops at Archangel 1918–19; Head of British Military Mission to Hungary 1920; Commander British Forces in Turkey 1920, and North Persia 1920–21; Quartermaster-General India 1933–36; Governor and Commander-in-Chief Gibraltar 1938–39; Chief of the Imperial General Staff 1939–40; Commander-in-Chief Home Forces May 1940; one of a small number of men who held general officer rank in both world wars.

Rufus **Isaacs**: *see* Lord Reading.

Hastings Lionel Ismay, Baron **Ismay** (1887–1964): served in India and Africa and then on the Committee of Imperial Defence; Chief of Staff to Winston Churchill and later to Clement Attlee 1940–46; Churchill's closest military adviser; participated in many important international conferences, including Moscow, Tehran and Yalta; first Secretary-General of NATO 1952–57.

Henry **Jackson** (1855–1929): First Sea Lord, replacing Fisher, May 1915 – December 1916.

Karol **Jaroszynski** (dates unknown): Ukrainian/Polish banker who purchased a string of banks and finance houses; a close associate of British agent Sidney Reilly, Jaroszynski was the leading advocate of a plan to form an Anglo-American syndicate to invest in post-Bolshevik Russia; considered by the British Consul-General in Odessa, John Picton Bagge, to be a possible 'Cecil Rhodes for eastern Europe'.

General Sir George Darrell **Jeffreys**, 1st Baron Jeffreys (1878–1960): infantry division commander in the 1914–18 war; Conservative MP for Petersfield 1941–51; Colonel of the Grenadier Guards 1952–60.

Harcourt 'Crinks' **Johnstone** (1895–1945): Liberal MP for Willesden East 1923–24, South Shields 1931–35, Middlesbrough West 1940–45; member of the Other Club and opponent of appeasement; a wealthy bachelor and great friend of both Sinclair and Churchill, he was mainly responsible, along with fellow Liberal MP Jimmy de Rothschild, for keeping the Liberal Party afloat financially during the 1930s; Secretary of Overseas Trade 1940–45 – not a great success as a minister, but in fine Liberal tradition he pushed a post-war free trade agenda during his time in government.

Stinton **Jones** (dates unknown): a British engineer working in Russia 1905–17; a witness to the Russian Revolution, after arriving back in Britain he published *Russia in Revolution* (Nast & Co., 1917).

Take **Jonescu** (dates unknown): former Romanian Prime Minister.

Air Chief Marshal Sir Philip Bennet **Joubert de la Ferte** (1887–1965): served in RFC and then RAF, from 1914; Air Adviser on Combined Operations, 1940; Assistant Chief of the Air Staff (Radio) 1940–41; Air Officer Commander-in-Chief, Coastal Command, 1941–43; well known for his commentaries on the progress of the war on the BBC and in national newspapers.

Alexander **Kerensky** (1881–1970): leading member of the Socialist Revolutionary Party; when the Tsar abdicated on 13 March 1917, a Provisional Government, headed by Prince George Lvov, was formed; Kerensky served as Minister of Justice and later Minister for War, and in July replaced Lvov as Prime Minister; with the deteriorating war situation Kerensky's government fell to a Bolshevik putsch (the October Revolution) and he fled to London; in the 1930s moved to the US and took up teaching.

Philip **Kerr**: *see* Lord Lothian.

William Lyon Mackenzie **King** (1874–1950): Leader of the Canadian Liberal Party 1919–48; Prime Minister of Canada 1921–26, 1926–30, 1935–48.

Herbert **Kitchener**, 1st Earl Kitchener (1850–1916): field marshal; Secretary of State for War, 1914–16, during which he organised manpower on a vast scale (the 'Kitchener armies').

General Alfred **Knox** (1870–1964): British Military Attaché in Petrograd from 1911; spoke Russian fluently and on the outbreak of the First World War became liaison officer to the Russian Army, working closely with George Buchanan, the British Ambassador; Chief of the British Military Mission to Siberia 1918–20; Conservative MP for Wycombe 1924–45.

Alexander Vasilevich **Kolchak** (1874–1920): Russian admiral; Commander of the Black Sea fleet during World War I; after the October Revolution became leader of the anti-Bolshevik White forces in Siberia, and in October 1918 proclaimed himself 'Supreme Ruler' of Russia; captured and executed by the Bolsheviks at Irkutsk in 1920.

Leonid **Krassin** (1870–1926): close ally of Lenin; Commissar for Foreign Trade 1918–22, sent to London to re-establish trade relations.

Alexander **Krivoshein** (1858–1921): political moderate; Minister of Agriculture 1908–15; dismissed because of his opposition to Tsar Nicholas II's decision to take personal command of the Russian Army; following the October Revolution of 1917 joined the White anti-Bolshevik Volunteer Army in the Crimea; after its defeat he fled into exile in France.

Bela **Kun** (1886–1936): Hungarian revolutionary, responsible for founding the world's second communist government, albeit short-lived, with the disintegration of the Austro-Hungarian Empire at the close of the First World War; forced from power in August 1919 by the right-wing nationalist Admiral Horthy; fled to Moscow, where he remained until purged by Stalin in 1936.

Sir William **Lambton** (1863–1936): Military Secretary to Sir John French, Commander-in-Chief, British Expeditionary Force, France 1914–15; Commander, 4th Division 1915–17; retired 1920.

Sir Henry Charles Keith Petty-Fitzmaurice, 5th Marquess of **Lansdowne** (1845–1937): Governor-General of Canada 1883–88; Viceroy of India 1888–93; left the Liberal Party for the Conservatives in 1893; Secretary of State for War 1895–1901; Foreign Secretary 1901–05; Minister without Portfolio 1915–16.

Walter Thomas **Layton**, 1st Baron Layton (1884–1966): politician and newspaperman; Editor, *The Economist* 1921–38; chair, Lloyd George's Committee of Industrial Inquiry, which produced the famous 'Yellow Book', *Britain's Industrial Future*; economic adviser to the League of Nations; Director of Programmes, Ministry of Supply 1940–42; Head of Joint War Production Staff 1942–43; created Baron Layton 1947.

Sir Trafford **Leigh-Mallory** (1892–1944): commanded fighter groups 1937–42; Commander-in-Chief Fighter Command 1942–44, commanded Allied expeditionary air forces for the Normandy invasion; appointed Commander-in-Chief Allied air forces in Southeast Asia, but was killed flying out to Burma in November 1944 to take up the post.

Vladimir Ilich Ulyanov ('**Lenin**') (1870–1924): led the Bolshevik wing of the Russian Social Democratic Workers' Party (later the Communist Party of the Soviet Union) after the split with the Mensheviks in 1903; returned to Russia from exile in western Europe in April 1917 and led the October Revolution; Chairman of the Council of People's Commissars (Prime Minister) from then until his death in 1924.

George **Leygues** (1857–1933): French politician during the Third Republic; Minister of Education, then Interior; Minister for the Colonies 1918–20; President of the Council of Ministers September 1920 – January 1921.

Prince Paul Ivan **Lieven** (1875–1963): Russian aristocrat, worked briefly as an engineer; senior Red Cross official during the Russo-Japanese War; commanded White Russian forces in the Baltic region 1918–19; increasingly disillusioned by the lack of British support, he turned to the local German commander, von der Goltz, for financial support; after the White collapse in late 1919 he fled to Paris, and subsequently lived in Germany, Belgium, and Ireland.

Frederick Alexander **Lindemann**: *see* Cherwell.

Victor Alexander John Hope **Linlithgow**, 2nd Marquess of Linlithgow (1887–1952): Civil Lord of the Admiralty 1922–24; Chairman of the joint select committee on

Indian constitutional reform on whose report was based the Government of India Act of 1935; Viceroy of India 1936–43; Chairman of Midland Bank 1943–52.

Sir Francis John **Linnell** (1892–1944): Controller of Research and Development, MAP, 1941–43: Deputy Air Officer Commander-in-Chief, RAF Middle East/ Middle East Command 1943–44; killed in a road accident in 1944.

Louis James **Lipsett** (1874–1918): Brigadier-General, attached to the Canadian Expeditionary Force; highly regarded by Churchill who described him to Beaverbrook as 'exceptional in his judgement and flair'.

Maxim **Litvinov** (1876–1951): appointed in November 1918 as the Bolshevik Government's representative in Britain; arrested by the British Government and held until exchanged for Bruce Lockhart, the British diplomat imprisoned in Russia; then employed as the Soviet Government's roaming ambassador; it was largely through his efforts that Britain agreed to end its economic blockade of the Soviet Union, and he also negotiated several trade agreements with European countries; Commissar for Foreign Affairs from 1930; in 1933 persuaded the United States to recognise the Soviet government; Ambassador to the United States 1941–43.

David **Lloyd George**, 1st Earl Lloyd George of Dwyfor (1863–1945): Liberal MP for Caernarvon Boroughs 1890–1945; President of the Board of Trade 1905–08; Chancellor of the Exchequer 1908–15; Minister of Munitions 1915–16; Secretary of State for War 1916; Prime Minister 1916–22; Leader of the Liberal Party 1926–31; ennobled 1945.

Gwilym **Lloyd-George**, 1st Viscount Tenby (1894–1967): second son of David Lloyd George; Liberal MP for Pembrokeshire 1922–24, 1929–50; the only Liberal MP to join the Chamberlain Government (as a junior minister) at the outbreak of war in September 1939; Minister of Fuel and Power 1942–45; Liberal and Conservative MP for Newcastle-on-Tyne North 1951–57; Minister of Food 1951–54; Home Secretary and Minister for Welsh Affairs 1954–57; ennobled 1957.

Megan **Lloyd George** (1902–66): daughter of David Lloyd George; Liberal and Independent Liberal MP for Anglesey 1929–51; Deputy Leader of the Liberal Party 1949–51; joined the Labour Party in 1955, Labour MP for Carmarthenshire 1957–66.

'Oliver' Godfrey **Locker-Lampson** (1875–1946): Conservative MP for Salisbury 1910–18 and for Wood Green 1918–35.

Air Chief Marshal Sir Arthur Murray **Longmore** (1885–1970): Air Officer Commander-in-Chief, Middle East Command, until June 1941.

Philip Kerr, Lord **Lothian** (1882–1940): Private Secretary to Lloyd George 1916–21, where he was active at the Paris Peace Conference, 1919; Chancellor of the Duchy of Lancaster August – October 1931; supporter of appeasement until 1939; Ambassador to US 1939–40; died in December 1940 following a common viral illness, his belief in Christian Science leading him to refuse simple medical treatment that would almost certainly have saved his life.

Edgar **Ludlow-Hewitt** (1886–1973): Commander in Chief, Bomber Command 1937–40; increasingly criticised, in particular for his insistence on the formation of more Operational Training Units at the expense of some front-line aircraft and crews; replaced by Sir Charles Portal in February 1940; Inspector-General of the RAF 1940–45.

Oliver **Lyttelton**, 1st Viscount Chandos (1893–1972): Conservative MP for Aldershot 1940–45, 1950–54; President of the Board of Trade 1940–41; Minister of State 1941–42; Minister of State Resident in Cairo 1942; Minister of State for War Production 1942–45; Secretary of State for the Colonies 1951–54; ennobled 1954.

Victor Alexander George **Lytton**, 2nd Earl of Lytton (1876–1947): Civil Lord of the Admiralty, 1916, 1919–20; Under-Secretary of State for India 1920–22; Governor of Bengal 1922–27; Head of League of Nations Mission to Manchuria 1932.

General Douglas **MacArthur** (1880–1964): Chief of Staff US Army 1930–35; commanded US forces in Philippines, 1941; Commander Allied forces, Southwest Pacific Theatre 1942–45; Commander, Allied occupation of Japan 1945–51; Commander, UN forces in Korean War 1950–51.

Jock **McDavid** (1897–1972): a Lieutenant in the 6th Royal Scots Fusiliers.

James Ramsay **MacDonald** (1866–1937): Secretary, Labour Representation Committee 1900–12 (negotiated MacDonald-Gladstone electoral pact with the Liberals); Labour MP for Leicester 1906–18, Aberavon 1922–29, Labour and National Labour MP for Seaham 1929–37; Leader of the Parliamentary Labour Party 1922–31; Foreign Secretary and Prime Minister 1924; Prime Minister 1931–35; the first Labour MP to be expelled by the party, following his decision to lead the National Government in 1931.

Lionel Douglas Dalzell **McKean** (1886–1963): pilot, RFC 1915–18; senior officer in RAF Training Command 1936–40; head of RAF Mission to Canada 1940–43, helping to set up the Commonwealth Air Training Plan.

Reginald **McKenna** (1863–1943): Liberal MP for North Monmouthshire 1895–1918; President of the Board of Education 1907–08; First Lord of the Admiralty 1908–11; Home Secretary 1911–15; Chancellor of the Exchequer 1915–16.

Sir Halford **Mackinder** (1861–1947): British High Commissioner in Southern Russia and a key liaison officer with General Denikin's White troops; argued that Britain's interests would be best served by splitting Russia into smaller states, and urged Curzon, the Foreign Secretary, to support the independence of Belarus, Ukraine, Georgia, Azerbaijan, Armenia and Chechnya; also recommended that Southern Russia, governed by the Whites, should be recognised as a separate state.

Maurice Harold **Macmillan**, 1st Earl of Stockton (1894–1986): Conservative MP for Stockton-on-Tees 1924–29, 1931–64; British representative in the Mediterranean, 1942–45; Minister of Housing 1951–54; Minister of Defence 1954–55; Foreign Secretary 1955; Chancellor of the Exchequer 1955–57; Prime Minister 1957–63; ennobled 1984.

Nestor **Makhno** (1889–1934): Ukrainian revolutionary and anarchist; jailed in 1908, released after the February 1917 revolution; returned to Ukraine and began organising against landlords and capitalists; when Ukraine was handed to Germany under the Treaty of Brest-Litovsk in 1918, formed partisan resistance groups, who united into the Revolutionary Insurrectionary Army of the Ukraine, also called the Black Army (fighting under the black flag of anarchism); successful against Germans, Ukrainian nationalists and Russian Whites in 1918–21, but defeated in 1921 by his former allies the Bolsheviks; fled into exile in France.

Geoffrey Le Mesurier **Mander** (1882–1962): Liberal MP for Wolverhampton East 1929–45; Parliamentary Private Secretary to Sir Archibald Sinclair 1942–45.

Carl Gustaf **Mannerheim** (1867–1951): Finnish soldier; Lieutenant-General, Russian Imperial Army; assumed command of white (anti-Bolshevik) forces in newly independent Finland in 1918 and defeated Finland's communists and Russian Bolsheviks; regent of Finland 1918–19, but defeated in Finland's first presidential election in 1919; tried to make Finland participate in the Russian counter-revolutionary military operations, but failed and retired to private life; Chairman of the Defence Council 1931–39; commanded the Finnish forces in the 'winter war' against Russia in 1939–40; joined Germans in attack on Soviet Union in 1941; President of Finland 1944–46, negotiated peace with Soviets in 1944; his greatest contribution was to maintain Finnish independence in the face of Russian aggression and German ambitions in the 1940s.

Henry David Reginald **Margesson**, 1st Viscount Margesson of Rugby (1890–1965): Conservative MP for West Ham 1922–23, Rugby 1924–42; Government Chief Whip 1931–40; Secretary of State for War 1940–42, sacked by Churchill following a series of severe military setbacks, including the loss of Singapore; ennobled 1942.

Eddie (Eddy) **Marsh** (1872–1953): Churchill's private secretary from December 1905 – November 1915; became private secretary to Asquith when Churchill left to fight in France.

George Catlett **Marshall** (1880–1959): US Army Chief of Staff 1939–45; Secretary of State 1947–49; proposed European Recovery Programme in 1947, later known as the Marshall Plan; Secretary of Defense 1950–51; received the Nobel Peace Prize in 1953.

James **Masterton-Smith** (1878–1938): Private Secretary to the First Lord of the Admiralty 1910–17.

Harrison Freeman **Matthews** (1899–1986): US Foreign Service officer, London Embassy 1941–45; Ambassador to Sweden 1947–50, Netherlands 1953–57, Austria 1957–62.

James **Maxton** (1885–1946): one of the 'Red Clydeside' leaders; a pacifist, opposed the First World War and imprisoned in 1916–17 for encouraging munitions workers to strike; Independent Labour Party (ILP) MP for Bridgend 1922–46; consistent critic of the Labour leadership and instrumental in persuading the ILP to break away from Labour after MacDonald formed the National Government in 1931; his pacifism led him to support Chamberlain's appeasement policies in the 1930s.

Charles **Maynard** (1870–1945): Major-General commanding Allied forces, Archangel, 1918–19.

Field Marshal Erhard **Milch** (1892–1972): State Secretary, Reich Aviation Ministry; oversaw the development of the Luftwaffe as part of the rearmament of Germany after 1933; Air Inspector General 1940–44, forced out by Göring after joining Goebbels and Himmler in attempting to convince Hitler to remove Göring from command of the Luftwaffe; found guilty of war crimes at Nuremberg, sentenced to life imprisonment but released in June 1954.

Air Chief Marshal Sir William **Mitchell** (1888–1944): Air Officer Commander-in-Chief, Middle East until May 1940; Inspector-General of the RAF 1940–41; Black Rod, House of Lords 1941–42; asked to return to service in mid-1942, became Commandant, London Command, Air Training Corps, until his death in 1944.

Walter Turner **Monckton**, 1st Viscount Monckton of Brenchley (1891–1965): Conservative MP for Bristol 1951–57; Minister of Labour 1951–55; Minister of Defence 1955–56; the only cabinet minister who disagreed with Eden's policy during the Suez Crisis, he was moved to be Paymaster-General 1956–57.

Sir Alfred Moritz **Mond**, 1st Baron Melchett of Blandford (1868–1930): Liberal MP for Chester 1906–10, Swansea Town 1910–18, Swansea West 1918–23, Liberal and Conservative MP for Carmarthen 1924–28; First Commissioner of Works 1916–21; Minister of Public Health 1921–22; joined Conservatives in 1926; helped to create ICI in 1926.

Edwin Samuel **Montagu** (1879–1924): Liberal MP for Cambridgeshire Chesterton 1906–18, Cambridgeshire 1918–22; Private Secretary to Asquith 1906–10; Chancellor of the Duchy of Lancaster 1915–16; Minister of Munitions 1916; Secretary of State for India 1917–22; in 1919 he was responsible for the Government of India Act, which provided India with wide powers of self-government.

Bernard Law **Montgomery**, 1st Viscount Montgomery of Alamein (1887–1976): arguably the best British field commander since Wellington; commanded 3rd Division in France, 1939–40; commanded 8th Army in Africa and Italy, 1942–43, under Alexander; won crucial battle of El Alamein, 1942; helped formulate the invasion plan for France, and in the Normandy campaign acted as field commander of all ground forces until August 1944, then led the 21st Army Group; commander British occupation forces in Germany 1945–46; Chief of the Imperial General Staff 1946–48; Deputy Supreme Commander of NATO forces in Europe 1951–58.

John **Moore-Brabazon**, 1st Lord Brabazon (1884–1964): first Englishman to pilot a heavier-than-air machine under power in England (1909); served in the Royal Flying Corps during First World War; Parliamentary Private Secretary to Winston Churchill 1919; Conservative MP for Chatham 1919–29, Wallasey 1931–42; Minister of Transport 1940–41; Minister of Aircraft Production 1941–42.

Herbert Stanley **Morrison**, Baron Morrison of Lambeth (1888–1965): Labour MP for South Hackney 1923–24, 1929–31, 1935–59; Minister of Transport 1929–31; Leader of London County Council 1933–40; Minister of Supply 1940; Home Secretary 1940–45; Deputy Prime Minister and Leader of the House of Commons 1945–51; Foreign Secretary 1951; ennobled 1959.

Sir Oswald Ernest **Mosley** (1896–1980): Conservative, Independent, and Labour MP for Harrow 1918–24, Labour then New Party MP for Smethwick 1928–31; in the 1920s seen as one of the rising stars at Westminster; Chancellor of Duchy of Lancaster 1929–30, resigned over government's failure to adopt his radical proposals to deal with unemployment; left Labour and founded New Party in 1931; founded British Union of Fascists in 1932.

Louis Francis Albert Victor Nicholas Battenberg, 1st Earl **Mountbatten** of Burma (1900–79): great-grandson of Queen Victoria; naval commander; chief of Combined Operations Command 1942–43; Supreme Allied Commander, South-East Asia, 1943–46; Viceroy of India 1947 (the last Viceroy), Governor-General 1947–48; First Sea Lord 1955–59; Chief of the Defence Staff 1959–65; killed by an IRA bomb on his boat at his holiday home in Ireland in 1979.

Robert **Munro**, Baron Alness (1868–1955): Liberal MP for Wick Burghs 1910–18, Roxburgh and Selkirk 1918–22; Lord Advocate of Scotland 1913–16; Secretary of State for Scotland 1916–22; created baron 1934.

Sir Ronald **Munro-Ferguson**, 1st Viscount Novar of Raith (1860–1934): Governor-General of Australia (1914–20); ennobled in 1920; Secretary of State for Scotland 1922–24.

Sir Archibald **Murray** (1860–1945): Chief of Staff to the British Expeditionary Force commander, Sir John French, 1914–15; suffered a nervous breakdown in early 1915 and replaced by Sir William Robertson; commanded imperial forces in Palestine and in March 1916 became British commander-in-chief Middle East; after twice failing to take Gaza, he was replaced by Edmund Allenby in June 1917.

Sir Cyril Louis Norton **Newall**, 1st Baron Newall (1886–1963): Director of Operations and Intelligence and Deputy Chief of the Air Staff 1926–31; Air Officer Commanding Middle East 1931–35; Air Member for Supply and Organisation 1935–37, where he oversaw the rapid growth of the RAF; Chief of the Air Staff (CAS) 1937–40, where he tried to ensure that the Home Air Force and Bomber Command units at least maintained parity with Germany; seen as hesitant and uninspiring, he was replaced in October 1940; Governor-General of New Zealand 1940–46; ennobled 1946.

Sir Harold George **Nicolson** (1886–1968): diplomat; journalist; active in Mosley's New Party 1931–32; National Labour MP for Leicester West 1935–45; Parliamentary Secretary, Ministry of Information 1940–41; author and biographer; his *Diaries and Letters* (Nigel Nicolson (ed.), Collins, 1971) are an invaluable source of information about political life between the wars.

Philip **Noel-Baker**, Lord Noel-Baker (1889–1982): commanded Quaker ambulance unit in First World War; Professor of International Relations, London University 1924–29; Labour MP for Coventry 1929–31, Derby 1936–50, Derby South 1950–70; Parliamentary Secretary to the Minister of War Transport 1942–45;

Secretary of State for Air 1946–47; entered the cabinet as Secretary of State for Commonwealth Relations 1947–50; demoted to Minister of Fuel and Power 1950–51; awarded Nobel Peace Prize in 1959 for his work on arms control and the regulation of conflict; ennobled 1977; Megan Lloyd George's lover from 1938.

Alfred Harmsworth, Viscount **Northcliffe** (1865–1922): founded *Daily Mail* in 1896, *Daily Mirror* in 1903; created Baron Northcliffe in 1905, the same year in which he purchased the *Observer*; in 1908 secured control of *The Times*; his papers, particularly the *Daily Mail*, were instrumental in exposing the army's shell shortage and in campaigning for the creation of a separate Ministry of Munitions; headed the British war mission to the United States in 1917; ennobled 1918.

Henry **Oliver** (1865–1965): Chief of the Admiralty War Staff, 1914–17.

Ignacy **Paderewski** (1860–1941): Prime Minister of Poland January – November 1919; Polish Representative at the League of Nations 1920–21.

Sylvia **Pankhurst** (1882–1960): daughter of Emmeline Pankhurst, the suffragette leader; a passionate supporter of the Soviet Union as a superior form of democracy to the parliamentary variety, she both visited and corresponded with Lenin and was regarded with deep suspicion by the British Government, which particularly disliked her pro-Communist articles in her newspaper *The Worker's Dreadnought*.

Sir Keith Rodney **Park** (1892–1975): Air Officer Commanding No 11 (Fighter) Group, 1940; commander RAF in Egypt 1941–42; Malta 1942–43; Air Officer Commander-in-Chief, Middle East Command, 1944; Allied Air Officer Commander-in-Chief, Air Command South East Asia, 1945.

Joseph **Paul-Boncour** (1873–1972): Prime Minister of France 1932–33; Permanent Delegate to the League of Nations 1932–36; Foreign Minister 1936–38; represented France at the San Francisco Conference which established the United Nations Charter in 1945.

Osbert **Peake**, 1st Viscount Ingleby (1897–1966): Conservative MP for Leeds North 1929–56; Parliamentary Under-Secretary of State to the Home Office 1939–44; Financial Secretary at the Treasury 1944–45; Minister of National Insurance 1951–53, for Pensions and National Insurance 1953–55.

Air Marshal Sir Richard Hallam **Peck** (1893–1952): Assistant Chief of the Air Staff.

Richard **Peirse** (1892–1970): Deputy Director of Operations and Intelligence, Air Ministry 1930–33; commanded British Forces in Palestine and Transjordan 1933–36;

Deputy Chief of Air Staff 1937–40; Commander-in-Chief Bomber Command 1940–42; Allied Air Commander-in-Chief, South East Asia Command 1943–44.

General John J. **Pershing** (1860–1948): Commander-in-Chief American Expeditionary Force, 1917–19; Chief of Staff, US Army, 1921–24.

Simon **Petlura** (1879–1926): Ukrainian political and military leader during Ukraine's unsuccessful war for independence in 1917–22; assassinated by a Bolshevik agent in Paris in 1926.

Jozef **Pilsudski** (1867–1935): leader of the Polish Socialist Party from 1892; declared Poland's independence in 1918, President of Poland 1918–22; Minister of War 1926–35; Prime Minister, 1927–28 and 1930.

Key **Pittman** (1872–1940): US politician and Democratic Senator 1913–40.

Sir Charles **Portal**, Baron Portal of Hungerford (1893–1971): Lieutenant Colonel, Royal Flying Corps, First World War; remained in RAF where he developed new approaches to improving bombing accuracy; in 1934 appointed Commander, British forces in Aden, where he tried to control the local tribesmen by air power; by 1939 a member of the Air Council and Director of Organisation in the Air Ministry; Commander-in-Chief, Bomber Command April–October 1940; advocated strategic area bombing against German industrial areas instead of bombing specific factories or plants, and gave the first order to bomb Berlin, on 25 August 1940; in response Göring ordered the Luftwaffe to bomb London instead of British airfields; Chief of Air Staff 1940–45; in January 1943, selected to coordinate US and British bomber forces in the bomber offensive against Germany; ennobled 1945; Controller of the Atomic Energy Authority 1946–51.

Admiral Sir Dudley **Pound** (1877–1943): First Sea Lord 1939–43.

Charles Gavan **Power** (1888–1968): Canadian MP 1917–55; Minister for National Defense for Air 1940–44, where he promoted the interests of Canadian air forces serving under British command and created Canadian squadrons in Europe; responsible for the local administration of the British Commonwealth Joint Air Training Plan which ran from April 1940 until March 1945 and turned out 131,553 pilots, navigators, bomb-aimers, wireless operators, air gunners and flight engineers.

Reginald **Purbrick** (dates unknown): Conservative MP for Walton, Cheshire 1929–45.

Percy Pollexfen de Blaquiere **Radcliffe** (1874–1934): Brigadier-General, General Staff, 1915–17; Director of Military Operations, War Office, 1918–22; appointed to mission to Poland in 1919 where he assisted General Weygand in reorganising the Polish Army; finished service as Commander-in-Chief, Southern Command, 1933–34.

Rufus Isaacs, Lord **Reading** (1860–1935): Liberal MP for Reading 1904–13; Attorney-General 1910–13; Lord Chief Justice 1913–21; Viceroy of India, 1921–26; Foreign Secretary for the first three months of MacDonald's National Government in 1931; Leader of the Liberal peers 1931–35.

Sidney **Reilly** (real name Georgi Rosenblum) (1874–1925): of 'Reilly, Ace of Spies' fame; Polish by birth, he spied on Germany and Russia for British Military Intelligence, and was regarded as Britain's most important secret agent; executed by the Russians on 5 November 1925.

Robert Burnham **Renwick** (1904–73): businessman who operated a number of factories in the Midlands producing equipment for the Ministry of Aircraft Production.

Lady Juliet **Rhys Williams** (1898–1964): Honorary Secretary, Women's Liberal Federation, 1943; joined the Conservative Party, 1945; Honorary Secretary, United Europe Movement, 1947–58, Chairman from 1958; opposed Treaty of Rome and campaigned vigorously against joining the Common Market, which she thought would hand over British sovereignty to Europe and betray the Commonwealth.

George **Riddell** (1865–1934): Chairman of the *News of the World* newspaper; Liaison Officer between the government and the press, 1914–18; close associate of Lloyd George.

Eugenio **Rignano** (1870–1930): Italian economist, built an international reputation on his proposal to make inheritance tax more progressive so that the tax rate on inherited property would be higher than the rate on self-created wealth; influential amongst Liberals like Sinclair because he argued that his proposals did not affect the incentives to work and save and would lead to gradual nationalisation of wealth, and hoped that his thinking would help bring about the reconciliation of socialism and liberalism.

William Robert **Robertson** (1860–1933): Chief of the Imperial General Staff 1915–18.

Mikhail Vladimirovich **Rodzianko** (1859–1924): served in the Tsarist army before turning to politics; President of the Duma 1912–17; monarchist and moderate reformer who was deeply opposed to both the Mensheviks and the Bolsheviks, he was an active leader of the White Russian forces in the Baltic area; sought exile in Yugoslavia in 1920 and died in Belgrade.

Bertram Henry Samuel **Romilly** (1878–1940): Churchill's brother-in-law (married to Nellie Hozier, Churchill's wife's sister); soldier, served in Sudan, the Boer War, and France in the Great War.

James de **Rothschild** (1878–1957): Liberal MP for Isle of Ely 1929–45; Parliamentary Secretary, Ministry of Supply March – May 1945; leading Zionist; a close friend of Sinclair's, he used his personal wealth to fund Liberal parliamentary activities during the period 1931–45.

Sir Herbert Samuel **Samuel**, 1st Viscount Samuel (1870–1963): Liberal MP for Cleveland 1902–18, Darwen 1929–35; Chancellor of the Duchy of Lancaster 1909–10, 1915–16; Postmaster-General 1910–14, 1915–16; President of the Local Government Board 1914–15; Home Secretary January–December 1916; High Commissioner for Palestine 1920–25; Chairman of the Commission of Inquiry into the Coal Industry 1925–26; Leader of the Liberal Party 1931–35; Home Secretary 1931–32; ennobled in 1937; Leader of the Liberal peers 1944–55; a leading New Liberal in his youth, he became a popular panellist on the radio programme *The Brains' Trust* and wrote several works of philosophy.

Duncan Edwin **Sandys**, 1st Baron Duncan-Sandys (1908–87): Churchill's son-in-law (married to Diana); Conservative MP for Lambeth 1935–45, Streatham 1950–74; Minister of Works 1944–45; Minister of Supply 1951–54; Minister of Housing 1954–57; Minister of Defence 1957–1960; Secretary of State for the Colonies and Commonwealth Relations 1960–64; sacked from the opposition front bench by Edward Heath in 1966 over his support for Ian Smith's Unilateral Declaration of Independence for Rhodesia; ennobled 1974; a strong supporter of European integration as a means of avoiding future conflict, he was involved in establishing the United Europe pressure group in the UK.

Maurice **Sarrail** (1856–1929): Commander-in-Chief of the Allied armies at Salonika.

Boris **Savinkoff** or Savinkov (1879–1925): anarchist, writer and anti-Tsarist member of the Socialist Revolutionary Party, he was transformed by the war into an ultra-patriot, becoming Deputy Minister for War under Kerensky in 1917; a bitter opponent of Lenin, he formed the Union for the Defence of the Motherland and Liberty as a White Russian umbrella organisation; his subsequent intriguing with the British and persistent insurgent activities against Soviet Russia ensured that when he was captured (having been tricked into returning to Russia to negotiate with the Soviets) there was little hesitation in arranging for him to fall to his death from a window in the Lubyanka prison.

Alexander MacCallum **Scott** (1874–1928): Liberal MP for Glasgow Bridgeton 1910–22; Parliamentary Private Secretary to Churchill, 1917–18; in 1924 left the Liberals to join the Labour Party; Churchill's first biographer, publishing in 1905 a flattering account of Churchill's first thirty years.

Charles Prestwich **Scott** (1846–1932): Editor of the *Manchester Guardian* 1872–1929; Liberal MP for Leigh 1895–1906; close friend and advisor to Lloyd George, and highly influential in Liberal circles.

John Edward Bernard ('Galloper Jack') **Seely**, Baron Mottistone (1868–1947): a Unionist free trader who followed Churchill in crossing the floor of the House of Commons to join the Liberals in 1904; Secretary of State for War, 1912–14, resigned over the handling of a potential mutiny of senior army officers at the Curragh in July 1914; commanded Canadian mounted brigade 1915–16; Under-Secretary of State to Churchill, Ministry of Munitions and Deputy Minister of Munitions, 1918; Secretary of State for Air, 1919; ennobled 1933.

Cecil Roundell Palmer, 3rd Earl of **Selborne** (1887–1971): Conservative MP for Newtown, Lancashire, 1910–18, Aldershot 1918–40; ally of Churchill in the struggle against the India Act of 1935; Director of Cement, Ministry of Works, 1940–42, responsible for the construction of anti-invasion pillboxes all over southern England; Minister of Economic Warfare 1942–45.

Count Carol **Sforza** (1873–1952): Italian diplomat; Minister for Foreign Affairs 1920–21; Italy's ambassador to France 1922; resigned after refusing to serve under Benito Mussolini; a strong anti-fascist, lived in voluntary exile in Belgium until 1939 and in the US 1940–43; returned to Italy after World War II to serve in various government posts, including Minister of Foreign Affairs 1947–51.

Eric James **Shearer** (1892–1980): Director of Military Intelligence in the Middle East 1940–42.

John **Sherwood-Kelly** (or Sherwood Kelly) (1880–1931): Lieutenant-Colonel, Norfolk Regiment, won the Victoria Cross whilst commanding 1st Battalion Royal Inniskilling Fusiliers in November 1917; served in Siberia 1918–19; court-martialled for publicly saying that he had 'formed the opinion that the puppet government set up by us in Archangel rested on no basis of public confidence and support, and would fall to pieces the moment the protection of British bayonets was withdrawn'.

William Philip **Sidney**, 1st Viscount De L'Isle (1909–91): Conservative MP 1944–45, succeeded to peerage 1945; Secretary of State for Air 1951–55; Governor-General of Australia 1961–66.

Sir John Allsebrook **Simon**, 1st Viscount Simon (1873–1954): Liberal MP for Walthamstow 1906–18, Liberal and Liberal National MP for Spen Valley 1922–40; Attorney-General 1913–15; Home Secretary 1915–16; split from the Liberal Party in 1931, and joined National Government; Foreign Secretary 1931–35; Home Secretary 1935–37; Chancellor of the Exchequer 1937–40; Lord Chancellor 1940–45.

Marigold **Sinclair** (née Forbes) (1898–1975): married Sir Archibald Sinclair on 18 May 1918.

Angus John **Sinclair** (1924–2003): Sinclair's second son; educated at Eton and Oxford; worked in the City as a fund manager, then enjoyed a career in the BBC including time as a studio production manager; never a political animal, he remained outside party politics.

Robin Macdonald **Sinclair**, 2nd Viscount Thurso (1922–95): Sinclair's elder son; educated at Eton, New College, Oxford and Edinburgh; RAF flight lieutenant during the Second World War, undertaking photo-reconnaissance missions in the Far East; Liberal county councillor (Caithness), town councillor (Thurso) and unsuccessful parliamentary candidate for East Aberdeenshire 1966; Lord Lieutenant of Caithness 1973–95; President of the Boys' Brigade 1985–93; close friend of the Queen Mother.

John **Singleton** (1885–1957): headed two wartime enquiries, the first on this issue of bombsights, the second on German Air Force strength.

Air Marshal Sir John Cotesworth **Slessor** (1897–1979): commanded No 5 Group, Bomber Command 1941; Assistant Chief of the Air Staff (Policy) 1942–43; Air Officer Commander-in-Chief Coastal Command 1943; Deputy Air Commander, Mediterranean Allied Air Forces, 1945; Air Member for Personnel 1945–47; Chief of the Air Staff 1950–53.

Frederick Edwin ('F.E.') **Smith** (1874–1930): Solicitor General, 1915; Attorney General, 1915–19; Lord Chancellor, 1919–22; Secretary for India, 1924–28; Created Baron Birkenhead, 1919, Viscount, 1921, Earl, 1922.

Philip **Snowden**, 1st Viscount Snowden (1864–1937): originally a Liberal but an early convert to the Independent Labour Party; Labour MP for Blackburn 1906–18, Colne Valley 1922–31; Chancellor of the Exchequer in both the first and second Labour Governments (1924 and 1929–31); followed MacDonald in the National Government where, as Chancellor, he introduced measures including a reduction in unemployment pay; ennobled 1931; Lord Privy Seal, 1931–32.

Carl A. **Spaatz** (1891–1974): General, US Air Force; Chief of the Air Force Combat Command 1941, began planning of the American air effort in Europe; Commander Allied Northwest African Air Forces 1943–44; Commander Strategic Air Force in Europe 1944–45, responsible for all deep bombing missions against Germany; Commander US Strategic Air Force in the Pacific 1945–46 – the atomic bombing of Hiroshima and Nagasaki took place under his command.

John **Spencer-Churchill**, Marquess of Blandford (1897–1972): son of Churchill's cousin, the 9th Duke of Marlborough.

Major General Edward Louis **Spiers** (changed surname to Spears) (1886–1974): Liaison Officer with French 10th Army 1915–16; based in Paris immediately after the war as head of the British Military Mission; National Liberal (Lloyd Georgite) MP 1922–24, Conservative MP 1931–45; remained a close friend of Churchill's throughout his life.

Sir Arthur Herbert Drummond Ramsay **Steel-Maitland** (1876–1935): Conservative MP for East Birmingham 1910–29, Tamworth 1929–35; Secretary for Overseas Trade at the Board of Trade, 1917–19; Minister for Labour, 1924–29.

Henry Lewis **Stimson** (1867–1930): US statesman (Republican), served in the administrations of five US Presidents from 1911 to 1945; Secretary of War 1911–13; Secretary of State 1929–33, when he denounced Japanese aggression in Manchuria (the 'Stimson Doctrine'); Secretary of War 1940–45.

George Granville **Sutherland**, 5th Duke of Sutherland (1888–1963): Under-Secretary of State for Air 1922–24; Paymaster-General 1925–28; Under-Secretary of State for War 1928–29; represented the Colonial Office in the House of Lords at the date of this letter.

Sir William **Sutherland** (1880–1949): Private Secretary to Lloyd George 1915–18; Coalition Liberal MP for Argyllshire 1918–24; Parliamentary Private Secretary to Lloyd George 1918-20; Junior Lord of the Treasury 1920–22; Chancellor of the Duchy of Lancaster 1922.

Colonel Frederick Hugh **Sykes** (1877–1954): Chief of Staff, Royal Flying Corps, 1914–16; air commander for the Dardanelles campaign; Assistant Adjutant-General, War Office 1916–17; Chief of Staff, Royal Air Force 1918–19; Controller of Civil Aviation 1919–22; Conservative MP, Sheffield Hallam 1922–28, Central Nottingham 1940–45; Chairman British Broadcasting Board 1923–27; Governor of Bombay 1928–33.

Sir Stephen George **Tallents** (1884–1958): civil servant; Irish Guards 1914–15; in 1919 appointed Chief British Delegate for Relief and Supply of Poland, and then British Commissioner for the Baltic Provinces, where he had some success in helping to restore order.

Tchitcherin: *see* Chicherin.

Arthur William **Tedder**, 1st Baron Tedder (1890–1967): Commander, RAF Far East Command 1936–38; Director, Research and Development 1938–40; Commander, RAF Middle East Command 1940–43; Deputy Supreme Allied Commander 1943–45, under Eisenhower – the two men worked closely together in planning the D-Day landings in June 1944; responsible for providing tactical air support and a strong advocate of destroying the German communication system during the invasion; ennobled and became Chief of the Air Staff in 1946.

James Henry 'Jimmy' **Thomas** (1874–1949): railway workers' union leader; Labour and National Labour MP for Derby 1910–36; Secretary of State for the Colonies 1924; Lord Privy Seal and Minister for Employment 1929–30; Secretary of State for the Dominions 1930–31; followed MacDonald into the National Government; Secretary of State for the Colonies and Dominions 1931–35; Secretary of State for the Colonies 1935–36.

Basil **Thomson** (1861–1939): trained as a barrister and joined the Colonial Office; served in Fiji and Tonga, where he was briefly Prime Minister; on returning to England joined the Prison Service and later served as Governor of Dartmoor Prison and Wormwood Scrubs; in 1913 became Deputy Commissioner of the Metropolitan Police and in 1918 head of the Special Branch; involved in some of the most sensational spying cases of the period and played pivotal roles in the investigations of Mati Hari and Roger Casement.

Sir John Anthony Cecil **Tilley** (1869–1952): career diplomat who served the Foreign Office in Constantinople before the First World War; became a Privy Councillor in 1920 and served as British Ambassador to Japan 1926–31.

Hugh Montague **Trenchard**, 1st Viscount Trenchard of Wolfeton (1873–1956): commanded the Royal Flying Corps from 1915; Chief of the Air Staff January – April 1918, when he helped establish the Royal Air Force, but resigned from office after a quarrel with Lord Rothermere, the Air Secretary; in February 1919, invited by Churchill to return as Chief of the Air Staff, a position he held until his retirement in 1929.

Lev Davidovich Bronstein ('Leon **Trotsky**') (1879–1940): joined the Mensheviks against Lenin in 1903, but returned to Russia in 1917 and aligned himself with

Lenin; appointed head of the Petrograd Soviet; military leader of the October Revolution; Soviet Commissar for Foreign Affairs 1917–18 and for Military Affairs 1918–25; expelled from the Communist Party by Stalin in 1927 and assassinated, on Stalin's orders, in Mexico in 1940.

Algernon **Trotter** (1870–1945): Lieutenant-Colonel, 2nd Life Guards, during 1916.

Alfred **Tyszkiewicz** (1882–1930): Lithuanian by birth (then part of Russia), served in the Russian army in the Russo-Japanese War (1904–05); subsequently worked in the Foreign Ministry and was secretary to the Russian embassy in London; transferred his allegiance to newly independent Lithuania in 1919, and attended the Paris Peace Conference; Lithuania's minister to Great Britain 1920–21.

Hoyt Sanford **Vandenberg** (1899–1954): US Deputy Chief of Air Staff 1943–44; Deputy Air Commander-in-Chief, Allied Expeditionary Forces, 1944; commander US 9th Air Force 1944–45; Director of Central Intelligence 1945–47; Vice Chief of Staff US Air Force 1947–48; Chief of Staff US Air Force 1948–53, succeeding General Spaatz.

Maxim **Vinaver** (1863–1926): Jewish lawyer and one of the founders of the Cadets.

Eleftherios **Venizelos** (1864–1936): Greek Prime Minister 1910–15, 1917–20, 1924, 1928–32, 1933; dismissed by King Constantine after inviting the Allied forces into Salonika, he established a provisional rival government and, with Allied support, forced the King's abdication in June 1917; at the Versailles Peace Conference, Greece won substantial territorial gains from Bulgaria and Turkey.

Gerald Lloyd **Verney** (1900–57): commander 2nd Battalion Irish Guards 1940–42, 6th Guards Armoured Brigade 1942–44, 7th Armoured Division 1944, 1st Brigade, Italy – Austria, 1945.

Ivo **Vesey** (1876–1974): Major, GHQ France, 1915–16.

Dimitri **Vladimiroffl** or Vladimirov (1896–1952): born into an aristocratic Russian family, originally called Dimitri von Prebsting-Cesarevsky; trained at Moscow's Bolshoi Theatre; an ardent monarchist, he rose to the rank of Lieutenant-Colonel in the Don Cossack Army during the Russian Civil War; fled Russia and moved to Toronto, where he established a successful ballet school.

John **Ward** (dates unknown): commanded 25th Battalion of the Middlesex Regiment, who at one time had the poet Wilfred Owen serving under him; the battalion fought on the Western Front for most of the war but in August 1918 was transferred to Siberia; Ward ended his war at Omsk in 1919; one of the founders of the organisation that became the Transport & General Workers' Union.

Archibald Percival **Wavell**, 1st Earl Wavell (1883–1950): British field marshal; Commander-in-Chief Middle East 1939–41, where he destroyed the numerically vastly superior Italian armies in North Africa but could not contain Rommel's Afrika Korps; Commander-in-Chief Southeast Asia 1941–43, defeated by Japanese in Malaya, Singapore and Burma; Viceroy of India 1943–47.

Vi Kuiyuin **Wellington Koo** (1887–1985): Chinese Nationalist diplomat, and at various times minister of foreign affairs and prime minister; delegate to the Paris Peace Conference in 1919 and then Chinese representative on the Council of the League of Nations.

Henry Graham **White** (1880–1965): Liberal MP 1922–45; a worthy and dedicated backbencher.

Aneurin **Williams** (1859–1924): barrister; Liberal MP for Plymouth January – December 1910, Durham Consett 1918–22.

Herbert G. **Williams** (dates unknown): Conservative MP for Croydon South 1931–45.

Sir Henry Hughes **Wilson** (1864–1922): Chief liaison officer with the French Army January 1915; commanded Fourth Corps 1916; Chief of the Imperial General Staff 1918–22; assassinated by Sinn Fein on the steps of his London house, 1922.

Henry Maitland **Wilson**, 1st Baron Wilson (1881–1964): Commander-in-Chief, Middle East, 1943; Supreme Allied Commander in the Mediterranean, 1944; popularly known as 'Jumbo' because of his great height and bulk.

Thomas Woodrow **Wilson** (1856–1924): 28th President of the United States (1913–21); creator and leading advocate of the League of Nations, for which he was awarded the 1919 Nobel Peace Prize; suffered a paralytic stroke while seeking American public support for the Treaty of Versailles (October 1919) which incapacitated him for the rest of his term of office; in 1919 US Senate failed to ratify the Treaty by seven votes.

Edward Frederick Lindley **Wood**: *see* Lord Halifax.

Piotr Nikolayevich **Wrangel** (1878–1928): former Tsarist officer who joined Denikin's forces in 1918, and assumed command of the anti-Bolshevik forces in southern Russia in 1920; launched a final offensive against the Bolsheviks in June

1920, but was forced to evacuate his forces from the Crimea in November 1920, bringing the Russian Civil War to an end; died in exile in Brussels.

Nikolai Nikolaevich **Yudenich** (1862–1933): Commander of the anti-Bolshevik North-Western Army against Petrograd in 1919; arrested by fellow White officers when his offensive failed, but released on British insistence and emigrated to Britain.

Appendix C

Abbreviations

AA	Anti-aircraft
ADGB	Air Defence of Great Britain
AFS	Assistant First Secretary to the War Office
AFV	Armoured fighting vehicle
AG	Adjutant General
AI	Aerial interception (airborne radar)
AM	Air Ministry
AMP	Air Member for Personnel (on the Air Council)
AMSO	Air Member for Supply and Organisation (on the Air Council)
Anvil	Codeword for the 1944 Allied invasion of southern France in the Toulon-Marseille area
AOC-in-C	Air Officer Commander-in-Chief
AP	Armour-piercing
ASU	Aircraft Storage Unit
ASV	Air to Surface Vessel (a type of radar)
Atfero	The Atlantic Ferry Organisation
BOAC	British Overseas Airways Corporation
Bolo	Bolshevik
CAS	Chief of the Air Staff
CIGS	Chief of the Imperial General Staff
CIU	Central Information Unit.
COS	Chiefs of Staff
CRA	Canadian Royal Artillery
DCIGS	Deputy Chief of the Imperial General Staff
DF	Direction Finding
DFC	Distinguished Flying Cross
DMI	Director of Military Intelligence
DMO	Director of Military Operations
DOT	Department of Overseas Trade
DPS	Deputy Permanent Secretary
DQMG	Deputy Quartermaster-General

DSO	Distinguished Service Order
FOO	Forward Observation Officer or Outpost
FOP	Future Operations Planning – a section of the Joint Planning Staff
FROZEN	Codeword for a secret telegram
GEE	Navigational aid for aircraft
GL	Gun-laying (radar)
GP	General purpose
GR	General reconnaissance
GS	General staff
H2S	Navigational aid for aircraft, the forerunner of ground-scanning radar
HE	High explosive
HLI	Highland Light Infantry
KBE	Knight Commander of the Order of the British Empire
LAM	Land Arm Mode (an automatic landing device)
LST	Local standard time
MAP	Ministry of Aircraft Production
MC	Medium-capacity (bombs)
MC	Military Cross
ME	Middle East
MEW	Ministry of Economic Warfare
MI	Military Intelligence
MI1	Office of the Director of Military Intelligence
MIR	Military Intelligence Research
MO5	Later known as MI5 – the branch of the secret service dealing with internal UK security matters
MT	Motor transport
Oboe	Blind-bombing device installed in aircraft but controlled from ground stations in England
OC	Officer commanding
OM	Order of Merit
OTU	Operational Training Unit
Overlord	Codeword for Allied invasion of Normandy
PAC	Parachute and Cable (rockets)
PFF	Pathfinder force
Priceless	Codeword for Allied support activities planned after the invasion of Sicily
PR	Photo-reconnaissance
PRU	Photographic reconnaissance unit
QMG	Quartermaster-General
RAC	Royal Automobile Club, Pall Mall
RAFNI	RAF Northern Ireland
RCAF	Royal Canadian Air Force

RDF	Radio Direction Finding
RIC	Royal Irish Constabulary
RND	Royal Naval Division
Round-up	Initial codeword used for the planned Allied invasion of the European continent
RTC	(Possibly) RAF (or Royal) Training Command
SA	South African
SAA	Small arms and ammunition (possibly)
SD4	A specialist part of Military Intelligence dealing with propaganda
SEAC	South East Asia Command
Sextant	Cairo-Tehran conferences, 22 November – 7 December 1943
Shingle	Codeword for the amphibious operation at Anzio, Italy in 1944
SNO	Senior Naval Officer
Starkey	Codeword for a planned assault on Boulogne in September 1943; never carried out
Super Gymnast	Code name for a projected US-British joint operation in North Africa that would combine an American landing at Casablanca with a British landing further eastward on the Mediterranean coast
TBR	Torpedo bomber reconnaissance
Torch	Codeword for the allied invasion of the North African French Colonies
UP	Unrotated projectile (rocket)
VCAS	Vice Chief of the Air Staff
Wee Frees	Originally the members of the minority of the Free Church of Scotland who refused to be joined with the United Free Church in 1900; later a popular way of referring to the Asquithian Liberals who refused to follow Lloyd George into coalition with the Conservatives in 1916

Index